P9-BZY-245

The
ALL AMERICANS

Also by Lars Anderson

The Proving Ground: A Season on the Fringe in NFL Europe

Pickup Artists: Street Basketball in America

This is for my dad, Commander Robert L. Anderson, JAGC, and all the other Americans who rest in honor at Arlington National Cemetery in Arlington, Virginia

CONTENTS

PART ONE

PART TWO

On November 29, 1941, Army played Navy in front of 98,942 fans. Eight days later, the Japanese attacked Pearl Harbor. This is the story of four players' journey from the football field to the battlefield.

He either fears his fate too much,
Or his deserts are small,
Who dare not put it to the touch,
To win or lose it all.

—EARL OF MONTROSE,
a seventeenth-century Scottish commander

The ALL AMERICANS

PART ONE

I

D-DAY

THE YOUNG MAN STOOD on the deck of the U.S.S. *Garfield*, looking across the English Channel, into darkness. It was just after midnight on June 6, 1944, and the defining hour of Henry Romanek's life was at hand. The *Garfield*, a transport ship, had just left the coast of England and was motoring south across the channel, its destination the waters off northern France, about ten miles outside of a quiet, enchanting beach the Allies called Omaha.

As Romanek gazed onto the black horizon, a cold wind dusting his cheeks, beams of moonlight filtered though the clouds to reveal an armada of ships so vast that it took his breath away. Over five thousand vessels were plowing through the whitecaps, the column of ships stretching as far as Romanek's eyes could see to the east and the west. The day of reckoning, D-day, had arrived. "Good God," Romanek said softly to himself, "Lord, have mercy on us."

The twenty-four-year-old Romanek was a platoon leader in the 149th Engineer Combat Battalion. Like all the soldiers in his company, he was dressed for battle. He wore a steel combat helmet that was outfitted with a fabric interlining. A life belt (a flotation device) was wrapped snugly around his waist. His first layer of clothing was a wool undershirt, wool underwear, and thick wool combat socks. On top of that were protective leggings, wool pants, a flannel shirt, an olive drab jacket, and waterproof jumpshoes. He also carried a field bag on his back that held a pancho, toilet articles, a towel, canned food, and a knife, fork, and spoon. A loaded carbine hung over his shoulder, and his dog tags dangled from his neck. On the ring finger of his left hand was his graduation ring from West Point, his dearest possession.

Romanek had received the ring a year earlier, and now as he looked down on it, the black onyx stone glittered in the moonlight. Romanek was in charge of a platoon of forty-five men, and they were constantly asking him to tell stories from his days at the military academy, especially what it was like to be an Army football player. Romanek had been a two-way standout at the Point in 1941 and '42, playing tackle on both offense and defense. The game he was most often questioned about was the '41 Army-Navy contest, which was played before 98,942 screaming fans at Philadelphia's Municipal Stadium. As Romanek drew closer to what he knew would be the bloodiest fight of his life, that game was still alive in his mind, its details burned into his memory. He must have told his men about that Army-Navy clash a hundred times, maybe more.

Though three and half years had passed since he last donned an Army football uniform, Romanek still looked like the strapping star he was. Barrel-chested and long-armed, Romanek, at 6' 2", 195 pounds, was more toned than muscular. He didn't seem to have an ounce of fat on his tight frame. He had a fair complexion, sleepy blue eyes, caramel-colored hair that was in a crew cut, and a soft, gentle smile that made ladies blush whenever he looked their way. He was, by all accounts, a dashing figure, the kind of clean-cut, riveting young man that people turned to stare at whenever he strolled into a room.

Yet the boys in his platoon—and to Romanek, they were *boys,* as most of them were still teenagers—looked up to Romanek not because of his handsome looks but because he was their leader. Romanek thought of his men as an extension of his own family, and he worried and fretted about them probably more than he should have. He spent every night after training reading all their V-mail letters that they were sending to loved ones back home. Because Romanek was the official censor in charge of screening all outgoing U.S. mail for his platoon, he came to know all of his men's deepest secrets and greatest fears. He talked to the men in his platoon about everything, from how they missed their sweethearts back home to the art of making a proper block on the football field. Even when Romanek was agitated, he rarely raised his voice when speaking with his men. Instead, in a firm and steady tone, he would simply lay out what needed to be done and how it would be accomplished. Then he always ended by saying how much he trusted everyone and how they should treat each other like they were blood brothers.

Romanek's soldiers were from the Midwest, mostly raised on farms and in small towns in Iowa, Missouri, and Nebraska, and they were as gritty as any soldiers Romanek had ever been around. Romanek cared deeply for them, which made him vulnerable on this early morning: Romanek knew that many of them wouldn't survive the coming day. "If all the soldiers on our side are as good as you guys," Romanek told his men a few days before the invasion, "the Germans don't have a chance."

Along with the rest of his battalion, Romanek and his men had sailed out of New York harbor on the early morning of December 29, 1943, and had spent the better part of six months on the south coast of England preparing for the invasion. The 149th practiced everything from landing on beaches to laying live mines to booby-trapping houses with explosives. The combat engineers had perhaps the most complex mission of any on D-day. They would be among the first to hit the beaches, and they were assigned multiple tasks. They were to identify and blow up any beach obstacle—most were large pieces of steel rail—that would interfere with the landing of troops as the tide began to rise. Then, as quickly as possible, they were to set up signs that would act as guideposts for incoming landing craft. Finally, if they were still alive, they were to clear roads from the beach and set up supply dumps.

Romanek had gone over the mission dozens of times with his men. He explained to them that the first assault waves on D-day were going to be DD tanks ("duplex drive" tanks that were modified M4 Sherman tanks, which could travel on water as well as land). These tanks would be rigged with rubber devices so—the hope was—they would float. The tanks would be followed by a wave of infantry and engineers. Romanek's engineering platoon was married to the 116th Infantry Regiment of the 29th Infantry Division. They would ride into Omaha Beach together on landing craft, and they would be among the first of the forty thousand men scheduled to land on Omaha, a beach that was about six miles long and slightly crescent-shaped. Romanek reminded his men over and over that what they really had to focus on was erecting the large marking panels for the D-3 exit so that subsequent landing craft would know where to go.

Now on the *Garfield*, the landings at Omaha just hours away, Romanek told his platoon to gather around him. When Romanek looked at his men, their eyes seemed to glow like full moons—wide-open and bursting with anticipation. "Now is our opportunity to participate in the greatest armada ever launched in history," Romanek said above the drone of the *Garfield*'s engines. "And history will be made by what we do here today. Now let's do our jobs and make our country proud." There were no replies from any of Romanek's men. They merely stared at their leader in silence.

At around two in the morning, when the *Garfield* was about twelve miles off the coast of France, the order was sounded; "Now hear this! All assault troops report to your debarkation areas."

Romanek made his way to the spot where he would descend onto a LCM (Landing Craft, Mechanized) that would ferry half of his platoon—approximately twenty-three men—and about eighty infantry personnel to the beach. Along with the hundred or so men on the LCM, there would also be explosive devices and marking panels on board, which Romanek and his platoon of engineers would erect. The marking panels were stored in twenty-foot-long polelike casings. The markers were large triangles that would be staked into the sand and would signify the D-3 exit at Les Moulins, an area on the beach that included a road that led inland to St. Laurent—a D-day objective for the infantry. Romanek carried one of the cases with him as he walked to the disembarkation point.

Boarding the LCMs was treacherous. The small vessels had already been lowered into the water and they were now bobbing up and down in the ten-foot swells.The men threw a rope net over the side of the *Garfield.* In a firm tone, Romanek told his men to go, to climb down the net and then jump into their LCM. "This won't be easy," Romanek said as men began to descend. "Don't lose your grip." Because the engineers were loaded down with weapons, ammo, rations, and a life preserver, mobility was limited. At the disembarking point, one of the men turned to Romanek. His face was white and he was so cold with fear he could hardly move. "Sir, I'm scared," he told Romanek.

"So am I," said Romanek, trying to calm the boy's spirit with encouraging words. "Listen, we're all apprehensive. But don't worry. I'll be by your side the whole way. Nothing will happen to you."

"But sir . . ."

"Come on, soldier, get in," Romanek said.

"Yes, sir."

As a parting salute before going over the side, Romanek took out an American-made glass bottle of beer from his pack. His wife Betsy had mailed the beer to Romanek while he was in England, and he took a big, hearty swig. He then handed it to his men and they each gulped a swallow and passed it along in silence.

Once everyone was on board, the engineers stood in the back of the LCM, the infantrymen in front. They were packed so tightly there was no room to sit. The LCM then pulled away from the *Garfield* and circled around to get in formation with the other landing craft. The moon had disappeared behind the clouds, and it was nearly as dark as blindness. The LCM continued to pitch sharply in the deep swells. Waves punished the sides of Romanek's LCM, sending sprays of water into the craft, quickly soaking the men. Within minutes, many of the men were vomiting as the LCM rocked up and down, side to side, up and down. Romanek had spent numerous days at sea in his young life, but now, for the first time, even he became seasick. This wasn't promising, this sad start to the invasion.

As Romanek tried his best to inflate the morale of his men, he noticed that one of the 116th infantry division's battalion commanders was in his LCM. Major Sidney V. Bingham Jr., was twenty-nine years old, but to Romanek he seemed like an old man, a savvy veteran. Glancing around at all the men on board, Romanek was struck by how young everyone looked. But not Major Bingham. Confidence seemed to radiate from his eyes, and it relaxed Romanek. He had seen this look before, many times before actually, on Earl "Red" Blaik, his football coach at Army. It was the dead-set-to-win expression that Blaik always wore on his face before a big game.

Raised in Rutherford, New Jersey, Romanek first became interested in West Point during his junior year at Rutherford High. Romanek was on the Rutherford football team that won the 1937 Group Three Northern New Jersey State Championship. Two weeks after capturing the state title, the team held a banquet dinner. The keynote speaker was an assistant coach from Army who delivered a pep talk to the players. He concluded by presenting all of the boys with gold footballs that commemorated their championship season.

Before he stepped down from the dais, the coach asked the players to raise their hands if they were A students. Romanek, along with two of his teammates, lifted his arm. The coach later chatted with Romanek one-on-one for a few minutes, eventually asking Romanek if he'd like to come visit the Point. A junior in high school, Romanek had never given serious consideration to the U.S. Military Academy, but he was possessed with a devouring curiosity—he could suck the information right out of a room—and so he said, "Sure, I'll visit. Why not?"

A few weeks later Romanek rode in a car with his coach, Eddie Tryon, to West Point. Not expecting anything, Romanek was awed by the place. The cadets in their sharp dress uniforms, the granite buildings, the broad green Plain, the granite-cliff shores of the Hudson, the motto of duty, honor, country—all of it stirred feelings inside him that he didn't even know existed. The assistant football coach chaperoned Romanek around campus and took him to the doctor's office for a physical. Romanek passed, and by the time he was shaking hands with the coach and preparing to get back into Tryon's car, both coach and player hoped that they'd meet each other again. Young Henry Romanek had seen his future.

Aside from his grades and athletic ability, what made Romanek such an attractive West Point candidate to the Army coaches was his leadership. His high school coaches marveled at how, when things went bad on the field, Romanek was the player everyone seemed to look to for answers. Even when he was a high school junior, in 1937, Romanek had a reassuring manner. This was evident when Rutherford hosted Passaic High at the end of the season. Rutherford was the state's Group Three champion, Passaic was New Jersey's Group Four champion. Held at Rutherford Senior High School Field on a snowy afternoon, the game was a defensive battle. Romanek, playing the line on both offense and defense with no substitutions, was a terror, ripping opening holes on offense for their star back Jimmy Blumenstock—who would later play for Fordahm and the New York Giants—and leading his team in tackles on defense. Passaic, however, pulled the game out late in the fourth quarter when their kicker drilled a 45-yard field goal in the snow to give his team a 3–0 win.

In the locker room afterwards Romanek walked from player to player, telling each one that he had nothing to be ashamed of, that they all had left their hearts out on the field. Romanek's performance against Passaic caught the attention of college coaches all around the tri-state area. Scholarship offers would soon come, but once he toured the grounds at West Point, his mind was made up: He wanted to go to the U.S. Military Academy.

Now it was 5:30 in the morning on D-day. As Romanek's LCM motored toward the beach, the loud thudding of the engine made it difficult to communicate. Nerves were tense, but the men were optimistic that the heavy naval gunfire of the Allies would destroy the Germans' shore defenses before they arrived at the beach. "That beach is going to be all torn up by the time we get there," said one solider in Romanek's platoon to another. "I bet we won't even see a single bullet!"

The LCM sped closer to the sand. At about 5:45 the first hint of daylight started to sliver across the eastern sky, and the Allied bombers began assaulting the German positions at Normandy. The Germans responded with antiaircraft fire, which from Romanek's position appeared to fill the sky with giant sparks. Here it was, he thought, the start of the D-day battle, two forces going at each other as mightily as angels and demons. Still Romanek and his men pushed forward to the beach.

The German shore batteries started firing on the naval fleet, the shells whizzing over the landing crafts. Seconds later, the fleet responded with a fury. As Romanek stood in the back of his LCM that was about four miles off shore, the air filled with the sound of a thousand thunderclaps bursting at once. Romanek could feel the noise in his chest—*thump, thump, thump*—with every breath. When he looked up into the still-dark sky, there were luminous streaks of flames shooting in every direction. There was no going back now.

Every gun in the Allied fleet was firing on the German shore batteries, pillboxes, fortified housing—anything that could pose a threat to the incoming landing craft. By 5:50 A.M., the first wave of landing crafts was closing in on the five beaches of Normandy. Once the LCTs (Landing Craft Tank) started deploying their DD tanks—the tanks that were designed to "swim" ashore with their rubber devices—the warships would lift their guns and begin shooting at targets inland. The first American troops were about to set foot in France on D-day, and the Allied fleet didn't want to take out any of its own with friendly fire.

Romanek could see the shoreline. But something wasn't right, and the sight made his skin feel numb. The DD tanks, which were supposed to provide cover for Romanek and his engineers, weren't swimming. In fact, they were sinking, dropping into the water like boulders. The swells were so high that the tanks simply disappeared into the water as they rolled off their LCTs. Romanek could see men desperately trying to crawl up through the hatches as the tanks sank, but most didn't make it out. Suddenly on Romanek's LCM, fear crept into everyone's heart.

Just as the first wave of Allied troops was about to hit the beaches, an Army teammate of Romanek's named Robin Olds was in the air above

Normandy, flying in his P-38 and prowling for Germans. Olds' orders were strict: He was only there to blast away at enemy planes should they appear. Olds had been firmly told by his commander that he wasn't to fire on anything on the ground. "We might accidentally take out our own guys," Olds was told in a briefing meeting before the invasion. "We're only there to keep enemy planes from strafing the ground."

As Olds buzzed over Normandy steady at 500 feet, he was overwhelmed by what he saw. It seemed as if every ship ever built was visible in the distance, firing on Normandy. Down below him the sea seemed to be crawling with large dark water bugs, all inching closer to land, every landing craft leaving a white wake in its trail. It would take Olds hours to count the number of vessels that were in his field of view. "Jesus Christ," Olds mumbled to himself. "It looks like the end of world down there."

Olds knew that his good friend Henry Romanek was somewhere below him, preparing to hit the beach. Over the last five years, Olds and Romanek had become the tightest of friends, almost as close as brothers. They attended prep school together in Washington, D.C., in 1939 for one year and they had played football together at West Point for three seasons. Among the Cadet players Romanek was known for his commanding presence and unflappability; Olds, a tackle who played on the line with Romanek, was renowned for being the toughest player on the squad. "If Robin ever wrestled an alligator," Romanek once told a friend, "I'd feel sorry for that alligator."

Olds' father, Major General Robert Olds, was a renowned pilot who had flown in World War I. Robert stayed in the service after the war to end all wars and taught aviation at Langley Airfield in Hampton, Virginia, where Robin grew up. As a boy, planes mesmerized Robin; he loved watching them take off and land at Langley. The sight of so much power always held his eyes, so much so that by age six he was already dreaming of one day flying a plane. "I'm going to become a pilot just like you," he announced to his father at dinner one evening.

"Well, you better be prepared to work for it," Robert Olds replied to his son. "Work hard and never back down to anybody, and you can do anything."

Some afternoons father and son would sit on their porch at their base home and watch the planes land. Little Robin liked to impress his father by identifying the approaching aircraft simply by listening to the distant sound of its engine. By age ten, he had such a discerning ear that he could tell the difference between the roar of the Pratt & Whitney radials in the Keystone bombers, the gentle hum of the Curtiss V-12 in the Curtiss P-6Es, and the loud belching and clacking of older planes, which were usually powered by antiquated Liberty engines.

At night, Robin enjoyed reading pulp magazines about World War I fighter aces, romantic as they were about how a battle unfolded. On these pages there was no mention of blood, or screams of horror, or grown men crying themselves to sleep at night. Inside these magazines were pictures and words that glorified the life and times of the fighter ace. His father tried to tell him what it was really like, that there was more to being a fighter pilot than winning medals and receiving kisses from beautiful blondes with heart-shaped mouths of red lipstick, but Robin had already made up his mind. He was going to follow in the footsteps of his father. This was one dream he wasn't going to let die on his pillow.

Other than flying with his dad, which Robin first did at the age of eight in an open cockpit byplane, Olds' other passion as a young boy was riding horses. Most days after school Robin would head to the stables at the base and tend to the horses that many of the officers rode. By age fifteen Robin had developed into a proficient rider himself, and a few officers at the base suggested that he'd make a fine candidate for the cavalry. But Olds paid no attention to them. Ever since he saw the 1934 movie *Flirtation Walk*, in which actor Dick Powell played a West Point officer, Olds had decided that his life path would lead to West Point. There on the Hudson Highlands he would become an officer, learn to fly and, if he could find the time, he might play football.

Olds reveled in the hand-to-hand combat that took place in the trenches of the football field. In 1937, his junior year at Hampton High and two years before he would go to prep school, Olds helped lead the team to the state title. By then, Olds had already developed a reputation for being the roughest player on the squad. At 6' 2", 190 pounds, Olds played tackle both on offense and defense. He even looked the part of a fierce player. With his short blond crew cut, his coat-hanger shoulders, and hands that were almost as big as catcher's mitts, he looked like he didn't even need to wear pads. His teammates often marveled at the intensity that flickered in his mischievous blue-gray eyes. He treated every play in practice—indeed, every drill in practice—like he was fighting with an enemy in a blood feud. When his temper reared, he had a mean streak that was so wicked even players on his own team feared him. Sometimes, it was as if a dark emotion suddenly sprang from the basement of his soul, and it usually left the person he was battling on the field wishing he'd never met Robin Olds. "Football ain't for sissies," Olds liked to tell his teammates. "You gotta be tough, and you gotta be a man. Don't ever back down, not to anyone."

Romanek looked at his watch. It read 6:30 A.M. Though his LCM was scheduled to land in a few minutes, they were still about six hundred yards from shore. Romanek eyed his men. Almost all of them were seasick, their faces as white as milk. They had been on the landing craft for about four hours and nearly everyone had vomited at least once. By this time Romanek's LCM had taken in so much water from the crashing of the waves that the men had to use their helmets to bail it out. Romanek and his men couldn't wait to get to the beach. Anything, they figured, was better than this.

They pushed closer. Through the black plumes of smoke that rose from the explosions on the beach, Romanek could see that the first wave of LCUPs had hit the beach—to his horror he saw that the infantry were being slaughtered. Entire LCUPs were getting blown to pieces by the German shore batteries, which clearly hadn't been disabled by naval gunfire. In a matter of heartbeats it was clear to Romanek that very little on Omaha Beach was going according to plan. Many of the rockets had fallen short of their targets, while others had simply missed. The Germans were firing artillery and machine guns from the bluff, and the soldiers on the beach were easy, inviting targets. Adding to the confusion were the rough seas and strong wind, which threw the landing crafts off course. Very few of the Allied units were landing where they were supposed to.

Romanek's landing craft continued to breast the waves, moving closer. At a distance of three hundred yards, Romanek could see that all the steel, X-shaped landing obstacles had been exposed because of the ebb tide. He looked up at the beach. The first wave of infantrymen, who had been scheduled to land three minutes ahead of Romanek's LCM, were instructed to gouge the German infantry. But instead, Romanek saw that many of the Americans had turned around and were diving for cover behind the obstacles. But there were few places to hide. They were under heavy machine-gun, mortar, rifle, and artillery fire. One after another, they fell to the sand, face-first.

As the LCM got within a hundred yards of the beach, Romanek noticed many soldiers were floating with the tide toward the beach, dead, their faces turned down to the water. He looked up at the beach and, through the haze of smoke from the grass fires that drifted down from the bluffs, could see that the beach had become a blood-stained killing field. Directly in front of Romanek, up on the cliffs, he saw a cherry red flicker of flame. A moment later there was a loud explosion on the beach, a black burst of smoke, then dozens of soldiers sprawled on the ground, all dead. "Everybody stay focused on what we need to do," Romanek yelled above the battle noise. "Let's just do our jobs and everything else will take care of itself."

Romanek and his men, who were all soaking wet, put on their assault gas masks. They expected a chemical attack, most likely the use of mustard gas, and a sealed mask would offer some protection. The infantrymen in the front of the LCM grabbed their rifles and machine guns and carbines. Romanek could hear the clack of bolts being drawn and rammed as the infantryman prepared to shoot. Incoming enemy fire started hitting the LCM—*ping, ping, ping*. The LCM began to slow.

At about fifty yards out, the LCM came to a stop, causing all the men to lurch forward. Several landing craft to Romanek's right and left were sinking or burning. The Coxswain in Romanek's LCM, a young coastguardsman, quickly moved from the protected tiller in the back of the LCM to the front to release the security clamps off the ramp. As he returned on the starboard upper walkway, bullets struck his head and chest. He fell, lifelessly, onto the troops in the LCM. He was the first man on Romanek's LCM to die on this day.

The square-faced ramp on the LCM came down. Everyone yelled, "Go, go, go!" But several German machine guns and artillery batteries were concentrating their fire on the ramp exit. Romanek and his men were still in the back of the LCM and now they could see their fellow soldiers being ripped apart by bullets. Blood and limbs and intestines flew through the air, the men falling forward in heaps. "We gotta get out of here," Romanek yelled to his engineers. Yet some of his men were frozen, unable to move. One soldier's head was blown off; another was killed when both of his legs were torn off his torso.

Romanek continued to yell to his men, telling them to push forward, to complete their mission. All the planning, all the months of training, all the miles they had traveled, it had all been done for this moment. But now? Now, even before Romanek had gotten off his LCM, more than half of his engineers and more than half of the infantrymen he'd been riding with were dead. Order was slipping away.

Still Romanek pushed forward. He could hear one bullet after the next clank off the metal sheeting of the LCM. "Get the hell out of here!" Romanek yelled again at his men. Many soldiers who'd been hit had fallen and were slumped over, draped in blankets of blood, impeding the path of Romanek and his engineers who were still alive. Finally, Romanek made it to the exit ramp. He was pulling several of the cases that stored the beach panel markers. He tossed them to a few of his men who'd made it to the water. Then Romanek, who was weighed down with about forty pounds of equipment and gear, jumped as fast and as far as he could into five feet of water.

In the closed cockpit of his P-38 Lightning, Olds couldn't stop looking down at the battle, his eyes drawn to the carnage taking place below. Flying low at about 500 feet, Olds and the other pilots from the 434th Fighter Squadron of the 479th Fighter Group buzzed over Omaha to protect the Allies in the sea and on the beach from attacks from the Luftwaffe, the German Air Force. But the Luftwaffe never appeared. "We're not doing anything up here," Olds said to another pilot over his radio. "Our boys are getting killed down there. God damn it, we've got to do something!"

"Remember our orders," Lt. Harold "Bud" Grenning, Olds' wingman, replied. "We're only here to take out the Luftwaffe. That's it."

"I know," said Olds, "but those are our boys down there."

Olds continued to roar over Normandy, flying through the clouds of smoke that billowed up from the battle. He itched to pull the trigger in his P-38, which was powered by two liquid-cooled engines, had a top speed of about 400 mph, and carried a 20 mm cannon and four machine guns in its nose. But Olds knew better than to disobey a direct order, so with an aching heart he just watched the destruction and deadly chaos unfold on Omaha beach. His frustration grew by the moment, knowing that guys like Henry Romanek, his friend and teammate, were down there dying.

The bullet pierced the left side of Romanek's chest even before he hit the water. It momentarily paralyzed him and robbed him of breath. It was as if a burning rod had just been shoved through his lungs. The gas mask container Romanek was wearing kept his head above the water, the air in it keeping his head afloat. He was in a daze. He couldn't focus on time, place, or purpose. His thoughts drifted through years of memories, with no order, like random dreams.

He knew that today was June 6, 1944. If there hadn't been a war—and if his course load hadn't been cut from four years to three at the U.S.

Military Academy—he knew that today would have been his graduation day from the Point. How he wished he could be back there right now, living in those crowded hours of happiness when he was a cadet and an Army football player. It seemed so long ago that he was lining up alongside Robin Olds in their leather helmets and crouching in a three-point stance. That was a different world and a different time when Romanek and Olds took on Navy and their star tailback Bill Busik in front of almost a hundred thousand fans in Philadelphia on an autumn afternoon in 1941. For a little more than two hours, Romanek and Olds were the biggest sports stars in America, as most of the nation had tuned their radios to the game and listened to the crackling account. Thinking about West Point caused Romanek to realize that he didn't want to lose his class ring, not here, not in five feet of freezing-cold water off the coast of France. His ring was as important to him as oxygen. He looked at his left hand in the water, saw the gleam of the thick gold band around his finger, and clenched his fist. "I can't lose my ring," he thought to himself. "I can't lose it. And I don't want to die here today."

After a few moments, Romanek began to regain his senses. He popped off his life belt so his feet could touch the sandy bottom of the water. He pulled off his gas mask container, stripped off his backpack and dropped most of his gear. He knew he had to get out of the water, but still felt sluggish, as if he could only move in slow motion. He could hear bullets hitting the water—*plop, plop, plop*—all around him. Every sound, every scent, seemed magnified. Romanek wanted to get to his men, his soldiers. He felt responsible for them; he could see many of them being cut down right before his eyes. Romanek had spent months talking to his platoon about the brotherhood of soldiering, about the kinship that bound all of them together, about the obligation each one had to look out for everyone in their band, but now Romanek was helpless to do that. "What's going to happen?" Romanek kept thinking to himself. "Who's going to show them where to go? Who's going to help them survive?"

Slowly, the fog lifted from his mind. Romanek marshalled his thoughts. He knew he had good sergeants; he trusted them, and he realized that they would take his place if he were to die here in the water now. That was the order of things. Ever since he first arrived at West Point, both in the classroom and on the football field, Romanek had been taught about the need for order, for preparedness. But now he was trapped in a situation that had no order, a situation that no man could really be prepared for.

Romanek tried to move his arms and legs and make his way to shore, but his strength had left him; it had leaked out through the holes in his chest and back. Still he tried to inch his way forward, but his body wouldn't respond to what his brain was telling it to do. He could now see blood—his own blood—rising up from the steel-gray water. "Oh God," he thought, "I *am* going to die here."

As Romanek wearily stood in five feet of water, running out of breath, a navy corpsman spotted him. Wearing a navy medic helmet that had a small red cross inside a white circle and a Red Cross armband, the corpsman came running from the beach and plowed into the water. There were numerous men floating in the sea who were already dead—too numerous to count—but there was Romanek, his head above water, gasping for air, still alive. The corpsman grabbed Romanek and, without a word, he put an arm around him and dragged him ashore. When they got to the beach, they lay huddled behind a metal beach obstacle as bullets continued to perforate the air around them. Romanek looked up at the corpsman, saw that his big eyes were wide with fear. He was a just a boy really, and even in Romanek's addled state he could tell that the young man was scared as all hell, as frightened as anyone Romanek had ever seen. "Let's head for cover," the corpsman yelled.

He grabbed Romanek's right hand and began to pull him across the gold, wet sand. Romanek tried to push with his legs as he was being dragged, but all of his strength was gone. They were trying to make it to the shingle, which was about two hundred yards away and would put them out of the line of machine-gun and mortar fire coming from the bluff, where the Germans had dug trenches. The shingle, named for the small stones that washed up there, was the first rise in the terrain. Located at the high water mark, the shingle on the western edge of Omaha Beach piled against a roadway that ranged in height up to five feet.

As the navy corpsman dragged Romanek across the open beach, they moved from beach obstacle to beach obstacle, ducking behind the steel rails to avoid being hit. Whenever they rested, both Romanek and the corpsman could hear the ping of slugs bouncing off the metal structures. They also heard the cries of the mortally wounded; some shrieked in pain, others pleaded for help. Body parts were scattered everywhere; arms, legs, and feet were lying in the sand.

While being pulled, all Romanek could do was watch the men behind him. Another wave of landing craft had just hit the beach, and, in some instances, not a single soldier had made it out of his boat. Men would fall as if they'd been hit by lightning as soon as their ramp came down; others would get blown into dozens of blood-splattering pieces. Romanek couldn't tell how many of his boys were now dead on the beach.

Supreme Allied Commander Dwight Eisenhower and his planners didn't know it, but the night before the attack, the Germans had reinforced the area with an extra division. On the night of June 5 the German 352nd Infantry Division had performed a training exercise at this precise location and were still there when the Allied troops invaded. Now death was everywhere; Romanek could even feel it tugging on his own soul. With every passing second he was losing more blood, and it was getting harder to breathe, harder to focus on anything but how badly he wanted to close his eyes and sleep.

The corpsman and Romanek finally reached the shingle. The corpsman laid Romanek down on the small rocks that had washed up there. Romanek, still struggling to take in air, again looked up at the corpsman's childish face and uttered his first words since being shot. "I played football at Army," Romanek said in a voice barely louder than a whisper. "I played in two Army-Navy games, and I never knew navy guys could be as nice as you. Thanks. The navy should be proud that they have a guy like you."

Moments later, Romanek was silent. He went into full-blown shock. He was swallowing his tongue and shaking violently, his body rattling with twitches. The corpsman, realizing what was happening, put a finger into Romanek's mouth, and pulled his tongue back. He then wrapped his arms tightly around him hoping to warm Romanek and save his life. This was all the corpsman could do, so he hugged Romanek as hard as he could. Still, Romanek stayed silent.

2

THE ARMY BOYS

FOUR YEARS EARLIER . . .

Carrying nothing but a wallet in his back pocket, the young man strode purposefully through the grimy catacombs of Penn Station in New York City. He had just stepped off the local train from Washington, D.C., and as he climbed the stairs that rose from the tracks below, he walked with the earnestness of someone who knew exactly where he was going—both in the next few minutes and in life. High above him, gold chandeliers hung from the vaulted ceiling. The morning sunshine rinsed through the station's towering arched windows, setting the station aglow in an almost heavenly light. Men in red caps flitted about the concourse, pushing carts of luggage past the Roman columns and the marble sculptures. Businessmen dressed in bowler hats and wing tips clawed their way through the rush-hour crush, many carrying a copy of the *New York Times*, whose front-page, triple-decker headline blared: RUSSIANS BATTLE RETIRING RUMANIANS; LAND TANKS FROM AIR IN OCCUPATION; CHAMBERLAIN DENOUNCES PEACE TALK. It was July 1, 1940, and on this Monday morning eighteen-year-old Robin Olds felt like he was about to step into a dream. The place he'd fantasized about ever since he was a little boy was just another fifty miles up the Hudson River Valley. He could hardly believe it: West Point was near.

As Olds wove his way toward the uptown subway train that would carry him toward a ferry that would take him across the Hudson River and drop him off at a train reserved for new cadets bound for West Point, Henry Romanek sat on the front steps at a friend's house in Fort Totten, Queens. For the past month Romanek, like Olds, had been counting down the days on the calendar, anticipating the arrival of this life-altering morning. The nineteen-year-old Romanek was waiting for his friend's father to come out of the house and drive him and his buddy to the Point.

"It's finally here," Romanek told his friend, Oliver Bucher, as they prepared to climb into the '38 Ford four door owned by Colonel Bucher. "I've got butterflies in my stomach."

Romanek and Olds both looked forward to renewing their friendship once they arrived at the Point. For six months of the previous year they had lived and studied together at Millard Prep in Washington, D.C., a school established to ready students for the entrance exams at the U.S. Military and Naval Academies. Founded by Homer B. Millard, a West Point graduate who fought in World War I, Millard Prep was an intense institution, a place that was as serious as a court room. Though the students didn't march and they weren't trained in firearms, they were given a taste of the disciplined lifestyle the service academies would demand. The days revolved around academic tutoring and studying; at night the lights went out in the dorms at precisely 10:00 P.M. The one reprieve came on Saturday evenings, when the school gates were opened and the students were free to leave campus. No student liked to skylark on Saturdays more than Olds, and when he and Romanek ventured off the campus and into the night, Olds often told his friend, "Let's see what kind of trouble we can rustle up."

Romanek and Olds both enrolled at Millard after graduating from high school, and they quickly bonded. They both loved sports—football in particular—and they both could talk for days about their hatred of Hitler. Their personalities, though opposite, meshed well: Romanek was steady and calm, and Olds was tempestuous and emotional. Eventually they started double-dating on the weekends, escorting their ladies to dances on the roof of the Army Navy Club in Arlington, Virginia. When they returned to campus, they'd invariably wind up wrestling in the hallway until someone—usually an irate teacher—told them to stop. Sometimes a whole group of boys would tussle, and more often than not, Olds and Romanek would be the last two standing. Their friendship never wavered, even as Olds and Romanek went after each other as if they were fighting a steel-cage match and the loser would be tossed to the lions.

When they got caught their punishment would be to do as many pushups as they could, right there on the spot. But neither minded this late-night exercise, because both Olds and Romanek enjoyed testing the limits of their physical strength the same way most people enjoyed a trip to the soda fountain. This was why they could raise so much hell on the football field, as the nation would soon find out.

Robin Olds was a hard-core, never-quit perfectionist, a trait he acquired from his father. Robin's mother died when he was four years old. As a single parent, Robert Olds taught his boy two lessons with drill-Sergeant intensity: always be tough and, no matter what the circumstances, always mind your manners. An imposing figure with big shoulders and a military-style crew cut, Colonel Olds' words were law, so Robin obeyed his father's demands without question. Consequently, around the airbase at Langley, young Robin had a reputation of being a courteous kid.

In his senior year of high school, Olds received a football scholarship offer from the Virginia Military Institute. Dartmouth also offered Olds a financial aid package if he would play football for them, but he turned both of them down to attend Millard and get ready for the West Point entrance exam. In his free time at Millard, Olds often listened to radio broadcasts of Hitler's speeches. He couldn't understand a lick of what he was saying, but the way he ranted and raved, Olds was convinced that Hitler was a madman.

One afternoon shortly after Germany invaded Poland in 1939, Olds got an idea. He was sitting in a classroom when the brainstorm came to him, and as soon as the bell rang he tore out of his seat and left the Millard campus with a wild hope in his heart: He wanted to become a pilot for the RCAF, the Royal Canadian Air Force. Olds figured this was the quickest way he could get overseas and join the fight. He walked into the recruiting office with a confident smile on his face and boldly asked where someone signed if he wanted to kill some Germans. He was handed an application, but as Olds filled it out an officer grew suspicious. Though Olds had a mature, developed physique, he still had a boyish face.

"How old are you, son?" asked the officer.

"Um, I'm twenty," he replied, even though he was actually eighteen.

"Sorry, son, you have to have a parent sign this consent form," Olds was told as the officer handed him the consent form. "Come back after you have a signature."

When Robin took the form to his father, the colonel hit the roof. "You're going to prep school and then the military academy," he told Robin. "End of discussion." Olds wanted to explain it all to his dad, how he had a plan, how he longed to fly in the war that raged in Europe, but instead he bit his lip and said nothing. It was no use trying to argue with his father. He'd have to wait until the United States got dragged into the conflict before he could begin his own personal battle with the Nazis. The only question was, how long would it be before that happened?

To make sure his boy won an appointment to the academy, Colonel Olds made several calls to congressmen asking them to support Robin's candidacy. (To gain entrance to both the U.S. Military and Naval Academies in the late 1930s, a prospective cadet or midshipman had to be appointed by a congressman—the same process that is still required today.) He finally found a representative from the state of Pennsylvania who agreed to make Robin his first alternate on the condition that Robin spend time living in his district. So after Olds graduated from Millard in the spring of 1940, he packed his bags and traveled alone to the southwestern corner of Pennsylvania, the heart of coal country, to a small burg called Uniontown, a place that to Olds seemed as remote as the dark side of the moon.

"It's awful," Olds told his dad over the phone after he arrived. "My God, it's the pits. It's going to be tough just to last a few weeks out here. There's nothing to do."

Olds lived in a tiny room at the YMCA and worked for an army recruiter. To earn extra money, he swept floors at various grocery stores. Sometimes on his way to work Olds saw miners who had just come up from the Pennsylvania earth, their faces plastered with dirt, their eyes devoid of hope. The place depressed Olds, and just when he thought he couldn't stand it one more day, he received a call from his father on the first of June. He had good news: Congressman Daniel Flood had decided to give Robin an appointment. His dad also said that he'd passed his entrance exam. "So it's official, son," Colonel Olds said, "You're going to West Point. You've been accepted."

Exactly one month after learning of his acceptance to the academy, Olds was making his way to West Point. After arriving in Penn Station, he took a subway uptown, then caught a ferry that took him across the Hudson River and dropped him off at the train station in Weehawken,

New Jersey. Because he'd grown up in a military family and because he knew as much about West Point as an outsider could, Olds didn't bother bringing any clothes or toiletries with him. The academy, he knew, would take care of all that.

In Weehawken, he boarded a reserved train for the last leg of his trip. As he took his seat, he noticed that one of his childhood friends, Gordon Steele, was sitting a few seats in front of him. Olds plopped down next to Steele, and the two of them talked excitedly of how these next four years would be the best of their lives. As the train rolled up the Hudson River Valley, past Bear Mountain, Olds knew West Point was close. In a matter of minutes he would become a Beast (meaning a new cadet) and he knew he'd be hazed by the upperclassmen. Some extremely difficult times awaited him, he understood that, but he was also sure of one other thing: He'd eat dirt before he would quit.

The four-door '38 Ford wove in and out of the midday traffic, motoring north up the Hudson River Valley along the Storm King Highway. It was approaching noon on a July afternoon that felt as hot as a kiln. As Henry Romanek sat in the backseat of the car, he looked out at the lush valley and silently wondered, "Will I ever go home again?" All Romanek had with him was a shaving kit in his right back pocket and a wallet in his left back pocket. Like Olds, he understood that once you stepped onto the grounds of the military academy, your civilian life was over. There was no point in packing a suitcase and bringing personal items. At the fighting factory of West Point, you were a body being molded into a solider. Period.

Romanek had been gearing up for this day ever since he first walked on the West Point grounds. A few months after that memorable stroll, Romanek joined the New Jersey National Guard at the age of eighteen during his senior year of high school, hoping it would make him a more attractive candidate. He was a whiz at math—it was as if numbers spoke secrets to him—so Romanek was assigned to an engineering regiment. He then began studying for the exam that would determine who would win the one appointment that the New Jersey National Guard could give out. Romanek hit the books for several weeks, but he didn't feel adequately prepared for the test, which would be administered at the beginning of the summer. But as he fretted, he was given some advice that would change the direction of his life: An officer at the national guard told Romanek that he should attend prep school at Millard in Washington. "It will help you win an appointment," the officer said. "They'll teach you everything you need to know to pass the entrance exam."

Romanek took his word. After he graduated from high school in June, Romanek rode a train to Washington and enrolled at Millard. One of the first students he met there was Robin Olds, who lived just down the hall in the same dorm.

As is the case with most kids, leaving home wasn't easy for Romanek. Carl Romanek, his father, immigrated to the United States from the Austrian Empire prior to World War I. When Henry was two, his father moved his family out of their home in Brooklyn to build a house in Rutherford, New Jersey, and a new life. It was a three-story home in which three families lived; the Romaneks (Henry, his father, mother, and three younger brothers) occupied the top floor. The three families—all Polish—had a business together building and selling wicker furniture. They didn't make great money during the Depression, but they got by better than most.

One day, when Henry was seventeen and hoping to attend the Military Academy, his mother Marianne asked him why he wanted to be a solider. "There's a war coming, Mom," he said. "I'd much rather be an officer than a private." This made sense to Romanek's mother, because she knew that there was trouble brewing with the Germans in her homeland. Born on a farm outside of Posnan, Poland, Marianne came to the United States at the age of fifteen to escape an arranged marriage. Her father died young, and Marianne was the oldest of six children. Because Marianne's family needed a man to work their farmland, the community leaders arranged for Marianne to marry a young Polish man who lived down the road. When Marianne's mother got wind of this plan, she was irate and quickly fired off a letter to her relatives in Brooklyn, begging them to take care of her oldest daughter. About a month later, Marianne was on a boat steaming for Ellis Island. She moved into her aunt's home in Brooklyn, which served as a boarding house for Italian, Polish, and German laborers. Most of these men, who were recruited to come to the States by the U.S. government, were paid a dollar a day. Some of the more naïve believed they were digging for gold under the streets of New York City; in reality, they were carving out space for New York's subway system.

Marianne's job at the boarding house was to make the beds and prepare the food. She kept in touch with her family that she'd left behind, occasionally sending money and bundles of goods to her mother and siblings. When the letters she received from home started detailing the German's aggression—in 1939, Hitler's army marched right over her family's farmland on its way to Warsaw—she knew that world stability was crumbling. She felt certain that one day the United States, and her boy, would be forced into action. So when she heard young Henry say that he wanted to be an officer rather than an enlisted man, she didn't argue with him. It made perfect sense.

All throughout high school, Romanek, like most kids in his neighborhood, held a few jobs to help his family make ends meet. He cleaned city rest rooms, painted lines on city tennis courts, and pumped gas for 16 cents an hour—which is exactly what a gallon of gas went for in 1937. Romanek's favorite job in high school was folding newspapers. Though the task was as exciting as watching paint dry, it was special to Romanek for one reason: He performed it with fifteen other members of the Rutherford High football team, his band of brothers.

Romanek hoped to play football at the U.S. Military Academy—and that goal suddenly seemed possible when, one afternoon in May 1940, Romanek received a letter from Senator William Barbour of New Jersey. Romanek had graduated from Millard just weeks earlier, and now, as he opened the letter, his hands were shaking visibly. "This is it," Romanek thought to himself. He then read the news: Senator Barbour was awarding his second appointment to Romanek. The letter also told him that he had passed the entrance exam and that his application had been accepted by the admissions office at the Point. Romanek had never felt so happy; he ran outside shouting to his neighbors that he was West Point bound. (Senator Barbour's first appointment, Romanek later found out, went to a young man named Ernie Barker, who in 1942 would become the first of Romanek's friends to be killed during pilot training.)

About a month after learning that he would become a cadet, Romanek sat in the back seat of his friend's car on his way to West Point. The car sped north along the Storm King Highway, winding along the Hudson River. The water sparkled and glistened in the summer sun. As he gazed out the window, Romanek's heart raced with anticipation. His boyhood was over, Romanek knew that, but now his life was teeming with possibility. The place that would transform him into a man was just a few odometer clicks away. The Point was close.

3

THE NAVY BOYS

AT THE CROWDED TRAIN depot in Pasadena, California, two young men gathered with their families. It was the morning of June 27, 1939, a morning fraught with beginnings and endings for Bill Busik and Hal Kauffman. In a few minutes the two nineteen-year-olds would step onto a train and leave their hometown, riding the rails across the country to the U.S. Naval Academy in Annapolis, Maryland. It seemed a universe away, which was why twenty friends and family members of Busik and Kauffman turned out to bid them farewell on this golden California morning. Their mothers, wearing their fanciest Sunday dresses and hats, were overwhelmed with sadness. Both holding Brownie cameras, which were made of molded plastic and were one of the first simplified cameras ever invented, they snapped one picture after the next of their young boys as they stood on the wooden platform, trying to freeze this moment in time.

As Busik and Kauffman waited at the whistle stop for the steam-engine train to push into town, each took comfort in the fact that they wouldn't be alone on their odyssey. They had met a year earlier at Meade Prep in San Marino, California. During their six months of intensive studying at Meade, a school much like Millard Prep in Washington, D.C., which was established to prepare students for the U.S. Military and Naval Academies, Busik and Kauffman became good friends. On the weekends they'd double date, escorting their ladies to movies like *You Can't Take it With You*, starring James Stewart, and *The Adventures of Robin Hood*, featuring Errol Flynn as the Prince of Thieves. Or they'd hop into Kauffman's '28 Ford convertible and take their dates on lazy moonlight drives down Pasadena's stately Orange Grove Boulevard, where some of the grandest hotels and mansions in all of America stood—the Wrigley Mansion, the Gamble House, and other breathtaking homes on Millionaires' Row. This majestic boulevard was a playground for the wealthy, a strip of asphalt that Busik and Kauffman liked to visit on Friday nights to see how the rich and powerful kicked back.

Bill Busik grew up in a working-class neighborhood in Pasadena on Atchison Street. His father, Jack, was a line-type operator for the *Pasadena Star News*. Jack had been an editor at a paper in Minnesota in his younger years, but when he and his wife, Lillian, honeymooned in Pasadena in 1909, they liked it so much they decided to stay. Pasadena in the early 1900's could do that to you. Once a farming community, Pasadena had plenty of wide-open spaces—and plenty of sunshine—for Midwesterners looking to escape a cold climate. Jack Busik was a farmer by nature and spoke as softly as a summer breeze, but he was also as tough as rawhide. He taught his four boys the lesson of responsibility at a young age by buying them a thousand fertilized chicken eggs and storing them in four large incubators down in their basement. It was up to Busik and his three brothers to handle the eggs and to turn them at the appropriate times. As soon as the eggs hatched, Busik and his brothers would move the chickadees to a barn across the street and care for them. When the chickens were old enough, the brothers Busik sold each one for a dime. They also hawked golden bantam corn that they raised in a field behind the barn. A dozen ears went for two bits, or 25 cents. At the end of one summer, young Bill had sold enough chickens and corn to have $5 worth of coins clanking in his pockets, which to him felt like more money than was possible to spend.

But around the neighborhood, Busik was known more for his love of sport than his salesmanship. By the time he was in high school, he had all the characteristics of a commanding athlete, even down to the way he walked. In the school hallways and on the sidelines of a football field, Busik moved along with the cool strut of a mountain lion, each step more effortless than the last. At 5' 11" and 185 pounds, Busik had the sturdy build of a blacksmith, and he was endowed with easy, graceful strength. Like most boys his age in California, Busik parted his dark brown hair to the side and slicked it back with pomade. He had big, shiny brown eyes. But the one thing that everyone noticed about Busik was that, no matter what the circumstances, he always seemed to be smiling, and his perfect white teeth had a way of catching the sun and reflecting his happiness. It was a wonderful smile—all of his classmates agreed—and when it flared it made girls weak in the knees.

One of Busik's best friends growing up was a skinny kid who lived a few blocks over named Jackie, who was black. Bill and Jackie first met when they were in kindergarten. At recess the two would often shoot marbles or kick around the soccer ball together. They were as inseparable as shadows. Pasadena in the 1920s had no segregation laws on the books, but the separation of races was still strict. The public swimming pool in Brookside Park, for example, was only open to blacks one day a week, and movie theaters had separate sections for blacks and whites. But the public schools weren't segregated, and as young boys Bill and Jackie simply saw each as that: young boys. Even though their families lived in segregated neighborhoods, young Bill and Jackie never once talked to each other about the color of their skin. To them, it simply wasn't an issue.

In their junior year at Pasadena Junior College, which was the equivalent of a four-year high school, Bill and Jackie tried out for the football team together. In preseason camp Jackie quickly emerged as the star of the squad. He had astonishing quickness; if you hesitated just for a moment as a defender, he'd cruise right by you. Playing tailback in the single wing, Jackie ran and juked like a cornered rabbit, and that's what they started calling him: Jack the Rabbit. But a week before Pasadena's first game in 1936, the Rabbit broke his ankle in a scrimmage. Bill, playing the same position as the Rabbit, had struggled during camp and was buried on the B squad. But when Jackie went down with his injury, Bill was elevated to the traveling squad. Still, he didn't expect to play in Pasadena's first game at Compton Junior College, a team that was the defending state champions.

When the first-string tailback failed to consistently move the ball on offense against Compton, the Pasadena coach benched him. Same thing happened to the second-stringer—and the third. All the while on this hot afternoon, Busik sat on the bench chewing orange slices and sucking on sugar cubes, typical energy food at the time which the trainer supplied the players on the sidelines. Finally, late in the second quarter, the coach told

Busik to stop eating and get in the game and return a punt. He grabbed his leather helmet, snapped his chinstrap, and excitedly ran onto the field. On the first play of his high school football career, Busik caught the punt cleanly at his own 1 yard line—he should have let it roll into the end zone—and returned the ball 10 yards. When he was tackled, one defender hit him high and one hit him low. The defender who dove at his feet had broken one of Busik's toes on his right foot. In spite of the pain, Busik stayed in the game at tailback and proceeded to astonish his coaches.

The tailback called the plays in Pasadena's version of the single wing, the prevailing offensive alignment in the late '30s and '40s that featured four backs—a tailback, fullback, quarterback, and wingback. The tailback lined up about 4 yards behind the center. The quarterback positioned himself a yard behind the tackle on the strong side. The fullback stood next to the tailback about 2 yards away; he could line up on either side of the tailback depending on the play call. All three backs crouched with their hands on their knees. The remaining back, the lone wingback, who gave the formation its name, set up in a three-point stance just off the tight end's outside foot. There were no wide receivers.

On his first play, Busik, now in at tailback, called his own number on an off-tackle run. He scampered for 20 yards—Pasadena's longest play of the day. Ten plays later Pasadena scored a touchdown. For the rest of the afternoon, Busik seemed to scorch the earth as he ran, sprinting around and through the Compton defense. With his running and passing, he went on to lead Pasadena to victory over the defending state champs.

When Jackie returned to the team at midseason, he and Bill were interchangeable at tailback and fullback. They were an unstoppable duo, tossing passes to each other and blocking for each other. At the end of the season, after Pasadena had been upset in the state playoffs, the team voted for its MVP. It wasn't even close: Bill won it over Jackie in a landslide.

After football season ended, Bill and Jackie often played baseball together, just the two of them. After school they'd head out to one of the many ballfields in the area and at first they'd just play catch. Though they received many quizzical looks as the two of them, each carrying a bucket of baseballs, walked side-by-side on the sidewalk—as in most parts of the country, blacks and whites didn't interact frequently in Pasadena—Bill and Jackie would just smile at whoever was making odd faces in their direction. The bond of their friendship, which was forged on the fields of sport, ran deeper than skin color, and they never allowed any of their friends or anyone else to undermine their special relationship.

Once they'd finally reached the ballfield, Bill would usually pitch to Jackie at bat. Bill loved pitching to Jackie; it was one of his favorite things to do when he was in high school. It wasn't that Bill enjoyed the fact that Jackie usually crushed the ball. It was that Bill knew he was witnessing something rare and he took pains to make sure that these images of Jackie hitting the horsehide became etched in his mind. It was as if Jackie was swinging a knight's sword, the way he wielded that baseball bat. And even after the sun had gone down, Bill and Jackie would stay on the field together, as Jackie would send one moonshot hissing into the dark after the next, no matter how fast, low, or high Bill pitched.

"You're one of the swellest guys I know," Jackie told Bill one day at Pasadena Junior College in 1938. "You're going to do terrific things in your life, Bill. I know you will."

"So will you, Jackie," Bill replied. "I believe in you. Just don't take any guff from anybody. Be yourself and everything will turn out fine for you."

Bill was right. Nine years later, in 1947, Bill's good friend Jackie Robinson would become the first black player in Major League Baseball history.

Ever since junior high, Busik had been interested in the U.S. Naval Academy. He often listened to their football games on the radio in his living room in Pasadena. Lying on the floor, Busik would close his eyes and imagine he was there in the stadium, watching the action, joining in with the roar of the crowd, seeing all the midshipmen in the stands in their dress whites. Just the name of the naval academy sounded glamorous to him; it conveyed some magical faraway place where everyone was smart and strong. Busik, like most boys in California his age, never considered the implications of combat. Unlike Robin Olds and Henry Romanek and other boys who lived on the East Coast, Busik and his buddies rarely talked about Hitler. There were fewer new European immigrants living in California in 1938, and so to Busik the rumblings being generated by Hitler seemed a distant thunder—a storm cloud that Busik and his family couldn't yet see on the horizon. When Busik was being recruited by Navy assistant coach Edgar "Rip" Miller to come to the academy and play football and basketball, war was the last thing on Busik's mind.

Busik knew all about Rip Miller. Every football fan in the country did. On October 18, 1924, Miller played on the offensive line for Notre Dame as the Irish faced Army at the Polo Grounds in Manhattan. Up in the press box that day was a newspaper writer for the *New York Herald Tribune* named Grantland Rice. After the game, which Notre Dame won 13–7, Rice penned what would become the most famous lead in the history of sportswriting. "Outlined against a blue-gray October sky, the Four Horsemen rode again," Rice wrote. "In dramatic lore they are known as Famine, Pestilence, Destruction and Death. These are only aliases. Their real names are Stuhldreher, Miller, Crowley and Layden."

The Four Horsemen were halfbacks Don Miller and Jim Crowley, quarterback Harry Stuhldreher, and fullback Elmer Layden. Rice also dubbed Notre Dame's offensive line as the "Seven Mules," which included Rip Miller at right tackle. Being a "mule" made Miller as recognizable as any college offensive lineman had ever been, and he liked to joke that the eleven starters on offense had repeatedly voted that the "Seven Mules" were more important than the "Four Horseman." "It's funny how that vote of those eleven guys turned out," Miller often said. "The Seven Mules always won over the Four Horsemen, by a count of roughly seven to four."

Miller graduated from Notre Dame in 1925 and spent the next season as an assistant coach at Indiana. The following year he joined the football staff at Annapolis. When he began recruiting Busik, he served as the team's offensive line coach. Miller didn't travel by rail to Pasadena to woo Busik; instead they corresponded by mail. "We think you would be a great addition to the naval academy," Miller wrote in one letter to Busik. "You're the kind of outstanding young man that, one day, will be a leader in our country."

Miller was a pigskin revolutionary, as he developed the first sophisticated recruiting operation in college football history. Called the Bird-Dog System, Miller relied on graduates of the U.S. Naval Academy, former sailors, and friends of his to act as his eyes and ears all over the nation. These scouts lived on the East Coast, the West Coast, the plains, the deep South, the Southwest—they were, simply, everywhere. If there was a good high school football player in their area who had the grades to get into the academy, Miller knew about him.

Most of Miller's scouts made their living in the sales business, including Abe Stacey. A 1922 graduate of the U.S. Naval Academy who worked for Wilson Sporting Goods in Pasadena, Stacey attended football games all over southern California. He carried a little black notebook in his back pocket and scribbled notes on the players he saw. Sometimes, when he saw a player who really impressed him, he'd write so feverishly that his hand would cramp. One such player who had him writing excitedly was Busik.

After watching a game at Pasadena Junior College, Stacey approached Busik, intrigued by his rugged running ability.

"What do you know about the naval academy?" Stacey asked Busik.

"I know a lot about the Army-Navy football game," replied Busik. "To me it's always the biggest game of the year."

"Let me tell you something," Stacey said. "If you want to go to the academy, and I think you're a good candidate, you need to study the right subjects and get yourself to prep school. Do that and you'll pass the entrance exam, and we'll help you get an appointment."

Busik was almost speechless. Hearing these words was like finding out he had a chance to guarantee his slot in heaven. Stacey also discussed the naval academy with Busik's family. Sitting in their living room, Stacey explained what the academy looked like, detailing its vast and beautiful lawns on the banks of the Severn River. He also assured the Busiks that the government would pay for the tuition. No one in the Busik clan had ever attended college before, so this sounded like a deal of a lifetime to Busik's parents. In fact, as John Busik sat there listening to Stacey with rapt attention, he smiled as broadly and as proudly as he ever had before. That his boy might be able to get a free college education made him feel as lucky as a man who just got dealt four aces in a game of poker.

In the late 1930s, there were two ways to gain admission to the U.S. Naval Academy after passing the entrance exam: A candidate could either be appointed by a congressman, or he could join the navy and try to win an appointment out of the fleet by taking a series of competitive examinations. Following Stacey's advice, Busik enrolled at Meade Prep after graduating from Pasadena Junior College and started taking his studies more seriously.

After Busik's father dropped him off at Meade, one of the first people he met was Hal Kauffman, who was assigned to the same dormitory as Busik. The two hit it off immediately. Kauffman, who was from Glendale, California, had read about Busik's exploits on the football field in the newspaper. "You and Robinson were a great one-two punch for Pasadena," Kauffman told Busik. "I'm surprised you guys didn't win the state championship. Maybe someday you and I will be playing together at Navy—if we can get in."

For six months, Busik and Kauffman prepared for the three-day entrance exam. Information tended to stick in Busik's mind like glue, and when he finally took the test at Los Angeles City Hall, it was a breeze. He passed, no problem. Busik had joined the marine reserve a year earlier, and soon after aceing the exam, he was awarded a fleet appointment. Finally, it became official: Bill Busik was going to the U.S. Naval Academy.

Hal Kauffman could be a tornado of a boy. Nearly every day after high school, at the urging of his father Vern, Hal would walk to the orange orchard located down the street and fight one of his classmates. Though Hal was as gentle and sweet as any boy in his eighth grade class, he raised his fists because his dad demanded that he go to the orchard and "toughen up." Hal got his share of black eyes and cracked ribs, but in the process he learned what it meant to be a man—just as his father had hoped.

Little Hal always had a strong will; if he hadn't, he would have died years earlier. When he was born in West Portal, Colorado, in 1920, baby Hal refused to drink the breast milk from his mother Rose. When she tried to give him cow's milk, he refused that as well. As he lay in his crib near death, his father Vern purchased a goat as a last resort. He milked the goat in his backyard, put it in a bottle, and then gave it to his baby son. Little Hal drank it, and for the first few months of his life, all Hal consumed was the milk of the goat that lived in his backyard.

Vern Kauffman was one of the preeminent engineers of his day. In the early 1920s he helped oversee the construction of the Moffat Tunnel in Colorado, which, when it opened in 1928, became the longest railroad tunnel in the western hemisphere. In 1927 the Kauffmans moved to Glendale, California, in a home that was a few miles away from the L.A. Coliseum, which had been built only four years earlier. Vern had been transferred to Los Angeles to help design the Pacific Coast Highway. It was an important job, but Vern considered his real calling to be raising his son. Whenever Hal came home bloodied from a fight in the orange orchard—Hal never would have raised his fists if his father hadn't told him to—his father would take him in the backyard and the two would box a few rounds in their bare knuckles. If my boy is going to get his ass kicked once today, the father told the son, then he may as well get a whuppin' twice. Vern was a small man, only 5' 5" and 160 pounds, but he could be as ornery as an aroused python when he fought his son. Soon, Hal quit losing fights in the orange orchard.

Unlike Busik, Kauffman was not a natural athlete. He ran track and played football at Glendale High, but he was an overachiever who got by on courage and determination rather than on inherited talent. At 5' 9" and 160 pounds, he had a thin frame. His brown eyes were the size of bullets and he had chubby cheeks, which gave him the appearance of someone who hadn't yet shed all of his baby fat. Though he didn't have movie-star good looks, Kauffman intrigued many girls—mostly because he had a tenor voice that the gentler sex loved to listen to.

On weekends during high school Kauffman's mother would drive him to downtown Los Angeles where he'd sing at different social events for teenagers. Kauffman was usually quiet, sensitive, and introspective, but once he stepped on stage all of his shyness left him. By the time he was a junior in high school, in 1937, he was performing songs that were popular on the radio, hits like "Pennies from Heaven," by Bing Crosby. Kauffman's sweet voice tugged on the heartstrings, and he glowed every time he stepped on the stage; people could see the happiness welling up and shining inside of him. He thought someday that he might become a professional singer, but that idea was quashed the moment his father found out about it. No son of his, he made quite clear to Hal, was going to be a sissy and sing for a living. And with that one pronouncement, Kauffman's hopes of a singing career came to an abrupt end.

What made Kauffman a special singer was the fact that he put his heart into every performance. Kauffman prided himself, in fact, on being big-hearted. In the summer of 1936, when he was fifteen years old, Kauffman's caring nature was put to the test. Always a determined young man, Kauffman had won a trip to Yosemite National Park by selling more *Saturday Evening Posts*, *Country Gentlemans*, and *Ladies Home Journals* than any other kid in the Los Angeles area. On the second day at the park, Kauffman was walking along the Merced River, enjoying the scenery and the serenity of the morning, when he heard a scream for help. Kauffman looked into the river, and what he saw caused his pulse to quicken: A little boy was bobbing up and down in the water, struggling to breathe. It was clear that the boy, who looked to be five or six, was drowning.

Kauffman tore off his shirt and darted into the cold water, sprinting as fast as he could. "Hang on, I'll get you!" Kauffman yelled to the boy. Kauffman quickly swam to the boy. The water wasn't very deep—it was only about six feet—but it was flowing rapidly. The boy was in the current and drifting downstream, struggling to keep his head above the water.

"Help me!" the boy screamed as he flailed his arms. "Mommy, help me!"

Kauffman kicked his legs furiously and plowed his arms through the water, performing the breaststroke. Just before Kauffman reached the boy, he went under again, this time sinking to the river bottom. Kauffman took a deep breath and dove, keeping his eyes open. Frantically, he looked all around where he thought the boy had gone down, but Kauffman was running out of air. He didn't want to pop back up for another gulp of oxygen—he feared that he'd never find the boy if he did that—so he continued his underwater search. Just as Kauffman was about to give up and surface, he saw the boy's body, limp and lifeless, on the river bottom. Kauffman quickly grabbed him and shot up to the surface.

"Come on, you're going to make it!" yelled Kauffman.

Moments later, while they were still in the water, the boy coughed, water squirting from his mouth. Kauffman put the boy on his back, told him to hang on tight, and towed him to the shore. Just as they crawled out of the water, the boy's parents came running up to Kauffman, concern etched on their faces. Kauffman explained what had happened, how he'd just plucked the boy from the wild river. But before he could finish, the parents hugged the breathless Kauffman.

After resting by the water for a long spell, Kauffman continued his walk, feeling like a new person. The experience of saving a life had given him a rush, almost like he'd taken a drug. It also made him respect the absolute power of water. When he returned home after his trip, he started spending more time at the beach, surfing or just sitting on the sand and staring out into the ocean, the crashing and receding of the tide as soothing to him as a lullaby. "Maybe I should join the navy," Kauffman often thought as he sat on the beach. "Or maybe I should go to the naval academy."

Two months after saving the boy, Kauffman was in his tenth grade English class on a Friday afternoon when he noticed a girl named Lois Bradburg sitting in a desk by the window. Bradburg was new to the school and Kauffman had never seen her before. As he looked at her, the sun bounced off her long blond hair, giving the appearance of an angelic light framing her flowing tresses. From his seat Kauffman could also see her eyes. They were the color of the bluest ocean, and right away Kauffman was bewitched. After class he convinced a friend to introduce him to Lois. For years after, Kauffman would swear it was the best day of his life.

In 1937, Kauffman, now a junior in high school, began visiting naval ships that were moored close to his home, trying to learn as much about life in the navy as possible. On these ships, he finally arrived at a decision about his future: He was going to apply to the naval academy. "I want to be an officer in the navy," Kauffman told his father. "I know it's a long way from home, but the naval academy just seems right for me." His dad told him he thought it was a fine idea.

To make himself an attractive candidate, he ran for senior class president of Glendale High in 1938—and won. He succeeded Frankie Albert, a star quarterback at Glendale who would later become an All-Pro with the San Francisco 49ers. An overwhelming majority of classmates voted for Kauffman because he had the reputation of being authentic. He had no enemies. Though he liked to keep to himself, it seemed as if everyone considered him a friend. Maybe this was because there was a sweetness to his character that was rare among the boys in his high school. At heart, he was still a singer who liked to croon about emotions. He figured he'd always be this way.

After graduating from Glendale High, Kauffman enrolled at Meade Prep to study for the Naval Academy entrance exam. While at Meade, Kauffman had only one regret. One evening, as he was taking a break from studying, Kauffman felt like he needed to burn some energy. He was feeling frisky and figured that a friendly sparring match with his buddy Bill Busik was just what he needed. So Kauffman ran up and down the halls yelling that he was challenging Busik to a boxing match, and if anyone cared to make a wager on the bout, well, he wouldn't stop him. This was all news to Busik, but never being one to shy away from some friendly competition, he met Kauffman later that night in the gymnasium, a night that neither of them would ever forget.

At first, both Kauffman and Busik thought they would just hit each other lightly, nothing serious. But moments after they raised their bare fists, with the adrenaline and testosterone flowing, things got serious. First Kauffman hit Busik with a light punch. Then Busik smacked Kauffman on the chin with a swing that nobody in attendance would have described as soft. The two traded a few more blows, hard punches all of them. The boys who were watching yelled in approval, prodding Busik and Kauffman to tear each other apart. But then, after just a minute or so of sparring, Busik landed a right on Kauffman's jaw that seemed to pack the power of a thunderbolt, knocking Kauffman out cold. Busik stood over his friend, blood dripping from nose, looking very much like a seasoned prizefighter.

"We're going to have a rematch when we get to the naval academy," Kauffman joked to Busik after coming to his senses. "How come I never saw that punch coming?"

Four months later, after they had both passed their entrance exams and won their appointments, the friends readied to board the train that would ferry them eastward. When the train finally arrived at the Pasadena depot, the conductor yelled, "All Aboard!" The boys smiled for a few more photos, hugged their mothers one last time, then stepped into their car. Sticking their heads out the windows, they waved good-bye to their friends and families who stood on the platform. Their mothers each waved white handkerchiefs above their heads and, with tears dripping from their eyes like candle wax, shook them frenetically. The train started pulling away. Busik and Kauffman kept waving. But soon their mothers were specks in the distance. Soon they could no longer see home.

When Pasadena finally faded from view, Busik and Kauffman took a long look at each other. They didn't have to say a word: The journey of their lives had begun.

4

ARRIVAL IN ANNAPOLIS

FOR FIVE DAYS and four nights, Bill Busik and Hal Kauffman rode an iron horse across the belly of the nation. Sitting next to each other in their crowded rail car, they broached almost every subject imaginable. They talked of how they both enjoyed the movie *Wuthering Heights*, which had hit theaters six weeks earlier. They chatted about how they each wished to visit the World's Fair going on in New York, to see a vision of the future that included nationwide television broadcasts, suburban homes built with plywood, and a transcontinental highway system. They also debated whether or not gangster Al Capone, who was up for parole in a few months but was now ill with third-stage syphilis, should be let out of the pokey. Yet no matter what twists and turns their conversations took, the stream of their thoughts always seemed to veer back to one topic: what the next few years would be like at the academy.

When they weren't talking they'd look out the window and watch the land flow by. On their first night they saw, there in the pale moon-light, the Western hills, which seemed to stretch all the way up to the North Pole. When they rolled across the prairie of Nebraska they spied farm houses with sagging porches, all looking as if an overweight farmer had spent too much time sitting on his rocker in the middle of the wooden planks. As they neared the Mississippi River, they saw what they swore was the greenest grass on earth, framed by a bright blue sky. And as the train crossed into western Virginia, they passed into the teeth of a summer storm, which sent sprays of lightning crackling to the ground all around the hurtling locomotive.

The train stopped every few hours at small towns and big cities alike to pick up and drop off passengers, which only made the cross-country journey seem longer than it really was. And it didn't speed up at night when both Busik and Kauffman struggled to fall asleep; their minds just wouldn't shut off. Though the train made a lulling sound as it swayed and chugged eastward on the slender iron lines, Busik and Kauffman were preoccupied with the fact that they had left the familiarity of home. No longer could they predict what the next day would bring, a realization that was as troubling as it was exciting. So at night, while the train clickety-clacked along the rails, they let their imaginations run wild, daydreaming about their new lives at the naval academy and how they'd fit in. In these quiet moments, as both Busik and Kauffman laid in a bunk in their sleeper car, they both made a promise to themselves: No matter what hardships the future threw at them, they wouldn't quit the academy. They both knew that in the U.S. Naval Academy Class of '39, which had graduated one month earlier, only two-thirds of its original members had made it through the rigors of the academy and received their officer's bars; the others either quit or were kicked out.

"I'd rather shoot myself than be forced to leave the academy," Busik said to Kauffman one evening. "I'll do whatever it takes." For the rest of that night Busik and Kauffman looked out the window, gazing at the clusters of stars that looked like a cooling fire against the dark sky.

Finally, on the afternoon of July 1, 1939, the train pulled into the station at Baltimore, Maryland. Busik and Kauffman both grabbed their small suitcases—unlike Olds and Romanek, they needed a few changes of clothes for the train ride—and then hopped on the Toonerville Trolley for the last leg of their journey. The trolley carried them out of Baltimore, across eastern Maryland, across the Severn River, down Main Street in Annapolis, and right into the Yard at the naval academy. This was the first time that either Busik or Kauffman had ever seen the academy in person, and the sight of the place made them go bug-eyed. As they panned the two hundred acres—about seventy city blocks—on the southern bank of the Severn River, they saw old stone buildings and sprawling lawns that were studded with oaks, maples, and walnut trees. To them, the academy represented greatness—and more important, the chance to achieve greatness. Maybe they were getting ahead of themselves, but at this moment, at this juncture in their young lives, if felt right to dream big about all they could someday do.

When they stepped off the trolley, Busik and Kauffman were greeted with a vigorous handshake extending from the arm of Rip Miller, the Navy assistant coach who had recruited Busik and who had told Kauffman he should try out for the team. Miller arranged for them to stay together in a local boarding house while they took their three-day physical exam. Busik and Kauffman had passed rigorous physicals before they had left California to make sure that the doctors at the naval academy wouldn't find anything that could lose them their appointment. So that night neither fretted about passing the exam as they were fed their first home-cooked meal in what felt like weeks. It was made by the head of the boarding house, a woman who was married to a former Annapolis graduate who had died in World War I. After their chicken and potatoes dinner, Busik and Kauffman retreated to separate bedrooms and had their first good night of sleep since leaving home.

The next morning the heat index in Annapolis rose rapidly. By the time Busik was walking over to Bancroft Hall for his physical, the blinding midday sun was cooking the academy's grounds. A California boy, Busik was accustomed to warm weather, but he wasn't used to the kind of heat that sticks to you. His physical was scheduled on the fourth floor of Bancroft, and by the time he climbed all those stairs, his shirt was soaked with sweat. Not only that, his heart rate was accelerated. When the doctor measured Busik's temperature, he looked at Busik as if he was in the wrong place, because no potential midshipman could have a temperature and blood pressure that high and hope to gain admittance. "I'm just nervous," Busik told the doctor. "And I've never felt heat like this."

The doctor then noticed that Busik had a deviated septum. Because the leather football helmet that he wore in high school didn't have a facemask or any bars that protected his face, Busik had broken his nose at least three times in games during his high school days. "Sorry son, but you won't be attending the naval academy with that nose," the doctor told Busik. "If you have a deviated septum, you can't pass this physical."

Terrified at the prospect of failing before he even started his naval career, Busik asked the doctor if he could use his phone. He called Rip Miller and, with his heart jackhammering, told him that he'd flunked his physical. "Don't worry," Miller said into the phone. "Go down to Franklin Street. It's a short walk. There's a doctor down there who's my friend. He'll check you over to see if you really have problems with your nose and your temperature."

Busik beat it down to Franklin Street. All kinds of terrible thoughts floated through his mind. "What if I have to get back on the train and go home? What will I tell my parents? What will my dad say? What will Jackie think?" When Busik finally walked through the door of the doctor's office, he'd convinced himself that his naval career was over. In the examination room the doctor told Busik to calm down and take some deep breaths. "Everything will be okay," the doctor told Busik in a parental voice. "I've got some advice for you. When you go back to Bancroft Hall, you'll get to the first deck and there's a scuttlebutt there. Use it."

"What's a deck and a scuttlebutt?" asked Busik, genuinely confused.

"The deck is the navy term for the floor you're on and a scuttlebutt is a drinking fountain," replied the doctor. "On the first deck drink that nice cold water from the scuttlebutt and rest. Then go up the ladder . . . er, the stairs, and on the second deck use the scuttlebutt there. Keep doing that until you get to the fourth deck."

Still feeling an anxious knot in his stomach, Busik followed the doctor's advice and returned to Bancroft Hall. He took sips from the water fountain on each level of the hall and by the time he reached the fourth floor his temperature and blood pressure were normal. But there was still the matter of the deviated septum. "I'm telling you son, this is a real problem," the naval academy doctor forcefully told Busik. "There's nothing I can do about this. My hands are tied by the regulations."

Nearly despondent, Busik once again called Miller. Just by Busik's quivering voice, Miller could tell that his young recruit was frightened. "Let me speak to the damn doctor," Miller said to Busik, who then handed the phone to the doctor.

"Hello, Rip," said the doctor, "how can I help you?"

"God damn it doc! I thought you *had* to have a deviated septum to get into the naval academy!" screamed Miller at the doctor, who was holding the phone six inches from his ear, allowing Busik to hear Miller's raised voice. "You should pass this boy, and you should pass him now!"

Minutes later, Busik walked out of the doctor's office and into the scorching summer afternoon. He had full clearance to be sworn into the naval academy in two days. As he strolled back to the boardinghouse, he felt energized, like an electrical current was passing through him.

"What a welcome to the naval academy," he thought to himself. At the very least, Busik took comfort knowing that Rip Miller was on his side. Now he knew that he had a friend in his corner, a friend he could stand shoulder-to-shoulder with for the next four years.

On the morning of July 3, 1939, under the blue-and-white flag of the U.S.S. *Chesapeake* in Memorial Hall, Busik, Kauffman and a room full of other first year students (called plebes) took an oath of allegiance to the United States and formally became midshipmen in the United States Navy. This was a take-your-breath-away moment for all of these young men, but especially so for Busik and Kauffman. Not only had they been preparing to take this oath for more than two years, but they also were two of just a handful of plebes from the West Coast. This meant they would not see their friends and family back home for at least a year—perhaps longer. But right now they didn't care about that. Right now they stood as straight as they could and, with their right hand raised, wedded their future to the United States Navy.

And with that, the hazing began. Suddenly the upperclassmen, who had moments ago seemed so friendly, now all treated the plebes as if they'd just personally insulted their mothers. As the plebes sat in a sweltering room in Memorial Hall and stenciled their names onto the uniforms and whiteworks they had been issued at the midshipmen's store, the upperclassmen showed no mercy. They employed two tactics of intimidation: verbal insults and physical punishment for inadequate responses to questions. The U.S. Naval Academy student handbook gave the upperclassmen permission to haze; it was all in writing.

"It is the duty of the upperclassman to impress upon the plebe that there is nothing that walks or crawls the earth that is lower than he," it was stated in the handbook. "He learns that as a plebe, he has no name, that he is 'Mister' to the members of every class but his own, and that 'Sir' is the word he will use most frequently. After a while, he becomes used to it, and learns one of his most valuable lessons—that to be able to command, one must know how to obey." It was, of course, the getting-used-to-it part that was so difficult for the plebes; some were so terrified of the upperclassmen that they feared getting out of bed each morning.

After receiving their gear and stenciling their names on every item, the plebes were assigned a roommate and led to their rooms. All the rooms in Bancroft Hall were identical. The spartan furnishings consisted of a rough wooden table with a reading lamp, two unpainted wooden chairs, two iron single beds, a radiator, a washbasin, and two lockers. A plebe was allowed to keep a photograph of his sweetheart pasted on the inside of his locker, and he could have a few books on his bookshelf other than textbooks, but all other personal items from home were prohibited.

After the plebes unpacked, they marched to the mess hall in Bankcroft for lunch. Once they came to a halt in the center of the vast room, the order of "Seats" was given and the plebes sat down, twenty to a table. Already, Busik had become friends with a fellow plebe named Gus Brady, his roommate. As they sat next to each other for their first meal at the academy, a midshipman officer sat at the head of the table. Midway through lunch, the officer, an upperclassman, looked at the plebe sitting directly to his right and yelled the question, "Mister, what are you famous for?"

Sitting on the other end of the table, Busik had no idea how to answer that query. Unlike most of his classmates, Busik hadn't memorized a book of sayings that had been sent to him months earlier in which all the answers to such questions had been given. Anxiously, he nudged his new roommate, asking him what he should say. The plebes were going around the table clockwise and attempting to answer the question. Most were failing and had to do forty-three pushups—because they were the '43 class—while the midshipman officer told them how pathetic they were. Others who answered incorrectly had their seats taken away, and were forced to endure the pain of assuming a seated position without the support of a stool.

As his turn got closer, Busik again asked his roommate for help. Busik figured that Brady—a boy from nearby Baltimore, who just had to be wise to the traditions of the naval academy—knew plenty of right answers.

"Just tell him that you're famous for tearing sheets of toilet paper in half," Brady whispered to Busik.

"Are you crazy?" replied Busik, a timber of fear in his voice.

"Just say it!" replied Brady.

Finally, it was Busik's turn. "Mister, why are you famous?" demanded the officer.

"Sir, I'm famous for tearing sheets of toilet paper in half, sir," Busik said with a straight face, though on the inside he was cringing and expecting the worst. The officer looked at Busik as if he had three eyes. He studied Busik carefully, slowly, looking at him up and down. He acted as though he was going to say something, to scream something, but then he just moved on to the next plebe, who happened to be Brady. When Brady got the question, he knew he couldn't say the same thing as Busik and so he answered, "Sir, I'm sorry, but I don't know." He then had his chair removed and was forced to squat in pain. For the rest of the meal, Brady shot dirty glances at Busik.

"What in the heck happened in there," Busik asked Brady after the two of them were back in their room.

"What happened is, thanks to me, you son of a gun, you outsmarted the officer," Brady replied.

"How?" asked Busik honestly.

"The officer knew that if he had asked, 'Why?' to your response, you could have nailed him," said Brady. "You could have said, 'Sir, I'm famous for tearing sheets of toilet paper in half for half-assed bastards like you."

Brilliant, Busik thought as he broke out in a fit of laughter. That night Busik started studying the thin handbook that had been issued to him earlier that summer. Even though all of his classmates that afternoon thought he was the sharpest guy around because of his ability to bewilder the class officer in the mess hall—all of them, that is, except Brady—Busik knew it was time to get serious about hitting the books. Next time a smart-ass reply might not be sitting right next to him.

For the remainder of July and August, Busik, Kauffman, and the rest of the plebes were worked to the bone. They went almost nonstop from the time that reveille sounded at 6:30 A.M. until taps was played at 10:05 P.M. Because Busik and Kauffman had matriculated at Meade Prep and had more experience in fundamental military drills than most of their classmates, they were frequently put in charge of squads. This elevated status meant that they weren't hazed as intensely as their classmates. This was a break, because both Busik and Kauffman saw some of their friends wilt in the summer heat, as one officer after the next jawed at them and had them do pushups until they vomited. For all of July and most of August, Busik and Kauffman were merely spectators to the hazing rituals. But all that changed in late August. That's when plebe football began.

At first, Busik wasn't going to play. Even though he'd had success in high school and had been named his team's MVP over Jackie Robinson, Busik decided to concentrate on his first love: basketball. Plebe summer had been so demanding that it sucked his passion for the sport right out of him; the idea of putting on pads and practicing in the scorching August heat was as appealing to Busik as doing more pushups just for the fun of it. Besides, Rip Miller had told Busik that as long as he played either football or basketball, he'd support him.

Two days before the tryouts for plebe football began, however, Busik changed his mind. Walking across campus, Busik and a classmate discussed football. The classmate told Busik that his older brother, who had graduated from the naval academy the previous June, was exactly Busik's size and that he hadn't been big enough to make the Navy plebe football team. "Are you kidding me?" replied Busik, adamantly. "Size doesn't make a difference. If you've ever played football, you know that there's a lot more to the game than bulk. There's quickness. Toughness. Intelligence. Desire. That's what makes a good football player."

"No way," replied the classmate, "size is the most important thing."

For the next fifteen minutes, the two argued, Busik's blood boiling. Finally, they made a bet. If Busik, who stood 5' 11" and weighed 185 pounds, made the plebe traveling squad—which consisted of the top four strings on the depth chart—then he'd win $2. If he didn't make it, he'd pay his classmate the same. To Busik, this was more about proving a point than making a team. But, goddamn it, he was going to win the bet and be a member of the traveling team. Suddenly, Busik had found his engine—the engine that would power his competitiveness for the next three years.

The tryouts began the afternoon of August 20. Football was the most popular sport at the U.S. Naval Academy, and almost half of the 833 plebes from the class of '43 appeared in the wrestling loft for the introductory meeting with head football coach Emery "Swede" Larson, who was set to begin his first season at Navy. At 6' 0" and 190 pounds, Larson seemed bigger and heavier than he actually was. That's because he had a presence, an air, that you could feel when he walked into a room, as if it brushed up against your body even if you were twenty feet away. Though he didn't have a booming voice or a heavy-set build, Larson commanded attention with his magnetizing persona. It was a trait he inherited from his father.

Back in 1895, Swede's father, A. T. Larson, had been the captain and guard on the University of Minnesota football team, an interior lineman who was as unrelenting as a crowbar. He had a bottomless passion for the game and he passed it on to his oldest boy, Emery, whom everyone called Swede because his father had emigrated from Sweden. A promising collegiate prospect in 1917, Swede played first string at West High School in Minneapolis, alternating between center and tackle. Largely because he understood the game more thoroughly than most coaches, Swede outwitted his opponents as much as he outmuscled them. His cerebral play earned him the admiration of his teammates, who voted him team captain his senior year. When it came time for Swede to decide where to go to college, his father figured that his son would follow his footsteps and play ball at Minnesota. But soon after high school graduation, Swede announced he was joining the marines and heading off to war.

"What's a marine?" his father asked.

"Well," Swede said, "it's something like a—"

"Soldier or sailor?" his father asked.

"Both," replied Swede.

"Don't make jokes," his father sternly replied. "No one can be both."

Though his father wasn't familiar with this relatively new branch of service called the marines, Swede enlisted anyway on May 18, 1917. Once he finished boot camp he was eager to get to France and join his American brothers in World War I, but instead he was assigned a Stateside post at Bear Mountain Station near West Point. Frustrated and disappointed, Larson especially missed football. Some friends of his in the Marine Corps mentioned that he'd be a great candidate for the naval academy, a place where he could pursue his twin dreams of national service and football. After writing several letters and taking a test, Larson was discharged from the Marine Corps on June 28, 1918, when Congressman Harold Knutson of Minnesota awarded him an appointment as a midshipman to the naval academy.

Right away, Larson went out for the football team. At the time plebes were eligible to play varsity and Larson, displaying the same kind of skill that made him the captain of his high school team, quickly worked his way up the depth chart. He was the second-string center by the time Navy took on its arch-rival, the Great Lakes Naval Training Station. Early in the game Navy's first-string center struggled, fumbling the ball twice. Gil Dobie, the Midshipmen's legendary coach, told Larson to start warming up, so Swede began running up and down the sideline. Problem was, Dobie quickly forgot about Swede and never put him in the game.

But that Great Lakes game in 1918 was a memorable one for Larson. From his spot on the sideline, he saw one of the most bizarre plays in college football history. Late in the fourth quarter, Navy led 6–0 when a Great Lakes running back broke free. He had outrun the Navy squad and, as he sprinted down the sideline, nothing stood between him and the goalline. Halfway to the endzone, however, a Navy player hopped off the bench and sprinted onto the field. Before anyone could stop him, he dove and tackled the Great Lakes runner at about the Navy 30-yard line.

The referees didn't know what to call, because such a play wasn't covered in the rulebook. The Great Lakes coaches thought they should be awarded a touchdown. The Navy coaches argued that the rules called for a penalty against the Midshipmen for illegal interference, but nothing more. The argument quickly heated up, as coaches and players on the field started shoving one another. That's when Admiral Eberle, the U.S. Naval Academy superintendent, intervened. He proclaimed that a touchdown be awarded to Great Lakes. After kicking the extra point, Great Lakes won the game, 7–6.

Larson went on to have a spectacular playing career at Navy, one that would glow in the consciousness of Navy football followers for a generation. In 1920, he was named on Walter Camp's second All-America team. He again made Camp's second team the following year in '21, while he was also serving as the lone team captain. The following spring he was named a first-team All-American in lacrosse. Because he was a standout in two sports, Larson won the Thompson Trophy Cup as Navy's outstanding athlete in '22. But his proudest moment came in his final football game as a Navy Midshipman. Facing Army at the sold-out Polo Grounds in New York, Swede helped Navy to a 7–0 victory in '21. Late in the game Swede was taken out so that his backup, Zeke Sanborn, could see some action. As Swede jogged to the bench he saw his father standing on the sideline. It was the only time his father had made the trip from Minneapolis to see him play. As he held a blanket for his son, his eyes flashed. "Boy," he told Swede as he wrapped the blanket around him, "this is the happiest day of my life."

After graduating and accepting a commission in the Marine Corps, Swede was stationed at Quantico, Virginia, for three years. There he coached and played on the Marine team. Like at the Naval Academy, Swede stood out. In December of 1922, playing against the 3rd Corps Area Army team in front of fifty thousand people at Baltimore's Municipal Stadium, Larson led his Marine team to a 13–12 victory. Swede's rival coach that afternoon was an aggressive young man named Dwight D. Eisenhower, and nine out of ten people who were there swore that Swede outcoached the future president.

During his itinerant career as a marine, Swede always found a way to teach football. In 1937, for example, he was assigned to the 2nd Marine Brigade in Shanghai, China. The Sino-Japanese conflict had just gotten off to a bloody start, but that didn't stop Swede from imparting some pigskin wisdom to the team of the 6th Marines that he coached. One afternoon, while practicing in Shanghai's City Park, a battle erupted all around them. With gunfire whistling directly over the park, Swede continued to work out his players, oblivious to the danger that was enveloping them. One player finally yelled to Swede, "Coach, all we want to hear you say is, 'No more workout today!' " Before Swede could respond, the entire team started running for cover. Swede quickly followed and no Americans were hurt.

The next year, in 1938, Larson was named the commanding officer of the Marine Detachment at the U.S. Naval Academy. He didn't have any official coaching duties, but he still kept his hands in the game. After working hours he'd head to a back lot where he'd give pointers to officers' kids who were playing sandlot football. While the kids played, Swede would stroll up and down the sideline, a slow, preoccupied walk that suggested a philosopher in deep thought. One afternoon in the spring of 1939, while Larson was at the lot, Navy's director of athletics approached. He had a broad smile on his face. "Larson, how would you like to coach Navy?" he asked.

Larson, who had always considered coaching Navy as the ultimate job, nearly fell over. He felt as if he'd been preparing for this position all of his life, and he immediately replied yes, he'd like to coach Navy. Now, three months later, he stood before the plebes, who had quieted down the moment Larson walked in. With his long, skinny face, his dark hair that was flecked with gray, his high cheek bones, and tan, weathered skin, he looked a bit like Abraham Lincoln without the beard. Some of the players even took to calling him Honest Abe, and honesty was what he started to talk about as he preached to his players. Swede told the young men in the wrestling loft that the tryouts would be fair and that he really liked kids who hustled and played with a mean streak. Larson spoke for twenty minutes, detailing his goals for Navy football, how he was going to build this team into a national power, and the plebes hung on his every word.

Larson spoke in a low and smooth voice—the kind of voice you didn't question. "You are the future of the varsity team," Swede told his players. "You are the guys who will someday lead this program to greatness. It will be a lot of work, I'm not gonna lie to you. In fact, we are going to work you harder than you have ever been worked before. But that's why, when it really matters, we'll be victorious. It all starts out there on the practice field. That's where we'll win games. Now let's get to work and do this together."

. . .

The first few days of the tryouts did not go well for Busik or Kauffman. Neither felt entirely comfortable in their new surroundings yet—they felt a twinge of homesickness—and it showed on the field. They made uncharacteristic mistakes, like missing tackles on defense and missing blocking assignments on offense, that dropped them both down to the fifth team after two weeks of practice. Busik figured he'd lose his bet. To make matters worse for Busik, he'd had an encounter with an upperclassman that had left him shaken. After all the upperclassmen had returned from their summer cruise in late August, Busik was walking into the academy rotunda one afternoon when a big, burly officer—who Busik assumed was a football player—saw Busik out of the corner of his eye. "Mister, into the room," said the officer to Busik, pointing to a broom closet. "Get that broom out of the closet and give it to me. Then, mister, assume the angle."

Following orders but very much wanting to punch the officer, Busik went into the closet and handed him the broom. He then bent over. The broomstick thwacked his behind. Again and again. In minutes Busik's buttocks started to bleed. As he was getting pummeled, Busik looked back and saw, on his aggressor's lapel, a nametag. It read: A. Bergner. That name seems familiar, Busik thought. After the hazing incident was over, as Busik gingerly walked out of the broom closet, Busik remembered that Allen Bergner was the captain of the football team. It was a name he wouldn't soon forget.

"He's mine on the football field," Busik thought to himself. "I'll make that bastard regret what he just did."

On the day before the annual plebe-varsity football game, played on August 30, all the plebes received shots. They were inoculated for influenza, small pox, and malaria, among other potential diseases they could contract while serving in the navy. The next afternoon, when Busik and Kauffman showed up at the practice field to prepare to play the varsity, they thought the game had been postponed, because only a few of their plebe teammates were on the field.

"Where is everybody?" Kauffman asked Busik.

"This place is a ghost town," replied Busik.

Most of the plebe players, it turned out, were sick in bed. Nearly half of the plebe team suffered a reaction to the shots and were in no condition to play football. But neither Busik nor Kauffman experienced the same negative reaction that many of their teammates had. Busik, who had been the sixth team tailback, suddenly was elevated to the first string. Out of nowhere, he had an opportunity thrust upon him—an opportunity to impress his coaches and, more important, a chance to get on the same playing field as A. Bergner.

The plebes had been training for two months, so they were in fine shape. The varsity players, because they had returned from their summer cruise just a week ago, weren't yet in football condition. This disparity showed right away. Operating out of the single wing with Busik calling the plays from his tailback position, the plebes moved the ball up and down the field. They stormed to a 12–0 lead early in the second quarter. That's when Busik noticed A. Bergner enter the game. Bergner played defensive tackle and his name was written on a piece of tape that was spread across the front of his leather helmet. Busik's eyes blazed with excitement. He had just spotted a bullseye.

"Okay gents, here's what we're gonna do," Busik told his team in the huddle. "We're going to run our 42 play over and over right at our friend, A. Bergner. Everyone hit him hard. We're going to do this until they haul his ass off the field."

Forty-two meant that the four-back (the tailback) ran the ball into the two-hole (the gap between the left guard and the left tackle). With offensive linemen Vito Vitucci, Gene Flathman, Moose McTighe, and Jake Laboon serving as Busik's front wall, the plebe team hammered away at Bergner, play after play. Whenever Bergner had a chance to make a tackle, Busik didn't elude him. He simply lowered his head like a bull and charged straight into Bergner, trying to inflict as much pain as possible. On a few occasions Busik sent Bergner flying into the air; he'd land on the ground with a thud. Watching this from the sideline, coach Larson started asking his assistants where this Busik kid had come from. He ran with a fury, a sense of purpose, that was as rare as dinosaur bones. After one particularly devastating collision with Bergner in the fourth quarter, Busik hopped up. Bergner didn't. He lay on the ground, motionless and unconsciousness, with Busik standing over him and smiling like a farm boy. Just as Busik had prophesied, Bergner was eventually taken off the field on a stretcher.

Midway through the fourth quarter, plebe coach Johnny Wilson benched all of the plebe starters. The plebe team held an 18–14 lead, and neither Wilson nor Larson wanted to demoralize his varsity players with a loss. The varsity wound up beating the plebes 21–18, but the fact that the first-year players had fared so well against the older, stronger players bode well for Navy's future. In fact, after the game, Larson privately admitted to friends that he thought these plebes, given time to grow and mature, could be a dominating group. Maybe he was being premature, but even before he coached his first game at Navy, Larson was already constructing a road map in his mind, a map that he believed would lead to the sweetest of destinations: the national championship.

5

WEST POINT 1940

AS SOON AS ROBIN OLDS stepped off the train at the small West Point depot, his welcome to the U.S. Military Academy rushed at him like a bucket of ice water to the face. Olds and the other young passengers were met by several cadet officers, who proceeded to vociferously herd them into groups. As they were being organized, the fresh-faced young men were reminded, in less-than-pleasant language, that their mommies were no longer around to care for them, and their daddies couldn't protect them any more. The words were hurled like sharpened spears, but Olds was unfazed. Frankly, he'd expected the torment to be much worse than this, but some of the kids who had no military background were in a near state of shock. Just wait until the Beast Detail gets ahold of them, Olds thought to himself as he glanced at a few of the future cadets who were already trembling with fear.

It was now approaching noon on July 1, 1940. All that was left in Olds' journey, which began in the predawn darkness at Washington's Union Station, was a four-hundred-yard walk up the Hudson Highlands. For weeks Olds had imagined himself joining the long gray line, and now as he left the train depot on the west bank of the river, he was minutes away from realizing a dream. He gazed up the hill and saw, outlined against the azure sky in front of him, the gray stone of the administration building, also known as base headquarters. To him, the building looked like a monstrous, impenetrable castle on a bluff, its massive stones glistening in the sunshine. The sight was awe-inspiring. There was an air of solidness, of importance to the place. Right then Olds thought the Point was the perfect place for him.

As the group continued to walk upward, they could see the tops of the trees on campus. No one talked. Olds could sense the anxiety level rising with each step. The group passed through the stone portal that led to the Plain. Still no one talked; all Olds could hear were the footfalls of all the young men who were now walking toward their futures. This was the same path that Douglas MacArthur had walked in 1899 after he arrived at the Point via the West Shore Railroad. Many of the young men were aware that General MacArthur, a former superintendent of the school, had once been here, and to them it was almost as if they could see MacArthur's image as they climbed the steep hill, step by agonizing step.

When the group finally reached the Plain, which from the river bluff stretched west for half a mile and housed all the academic buildings, barracks, and the parade ground, they were guided into the open quadrangle of the cadet barracks. Then they were handed over to the Beast Detail—cadets who were in charge of indoctrinating the new plebes into what were gently called the "traditions" of the academy. And that was when all hell broke out. If any of the young men had any romantic notions about life at West Point, they were about to be dashed.

"Pull in that chin, mister!"

"Stand up straight, mister!"

"You have no chance of surviving here! You will not make it, mister!"

"You think you're tough? We'll show you tough, mister!"

"You are a disgrace, mister!"

And on and on it went for most of the afternoon, the white-gloved upperclassman acting like wolves chasing sheep. After their initial berating, the young men were issued uniforms, and then they were taken to the campus barber to have their hair shaved to a quarter inch from the scalp. While waiting in line to have his trim, Olds locked eyes with Henry Romanek, his old friend from Millard Prep in D.C., who was also waiting in line. Romanek had arrived an hour or so before Olds and had been dropped off by his father's friend. All morning Romanek had been screamed at and told how pathetic he was, and now seeing the familiar face of Olds brought a smile to his face.

"I didn't know if you'd actually show up," Romanek joked to Olds. "But it's good to see you."

"You never need to worry about me, Henry, I can take care of myself just fine," Olds replied with a smile. "You're the one who's going to be hauled out of here on a stretcher."

Around 5:00 P.M., the Beasts were shepherded out to a place called Trophy Point, which overlooked a bend in the dark, glittering river, and they were asked to raise their right hand. There's no going back now, Olds thought to himself as he lifted his right hand skyward. Amid the lengthening afternoon shadows, the Beasts swore allegiance to the United States. It had been a long day, but finally Robin Olds and Henry Romanek were Army cadets.

Every Beast knew war was coming. President Roosevelt was already warning the American people that there would be no compromise with Germany and Italy, which he called "the new corporate governments" of the world. "The new governments generally destroy the legislative and judicial branches and delegate all powers to an executive or dictator, thus striking at the heart of fundamental liberties by which men should and must live," the President told reporters at a press conference on the same afternoon that Olds and Romanek arrived at West Point.

Days earlier, France had surrendered to Germany. General Charles Huntziger had signed away France's freedom in the same railway car in Versailles in which the Germans were forced to sign the surrender at the end of World War I. The terms of the capitulation were mild but troubling: Any German national was to be handed over to the German authorities on demand; and any French national caught fighting for the British was to be treated as an insurgent. A day after the surrender was signed, a picture of Hitler standing in front of the Eiffel Tower ran in newspapers around the world, and accompanying stories discussed Hitler's likely next move: the invasion of England.

The dominoes were beginning to fall. Romanek and Olds both understood that. Days after France had lost her freedom President Roosevelt asked Congress for the largest defense budget in U.S. history. Roosevelt needed the money for two main reasons: to fund a 1.2 million man army and to build fifteen thousand new planes.

. . .

In spite of the school's rich football tradition, Army was not considered a powerhouse in the summer of 1940. The previous season, 1939, had been catastrophic. The Cadets stumbled to a 3–4–2 record with a squad coached by William Wood, Army's first losing season since 1906. Worse, the Cadets had been shut out in three of their last four games of the '39 season. The team's sagging football fortunes put an intense amount of pressure on Wood, a 1925 graduate who had collected twelve varsity letters. He knew the future success of Army football would be tied to this freshman (plebe) class—he planned on playing many of them once they became eligible the next season—and so when the tryouts for plebe football commenced in mid-August of 1940, he watched all of his young players with careful, critical eyes.

The practices were unlike anything Olds and Romanek had ever experienced. They weren't overly long—they started at 3:15 and lasted until 5:30—but the players weren't allowed to take a single break. Before and after each practice, the team trainer, Beaver Beaven, weighed each team member. It wasn't unusual for some of the bigger players (such as Olds) to sweat off eight to fifteen pounds during their 2 hour and 15 minute sessions. Coach Wood wanted his team to be as physically fit as any in the nation, and he wanted his players to dominate in the fourth quarter, so he tried to make his practices more difficult, more demanding, than anything his players would face all season. The downside to this approach was that after a few weeks, the players were worn down and physically deflated. Olds played offensive and defensive tackle, and by the end of most practices he'd feel as if he'd just pushed a boulder up a mountain. Once the whistle blew and practices were over, Olds would spend at least 30 minutes in the whirlpool, trying to soothe his aching muscles. A few times, Romanek, who played next to Olds on the line, jumped into the swimming pool to cool down with his pads still on after practice, too exhausted to peel them off.

Once the plebe season started, the team was predictably flat, as the players had no freshness in their legs. After losing their first three games, the Army plebes hosted Fordham's freshman squad on a cold, rainy afternoon at West Point. Against the Rams, Olds and Romanek played both ways on the mud-drenched field for the full 60 minutes. By the time the game was over—final score: 0–0—Romanek was so sore he was hobbling like an eighty-year-old man. After a hot shower in the locker room, he headed straight for bed, skipping dinner.

The next morning the pain and stiffness still had a grip on him—head to toe. When Romanek awoke, it hurt just to get out of bed. But Romanek grabbed his gray overcoat and staggered out to ranks. He made it there by first call, which was 5 minutes before assembly. As he stood there in a cold, driving rain, his squad leader strolled up. He was a varsity football player and he took it personally that the plebes hadn't defeated Fordham. The squad leader figured Romanek, like all the plebe players, needed some toughening up.

"Pull in your crock right now," he yelled as he put his face within a few inches of Romanek's.

"Yes, sir," Romanek replied.

"More!" screamed the squad leader.

"Yes, sir," said Romanek.

"More, god damn it!" again yelled the squad leader.

Romanek pulled in his chin as tightly as he'd ever done before. He stood ramrod straight, but then, seconds later, he fell to the ground. Passed out cold.

"Get a medic!" yelled one plebe that had seen Romanek tumble to the earth. No one was terribly worried about Romanek's condition because several plebes had passed out during Beast Barracks. In Romanek's case, tucking his chin tightly into his chest cut off the blood flow to his brain—an all too common occurrence among the Beasts. After a few moments, he opened his eyes and asked what had happened. When he figured it out, he silently wished for the same thing that Bill Busik had when he got hazed at Navy: an opportunity to go one-on-one on the football field with his aggressor.

The plebe football players who had seen this incident were irate. "You're a mean bastard," one yelled at the squad leader as Romanek awoke.

"You'll get it for this," shouted another plebe player.

As Romanek struggled to his feet, he was comforted by the fact that his young teammates were sticking up for him. Maybe, he thought to himself, there was hope for this team after all.

The 1940 season was one long, waking nightmare for varsity coach William Wood. Though he was pleased with his plebe team in spite of their slow start—his young boys, led by Olds and Romanek, had gotten progressively stronger throughout the season and finished with a record of 3–4–1—his varsity squad limped to a 1–7–1 record. It was the worst season in the fifty-one years that Army had been playing football. The low-point came on November 16 at Franklin Field in Philadelphia against the University of Pennsylvania. One of the spectators in attendance that afternoon was General Robert L. Eichelberger, who had just been named to succeed General Jay Benedict as superintendent of the U.S. Military Academy. Eichelberger would officially assume the position on the following Monday, and he wanted to get a first-hand look at the state of the school's football team. What he saw was the worst defeat in Army history, as Penn routed the Academy, 48–0. Eichelberger knew that something drastic had to be done to revive the flagging program, and he had a bold idea.

On the following Monday, in his first official act as superintendent, Eichelberger called a meeting of the athletic board. "I was impressed Saturday by the way the cadets cheered our team right to the end," he told the board. "It looks as if we are developing the finest bunch of losers in the world. By the gods, I believe the cadets deserve a football team which will teach them how to be good winners. Our graduate officer–head coach system has long been outmoded. I propose to ditch it, and, if I can, get Red Blaik back here from Dartmouth."

Dating back to 1890, Army always had a graduate officer serve as its head football coach. Eichelberger believed that this was the reason why the program had fallen into decay, and he made it his top priority as superintendent to rescind this unwritten policy and hire a coach with an off-the-charts football IQ. After his meeting with the board, he went to his office and personally typed a letter to Blaik, who was the head coach at Dartmouth and a 1919 West Point graduate. No longer in the army, Blaik was in the process of leading the Big Green to a 5–4 record in 1940. "If you have not signed a new contract," Eichelberger wrote, "don't sign any until you have talked to me first."

Once he received the missive, Blaik quickly replied with his own telegram. "I understand what you mean," Blaik wrote. "I will see you next week at the Army-Navy game."

So on the eve of the 1940 Army-Navy contest, Eichelberger and Blaik met in the general's suite in Philadelphia's Benjamin Franklin Hotel. For more than two hours, Eichelberger explained how the U.S. Military Academy needed Blaik to restore luster to its football team. Eichelberger said he would abolish the graduate officer rule and that he'd give Blaik all the resources he needed to turn around the football team. Blaik asked for time to weigh the offer.

"Take all the time you want, Earl," said Eichelberger. "But just remember one thing: West Point needs you."

For nearly a month, those last four words echoed in Blaik's mind. The colors had called him. He knew, deep inside, he couldn't turn that down.

Born to Scottish parents in Detroit, Michigan, in 1897, little Earl Blaik had a mop of copper-colored hair—everyone called him "Red"—and he played the role of the rambunctious redhead to a T. In school he sassed his teachers, telling them how things ought to be. He often got the paddle after class, but that did little to calm this tempest of a boy. He found that the best place to channel his energy was on the athletic fields, where he could dominate boys nearly twice his size simply because they couldn't match his intensity.

When he was ten years old in 1907, Blaik formed a neighborhood football team and appointed himself coach. He named the team the "Riverdale Rovers," after the *Rover Boys* books he liked to read at night before bed. The Rovers played with a round, black ball that more closely resembled a soccer ball than a football, which made it almost impossible to pass. Even though the forward pass had been legalized in 1906, Blaik as a young boy didn't care much for an air attack. He never would, in fact, mainly because of what he learned on the sandlots while playing with the Rovers. He found that the ground game was much more reliable than the pass, and that if you could dominate your opponent running the ball, you could break his spirit as easily as a carrot stick.

The Riverdale Rovers played other neighborhood teams after school, and the games more often than not devolved into rock fights. One Thanksgiving, young Red showed up for dinner two hours late and was in no condition to sit down at the table with his family. His face was scratched, his clothes were torn, and dirt covered a good portion of the clothes that weren't ripped. His father William, who saw no future in football, was about to ban his son from ever playing the sport again when one of Red's friends spoke up. "But Mr. Blaik," the young voice said. "He won the game!"

Blaik was never one of the biggest boys around—by age eighteen he was 5' 9" and 135 pounds—but from his father he inherited the gift of raw strength. William Blaik came to the United States from Glasgow, Scotland, in 1883. Three years later he opened a blacksmith and carriage shop on Twelfth Street in Detroit, and he quickly acquired a reputation as being one of the most reliable blacksmiths in town. William was a considerate man, but the one thing that really upset him was when Henry

Ford came around. The elder Blaik could always hear Ford before he saw him, because Ford was experimenting with a horseless carriage, and when he ran his "contraption" down Twelfth Street it made such a racket that it riled the horses. In some cases, it caused them to bolt out of their stalls, agitated, and sprint down the dusty streets. When Ford's cart broke down—as it often did—the blacksmiths along Twelfth Street all whooped and hollered in approval right in front of Ford's face. Yet when Ford went to William Blaik and asked to borrow some tools for repairs, Blaik never once refused. Even though he didn't like what Ford's cart potentially could mean to his future livelihood, William Blaik never hesitated in opening his shop up to Ford. Like most immigrants, Blaik had an appreciation for what it meant to lend—and to receive—a helping hand.

In 1901 William Blaik sold his business to become the Ohio and Kentucky sales representative for the Capwell Horseshoe Company. He moved his family to Dayton, Ohio, and it was there that young Red experienced the defining event of his childhood. On March 25, 1913, when Red was sixteen, one of the most disastrous floods in the history of the United States swallowed a good portion of Dayton. On the morning of the catastrophe, police and fire alarms awoke Red at 4:00 A.M. Five days of constant rain had swollen the Great Miami River, and now the threat of a massive flood was high. At 7:30 the levees above the Herman Avenue Bridge broke and water rushed down the streets. By 8:30 the raging channels reached the front steps of the Blaik household. Minutes later the Blaiks—father, mother, Red and his brother and sister—linked hands and waded into the rising, rapid waters. After two horrifying hours, they made it to higher ground at the Forest Avenue Presbyterian Church, which is where they stayed for the next few days.

Others weren't as lucky. Because several bridges had been washed out and the lines of communication were dead, many people were stranded on their rooftops, paralyzed with fear. Entire houses were being swept away and, from his spot at the church, Red Blaik could hear the screams of people struggling to stay afloat in the rapid waters. At the flood's crest, Dayton lay under fourteen feet of muddy water. Young Red saw it all, and couldn't help but wonder: Why wasn't the city prepared for this? Why didn't the city have a plan? When nightfall came, Blaik and his family saw a fire break out in a downtown office building. The fire soon engulfed an entire block. When it reached a paint company, explosions shot high into the sky. In the afterglow of the blasts, Blaik could see people stranded on their rooftops, frantically trying to find help.

After four days, the water began to recede. Red was one of the first people to get to the downtown area and what he saw left him speechless. It looked as if the apocalypse had dawned. Many buildings were burned out; others had been completely washed away. An eight-inch layer of mud covered everything. Bloated carcasses of hundreds of dead horses were strewn in the streets, reeking of decomposing flesh. Again Red thought to himself: Why wasn't the town ready for this? Over one thousand homes and buildings had been demolished and more than three hundred people had died in the disaster. To Red, it seemed an utter waste. A lack of coordination and foresight had made the flood worse that it should have been, and Blaik would never forget this. This partly explained why, years later, he would become the most meticulous, organized, detail-oriented coach of his time—a coach who would revolutionize the sport of football with his approach to the game.

Blaik attended the University of Miami at Oxford, Ohio, where he starred at end for three seasons. Like some other college football players of his time, Blaik got to start his college football career over again when he was accepted to West Point after graduating from Miami. Army didn't recognize the three-year eligibility rule until 1930—an intercollege athletic rule that stated, in effect, that a player only had a total of three years of varsity eligibility—so when Blaik arrived at the Point in the summer of 1918, he joined the plebe squad. The next year, when he was elevated to the varsity, Blaik became a favorite of General Douglas MacArthur, who at the time was superintendent at the school. MacArthur so enjoyed watching the football team play that on many autumn afternoons he put aside his responsibilities and attended football practice. There he would stomp up and down the sidelines, his riding crop stuck under his arm, and encourage the young cadets to play stronger, to run faster, to hit harder. MacArthur always believed that there was a strong correlation between sports and war, and before he left his post as superintendent for the Philippine Islands in 1922, his thoughts on the subject were inscribed over the entrance to the Physical Education office in the South Gym:

> UPON THE FIELDS OF FRIENDLY STRIFE
> ARE SOWN THE SEEDS THAT,
> UPON OTHER FIELDS, ON OTHER DAYS
> WILL BEAR THE FRUITS OF VICTORY

MacArthur had always dreamed of playing football for Army, but when he arrived at the academy in 1899, he was just 5' 11" and 133 pounds. He was also something of a mama's boy, and Mary MacArthur didn't want her son getting hurt playing football. For four years Mary MacArthur lived in the West Point Hotel. From her vantage point in the hotel, she had an unobstructed view of Room 1123 in the barracks. At night if she didn't see young Doug with his head buried in a circle of lamplight, she'd talk to him the following day about why he wasn't studying. Finally, in his first class year (his senior year), MacArthur found a way to accommodate both his mother's desire that he not play football and his desire to be connected to the football team: He became the equipment manager.

When MacArthur was superintendent in 1919, no cadet impressed him more than Blaik. Playing end, Blaik was named to Walter Camp's third string All-America team and won the saber as the best athlete in his class. After graduation in 1920 Blaik hoped to be stationed in Europe, but instead he was sent to the Mexican border with the 8th Cavalry. Three years later, with World War I over and the Army poised to reduce its number of troops, Blaik resigned his commission to join his father's real estate and contracting business in Dayton. He felt ready to begin a normal life.

Blaik married a local Dayton girl and for the next few years he led a perfectly ordinary life. He worked nine to five, mowed his lawn on the weekend, and started a family. In 1922 he received a surprise letter from MacArthur, who had just been given a new command in the Philippines. MacArthur invited Blaik to become his aide-de-camp. But MacArthur didn't know that Blaik had already resigned his commission, so the offer was moot. Later MacArthur took to Manila another former West Point football player, Dwight Eisenhower.

Working with his father in Dayton, Blaik was content except for one thing: He missed football terribly. It wasn't that he didn't like his job at the firm of W. E. & E. H. Blaik, but he thought of football as his first love, and he couldn't get his strong feelings for the sport out of his heart. So he started looking for ways to get back into the game—just on a part-time basis. In 1926 he landed a coaching job as an unpaid assistant at Wisconsin. The next season he traveled to West Point to help out with the team, still as an unpaid assistant. He always returned to his job in Dayton after the season ended, but for seven straight years he coached at West Point in the fall, learning as much as he could and quietly formulating his own strategy that he would one day implement when he became a head coach. That day came in 1934. Blaik announced that he was leaving his father's business for good in order to seek a job as a head coach of a college team.

Army couldn't hire him because of the regulation barring civilians from being its head coach, but Blaik got an offer from Dartmouth. He then led the Big Green to it first-ever victory over Yale in 1935 and to Ivy League titles in 1936 and 1937. Blaik had his players run the single-wing almost to perfection, and his reputation grew by the year. When Eichelberger offered him the Army job the night before the Army-Navy game in 1940, Blaik said he would only consider leaving Dartmouth if two conditions were met: He wanted to bring all of his assistants to West Point and he wanted Army to abolish its weight and height restrictions. The restrictions were implemented in 1931, when the Surgeon General issued a directive stating that overweight candidates would not get a waiver to attend the U.S. Military Academy. Based on the theory that slimmer men have a greater life expectancy, the Surgeon General instructed the examining boards to strictly adhere to an age-height-weight chart. According to the chart, a candidate who was 6' 4", for example, could weigh no more than 198 pounds. Blaik, like many at West Point, believed these restrictions were undercutting any chance that Army had to be competitive in football, and he told Eichelberger that he wouldn't coach the team unless Eichelberger did something about it. Eichelberger said he'd look into it after the game.

About 265 miles to the southwest of West Point, the state of affairs at the naval academy were much more settled in the autumn of 1940—thanks in large part to a young player named Bill Busik. Just as Navy coach Swede Larson had hoped, his 1940 varsity squad was bolstered by the additions of several players who had shined on the '39 plebe team. The biggest surprise was Busik. In the first scrimmage held in September 1940, Busik lead the team in rushing and passing. Whenever Busik busted into the open field, he ran like a man who was bolting from a jailhouse, leaving defenders in a swirl of dust. His strong performance prompted Larson to breathlessly compare Busik to Buzz Borries, a bowlegged running back who had been an All-American for Navy in 1934.

Larson knew Borries's skills well. In 1936 Larson coached the football team aboard the U.S.S. *Pennsylvania*. Their chief rival was the team on the U.S.S. *Arizona*. In November of '36, after the *Arizona* and *Pennsylvania* had been out at sea for a few months, both ships came to port in San Pedro, California, which was where one of the American fleet's bases was located in the mid-1930s. By the time each ship had docked, the football players had enough pent-up testosterone to raise the dead. The *Arizona* and *Pennsylvania* teams, which had been practicing aboard ship for months, faced off in a dilapidated, rickety baseball stadium in San Pedro. A football field was marked off with paint and a few thousand fans showed up and watched Borries put on a show. Operating out of *Arizona*'s single wing, Borries ran both inside and out, with quickness, power, and guile. Even though Borries rushed for nearly 100 yards, the *Pennsylvania* squad won the game—and the fleet championship—because Larson had them playing disciplined, smart, savvy football. Yet Borries's performance left a lasting impression on Larson, who often said that Borries was the best back he'd ever faced. So when Larson compared Busik to Borries, it was the highest of praise.

The fastest player on the Navy team and also one of its strongest, Busik in the preseason of 1940 had worked his way up from sixth-string to first by the time the Midshipmen opened the season against William and Mary. He quickly developed into a triple threat in Navy's single-wing offense. Not only did he call the plays, but he also was charged with being the team's primary runner, passer, and punter, and he led the Midshipmen to a 5–3 record in their first eight games of the '40 season. Their season finale came against Army on November 29, 1940, the fiftieth anniversary of the first Army-Navy rivalry, a game that Romanek and Olds—both Cadet plebes—would have to watch from the stands.

"Number 63 (Busik) is the guy that makes their entire team go," coach Wood told his players at Army's final practice before they boarded a train and traveled to Philadelphia for the Navy game. "Busik is the guy we always need to be aware of. He's the guy we're going to have to stop."

Midway through that '40 season, as it became increasingly clear that Busik was the team's top player, sportswriters started calling him "Barnacle Bill." The nickname stemmed from a popular Betty Boop black-and-white cartoon in 1930 named *Barnacle Bill*, which was based on the song "Barnacle Bill the Sailor." In one version of the song—and there were several—the first two verses went:

It's only me from over the sea,
Said Barnacle Bill the Sailor;
I'm all lit up like a Christmas tree,
Said Barnacle Bill the Sailor.

I'll sail the sea until I croak,
Drink my whiskey, swear, and smoke,
But I can't swim a bloody stroke,
Said Barnacle Bill the Sailor.

Though Busik had little in common with the Barnacle Bill in the song—Busik never drank or smoked, and he could swim like a fish—Busik didn't mind the nickname. He figured he must have been doing something right to have earned the admiration of the press. And the sobriquet made him think of the Rabbit, Jackie Robinson. Ever since Busik had left southern California, he and Robinson corresponded through letters. Robinson was now at UCLA and, like Busik, he was rapidly developing into a star football player. The two followed each other's success on the field as closely as they could, writing about once every two months, keeping each other up to date with how the plot of their young lives was evolving.

Thirty minutes before the kickoff of the Golden Anniversary game between the U.S. Naval and Military Academies, Robin Olds and Henry Romanek walked onto the field at Philadelphia's Municipal Stadium. Wearing their dress uniforms, they marched in formation through the field gates with the rest of the plebes and nonvarsity football players. The crowd greeted the Cadets with a mighty roar. As Olds and Romanek looked up into the sold-out stands, the 102,311 fans seemed to stretch from sideline to skyline, all their hands vigorously clapping. Neither of them had ever heard such a booming noise at a football stadium before.

The Army and Navy regimental commanders then met at midfield and shook hands. A crackling voice came over the public address system. "This shaking of hands symbolizes the unity of Army and Navy in the common cause of national defense." Again the crowd belched a roar, cheering so loudly that it seemed to Romanek and Olds as if everyone in the stands was screaming at the top of his or her lungs. After the game Philadelphia's *Evening Public Ledger* noted, "The spirit of unity that is massing a nation . . . electrified the crowd today."

Navy was the three-to-one favorite over Army. The Midshipmen's record stood at 5–3; Army was 1–6–1, its lone highlight holding Notre Dame to one touchdown in a 7–0 loss to the Irish on November 7. Most everyone expected a blowout. On the eve of the game, one reporter in the *Baltimore Sun* joked in print, "If Navy doesn't beat the Army decisively, it means it has gone backward faster through November than any good football team in history and there should be a congressional investigation."

Red Blaik sat behind the Army bench with Eichelberger. Blaik was eager to see the talent level of the Cadets, to gauge whether or not he could cobble together a winning team in just one season—if he decided to take the job. Army received the opening kickoff, but was forced to punt after three plays. Busik returned the punt from his own 36 to the Cadet's 42. On Navy's first offensive play, Busik floated a pass to Everett Malcom, who was pushed out of bounds at Army's 18-yard line. Three plays later Busik scored on a 2-yard plunge into the endzone. After the extra point, Navy led 7–0 just 6 minutes into the game. Busik, the Cadets quickly found out, was as good as all the sportswriters were saying.

It was right about this time that President Roosevelt, who was listening to the game on a radio in the Oval Office, phoned Secretary of War Henry Stimson, who was sitting in a box on the Army side of the field. Roosevelt not only wanted an eyewitness account of what was transpiring at the stadium, but he also wanted to keep Stimson informed of the latest developments in Europe. Earlier that morning the Associated Press, citing an unnamed source, reported that Hitler's Germany was planning to invade Great Britain within the next three weeks. Roosevelt discussed this report with Stimson. But when the two weren't talking about foreign affairs, they chatted about the game. Roosevelt, a former assistant secretary of the navy, was no doubt thrilled that Busik and the Midshipmen had taken the early lead.

One person who wasn't pleased with the events on the field was Olds. "I wish I was out there to stop Busik," Olds told his plebe teammates as they watched the action from the stands. "I think I could make a difference. I think quite of few of us could make a difference." Seated a few feet away from Olds, Romanek felt the same way. "Next year, boys," he said over and over to his teammates. "Next year."

The Cadets, who were outweighed and outmanned, lost 14–0. In the closing minutes of the game, as the Midshipmen were trying to run out the clock, the school bands assembled behind the north goal. As soon as the final gun sounded, the bands started to belt out the first strains of the "Star Spangled Banner." The music echoed throughout the hushed stadium, as everyone in attendance stood and sang in unison. But a few excited Midshipmen had already run onto the field and were tearing down the wooden goalpost in the south endzone. Once they realized that everyone was singing the "Star Spangled Banner," they stopped. A few Middies

sat on the crossbar as they saluted the flag, all of them unable to conceal their canary-swallowing grins. As soon as the music was over, the goalpost came tumbling down.

"This is obviously the highlight of my season," Busik told reporters after Navy's victory. "There was just so much excitement in the stadium today. Running out onto the field and seeing all those people was just incredible, something I'll never forget. I've never experienced anything like it. I can't wait to play Army again next year."

As soon as Busik was done talking to the reporters, one of the first players to congratulate him on his stellar performance was Hal Kauffman, who had suited up for the game but didn't see any action. Yet even though he hadn't stepped onto the playing field, Kauffman, who was buried on the depth chart, felt like he was a big part of the victory. He'd played on the scout team in practice and, on the sideline, provided constant encouragement. Unlike some young men, Kauffman understood that not every player is destined to be a football star—he certainly wasn't—but that didn't diminish the joy of the moment for him.

"You were terrific, Bill," Kauffman said after the game. "But all of us knew you would be. Good golly, you looked like a pro out there." With that, the two friends from Pasadena shook hands. A few years later, half a world away and under dramatically different circumstances, they'd recall this moment, and how simple and sweet their lives had been when all that mattered was beating Army.

After watching the Cadets fall to the Midshipmen, General Eichelberger became even more determined to get Red Blaik to coach at the Point. Shortly after the game Eichelberger contacted the surgeon general and asked him to ease the age-height-weight restrictions. Eichelberger wanted the chart to be more of a suggestion than a strict rule. After all, Eichelberger noted, sometimes the chart said a man was obese when, in reality, he simply had a stout, athletic build. Eichelberger also convinced General Edwin Watson, President Roosevelt's aide-de-camp and a West Point grad, to lobby the surgeon general. Watson was more than happy to put a call into the surgeon general. Watson, like many high-powered West Point graduates in Washington, was tired of losing bets on Army-Navy games to high-ranking navy officials. Finally the surgeon general, after much verbal sparring with Eichelberger and Watson, relented and loosened the restrictions.

A month after the Army-Navy game, Blaik still hadn't made up his mind. His biggest reservation was that he didn't know how he'd be received

being the first graduate head coach not in the service. In mid-December Blaik traveled to West Point and articulated this feeling to Eichelberger, who in turn had a strange request for Blaik. "Go over to the Officer's Club," Eichelberger said, "and get your hair cut by Tom Impel. When you get back, let me know how long it took."

Blaik did as he was told. Impel was known around West Point to dole out conversation in direct proportion to the importance of the customer in his chair. When Blaik sat down and introduced himself, Impel let the words fly. He slathered Blaik's face with shaving cream and fired one question at him after the next. About 45 minutes later, Blaik returned to Eichelberger's office, his hair freshly shorn and his face as smooth as the skin of an apple. "How long did Tom have you in his chair?" asked Eichelberger.

"About forty-five minutes," Blaik answered.

"A shave and haircut for a second lieutenant takes Tom about five minutes," Eichelberger replied. "The superintendent usually gets forty-five minutes of cutting and conversation. Right now you're the second ranking person on the post. You'd better take the job, Red."

On December 22, 1940, Blaik did. He met General Eichelberger at a hotel in midtown Manhattan and told him he accepted the offer. Blaik's orders were to come up with a "crash" program to restore Army football. He was bestowed the rank of full colonel and appointed athletic director. The program was completely his. Change—badly needed change—had arrived at the Point, and football at the Military Academy would never be the same.

6

PRESEASON 1941

THREE WEEKS AFTER ACCEPTING THE head coaching position at Army, Blaik summoned Ray Murphy to his office. Blaik had not yet spoken to any of his players and he figured that Murphy was the logical player to call in first. Two months earlier, Murphy, an interior lineman who played both ways, had been one of a handful of players nominated to be team captain of the '41 squad. The vote took place the evening after Army's loss to Navy. Just outside of Newark, New Jersey, as the team's locomotive chugged north through the autumn twilight, the three candidates stood in the front of a rail car. An assistant coach then asked everyone on the team to raise his hand if he wanted the first candidate, Murphy, to be captain. With Manhattan glowing outside the windows like a giant orange torch, about 90 percent of the players raised their arms. Murphy, it was quickly decided, would be the team's lone captain for the 1941 season.

Murphy was from Anaconda, Montana, a gritty mining town located in the foothills of the Rocky Mountains. At Anaconda High Murphy was a bear of a lineman, and when he played he had an air of ruthlessness about him. He was so talented that he became the rare Montana high school player who got recruited by several Division I schools. What helped make him such a menacing interior player, according to his coaches, was that he worked year-round as a logger. On the weekends and after school he'd cut down trees, haul timber, and occasionally help build log cabins. The labor was strenuous, but because Murphy had forearms as thick as fence-posts, he often did the work of two men. Murphy would have been perfectly content spending his entire life chopping wood and breathing the cool Montana air that was tinged with the scent of pine needles and wood smoke, but then he started listening to Army football games on the radio and his ambition got redirected, as if a giant hand had swooped down from the sky, tapped him on the shoulder, and pointed to West Point. In the late '30s, this was happening to boys all over the nation, especially to country boys like Murphy.

By the time he was fourteen, Murphy would come home from work on fall weekends and sit in the living room with his father. Together they would listen to play-by-play radio broadcasts of Army football games. Murphy had to adjust the directional antenna every few minutes because the reception failed, but that never stopped him from being captivated by the static-filled accounts. Before long, those faraway Cadet players became Murphy's gridiron heroes. As the games played out in the world of his imagination, Murphy believed that the players must surely have glowed in the dark each time they donned the black and gold Army uniform. They were America's heroes. How he wished to be one of them.

Five years later, he *was* one of them. Yet there was nothing epic or lyrical about going 1–7–1. Murphy had heard from teammates that Blaik had turned around the program at Dartmouth, so he was optimistic that Blaik could work that same magic at the military academy. But in just one season? Murphy's eligibility would be over at the end of the '41 season, and he wanted to be on at least one Army team that had a winning season. "Things are going to be completely different from now on," Blaik told Murphy in their initial meeting. "We are going to work like you've never worked before. No team in the United States will be as fit as us. That's why we'll win games next year. In fact, we'll win a lot of games."

Blaik continued. "I don't care what you did last year, every position is up for grabs," he said. "You'll have to earn the right to start. I'll give everyone a fair chance, but just know that what you did last year or two years ago no longer matters. All that matters is what you do from right now until the first kickoff of the season."

Instead of waiting until March to begin spring practice—which is what virtually every other team in the nation did—Blaik told his players to meet him in the fieldhouse on a late afternoon at the end of January. Snow swirled on the plain in the winter winds as the Cadet football players, all wearing their long gray coats, trudged through the blistering dusk to meet their new coach. Once they opened the fieldhouse doors, there stood Blaik in the entry. He cut an imposing figure. At 6' 2", 190 pounds, he was in excellent shape. He had bronze hair and piercing pale blue eyes—eyes that seemed to indicate that he was all business, all the time. He always stood perfectly straight—it was as if the man had steel in his spine—and now he wore a serious look on his face. The coach knew that the air had leaked out of his players' football dreams, and he understood that it was his job to inflate those dreams once again. That process was about to begin.

Once the entire team was present, Blaik began speaking. "Gentlemen, we have a lot of work to do in the next few months," he said. "We are going to master the fundamentals of this game before we move on to anything else. I believe we can have a winning team this year if we work harder than any other team in the nation." Blaik continued speaking for about another 30 minutes, emphasizing to his players that the only way they were going to get better was to trust each other and the coaches. At the end of his talk, Blaik had a surprise for the players. Though none of them had brought their cleats to the meeting—they expected this to be nothing more than a get-to-know-you session with their new coach—Blaik ended his remarks by telling the squad, "Practice starts right now. Everyone out to the field." In the early '40s there were no rules restricting the number of practices a team could hold in the winter and spring, so Blaik, being the impatient man that he was, put his boys to work even though snow and ice covered the ground.

In reviewing film from the '40 season, Blaik determined that Army's biggest weaknesses were blocking and tackling, the two most fundamental skills in football. Starting at the end of January and continuing until the beginning of June, Blaik had his players work on blocking and tackling almost every day from 3:45 to 5:15. Only occasionally during these eighteen weeks of practice did Army work on actual plays. Instead, Blaik drilled his players in rudiments of the game. The typical drill pitted two players against one. A coach would toss the ball to an offensive player, who was given a simple command: He was to try to push forward and gain as many yards as possible against the two defenders, both of whom were in three-point stances directly in front of him. With the coaches watching closely, the two defenders had to display perfect technique in making the tackle before they'd be given a breather.

Of course, these sessions were particularly brutal for the backs and receivers. Archie Hill, a back out of New Mexico, had his appendix removed two weeks before Blaik had started "spring" practice. Wanting to impress the coaches, Hill didn't tell the coaches about his surgery and began practicing with his teammates. But after three days of nonstop pummelings, Hill was taken to the hospital because of internal bleeding. When Blaik discovered that Hill was still recuperating from an appendectomy, he couldn't help but be impressed. Hill was his kind of player: tough, relentless, and willing to play with pain. If he had a team full of Archie Hills, Blaik commented to several players, then he was sure that Army would win the national championship. Not in three seasons. Not in two. But next season, with most of the same players who couldn't even win two games in 1940.

Blaik also believed that changing the mindset of his players was just as important as improving their fundamentals. This became clear to Blaik during one of his first meetings with the entire team. Standing in front of a chalkboard in a classroom, Blaik diagrammed a running play and then turned to his players, who were seated at desks. "Boys, the most important part of football is line play," Blaik said. "Football games are lost because of poor line play and . . ." Just then, Blaik noticed a player in the back of the room who was dozing off.

"Mister," Blaik yelled, "where are most games lost?"

Startled, the player opened his eyes and saw Blaik, red with anger, staring at him. "Uh," the player stammered, "right here at West Point?"

The players in the field house wanted to laugh, but they kept their feelings muted for fear of further upsetting Blaik. There was nothing funny about that comment, Blaik told his team. He went on to deliver a sermon about what it takes to win—not only on the field of football, but also on the field of combat. "There's a bigger battle going on in the world right now, and everything we do here as a team will help you get ready for the obstacles that you'll be facing once you leave the academy," Blaik told his players that day. "Let's never lose our focus and try to get better each and every day. This will make you a better player and a better soldier."

During these four months of "spring" practice, Blaik usually arrived at the south gym by 8:00 A.M. He'd ride an elevator to the top floor and then walk up another flight of stairs to his office in the tower. Blaik's office was his second home, as he spent more time in there than he did under the roof that he shared with his wife. On one wall hung a West Point coat of arms. Behind Blaik's mahogany desk was a framed photograph of a saluting MacArthur, his hero and role model. Every morning, in the soft, amber light of his office, Blaik would plan in painstaking detail every minute of practice. From the moment that the players left the dressing room at 3:45 until the final whistle sounded at 5:15, Blaik scripted everything. He set times for all the drills and for learning new plays. Blaik memorized every practice schedule and all the players' assignments in every play so he wouldn't need to bring notes to practice; he expected his assistants to do the same, because he believed it sent a good message to the players. Indeed, coaches all across the nation talked about the importance of preparation, but Blaik took it to another level. Years later one of Blaik's assistants, a young coach named Vince Lombardi, would be so impressed with Blaik's preparedness and attention to detail that Lombardi would copy Blaik's approach to the game when, at the age of forty-five, he became the head coach of the Green Bay Packers in late 1958.

Blaik held a daily staff meeting that usually began at nine and lasted until two in the afternoon, with a brief break for lunch. After practice the staff would reconvene and often the meetings would go deep into the night. The most time-consuming aspect of the staff's job was watching film. Blaik, without question, watched more film than any coach in the country. He had a projector in his office and it ran continually, spitting out grainy, black-and-white images of upcoming opponents. Blaik charted opposing team's tendencies based on the down, distance, and field position, and he was one of the first coaches to grade his own players on their effectiveness on each play. By the time he'd be done watching a film, Blaik would have a mountain of notes. But part of Blaik's genius as a football coach was that, after film study, he'd distill those notes into a simple, well-crafted, well-oiled game plan that was easy for his players to digest and comprehend.

Coaches all across the country watched film, but no staff in America took film study as seriously as Blaik's. Even as early as January 1941, Blaik was watching the films of the teams Army would be facing nine months later once the '41 season kicked off. He paid particularly close attention to the games that featured the naval academy. Blaik knew that, even if Army lost every game but managed to defeat the Midshipmen, the year would be judged as a success by his superiors. So Blaik and his assistants all studied film—both of Army's practices and of past games of their upcoming opponents—as if their jobs depended on it, which, in a way, they did.

Blaik got so caught up in viewing film, in fact, that it made a dent in his social life. A few times during these four months of practice, Blaik's wife, Merle, hosted cocktail parties on Friday evenings. Much to his wife's displeasure, Blaik often showed up late because he got bogged down viewing film. One time when he arrived mid-party he didn't understand why so many people were in his house. He'd forgotten all about the party his wife had been planning for weeks. Not only was football the man's livelihood, it was also his life.

For the players, it was hard to concentrate on football, with all that was going on in the world. In late 1940, Franklin Roosevelt became the first man in the history of the United States to be elected president for a third time. Roosevelt defeated Republican Wendell Wilkie in a landslide, and the consequences of Roosevelt's victory were significant. Roosevelt had spent months warning the American public about the evils of fascism. FDR believed that the United States couldn't remain isolationist forever, but he always chose his words carefully because he didn't want to alienate the "America Firsters," those voters who were passionate in wanting the United States to remain a bystander in the growing global conflict. But with Roosevelt securely in office for a third term, he almost immediately strengthened the United States' ties with England. "We should do everything to help the British Empire defend itself," Roosevelt said after the election.

By early 1941, the attitude of the American public toward the possibility of entering the war was beginning to change. A poll in *Fortune* magazine showed that a year earlier American businessmen were unsympathetic with the plight of Britain and France. Now the majority supported assisting both counties in defeating Hitler, even though most hoped they themselves wouldn't have to fight. Roosevelt used a metaphor to describe the situation: If your neighbor's house is on fire, Roosevelt said, and he wants to borrow your garden hose, you don't ask to be paid, you just want your hose back. "There is far less chance of the United States getting into war if we do all what we can now to support the nations defending themselves against the attack by the Axis than if we acquiesce in their defeat," Roosevelt told the nation over the radio in a fireside chat.

In mid-May of '41, with many players poised to quit the Army team because they were so run down from the nonstop blocking and tackling drills, Blaik finally had his team start practicing basic plays. One of Blaik's staple plays was "41 Pitch," a simple pitch sweep to a back. Blaik told his team that this would be one of the primary offensive plays that they'd run throughout the season. This meant that his players had to master it to perfection before they could start learning other plays. "Precision, precision, precision," Blaik repeatedly told his team as they worked on perfecting the one play they were taught.

Robin Olds quickly grew to detest "41 Pitch." Even though he would only be a sophomore (second class) next season, Olds had quickly worked his way into the starting lineup. By May he was a first-string offensive and defensive tackle on the varsity. When he was on offense, his assignment on "41 pitch" was to block a defensive tackle named James McKinney. Before he'd arrived at West Point, McKinney had worked as an attendant at a sanitarium. One of his duties was to keep the patients in line. If, for example, a patient became physical with another patient or a staff member, it was McKinney's job to subdue that patient. This meant that McKinney, who stood 6' 0" and weighed 220 pounds, had a lot of experience in grappling with people one-on-one. McKinney also had a wild streak—he was known to deliver more than a few late hits—and occasionally acted as if he should be living *in* an asylum rather than working at one. "I've been thinking about hitting you all day long," McKinney would sometimes tell Olds before they lined up. "I got a lot of anger I need to take out on you."

In spite of his heated talk, nine times out of ten Olds prevented McKinney from making the tackle—or even disrupting the flow of the play. But the leather helmet that Olds wore didn't protect his ears, and McKinney frequently smacked Olds' ears when he'd club Olds with his forearms in an attempt to knock him off balance. After a week, Olds' right ear was so cauliflowered that he had to go to the campus infirmary to have it pierced and drained. A few days later, he started to lose hearing out of that ear.

"Coach, could we at least mix the plays up so the defense doesn't know what we're running all the time?" Olds asked Blaik after practice one afternoon. "They're beating us up out there because they know exactly how we're going to block them. Could we at least run it in the other direction?"

"We can't do that," replied Blaik. "We're making this as hard as possible on you, Robin, because once we run this play in a game against a team that doesn't know it's coming, you shouldn't have any problems making the right blocks."

When he spoke during practice, Blaik rarely raised his voice. Always wearing his Army baseball cap, sweatshirt, football pants that were cut off below the knee, wool socks, and black cleats, Blaik stood alone as he watched his players perform one drill after the next. If he saw something that bothered him on the practice field, he sometimes blurted out, "Jesus Katy!" but usually he would stand stoically off to the side, a liquid glimmer of intensity flickering in his eyes as he scanned the field, absorbing the action. If he did need to correct a player, Blaik would calmly call him over and quietly explain what he did wrong, leaning over close to his ear. Blaik was a literalist, not a storyteller who had a gift with words, and he always cut straight to the chase, no matter what the setting.

Along with Blaik's outwardly detached demeanor—Henry Romanek once remarked to a teammate that Blaik was as "warm as a cold bottle of piss"—he also had a bullish aura. The players never challenged him, though several came close to saying something to him about his method for conditioning the team. Blaik always saved his toughest drill for the end of practice. He wanted the players' legs to be already burning when he instructed his boys to line up on the goal line and try to make a series of goal-line stands. These were often the most intensive few minutes of practice. Standing on the goal line with a whistle in his mouth, Blaik would ask his players to dig deep, to find that last kernel of energy and give all that they had for just a few more plays. He would tell his players to imagine that it was the fourth quarter against Navy and all that stood between a victory and a loss was a mere three yards. *Do you have what it takes to stop them?* Blaik asked. *Are you strong enough? Are you man enough?* "Give me your all right now!" he'd yell to his squad.

To the players, it sometimes felt like Blaik and his assistants were the Hounds of Hell, always snapping at their ankles, chasing them around the practice field, barking one directive after the next. But the staff's intensive approach worked. Because by the time October rolled around and Army was preparing to play its first game against the Citadel, the Cadet players had been transformed. The spring practice that began in the chill of January, continued through the sleets of March, and concluded in the heat of August had succeeded in changing the attitude, the conditioning, and the skill level of the players. This was a team that had been remade in Blaik's image: They were fundamentally sound, mentally tough, and emotionally starving for success. "I like this team," Blaik told Murphy one afternoon before the season opener. "I like it because no one knows how good we're going to be. This means we've got something that our opponents don't: the element of surprise."

Down at Navy, on August 18, Swede Larson held the initial team meeting of the Midshipmen's 1941 season. Wearing a dark sweatshirt, gray sweatpants and football knickers, Larson spoke to his team in the wrestling loft. Larson was normally an upbeat person—he constantly had a piano-key smile on his face—but he was also famous for his Midwestern reserve, so he rarely let his emotions bubble up to the surface. Yet now as he prepared to speak to the hundred players who were trying out for the team, he couldn't stop himself from getting excited. There was promise in the air. Larson knew that, unlike many of their upcoming opponents, graduation hadn't hit the Middies hard. They had lost only eight lettermen from the top two strings. So as Larson looked out at his players, he knew he was staring at a team that could seriously challenge for the national championship, and he told his players as much.

"We have a chance to be one of the best Navy teams in the history of Navy football," said Larson. "But at this point, it's just a chance. We have to work hard and stay focused from now until the season is over."

Before the 1941 season began, the era of single platoon football came to an end when the NCAA passed a rule allowing free player substitutions except during the last two minutes of the first half. Up until then, player substitutions could only be made between quarters. Larson liked the idea of single platoon football, and in 1940 he had successfully employed what he called "The Two Ocean Navy." Because Larson felt he had an abundance of talented players, he typically played his first string in the first and fourth quarters and his second string in the second and third. Even though all the players played both offense and defense, they didn't get fatigued because they only played half the game. The majority of college coaches were opposed to the new substitution rule of '41, believing that football players should be all-around talents and be good on both sides of the ball. Most coaches also felt that the rule rewarded specialization. In spite of the new rule, Larson told his team that they'd again be operating "The Two Ocean Navy."

Larson also announced to his players that they'd be wearing a new type of helmet for the '41 season. Instead of donning leather caps, the Middies would be wearing a plastic helmet with a blue stripe down the middle. Larson noted to his players that in 1940 a few college teams had worn these helmets—which didn't include face guards—and they had dramatically reduced the number of head injuries that the players had suffered. All of this made sense to Busik, Kauffman, and the others in the room, even if the helmets did, in their estimation, look a little like something Buck Rogers would wear.

The other cosmetic change that Larson told his players about was the numbering system. Instead of allowing players to wear whatever number they desired, the NCAA had recently issued guidelines for a player's number based on the position that he played. Wingbacks were to be numbered 10 to 19, blocking backs 20 to 29, fullbacks 30 to 39, tailbacks 40 to 49, centers 50 to 59, guards 60 to 69, tackles 70 to 79, and ends 80 to 89. These new requirements didn't sit well with a number of the returning players, especially those who felt that their old numbers had brought them good luck. Larson, not wanting anyone to feel jinxed, allowed his returning lettermen to keep their number if they desired, but all the new players had to abide by the NCAA guidelines. Busik was relieved. As tailback, he wore number 63. It didn't make sense to him to don a jersey that had a number in the forties. "It looks funny when I don't wear 63," Busik told a teammate. "That's my number, simple as that."

When the Navy team finally hit the practice field during the last days of August, Larson wasn't disappointed. As he walked from one group of players performing a drill to the next, he was pleased with the effort and talent level that he saw. Unlike Army's Blaik, Larson left much of the actual coaching to his stable of assistants. Larson's top lieutenant was Rip Miller. A hearty, amiable man, Miller coached Navy's offensive and defensive lines. Many of the players considered him a surrogate father, mostly because he was the reason that nearly all of them were there. Miller, who also served as Navy's recruiting coordinator, was a noted ball-player bloodhound who could sniff talent from thousands of miles away. By 1941, his Bird-Dog recruiting system—having dozens of scouts across the country on the prowl for talent—was starting to be copied by schools all across the country. But no one in the recruiting game was as plugged in as Miller, whose connections extended all the way to the White House.

Throughout the late '30s and early '40s, Miller made several trips to visit President Roosevelt, who was a rabid Navy football fan. Roosevelt kept a miniature wheel of a ship on his desk in the oval office and he was always snooping around for inside information on the Midshipmen football team. On numerous occasions during his trips to Washington, Miller would bring a silent reel of film from the most recent Army-Navy contest and, usually in the president's private quarters, the two would sit and watch the game. Miller would narrate the action to the President, but he was always careful with his words. Because the President could issue ten appointments to each academy, Miller stressed to Roosevelt that it would greatly help the Navy program if the President doled out his appointments to potential football players. One time, on the tape, Navy was outfitted in white uniforms and Army was dressed in black—on the video, black always made the players look bigger than they actually were—and Miller tried to pull the wool over the President's eyes, noting to Roosevelt, "Look, Mr. President. Just look at how much bigger those Army boys are than us. We have a hell of time beating them."

"Well, Rip, what do you plan to do about it?" the President asked.

"That's where we were hoping you'd come in, sir," Miller replied. "We could really use your ten appointments. I've got boys all around the country lined up, but it's tough to get all of them congressional appointments."

Rip's plan worked. "Well, Rip," replied the President, after considering the situation, "I'll tell you what I'll do. I'll do my best to give you all ten. We gotta do whatever it takes to beat Army."

On the practice field, Miller often lined up against his players. Miller believed that the best way to teach proper blocking and tackling technique was through example, and he relished putting on the pads and mixing it up with lineman who were twenty years his junior. Miller was so passionate about line play that he wrote a two thousand word article on the subject in the November 1926 edition of *The Athletic Journal.* "The main objective of the offensive lineman," wrote Miller, "is to obtain quick contact and above all things to keep that contact. Whether a lineman uses a shoulder charge to drive a man out of the way of a play, or whether he reverts to a body block to prevent a drifting defensive opponent from slicing into a play, or whether he runs interference in the open field, the thing uppermost in his mind at all times is—to keep contact. Too many offensive lineman give up easily."

As Miller coached the offensive line, telling his players over and over at practice, "Damn it, you gotta be tough," Keith Molesworth was busy teaching both the offensive and defensive backs. Molesworth had been a star quarterback with the Chicago Bears from 1931 to '37 and his success in the NFL gave him instant credibility among the Navy players. When he talked to them, it was as if his words came thundering down from

Mt. Olympus, so attentive were the players to his every suggestion and command. Larson felt comfortable letting Miller and Molesworth oversee the Xs and Os of the game; Larson was more at ease acting as the leader who made the big-picture decisions. So at practices Larson floated from one group to the next, a serious look etched on his face, imploring his kids to work harder, but rarely did he delve into the nuances of the game with them.

As Navy's first game against William & Mary approached on September 27, the players badly wanted to win for their coaches—especially their head coach. Because even though Larson hadn't told them yet, the players figured that this was going to be his last season as Navy's coach. The clouds of war were gathering, and they knew Larson would soon have to fight in the approaching storm.

That storm was intensifying by the day. In late June of '41, as the Navy boys continued practicing in Annapolis, Germany attacked Russia, its former ally. Speaking on a radio broadcast on the morning after the invasion, Hitler boasted that Germany's army movements were "the greatest the world has ever seen."

Days later Japan conscripted a million men into its army and recalled all of its merchant ships from the Atlantic. The Japanese government was preparing for a possible war against Britain and the United States over Indochina, which Japan had invaded in September 1940 and by June of '41 had established control over the entire country. On the afternoon of the announcement of troops being called up, the war minister, Hideki Tojo, made a rare appearance at an imperial conference. He emphatically told the Japanese cabinet that the time for action had come. Based on Germany's success in Europe, the war minister insisted that the Japanese empire needed to expand immediately—or risk missing a rare opportunity in history.

The British and U.S. governments responded by signing the Atlantic Charter. Meeting in secrecy on board the American cruiser *Augusta* and British battleship *Prince of Wales* at Placentia Bay in Newfoundland, President Roosevelt and Prime Minister Winston Churchill signed a joint declaration of common principles. The two countries were bound together like family, and both Roosevelt and Churchill insisted that, no matter what the outcome of the approaching storm, neither country would seek territorial gains from the war.

. . .

Like most high school, college, and pro football teams in 1941, Army and Navy both ran the single wing offense. In the Cadets' and the Midshipmen's versions of the single wings, the center could snap the ball to the tailback, fullback, quarterback, or wingback in motion. The center had to be one of the most skilled players on the offense, because he was required to accurately hike the ball in different directions based on the play call. The center usually looked through his legs when he made the snap, which left him vulnerable to a hard-charging defensive lineman. But even more important than the center in the single wing was the tailback, because he received the majority of the snaps and then either ran, passed, or punted. Indeed, most of the great triple threats in football history were single-wing tailbacks, players such as Red Grange, George Gipp, Sammy Baugh, Tom Harmon, and Doak Walker.

Sometimes after receiving the ball the tailback would hand the ball to the fullback, who would take a step forward and then spin 180 degrees. With his back to the line, the fullback had several options: He could hand off to another back, fake a handoff and run, or turn back toward the line of scrimmage and run straight into the middle of the line. The quarterback, for his part, rarely touched the ball. His most important role was to be the lead blocker, which made him more of a glorified guard than anything else.

What made the offense so hard to defend was that all the backs in the single wing were constantly spinning, reversing, faking handoffs, making handoffs, running the ball, passing the ball, blocking, and receiving. Confusing the defense was what Pop Warner had in mind when he devised the offense in 1906 while he was the coach at Carlisle (Pennsylvania) Indian School. In 1912, Warner wrote a book on the formation and its popularity spread quickly. Blaik and Larson had by now tweaked the offense, but the single wing was the dominant formation that each squad practiced prior to the '41 season kickoff.

"The offense is hard to defend because of its deception," Larson told reporters one day during preseason practice. "I know some teams are starting to get away from the single wing, but we'll still use it. After all, we've got a tailback named Bill Busik, and I'd be crazy not to run the single wing with him."

7

THE 1941 SEASON

ON THE PORTABLE RADIOS that many of the Cadets and Midshipmen kept in their rooms, the sports news crackled out, story after story in the summer of '41. Joe DiMaggio, the Yankee Clipper, hit safely in fifty-six straight games. The Red Sox's Ted Williams, the sweet swingin' lefty, was hitting .400 heading into the final day of baseball's regular season. Instead of protecting that magical number by sitting on the bench that last day, Williams played in both games of a double-header against Cleveland. He went six for nine, leaving his season-ending average at .406.

There was more. On June 18, Billy Conn, known as the "Pittsburgh Kid," met Joe Louis in a boxing ring at the Polo Grounds in New York. Conn was the definition of an underdog. He weighed 168 pounds. Louis, the champ, already an American folk hero, checked in at 202 pounds. But through the first ten rounds of the bout, Conn was clubbing Louis, winning on all three of the judges' cards. At the end of the twelfth, Conn landed a devastating right that nailed Louis flush in the face. After the round Conn boldly told his corner that he was going to be the first man to knock the great Joe Louis out. Conn's corner begged their fighter to stay away, telling him that he had the fight won on points but Conn, sensing a historic KO, didn't listen.

Conn came out in the thirteenth firing one punch after the next, tiring with each shot. Louis waited and waited, taking the punishment, absorbing all that the challenger could give, then . . . *BAM!* Louis unleashed a right-hand cross that hit Conn square in the jaw. For the first time all night, the challenger, having just spent so much energy trying to flatten the champ, staggered. Louis followed with seven straight punches—all of them connected. The eighth punch, another right to the jaw, was enough. It sent Conn sprawling onto the canvas. He was counted out. After he came to his senses, Conn, who was as Irish as a shamrock, was asked why he didn't try to win the bout on points. Without missing a beat, he replied, "What's the sense of being Irish if you can't be dumb?"

Then there was Whirlaway, the handsome little red colt that captivated the imagination of racing fans across the nation. Nicknamed Mr. Longtail because of his uncommonly long, flowing black tail that shot up at a 90-degree angle when he ran, Whirlaway had a hard-charging, come-from-behind style not seen since the great Seabiscuit from the late '30s. In the '41 Kentucky Derby, Whirlaway, ridden by jockey Eddie Arcaro, was foundering at the back of the pack with a quarter mile left—but then blazed to victory, winning by eight lengths. In the Preakness, he again started slowly, closed in the last quarter and won by five and a half lengths. And in the Belmont, he broke out of the gate quickly, opened up a seven-length lead and won by two and a half lengths to capture the Triple Crown. The horse was a little nuts—he often veered wildly all over the track until trainer Ben Jones fashioned a special hood with a one-eyed blinker that kept the colt from bearing to the outside—but by the end of the summer Whirlaway was as beloved as any thoroughbred of his time. "There may be better horses," Ben Jones said after winning the Triple Crown, "but there can be only one Whirlaway."

None of these riveting stories was lost on Robin Olds or Henry Romanek. It seemed that in sport anything was possible in the summer of '41, so why not a rebirth of Army football? From listening to the radio and reading the newspapers, Olds and Romanek knew that DiMaggio had done the unexpected, as had Williams, as had Whirlaway, as had the Pittsburgh Kid. To Romanek and Olds, it was now Army's turn. Certainly, the Cadets had worked harder than any college or pro team since the start of the year. They also had Earl "Red" Blaik, who, like a Baptist preacher, had won a squad full of converts. Indeed, in the summer of '41, for the first time since Olds and Romanek got their first stains on their Army football uniforms, hope was rolling high at the Point.

Half a world away during this stellar summer of sport, Japanese Admiral Isokyro Yamamoto sat in his cabin aboard the 42,000-ton battleship *Nagato*. The date was August 10, 1941. Though he was the commander in chief of Japan's Combined Fleet, Yamamoto was not an imposing figure. At 5' 3" Yamamoto, even by Japanese standards, was considered short. He had a straight, large nose and pointed eyebrows, which usually gave Yamamoto the appearance of having a inquisitive look. On this morning the commander's dress uniform overflowed with medals and honors.

Aboard the *Nagato*, which was anchored in Saeki Bay, Yamamoto summoned one of his old friends, Admiral Zengo Yoshida, to his cabin. In their younger days Yamamoto and Yoshida had been classmates, and they trusted each other without question. Once Yoshida walked into the cabin, the commander told his old classmate about a secret plan that he'd been crafting for months. "Japan must deal the U.S. Navy a fatal blow at the outset of the war," Yamamoto told Yoshida in Japanese. "It is the only way she can fight with any reasonable prospect of success. An attack is necessary to give Japan a free hand in the southern operation."

"How will it be possible to send a task force so far from Japan with the present radius of action of the fleet?" asked Yoshida.

"The task force will refuel at sea," replied Yamamoto. "Prospects are favorable for its success."

Army opened the 1941 season by pounding the Citadel, 19–6. The next week the Cadets squeaked past VMI, 27–20. By the time Army faced an undefeated Notre Dame team at Yankee Stadium on November 1, the Cadets were 4–0 and the surprise team of the nation. In just over a month, Army, a team that began the season unranked, had risen to Number 14 in the AP poll. "There's no reason we can't beat Notre Dame," Olds told reporters a few days before Army traveled to New York. "Sure, they're a great team, but we've been through so much together already that we feel like we can conquer any challenge."

"This team has come along fast," added Blaik. "Actually, it's come along even faster than I expected. Right now, I think we can give anyone in the country a great battle."

Army's quick start had all of West Point abuzz. After their 20–7 win at Yale on October 18 in New Haven, hundreds of cadets met the team at the train depot on the Hudson. The cadets ushered the players into horse-drawn carts. But instead of having horses pull the players, the plebes grabbed the carts and dragged the team up the steep hill and into the central area of the campus for a celebratory pep rally. The plebes in particular were ecstatic over Army's four wins to begin the season. When the Cadets were victorious, the plebes were afforded the luxury of falling out for the next week, meaning they weren't hazed for six whole days after the game. The prospect of falling out always prompted the plebes to cheer like they were in a shouting contest whenever they sat in the stands at games, many screaming so loudly they became hoarse for days afterward.

With the team undefeated, cadets began gathering at the old parade grounds to watch practice. Standing in groups of ten and twenty along the marked-off sideline, the cadets constantly encouraged the players to hit harder, to play well for the entire army. The Corp also started cheering the team each night at mess hall, the yells of support loudly reverberating off the hall's concrete walls. The student-body excitement reached a crescendo on October 31, the eve of the Notre Dame game at Yankee Stadium in New York City. Before the squad left for the Knollwood Country Club in White Plains, New York, the eighteen hundred cadets held a boisterous mess-hall rally. Then they marched outside and had a torch-lit parade, capped by a bonfire on the practice field. As the tongues of flames licked the autumn sky on this Halloween night, the entire school seemed reinvigorated by its football team. The student body chanted that they wanted to squash Notre Dame, that they wanted to flatten the Fighting Irish. This kind of school spirit was exactly what Eichelberger had hoped Blaik would generate when he hired him away from Dartmouth, but not even Eichelberger thought Blaik could fashion a winning team at Army so quickly. His wildest dreams never reached that far.

The next day newspaper men from around the country traveled to Yankee Stadium for the Army-Notre Dame contest, which was billed by many as the best game to date of the 1941 college football season. "While over two-hundred games will splash across the gridirons of this broad land today, none compares in public interest and enthusiasm with the meeting of the Cadets and Irish," stated the *New York Daily News*. Dating back to 1923, when Army and Notre Dame first played each other at Ebbets Field in Brooklyn, this game had been the showpiece of New York football. Big Apple businessmen had long used it as an opportunity to invite out-of-town customers to Gotham. And even fans who only had a moderate interest in football—including scores of women—marked it on their calendars months in advance. This was as much a social event as it was a football game, and New York blue bloods, dressed in their mink coats and tailored suits, wouldn't dream of being no-shows.

On the morning of the game, which had a 12:30 P.M. kickoff, the skies over the South Bronx turned dark. The rain started at 11:00 A.M. and wouldn't stop for some ten hours. Nonetheless, a capacity crowd of seventy-six thousand filled Yankee Stadium. The stands and boxes were an ocean of umbrellas, oilskins, cellophane coverings, and plastic ponchos. Most fans carried a thermos of hot cocoa—some spiked it with mint schnapps—and the drinks helped the fans stay warm on this miserable afternoon.

When the Notre Dame players ran out from their locker room and into the gloom, they made football history: The Irish became the first college team to wear nylon football pants. Notre Dame coach Frank Leahy, in his first year on the job, made the decision to have his players wear these newfangled pants once he learned that the weather forecast called for thunderstorms. The gold nylon pants, which weighed only four and a half ounces—or half the weight of the standard cotton football pants—shed water rather than absorbed it. Notre Dame had always been considered the sartorial leader of the gridiron, but to Leahy, this was about football strategy, not about making a fashion statement.

Even though a tarp covered the field until just minutes before kickoff, the field quickly became a large pit of mud. The poor playing conditions favored Army. The slow, slick field helped mitigate Notre Dame's size advantage: The Irish outweighed the Cadets by an average of fifteen pounds per man on both the offensive and defensive lines. Ranked sixth in the nation in the AP poll, Notre Dame entered the game as a three-to-one favorite over the fourteenth ranked Cadets, yet Army threatened to score first. Late in the first period the Irish's Dippy Evans, lining up to punt at his own 21-yard line, had the ball slide off the side of his foot as he went to kick; the ball fluttered out of bounds 13 yards beyond the line of scrimmage at Notre Dame's 34. Army suddenly had an opportunity to gain the early advantage.

After a few runs by the Cadets' Hank Mazur, Army faced a fourth and one at the Irish 10-yard line. All throughout the first quarter Mazur had been brilliant, running through the slop like a gifted mudder at Churchill Downs. A native of Lowell, Massachusetts, Mazur had attended Boston College for two years before enrolling at West Point. He was considered one of the best backs in the nation by most newspapermen and, if the season went well, a darkhorse candidate for the Heisman Trophy. Now on fourth and one, Mazur took the handoff, ran off tackle and gained two yards. First down. But then Mazur noticed a yellow flag laying on the sloppy field: Army was offside. On fourth and six, Blaik chose to go for it again, to gamble and try to get an early touchdown. He called for another off-tackle run—Army had had success with this play—but the Irish held Army to only a 2-yard gain. After the Cadets gave up possession, Blaik looked like a man in search of a wall to punch as he paced back and forth on the sideline. He knew a precious opportunity had slipped away. Worse, it had slipped away because of a mental error.

But Notre Dame, led by star runner and passer Angelo Bertelli, couldn't seize the momentum. Not only was the muddy field slowing down the Irish, but Notre Dame's offensive line couldn't consistently block Robin Olds, who was having the best game of his life. Playing the full 60 minutes on both the offensive and defensive lines, Olds made about a dozen tackles. That Olds could have such an impact on the game was a testament to his toughness. A few weeks before fall practice began, Olds and a few friends spent a lazy afternoon at Delafield Pond, a popular swimming hole just north of West Point. Delafield had three diving platforms and Olds decided to attempt a simple swan dive off the highest platform. But he hit the water at an awkward angle—it was one of the first times in his life that he looked woefully unathletic—and both of his arms were pushed back behind his head. Pain immediately pulsed through his body. Underwater, Olds couldn't move either of his arms. He kicked his legs, pushing himself above the surface. He took a big gulp of air, relieved that he didn't drown, then kicked his way to the beach.

Later that night, his arms were still numb, almost lifeless. In the mess hall the next day he couldn't even lift a pitcher of water off the table with his right hand. Olds never told Blaik about the injury, fearing that he'd lose his starting position, but often in practice and in games his right arm would go dead if he took a direct shot to the arm. Midway through the second quarter against Notre Dame this happened—the hit sent a shot of pain that flowed to every part of his body—and for the rest of the game Olds essentially played with only one good arm.

Olds' teammates knew that he was injured. They saw him in the hot tub after every practice, nursing his sore right shoulder. And they saw him struggle simply to lift his right arm when he was putting on his shirt. Seeing this, his teammates came to view Olds with renewed respect. Even though he was in his first year on the varsity squad, whenever Olds rose to speak in the locker room, his teammates would quiet down and listen as intently as if Coach Blaik was talking. The respect Olds commanded was deep, and he never held his tongue when he had something on his mind. His teammates were reminded of this in the third quarter against the Irish, the score still 0–0, when Olds nearly blew a gasket in the huddle.

Army faced a first and ten from its own two yard line. Olds, like all of his linemates, was now completely slathered in mud; the fans were unable even to see his uniform number of 75. All you could see was the whites of his eyes. "I feel like a goddamn pig," Olds told one of his teammates in the huddle. "But this is fun."

With the ball on their own two-yard line in the third quarter, Blaik sent in a backup tailback, whose uniform was spotless because he hadn't played all day. The tailback was charged with making the play call and he decided to open the series with a reverse, a risky play given Army's field position and the poor playing conditions. "Like hell we're going to run that play," Olds yelled in the huddle. "We've busted our asses all afternoon, and we're not going to throw away this game with that stupid play call of yours."

"Shut up, Olds, or I'll throw your ass off the field," replied the tailback.

"You and who else," countered Olds.

But that's as far as the argument went. In spite of Olds' objections, the Cadets went ahead and ran the reverse. If not for a last-second lunge by end James Kelleher, the Irish would have tackled Kelleher in the end zone for a safety. But as it stood, Army faced a second and 11 from its own 2-inch line. Instead of risking a safety by running another play, Blaik opted to punt on second down. That near safety, it turned out, was the closest that either team would come to scoring all afternoon. The game ended in a 0–0 tie. Army had more first downs than the Irish (5 to 4) and more total yards of offense (120 to 96), but neither team even attempted a field goal. Though Blaik wouldn't admit it, the tie amounted to a moral victory for the underdog Cadets. It proved that they could play with any team in the nation, and it proved that Blaik had his team moving in the right direction.

"Army doesn't like ties," Blaik said tersely to the press after the game outside the locker room. Blaik then walked away from the newspapermen, anxious to return to West Point and study the game film of their next opponent, Harvard. Blaik feared his team would suffer an emotional letdown against the Crimson; he knew that his Cadets were beat-up and exhausted. But for the first time since he took over the Army program, Blaik privately experienced an emotion for his players that he hadn't experienced since his days at Dartmouth: He was proud. Damn proud, in fact. Even Blaik, a natural-born pessimist, started to believe in his boys, believe that they could do something special in '41.

Before the 1941 season kicked off, the Cadet and Midshipmen football players were given some sobering news: Because of the increasingly volatile situations in Europe and the Far East, academic programs at both academies would be accelerated. The demand for more army and navy officers was rapidly growing, and the quickest way to fill that need was to expedite the pace of study at the academies. This meant that Olds and Romanek, for example, would graduate after only three years at the school in June 1943 instead of June 1944. Busik and Kauffman, meanwhile, would finish their studies in June 1942 instead of June 1943. This eliminated one year of football eligibility from every player at the academics, so they all knew that they had to make this season count, that they had to pack two years worth of dreams into one season. This redlined everyone's intensity.

Before Navy's third game of the 1941 season against Lafayette, which was played on a warm early October day in Annapolis, that sense of intensity was written all over the face of Swede Larson. Navy had blown out its first two opponents of the season, William & Mary (34–0) and West Virginia (40–0), but that didn't offer much comfort to Larson in the moments before the Lafayette game. As Larson put on his sports jacket and gray felt fedora in the coach's locker room, he smoked one Lucky Strike after the next. Larson made it a point not to smoke during games and practices, but he felt that having a cigarette before the game—or, hell, half a pack on occasion—helped calm his nerves. Once dressed, Larson then met with his team in the wrestling loft an hour before kickoff. "Go out there and fight like your life depends on it," Larson emphatically told his boys. "Go out and do the things that we practiced and be disciplined and this game is ours. Now let's do it!"

Larson led his boys on their long walk across campus to the football stadium. Many midshipmen and local fans walked with the players to the field, slapping the players on their shoulder pads and shouting encouragement. Once they reached the stadium, the 21,660 fans—which included Vice President Henry A. Wallace—gave the Middies a standing ovation. From his seat in a box, Wallace appeared to be in especially high spirits.

A smile stretched across his face like a rubber band as he watched Navy exert its dominance right away. Busik led the Midshipmen on three pile-driving touchdown marches to give Navy a 21–0 lead midway through the second quarter. The Midshipmen were a heavy favorite, and several marines who were in attendance had bet that Navy would shut out the undermanned Lafayette squad. For most of the first half, those bets looked as safe as a bar of gold in Fort Knox. But then Busik fielded a punt on his own one yard line. Instead of pushing forward for an easy five yards, Busik stepped back two yards while he cut to his left, thinking that he had a wall of blockers set up for him. But just as he was making the turn upfield, he was tackled by Lafayette's Bob Leopard for a safety. After the game, which Navy won 41–2, the marines accosted Busik as he walked back across campus to the locker room, telling him that his mistake had cost them a thick wad of bills.

"I'm just trying to do my best, fellas," Busik told the angry marines. "Sorry about your bet, but even if I had known about it, I wouldn't have changed a thing. If you got a problem with it, tough luck."

Busik then stopped in his tracks and coldly eyed the group of marines. He said nothing for a full minute, daring one of the marines to offer a challenge. When none was proffered, Busik turned and slowly walked away, his head held high.

On the Monday evening after the Lafayette victory—like every Monday evening after a game—the Navy team gathered in the team's projection room to watch the eight-millimeter, black-and-white film of Saturday's contest. Holding narrow wooden sticks that served as their pointers, Larson and his lieutenants went over every play in excruciating detail. After Larson gave his initial remarks on the play, the position coaches would point out what each of the Middies did well and what they did poorly on the play. A few Navy staffers were assigned to take still photographs during the game, and these were analyzed on Monday nights with the same intensity as the film. By the end of the 90-minute session following the Lafayette game, it was clear to the coaches and the rest of the team that Busik was playing better than any back in the country. "Busik is the most well-rounded tailback I've ever coached," Larson told reporters shortly after the Lafayette game. "There's really not anything he can't do. He can run inside, outside, and boy, he can really wing the ball when we have to pass."

The next week Navy beat Cornell, 14–0. Seven days later the Middies traveled to Cambridge, Massachusetts, to face Harvard. Many columnists in the East had Navy sitting atop their national poll. Jesse A. Linthicum of the *Baltimore Sun*, for example, ranked Navy number one, Minnesota two, and Michigan three. Because of Navy's growing reputation, the Middies were a four-to-one favorite over Harvard, but all week prior to the game Larson was as worried as an expectant father on his baby's due date. He repeatedly told his team to be wary of the Crimson, mainly because they were coached by Dick Harlow, who was one of the most cunning coaches of his time. Harlow often developed off-beat, wild gameplans that employed strategies and formations that no other coach in the nation used, such as the slanting line defense. As the *New York Sun* put it a day before the game, "Harlow . . . is noted for his ability to harness the power of a stronger opponent and occasionally upset a rival by means of ambuscade, surprise, and everything but fifth-column activity."

On the eve of the game, Larson took his players to a movie theater in Boston and showed them a motion picture of the 1937 Harvard-Navy game. The players munched on popcorn and drank soda in the dark as they watched the game end in a scoreless tie. "We need to execute, execute, and execute some more to make sure that what happened to Navy in 1937 doesn't happen in 1941," Larson told his players after watching the film. "Every man will win his own individual battle on every play, and then we'll have no problem winning the team battle."

But the next afternoon, just as Larson had anticipated, Harvard coach Dick Harlow did have a surprise for the Middies. Moments before the Navy offense hiked the ball, the Crimson defense shifted multiple players, trying to confuse the Midshipmen. What's more, on almost every defensive play both of Harvard's ends looped to the outside of their blockers in an effort to force all the plays to the inside. In their scouting and film study, Navy had never seen Harvard play this kind of defense. It rattled the Midshipmen—especially Busik. He fumbled three times and had one punt sail off the side of his foot, a shank that only traveled 10 yards. This was by far the worst, and most embarrassing, game of Busik's career. The final score, just like in '37, was 0–0.

In the locker room Larson consoled his players by telling them that the 1926 Navy team had won the national title even though they had tied a game. This team could repeat that feat, Larson said over and over as he shook the hand of each player in the locker room. Then, as was his custom, Larson walked over to the Harvard locker room and congratulated the Crimson. He rarely left the opponents' locker room until he had shaken the hand of every player, from the star tailback who played all 60 minutes to the lowest reserve who didn't even make it onto the field.

Three days after the Harvard game, Larson traveled to New York to attend a luncheon for New York football writers. As he nibbled on a steak, he received a telegram stating that Rose Bowl officials had offered the naval academy a bid to play in their New Year's Day game. Larson was stunned—and not just because his team hadn't played in a bowl game in seventeen years. Larson was surprised by the bid because Navy was only halfway through its schedule—the three giants of Pennsylvania, Notre Dame, and Army still remained—but already his boys were attracting nationwide attention.

"We are still seeking to instill confidence in the boys for any and every situation which must face them," Larson said at the luncheon after he had time to put some perspective on the Rose Bowl invite. "I certainly hope we go through the season unbeaten, because I'd like to see the boys get a chance to play in such a game as the Rose Bowl. We have four games left to play and even if we win them, we have another difficulty to overcome. We're on an accelerated academic program because there's a war coming. And our boys are going to fight."

During the luncheon, Larson also was peppered with questions about a rumor that suggested he was going to become the next commissioner of the NFL. Washington Redskins' owner George Marshall had been touting Larson's credentials for weeks. But Larson, wearing a coat and tie, told the writers that his future was tied to the armed forces. "I don't have time to think about a job in the NFL," Larson said, "I've got a football team and a war to worry about."

On November 1, the same rainstorm that fell on New York City as Army played Notre Dame also drenched Philadelphia, where the Midshipmen were facing Penn. The constant rain swirled in the cross-wind at Franklin Field, forcing many of the 73,391 fans to watch the game from the covered runways in the doubled-decked, horseshoe stadium. But nearly everyone stayed in the stadium because this was the first time since the series between Navy and Penn originated in 1922 that both teams entered the game ranked in the Eastern rankings' Top 10 (Penn was second, Navy was third) and in the Top 20 in the AP national rankings (Penn was eighth; Navy was eleventh).

Navy struck first. The Middies marched 51 yards on their first drive to score a touchdown on a 12-yard pass from Busik to Sammy Booth. For the rest of the first half and seven minutes into the third quarter, neither team could push the ball into the end zone. Navy had only given up two points all season—and that was on Busik's safety against Lafayette—so the defense was virtually impenetrable. Then midway through the third the Middies got some breathing room; back Archie Clarke took a pitch from Busik and crossed over the goal line. The point after sailed wide right, but Navy had a 13–0 lead.

When the Middies got the ball back after a Penn punt, they again began to move the ball. Facing a third and three early in the fourth quarter, Busik took the center snap, spun, and ran to his right. After getting the first down, he was tackled by a Penn lineman. With Busik lying prone on the ground in front of the Navy bench, another out-of-control Quaker player jumped on Busik, hitting him with a flying elbow to the head, knocking Busik out cold. None of the referees saw the cheap shot, but Navy assistant Rip Miller did.

"Laboon!" Miller yelled down the bench. He wanted Jake Laboon, a strapping, 6' 4", 220-pound sophomore tackle. Laboon grabbed his helmet and sprinted toward Miller.

"Laboon, did you see what just happened to Busik?" Miller shouted.

"Yes sir!" replied Laboon.

"Well, you get in there and I don't want that end to be in this game much longer. Do you understand me, Laboon?" Miller asked.

"Yes sir!" again replied Laboon, who then jogged onto the soggy field.

Busik still lay on the ground, motionless. The elbow blow had hit him in the forehead, which was left exposed by his plastic helmet. Finally, after a few minutes, he groggily got up and was helped to the bench. In the huddle all the Navy players knew Laboon's mission. They didn't say anything outright; they just looked at Laboon and nodded their heads. When Navy broke the huddle and approached the line of scrimmage, Laboon sized up the end he was told to take out, his nostrils flaring. A few of Laboon's teammates later swore they'd never seen a scarier face.

The ball was snapped. Laboon grabbed a fistful of mud and slung it in the end's face. As the play drifted to the opposite side of the field, leaving Laboon and the end standing face-to-face some twenty yards from the action, Laboon drew a fist. The end was trying to get the mud off of his face, his hands rubbing his eyes. Laboon then threw a haymaker, hitting the player in the nose with all his might. The Penn player fell to the ground, sprawled out in a whirling daze. His nose was broken and his face, which was already covered in mud, quickly reddened as a reservoir of blood pooled. He tried to get up, but he swayed like a tall wheat stalk in the wind, and fell back to the ground. The officials—and most of the fans—had seen this retaliatory act, and Laboon was tossed out of the game. He walked to the sideline, took off his helmet, and spoke to Miller. Now in the cool and wet air smoke rose off Laboon's head as if from a smoldering camp fire.

"Laboon, I didn't tell you to take him out in front of everybody," Miller told Laboon as the assistant coach escorted his player to the locker room. "I meant for you to be a little more subtle about it."

"Sorry coach," replied Laboon.

"It's okay, Jake," said Miller. "You did good. You protected our star."

Late in the third quarter Penn scored, but Navy won the game, 13–6. The Fighting Irish, who earlier on this day had tied Army, were up next.

At precisely the same time that the Navy players were slugging it out with the boys from Penn, a ship named the *Taiyo Maru* eased into Honolulu Harbor. The *Taiyo Maru* was a passenger vessel from Japan, and the U.S. government allowed her to enter the waters of Hawaii in the hope of deflating the growing tensions between the United States and Japan. (On this very day, Joseph C. Grew, the U.S. ambassador to Japan, sent a telegram to President Roosevelt from Tokyo. In it Grew warned Roosevelt that the Japanese may be planning a "surprise attack.")

On the bridge of the *Taiyo Maru*, with binoculars held to their eyes, were what appeared to be two Japanese tourists. Suguru Suzuki and Toshihide Maejima each looked at the Navy port on Oahu carefully, as if they were studying a piece of art from afar. They were particularly interested in the ship and personnel movements at Pearl Harbor. It was 8:30 A.M. local time and on this crystal-clear Saturday Suzuki and Maejima were afforded an almost perfect perspective on what the early morning conditions around Pearl Harbor looked like on the weekend. Most of the base appeared to be resting, the two Japanese men said to each other.

The U.S. government didn't know it, but Suzuki was a lieutenant in the Japanese Air Force, Maejima a submarine expert in the Japanese Navy. They were spies.

In the Navy locker room after defeating Penn, at about the same time that Suzuki and Maejima were peering though their binoculars at Pearl, the Midshipmen coaches and players slapped Laboon on the back and congratulated him on obeying the instructions of his coach. Yet Laboon was deeply disturbed by his action. One of the most popular Midshipmen at the naval academy, Laboon had a clear idea of the line between right and wrong, and he felt he had crossed it. A native of Pittsburgh, Pennsylvania, Laboon came from a deeply religious Catholic family. The first day he arrived at the academy, Laboon joined the Newman Club (a Catholic club) and every Sunday morning he led all the Catholic midshipmen in the mile-long march to St. Mary's, an old brick church where they would attend mass. Laboon had a notion that he might one day pursue the priesthood, but like most young men, he wasn't sure what the future held for him. "I really like helping others," Laboon told his roommate William Leahy one day during their plebe year. "I just need to figure out what's the best way to do that."

Even though Laboon sucker-punched the Penn player—and even though he often liked to blow off steam by banging his fists into walls—there was a sweetness in his character that endeared him to admirals, midshipmen, and janitors alike. He talked to everybody about everything; no subjects were off limits. *Is Jackson Pollack the greatest living painter? Is Spam, that new kind of canned meat, as tasty as everyone says? Is Rita Hayworth, the movies' Love Goddess, the sexiest woman alive?* Always with an ear-to-ear grin on his face, Laboon flapped his gums on all these topics, and his teammates quickly came to regard him as the biggest talker on the team.

The very large Laboon, who was also an All-American lacrosse player, decided in his first year at the academy that he would enter the Naval branch of submarines after he graduated from Annapolis. Laboon figured since he was already ducking every time he walked inside a naval academy building, life in a sub wouldn't be that drastic of a change. "Subs fascinate me," Laboon told his friend Leahy. "And mark my words: They're going to be critical in the war."

The decision to join the subs would ultimately be the most important of his life. Because in a few years, while out at sea, Jake Laboon would do something that sailors would end up talking about for decades, an act that would seal Laboon's fate.

The Navy players considered Notre Dame their second-biggest game of the season, right behind their blood feud with Army. In the days before taking on the Fighting Irish, Larson told reporters that he was most concerned about stopping Notre Dame's Angelo Bertelli, one of the best passers in college football. When the Irish played Army the previous week at muddy Yankee Stadium, the poor playing conditions had limited what Bertelli could do. Larson now fretted that Bertelli was due, but he still believed the Navy defense could shut him down.

"If our plans centering around Mr. Bertelli work out, I think there's a good chance we'll win this game," Larson said. "Anyway, we expect to do some scoring. Maybe people think we play defensive football, but we spend far more time on our offense, and I hope our attack will really get going on Saturday."

Though Navy hadn't defeated the Irish since 1936, the Midshipmen exuded an air of confidence as they practiced and prepared for Notre Dame. Hundreds of midshipmen attended each practice, sometimes sitting in the rain to watch and support their football team. There was plenty to see, because Larson put his team through three scrimmages in the five days before the game. About a dozen reporters attended the scrimmages, and though none of them noted it in their columns, Hal Kauffman once again proved his value as a sixth-string back. Working on the scout team, Kauffman impersonated Notre Dame's Dippy Evans, a small, fast back who was a threat to go the distance whenever he touched the ball.

Every time Kauffman's number was called, the Midshipmen's first-string defense pounded him. But Kauffman always popped up after being tackled and congratulated his teammates on their powerful defense. Kauffman knew he wouldn't play a single down against the Irish, so he treated these scrimmages as his game, his moment to shine. Showing as much courage as anyone on the team, Kauffman was still as introspective off the field as he was when he was in high school. But once he stepped between the lines, he ran the ball as furiously as Busik—even though he wasn't as big or as fast as his buddy from Pasadena.

Kauffman was a coach's dream. He wasn't listed on the official team roster, but Kauffman was one of a handful of Midshipmen who was allowed to practice with the team because he showed as much heart on the field as Larson had ever seen. As a reward for his hard work, Larson promised Kauffman something that, to Kauffman, was more delicious than chocolate: An opportunity to suit up and stand on the sideline for the Army game.

"You've got to be the best scout-back in America," Busik told Kauffman once. "Nobody works harder in practice than you."

"I just like playing," Kauffman replied. "I feel free out there on the field."

Two and half years since arriving at Annapolis, Busik and Kauffman

remained close. Though there was little time for socializing, they still double-dated every so often, taking their ladies to formal hop dances at the academy on Saturday nights after football games. The two friends also talked frequently about the future, and where they'd end up. "It's time for the Germans to be stopped," Kauffman told Busik one afternoon after practice. "And I think the Japanese are going to have to be dealt with at some point as well. I don't know about you, but I'm ready to fight."

"So am I," said Busik. "But I'd sure like to win a national championship before we go overseas. That would be the perfect way to end our football careers."

A cold front blew into Baltimore on the morning of kickoff of the Notre Dame game, dropping the temperature into the high thirties. But the sun shone brightly and more than seventy-six thousand filled Baltimore's Municipal Stadium, including a third of the president's cabinet who had arrived via train from Washington. Notre Dame brought with them their one-hundred-piece band, and they entertained the crowd before the game by playing an assortment of tunes, including repeated renditions of the Irish fight song, "Notre Dame Victory March." Football fans from across the country tuned into NBC radio to hear the broadcast. Out in California a dozen Rose Bowl representatives adjusted their radio dials to listen to the game, anxious to see if Navy could keep its unbeaten record.

Notre Dame, a slight underdog, won the toss and elected to kick. The Middies' Johnny Harrell returned the ball to the 25. On first down Navy ran for 3 yards; on second down they were flagged for offsides. After the penalty, the Middies faced a second and 12 from their 23. Busik called for a quick-kick, and it worked to near perfection: The ball covered 56 yards, rolling out of bounds at Notre Dame's 21-yard line. After two ineffectual plays, the Irish also quick-kicked. Busik, playing deep, returned the ball to his own 48-yard line. It was early, but Navy was winning the battle for field position.

But in the second quarter, Bertelli got on a roll. After receiving the snap, Bertelli would often drop 10 to 15 yards behind the line of scrimmage before he'd look downfield for a prospective receiver. Only a few teams in the country relied so much on down-the-field passes. Even though Navy had spent the entire week preparing for it, now that they were facing this novel kind of offensive attack, they couldn't stop it. Bertelli's skinny right arm propelled the Irish on two touchdown drives in the second quarter as Notre Dame stormed to a 13–7 halftime lead. Navy

kept the game close in the second half, but lost 20–13. Bertelli completed 12 of his 18 passes for 232 yards—by far the most passing yards Navy had given up in more than three years.

After the game, Swede Larson's wife jumped out of her seat and ran onto the field. Upset over Navy's loss, she was especially irate with Navy tackle Gene Flathman for playing a poor game, in her opinion. Dressed in a fur coat and wearing high heels, Mrs. Larson, a petite brunette, nearly stumbled as she approached Flathman. Away from the football field, Mrs. Larson was as warm as hot cocoa on Christmas morning. On Sundays she invited the entire team to her house for cake, cookies, and milk. Swede occasionally talked football to his players as they munched on Mrs. Larson's treats, but that wasn't the real purpose of these gatherings. Rather, Mrs. Larson wanted the players to feel as if she was a second mother to them, and she tried to make her home as welcoming as possible. Many of the players even took to calling her "Mama Larson," and they never left her home without giving her a big hug.

But once Mama Larson walked into the stadium and started watching a game, she yelled louder than any midshipman and she took the losses just as hard as her husband. When she finally found Flathman on the field after the Notre Dame game, Mama Larson grabbed him by the jersey, pulling his face close to hers. "Why didn't you play better?" she screamed at the 6' 4", 220-pound Flathman. "We could have won the game if you had played better." The diatribe continued for a few minutes, and it left Flathman near tears.

In the locker room, Larson was much more composed than his wife. He spoke calmly and with a reassuring tone, like a father telling his kids that everything will be okay. "It just wasn't our day today, boys," Larson said. "But our season is not over. We have Princeton and Army left. You know and I know that all that really matters is beating Army. We'll get them in a few weeks. But now let's just prepare real hard to play Princeton next week and we'll worry about Army later. Forget what the scoreboard says. I'm proud of you boys."

While Larson was speaking to his players, Red Blaik was giving a similar speech to the Army players at Cambridge. Blaik's worst fears had come true: his players, still recovering physically from the game in the mud against Notre Dame, seemed a step slower against Harvard. In front of a crowd of fifty-three thousand at Harvard Stadium—the largest attendance total since 1937—the Crimson thoroughly dominated the battered

Cadets, winning 20–6. Army couldn't consistently stop Harvard's modified T-formation on offense. And it didn't help that both Olds and Romanek were still sore from the previous week's game. Both had trouble making blocks on offense and shedding blockers on defense.

"We will get over this loss," Blaik said sternly in the locker room. "We will go back and we will practice and we will improve. We've still got some football to play this season. And, remember, we've still got Navy. Never forget that."

In Washington, relations with Japan continued to cool. Five days after Army's loss to Harvard, President Roosevelt rejected a peace proposal from Japanese Premier Hideki Tojo. United States Secretary of State Cordell Hull said that U.S. acceptance would be tantamount to "aiding and abetting Japan in her efforts to create a Japanese hegemony in and over the western Pacific."

Few around the world were surprised by the Secretary's dismissive attitude. After all, Japan's proposed peace agreement with the United States called for the United States to lift its oil embargo on Japan, supply Japan with one million tons of aviation fuel each month, and help the country acquire whatever oil it needed from the Dutch East Indies. Japan was desperate for oil. The United States and Britain imposed an embargo after Japan invaded Indochina. Japan imported 88 percent of her oil—and its supply was dwindling. Her need was growing by the hour.

The Midshipmen did not overlook their next opponent, Princeton. Before a crowd of forty-two thousand at Tiger Stadium—which included Secretary of the Navy Frank Knox—Navy played its best game of the season, defeating the Tigers 23–0 on November 22. Busik ripped off runs of 46, 35, and 20 yards in leading the Midshipmen to their fourth shutout victory of 1941.

After the game, the white-capped Midshipmen stormed out of the stands and onto the field to congratulate their players. They were met by hundreds of Tiger fans who also poured onto the field. A few brawls started and just when it appeared to the fans remaining in the stands—including Secretary Knox—that a full-scale melee would break out, the Navy band, hoping to diffuse the situation, struck into "The Star Spangled Banner." The Midshipmen and the Tiger fans quickly came to attention, and the fighting ceased. When the song was over, no one had the spirit to raise their fists. Everyone left the field in peace.

"We knew we couldn't look ahead to the Army game," Busik told reporters after the game. "We had to focus all of our attention on Princeton because we thought they would be tough. But now, finally, we can think about Army and Army alone. It's going to be my last game for Navy, and I plan on making it memorable. I'll be heading overseas soon, and I want to be able to tell everyone I serve with about how we beat Army in my last game."

After losing to Harvard, Blaik took it easy on his Army players during practice. He had no other choice. With five starters nursing injuries and several second-team players also hurt, Blaik didn't hold a single scrimmage in the days before the Cadets hosted Pennsylvania.

On the eve of the game Blaik reminded his team that the Quakers had embarrassed Army last season, defeating the Cadets 48–0. "Remember what happened last year," Blaik said, his voice rising. "Let's make up for that tomorrow. We may be a little banged up right now, but remember how hard we've worked. Remember when we were out there in the cold and practicing in January. No team has worked harder than us this year. Let's make all of that work pay off for us tomorrow."

In spite of Blaik's passionate words, the next day the injury-riddled Cadets couldn't consistently move the ball on offense and lost 14–7—a 41-point improvement in the outcome from the previous year. The next week Army again struggled, but hung on to down West Virginia, 7–6. Navy had destroyed the Mountaineers 40–0 earlier in the season—a fact that many of the Cadet players talked about in the locker room after the game.

"I don't care how many points Navy beat West Virginia by, I think we have a real good chance at beating the guys from Navy next week," Olds told reporters. "We're starting to get healthy again and when we're healthy, we feel like we can beat anybody in the nation. Even Navy."

"I know two things," Romanek told anyone with a press badge and a notebook. "One, we'll show up to play next Saturday. And two, we'll give it our all. Navy has a way of bringing out the best in us."

The 1941 Army-Navy game was seven days away.

8

THE BUILDUP

FIVE DAYS BEFORE the Army-Navy game kicked off, clerks at Philadelphia's Municipal Stadium were besieged with mail. More than two thousand requests for tickets from all corners of the country piled up in the stadium box office. Municipal could hold a standing room crowd of more than 102,000 fans, but the game had been sold out for months. Thus, the clerks spent much of the week sending out preprinted forms regretting that the ticket supply had run dry long ago. This overwhelming demand for tickets underscored the fact that, even though neither team was undefeated, the nationwide interest in the game was as high as it'd ever been since the two teams first played each other in 1890. A few days before kickoff, the *Philadelphia Sun* captured the magnitude of this Army-Navy matchup when the paper reported, "There probably never was a time when interest in the game was greater than it is today, the international situation being as it is, the eyes of this nation being on its young men in the military and naval academies."

Trying to capitalize on the demand to see the game, a local television station in Philadelphia decided to broadcast the game on closed-circuit television—one of the first times in college football history that this bold new innovation was used. At two different locations in Philly, fans could pay $2 to watch the game on a TV screen. "The entire country and our armed forces around the world will be following this game," Larson told his players early in the week. "Remember that you're not playing for yourself or for this team. You're playing for the entire navy."

At both academies, the week of the game was unlike any other. Pep rallies were held every day on both campuses. In Annapolis, the Middies hung posters and bed sheets with painted words on them all around Bancroft Hall urging their team to defeat Army. A large sign at the main entrance to Bancroft read: BEAT ARMY! Every evening at dusk those words above Bancroft's entrance became illuminated by electrical lights, serving as a late-night reminder of what was truly important at the naval academy this week. The Middies also posted a sign in the gymnasium, which was changed daily, that counted down the days to kickoff, FIVE DAYS ARMY, FOUR DAYS ARMY, THREE DAYS ARMY.

At West Point, the cadets were just as juiced. Though Blaik had closed practices both to the media and to the corps for fear of spy scouts, the players were greeted by hundreds of cadets each time they walked off the practice field. The energy on campus hung in the air like a mist, and the cadets were so excited that they hardly needed sleep to get through this week. The scream of "Beat Navy" could be heard echoing off the stone buildings and pines several times a day, and whenever Romanek and Olds walked to class several of their fellow cadets would always pat them on the back, telling them that it was Army's turn to win the big game. Everyone on campus knew the recent history: The Cadets had not beaten Navy in three years—their longest winless streak against the Midshipmen since 1921. This fostered such a sense of urgency at the Point that even those few cadets who didn't know a first down from a touchdown could detect the immensity of this particular Army-Navy game.

"Army has one of its best teams in years," Larson told reporters four days before kickoff. "Army is offensively minded and has a diversified attack. There are sixteen letter winners from last year, they're all six-footers with the exception of two, and they're going to give us all the trouble anybody can handle for one afternoon."

Larson had an intimate understanding of Army's team. Navy had sent at least one scout to every game that the Cadets had played. The scouts took notes on Army's coaching tendencies and its players' strengths and weaknesses. Based on all the information that he'd accumulated over the course of the season, Larson felt that Navy would have success running the ball straight at the Army defense. The Midshipmen had a decided size advantage on the line, and Busik had flourished all season when he put his head down and bulldozed between the tackles.

Out on the Navy practice field this week was a special block of wood. It was the remains of one of the goalposts that had been torn down after the '40 game, and a few players made sure to touch it for good luck at the end of every practice. One late afternoon, as several players made their way toward the wood after the final whistle of practice had sounded, Rip Miller noticed a man on the sideline whom he'd never seen before. The Navy practices were open to reporters, but Miller didn't think this man dressed in a trenchcoat was a reporter. "Look at him, he's a spy from West Point," Miller told a player as he subtly pointed toward the man. The next day the mysterious man appeared again. But this time as Miller walked off the field he purposely dropped Navy's playbook within eyeshot of the stranger. Miller had spent part of the morning drawing up a bogus playbook, complete with formations, terminology, and plays that Navy never used. Later that night Miller returned to the practice field to see if the phony playbook still lay in the grass. Much to his delight, it was gone.

On Wednesday morning, a bulletin was issued to all of America's armed forces. REPEAT. PACIFIC, NOVEMBER 26, 1941: JAPANESE CARRIER FORCE LEAVES BASE, MOVING EAST . . .

At 6:00 A.M. Japan time on November 26—which was 11:00 A.M. November 25 at Pearl Harbor—the task force pulled out of Hitokappu Bay, the task force's assembly point off the coast of Japan. Amid snow that blew over the cold and choppy water, thirty vessels set sail in the half light, their destination thirty-five hundred miles across the Pacific. The armada boasted six carriers, led by the flagship, the *Akagi;* four hundred warplanes; two battleships; three cruisers; nine destroyers; and ten other surface ships. They would travel at an average of thirteen knots. Its orders stated that "in the event an agreement is reached in the negotiations with the United States, the task force will immediately return to Japan," but none of the officers on board these thirty ships expected to be turning around.

On Thursday afternoon the Midshipmen boarded a train for Philadelphia. They were sent off like princes, as the entire regiment gathered for a rally in the Yard. Larson said a few words, thanking everyone for their support, then the team hopped on the Toonerville Trolley. On the ride to Philly the players were uncharacteristically quiet, everyone deep in thought. The game was still 48 hours away, but already the players had begun their pregame routine. Most simply looked out the window and watched the countryside fly by as the train jiggled northward.

Army also left for Philly on Thursday afternoon. Like the Navy squad, they were given a hero's sendoff as they stepped onto the train at the Hudson River depot. It had already been a remarkable season for the Cadets, and even though they had lost two of their last three games, the players now reflected the quiet confidence of their coach. With Blaik, it seemed that anything was possible, that Army could beat any team on any day, and this was the attitude the players took with them as the train pulled out of the depot and began to snake its way southward along the river. They had nothing to lose, the players figured, because they'd already accomplished more in the 1941 season than anyone could have possibly predicted. This relaxed the players, and now 48 hours before kickoff, many of them took naps as they sat in their rail cars.

Navy stayed at a country club located on the northern outskirts of Philadelphia. After checking into their rooms, Larson met the players on an open grass field behind the hotel that was surrounded by trees turned golden by autumn. The team held a quick, padless workout. What really caught the attention of the players was how quiet it was as the team practiced. Aside from the squawks of a few blackbirds, the only sounds were the voices of the coaches and the grunts of the players as they went over a few basic plays. It was oddly peaceful. At the end of session, just as the late-November sun bled across the western sky, Larson asked his players to gather around. "Let's use this time out here to focus on what we need to do on Saturday," he said. "You'll remember this game for the rest of your lives, I promise you."

Army was quartered at a hotel on the southern outskirts of Philadelphia. Their special train was delayed arriving into Philly, which meant that the players didn't check into their rooms until 7:00 P.M. Instead of holding a workout, the cadets ate dinner and were in bed by 10:00 P.M. The next morning the team rode on two buses to Municipal Stadium for a light practice. As Olds and Romanek walked into the empty stadium, it appeared bigger to them than it had last year when they attended the game as plebes and sat in the stands. Then it was full of screaming fans. Now the wind howled and whipped around the vacant horseshoe structure. Olds imagined what the place would be like tomorrow, and the mere thought of it gave him a rush of adrenaline. Like every other Army player, Olds didn't think gameday could come fast enough.

Early that evening the two teams went to different local theaters. Before either movie came on, though, both teams were shown newsreels that depicted the deteriorating situations in the Far East and Europe. As they munched on buttery popcorn, the players sat wide-eyed as they watched the news unfold, fantasizing not about what would transpire the next day on the football field, but what would happen once they entered the field of combat. For the 10 minutes that the black-and-white images flickered on the big screens, not one player on either team uttered a word. They were all transfixed by the images that unspooled before them, which included pictures of innocent civilians already dead in the growing conflict. The players understood that tomorrow's game meant nothing compared to the war overseas, and seeing these newsreels reminded every Cadet and every Midshipmen that they were bound together by a cause bigger than the game.

"Boy, I can't wait to start fighting," Olds told a teammate. "I say we kill every one of those goddamn Nazis."

About forty-eight hours before kickoff, the War Department sent Pearl Harbor and other American outposts around the world a "war warning." "Negotiations with Japan appear to be terminated to all practical purposes," said the message from George Marshall, the army chief of staff. "Japanese future action is unpredictable but hostile action possible at any moment. . . . You are directed to undertake such reconnaissance and other measures as you deem necessary, but these measures should be carried out so as not, repeat, not to alarm civil population or disclose intent."

The commanding officers at Pearl Harbor responded to the warning by taking steps to avoid sabotage, like locking up all ammunition supplies. When these antisabotage measures were reported to the War Department, Marshall felt satisfied that the commanding officers at Pearl had adequately fulfilled his request.

On the eve of the game the players on both teams had their lights out by 8:45. Tomorrow would be a long day—one that would go down in American history as one of the last carefree afternoons before America entered World War II. But before the players retired for the evening, both Blaik and Larson read to their players a statement that the president had made to the American public that afternoon.

> *"Thinking about people in other countries that have been overrun and about those who have been doing the attacking, I think we can offer up a little silent prayer that those people, we hope, next year will be able to hold a Thanksgiving more like an American Thanksgiving," Roosevelt said. "That is something to dream about perhaps. In days like these it is always possible that our boys who are now at the naval and military academies may be actually fighting for the defense of these American institutions of ours. . . . Great games run in the spirit of peoples and the right kind of national spirit of peace is necessary for that Army-Navy game. How many other countries have things like that going on now?*

The next morning at the country club, after a steak-and-potatoes breakfast, Larson told his Navy players to walk around the golf course and clear their heads. Busik and Kauffman strolled along a fairway and each privately marveled at how far they'd come since that May day in 1939 when they boarded the train in Pasadena. Busik was now a national sports figure—nearly everywhere he went, little boys would ask for his autograph—but in many ways he was still the same California kid who rode the train across the nation. He still was as friendly as a favorite uncle, and he still never got too upset or too overjoyed at anything. The biggest change in Busik was that he was now hardened. Like many in his class, the sense of optimism about the future that he brought to the academy had eroded. He once thought he could change the world; now he felt he'd be lucky if he survived the next five years.

Hal Kauffman had also changed. Though he still daydreamed of being a professional singer—a dream that he never shared with his classmates—Kauffman was no longer the overly sensitive boy who had stepped onto the train with Busik. Since arriving at the naval academy, Kauffman had emerged from his shell, becoming more talkative and animated. He now was as confident as any of his classmates in his ability to accomplish whatever task was before him. This newfound certainty in him stemmed from the fact that Kauffman had steadily climbed the class rank ladder, and now he was one of the top academic students at the academy. One day he hoped to be the captain of a destroyer, and based on his performance at the academy, his instructors thought it was just a matter of time before that happened.

Indeed, Busik and Kauffman had grown up. Their last game as Midshipmen was hours away, and then they didn't know where they'd be off to. Perhaps the Atlantic. Maybe the Pacific. All they really knew was that their futures were clouded and suffused with peril. But on this morning, as they strolled on the golf course through the cool and fresh November air, life was peaceful. They were Navy football players, and in a few hours the ears of a nation and the eyes of one hundred thousand fans would be riveted on the game. As Busik and Kauffman and a few other players tossed a football around in the quiet of the golf course, it felt to them as if they were standing on the summit of life.

9

THE ARRIVAL

FROM ALL ACROSS the Eastern Seaboard, they came by plane, train, and automobile to the great concrete horseshoe that stood on the marshy flats of the Delaware River. Located on the south side of Philadelphia, at the corner of Broad and Pattison, Municipal Stadium was a sprawling, single-deck ballyard that could seat 98,620 people—with standing room only, the crowd could swell to 102,000. On this cool, still, foggy morning, fans started arriving at the stadium at 7:30 A.M. for the 1:30 kickoff. Like an electrical storm, anticipation charged the air.

For two days, long lines of reserved trains carrying football fans from New York and Washington, all of whom were packed tight in the compartments, creaked along the rusty rails that led into the heart of Philly. On this Saturday after Thanksgiving—the Army-Navy game's traditional date—the trains dropped off passengers right at the gates of the stadium.

For the 1936 Army-Navy contest, the Pennsylvania Railroad had scheduled thirty-eight special trains. By '41 the Pennsy, as it was called, ran forty-two special locomotives—making this one of the most complex single-day operations in passenger railroad history. Railroad executives held planning sessions for this one event throughout the year to nail down the logistics. In the days leading up to kickoff all the railcars were repaired and cleaned; the trains' exteriors were waxed and polished. On game day wreck crews were deployed up and down the Eastern Seaboard, just in case, and extra crew members were added to all the locomotives.

For those passengers who arrived the night before the game, they found downtown Philadelphia teeming with Army and Navy fans. All the hotels were booked. Restaurants turned away customers and the pubs overflowed with revelers. Indeed, the city was transformed into a rollicking festival that surged with patriotism; Army's colors of black, gold, and gray and Navy's blue and gold bathed the entire area. In the crowd at the Benjamin Franklin Hotel, where the Army backers made their headquarters, were ranking officers from both Washington and from forts and camps all over the country—officers, who, somehow, had arranged to get leave for the game. At the Bellevue Stratford, where the Midshipmen supporters were staying, were navy officers from ships and ports all over the world. And from Iceland to the Straits of Singapore, from Alaska to the West Indies and beyond, soldiers, sailors, and marines huddled around short-wave radios to catch broadcasts of the game.

Perhaps no one in the world, though, looked forward to this game more than Alan Shapley, who was stationed aboard the U.S.S. *Arizona* off the coast of Oahu Island. When Shapley was at the naval academy from 1923 to '26, he earned twelve varsity letters in the three major sports of football, basketball, and track—a mark that has never been equaled. Of all the sports he played, though, his favorite was football. A four-year starting quarterback, Shapley helped the '23 team capture a 14–14 tie against the University of Washington in the Rose Bowl. Three years later, in his final season at the academy, he led Navy straight into the history books, guiding the Midshipmen to their first and only national championship.

Navy bolted to a 9–0 start in 1926 behind Shapley's passing and running. All that remained was a game against Army at recently finished Soldier Field in Chicago. The game, the first-ever gridiron contest held at Soldier Field, also marked the first time that Army and Navy had ever played each other in the Midwest. The lure of the game was so strong in the heartland that more than half a million people requested tickets. Notre Dame coach Knute Rockne even abandoned his team on game day—the Irish played Carnegie Tech on the same afternoon—to sit in the stands and watch the Army-Navy matchup. (Without their coach, Notre Dame wound up getting upset by Carnegie Tech 19–0).

More than 110,000 fans filled Soldier Field. Army's first-year coach Biff Jones tried to surprise Navy by starting his second-team unit. The plan backfired: The Middies stormed to a 14–0 lead. But Army came back, and late in the fourth quarter, with about four minutes to play, it led the Midshipmen 21–14. The Cadets now had the ball and were trying to kill the clock, but Navy intercepted a pass with less than two minutes left and got the ball back on its own 35-yard line. Pointing to the end zone 65 yards away, Shapley told his teammates in the huddle, "We're going to cross the line."

As Navy moved the ball down the field, it started to get dark. The field was rimmed with snow and the players were covered in mud, making it difficult for fans to discern what players belonged to which team. Finally, Navy faced a fourth and goal from the eight-yard line. The Middies called a double reverse. Halfback Howard Ransford faked a run to the right and slipped the ball to Shapley, who broke a tackle and pushed the ball over the goal line with just seconds to play. A hush fell over the crowd as Shapley dropkicked the ball through the goal posts to tie the game at 21–21, which would be the final score. The Navy boys were ecstatic over the tie; because they were the only unbeaten team in the country, it meant they'd won the national championship. That evening Shapley was the toast of the town in Chicago, as he and his teammates met up with their dates who had traveled to the Windy City from different towns in the Midwest. Together, they danced to tunes such as "Bye, Bye Blackbird," by Ray Henderson and Mort Dixon, and, "When the Red, Red Robin Comes, Bob, Bob, Bobbin' Along" by Harry Woods. It was one of those special nights that they'd all talk about for the rest of their lives.

Fifteen years later, Shapley could still vividly recall that 1926 Army game in his mind. He could tell anyone who was interested all about that chilly late-afternoon in the Windy City. Now he was aboard the U.S.S. *Arizona*, and Shapley still followed the team as if he were living in Bancroft Hall. On this late November day in 1941, the *Arizona* was running drills and playing war. In a few days she would dock at Pearl Harbor. But now, out in the blue ocean, Shapley arranged for the broadcast of the Army-Navy game to be piped through the ship's public address system. He had to hear it, and he was the kind of person who made things happen.

Shapley was the commanding officer of the marine detachment aboard the *Arizona*. He was also a close friend to Navy assistant coach Rip Miller. Whenever Shapley got the chance, he'd phone or telegram Miller and ask for information on the current state of the Navy football team. He was always looking for scouting reports and inside information—just like he did when he was a player. Back when he was the golden boy of Annapolis, Shapley, a sandy-haired, handsome midshipmen, was known for his strong right arm and quick thinking on the field. Those same characteristics still held true fifteen years later. On the *Arizona* he often threw a football around with his marines, and he was the coach of the marines' whaleboat race-team. When his marine whaleboat team beat all the other teams on the *Arizona*, Shapley approached the *Arizona*'s Captain, Van Valkenburgh, and asked that his marines represent the ship in future competitions with other ships rather than assembling an all-star team, which was what had been done in the past. Valkenburgh reluctantly agreed, and each morning while nearly everyone else on the ship was still sleeping, Shapley and his marines were up and practicing rowing their whaleboat in the gray, early-morning light. The work ethic he learned playing football at Navy was still with him.

Though Shapley didn't know it, the battleship *Arizona* was featured in a picture in the 212-page 1941 Army-Navy game program, which cost 50 cents. On page 180 the *Arizona* was shown plowing into a huge swell. The caption read: "It is significant that, despite the claims of air enthusiasts, no battleship has yet been sunk by bombs."

In its heyday, Municipal Stadium held concerts and sporting events that attracted more than one hundred thousand people. On September 23, 1926, 120,757 packed into the massive venue to watch Gene Tunney's heavyweight title victory over Jack Dempsey. Only Chicago's Soldier Field and the Memorial Coliseum in Los Angeles could hold a larger crowd than Municipal. And for two reasons the stadium's sixty-acre site was the logical choice to host the Army-Navy game: It was big enough to accommodate the intense interest in the game and it was located between Annapolis, Maryland, and West Point, New York.

Situated at 2601 South Broad Street, Municipal was fifteen years old in 1941 and still living on an allowance from the taxpayers. The stadium was built in connection with Philadelphia's Sesquicentennial celebration and in its first years was under the control of the Sesquicentennial Association. Planned to give the city the "biggest stadium in the world," one that was suitable for the staging of Olympic Games and other marquee events, construction of the stadium was authorized by the City Council on March 3, 1925. It was completed on May 15, 1926, at a cost nearly twice the original estimate of $2 million. Financing was done with miscellaneous city funds plus a fifty-year bond issue of more than $2 million.

In 1941, small cracks in the stadium's concrete facade pinstriped the outer walls. Many fans pointed to these cracks as they entered the stadium, wondering aloud if the venue was safe to hold a standing-room-only crowd of more than one hundred thousand. A few fans went so far as to ask ushers if they thought the whole place was going to buckle. Still, even with cracks spiderwebbing toward the sky in some places at Municipal, fans arrived in droves on November 29. At 10:45 A.M., a squad of thirty men began removing the eight tarpaulins that covered the entire playing field. The stadium slowly began to fill up. Among the first in the stadium were two navy enlisted men who were assigned a most peculiar task: They were to warm the seat cushions of a few high-ranking navy officers who weren't scheduled to arrive at the field for another two hours. So, following orders, the two enlisted men wiggled their backsides on the officers's seat cushions, moving side to side in their wool pants, keeping the cushions cozy for the navy brass hats, as the enlisted men called them.

At 11:00, the early-morning fog lifted and soft beams of sunlight burst though the torn sky. Suddenly, it was a perfect afternoon for football. A mild breeze fluttered the flags on the rim of the stadium and it strummed the bunting that was draped on the stands surrounding the field. The temperature was a comfortable 61 degrees. If this late November afternoon had been a painting, the brushstrokes on the canvas couldn't have been more beautiful.

The security on this day was unprecedented for a sporting event. Outside the stadium, more than one hundred patrolmen were on duty. Inside, one hundred and fifty police officers had been assigned to various posts. There were also seven hundred Pinkerton men, several hundred schoolboy ushers, and dozens of detectives stationed inside the stadium. Sixty Internal Revenue agents, most from Washington, D.C., were on hand to make sure that the scalpers didn't sell any tickets for more than the $4.40 face value and to spot counterfeit tickets. In the first aid room, located in the bowels of the stadium, four hospital cots stood ready for any game-day casualties. Chief Police Surgeon Mike Keegan and eleven other police surgeons manned the first aid room. During the previous year's game some fifty cases were treated; most were fans who'd had a little too much beer with their cheer.

Outside the stadium, merchandise and concessions sales were stellar.

The thick glossy programs, which weighed almost two pounds, were being nabbed up quickly. At 8:30 A.M., Irving Fried, the senior partner of Fried and Gerber Concessionaires, hauled truckloads of hot dogs, soft drinks, and sandwiches into the stadium. About three hundred members of Fried's staff were local high school boys employed for the day, who were, according to Fried, "jumping out of their socks for a chance to see the game."

At the Navy Stock Yard, which stood adjacent to the stadium, a vendor sold his supply of five hundred blue-and-gold Navy buttons to workers entering the main gate by 7:00 A.M., clearing his inventory in less than an hour. The men who bought the buttons proudly pinned them to their work overalls, trying to do their part to support their team, and they didn't take the buttons off as they worked on the ships in the Yard. The Navy Yard's twenty-five thousand employees only worked a 6-hour shift on the day of the game, in order to avert congestion of northbound traffic on Broad Street. Everybody went to work 15 minutes early, with orders to quit 2 hours early. This meant they would be able to listen to the game on the radio and cheer for their beloved Midshipmen.

As Army officers left the Benjamin Franklin hotel, they were given box lunches, which were stacked high in the lobby, that included a ham sandwich and an apple. Weaving their way to the stadium, many officers bought chrysanthemums at local flower shops, which sold for $1.25 a piece. Two hours before kickoff, more than thirty people stood in line to buy the flowers from a street vendor on Broad. The officers either affixed the chrysanthemums to their overcoats or gave them to their girls. In just a few hours, flower merchants all around the stadium made a week's worth of profit.

Finally, at precisely 12:15 in the afternoon, the castle-like gates at the northeast end of the stadium swung open and the boys from the academies who weren't football players made a Caesar-entering-Rome kind of entrance. Since Army was the host team, the Midshipmen marched into the stadium first. Many of the Midshipmen had been standing on the rise just outside the gate, and now the seventy-five-piece Navy band led them inside, playing "Anchors Aweigh." The song's booming notes split the air, bouncing off every corner of the colossal, echoing bowl as the entire navy academy complement—3,110 midshipmen—confidently marched in.

At first, the fans in the crowd were hushed as the Middies appeared before their eyes. Then applause erupted, as the men, women, and children in the stands rose to their feet and shouted their support—not just for Navy, but for America. The twenty midshipmen companies marched around the track and past the Army stands. Company by company filed onto the field and then, arriving at their designated position on the field, stood as still as statues beneath the north goal posts while the band played.

At 12:40 the army cadets entered the stadium. Dressed in service grays, eighteen hundred cadets and a ninety-two-piece enlisted men's band marched in. The band first played "Anchors Aweigh" as a mark of courtesy to the navy, but then it broke into, "Fight On, Old Army Team," as the cadets marched past the Navy stands. By 12:50, the cadets and midshipmen were all in their seats. Now it was time for the real pageantry to begin.

Upon arriving at the railroad station south of the stadium, Eleanor Roosevelt, accompanied by Vice President Henry Wallace, rode in a car to the stadium. The First Lady, who was guarded by two secret service agents, was helped out of the vehicle at the stadium entrance and then walked in, strolling onto the field. First she looked to the Navy side and bowed and waved to Rear Admiral Russell Wilson, the superintendent of the naval academy. Wearing a black wool suit with a blue skirt, a fur coat, and a black felt hat with a shallow crown, she slowly walked around the south end of the field, accompanied by Major General Robert L. Eichelberger, superintendent of the military academy, and other army officers, to view the first half of the game. The First Lady planned to watch the first two quarters on the Army side of the field with British Ambassador Lord Halifax. Not wanting to appear partial, she would then move to the Navy side for the game's second half.

Forty years earlier, in 1901, President Theodore Roosevelt also tried to act like he didn't care who won the Army-Navy game at Franklin Field in Philadelphia. In the first half, Roosevelt sat on the Midshipmen's side; at halftime, he switched over to the Army bleachers. But when Navy tied the score 5–5 in the fourth quarter, Roosevelt, who had been assistant secretary of the navy under President McKinley, couldn't contain his enthusiasm. He rose from his box seat, ran past his Secret Service guards, leaped over a railing and jogged to the Navy bench to congratulate the players. The president whooped and hollered the entire time, as he shed all appearances of impartiality. But as happy as the president was when the Midshipmen tied the score, he was equally dejected when Army scored a late touchdown and won the game, 11–5.

. . .

A few hours before kickoff of the 1941 game, Franklin Roosevelt was on the tail end of a nineteen-hour train and car trip from Washington to Warm Springs, Georgia, where the president would enjoy a brief vacation. The president had wanted to come to Warm Springs for more than a week, but felt that he couldn't leave the White House with America's immediate future in such a fragile state. But on the evening of November 28, the president and his staff decided he should take a break and head to Warm Springs for a few days. Special arrangements were made so that the president could respond quickly to a sudden crisis. When the president's train stopped in Atlanta for 10 minutes, a secret telephone was connected to his vehicle in the motorcade that was being transported on the train so that he could be kept abreast of breaking international developments once he got off the train. Contrary to custom, the journey was interrupted at Newman, Georgia, where the presidential party left the train and drove by car the remaining forty-three miles to Warm Springs. Under a cloudless sky on the morning of November 29, the motorcade sped past scrubby pinewoods and fields of cotton, traveling deep into the Georgia countryside. When the President finally reached his cottage on a hilltop in Warm Springs, he wanted to do just one thing: get in his car, turn on the radio, and listen to the game.

To relax while he listened, the president spent the afternoon being driven in his own car through Warm Springs. He tuned the radio to the game, straining to hear every drip of information that was coming out of the speakers. He listened as the car tooled though the pleasant land of white houses and ploughed fields, all the while imagining what the action on the field looked like. Hours later the president related to reporters what raced through his mind as he took in the action from Philadelphia. "The game was run in the spirit of peace, and the spirit of peace is necessary for this game," he said. "I think we ought to be thankful that since 1918 we have been able to hold our gains—in health and education and in a great many volunteer lines. We're one of the largest nations of the world and nearly all other large nations are at war or defending themselves or conquered."

A few hours after making this statement, presidential advisers announced to reporters that the president's vacation would be cut short. That evening the president received a phone call from Secretary of State Cordell Hull. Hull had received some extracts of a speech that Premier Tojo of Japan was scheduled to deliver the following day. Tojo was going to say that his country was taking steps to wipe out the "exploitation" in the Far East being perpetrated by the United States and Britain. Hull informed Roosevelt of the inflammatory speech and stressed "the imminent danger of a Japanese attack." Hull asked the president to cut his trip short and return to Washington to consult with his advisers. The president agreed to return on December 1. World civilization, slowly but surely, was falling apart.

Robin Olds, West Point Class of June '43 *(U.S. Military Academy Library, Special Collections and Archives Division, National Archives Record Group 404, White Studio Collection)*

Henry Romanek, West Point Class of June '43 *(U.S. Military Academy Library, Special Collections and Archives Division, National Archives Record Group 404, White Studio Collection)*

Hal Kauffman, Naval Academy Class of '43 *(Naval Academy Special Collections and Archives)*

William S. Busik, Naval Academy Class of '43 *(Naval Academy Special Collections and Archives)*

Navy player Bill Chewning. He wouldn't survive the war. *(Courtesy Chewning family)*

John Frances Laboon, Naval Academy Class of '44 *(Naval Academy Special Collections and Archives)*

William Francis Leahy, Naval Academy Class of '44 *(Naval Academy Special Collections and Archives)*

Alan Shapley, Naval Academy Class of '27 *(Naval Academy Special Collections and Archives)*

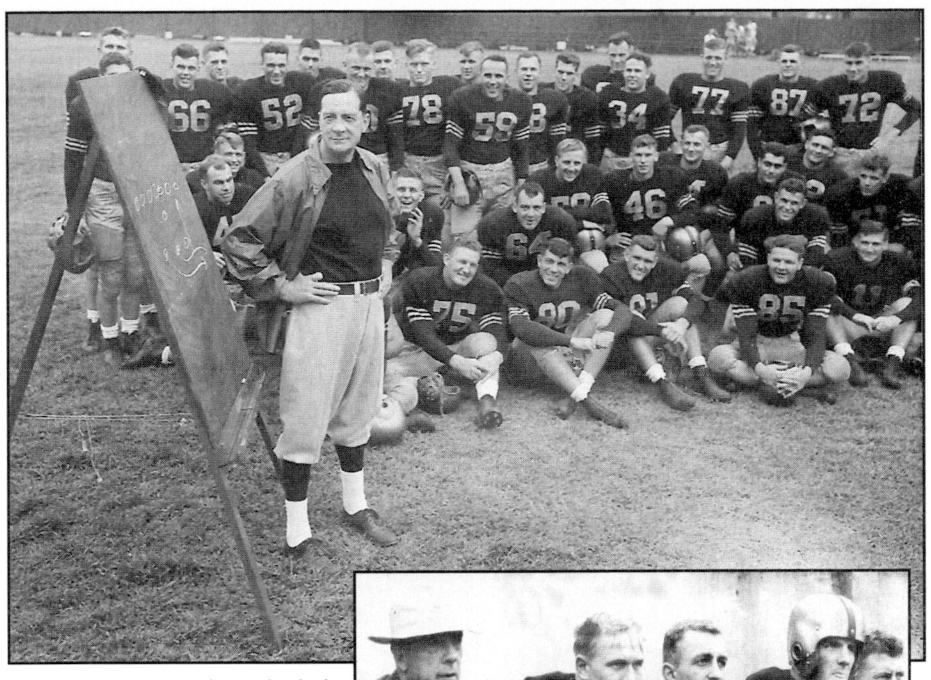

Army coach Red Blaik diagrams plays for his team.

Coach Blaik *(far left)* on the sideline during a game

(U.S. Military Academy Library, Special Collections and Archives Division, National Archives Record Group 404, White Studio Collection)

Navy coach Swede Larson *(far left)* with assistants Keith Moelsworth *(center)* and Rip Miller *(right)* in 1940 *(Courtesy Swede Larson, Jr.)*

A 1940 intrasquad scrimmage at the Naval Academy *(L. McNally, Baltimore News Post)*

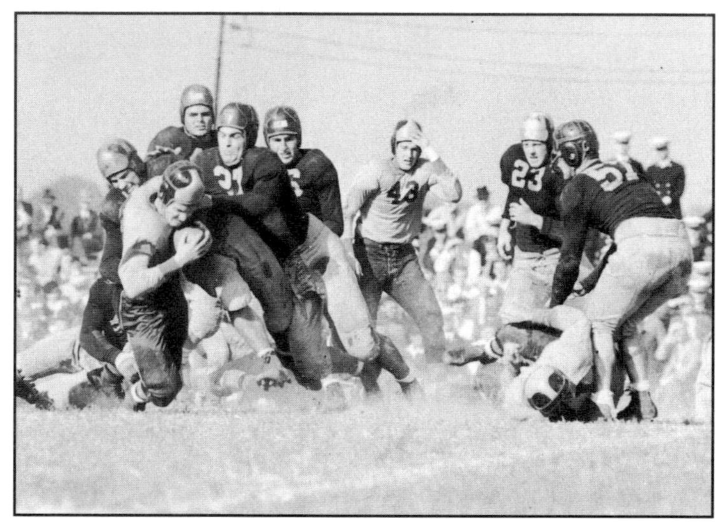

Bill Busik *(with ball)* struggles for yards in a 1940 intrasquad scrimmage. *(L. McNally, Baltimore News Post)*

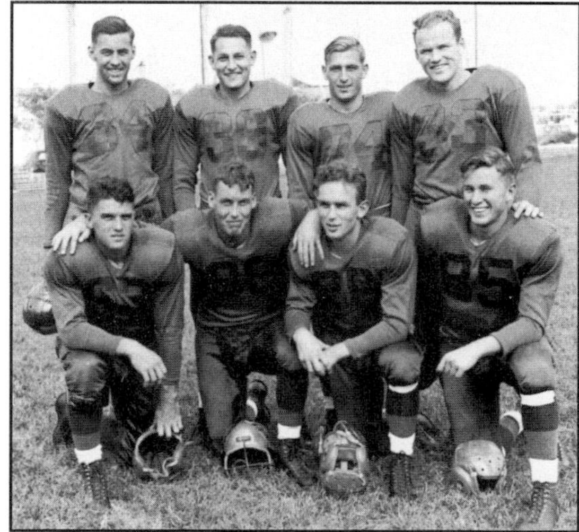

Bill Busik *(bottom left)* with several of his Navy teammates after a practice in 1940 *(Courtesy Bill Busik)*

Navy's Bill Busik in the fall of 1941 *(Naval Academy Special Collections and Archives)*

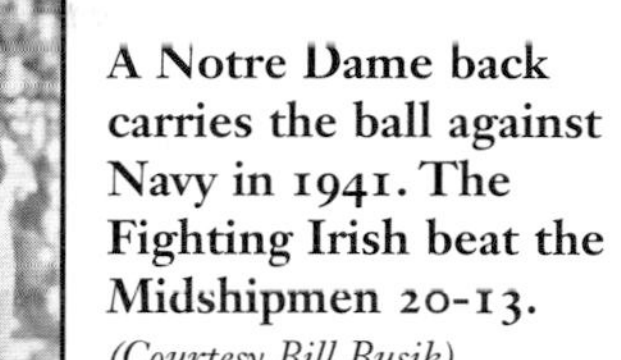

A Notre Dame back carries the ball against Navy in 1941. The Fighting Irish beat the Midshipmen 20-13. *(Courtesy Bill Busik)*

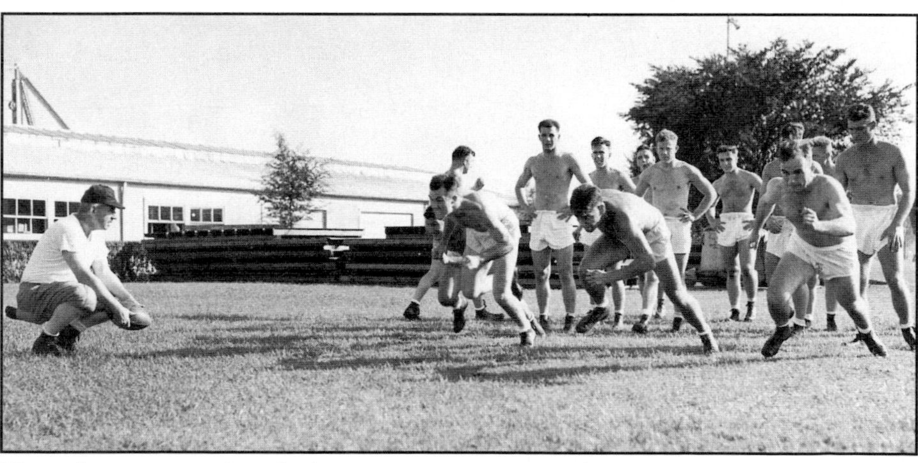

Navy players run sprints during 1941 preseason practice. *(Naval Academy Special Collections and Archives)*

Both Academies march on the field prior to the 1941 Army-Navy game. *(Naval Academy Special Collections and Archives)*

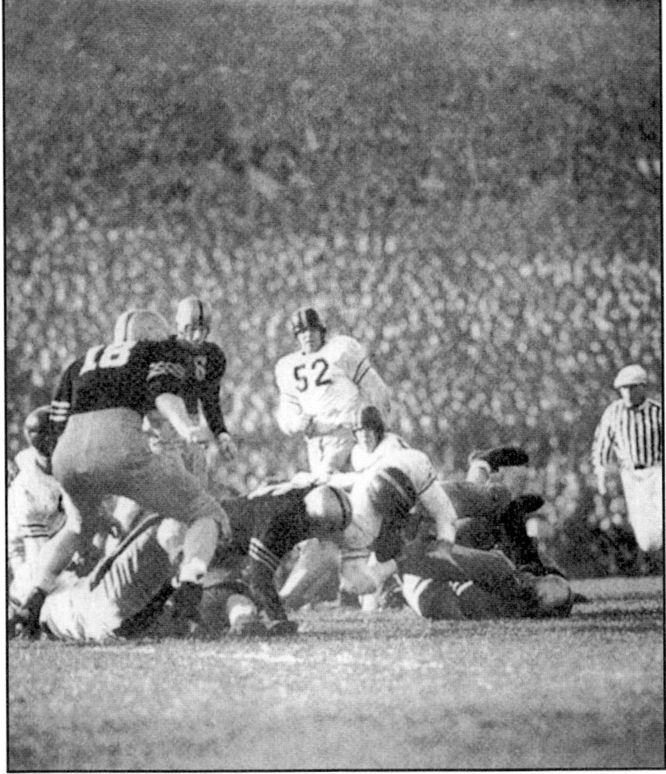

Bill Busik carries the ball against Army during the 1941 game. *(Naval Academy Special Collections and Archives)*

Program from the 1941 Army-Navy football game
(Naval Academy Special Collections and Archives)

A day after the big game, Swede Larson is surrounded by Annapolis locals and midshipmen as he rings the Gokokuji Bell to celebrate Navy's 14-6 victory over Army.
(Courtesy Swede Larson, Jr.)

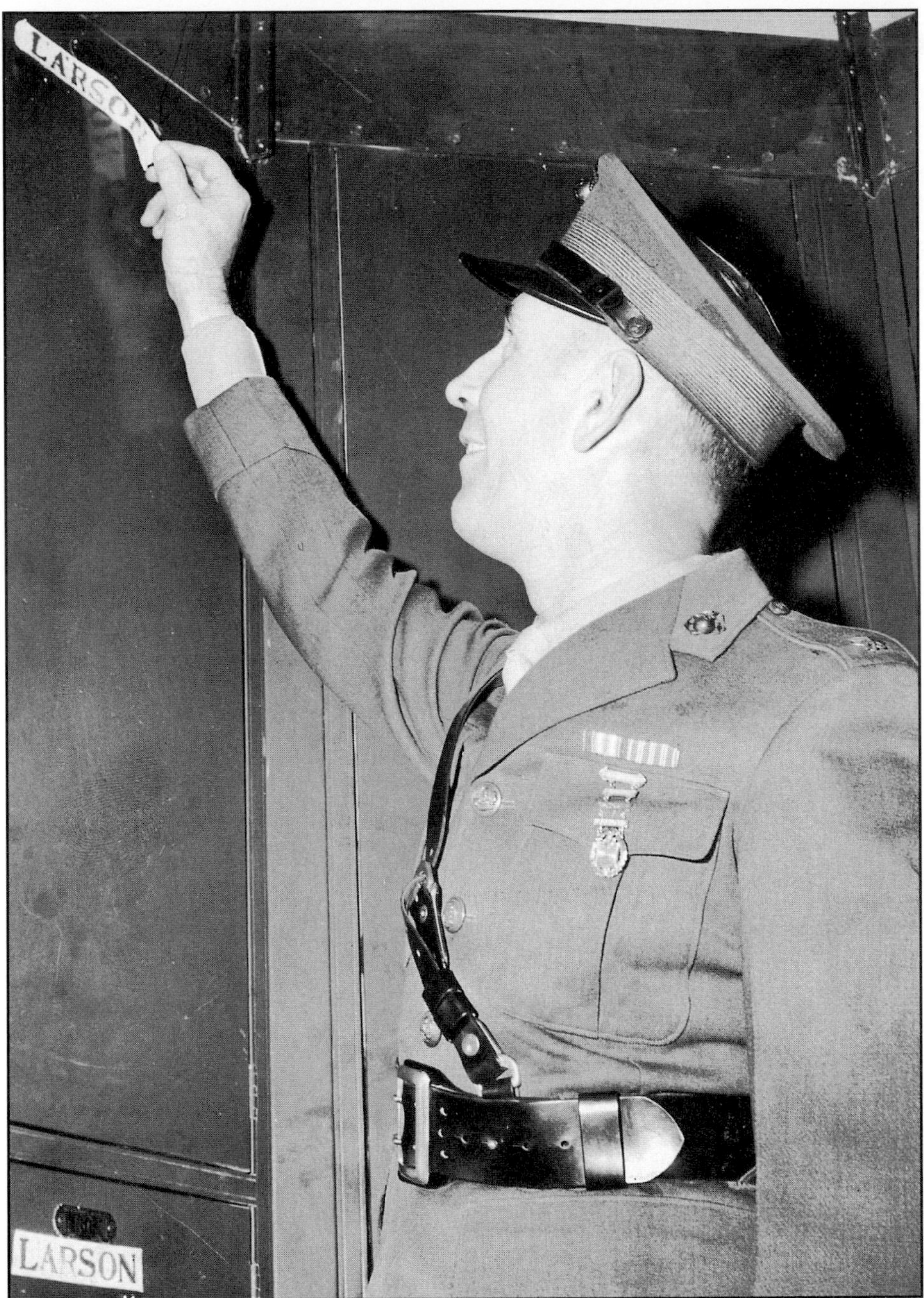

Swede Larson, in his Marine Corps uniform, removes his name tag from his locker for the final time as he heads off to war. He would lose his life in November, 1945.
(Courtesy Swede Larson, Jr.)

10

THE GAME

WITH SIRENS WAILING, two police cars escorted the two yellow school buses full of Navy players and coaches down Broad Street. As the cavalcade motored through heavy traffic, fans on the sidewalks shouted encouragement and pounded their hands on the sides of the buses. A few players stuck their heads out the windows and shook hands with the fans as if they were running for governor. Kickoff was still three hours away, but already the Navy players could sense the building emotion of the gathering crowd. Even fans wearing Army black and gold cheered the Navy buses as they slowly rolled through the bright sunshine toward the stadium.

To the Navy players, this was an overwhelming sight, seeing Army fans stopping in their tracks and zealously cheering as the buses of Midshipmen approached. The whole town seemed to be performing a human drum roll as the buses inched their way to the stadium for the big showdown. Men, women, and small children waved American flags at the buses. A few old men held their canes—which had red, white, and blue streamers flowing from them—up high as the boys from Annapolis went by. Many fans blew on horns, whistles, and trumpets; others shook rattles and large brass hand bells.

Army was the first team to arrive at the stadium. Before having his team dress and don their pads and uniforms, Blaik led them through the locker room and out onto the field. Kickoff was two and a half hours away, but already a smattering of hard-core fans had taken their seats. Blaik wanted his team to get familiar with the field, and he instructed his players to walk around and acquire a feel for the grass and the footing. He also told his players to imagine what they'd be doing once the whistle blew and the game started. The crowd will be deafening, he warned them, but don't let that blur your focus. Some players, as they strolled down the sidelines, looked up into the mostly empty stands, which stretched up and up and up, like the floor of heaven rested just above the top rim of the stadium. None of the players said it, but all of them knew it: Their moment was at hand.

Around the time the Army players retreated to the locker room to put on their uniforms, the Navy buses pulled into the stadium parking lot. The players went straight to the locker room, where Larson gave his team 45 minutes to suit up and take care of whatever pregame business they needed to attend to—doing some extra stretching, studying their plays, or just concentrating on what they needed to do to be successful. Larson didn't script his players' pregame activities as thoroughly as Blaik, who planned every minute of his players' actions for the two hours before kickoff, because Larson insisted on putting a lot of faith in his players' ability to get ready on their own. "I figure I've got some of the most responsible young men in the country," Larson once told a friend, "so I trust them to do what's right until they prove me wrong. And you know what? They never do."

By the time the Midshipmen were ready to jog out onto the field and warm up, the stadium was almost half full. Navy hadn't stepped foot on the Municipal Stadium field since 1940—they had practiced at Temple the day before—so when the boys ran out of the locker room and into the late-fall afternoon they were overwhelmed by what greeted them. It was as if a powder keg of excitement had burst. Even Busik, who had played in the game the year before, didn't expect the hyped atmosphere that he and his teammates now stood in the middle of. The crowd was producing thunder, and the noise rattled around the concrete horseshoe. Unlike many of the stadiums in which Navy had played, the fans at Municipal seemed right on top of the field. Municipal was built with watching football in mind; there was an unusually high tilt to the bleachers. The fans also appeared more animated than the previous year. Very few sat and many fans brought large signs that they placed all around the stadium. Already, some thirty minutes before kickoff, the place seemed to be rumbling.

"This is the most amazing thing I've ever seen," Busik told a teammate on the field. "This is something I'll never forget."

A few minutes later, the Cadets came out for their warm-ups and were given a similar greeting. As the players stretched, Blaik and Larson met at midfield. The two coaches shook hands and congratulated each other on their seasons. Though neither coach was a small-talker, the topic of the crowd made for an easy, free-flowing conversation. There was a hum in the stadium even as the teams sat on the ground and stretched. In all their years on the sidelines, neither coach had ever been swaddled in a more robust football atmosphere than what they were standing in the midst of just then. A few minutes later, the two shook hands again and parted.

After warm-ups, both teams retreated to their respective locker rooms one final time before kickoff. Coach Blaik, looking into the eyes of his players, felt that they were too anxious, wound a little too tight. To settle his team down, Blaik told everyone to lie down on the floor. He wanted his players to take deep breaths and visualize what they were going to do on the field. This yoga-style exercise was before its time, and many of the players thought it was odd, including Olds. As he lay on the cold concrete floor of the locker room, Olds suspected that Navy was going to try to run right at him. As a result of the diving accident months earlier, he still had trouble raising his right arm, and he figured that the Midshipmen had noticed that in their film studies. Nonetheless, Olds couldn't wait to get on the field. It was something he'd been thinking about almost every day since he sat in the stands and watched Navy beat Army last year 14–0.

A similar thought floated through Romanek's head. With his eyes closed, Romanek visualized making strong, solid blocks on offense and sure-handed tackles on defense. He knew that if unranked Army was going to have a chance to upset the eleventh-ranked Midshipmen—Navy was a four-to-one favorite—then the Cadets needed to control the line of scrimmage on both sides of the ball. It was as simple as that. As Romanek and Olds lay there, the stadium seemed to shake above them, the crowd sizzling with an emotional fever.

Across the field, in the Navy locker room, Larson made a stunning announcement to his players: This was going to be his last game as Navy's coach. "There's a war coming boys, and like all of you, I'm going to go fight in it," Larson said. "All of us in this room have a more important duty than playing football." As Larson spoke, he appeared as serious as he'd ever been. Many of the Navy boys felt the urge to run up and hug their coach, but instead they all stayed sitting on the benches in front of the lockers, unsure of how to react. The players had suspected that this might be Larson's last game, but none of them thought he'd make the announcement right before kickoff. In the long history of pregame speeches, no five words—not even, "Win one for the Gipper," which Notre Dame's Knute Rockne uttered in 1928 before the Irish's game against Army—had a more meaningful impact than Larson's, "I'm going to go fight." As soon as those words floated from his lips, the boys in the locker room were prepared to do whatever it took to win this last game for their beloved coach, to send him out with a victory.

Larson went on to tell his players that he'd never lost to Army. As a Midshipman player back in the '20s, Larson went 3–0 against the Cadets. In his first two seasons as a coach, he'd defeated Army both seasons. Now just 60 minutes of football stood between him and a perfect record against his rivals from West Point.

After speaking for a few minutes about how much this final game meant to him, Larson then took his team on a trip back through the mists of time, giving them a crash-course history lesson on the Army-Navy game—a history that dated back fifty-one years to the day, when on November 29, 1890, the schools first met on a cool autumn afternoon at the Point . . .

On that chilly November afternoon in 1890, Dennis Michie paced back and forth up on the cliffs at West Point, looking out across the Hudson River. Michie, a cadet, had been waiting for this day for more than a year. Then, in the distance, Michie saw them: On a wooden ferryboat, the naval academy football team was chugging across the river. Minutes earlier the Midshipmen had arrived on a train at the rail station directly across from West Point on the East side of the Hudson. Then the Navy players, who were all carrying a canvas bag that contained a football uniform, boarded the ferryboat for West Point. The first football game between the schools was minutes away.

Michie was the driving force behind this historical matchup; he had spent much of that fall trying to organize a game. Now a crowd of more than 1,000 people—which included cadets, the army band, a few dozen

West Point officers (many of whom had fought in the Civil War), their wives, visitors from outside the post, and a group of navy officers—had already gathered around a makeshift football field that had been laid out on the southeast corner of the parade grounds.

Months earlier, in the summer of 1890, Michie was one of only three cadets at the military academy who had ever played in an organized football game. In the 1880s the sport had been revolutionized by Walter Camp, an advisory coach at Yale who created rules such as the play from scrimmage and the eleven player on-field limit for each team. By laying out a standardized set of rules, Camp ended much of the chaos in the game. (But it was still a brutal sport; after the 1905 season President Theodore Roosevelt suggested that colleges ban it after eighteen players died as a result of collisions in a game.)

Because of Camp's alterations, football had become popular at eastern colleges such as Yale, Harvard, and Princeton by 1890, but it was slow to catch on at West Point. Navy, conversely, had a comparatively rich tradition. The Middies had played their first game in 1879, and by the beginning of 1890 had a cumulative record of 14–12–2. Bill Maxwell, who was a Midshipman in 1879 and served as the team's captain that season, had been credited by Camp with developing the first football uniform. Maxwell fashioned some athletic wear for his team only after he learned that the squad from the Baltimore Athletic Club, the only opponent of the Naval Academy in 1879, outweighed the Midshipmen by an average of ten pounds per player. Determined to make his players heavier for that game, Maxwell visited the academy's tailor, who proceeded to make heavy sleeveless jackets for the players. They consisted of double-lined canvas and were laced down the front and drawn tightly to fit snugly around a player's body. The Midshipmen, wearing these strange, heavy, newfangled getups, wound up tying the team from the Baltimore Athletic Club, 0–0.

At West Point Michie was one of the few cadets who even knew the rules of football. Nonetheless, he wanted to found a football team at West Point, and he figured there was only one way to do it: Get the boys at Navy to challenge Army to a football game. This way the power brokers at Army, with their pride on the line, would be forced to accept the matchup. Weeks later, after Michie had written a few clandestine letters to midshipmen that he knew, a letter arrived for him from Annapolis. The missive was a formal challenge to a football game. Michie took the letter to his father, Lieutenant Colonel Peter Michie, a philosophy instructor at West Point who had served in the Civil War. With his father backing him, Michie didn't have to ask twice to get permission from Superintendent Colonel John Wilson to accept the challenge.

Not everyone was pleased that this game was going to take place. Two months before the showdown, the *New York Times* ran a story on faculty upheaval at West Point. Many instructors argued that it made no sense for young cadets and midshipmen to hit and bloody each other on a football field, given that someday they may have to rely on each other in the field of combat. Yet in spite of these objections, Michie and his father kept lobbying the superintendent and others that the game would ultimately benefit both the academies and bring them closer together. The superintendent agreed with the Michies, and he refused to stop the game.

Now all young Michie had to do was assemble a twenty-one-man team, tutor the players in the essentials of the game, and whip them into playing shape. A classmate of Michie's, John A. Palmer, later recalled what those first weeks of Army football were like in *The Assembly*, a U.S. Army magazine.

> *"Dennis now had his hands full. He was captain, coach, trainer, and business manager of a nonexistent team that must play a championship game at the end of eight weeks. Dennis had scant time to teach the simplest fundamentals to his raw recruits. They had no practices except for a few riotous scrimmages against an even more inexperienced second team. There was no time for coaching except in the brief intervals between military duties.*
>
> *"Only on Saturday afternoons when the weather was too bad for drill and dress parade could Dennis count on any time for continuous practice. Dennis was able to rouse his teammates at 5:30 A.M., half an hour before reveille, for a run around the Plain, down and back Flirtation Walk, over past Thayer Hall, around the Supe's headquarters, and then back to the barracks in time for reveille."*

When the naval academy squad finally arrived on the West Bank of the Hudson on their ferryboat, the Middies were in high spirits. Many town residents of West Point stood in their front yards and chatted with the young Navy players as they made their way up to the Plain.

Once the Navy players finally made it to the football field, they were surprised to see several New York newspaper men, all clutching a notebook and a pencil, waiting to ask them questions. Beyond them were hundreds of people, all circled around the field, curious to see what this relatively new game of football was all about. In the front were scores of women, all wearing their finest Sunday dresses and sitting on folding chairs that had been swiped from classrooms. Everyone else stood around the field, in some cases three deep. When the two teams jogged out for the opening kickoff, virtually the entire crowd leaned inward, all anxious to see if the young men from West Point could give Navy a run for their money.

Then the referees, who all had on big black hats, signaled that it was time to start the game. Army kicked the ball. Navy's Charles Emerich, behind a V-formation, caught the ball and headed straight upfield. What followed was a massive collision, as the two teams—all the Navy players wore wool caps, the Army players were bareheaded—ran into each other at full speed. To the fans, it sounded like concrete slabs ramming into each other. Immediately, a few players from each team dropped to the earth, as if they'd suddenly been rendered unconscious. Many in the crowd gasped and yelled for Army to make the tackle, but Emerich broke free from the pileup and scampered 20 more yards before he was tackled by a group of Army players led by Michie. The opening kickoff turned out to be a preview of coming attractions: Navy was better in all phases of the game and won 24–0.

It wasn't until the matchup was over that everyone involved realized the savagery of the game. One Army player lost three teeth. Another Cadet had a piece of his ear bitten off while yet another Army player had his nose broken. The next day the *New York Times* placed their story of the game on the front page, hailing the contest as "the greatest victory the Navy has achieved since Decatur and John Paul Jones . . . The result was watched with national interest . . . It was generally regarded as the beginning of new era in the athletic training of two institutions."

This new era, however, almost ended before it could gather steam. By 1893 the game had grown progressively more violent. Not only were fights common on the field, but also skirmishes along the sidelines frequently broke out between cadets and midshipmen. A few hours after the game in 1893 the rivalry between the two institutions was so white-hot that a general and an admiral challenged each other to a duel at the Army-Navy Club in Washington, D.C. The duel was averted, but clearly something needed to be done about the mounting animosity between the two schools.

"The excitement attending [the game] exceeds all reasonable limits," said Major Oswald Ernst, who had replaced Wilson as the military academy's superintendent.

At the urging of Ernst and others, President Grover Cleveland convened a special Cabinet meeting to discuss Army-Navy football in February 1894. Shortly after the Cabinet meeting was over, both the secretaries of the army and the navy issued edicts that, in effect, canceled the game. Not until 1899 was it resumed on an annual basis. But by then, Michie, who had been the key figure in organizing the first Army-Navy game, was dead. He'd been killed in the Spanish-American War in 1898. The only Naval officer killed in that conflict was Worth Bagley—a four-year letterman for Navy's football team. Michie and Bagley were two of the first football players from Army or Navy to die in combat on foreign soil.

After Larson delivered his history lesson, he told his boys to get out on the field and make the entire Navy proud. Let's play like this is the last game of our lives, Larson told his team. The players then bolted out of the locker room, primed for the challenge.

Navy was the first team on the Municipal Stadium field. The Middies were clad in white jerseys with blue numbers, their pants gold. Less than a minute later the Army players, adorned in black jerseys with gold numbers and also outfitted with gold pants, jogged to their sideline. Each team's offense practiced a few plays in their single-wing formations while the captains were beckoned to the center of the field. There, Army's Ray Murphy and Navy's Bob Froude shook hands and made a friendly wager: The losing captain would have to give the winner his football helmet. The regiments had been making bets against each other all week long. Bathrobes, sweaters, cuff links, even full uniforms were put on the line between cadets and midshipmen. These items carried little monetary value, but their symbolic and personal worth would be priceless to the winners, as precious as family heirlooms packed in a cedar chest.

Army won the toss and elected to kick off—as most teams did in 1941 in the hope of acquiring superior field position. As the players lined up in kickoff formation, a burr of expectation filled the stadium, which was now stuffed to capacity, making this game the most heavily attended football, baseball, or basketball contest of 1941. Over one hundred writers in the press box grabbed their pencils and prepared to take notes. Broadcasters from three separate radio networks—National, Columbia, and Mutual—all cleared their throats as they readied to speak to national audiences, and in some cases global. Calling the game on NBC radio were Fort Pearson, who gave the color description, and Bill Stern, who handled the play-by-play duties. Both Pearson and Stern were considered two of the top football announcers of their time, and this game was the plummiest assignment anyone in sports radio could land. In the pregame portion of their broadcast Pearson and Stern interviewed former Notre Dame coach Elmer Layden, Columbia coach Lou Little, Minnesota coach Bernie Bierman, Colgate coach Andy Kerr, and sportswriter Grantland Rice. All the guests agreed that Army would have to play a near-perfect game to beat Navy, a team that simply was bigger and had more experience than the Cadets.

With the fans standing on their feet in the grandstands, which were a sea of black, brown, and gray fedoras, Army's John Roberts, using a straight-on approach, kicked off. The ball sailed low and rolled out of bounds at Navy's 35-yard line. In the Navy huddle Busik called for a run up the middle on the Middies' first play. Larson had told Busik all week long that he wanted to wear down the Cadet lineman, and to accomplish that Larson instructed Busik to hammer the ball between the tackles. But three straight runs into the line produced only five yards. On fourth and 5, Busik punted the ball to the Army 35-yard line, where it rolled out of bounds. Now Army's offense got its first shot.

On first down, Hank Mazur, the left back, received the direct snap and plowed straight over the left tackle for 2 yards. On second down Mazur, lined up 7 yards behind the left tackle, again received the direct snap. Instead of running, though, he quick-kicked the ball. The surprise worked, as the ball rolled to a stop at the Navy 16-yard line. The 47-yard kick prompted a clapping of the hands from Coach Blaik on the sideline. It was blue-moon rare for coaches to call plays in 1941—they usually left it up to their star back—but during the previous week in practice Blaik repeatedly told Mazur that he should be conservative with his play-calling on offense. This meant, Blaik said, that in many cases the best play call on a second and long would be a quick kick.

Navy's offense began its second series. On first down Busik took the direct snap and ran to his right. Not seeing any daylight, he put his head down and bulled forward. Just as he was falling to the ground, Romanek slid over from his defensive end position and put a wicked helmet-to-helmet shot on Busik. For a split second, Busik, who had lost a yard on the play, didn't know where he was. But he quickly regained his wits and was able to get up without any help.

In the huddle, Busik was frustrated. He felt like he'd just run into a stone wall and he wasn't getting any help from his blockers. Tired of being pummeled, he called for another quick kick with the ball on the 15-yard line. The Army defensive backs had anticipated the play, but Busik uncorked the best kick of his life. After receiving the direct snap 8 yards behind the line of scrimmage, Busik took one step back with his left foot, then one forward with his left foot, then dropped the ball. His right foot swung up like a massive pendulum in motion and connected with the sweet spot of the ball. The Army backs, in full sprint, were at midfield when they looked up into the cobalt-blue sky and saw the football some 20 yards directly above them. The ball landed on the Army 20 and then it rolled. It came to a dead stop at the Cadet one-foot line. Busik had out-kicked not only his coverage, but also Army's returners. The ball sat perfectly stone-still for a couple of seconds before anyone on the field could reach it. The punt had traveled 85 yards, by far the longest in Navy history.

Busik was taught how to punt by Snede Schmidt, a Navy assistant coach who had graduated from the academy in 1936. After practice, Schmidt, Busik, and the team's center would often stay until darkness fell to work on their quick-kicks. Holding a stopwatch, Schmidt would chart the amount of time it took Busik to get each punt off. When Busik was a plebe, Schmidt thought that Busik, who was using a two-step approach, was taking too much time. So Schmidt taught his young pupil the rocker step. Busik would line up 8 yards behind the line of scrimmage with his legs together. Once he was hiked the ball, he'd take one step back with his left foot, then a step forward with his left foot, and then kick the ball with his right foot. Busik could tell when he unleashed a good kick by the fact that he wouldn't feel or hear the punt. Schmidt instructed Busik to drive the ball and not to worry about hang time, because all he needed to do was get the ball beyond the defense's deep safety and let it roll. But against Army, Busik had driven the ball and booted it high enough so that it traveled the arc of a big, beautiful rainbow. "The perfect punt," was how Larson would later describe it.

At first, the crowd reacted quietly to this "perfect" punt. As soon as the ball left Busik's foot, it was so hushed in the stadium that Busik could hear his cleats crunch against the thick green grass as he ran upfield. The crowd seemed to be in momentary disbelief, as if they'd never seen a ball travel so high into the sky before. But when the ball began its descent, the crowd came alive. This was the first big play of the game, and the fans had been waiting for nearly a quarter to roar. Now, they let it all out. By the time the ball rolled to a stop, the noise in Municipal Stadium could practically be heard on the other side of town. Busik, like most of his teammates, jumped wildly up and down as he ran to take his position on defense. The Midshipmen on the sideline were also ecstatic. Hal Kauffman had often stayed after practice and shagged balls for Busik as he worked on his punting. Now Kauffman yelled to his friend to keep the pressure on Army. Kauffman knew it would take an act of divine intervention for him to play in the game, but he felt like he played a small part in Busik's magical punt. It wasn't much, but it was something he was proud of.

On first down, backed up to their one-foot line, Army's Mazur didn't want to risk a safety or a turnover deep in Army territory, so he quick-kicked the ball back to Navy. Under the circumstances, it was a splendid kick. Busik caught the ball at Army's 48-yard line and, making a few deft cuts, returned it to the 31, where he slipped and fell. On first down, Busik received the snap, gyrated, faked a pass, then ran around the right end for 8 yards. It was early, but Navy already appeared to be taking control of the line of scrimmage. In the huddle Busik called for a sweep to the left side. But as the snap was centered to him, Busik looked up before the ball was in his hands. There was a gaping hole he could have run through—perhaps he even could have scored—but he never gained control of the ball. It fell to the ground and bounced away from him. Army's George Seip, who had been blocked and was out of position to make the tackle, was in perfect position to recover the fumble, which he did on the 28-yard line. The play prompted almost every Midshipmen in the stands to either stomp his foot or put his hands on his head in utter exasperation.

The rest of the first quarter was a defensive struggle. After four punts were exchanged, Navy faced a third and one from Army's 48. Busik had yet to attempt a pass, and he thought that switching to an aerial game would surprise the Cadets. He dropped back into the pocket and saw one of his ends cutting across the middle of the field. Busik lofted the ball, but Army's Robert Evans, who was the team's middle guard, had dropped off the line and back into coverage. Evans leaped high into the air, tipped the ball, and made a spectacular interception. For an interior lineman, it was an unexpectedly athletic play—exactly the type of effort that Coach Blaik knew he'd need to win this game. The Cadets in the stands yelled as Evans returned the ball to Navy's 44-yard line. At the end of the play, the whistle blew, signaling the end of the first quarter.

Earlier in the day, the Japanese consulate in San Francisco received an important message from their Foreign Ministry back in Tokyo. The consulate was to make full reports of the name, nationality, port of departure, port of destination, and departure date "of all foreign commercial and war ships now in the Pacific, Indian Ocean, and South China Sea." Four days had passed since the task force of thirty ships sailed away from Hitokappu Bay, and officials in Tokyo wanted to know if any foreign vessels leaving the port of San Francisco might sail within sight of Japan's war ships.

As the boys from Army and Navy fought it out on the football field, the Japanese ships had sailed about a third of the distance to Pearl Harbor, creeping closer toward their date with history.

As the teams switched ends of the field after the first quarter, Larson called all of his players over to him. He was going to insert his entire second team for the second quarter—earlier in the week he had contemplated playing only his first string in the game, but eventually decided he didn't want to stray from the substitution pattern he'd employed all season. But before the second team went onto the field, he wanted to give them a pep talk. "Everybody do your job and trust your teammates," Larson told his players. "We will wear this team out because we have better depth and we're bigger. Just stay patient."

Over on the Army sideline, Coach Blaik wasn't talking. In fact, he didn't say a word to his players because he was reasonably pleased with how his team had performed in the first quarter. Before the game he was concerned that Navy might jump all over his boys early because they had more experience in big games. But now that fear had been allayed, and Coach Blaik felt like the game was anybody's to win.

Facing Navy's second team at the start of the second quarter, Army still couldn't move the ball. Three runs into the line netted just 5 yards, forcing Mazur to punt again; this time the ball bounced into the end zone. Fearful of making a mistake, Navy punted the ball back on second down, giving Army the ball back on its own 47. Two plays later, Mazur made the first big offensive play of the game. Receiving the snap, Mazur faked a run into the line, then dropped 15 yards behind the line of scrimmage to pass. He fired a long bomb to James Kelleher, who made a graceful leaping catch at the Navy 15. It was Mazur's first pass of the afternoon, and not a single Midshipman lineman got within five yards of Mazur when he dropped back in the pocket. Olds, Romanek, and the rest of the line neutralized the Navy rush, giving Mazur all the time he needed to find the open receiver.

Navy's defense quickly stiffened. Three plays after the long pass, Army faced a fourth and 10 from the 15. Instead of attempting a fairly easy field goal, Coach Blaik opted to go for it. He steadfastly believed that field position was almost as important as points, so even if his team didn't convert the fourth down, his thinking went, Navy would still be pinned deep in their own territory. On fourth down Mazur again had a few seconds to pass, but this time he overthrew his intended receiver. Navy got the ball back on downs.

The next 5 minutes of the second quarter was a festival of punts. Navy kicked the ball three times, Army twice. But before Navy's third kick, late in the second quarter, Coach Blaik instructed his returners to run a trick play that they'd practiced all week. In film study Coach Blaik noticed that one of the things that the Midshipmen did very well on punt coverage was to pursue the ball carrier. The Navy players went after the returner like bulls to a red-waving flag, and Blaik thought that a well-conceived reverse on a punt return could be successful because the Midshipmen, at least initially, would be zeroed in on the wrong player. After a week of practices, the Army return team had perfected this trick return.

With a little less than 5 minutes remaining in the first half, Mazur received the punt on his own 20 near the Army sideline. He immediately sprinted to the other side of the field, drawing to him all the Navy defenders, who were hurtling in his direction. Running down the Navy sideline in the direction of Mazur was Cadet wingback Ralph Hill, one of the fastest players on the Army team. Just before Mazur got tackled, he flipped the ball to Hill. The reverse fooled the Midshipmen. As soon as Hill got the ball, he appeared to be startled by how much open field lay in front of him. He nearly tripped, but regained his balance as he eyed the end zone. The crowd rose to its feet as he sprinted up the Army sideline.

Hill was at midfield. Still no Navy defender around. He was at the 40. The 30. He was running as hard as he could, his legs pumping like pistons. Finally, at the 22-yard line, a Midshipman who had gained ground on Hill only because he had the angle, pushed him out of bounds. Now the momentum was with the Cadets. Feeling confident, Coach Blaik ordered his team to operate out of the T-formation—something he'd never done before at Army. The Cadets had only practiced it for a few days, but that was also why Blaik thought it could be effective: Blaik knew that Navy hadn't had a chance to prepare for it in their pregame practices. And, sure enough, the switch in formations confused the Midshipmen. On first down, Kelleher gained 5 yards on an end around. On second down Mazur ran for 11. Three plays later, fullback Jim Watkins plowed through the center of the line for a 1-yard touchdown plunge. The

Cadets in the stands went delirious, producing a noise that echoed throughout the concrete horseshoe. Suddenly, an upset seemed possible.

Yet the Navy players were a reflection of Larson—their emotional equilibrium never got too out of whack, no matter what the circumstances—and as the teams lined up for the extra point, Navy lineman Arthur Knox nudged Dick Fedon, also an interior lineman for the Midshipmen. The two made eye contact and flashed each other a knowing nod. Ever since Knox was in prep school, he excelled at what he called "pulling the center," which years later would be deemed holding. An accomplished wrestler, Knox lined up over the center on extra points. As soon as the ball was centered, he'd perform the move: First he'd leap and grab the center by his shoulder pads. Then, holding onto the center's pads, Knox would twist and throw his feet up off the ground so that the center would be holding all of Knox's weight. Using his leverage, Knox would then pull the center to his left. Once the center was out of the way, a teammate—in this case Fedon—would loop behind Knox and have a straight shot at the kicker.

Against Army the move worked to perfection. Knox fired off the line of scrimmage, grabbed the center, twisted, then threw him out of the way. Fedon slid into the gaping hole and smothered the kick. He arrived at the ball at almost the same time as the kicker. As soon as the kick was blocked, the Navy sideline, where most of the players and coaches had been sitting on folding chairs, erupted. "I knew we could get 'em on that one," Knox shouted to Fedon as they jogged to the sideline. "It's the oldest trick in the book." Other than Busik's long punt, this was the first game-altering play Navy had made all afternoon, and it injected the team with a shot of confidence. The scoreboard read: Army 6, Navy 0.

Navy's second-string offensive unit had time for one more drive before halftime. On a second-down play from their own 11-yard line, Alex Zechella caught a pass over the middle from Sherwood Werner. Just as Zechella was being tackled at the Navy 20-yard line, he lateraled the ball to teammate Bob Woods, who then ran up the Navy sideline to the Cadets' 45. Less than one minute remained in the half. Back Howie Clark, who was the second team player in charge of play-calling, opted to try another pass. As he dropped back deep into the pocket, though, Romanek beat his man off the right edge. Coming from Clark's blind side, Romanek had a clear shot at making the sack. But instead of going strictly for Clark, Romanek went for the ball, stripping it cleanly, swiping the pigskin directly out of Clark's arms. The Army players on the sideline leapt from their chairs, screaming for Romanek to run.

Romanek saw no one between him and the end zone, 40 yards away. The Cadets in the stands yelled deliriously. If Army could score here, it would be a devastating blow to Navy. But just as Romanek secured the ball and started to run—just as the vision of him scoring a touchdown began to gloriously unfold in his mind—Clark lunged at Romanek and poked the ball just hard enough to jar it loose from Romanek's grasp. Army ultimately recovered the fumble, but failed to advance the ball any farther upfield. Only seconds remained in the half.

The Cadets ran one play and then let the clock expire. As Romanek headed off the field for the locker room, he couldn't believe he hadn't return the fumble for a touchdown. He figured that play would haunt him for the rest of his life. "I should have scored," he muttered to himself over and over as he neared the locker room. "Goddamn it, I should have scored."

In the Navy locker room, the overwhelming sentiment was anger. The players felt like they'd played their worst half of football of the season. They let Army dictate the tempo and flow of the game on both sides of the ball and, worse, they seemed to be playing as if they were afraid to lose rather than wanting to win. Larson nervously paced back and forth from one end of the locker room to the other, trying to figure out what he should say to his team. He was searching for magical words, for a few sentences that would make his boys play to the top of their potential in the last 30 minutes of the game—the last 30 minutes of his coaching career. Then it came to him.

"Boys, today is our last war together," said Coach Larson. "We have a chance to win this war together on this battlefield. Now listen, you boys are fine football players, and you will make even better officers. The nation will need you. You will need each other. In these last 30 minutes, let's show the nation what kind of football players you are and what kind of officers you will be." Larson's voice grew louder. "Let's play these last 30 minutes of football like they're the last 30 minutes of our lives, because what you do right now you will remember for the rest of your lives. Now let's go get 'em."

As soon as Larson stopped speaking, every player in the locker room jumped from his seat on the bench and yelled. Never before had they seen their coach so passionate and intense. They were so ready for action that they would have run through barbed wire to get out of the locker room, if that's what it took to get back on that field and get another crack at Army.

As fire and brimstone flew from Larson's lips in the Navy quarters, Coach Blaik was coolly assessing the situation with his assistants in the opposite locker room. The consensus was that their boys had played their best half of football of the season. Blaik hadn't expected to move the ball much on offense, and that was holding true. Blaik believed that the only way the Cadets would maintain their lead was if they could continue to win the minigame of field position and make one more game-changing play on special teams. Blaik knew that the more talented players resided on the other side of the field, which meant he needed to outfox Larson in the second half. "We're doing great," Coach Blaik calmly told his team. "Let's just keep being precise in everything we do—with our blocking, tackling, and running—and we'll win this game."

During halftime, Mrs. Roosevelt and her entourage slowly walked across the field to take their seats on the Navy side of the stadium. Because of her husband's long-standing interest in the Army-Navy clash, the First Lady had a good grasp of the rules of the game and was well versed in its nuances. As she strolled across the field she waved to the Navy fans, all of whom gave her an enthusiastic welcome. Some in the stands even figured she'd bring the Midshipmen good luck. After all, they figured, the underdog Cadets did score a touchdown when she sat on *their* side.

Navy had the option to kick or receive to begin the second half, and Larson chose to go on offense first. His best player was Busik, and he wanted the ball in Busik's hands for as much of the second half as possible. When Busik received the kickoff at his goal line, he sprinted upfield, broke two tackles, and was finally dragged down on Navy's 32-yard line. Before calling the first play of the drive, Busik looked around in the huddle, locking eyes with his teammates. "This is why we play football, fellas," Busik said above the crowd noise, "for moments like this. Let's do what we have to and win this game for coach."

Busik then called his own number—as he did for eight of the next nine plays. None of these runs or passes was particularly spectacular, but each time Busik made positive gains. He'd get 3 yards running up the middle. Then 5 to the outside. Then 3 more up the middle in a cloud of dust. Then 6 on a pass to the Army sideline. Eventually, Busik led the

Midshipmen to the Army 16-yard line, where Navy faced a fourth and 6. The key moment of the game—up to this point—had arrived.

On the sideline, Larson knew exactly what Busik should call: a run around the right end. But the play call was Busik's. Larson, though, was so sure that he knew the right play to call that, suddenly, he yelled at the top of his lungs, "Gebert!" Tackle Wes Gebert quickly got up off his metal folding chair, grabbed his helmet, and sprinted up to his coach. Larson told Gebert what play he wanted Busik to run and then he pushed Gebert out onto the field, subbing him in for another tackle. Even though a rule was implemented at the beginning of the 1941 season that allowed coaches to shuttle players and play calls in from the sideline, Larson had never done it before. He trusted his players on the field to make the play calls. Larson figured they had a better feel for what would work because they were more intimately involved in the action. But this was such an important moment in the game that Larson made the snap decision to send in his first midquarter substitution of the season and call the first play of his coaching career. He felt, right now, that he had a golden touch, a sure thing, and he obeyed his instincts.

When Gebert got to the huddle and relayed the information, Busik was shocked. He looked to coach Larson on the sideline, who nodded his head and motioned that Busik should get to the line of scrimmage. The Army players were equally surprised to see Gebert run onto the field. A few players thought that a trick play was coming; others thought that Gebert would attempt a field goal. The confusion on the Cadet side seemed to linger once Busik was hiked the ball. He sprinted around the right end—it was almost as if he were flying—and he gained 15 yards to the Army 1-foot line. On the next play, backup Phil Hurt bulled through the middle to score Navy's first touchdown of the afternoon. The extra point was good and 8 minutes into the third quarter Navy held a 7–6 lead. The fans on the Navy side of the field were in a frenzy, shouting at the top of their lungs.

On the Army sideline, Coach Blaik weighed his options for what to do next. According to the rules in 1941, once a team surrendered a touchdown it had the choice of either receiving the ball or kicking off for a second straight time. It was virtually unheard of for a coach to use this rule and kick off after his team was just scored upon, but the idea intrigued Blaik. He figured Navy's offense was just as tired as his defense, and if they could hold the Midshipmen inside their 30, then the Cadets would be able to acquire good field position. With his team gathered around him on the sideline, Coach Blaik quickly made up his mind: He called for the kickoff squad to get back on the field. Many of his players looked at Blaik like he'd gone made, but again Blaik barked his instructions.

The Navy players were as surprised by Blaik's decision as the Army players. The Midshipmen kickoff team was already on the field when the referee signaled that the Cadets would be kicking off. Many fans didn't understand the move either, as a quizzical groan emanated from Army supporters in the stands. Nonetheless, Blaik saw this as a chance to eventually put his offense in a favorable position to score, which to Blaik was the key to the game. He didn't think his offense could drive the ball any distance and push the ball into the end zone.

Again Busik returned the ball and again he advanced it to Navy's 32-yard line. On the sideline before the kick, Larson had told Busik to pound the ball, really pound it, between the tackles. Larson added that 37 Buck, which was a fullback plunge up the middle, would be a good play to run. Larson thought the play would further wear down the undersized Cadets, and Larson was right. Mixing 37 Buck with an assortment of short passes, the Midshipmen moved the ball methodically down the field. They faced only one third down—a third and two at Army's 37—and converted it with a 12-yard run by Busik.

One of the players that Navy was successfully blocking was Olds. When healthy, Olds had all-American potential. He thought the adrenaline rush brought on by the game would propel him for four quarters, would make his pain go away, but by now his right shoulder had been hit so many times that his entire right arm was virtually limp. If he had two good arms, Olds may have been able to stop the Midshipmen on the drive that they were now embarking on—Olds was that talented, no question—but not by playing at only 50 percent. Navy knew that Olds was injured, and the Midshipmen didn't hesitate running the ball in his direction, a tactic they never would have pursued had Olds not been hurt.

The twelve-play drive concluded with another 1-yard touchdown run, this one by back Howie Clark. The extra point kicked by Bob Leonard split the uprights and, with less than a minute remaining in the third quarter, Navy had a 14–6 lead. The Midshipmen in the stands, sensing that their team was closing in on victory, celebrated exuberantly. If the Navy fans had been worn out by the nearly three quarters of tense football, it didn't show, because they continued to yell like their pants were on fire.

This time Blaik didn't elect to kick off. Mazur, who felt like he hadn't had the ball in his hands for hours, received the kick at the goal line and returned it 36 yards. Playing with a sense of urgency, Mazur on first down threw deep over the middle. The pass was incomplete, but Navy was flagged for interference, giving the Cadets a 22-yard gain to Navy's 42. After the referees marched off the penalty yards, the quarter came to an end. Fifteen minutes of football remained.

Coach Larson asked the entire Navy squad to gather around him on the sideline. "This is it, one more quarter," Larson yelled. "Give it your all right now, and we'll win this game."

After the teams changed sides, Mazur threw another beautiful long pass. He hit Ralph Hill in stride as Hill streaked down the Navy sideline. Hill was pushed out of bounds at the Middies' 17-yard line. Suddenly, the Cadets in the stands were bouncing up and down again. The game, which had seemed like a lost cause just moments ago, suddenly was exciting again. Trying to capitalize on his hot hand, Mazur called for another pass play in the huddle. He dropped back 10 yards behind the line of scrimmage, sprinted to his left, then saw what he believed to be an open man cutting across the field at Navy's 5-yard line. Mazur threw the ball as hard as could, trying to squeeze it between two defenders, but Busik, playing defensive back, reacted quickly and intercepted the ball at the 5. He returned it 6 yards to the 11, where he was pushed out of bounds. Some 13 minutes remained in the game, but to Larson and to everyone else who was on the Navy sideline this appeared to be the play of the game.

When Busik came to the bench—the second team was now in on offense—the first player to greet him was Hal Kauffman. All game long Kauffman had intensely watched the game from the bench. He had agonized over every play, every block, and now his buddy from California had at least momentarily saved the game. They embraced on the sideline—a long, tight, heart-felt embrace. Right now Kauffman almost felt like he was a brother to Busik, so proud was he of his friend.

Navy again ran the ball between the tackles, trying to bleed as much time off the clock as possible. They gained two first downs before Army finally forced a punt. But when the Cadets got the ball back at their own 25 with 6 minutes to play, they were a demoralized—and a dog tired—squad. Mazur ran for one first down, but the Navy defense stiffened and forced another punt. When the Middies gained possession of the ball only 3 minutes remained. Now the Navy supporters in the stands were in full-scale party-mode, as they smiled and hugged and laughed in the bleachers.

On the other side of the stadium it was perfectly quiet. Some fans cried while others consoled. Yet not a single fan filed out of the stadium.

Navy slammed the ball between the tackles on three straight plays and gained a first down. Then the final gun sounded. The game was over. The undermanned Cadet players had fought as hard as Vikings, but the Midshipmen prevailed 14–6.

As Army and Navy players began to walk across the field, the Midshipmen band struck into its alma mater song, causing players from both teams to stand at attention. Cadets, holding their helmets under their arms, wept as the Midshipmen players all proudly sang along. Minutes later, the Cadet band broke into its alma mater song, and the Navy players stood at attention out of respect for Army. Up in the stands, men, women, and children all teared up as they watched the young men on the field, standing shoulder-to-shoulder in the growing afternoon shadows.

It took Larson about ten minutes to reach Navy's locker room. After the playing of the alma mater songs, fans spilled onto the field, impeding Larson's route. The Midshipmen fans climbed on top of both goalposts and, as both bands now played the "Star Spangled Banner," the posts tipped down until their roots were unearthed. After the national anthem was over—the entire stadium had sung together—Larson shook hands with Coach Blaik and several of the Army players and then waded through the crush of fans that had congregated on the field. A full 20 minutes after the game was over, the stadium was still packed. No one wanted to leave. Everyone understood that this was one memory worth stretching out as long as possible.

A group of reporters was waiting for Larson when he walked into the locker room. Now a big smile lighted Larson's long, slender face. "Those Army lads were as hot as firecrackers!" Larson shouted. "But we showed them a few plays they hadn't seen before."

Just then, tackle Bill Chewning, his uniform smeared with dirt, blood, and grass stains, approached Larson with the game ball. "Here you are, coach," said Chewning as he handed Larson the ball.

"Thanks, Billy," replied Larson. "You played a marvelous game."

On the other side of the stadium, in the corridor just outside the Army locker room, Blaik stood straight and tall. Though his heart was sick, he still looked all the reporters in the eye. "If we had a few boys to stick in that backfield, we could have done better," he said. "You saw how it was. Navy not only had two lines but two backfields. I'm definitely not satisfied. I'm a bad loser. I thought we might upset them. We had them on the run for awhile, but a few little things in there hurt us and helped Navy."

That night players from both teams celebrated the end of their seasons. Most the Midshipmen attended a party at the Bellevue Hotel and gorged on the nectar of glory. They danced with their dates until the sun peeked over the horizon, moving their feet to songs like "Waltzing Matilda," by Banjo Patterson. The scene was similar at the Franklin Hotel. Even though the Cadets had lost a heartbreaking game, most of the players were still in a festive mood. "You can't cry all day," Romanek told a few of his teammates who were crestfallen and holding pity parties in their rooms at the hotel. "You gotta move on. After all, who knows where we'll be in the next month, the next year, or the next two years."

In the morning each team made its way back to its respective campus. At West Point, their fellow classmates and a few hundred locals greeted the Cadet players at the train depot. Everyone cheered as the team stepped off the train. This one last show of support by their fans somehow made the loss bearable.

At the naval academy, it seemed that the entire city of Annapolis turned out to meet the Middies. The Toonerville Trolley carried the team straight into the Yard. From there, players and fans walked over to Tecumseh Court and rang the Gokokuji Bell. The bell, which Commodore Matthew Perry brought to the United States in 1854 from Japan, tolled only after a Navy victory over Army. And now each player and coach rang the bell fourteen times—for the fourteen points they scored against the Cadets—as the throng of midshipmen and fans cheered. The bell clanged and clattered deep into the night, the sounds echoing through the trees and all across campus.

"I'm glad I decided to play football," Busik told a teammate as they waited their turn. "It's probably one of the best decisions I ever made. I'll never forget this win."

The date was November 30, 1941. For the next few days, Busik and his teammates would swap tales—some a little taller than others—about their exploits from that dream day. For seven days the glory of the game seemed to lighten everyone's spirit at the naval academy. Fellow midshipmen and Annapolis locals alike all sought out Busik, greeting him like a conquering hero and asking him for an autograph. Even the academy instructors went out of their way to congratulate the players, even guys like Hal Kauffman who didn't get into the game.

Indeed, these were golden moments for Busik and Kauffman. Graduation was just months away, and then they'd be sent off into the real world as officers in the United States Navy. But for now, for the next few days, they reveled in the warm glow of victory.

II

PEARL HARBOR

AFTER THE NAVY VICTORY Alan Shapley took every opportunity to chat about the game. Whenever he so much as bumped into one of the eighty-seven marines he was in charge of aboard the U.S.S. *Arizona* who hadn't paid close attention to the radio broadcast of the Army-Navy contest, Shapley would put a hand on his shoulder and tell him all about it, sparring no detail. Normally stingy with his words, Shapley would talk a blue streak when it came to discussing Navy football—particularly when it involved beating Army. The Midshipmen's victory over the Cadets on November 29 had tickled his heart, filling Shapley with so much pride that it was as if his own blood brothers had won the game.

Now, on the morning of December 7, 1941, as Shapley walked into the *Arizona*'s wardroom for breakfast, he was still beaming. The widest of smiles illuminated his angular face. With his sandy-hair, big blue eyes, and athletic, slender build, Shapley still could be taken for the Big Man On Campus, even though it had been fifteen years since he led the Midshipmen to the 1926 national title. Now Shapley took a seat. The *Arizona* was moored in the still waters of Pearl Harbor. Along with the *Arizona*, there were seven other battleships, eight cruisers, thirty destroyers, and four submarines resting at the Navy base.

Outside it was a peaceful, quiet morning. The air was moist and mild. Blue waves glistened in the winter sunshine. A soft breeze fluffed the palm trees on the island. Sunday was generally regarded as a day of leisure at Pearl, so there was little activity at the base. Inside the *Arizona*, Shapley had more than just Navy's victory over Army to be happy about. The previous afternoon he had been promoted to major. His new orders were to report to the First Marine Amphibious Corps at Camp Elliot, located outside of San Diego, as soon as possible. Though he had been relieved of his duties aboard the *Arizona*, which had recently returned to Pearl Harbor after performing exercises in the Pacific, the next transportation ship back to California wasn't scheduled to leave until the morning of December 8, a Monday. The delay suited Shapley just fine. He was both the coach and first baseman of the *Arizona*'s baseball team, and on this Sunday morning the U.S.S. *Arizona* had a game scheduled against the U.S.S. *Enterprise*. But Shapley had time to enjoy his breakfast because the *Enterprise* was still due in from Wake Island, an atoll in the North Pacific Ocean where she had delivered planes to reinforce the Marine garrison. So Shapley was in no hurry as he drank coffee and ate eggs and hot cakes with two dozen other officers in the wardroom.

At about 7:50, Shapley rose from his seat and stretched his legs. He walked outside the wardroom and started chatting with a few other officers. He explained to them that he had mixed feelings about leaving. On one hand, he was thrilled that he'd see his wife and two young children once he made it stateside. They lived in Detroit, some five thousand miles away from Pearl Harbor. Shapley, like many officers stationed at Pearl, chose to leave his family in the States out of concern for a possible war erupting in the Pacific. But as happy as Shapley was that he'd get to see his loved ones, he was heartbroken that he'd have to leave his men. "They're like family to me," Shapley said on numerous occasions of his marines. "It just doesn't seem right leaving them."

The marine detachment of eighty-seven men on the *Arizona*, which had a total crew of 1,731, was charged with several duties. They acted as orderlies and messengers for the senior officers on board. They stood watch at the brig in four-hour shifts. They served as gun crews and they performed ceremonial duties, such as keeping track of the time of day by ringing the ship's bell. And the marines were the only ones aboard the ship who carried loaded guns—an old tradition based on the theory that the marines were present to protect the senior officers in the event of a mutiny. When the marines weren't on duty, they spent a good deal of their free time shining shoes, pressing their uniforms, and polishing their belt buckles. This wasn't a particularly glamorous way of life, but Shapley—ever the quarterback, the leader of his team—tried to make his men feel important. One of the first things that Shapley did when he assumed command of the detachment was to memorize as well as he could the biographies of all his men. He then took a genuine interest in all of them and talked to each of them about his family, his hopes, his dreams, his fears. This fostered a closeness between Shapley and his men that was rare in the world of marine detachments.

At approximately 7:56, Shapley left the officers standing outside the wardroom and began walking to his stateroom, his living quarters. There he planned to put on his baseball uniform and, if he had time, pack his bags for his transfer to the States. But just as he turned to start walking he felt a jolt, which rocked the ship and forced him to put his hands on the wall to keep his balance. A loud thud followed. He figured that perhaps one of the forty-foot boats had been accidentally dropped off the crane onto the stern of the ship.

Alarmed but hardly panicked, Shapley climbed the ladder to the deck just to make sure that everything was okay. There he saw a group of sailors standing on the rail and peering across the harbor at the big Number 1 dry dock. In the dry dock were the flagship U.S.S. *Pennsylvania* and two destroyers, the U.S.S. *Cassin* and the U.S.S. *Downs*. The sailors were watching dozens of airplanes zoom over the Pearl Harbor shipyard. "This is the best damn drill that the Army Air Force has ever put on," remarked one sailor to Shapley as Shapley kept his gaze fastened on the harbor. A few seconds later, to everyone's horror, one of the destroyers burst into flames. A mushroom cloud of black, brackish smoke swelled into the sky. The boom of the explosion shot across the water; it was so strong that Shapley and the others could feel a sharp thump in their chests. A voice shouted over the *Arizona*'s loudspeaker for all disengaged personnel to get below the third deck, where they would have the protection of armor plating. Moments later, the flagship *Pennsylvania*, which was now engulfed in flames, countermanded, which overruled the last order, and ran up the signal for general quarters, signaling for everyone to get to their battle stations. They were under attack.

Shapley immediately recognized the planes as Japanese, since the red ball on the underside of the wings was a telltale marking. Shapley's battlestation for general quarters, along with thirteen enlisted Marines and one of his lieutenants, was to man the gunnery director station up in the Arizona's mainmast and, if necessary, the two .50 caliber machine guns that were fastened at the very top of the mast in a post known as the "bird bath," which sat more than one hundred feet above the waterline. The *Arizona*'s mainmast—the ship's tallest mast—had three positions that could be manned. The first was the searchlight platform, which was forty feet in the air. The next was the gunnery director station, which was ninety feet up. The third was the "bird bath," fifteen feet above the gunnery station. Shapley headed for the gunnery station, on the double.

On the deck, men were running in all directions, trying to get either to their battle stations or into the belly of the ship for protection. Some of the younger men—some weren't even shaving yet—looked panicked, unsure of what to do, as they frantically scrambled around the deck. As Shapley ran toward the ladder that led up to the bird bath, he saw Second Lieutenant Carleton Simensen, a graduate of North Dakota University and one of the junior officers in the detachment. Simensen had already rounded up a group of marines and they were all running to the tripod mainmast. Shapley calmly told everyone to remember their training. This, he reminded everyone in a loud voice, was the real thing.

Simensen was the first marine to reach the metal ladder. Hand over hand, he began climbing. Shapley was next. As they moved upward, more planes appeared, dotting the sky like a swarm of killer bees. The planes bore down on the ships, releasing bombs that whistled as they fell and detonated with a thunder when they blew gaping holes into the ships. As Shapley climbed, he could see that the planes were also strafing the men who were topside on the ships with machine guns; men would fall in an eyeblink once they were struck. Torpedoes also rained from the sky. Once they hit the water, they moved like sharks after meat toward their intended targets. Shapley felt each explosion reverberate against him as he continued the push to his battlestation.

Just as Simensen, the lead climber, reached for the last rung before the searchlight platform—forty feet in the air—he lost his grasp. He fell backward onto Shapley, lifeless as a rag doll. With one hand gripping a rung, Shapley caught hold of Simensen with his free arm. Shapley pushed him across his shoulders and, exerting all the strength he had, managed to carry Simensen up three feet and lay him on the searchlight platform. Out of breath, Shapley quickly inspected Simensen. His shirtfront was soaked with blood, and he wasn't breathing. Simensen had been hit by machine gun fire, killed instantly. Shapley looked down the ladder and saw that four other marines had also been struck and fallen off the ladder. They were all dead.

In a firm voice, Shapley instructed his men who were still alive that they had to keep climbing; they had to reach their battlestation. They continued to climb, up, up, up. Shapley and his eight marines could see some of the faces of the Japanese pilots as they whizzed by. Many of the planes had their canopies open, and Shapley was so close to one pilot that their eyes met. For a moment that seemed to occur in slow motion, Shapley and the pilot looked hard at each other. It was almost like they were communicating . . . then, in a flash, the pilot and the plane were out of sight, gone to drop more death on Pearl.

When Shapley and eight of his men finally finished the climb to the director platform, they went to man the five-inch guns—but it was a futile task. The guns weren't designed to blast enemy aircraft; they were made to shoot at other ships. Shapley and his men desperately tried to elevate the guns so they could target the planes that circled Pearl like buzzards, but they wouldn't budge. All Shapley and his men could do was watch the destruction. From their perch they saw a torpedo ram into the U.S.S. *Oklahoma*, which was moored just ahead of the *Arizona* in Battleship Row. The blast caused the *Oklahoma* to roll over on her back and pitch hundreds of her crew into the water. Shapley and his men watched dozens of injured men drown within a few feet of land.

The whole scene had a dreamlike unreal feel to it. In the distance Shapley and his men could see Hickem Field, which was an Army Air Force base, and closer by was Ford Island, where a naval air station was located. Japanese aircraft were attacking both. As they witnessed the destruction with their panoramic view of Pearl, chips of metal and paint struck Shapley and his men, the result of enemy gunfire hitting the ship. Realizing there was nothing they could do at their battlestation, Shapley looked for a clear path down. He examined each of the tripod legs, but each one led directly into a towering ball of flames. For the moment, there was no way out. The ship was burning from bow to stern and, after spending about 10 minutes up in the director platform, the heat was becoming unbearable.

"We're cooking up here," a sergeant told Shapley.

"I'll get you out of this," Shapley replied, his hair standing on edge from the nonstop concussions of shock waves that were being produced by the explosions. "I promise I'll get you out of this. We're not going to die."

Just then, Shapley noticed that one of the tripod legs of the mainmast had become clear of flames. This was their opportunity to get to the main deck and abandon ship, and he ordered his men to start the descent. The metal ladder was now so hot that it burned their hands when they touched it, but Shapley encouraged his men by telling them that burned hands and burned feet will heal. Shapley was the last to leave the platform and he climbed down as fast as he could. When he reached the searchlight platform he again checked the status of Simensen, confirming he was dead. As Shapley got back on the ladder and started his final descent, he looked up and saw a bomb fall from the sky, heading straight for the *Arizona*. Shapley—and the rest of his men who saw this bomb coming—took a deep breath and braced for the explosion, clenching their teeth and wrapping their hands tight around the hot metal ladder.

The 1,760-pound armor-piercing shell struck the *Arizona* near the Number 2 turret, igniting a fire. The flames spread quickly through a hatch that the men inside the *Arizona* didn't have time to shut. Within seconds the fire reached the ship's munitions rooms where one hundred tons of gunpowder rested. First there was a silent white flash, then a blast erupted like a volcano from inside of the ship. In an instant, more than two-thirds of the crew were dead.

A putrid rush of air came at Shapley, who was still on the ladder, forty feet above the water line. Then the explosion lifted him off the ladder, throwing him high into the air. He landed in the water some thirty feet from the ship, unconscious. All around him debris fell from the sky and plopped into the water—parts of the ship, human body parts, and charred sailors. As Shapley started to sink, he came to and—miraculously—he was physically unharmed except that he felt sick to his stomach. All of his clothes either burned or blew off and he was momentarily deafened by the blast—but he was still alive.

When Shapley emerged from beneath the water, he took a gasping breath of air. Looking around him, it was as if he was glimpsing a boiling, screaming hell. Men were splashing in their own blood, crying for help. Others were swallowed in flames. Much of the surface of the water was on fire; the *Arizona* had some ninety-three thousand barrels of oil aboard, and when she was hit the fuel spewed out and ignited.

In the distance Shapley saw five of his marines in the water, most struggling to stay afloat. Shapley always was a strong swimmer and he kicked and paddled to his men, gliding by several body parts and charred bodies that were floating in the water. When he reached his marines—like Shapley, they were all covered in oil—Shapley explained to them how they should swim through burning water. He told them to swim underwater and then, when they had to come up for air, they were to perform a quick twirl to keep from catching on fire. Then, Shapley told them, they should get back under water as quickly as they could. Shapley also said that they should swim directly into the breeze when possible, because that made them less likely to catch fire when they bobbed up for air. Shapley then lead five men toward a water-supply pipeline that was about halfway between them and Ford Island, which was about 150 yards away.

As the group swam though the oily water, Shapley shouted encouragement. "We can do this," he told them. "All of us can. We've trained and we can do this. All of us will make it." When Shapley noticed that Russ McCurdy, one of his marines, was struggling, Shapley swam over to him and told McCurdy not to give up. "You're a great whaleboat man so I know you can do this," Shapley told his marine, who he also coached on the whaleboat team. "Be strong. Just be strong."

Bombs continued to fall from the sky like hail, one after the other, as Shapley and his men swam. From their perspective, when they looked up it seemed as if each bomb was headed straight for them, as if they had bull's-eyes tattooed on their foreheads. Whenever a bomb detonated in the water, the reverberation was so great that it jiggled the men's flesh. About halfway to the pipeline, Shapley saw that corporal Earl Nightengale, who was swimming nearby, was losing strength. Shapley maneuvered close to Nightengale and told him, "Come on, son, you can do it. We'll get out of this together. Keep fighting."

But Nightengale's strength was completely sapped. He told Shapley to go on without him. "Grab my shoulders," Shapley said. Though he was a dozen years older than most of his men, Shapley was still more athletic than any of them. His natural endurance helped him now as he attempted to tow Nightengale to the pipeline, which was still some twenty yards away.

For the first few yards, Shapley felt as if he and Nightengale would make it. But then, as quick as a room light being turned off, a wave of fatigue overwhelmed him. It felt as if lead weights were draped around his legs. He started bobbing in the water. Nightengale let go. He told Shapley to save himself, that he was ready to die. Shapley looked up at the pipeline and it was still ten yards away, but to him it seemed on the other side of the ocean. Shapley told his men that he was letting go as well. Nightengale, just before he disappeared beneath the water, brought his trembling fingers to his forehead, his final salute to a commanding officer.

Shapley then descended into the water, dropping like a bag of rocks, all hope lost. But suddenly, eight feet down, his feet touched the bottom. Shapley was shocked. He had figured the water was much deeper. He tapped his feet on the muddy surface, just to make sure he was actually feeling the bottom. Revitalized and refueled with hope, he bolted back up above the water, pushing with his legs, and resumed the struggle.

When the men saw Shapley fighting to stay alive, it lifted their spirits. After coming up for a breath of air, Shapley dove back down, grabbed Nightengale by the shirt, and yanked him back up. Gritting his teeth, Shapley dragged Nightengale the rest of the way to the pipeline. Soon the other men joined. They were now about halfway to Ford Island, where they could find safety in a bomb shelter. Behind them the *Arizona* was sunk, though a thick stream of black smoke still poured out of part of the ship's superstructure that was above the surface. "Let's make this a quick rest and then we'll move on," Shapley told his men as they all clung to the pipeline. "We're going to do this."

After a few minutes, the group began the final leg of their swim. The bombs kept falling and planes peppered the water with bullets. One bomb whose target was apparently the U.S.S. *Nevada* strayed far off course. It landed about fifty feet from the men, and the vibration in the water was so great that the men felt as if the flesh and muscle was being pulled off their bodies. Shapley, though, never lost his focus. As the group got closer and closer to Ford Island, he continued to shout encouragement to his men. Finally, after about 30 minutes of swimming, the entire group reached Ford Island. As Shapley got out of the water, he was in a daze, not really sure what had just happened to him. For a few moments he wandered around the island with a confused look on his face, but he was eventually recognized by a chief petty officer. The officer gave Shapley an official boat cloak and a bottle of whiskey, which he had taken out of the officers' club. Shapley took a big swig, and then, along with the other men he was in the water with, was escorted to the bomb shelter. Shapley stayed there for about 90 minutes, dazed but sure of one thing: The Japanese would one day pay dearly for this attack.

Some six thousand miles away, an hour after the first bomb had exploded at Pearl Harbor, hordes of fans were pushing their way through the turnstiles at Washington D.C.'s Griffith Stadium. The final pro football game of the 1941 season for the Washington Redskins and Philadelphia Eagles was scheduled to kick off at 2:00 P.M. local time—9:00 A.M. in Hawaii. More than twenty-seven thousand fans filled Washington's old ballpark at Seventh Street and V Street NW. Many of the men wore suits and ties under their overcoats while most of the women were decked out in long dresses and furs. It was a chilly December morning—in the cold air, everyone's breath burst out of their mouths in white puffs—but the weather didn't bother members of the Navy B squad (the backup players) who had made the trip from Annapolis to see the game. They were just thrilled to witness an NFL contest, which for most of the players was a first.

William Leahy, a second-year reserve player at Navy who in less than four years would play a pivotal role in D-day, was especially enthralled. A native of Philadelphia, Leahy liked the Eagles even more than cake when he was growing up in the City of Brotherly Love. The Eagles were the heroes of his youth, players like quarterback Davey O'Brien (an Eagle in 1939–40), end Don Looney (1940), and running back Swede Hanson (1933–37). On this afternoon Leahy was interested in seeing if the Philadelphia defense could slow down the Washington offense, which was led by Slingin' Sammy Baugh. As the Redskins' tobacco-juice-spitting quarterback, Baugh threw a pretty ball, and he could chuck it better than any other player of his day. Though neither the Redskins nor the Eagles were going to advance to the playoffs, Leahy considered this game to be as important as the NFL Championship. After all, this was the first time that Leahy had gotten a chance to see his beloved Eagles play all season.

After traveling to the stadium on a school bus, the Navy B squad players took their seats behind the visitor's bench at about the 30-yard line. Just before kickoff, high above them in the press box, a reporter for the Associated Press named Pat O'Brien received a message from his editor ordering him to keep his story short. When O'Brien complained, he received a second message: "The Japanese have kicked off. War Now!" O'Brien was shocked. He ran up and down the press box announcing that the Japanese had attacked the United States. O'Brien relayed the information to Redskins President George Marshall and General Manager Jack Espey. By this time the game had already started and, midway through the first quarter, Philadelphia held a 7-0 lead. After considering what they should do for a few minutes, Marshall and Espey decided not to inform the crowd of the events at Pear Harbor, fearing that panicked fans could injure each other as they stampeded for the exits. "We don't want to contribute to any hysteria," said Espey. A few moments later, in a box on the 50-yard line, Jesse Jones, the secretary of commerce, was handed a message and quickly departed from the game.

Even without the official announcement, it soon became clear to the fans that something monumental had happened. Every few minutes a voice would come over the public address system and announce that a certain admiral or major was being summoned to his office. "Admiral W. H. P. Blandy is asked to report to his office at once!" said the PA announcer midway through the first quarter. "The Resident Commissioner of the Philippines, Mr. Joaquin Elizalde, is urged to report to his office immediately!" came another announcement. By the end of the first half, after more than a dozen people had been urgently paged, a rumor had spread through the crowd that most of the United States' Pacific Fleet had been destroyed at Pearl Harbor.

In the press box, only a few reporters remained. Editors from the *Washington Post* and the *Washington Times Herald*—D.C.'s two morning newspapers—had been frantically calling the press box ever since the opening kickoff. They needed all of their reporters back in the office so they could help put out a special afternoon edition. One wife of a reporter took matters into her own hands. She instructed Western Union to deliver a telegram to Section P, Top Row, Seat 27, opposite 25-yard line, on the east side that read: "War with Japan. Get to office." Down on the field, only one photographer remained. The rest had been told to go to the Japanese Embassy or to the White House or to Capitol Hill.

Midway through the third quarter the most pressing announcement of the day was made: All military personnel, whether on leave or just away from their stations, were to report to their stations immediately. Upon hearing this, Leahy and all the other Midshipmen quickly rose from their seats and headed for the exit. But as soon as Leahy got to the aisle, one female fan after the next rushed up to him and gave him a hug and a kiss on the cheek. Leahy looked around and saw that the same thing was happening to his teammates. "That was the most attention I've ever gotten," Leahy told one of his teammates when they finally reached the bus. "I've never been kissed that much in my whole life!"

The B squad didn't get a chance to see the finish of the game. Late in the fourth quarter, Baugh threw his third touchdown pass of the day to rookie end Joe Aguirre to cement the Redskins' 20–14 victory. After the game, exuberant Washington fans rushed the field and tore down the goal posts. It marked the last football celebration of an era. Just outside the stadium, newsboys held swag sacks that were full of special-edition papers. These boys were screaming the most important news in the western hemisphere since November 11, 1918, when the armistice ended World War I. "United States attacked!" the boys shouted. "United States attacked!"

Forty-five miles northeast of Washington, the party at the superintendent's quarters in Annapolis was just getting into full swing when the Redskins and Eagles kicked off. The superintendent at Navy had promised the Navy varsity players that if they beat Army he'd invite them over to celebrate. When the players arrived attired in their dress uniforms with their drags (dates) on their arms, they saw a mouth-watering spread of food. Various meats, fruits, vegetables, cheeses, and desserts were laid out on several tables. The food perfumed the air, and the players couldn't wait to dig in.

At the party, Busik shared some surprising news with his teammates: Two days earlier he had received a telegram from Earl (Curly) Lambeau, the head coach of the Green Bay Packers. Lambeau had listened to the Army-Navy game and he had been mighty impressed with Busik's all-around play. Even though he'd never seen any tape of Busik, Lambeau still wanted to offer Busik a tryout with the Packers. In the telegram, Lambeau said that the Packers were interested in Busik both as a back and as a punter. "Can you believe that the Packers actually want me to try out?" Busik laughed as he discussed the matter with a few teammates, including Hal Kauffman, at the superintendent's party. "Don't they realize that I'm committed to the navy? But maybe someday I'll give it a try, who knows?"

Thirty minutes into the party, at about 2:30 local time, a waiter informed the superintendent that he had an important telephone call. The urgency and quaver in the waiter's voice caught everyone's attention. Conversations stopped and every set of eyes followed the superintendent as he went to the top of a winding stairway to speak in private. The teammates moved toward the base of the stairs with a premonition that something was terribly wrong. When the superintendent hung up the phone and came back down the stairs, his face was ashen, his eyes wide with alarm. He informed the team that Pearl Harbor had been attacked and that thousands of Americans were dead. Several recent academy graduates, more than likely, were also dead. "We are now at war, gentlemen," the superintendent told the players. "Return to quarters and await further orders."

At first Busik and Kauffman, like most of the players, were too numb to move. By the time that the boys reached Bancroft Hall, armed guards were already standing outside the entrance of the dorm. Busik and Kauffman were both shaken. Suddenly, combat was no longer something that existed only in the abstract, on the pages of books. Now it was something they'd wake up to every day, and soon be face to face with. In an instant, the world had changed.

At West Point, Henry Romanek sat crosslegged on a folding chair in the gymnasium theater. He and several other cadets were spending their Sunday afternoon watching a movie. When Romanek walked out of the theater, he saw several cadets running wildly around the campus, screaming something he couldn't understand. When he finally cornered one of them, he was told about Pearl Harbor. "Isn't this great?!" the cadet gleefully shouted at Romanek. "Now we get to graduate early. We'll be off to war before you know it!"

Romanek didn't think it was great. Neither did John Buckner, one of Romanek's teammates. He was down near the Hudson River on a flat path known as Flirtation Walk. This was a popular place to bring dates, which was what Buckner did on this December afternoon. He and his honey were sitting on a rock. They looked across the Hudson, watching the dappled sunlight bounce off the water, and they were listening to a hand-held radio when the announcement came over the airwaves. Both Buckner and his date turned to look at each other, overwhelmed by the news. She started crying uncontrollably, saying how much she didn't want him to leave. Buckner tried to console her, softly and sweetly telling her that everything would be okay. What he didn't tell her was that he also couldn't wait to get overseas. He'd been in flight training for more than two years and now he felt it was time for the United States to flex its military muscle. "Everything will be just fine," Buckner told his date. "Don't worry, nobody's going to kill *me*."

At mess hall the next evening, the administrators at West Point piped into the PA system the president's war message to Congress. As soon as the President uttered his first sentence, no one at West Point spoke or ate. Every cadet was transfixed by the president's words, which were delivered in a clear, confident voice, a voice that was perfect for radio.

> *Mr. Vice President, Mr. Speaker, members of the Senate and of the House of Representatives. Yesterday, December 7, 1941, a date which*

> *will live in infamy, the United States of America was suddenly and deliberately attacked by naval and air forces of the Empire of Japan. The United States was at peace with that nation and at the solicitation of Japan, was still in conversation with its government and its emperor looking toward the maintenance of peace in the Pacific . . .*
>
> *The attack yesterday on the Hawaiian Islands has caused severe damage to American naval and military forces. I regret to tell you that many American lives have been lost. In addition, American ships have been reported torpedoed on the high seas between San Francisco and Honolulu . . .*
>
> *No matter how long it may take us to overcome this premeditated invasion, the American people in their righteous might will win a thorough to absolute victory. I believe I interpret the will of the Congress and of the people when I assert that we will not only defend ourselves to the uttermost but will make it very certain that this form of treachery shall never again endanger us.*
>
> *Hostilities exist. There is no blinking at the fact that our people, our territory, and our interests are in grave danger. With confidence in our armed forces, with the unbounding determination of our people, we will gain the inevitable triumph—so help us God.*
>
> *I ask that the Congress declare that since the unprovoked and dastardly attack by Japan on Sunday, December 7, a state of war has existed between the United States and the Japanese empire.*

As soon as the president finished speaking, the mess hall at West Point erupted. The winds of war were blowing, and every cadet in the hall—even the quietest of them all—stood on his feet and clapped, some applauding so hard that they bruised their palms. The emotion and energy in the room bounced off the walls, the intensity of this moment unlike anything any of these young men had ever experienced before. A similar outburst occurred at the naval academy, where many of the midshipmen also listened to the speech in their mess hall.

For Busik, Kauffman, Olds, and Romanek, the direction of their lives had just taken an unexpected turn. The battle was joined.

PART TWO

12

THE *MEREDITH*

AS HAL KAUFFMAN SLOWLY walked along the topside of the destroyer U.S.S. *Meredith* on the morning of October 15, 1942, he enjoyed a beautiful sunrise. The first blush of pink light danced over the rippling waters of the South Pacific Ocean and, for a brief moment, Kauffman allowed himself to forget where he was. Nearly eleven months had passed since the attack on Pearl Harbor, but to Kauffman it seemed like decades since he was carrying his books around the leafy Annapolis campus and taking out his frustrations at football practice. Now aboard the *Meredith*, a destroyer that was commissioned on March 4, 1941, Kauffman and his shipmates were pushing straight into the heart of one of the most volatile regions on the planet. The *Meredith* was escorting ships between Espiritu Santo—an Island in the Coral Sea controlled by Allied Forces—and Guadalcanal. Known as "Bloody Guad" because of the fierce fighting taking place on the island, Guadalcanal lay east of the southern tip of New Guinea. On this clear, bright morning, the *Meredith* was escorting a convoy of troop carriers and a tug with two barges filled with aviation gasoline.

As Kauffman continued to stroll on the deck of the *Meredith*, he marveled at how much his life had changed in the four months since he and 610 other midshipmen graduated from the Academy and became officers in the navy. On June 19, 1942, Admiral Ernest J. King, the commander in chief of the United States fleet, welcomed the largest class in the ninety-seven-year history of the naval academy to the brotherhood of naval officers. Speaking to the class at Dahlgren Hall, which overflowed with classmates, friends, and family, Admiral King began his remarks by saying it was an appropriate time to recall Prime Minister Winston Churchill's notable phrase, "I have nothing to offer you but blood, toil, sweat, and tears." Admiral King then added that victory would come only at the cost of "unremitting labor and a multitude of heartaches and sacrifices such as this country has never known before."

Sitting close to Bill Busik and several other of his football teammates, Kauffman was surprised by the brutal frankness of the Admiral's words—as were many of the family members in attendance. A few of the mothers in the crowd began to weep as the Admiral continued to talk, crying out of joy and fear for their sons. "Victory will bring us not only the preservation of your own freedom and the restoration of the lost liberties of uncounted millions," the Admiral said, "but also the firm confidence that when we have won this war, we Americans—under the leadership of the president—will take steps to see to it that the ability of any person or of any people to enslave others physically or mentally or spiritually, shall forever be destroyed."

The ceremony concluded with the traditional singing by the graduates of the "Navy Blue and Gold" alma mater song, followed by a cheer of the regiment "for those about to leave," a cheer for "those we leave behind," and the tossing of the graduates' white midshipmen caps into the air. Each cap immediately became the center of a scrum, as every Middie wanted to save one as a momento. From Dahlgren Hall, the graduates marched to Bancroft Hall to take the officers' oath. Many of the graduates had their new bars and officers' shoulder boards pinned on by their mothers and sweethearts. After their oath, they were told that they had ten days to report to active duty. Every newly minted officer in attendance planned to pack as much fun in the next ten days as possible, as they all knew that these could be the last ten unfettered days for a long time.

Busik's and Kauffman's last months at the Academy were frantic. Because their course of study had been truncated from four to three years, the instructors overloaded the midshipmen with work. There was so much to study. The soon-to-be-officers learned all they could about new weapons systems (such as gun directors) that were being added to many of the ships. They also were tutored on the rapidly developing technology known as radar, which the instructors said would one day play a critical role in the war. Busik and Kauffman absorbed as much as they could, often studying until four in the morning.

In these months Busik and Kauffman also began to view themselves differently. Soon they would be officers. They would be in charge of many young men and making decisions that would impact hundreds of lives. People had always looked up to Busik because of his superior athletic ability, but in war men would look to him for answers because of the bars on his shoulders. Busik and Kauffman frequently talked about this awesome responsibility in late-night bull sessions with friends, and Busik became more earnest in everything he did. If you're going to be a leader, Busik told his friends one night, you need to act like one all the time. His words may have sounded hokey in different, more peaceful times, but not one of his friends disagreed with what he said.

Kauffman felt the same way. Though he was the senior class president of his high school, Kauffman was never as sought-after as Busik. His natural tendency was to shy away from people rather than seek them out, but he was much more outgoing now than when he arrived at the academy in July of 1939. Like Busik, Kauffman grew more serious-minded as his time in Annapolis dwindled.

Part of the reason why Busik and Kauffman had changed was because of the mail they received during their final spring at the academy. Almost every day a frightening letter from a former classmate would arrive that detailed the cold reality of combat. In these missives Busik and Kauffman read about what it was like to have a man die in your arms, and what it was like to take the life of a stranger. These were troubling letters, yes, but they also emboldened the young, would-be sailors. By the time they graduated, Busik and Kauffman were anxious to join their friends and fellow Americans on the battlefield. This was their destiny, and they wanted to fight, consequences be damned.

A few hours after graduation, with his friends and family watching from the pews in the Naval Academy Chapel, the kiss sparked a small fire in Hal Kauffman. Kauffman had fantasized about this kiss ever since he first laid eyes on Lois Bradburg, that pretty girl in his tenth grade English class at Glendale High in California. They had started dating shortly after he first saw her, and Kauffman often took her to the beach, to weekend dances, and on daytrips to Hollywood. Now, the day after his graduation from the naval academy, Kauffman stood at the altar of the academy chapel wearing his white officers' uniform. As Bradburg glided down the aisle in a traditional satin white wedding dress, Busik sat near the front of the chapel, nodding in approval at the groom.

Kauffman and Bradburg were one of 180 couples to tie the knot at the academy chapel in the days following graduation. A few months earlier the Navy Department rescinded a rule that forbade newly commissioned officers from marrying in their first two years of service. As soon as Kauffman learned that the rule was no longer in effect, he wrote Bradburg a letter asking for her hand. A week later, Kauffman received a note with her one-word answer: Yes.

Now aboard the U.S.S. *Meredith* as she headed toward Guadalcanal, the memory of that special day rose in Kauffman's mind. They had spent their honeymoon in a private cabin on a train that took them back across the United States to California. For a week and a half, the two were inseparable, constantly by each other's sides and holding hands. After only ten days of marriage, Kauffman reported for duty aboard the *Meredith* in San Diego. Before stepping on board, he kissed and hugged his wife good-bye, promising her that he would one day come back to her.

"Saying good-bye to you is the hardest thing I've ever done," Kauffman told his new bride as they embraced for the last time.

On the *Meredith*, Kauffman often lost himself in those memories, especially during the quiet, early morning hours when he'd watch the red sun slink into the sky over the South Pacific. After seeing the horizon light up on October 15, 1942, Kauffman, an ensign, chatted with several of the sailors. The men on the *Meredith*, whose crew of 260 mostly came from the New England states, were uneasy. Their mission to Guadalcanal, which sits in the Solomon Islands about twelve hundred miles northeast of Australia, was significant: Henderson Field, the U.S.-controlled airbase on Guadalcanal, had only three hours of aviation gasoline left in reserve, which forced all the American planes based on Guadalcanal to be grounded. Ever since August 1942 when a division of marines had landed on Guadalcanal and seized the airfield that the Japanese were building, intense fighting had ensued on the over-two-thousand-square-mile island. The Japanese had reacted violently to the unexpected attack on their airbase—it was the first major American offensive in the Pacific—and both sides poured reinforcements into the area.

The Japanese, operating from their massive bases at Rabaul and Truk, made repeated, aggressive attempts to cut up American supply convoys that motored for the island. The jungle airstrip on Guadalcanal was vital to both sides; it was one of the few useable airfields on the islands of the South Pacific. And now it was one of the most fiercely fought-after pieces of land in the world. Admiral Chester Nimitz had recently said of the situation on Guadalcanal, "It now appears that we are unable to control the sea in the Guadalcanal area. Resupplying the positions [on Guadalcanal] will only be done at great expense to us."

The captain of the *Meredith*, Harry E. Hubbard, had warned his crew that they were headed into dangerous waters. On the morning of October 15, Hubbard had been informed that five Japanese transport ships had landed on Guadalcanal and deployed several thousand new troops west of Lunga Point. Hubbard figured that the American forces on Guadalcanal would be doomed unless they were quickly reinforced and resupplied. Hubbard had also received intelligence that stated enemy ships were closing in on the *Meredith*'s advancing position. Explaining this dicey situation to the ship's officers—including Kauffman—Hubbard said they had no choice but to press forward and try to help the soldiers on Guadalcanal. The troop carriers in the convoy turned around, but the *Meredith* and the U.S.S. *Vireo*, the tug in the convoy that controlled one of the barges, maintained their original course, hoping to deliver their cargo of five hundred quarter-ton bombs and ten thousand gallons of aviation gasoline to the marines on Guadalcanal.

"We're in for a difficult time," Hubbard had told Kauffman and a few other officers. "We're going to be vulnerable."

The morning passed slowly. Kauffman stood on the bridge and, using binoculars, scanned in all directions, hoping not to spot anything. At first, he didn't. But then at 10:45 A.M., with the ship about 130 miles southeast of Guadalcanal, Kauffman zeroed in on a sight that made his heart pound: Two enemy carrier planes were flying low and slow through the golden morning light. Kauffman quickly relayed the sighting to Captain Hubbard. After consulting with other officers, Hubbard, who had graduated at the top of his class at the naval academy in 1925, ordered the crew aboard the *Vireo* to prepare to come aboard the *Meredith* because the *Vireo* lacked the firepower to defend herself. As Hubbard transmitted this message, a friendly plane, a PBY seaplane, approached the *Meredith* and flashed this simple message: TWO EMEMY CRUISERS 20 MILES WEST AND HEADING YOUR WAY AT HIGH SPEED.

At 11:40 A.M., radar aboard the *Meredith* came alive with pips, detecting a large group of unidentified planes forty-five miles north. The bogies appeared to be gunning for the *Meredith* and the *Vireo*, but they soon disappeared from the screen. It could only be assumed that they were going after the U.S.S. *Hornet*, an aircraft carrier, and her escorts; they were about two hundred miles away from the *Meredith* and heading away to the southeast. Captain Hubbard quickly moved the *Meredith* alongside the tug and asked the *Vireo* crew if they wanted to come on board. The tugboat skipper was hesitant to leave his ship and his command, but the protection that the destroyer offered was far superior to any defense the tug could mount should the Japanese appear, so he reluctantly ordered his men aboard the *Meredith*.

As soon as the *Meredith* had safely picked up the *Vireo* crew, Captain Hubbard reversed course and ordered full speed ahead, hoping to get closer to air support. As it stood, the *Meredith* was naked: They had no air cover and the U.S.S. *Hornet* and the other ships were too far away to provide any assistance should the Japanese attack. "We need to be ready for anything," the captain told a few of his officers. "We're on our own."

The *Meredith* increased her speed. Kauffman moved from the bridge to the gun director deck, which was located above the pilothouse, still holding binoculars. He glanced at his watch. It read 12:15 P.M. Then he heard a noise directly above him; he titled his neck. Diving down out of the bright sunshine, Kauffman saw the silvery wings of two Japanese bombers, barreling straight toward the ship. "Holy fucking shit!" Kauffman yelled, as enemy aircraft approached. The dive-bombers had flown at an altitude that was too high for the *Meredith*'s radar, which was only a surface search-unit, to detect. Then, in the distance, more Japanese planes appeared. They were low-level bombers, torpedo planes and fighters that had skimmed along the wave tops, just underneath the *Meredith*'s range of detection. Within seconds, a total of thirty-eight planes, which had taken off from the Japanese carrier *Zuikaku*, swarmed the *Meredith*. The Captain urgently ordered, "Battle stations prepare for surface action."

Kauffman knew what would come next. When the Japanese attacked like this—dozens of planes flying low and high—it meant they were on a hunt to kill. The *Meredith* made for a delicious target. Without any aerial support, she would have to defend herself against the enemy planes that kept appearing, one after the next.

The *Meredith*'s 5 inch guns opened fire on the lead bomber, but the pilot still bore down on the ship, the sound of the plane's engine growing louder and louder. Only seconds had passed since Kauffman first spotted the plane diving out of the sun, and suddenly it was only five hundred feet away and closing in. Kauffman immediately sprinted toward the bridge to speak with the captain. When he looked up again he saw the plane release a bomb. It looked like the pilot would slam into the ship's superstructure, but he pulled up just in time.

Kauffman could tell right away that this first bomb was going to be a direct hit. It landed on the bridge, passed through the spot where the helmsman had been standing moments earlier and penetrated to the next deck below. Kauffman hit the ground. The bomb exploded. Deck plates and gratings flew in all directions. The blast threw Kauffman fifteen feet in the air. He landed on his hands and knees almost where he'd been standing before, dazed. He looked around and saw several of his shipmates also lying on the deck, badly burned. Kauffman struggled to find his breath—the wind had been knocked out of him—then staggered to his feet. As smoke cleared, he realized that dozens had been killed by the initial blast, including everyone on the bridge deck except Captain Hubbard, who was severely burned, the ship's doctor, and a few enlisted men.

The bomb severely disabled the ship. All telephone communications, the ship's gun controls, and steering controls were destroyed. The fuel tanks had also been blown open, scattering heavy fuel over the decks and surrounding water. Many of the men were now covered in fuel as everyone tried to maintain their composure and get to their battle stations.

Moments later, another bomb fell out of the bright sunshine, striking the port side of the ship a few feet in front of the bridge. The explosion rocked the ship, nearly breaking it in two. The blast sent dozens of men overboard. Kauffman was knocked down when the second-bomb erupted, but he got back on his feet. Dozens of planes were still overhead, buzzing in the sky. A torpedoman, John Hunter, yelled to Kauffman, "Come on, Mr. Kauffman, let's get us a machine gun and shoot those bastards down!" As soon as the word "down" flew from Hunter's lips, a torpedo struck the *Meredith*, throwing both Kauffman and Hunter into the air, hurtling them overboard. In the water, Kauffman lost consciousness.

Chaos broke out on the ship. Men were running in all directions, panicked. The torpedo had exploded near the ammunition ready locker. The blast ignited star shells and flares, which set the oil on the water's surface on fire. Down in the engine room, men made frantic, desperate efforts to restore power. Up on the decks, gunners scrambled to get to their weapons. A few fired their .50 caliber machine guns, but they were no match for the Japanese onslaught. These Japanese fighters had failed to locate any carriers in the region, so they focused all their firepower and ferocity on the *Meredith*.

The assault continued. Only three minutes had passed since Kauffman saw the first plane in the sky, but the *Meredith* was already sinking. Bombs and torpedoes kept hitting; each explosion slightly lifted the *Meredith* out of the water and tipped her to the side. Near misses threw the flaming oil that was on the water all over the ship, which burned many of the men. The air was now heavy with the smell of flames, sizzling steel, and salt water.

Captain Hubbard, lying on the bridge with severe burns on his face, neck and arms, still tried to shout out orders. He implored the machine gunners to keep shooting, and told his men to maintain order. The gunners did knock seven of the enemy fighters out of the sky, but this was a one-sided fight: In less than 5 minutes of coordinated bombing, thirty-eight Japanese fighter planes made hits with an estimated fourteen bombs and seven torpedoes, ripping the ship apart.

Things were happening so fast that the men on the *Meredith* didn't have time to even consider what their lives had meant, to review who they'd loved, to consider the fate that threatened them. Oil fires burned on the inside and there were gaping holes in the *Meredith*'s sides and decks. On the bridge Captain Hubbard, despite being injured, stayed calm. He called out, "Send a message: '*Meredith* sinking,'" but the radio room had been destroyed. Finally Hubbard, as torpedo planes strafed the bridge, gave the order for his crew to abandon ship. Ten minutes had passed since the first bomb had struck.

For those inside the engine room, raging floods made it nearly impossible to get out. Up on deck, as soon as the call to abandon ship had been made, lifeboats were launched. The two motorized whaleboats had been damaged in the attack and could not be released from their cradles, which meant that the crew had to share the small non-motorized lifeboats—rafts, basically—that could hold ten to fifteen people. With Japanese zooming over the *Meredith* and spraying her with machine gun fire, Botswain Kevin Singletary cut the lashings to the lifeboats. The lifeboats slid overboard and into waters that were being stirred by a suddenly strong wind. The *Meredith* continued to sink. Thirteen minutes had passed since the first attack. Now those who were still alive had only one chance for survival: They had to swim to their rafts.

In the water, Kauffman opened his eyes. He'd blacked out, but now, wearing a life jacket and floating face up, he was twenty feet from the ship. Crewmates were all around him, many floating face down, others burned so badly that Kauffman couldn't recognize them. Still in a daze, Kauffman couldn't detect any sounds; the loud explosions had momentarily dulled his hearing. He looked back at the ship, saw that it had begun to roll over. He turned his head and in the distance there was a liferaft. He started swimming in its direction. As he pushed through the water, Kauffman again looked back at the ship, just to make sure it really was sinking, that he wasn't hallucinating. The *Meredith*'s propellers were lifted in the air, still spinning. Kauffman saw that the men in the engine room were still trying to perform their jobs even as they were descending to their graves.

At just past one in the afternoon, as Kauffman continued to swim for his life, the *Meredith* slid down bow-first into the whitecaps. The last man seen on the ship was Joe Oban. He was firing a 20 mm gun into the sky at planes overhead. He was still strapped in the harness, which kept him from being kicked off the gun each time it fired, when the *Meredith* disappeared into the water. Oban had once made a statement that he'd never leave his gun until he shot down a plane. Now he honored that statement to his death, firing his gun at the Japanese planes that were strafing his helpless shipmates in the water.

"Godamn, Japs," Kauffman said to himself as he swam. "I'll kill every one of them if I get a chance." Many of Kauffman's shipmates—including a few of his good friends on board—were clinging to pieces of floating wreckage. Kauffman would never see them again.

As Kauffman and other survivors swam for the rafts, several Japanese planes dove, heading right for them. "Look out!" Kauffman heard someone yell. As he looked up, a few planes came bearing down on him, machine guns ablaze. The planes buzzed just above the water, spraying the area with bullets, deliberately shooting survivors even after the ship was gone. Kauffman had never seen this kind of evil. The United States Navy had a policy that outlawed such cruelty as shooting defenseless enemy soldiers. Kauffman had never hated anything in his life—at his core, he was a softie who enjoyed nothing more than singing a tune—but now enmity filled his heart. Kauffman dove into the water as the planes whizzed overhead and unloaded their machine guns. When Kauffman came to the surface, several of the men who had been swimming right next to him had been shot, blood gurgling out of their mouths. Kauffman checked on a few of the wounded, but there wasn't much he could do. Most were dead within minutes.

In the distance, Kauffman could see four rafts tied together, about seventy-five yards away. He wasn't sure what to do. If the Japanese planes returned—they had just flown out of view—Kauffman figured they would concentrate their machine gun fire on those rafts. But then Kauffman saw several men swimming toward the rafts. Thinking that it was better to be with his shipmates than alone, Kauffman started kicking his way toward the rafts. When he passed over the spot where the ship had gone down, an explosion reverberated up through the water; a powerful jolt hit his feet and buttocks, slightly lifting him up. The explosion was probably a depth-charge on the ship that had detonated at its set depth. Once again, Kauffman wasn't injured.

Six rafts had floated off the *Meredith* and into the water. The first raft quickly filled up with six men. The men on this raft made a snap decision: They'd try to make it to the tug *Vireo,* which had been damaged by the Japanese but was still adrift a mile away. The men started paddling with their arms and one wooden paddle.

Near the spot where the *Meredith* went down, four rafts were tied together, while a fifth drifted away. Each of the *Meredith*'s life rafts had rations lashed to the plywood grating that formed the bottom of the raft. The rations included cans of meat, malted milk tablets, two canteens of fresh water, first aid supplies, maps, signal flags, and flares. A total of 141 crewmen had survived the initial attack—a little more than half of those on board. Six were on the raft that was making a run to *Vireo;* thirty-four were struggling to stay close to the raft that had drifted away; and the remainder were near the four rafts that were tied together.

In this last group there wasn't enough room on the rafts for all the men, so most of the sailors who weren't wounded—including Kauffman—remained in the water, clinging to the rafts' lifelines. Everyone was covered in oil; the whites of everyone's eyes sticking out like those of a hobgoblin. Most were naked; their clothes had been either blown or burned off.

After drifting together on the four rafts for about 30 minutes, Ensign Dan Haible told Kauffman and a few other officers that he was going to swim to *Vireo,* which was more than a mile away. Haible explained that he would board the *Vireo* and bring back the ship's motorized whaleboat and search for more survivors. Kauffman asked Haible if he thought he could make it, and Haible replied with an emphatic, "Yes, Sir!" Haible, a former star swimmer at the University of Colorado, then unbuttoned his life jacket, tossed it aside, and started swimming the breast stroke. Six hours later, around 7:00 P.M., Haible was helped on board the tug by the five men on the first raft who had reached the *Vireo*. Once he was pulled up on the ship, Haible collapsed, so weak that he couldn't even walk for about 30 minutes.

Despite his life-threatening injuries, Captain Hubbard made it to a raft. He was lying in one of the four rafts that was tied together when Kauffman first saw him. The captain was in bad shape. His face and arms were swollen from burns, and he couldn't see. The men regarded their captain the same way Catholics regard the Pope, and so his condition was terrifyingly upsetting to the crew. "I'm badly burned," Hubbard told the ship's doctor, Michael Bowers, who was on the raft with Kauffman and the captain. "You sure were right about those flash burns." Days earlier the doctor and the captain had talked about the dangers of flash burns—a burn due to brief exposure to intense radiant heat—and now they were slowly killing the captain.

As the doctor tried to comfort Hubbard, someone yelled, "There's a flying fort!" Kauffman looked up and, there in the mid-afternoon light, was a B-17 flying overhead at about twelve thousand feet. The men screamed wildly, hoping to catch the pilot's attention. But the B-17 gave no signal that it had seen any of the life rafts, and the plane soon melted into the horizon. An hour later—some two hours after the *Meredith* had been sunk—the survivors heard another roar in the distance. They all looked up into the sky again, but this time they saw several Japanese planes, seemingly headed right at them. Some men ducked, others jumped into the water, afraid that the rafts would be strafed. But just as some men were swimming away, the planes peeled off in another direction.

The officers in the water knew that a U.S. carrier and other surface ships, which were greatly outnumbered in the region, had been directed to the southeast of their present position in order to avoid a confrontation with the superior Japanese forces. This meant that the *Meredith* and the *Vireo* were the only U.S. ships in the area, and that a rescue might not happen for quite some time. Realizing this, Kauffman, the doctor and a few other able officers, began to take charge. One of the first navigational decisions made aboard the life rafts was to stay in the oil slick that the *Meredith* had left behind. Instead of trying to paddle to the *Vireo*, which the other raft had done, the men on the four rafts that were tied together opted to hold their ground, afraid that the Japanese would return and sink the defenseless *Vireo*. Meanwhile, aboard the *Vireo*, ensign Haible and his five shipmates suffered a devastating blow: While lowering the motorized whaleboat by hand, it slipped and the bottom was punctured. The boat could be fixed, but the six shipmates figured it would take about five hours. They just hoped that the sailors floating in the oil slick could hold on that long. Many had burns that required immediate care.

While in the oil slick, Doctor Bowers calmly told everyone who was suffering from a burn that they should apply the heavy, emulsified oil to their wounds. Though it would initially sting, the doctor said, it would also protect the skin from the sun, which on this October afternoon in 1942 shone brightly. Eventually, Doctor Bowers also convinced those with deep wounds to pack their cuts and gashes with fuel oil. The men screamed in agony when they did this, but the act slowed the loss of blood and helped save their lives—at least momentarily.

As Kauffman hung onto a lifeline while floating in the water, he looked into the raft and couldn't even recognize a few of his shipmates. With their crushed features and charred bodies, Kauffman was surprised that they had lasted this long. Late in the afternoon, the ship's chief storekeeper, a sailor that everyone simply called "Silva," started to have difficulty breathing. Burns and blood covered most of his body and, after about 10 minutes of taking labored breaths, he stopped breathing altogether. The doctor moved over and examined Silva; he could feel no pulse or heartbeat. A few of the stronger shipmates who were in the water—including Kauffman—pulled Silva to the side of the raft, removed his identification tag, cut off his life jacket, dragged him out of the raft, then swam him out a short distance before letting him go. Kauffman wanted to say something profound as Silva dropped into the blue ocean, but no words came to him.

After Silva died, Kauffman returned to a spot beside the rafts. The sun was beginning to go down—it was about 6:00 P.M.—and Kauffman thought many of the men wouldn't survive the coming night. Some men were burned so severely that the hair on their heads was gone. Others suffered broken legs, arms, and ribs. The groans of the dying and the steady lapping of the waves against the four rafts—*plooop, plooop, plooop*—were the only sounds that rose though the humid, heavy air. Though the men reeked of oil and sweat, the aroma of burnt flesh hovered over the men like a cloud. Even the uninjured sailors were growing tired. The healthy men had been in the water and hanging onto the rafts for several hours, and it was a grueling activity. The arms of even the strongest survivors were becoming weak, their legs cramping. There were about one hundred sailors on or near the four rafts. Each raft could hold about ten men before it started to take on water, which meant that about sixty men were in the water the entire time.

Realizing that a routine needed to be set up, Kauffman and a few other officers organized a "waterbuddy" system: Each man would have a waterbuddy with whom he could switch places between the raft and the water. The badly wounded would stay inside a raft at all times; everyone else was assigned a waterbuddy and would trade places every few hours. In the raft, the men were to try to sleep. "We might be out here for days," Kauffman warned the men, "so we need to rest whenever we can."

A mile away from the four rafts, the men aboard the *Vireo* finished repairing the punctured whaleboat around 10:00 P.M. Instead of launching the motorized boat in the darkness, the sailors decided to stay on the tug until dawn. At that point they'd hunt for survivors.

Throughout the night, the minutes continued to pass slowly for the men on the four rafts that were clustered together. A quarter moon glowed in the clear sky like a giant comma, radiating a faint, milky light that fell on the ocean. Stars dotted the black roof of the universe; occasionally, one would shoot across the sky, leaving a luminous streak in its wake that would disappear a heartbeat later. The men rarely talked, but every so often Kauffman would hear cries for help in the dark distance. These desperate pleas came from the voices of men who had been on the outside of the raft and had lost their strength—or had fallen asleep—and floated away in the current. None of the able-bodied men dared to go after these drifters because it would have been virtually impossible to locate them in the darkness. After a few minutes, the cries that shot across the oil-covered water would fall eerily silent.

Later in the night one man jumped off the raft and began to swim, believing he could see land. Kauffman and other healthy crewman tried to save him, but the addled sailor was adamant that an island was just twenty yards away. He was never seen again. Another deranged sailor stood up in the night and announced that he was going to "go below decks." Before anyone could stop him, he dove head-first into the water—he also was never seen again.

When Kauffman switched places with his water buddy in the middle of the night, he saw that the captain was shaking uncontrollably. The doctor huddled over him and wrapped his arms around the captain trying to keep him warm, but Kauffman didn't think the captain would last much longer. It hurt just to look at the captain, whose face was now black with burns. A few men remarked on the captain's deteriorating condition, but other than that, all conversations were centered on one topic: When would the rescue ships pick them up?

The most valued possessions this night were the five-gallon water casks that had been stored on each raft. When the wounded got very thirsty, they were given a sip of water. Kauffman and the other officers didn't know how long they'd be drifting at sea, so they were careful to ration the water. Yet some men, not wanting to appear weak, refused their water and asked that their portion be given to the wounded. Others tried to drink saltwater. They'd take a mouthful, hold it in their mouths for a few seconds, then spit it out, hoping that they would absorb some drips of moisture. A few men tried an old Boy Scout trick of placing a shirt button under their tongues in the hope of inducing salivation. But their bodies were beyond parched, so this rarely worked. For food, a few of the men on this first night tried to eat the oil-covered cookies and malted milk wafers that they had in their provisions. Those who did eat two or three cookies vomited them up in minutes, unable to digest the oil.

Late in the night the men heard a loud rumbling sound. As it grew closer, a few claimed that it was an advancing ship. "We're rescued!" one sailor shouted. He then jumped into the water and started swimming furiously toward the noise. But it wasn't a ship; a sudden thunderstorm was blowing in. The men on the rafts yelled to the sailor who was now swimming toward the squall, but it was too late; the sailor disappeared in the distance. Once the storm was over the rafts, the men lay on their backs with their mouths agape, trying to catch the fresh water.

Over the next several hours many more men died from their burns. Kauffman, realizing that he was as healthy as anyone, put himself in charge of disposing the dead. He'd remove their life jackets, tow them out a few yards from the raft, then let them go. Then he'd tell one of the men in the water to take the spot in the raft that was open. During the small hours of the night, several died on the rafts. The deaths started to become so routine that the men stopped saying anything once somebody died. Kauffman would simply remove the body in silence, and the dead sailor's spot would be taken by another man.

When the sky began to lighten early the next morning, the captain was struggling to breathe. Around 8:00 A.M.—about twenty hours after the attack—the captain died from burns and blood loss. The doctor cut off his tags and life jacket and Kauffman led him away from the raft. When he was let go, a gunnery officer said, "We are giving them a good man this time." After that no one said a word. They just looked in silence as their captain floated away on his back, his face and hands burned black.

At daybreak on the second morning the six men who had reached the *Vireo* the night before and repaired the whaleboat began the search for their shipmates. First, one of the sailors climbed up to the tug's top deck and scanned the horizon for signs of life. No rafts were visible. The six men tried to pinpoint their starting point before drifting, but that was as specific as they could get.

They hopped in the whaleboat, turned on the motor, and pushed away from the tug. The men looked in all directions as they darted through the water, but the first five hours turned up nothing. At noon they heard a noise in the sky; a Japanese scout plane was crisscrossing the area. They assumed that the plane was looking for the pilots that gunners on the *Meredith* had shot down. Not wanting to be seen, the men quickly guided the whaleboat behind the *Vireo* to stay out of the scout plane's field of view. Then they boarded the tug and loaded as much food, water, and gasoline onto the whaleboat as it could hold. They also took the ship's compass and navigation chart. At this point they believed that they were the only survivors of the *Meredith*, and once the scout plane had disappeared, they boarded the whaleboat and prepared to make a run for Espiritu Santo Island, which they figured about four hundred miles to the south.

As the sun grew hotter on Day 2—the date was October 16—the men on the four clustered rafts smeared more oil on their faces, necks, and arms to prevent sunburn. Even though they had just endured a horrific night in which many men had gone delirious and died, there was a sense of optimism among the survivors. During the daylight hours a rescue plane or ship would find them—they were certain of that—and that they wouldn't have to face another night alone floating in oblivion.

Indeed, for the first few hours of the morning, the men appeared relatively upbeat to Kauffman. A few talked of the first thing they would do when they were rescued—the consensus was to drink a gallon of water—while others spoke about how they would tell everyone how brave their captain had been. A handful of men even felt so good that they went for a playful swim just to cool down. At noon, however, the mood changed when one word was shouted. A sailor floating fifteen feet from the rafts spotted several large dorsal fins circling around him in the water. He screamed, "Sharks!" and then frantically kicked back to the raft. But halfway to safety, a six-foot tiger shark attacked, chomping several bites out of his legs. "A shark's eating me!" the sailor yelled. Two men in the rafts jumped into the water and pulled the wounded sailor onto the raft. The sailor, missing part of one leg, was in shock. Blood spurted out of his legs like soda out of a shaken can as he screamed in agony. He'd be dead within hours.

To most of the young men in the water and on the four rafts, sharks were the stuff of myths. In fact, many of the men had never given sharks a second thought until now. Navy lore was full of stories of what one should do when a shark attacks, but only a few on these rafts had really paid attention to those hypothetical situations. Some had learned in their training that they should kick their legs as furiously as possible to deter the "hyenas of the sea," as sharks were often called by the sailors, but most of the men had no clue how to repel the aggressive, blood-thirsty predators.

The group of tiger sharks, which numbered in the fifties, now circled the rafts. They had likely been following the U.S.S. *Meredith* even before she was sunk. Sharks frequently track ships and feed on the refuse that is hurled overboard. Made of steel, the *Meredith* also emitted low-grade electrical currents that could have attracted the sharks. Tiger sharks, which typically range ten to fourteen feet long and weigh 850 to 1,400 pounds, have a very good sense of smell and keen eyesight, which meant that the sailors at the greatest risk were those who were naked or only partially clothed. The tigers likely focused on color contrasts, such as that between a white-skinned body and a dark blue sea.

Swimming at an average speed of 2.4 mph but able to burst up to 43 mph over very short distances, the shark has dark, tiger-like stripes on its back. It has a large, thick body with a blunt snout. The tiger's teeth are serrated and razor-sharp. Most biologist aren't sure why tiger sharks attack humans, but the fish also eats turtles, seagulls, other sharks and, at various times, have been found to ingest tin cans, goats, sheep, snakes, reindeer, and monkeys. They often attack using what is known as "bump and bite" maneuvers. First they'll bump their victims to disorient them, then they'll rip away chunks of flesh with their teeth. This was the attack of choice for many of the sharks on this horrifying afternoon.

Kauffman tried to calm the men. As soon as the first dorsal fin appeared, panic spread like a poisonous gas among the sailors. Kauffman had learned almost everything there was to know about tiger sharks when he was a midshipman, and he knew that these were menacing creatures. From his spot in the water—he was holding onto a lifeline—he told the sailors that they needed to be brave. He boldly shouted to the men, Either fight or die.

This was the moment that Kauffman had spent much of his young life preparing for. Ever since he had plucked that drowning boy out of the Merced River seven years earlier, Kauffman had never been afraid of water. He was an excellent swimmer and still as fit as he was when he played football. He didn't allow himself to be scared, because he didn't want the men to see fear in his eyes. "I've got to be strong," Kauffman told himself. "I'm going to get these guys through this."

The tiger sharks were as big as men, and Kauffman told the sailors—especially those who were still in the water with him—to think of the sharks as if they had two arms and two feet. "You *know* you can kill another man," Kauffman yelled, "together we will overcome this." Kauffman instructed the men to keep their legs tucked tightly underneath them as they floated in the water.

Kauffman then reached for his belt—he was wearing a white T-shirt that had been stained black by the oil, a life jacket, khaki pants, underwear, and a belt—and unsnapped a six-inch hunting knife. A few months earlier a group of Boy Scouts had sent the crew of the *Meredith* hunting knives. Many carried them on their belts at all times, and now Kauffman's knife became an essential weapon. "These sharks don't like to be cut up," Kauffman told the crew. "You've got to send them a message that you're going to fight back if they come after you."

After the first attack, the school of tiger sharks circled the four rafts at a range of ten to fifty yards out, stalking their prey. The men in the water all gripped their lifelines tight, staying as close to the rafts as possible. They all wanted to climb into the rafts to safety, but they knew the rafts would sink if they did this. Holding his knife in his right hand and his lifeline in his left, Kauffman prepared to lunge—knife first—if a shark got close. It was now 2:00 P.M. on Day 2.

Just as Kauffman began to think that the sharks might not attack, a sailor five feet away screamed in agony. The yell was cut short as the shark pulled the sailor under water. A few men dove trying to save the sailor, but they couldn't locate him or the shark in the dark water. Within minutes, the sailor's blood floated up to the surface, coloring the water red. The sailor was never seen again. Kauffman again urged the men to stay calm. "Let's keep our cool and work through this together," Kauffman said. "We have no other choice."

Later in the afternoon, the sharks grew more aggressive. One sailor who was sitting on the edge of a raft had his buttocks torn off. Another let out a blood-curdling scream and then held up the stump of his arm, which had been bitten off at the elbow. When a shark closed in on Kauffman, he did exactly what he told his shipmates to do: He fought. Kauffman jumped at the beast and stabbed him in the eyes with his knife. "Take that you son of a bitch!" Kauffman yelled as he drove the knife into the shark's skin. The shark retreated, hemorrhaging blood. A few shipmates hollered in approval. "Let's kill all of 'em!" one sailor shouted in Kauffman's direction.

By late afternoon, the sharks began targeting the weakest of the men who were in the water, the ones who offered the least resistance. Kauffman saw five of his shipmates get pulled under—all of them were either so tired or weak that they didn't even say anything as they were dragged to their death. The sharks, attracted to the scent of blood, also started going after the men with open wounds. The sailors had tried to pack their wounds with oil to stem the loss of blood, but if just a little bit of blood seeped out of the wound, a shark would track it.

By this time Kauffman and a few other officers had devised a plan to ward off the sharks: Two men in the water were to put their backs to the raft and, with their arms interlocked, they'd stick their arms and legs outward. When the sharks approached, the men kicked and splashed the water in unison, which usually succeeding in scaring the sharks off.

Later in the afternoon, just as the flaming yellow sun was starting to fall out of the sky, Kauffman changed places with his waterbuddy and took a seat in the raft. He shut his eyes and let his mind go electric with visions. He daydreamed of his new wife, of how she had smiled up at him and batted her blue eyes as they stood at the altar. His mind rewound to his carefree days at the naval academy, how he enjoyed nothing more than strapping on his leather helmet and practicing with the guys on the football team. He went back to that November afternoon in Philadelphia in '41—it wasn't even a year ago—and he could still hear the hum of the crowd as they watched Navy play Army. He remembered running onto the field and giving his buddy, Bill Busik, a big hug after Busik had made the game-saving interception. He recalled how he and Bill celebrated until dawn, having the time of their lives. He thought about . . .

"Holy Shit!" a sailor screamed.

Stirred from his reverie, Kauffman opened his eyes and was shocked at what lay two feet in front of him in the middle of the raft: A seven-foot shark, his mouth open. It had leapt into the raft moments before. A few of Kauffman's crewmates had opened a canister of dry food, which evidently attracted the shark. Before anyone knew what was going on, the shark took a bite out of the thigh of a lieutenant. Without hesitating, Kauffman jumped on the shark, driving his knife into its back. Kauffman then grabbed the shark by the tail and flung him about five feet overboard. "Get the hell out of here!" Kauffman screamed as he tossed the shark back into the water. He then looked at the lieutenant. Blood spilled out of his thigh. Kauffman took his shirt off and tried to put a tourniquet on the lieutenant's leg, but it was too late. The lieutenant soon became delirious and died four hours later.

After the sun went down, the condition of many men on the four rafts continued to deteriorate rapidly. The majority suffered from sharp abdominal cramps. Everyone was nauseous and most were vomiting regularly. When the men would fall into a light sleep, they would have fantastic dreams, usually about a rescue ship. When a few men woke up from these dreams they were so despondent that they leapt overboard and tried to swim to an imaginary boat. Mentally stable men were usually successful in catching a delusional crewmate and pulling him back on the raft, but not always.

Late in Night 2, with a rescue seeming as if it would never happen, a few men lost their grip on reality. Some started eating the raft's wood crating. One young man, who was badly burned and whose flesh was peeling off, thought he was back home on his farm in the west. He wanted everyone to get off the raft. When he started taking swings at the crewmates, they had no choice but to beat him unconscious. Later a lieutenant commander stood up and said to his shipmates, "I think I will go get some cigarettes." He then jumped out of the raft and never returned.

By midafternoon on Day 3 the group of four rafts had split into two groups of two, which were several hundred yards away from each other. Another single raft that had been alone ever since the *Meredith* went down had drifted a considerable distance from the other two groups.

In Kauffman's group, there had been little dissension. The rations were shared equally among the healthy men and a greater proportion of water was given to the weakest. The men still honored the water-buddy system and everyone generally looked after each other like family. Late in the day a wounded man in the group feared that he was being a burden on his shipmates. So, using all the energy he had, he crawled out of the raft and swam silently away from the group, giving up his life so that the shipmates would have a better chance at surviving. Kauffman tried to coax him back, telling him that he would help him get through this ordeal, but the sailor didn't return.

The sharks continued to circle the rafts all day, but they didn't attack until twilight. First a shark jumped up and bit off the finger of a sailor who was sitting on the edge of the raft. The shark came back a few minutes later and ripped a chunk out of his thigh. The sailor fell into the water, and a moment later the shark returned a third time and snatched his entire body. After witnessing this gruesome event, a few of the men started to babble and cry uncontrollably. Two men jumped into the water, while others sat as still as mannequins, comatose with fear.

The third night was a more vivid nightmare than the first two. Hallucinations were as rampant as the sharks. Some men, thinking that an enemy sub was approaching, dove into the water to try to fight it. Others jumped into the ocean thinking their bunks were beneath their raft. Still others believed that a scuttlebutt—a drinking fountain—was also located just beneath the life raft. The mentally stable men were often able to retrieve those who believed something existed underneath the raft, but again, not always.

Even men who were relatively uninjured were beginning to see things and lose grasp of reality. Some believed that they were smoking cigarettes and they asked their shipmates for a light; others thought they were back in their houses in the United States and wondered why their moms weren't home.

Kauffman was still perfectly sane, and his mind was preoccupied with one topic: water. The men were running out of drinking water. Sailors who at first declined to take a drink were now accepting every time a sip was offered. As Kauffman eyed the men in the raft as they laid in the moonlight in their ripped, oil-stained clothes, most were so weak that they couldn't stand. Kauffman figured that maybe the strongest could survive another 48 hours, but not much longer. The weakest? They could go at any minute. Most of the sailors had given up hope, and they had quit talking about being rescued. Some even appeared happily resigned to the fact that their fate was to perish on a raft in the South Pacific. The men were tired of fighting the sharks and tired of just fighting to survive. They had seen would-be rescuers come and go throughout the third day—a few U.S. planes had flown over the rafts, but they were too high to see them floating in the middle of the ocean—and most of them believed that the navy had forgotten about the U.S.S. *Meredith*.

During this chilly third night, men who hadn't prayed since childhood were now reciting psalms and scriptures that they had learned years ago in Sunday Bible study. One of the most frequently uttered was Psalm 23:

> *"Though I walk through the valley*
> *of the shadow of death*
> *I will fear no evil*
> *For Thou art with me . . ."*

Reciting these lines of scripture steadied the men. Saying the words in a cool, soft voice made them momentarily forget the hopelessness of their situation. But Kauffman never could forget it. He dreaded the coming morning. He didn't want to count how many familiar faces had disappeared during the night.

Kauffman tried to shut his eyes and lose consciousness, but sleeping was hard. Even though he was as fatigued as he'd ever been, he could only sleep in two minute spurts, then he would jolt awake, fear rushing through his body like a electrical shock.

When the sun rose over eastern waters to mark Day 4, Kauffman was wide-awake, his swollen eyes alert. He anxiously scanned the sky—unlike most of the men, Kauffman still held a flicker of hope of being rescued—for an American plane. At first, as usual, he saw nothing, just blue sky and a few white puffs of clouds. But then it appeared like an answered prayer: a U.S. PBY Catalina seaplane cruising through the bronze morning light at five thousand feet.

Upon seeing the plane, the spirits of the men on the rafts rose all the way to heaven. The plane was on a reconnaissance mission in search of information on the whereabouts of the Japanese fleet. Once the plane's crew spotted the oil slick, they dropped to an altitude of fifty feet to investigate. The crew was shocked to see, there in the patches of oil, men on life rafts frantically waving their arms. Because the men were covered in oil, the crew at first couldn't discern if they were Americans or Japanese. On their next trip over the men, the crew determined that the flailing men were, in fact, star-spangled soldiers. Just then, for the first time in about 48 hours, the sharks dispersed and dove to deeper water, scared off by the noise that the plane and the *Meredith* crew were making.

The PBY circled back again. It flashed its lights and rocked its wings, signaling that a rescue ship would be coming shortly. The plane deployed smoke floats to mark the position of the survivors; it also dropped emergency life rafts equipped with supplies. The plane turned and flew away from the men. Just before it sank over the horizon, the men on the raft saw the plane drop a lifejacket into the water. Below the plane, a few miles away from Kauffman's raft, was Chief Lamont Norwood, who had swum off alone after he thought he saw land. A school of sharks, their fins sticking out of the water, trailed Norwood by ten yards—and were closing in on him. The plane crew considered shooting the sharks, but were afraid they'd accidentally hit Norwood. With no way to help Norwood, the plane cruised out of the survivor's field of sight, leaving Norwood to fight off the sharks by himself.

The U.S.S. *Grayson*, *Gwin*, and *Seminole* were about thirty miles away from the survivors. Using an Aldis Lamp, the PBY signaled to the ships, "Follow my course, men in water." An hour later, the *Grayson* and the *Gwin* had reached the survivors. The *Gwin* launched small motorized boats into the water that were driven by rescue personnel. The rescuers had expected to find men with open wounds and broken bones. But, much to their surprise, no such men existed on the life rafts. Anyone injured was already dead—or had been eaten by sharks.

As the *Grayson* approached Kauffman's group, sailors on board threw cargo nets and rope ladders over the ship's sides. Yet most of the men in Kauffman's group were too weak to climb—some couldn't even stand. On Kauffman's raft a few drops of water still remained in one of the water kegs. Before leaving the raft, one survivor held up the remaining water keg. Most of the survivors were now on the deck of the *Grayson*, looking down at the last man in the raft. As the sailor looked at the water keg, he glanced up at the men, smiled, then proudly dumped its remnants into the sea, as if to say, "We won." Seeing this, Kauffman started chanting in a weak, trembling voice, "*Meredith—Meredith—Meredith.*" His shipmates soon joined in. Then they all started to softly cry.

. . .

After the survivors were aboard the three ships, a sailor on the *Grayson* saw through his telescope a man swimming toward the ship. It was Norwood, the lone swimmer, and he was the last of the eighty-seven survivors to be hauled aboard and rescued. Four days ago there had been 260 men aboard the *Meredith*.

Once safely aboard the *Grayson*, Kauffman was handed a shot-glass full of scotch whiskey, which he promptly vomited. He then walked to the shower and scrubbed the oil off his skin. He put on a T-shirt and shorts and ate a bowl of chicken noodle soup. He then ambled to a bunk, and plopped down. He lay flat on his back, shut his eyes, and then didn't move for 15 hours except to breathe slow and steady.

Of all the survivors, Kauffman was the only one able to bathe himself, eat for himself, and walk himself to a bunk. In the last four days he never had felt the cold finger of death tapping on his shoulder. Now, as he laid still throughout the night, he dreamed of better days.

The next day a doctor examined the survivors. In each case, the doctor reached the same conclusion: This man should be dead. All had suffered significant weight loss, in many cases up to twenty pounds. Their ear drums had been pierced with hundreds of tiny holes. Fillings in their teeth had been jarred loose or lost. White water-blisters covered them. Many burns and puncture wounds had become gangrenous. Nonmalignant growths often appeared around nerve centers. Most men suffered from rasping coughs and upper respiratory infections. They had oil forced into body openings as a result of the explosions. Several had developed sties in their eyes. And everyone had lower back pain.

As soon as they were strong enough, the survivors who were on the U.S.S. *Grayson* started talking to each other about their experience. They congratulated one another on surviving, but many also felt profound guilt for still being alive while so many of their shipmates had been lost in the battle. Over the next few days, as the survivors struggled to make sense of it all, hundreds of stories were exchanged about their fallen friends.

For many of the men, the worst was yet to come. Three days after the rescue, the captain of the *Grayson*, which had taken on sixty-three of the eighty-seven survivors (three more would die aboard the rescue ships), spotted a Japanese bomber and opened fire. Though the Japanese plane got away, when the general alarm sounded and the guns started blasting, the ship shook—an agonizing experience for the survivors. They were below deck and locked in watertight compartments. When they heard the guns firing, many leapt out of their beds and became delirious with shock. Six men fainted and about a dozen became hysterical. Many had to be physically restrained.

A few days later, the *Grayson* stopped at a secured port on a South Pacific island to drop off several of the survivors at a base hospital. Many had infections from shrapnel and required immediate attention. While there, Kauffman noticed that the U.S.S. *Shaw* was also moored in the port. Wearing sandals that he'd fashioned out of rope and rubber and dressed in some tattered clothes that a sailor aboard the *Grayson* had given him, Kauffman boarded the Shaw. There he knocked on the cabin door of one of his best friends from the naval academy.

"You look awful," Bill Busik told Kauffman when he saw him. "What the heck happened?"

13

1942

ON THE SAME OCTOBER AFTERNOON that the *Meredith* plunged into the blue darkness of the South Pacific, some eye-grabbing sports news leaked out of Washington: President Roosevelt decided that the Army-Navy game of 1942 would not be played in Philadelphia. An Associated Press report on October 15 stated that the President ruled out the City of Brotherly Love as the host site for the game because it would require too much travel for both of the schools. There was a nationwide ban on all nonessential travel in the States to conserve gas, and the President decreed that the Army-Navy game would have to be played with that restriction in mind—if the game would be played at all.

The last time the United States had been engaged in a world war, the Army-Navy matchups were called off in 1917 and '18. In the fall of '42 a handful of officials at both academies argued strongly that the game should be canceled again, believing the contest would divide military men who were stationed overseas. In pubs and on street corners up and down the Eastern Seaboard—indeed, in spots all around the country—the debate raged: Should the service boys play? Many considered this game the gold standard of American sport. In some ways it was even bigger than war, and those who wanted the game to go on thought that canceling it would send a signal of weakness overseas. Others were adamant that the game should be called off, saying that it was just a distraction and a waste of resources.

Finally, on October 22—the same day that Kauffman detailed his chilling experience to Busik aboard the U.S.S. *Shaw*—the White House reached its decision: The game would go on, and it would be held at the navel academy's Thompson Stadium. The next day the announcement was splashed on front pages of newspapers across the nation, one of the few times during the war that a sports story crept onto the lead page of the country's top papers. Even the Old Gray Lady, the *New York Times*, gave the story a prominent position.

> *"Since no railroad facilities afford the means of transportation to Annapolis on regularly operated lines and since there is a compelling need to save gasoline and rubber, tickets will be issued only to residents of Annapolis—not to outsiders," the White House announced in a statement. "Only the members of the Army team and such other officials whose presence is needed for the actual playing of the game will go from West Point to Annapolis. Every precaution will be taken to prevent persons living outside of Annapolis—in Washington or Baltimore or other nearby places—from securing tickets to the game. . . . The fact that the game was scheduled before the war was declared and its cancellation at this late date undoubtedly would cause great disappointment throughout the armed forces, in and out of the United States, was discussed at length before the decision was reached to permit the holding of the game this year."*

In Annapolis, midshipmen and locals alike were ecstatic that the game would be played on their home turf. For one autumn afternoon, the town would be the center of the sports universe. One Annapolis resident, Virginia Russell, a legal secretary, couldn't contain her enthusiasm, telling a local paper, "Just imagine how exclusive we're going to be, and how the rest of the country will envy us." At West Point, the news arrived like an early Christmas present. Olds and Romanek still had one season of football left before they marched off to war—they were a class behind Busik and Kauffman—and both craved a second chance to beat the Middies. They didn't care where they played Navy or even if anybody watched. They just wanted a chance to prove to themselves that they had the talent to topple the Midshipmen.

The game also presented the Army players an opportunity to salvage their season, which had been a disappointment. Though Army won its first four games in '42 by an average of nineteen points, the team slumped in midseason, losing two straight to Penn and Notre Dame. Nonetheless, in the days leading up to the '42 Army-Navy showdown, the Cadets were listed as a two-touchdown favorite over the Middies, whose record heading into the game was 4–4.

The '42 game would be unlike any other in Army-Navy history. To purchase a ticket, which cost $4.40, citizens had to travel to the naval academy and sign an application swearing that they lived within a ten-mile radius of the State House in Annapolis. The only exemptions were granted to naval academy employees, to girlfriends of midshipmen who planned on attending the academy dance the night before the game, and to the 210 newspaper reporters, radio announcers, photographers, and telegraph operators who were covering the game. Even Navy's football players had to apply for admission to the stadium. The First Lady, Eleanor Roosevelt, a regular at the Army-Navy games, wasn't allowed to attend because she lived outside the ten-mile boundary.

About a week before kickoff, Army and Navy officials made a controversial decision: The Corp of Cadets would not be allowed to make the trip down from West Point to attend the game. Subsequently, the superintendent of the naval academy ordered all third and fourth class midshipmen to sit behind the Army bench and to cheer for the Cadets. These were going to be the fill-in fans for Army. Though they wouldn't be forced to wear West Point colors and wave Army flags, these young midshipmen were told that they had to yell and clap just as loudly for the boys from West Point as they would their own team. Many midshipmen snickered when they were first given this order, but they had no choice but to follow it.

To learn the Army cheers and fight song, Navy sent two of its cheerleaders up to West Point a few days before the game, where they were taught a crash course in Army cheering. The Cadets' cheerleaders went over the proper cadence of the cheers and songs and gave the two midshipmen several hundred copies of a "Song Book" that listed all the cheers and songs. On the back page of the Song Book, which was distributed to all the third and fourth class midshipmen, was a note from the Corps of Cadets. "The Corps of Cadets desires to express its appreciation to the

Regiment of Midshipmen for its good sportsmanship in furnishing a cheering section to support the Army team. This demonstration of good will and cooperation will do much to cement the feeling of *friendly rivalry* that must always exist when Army and Navy teams meet."

Two days before kickoff, Olds, Romanek, and the rest of the Cadet football team boarded a steam-powered riverboat on a Thursday morning and traveled down the Hudson. Instead of riding a train to Annapolis, the Army team was ordered by Washington to travel by boat so that the rails could be kept open to transport war-related resources. The change in plans suited the players just fine, because as the riverboat floated down the Hudson and under the George Washington Bridge, past the towering buildings of midtown Manhattan, past the Statue of Liberty, and then out into the Atlantic for a trip down the coast, Olds, Romanek and the rest of the Cadets were able to relax. Wearing their long gray coats, they ate box lunches of roast-beef sandwiches and enjoyed the scenery, talking of how they were going to make the most of this last opportunity to beat Navy.

"We've been waiting for this game ever since we got to West Point," Olds told a few of his teammates on the river boat. "It's our turn to win one of these dadgum games."

For Olds, it had been a whirlwind few months. A few weeks after the '41 Army-Navy game he had decided, once and for all, that he would become a pilot like his father, so he joined the Army Air Corp. In the fall of '42, during the heart of football season, Olds spent about a third of his time at Stewart Airfield, located just north of the Academy, where he studied and trained. In a typical two-day period, Olds would have a class at the Point in the morning, then board a bus and travel seventeen miles to the air base and fly that afternoon. He'd spend the night at Stewart and fly again the next morning. After that he'd hop back on a bus and return to the academy, where he'd have classes all afternoon and, later on, football practice. The next morning the schedule started over again with morning classes at the academy. With his life overflowing with responsibilities, Olds often couldn't find time to study during the day. So many nights, after the lights went out at 9:30, Olds would sneak into a bathroom and, sitting on a toilet while holding a flashlight, he'd read his textbooks and take notes until two or three in the morning.

A month into the football season, Olds' schedule grew even more compacted when he started practicing night flying. He'd spend up to three hours each night flying up and down the Hudson River Valley, zooming through the darkness, dogfighting an imaginary enemy. The drone of these planes was so loud it often kept Coach Blaik up at night in his West Point quarters, where he'd lie in bed and worry about whether or not his players who flew would be alive for the next afternoon's practice.

Blaik had reason to worry. Five of Olds' classmates perished while training at Stewart, which was roughly an L-shaped airfield. Olds saw one classmate die when he slammed into a mountain. Two others were killed in spin-related accidents, while two more lost their lives in landing accidents. Olds, considered by the instructors as one of the top pilots of his class, tried not to think of the scary odds whenever he witnessed a classmate crash in a ball of flames. Like most great aviators, Olds didn't lack confidence. He talked and acted as if he was the best young pilot at the academy, and when a classmate got in an accident he didn't brood over it. He simply believed that the reason a classmate had crashed was because he'd made a mistake. "If you make just one dumb move, you won't be around very long," Olds told a friend.

On the riverboat, Olds peered out at the New Jersey shore. Because of the trip to Annapolis, he was given four days off from pilot training, and now he tried to forget about combat. Like all the cadets, the war usually dominated Olds' thoughts. Almost every week a new story of a recent graduate being wounded or killed in combat circulated through West Point. Olds had wanted to join the fight overseas ever since he was in prep school, and that day was rapidly approaching. Though he was still as tough and resilient as anyone who'd ever stepped onto the academy grounds—his teammates all believed that—Olds no longer boasted the reckless, devil-may-care attitude that he brought to the Point. Two-and-half years of academy training had infused him with discipline and responsibility. He knew that other pilots would soon be trusting him with their lives, and this grave realization made Olds more circumspect in all areas of his life. In the classroom, on the football field, and up in the air, Olds didn't take as many chances as he used to—his way of preparing for war.

Romanek also was girding for combat. His mother had sent him dozens of letters relaying the hardships that people in Poland—including Romanek's relatives—were enduring at the hands of Hitler. With the arrival of every new letter, Romanek grew more determined to fight. Ever since he was a junior in high school, Romanek had been refining his soldiering and leadership skills. Now, as graduation approached, he felt prepared to assume command of other men. Romanek had originally wanted to join the Army Air Corps, but failed the eye exam. So, like many of the top students at West Point—Romanek would graduate near the top of his class—he entered the Corps of Engineers. "That's where all the smart guys are," he joked to Olds. "Besides, it'll be safer on the ground than in the air."

Romanek didn't really believe that. He knew that the engineers were often on the front lines in major assaults, clearing areas of mines and other obstacles, building roads, and performing other essential duties in the initial phases of a ground attack. His time at the academy had taught Romanek that one of the keys to leadership was to always exude an air of confidence—and now he did. You could almost see his self-assuredness when he walked into a room, his posture as straight as an ironing board, his chest pushed out. It wasn't cockiness or arrogance that Romanek radiated, just a belief in himself that he'd accomplish—somehow, some way—whatever needed to be done. He had to, if he wanted to stay alive. With graduation seven months away, Romanek, like many of his classmates, bore the earmarks of an outstanding officer.

The morning of November 28, 1942 broke clear and cold in Annapolis. A whisper of wind blew from the north. Because of the wartime restrictions, only 11,700 people made the pilgrimage to Thompson Stadium—the smallest crowd to attend in Army-Navy game since 1893, the last time Army and Navy played in Annapolis, when a crowd of about six thousand watched the players in knit caps slug it out. Most in the stands in '42 bought a game program, which included a note from President Roosevelt, who praised former Cadets and Midshipmen football players now fighting around the world. "On battlefields and on seas throughout the world," the President wrote of the former football players, "they are knitting still more firmly the ties of comradeship which they first formed on the playing fields of their homeland."

The Army team occupied the visitor's locker room, which had no heat or hot water. It was so frigid in the locker room that as the players dressed, they could see their breath, and many players wrapped blankets around their shoulders. Blaik, sensing that his players wanted to get out to the field to run around and warm up, was brief in his pregame speech. "We know what we have to do," Blaik told his players. "Execute, execute, execute. If we do that, we'll walk out of here with a win."

Just as Army was about to kick off, Bill Busik huddled close to his shortwave radio aboard the U.S.S. *Shaw*, which was motoring through choppy waters in the Guadalcanal area. More than a month had passed since his buddy Hal Kauffman had appeared on his ship, with his body gaunt, bruised, and cut up. Busik immediately gave Kauffman one of his extra uniforms to wear and they talked for hours not only about Kauffman's struggle to stay alive, but also about the good times they shared as teammates. After a few hours, Busik relayed some good news: He'd met a girl and gotten married. "I got to know her only a few days before I reported to duty on the *Shaw*," Busik told Kauffman. "She's a vision."

A week after graduating from the naval academy, Busik sat in the officers' club in San Francisco chatting with friends when a waitress named Margaret Andrus asked for his order. Once Margaret's shift was done, she and Busik talked for hours. Even though Margaret wasn't a big football fan, she'd heard of Busik and knew that he'd played football for Navy. Three days later Busik boarded the U.S.S *Shaw*, but he wrote a letter to Margaret—he called her Midge—almost every day. After a few months at sea, Busik, still burning hard for Midge, asked her to marry him in a letter. She wrote him back and accepted his proposal, and they tied the knot at a chapel in San Francisco when Busik was there on a ten-day shore leave.

"She's the best thing that ever happened to me," Busik told Kauffman. "I just want to get this war over with so I can get back to her."

A month after sharing the news of his nuptials with Kauffman, Busik prepared to listen to the '42 Army-Navy game. A war was going on all around him, but for the next two hours Busik, as he sat in his tiny quarters, would be transported halfway around the world, to a place where all that mattered was a game. To Busik, listening to this broadcast would be as satisfying as a home-cooked meal of fried chicken and apple pie served hot.

Navy received the opening kickoff, beginning their initial drive on their own 28-yard line. The tone of the game was set on the first play from scrimmage when the Midshipmen gained 8 yards on a sweep to the left side of the field. During the run, three Navy lineman had hit Army players with either an elbow or fist to the face. The three Cadets tumbled to the ground. In the defensive huddle following the first play, the Army players felt that the Midshipmen had just pulled an orchestrated, low-down dirty trick. On the sideline Blaik was irate. After Navy quickly gained three first downs, Blaik called a timeout and motioned his defense over to the sideline. "Keep your heads in the game," Blaik said. "I'll let the officials know what's going on and the illegal tactics will stop."

After the timeout, Army's defense stiffened and forced a punt. The first quarter ended in a scoreless tie, and after 15 minutes of action it was clear to everyone in the stands that the game was quickly getting out of hand. Both sides were playing more aggressively than any Army-Navy game in recent memory. All the anxiousness that the players felt about what the coming months would be like, all the fear that the players tried to keep at bay, all the frustration that they felt because of the war-time restrictions—it all boiled over onto the field. The players channeled everything they felt into this game, and the result was a bloody fight.

When the second quarter began, Olds' temper was about to erupt. On several plays on defense he'd been smacked in the face or clipped from behind—which he interpreted as cheap shots. Five minutes into the second quarter, Olds fought back. As Navy's Hal Hamberg dropped back to pass, Olds beat his man at the point of attack and broke through the line of scrimmage. But just as he neared Hamberg, a Navy blocking back delivered a vicious forearm shiver to Olds' mouth. Olds fell to the ground, and as he lay writhing on the grass in pain, he raised his right hand to his mouth to rub his teeth. His mouth felt like it'd just been hit by a baseball bat, and he quickly realized that his two front teeth had been knocked out. Blood pouring from his mouth, Olds crawled around on the ground, searching for his teeth. Frank Marriet, an Army defensive lineman, kneeled down and asked Olds what he was doing.

"I think I lost some teeth," Olds said. "Help me find them."

"You need to get out of here, Robin," replied Marriet. "You're in really bad shape. You need a doctor right now."

"But I gotta find my teeth," Olds said.

"Why?" asked Marriet.

"I don't know, I just do," said Olds.

But after more prodding, Olds got up and, still bleeding like a man chewing on glass shards, was led off the field. He walked right past Romanek, who was standing on the sideline and strapping on his leather helmet. Romanek was serving as Olds' backup for this game and, after seeing what had happened to his friend, gusts of rage shook Romanek. "Play smart," Blaik instructed Romanek. "Don't do anything that will hurt the team. I'm telling you, play smart!"

Romanek didn't listen. He flew recklessly around the field. Over the next several plays, he hit players in the jaw, he clipped a few Midshipmen, and eventually he was flagged for a personal foul. As soon as that flag was thrown, Blaik pushed a substitute onto the field for Romanek. As Romanek jogged to the sideline, Blaik, screaming, demanded that Romanek stand right in front of him.

"What the hell was that?" Blaik asked Romanek. "If you ever do that again, you'll never play football for Army again."

Olds laid on a table in the locker room. In two separate places his teeth had stabbed through his upper lip, which was badly swollen. Captain Ollie Neiss, the team's doctor, worked for 10 minutes sewing up Olds, giving him 34 stitches. When Neiss was finally finished, Olds looked as if he'd been in a car accident. Cotton was jammed up his nose, and blood was splattered all over his face and uniform. Nonetheless, when Neiss was finished, Olds hopped off the table, grabbed his helmet, and ran back onto the field. He wanted payback.

A single crossbar made of heavy plastic had been affixed to his helmet, a device that served as a temporary facemask to protect his mouth. Olds ran directly to Coach Blaik, staring at his coach with intensity shining in his eyes. Using his hands and grunting like a cavemen, Olds motioned that he wanted to get back in the game. Blaik asked the team doctor for his opinion. "He'll be all right," replied Neiss, "if he can stand it." Olds signified that there wouldn't be a problem, that he was fit to play. "Okay, Robin, go get 'em," Blaik told Olds with a grin.

When Olds ran onto the field, he scanned the Navy huddle for the blocking back who had knocked out his teeth. Olds couldn't speak very well, but as soon as he saw the back he growled like a monster, spitting blood. The Midshipmen lined up and pitched the ball to a back on a sweep to the opposite side of Olds for a 4-yard gain. On Olds' second play, Navy ran directly at him. Shedding his initial block, Olds was suddenly face to face with the blocking back who'd hurt him. Olds shoved him to the ground, then jumped in the air and came down, right knee first, directly onto the player's rib cage. The blow knocked the wind out of the blocking back and broke two of his ribs. "How's that feel?" Olds grumbled as he stood on the player, who was eventually hauled off the field on a stretcher and wouldn't reenter the game.

At halftime, the score was tied 0–0. But five minutes into the second half Navy's Joe Sullivan, a running back, broke through the line of scrimmage and raced 40 yards for a touchdown. The extra point was good, and the underdog Midshipmen had a 7–0 lead. Blaik paced up and down the sideline, upset that his players were losing their cool. They were committing penalties and ignoring their assignments, more interested in trying to hurt a Midshipman than doing what it took to win the game.

As the clock counted down, Olds didn't miss a play on either offense or defense, and two more Navy players were helped off the field after absorbing a blow from Olds. Olds' valiant effort even impressed the Midshipmen in the stands who sat behind the Army bench—the Cadets performed the West Point cheers and sang the Army fight song just like they were taught—but Olds alone couldn't carry Army to victory. Navy won 14–0.

"Robin, I'm sorry about you losing your teeth," Blaik told Olds on the boat ride back to West Point.

"That's all right," Olds replied with a swollen smile. "I always wondered how I'd look without them."

Two decades later, Blaik would call the performance that Olds gave on that cold afternoon in November of 1942 the most courageous he'd ever seen on a football field, and later that year sportswriter Grantland Rice would name Olds to his 1942 All-America team. For the record: Olds never did find his teeth.

14

ARMY

THE PHONE CALL CAME EARLY on an April morning in 1943. Two months shy of his graduation from the Point—and five months after he had played in his final college football game—Robin Olds was walking across the Plain when a stone-faced administrator approached him. The words he spoke thundered in Olds' ears. "Robin, your dad is asking for you," the administrator told Olds. "He's not well."

Robert Olds, now a two-star general, lay dying in a Tucson, Arizona, hospital room from the sudden onset of periocardial disease, a hardening of the lining around the heart. Ever since he'd entered the Army Air Corps, Robin had thought often of his father, of how they used to watch the planes take off and land at Langley Airbase when Robin was a boy. And now, whenever Robin flew, he could feel his father's courage and spirit rising up in him every time he strapped himself into the cockpit.

One of Olds' instructors at West Point, Lieutenant John Hacker, recognized early on that Robin had the ideal makeup of a great fighter pilot. He possessed just the right ratio of brains, ego, and guts. One night, the lieutenant decided that he and his pupil should have some fun together, just the two of them. Taking off from Stewart Airfield, the two flew Beech AT-10s, twin-engine trainer planes of all-wood construction, and pretended they were in a nighttime dogfight. First they tore south through the darkness down the Hudson River to New York City. After zipping by the Statue of Liberty, whose torch lit up New York harbor, they made a U-turn and proceeded to fly north under the George Washington Bridge. Over the next hour they buzzed under every bridge on the Hudson River from New York City to Albany, laughing the entire way like kids sharing a secret joke. Hacker and Olds never told anyone at the academy what they had done, but that evening the instructor knew it was only a matter of time before his student would be able to teach him a few flying lessons.

But now Olds' heart grew heavy with the news that his father was gravely ill. He and his little brother Steven, who was a plebe at the academy, hopped on a B-17 that was already scheduled to fly to Tucson and hitched a ride. Because his father was a two-star general, Olds and his brother received special permission to leave the academy for a few days. Their father had fallen sick quickly, and when Olds arrived at the hospital the doctors told him that his father didn't have long to live and that it was time to say final prayers and good-bye. Kneeling at his father's bedside and cradling his hand, Olds told his father for the first time that he was going to become a fighter pilot. His father smiled and told his son, "I never went up in the air without learning something new, so never think you know it all."

A few hours later, with Robin still grasping his father's hand, Robert Olds died at age forty-seven. Both sons were devastated, especially Robin. He'd always viewed his father as a man made of iron, a man who could never melt away. Standing over his father, young Robin made a promise to himself: He would make this man proud of him as a pilot in the war.

On May 30, the day before graduation, the cadets who had successfully completed their air corp training assembled on Trophy Point. It was a splendid spring morning; a refreshing breeze blew up off the river. General Henry H. Arnold, the commanding general of the Army Air Force, addressed the 206 cadets. "How you boys perform in the next few weeks, the next few months, will be critically important to our country's safety," the General said. "Congratulations. Now make us all proud." The general then approached each cadet, shook the cadet's hand, and pinned on his wings. After the general moved past him, Olds couldn't stop himself from glancing down at the silver-plated wings every few seconds. Even when the ceremony was over and Olds was walking across the parade ground to the barracks, he still kept sneaking peeks at his shiny wings.

The next morning the commencement speaker was General Arnold, the architect of America's Air Force. A steady patter of rain fell on the Field House as the General delivered his remarks to the June Class of '43. A total of 514 Cadets—the largest class in West Point history—now sat in the Field House, minutes away from becoming officers. Because of the gasoline shortage, few visitors arrived by car. Instead, the majority of the girlfriends and parents came by train to West Point for the ceremony. The most determined visitor might have been Mrs. John W. Rhea, who had traveled from Waldo, Arkansas, to see her son graduate. Four days before commencement, she injured her hip when she fell while walking on the academy grounds. A frail woman, she was carried on a stretcher from the post hospital to the Field House for the graduation ceremony, where she saw the exercises from a balcony near the main platform. She figured it might be one of the last times she'd ever see her only boy, F. W. Rhea, who at age twenty was one of the youngest men ever to graduate from the Point.

In somber tones, General Arnold told the graduates that they would be "commanding and leading troop batteries, companies, or squadrons in actual combat within six months." He demanded that the men be tough, and characterized the Japanese as "uncivilized savages" who must be exterminated "like termites." "War is a ruthless business," the General said. "But I believe we are now ready for a decisive year."

At 3:00 P.M., some 5 hours after General Arnold concluded his remarks, Henry Romanek stood at the altar of the Catholic Chapel, watching his bride to be, Betsy Wells, stride down the aisle. They had met four years earlier when Romanek was in prep school in Washington, D.C. on a blind date. They went to a Saturday night dance at the Army-Navy Country Club in Arlington, Virginia, and Romanek was smitten within seconds. Betsy was a traffic-stopping blonde with hazel eyes, and right away, the air was electric between them. They had so much in common. Betsy's father was a major in the War Department in Washington, and she always respected men in uniform. During the three years Romanek attended West Point, the couple wrote letters to each other frequently. Romanek eventually invited Betsy up to West Point for Christmas vacation during his plebe year, and that's when he knew he wanted to marry the girl of his dreams.

The day after they married, Romanek and his new bride visited New York City, and then took a train south to Virginia Beach for their honeymoon. Like everyone else at the Point who had entered the Corp of Engineers, Romanek was given a month's leave—and he planned to get as much enjoyment out of the next thirty days as possible. At Virginia Beach, Romanek and his wife went on moonlight walks along the beach and danced at a local officers' club. One evening at the Navy Beach Club they bumped into Robin Olds, who was also enjoying some R&R before going to war. A bachelor who didn't mind an occasional belt of whiskey, Olds and his fly-boy buddies were quite a sight as they sat around a table and talked of killing Germans and Japanese. Olds even sneaked in a few dances with Romanek's wife, Betsy.

After a few days in Virginia Beach, Romanek shook Olds' hand, wished him luck, then boarded a train with Betsy. They spent the next few weeks at Romanek's home in New Jersey and with Betsy's parents in Washington. On July 1, Romanek reported to the base at Fort Pierce, Florida, where he was schooled in beach landings. Weeks later his engineering battalion was moved to a base outside of Norfolk, Virginia. In the Chesapeake Bay, they trained to be amphibious engineers, practicing loading and unloading landing ships with equipment. Romanek didn't know it, but his platoon was preparing for what would be the key moment of the world's second great war. They were training to storm the beach at Normandy.

15

BARNACLE BILL

ON A COOL JANUARY MORNING in 1944—six months after Robin Olds and Henry Romanek graduated from the Point—Margaret Busik sat down at the kitchen table in her San Francisco apartment to read the *San Francisco Chronicle.* Sipping hot coffee and nibbling buttered toast, she flipped through the paper, anxious to find out as much war news as possible. She and her husband Bill wrote almost every day, but often weeks went by before their letters reached each other's hands. She missed him desperately—she spent many late nights thumbing through their wedding pictures—and prayed each day for the war to end.

She opened the paper, hoping to find a mention of the U.S.S. *Shaw,* the ship her husband was on. She knew that the *Shaw* was somewhere in the South Pacific fighting the Japanese, but Bill wasn't allowed to mention any specific ship movements in his letters, so she wasn't aware of the precise location. Now she read about how actor Jimmy Stewart, one of the stars of *The Philadelphia Story,* had recently completed a daylight bombing mission on Ludwigshaven in Germany, flying with forty-seven other bombers of the 445th Group based in Norfolk, England.

She continued to scan the newsprint, smudging her fingers. She learned that British and American forces had broken through the Germans' winter defense line in Italy, as the Allies had recently taken the village of San Vittorio and now hoped to "romp to Rome." In the Pacific theater, the U.S. 6th Army had recently landed on New Guinea's north coast and taken Saidor, a Japanese supply depot. General Douglass MacArthur now seemed on his way to driving the Japanese off of New Guinea. Indeed, on this morning, the war seemed to be going reasonably well.

Margaret flipped another page, and a story about a former Navy football star leapt out at her like a burglar from the bushes: Bill Busik, the paper reported, had gone overboard on the U.S.S. *Shaw*. He was now missing—and presumed dead.

Three weeks before Margaret had read those heart-wrenching words, her husband was up in the gun director of the *Shaw*, standing about fifty feet above the water. Holding binoculars to his eyes, he scanned the cloudy horizon, looking for enemy aircraft. The date was December 26, 1943, and the *Shaw* was patrolling at ten knots about six miles to the northeast of Cape Gloucester, located at the western end of New Britain, a tiny island in the Solomon Sea off the coast of New Guinea. The *Shaw* had been providing support for the troop landings at Hollandia, a town on the north coast of New Guinea. The *Shaw*'s guns provided cover for the advancing Allied soldiers and bombarded the enemy on the shore. The previous few days had been relatively uneventful for the boys on the *Shaw*. Enemy planes occasionally showed up on radar, but the destroyer never took any hits.

On the afternoon of December 26, the sea was calm. Up in the director, Busik was still laughing about a request he'd received from an officer sitting next to him at breakfast: Could Busik tell the table a Navy football story? It was a familiar question, because everyone aboard the ship, from the lowest-ranking enlisted man to the captain, knew Busik's biography. Just a month ago, they had all listened to the '43 Army-Navy game together—for the fifth straight year, the Middies beat Army, this time 13–0 at West Point's Michie Stadium. Many of the sailors and officers on the destroyer had also tuned in to the radio broadcast of the '41 Army-Navy game, when Busik had thrilled them all with his running, passing, and defense.

In fact, when Busik reported to the *Shaw* on July 1, 1942, for active duty, he was treated differently than the other officers. He had star power, and it burned brightly in everyone's imagination. Busik's shipmates frequently asked for his autograph and there always seemed to be someone begging him to tell a football tale. Busik obliged every time, and he was so good at spinning yarns that he made his listeners feel as if they were with him in the huddle and on the field, surrounded by one hundred thousand fans.

Busik's past endowed him with a special power, and the first time he used it was three months after he graduated. He'd been on the *Shaw* for about sixty days when she was in the battle of the Santa Cruz Islands, Busik's first interaction with an enemy. The battle, which took place on October 26, 1942, would be the last of the carrier battles around Guadalcanal. The *Shaw* was one of fourteen U.S. destroyers involved in the engagement. Her mission was to provide cover for one of the two U.S. carriers in the area. Busik, at the time, was a damage control officer, and his battle station was the forward battery, meaning he was in charge of the forward guns. Using binoculars, he'd tell the men on the guns when and where to fire. On the morning of October 26, Busik was in the forward battery, scanning the horizon, looking for dots in the sky. For the first few hours of the day, there was nothing out there, just blue sky and a few clouds.

The ship next to the *Shaw* in the screen around the carrier was the U.S.S. *Porter*. At 10:55 A.M., Busik, while sipping on a cup of coffee, again scanned the horizon for enemy aircraft. Suddenly it appeared: A Japanese plane was dropping out of the sky, having approached the Task Force at a high altitude. Within seconds of spotting the plane, Busik telephoned his captain, requesting permission to fire. Before he heard back, Busik saw the plane drop a torpedo in the water. Busik again telephoned the Captain, this time telling him that a torpedo was in the water. Busik could see the wake of the torpedo several hundred yards away and heading in their direction. The captain ordered the engine room to back down on the power. The torpedo would have intercepted the ship had the *Shaw* not slowed down. Seconds later, the torpedo whizzed in front of the bow of the ship—and headed directly into the belly of the U.S.S. *Porter*, which had stopped to pick up a downed U.S. pilot. The torpedo exploded midship into the *Porter*'s port side, flooding its fire rooms. The *Shaw* then dodged another torpedo—this one missed the disabled *Porter*—and circled the *Porter* to inspect her. At 11:30 the commander of the Task Force ordered the *Shaw* to rescue the crew of three hundred people aboard the disabled *Porter*.

As Busik helped the crew of the *Porter* come on board, he was terrified to see the condition of the survivors. This was the first time in the war he'd seen men injured, and these poor boys were tough to look at. Many were covered in blood. Others were so burned that their faces had seemed to melt like ice cream, while still more suffered from life-threatening shrapnel wounds. In the months that he'd been on the *Shaw* Busik often felt as if he'd been fighting a phantom enemy that never materialized. But now the awful reality of the enemy's firepower was spread before Busik's eyes.

Busik's stateroom was located next to the wardroom, which sailors aboard the *Shaw* quickly converted into an emergency medical room. As soon as this medical room filled up, Busik began escorting the wounded to officers' bunks, including his own. The *Shaw* only had one doctor and one hospital corpsmen aboard ship, and there was little they could do for the men other than give them shots of morphine. When all the wounded had been moved, Busik tried to comfort the men.

"I wish there was more I could do for you, sailor," Busik told one boy who was seriously burned.

"Tell me a story," the sailor replied. "You're Bill Busik from the Navy football team, right?" the sailor asked.

"Correct," replied Busik.

"Tell me something about it,"

Busik began talking, detailing all that he could remember from his big Army-Navy showdowns. The Navy football legend tried to get their thoughts focused on football rather than pain. He told these dying boys about the crowd at the '41 Army-Navy game, about what it was like to have thousands of eyes locked on your every move, about how even Army fans had cheered for the Navy players. He told them everything he could remember about those bright days of being a Midshipman football player, trying to mentally transport the wounded away from the place they were in now, and the sailors were held spellbound by his stories. Some of the boys even smiled through their suffering.

One boy was in particularly bad shape. He was young, maybe nineteen years old, and he was lying in Busik's bunk, shaking uncontrollably. Burns covered his head and chest; he was in shock. Busik called for the doctor, and he soon appeared with a syringe of morphine. The doctor asked Busik to hold the boy down so he could stick the needle in his arm. Busik cradled the boy's face with his hands, trying to comfort him, telling him in a voice that was as soothing as a prayer that everything was going

to be fine, that he was safe now. The doctor gave him the shot. As Busik lifted his hands away, the boys' ears stuck to Busik's hands. They'd peeled right off his head. Less than an hour later the boy was dead.

Like all the men aboard, Busik was proud to serve on the *Shaw*. Among the ships in the Pacific Fleet, the *Shaw* was symbolically significant. She had been in dry dock at Pearl Harbor when the Japanese dropped three bombs on the front section of the ship, causing a fire that exploded her ammunition magazines and practically demolished her from the mast forward. When the magazines exploded the entire fore section of the *Shaw* was lifted high into the air, and it shattered into several pieces. A photograph of the explosion was published throughout the world; it became *the* picture of the attack.

After December 7 the *Shaw* was considered a total loss, as were her sister ships, the U.S.S. *Cassin* and the U.S.S. *Downs*. The Japanese even announced that the *Shaw* had been sunk. For ten days following the attack no one knew what exactly to do with the twisted, blackened destroyer. The *Shaw*'s skipper, commander W. G. Jones, said he "wouldn't have given a nickel for it." To Jones's surprise, on December 18, 1941, he received an order to "take the *Shaw* back to mainland United States and get her cleaned up." For the next three weeks, working day and night, civilians from Hawaii and members of the *Shaw* crew repaired the ship. A temporary bridge was built. A sturdy blunt bow—basically, a metal nose to the ship—was installed. And then, under her own power and with the same engines it had before the attack, the *Shaw* sailed away from Hawaii to the Navy Yard on Mare Island near San Francisco.

The journey wasn't easy. The ship was stiff and light. When she ran into stormy weather, waves engulfed the vessel. She tossed and turned and, at one point, nearly capsized. The men slept little, and after ten days the slow voyage was completed. Once in San Francisco, the *Shaw* underwent six more months of repairs. Busik joined the ship a few days before she once again set sail on July 4, 1942. "We're better than ever," said Commander Jones as the *Shaw*—the ship with nine lives (or at least two)—rolled back into the sea.

Eighteen months after being rechristened, the *Shaw* patrolled the waters off of New Guinea. Up in the gun director's deck, which was about sixty feet above the water, Busik held binoculars to his eyes, scanning the clouds. It was precisely 4:38 in the afternoon of December 26, 1943. It

had been a quiet day, but then Busik spotted several dark specks circling high in the sky. Immediately recognizing the specks as Japanese fighters, Busik telephoned the ship's captain, asking him for permission to give the order to fire. Busik wanted to spray the sky with bullets before the planes started peeling off and diving down. But the captain was delayed in responding to Busik. Without hearing back from the captain, Busik gave the order to shoot anyway. "We're going to get these guys before they get us," Busik said.

Just as the *Shaw*'s guns began blazing, the first plane dove, heading at the *Shaw* in a fifty-degree dive. When the dive-bomber got within about one thousand feet of the *Shaw*, the plane burst into flames, hit by the *Shaw*'s gunfire, and went out of control. The plane crashed into the sea about fifteen hundred yards to the port side without dropping any bombs near the vessel. Busik felt vindicated. In his training at the naval academy he was schooled in all the nuances of when to engage the enemy, and he was taught to pepper enemy aircraft with fire as soon as he thought they were about to attack the ship. Sure, he didn't have the authorization of the captain, but he went with his own instincts. It was a split-second decision, and it proved to be the right one: Moments after the ship's gunfire had knocked it down, the plane started sinking into the ocean.

Then a second plane dove. Busik again gave the order to fire. Seconds later, shells hit the plane at about fifteen hundred feet, and smoke spewed out as the plane descended toward the *Shaw*. But this time, the Japanese pilot didn't lose control. At about one thousand feet in the air, the aircraft released one five-hundred-pound bomb. A fraction of a second later, it released two smaller one-hundred-pound bombs. From Busik's position in the director, it looked like the bombs were heading directly at him; he could even see the circular nose of the five-hundred-pounder bearing down on the spot where he stood. He thought he was a dead man. He braced himself against the railing of the gun director's deck, expecting to get blown into past tense. He took a deep breath and closed his eyes, ready for heaven.

The five hundred-pound bomb struck the water about ten feet off the starboard side and about fifteen feet forward of the bridge. The two smaller bombs smacked the water on the port side, about ninety feet from the ship. All three bombs then burst. Shrapnel and water flew everywhere. More than 110 holes were instantly cut into the port side of the ship, three feet of water had been thrown onto the ship, and dozens of men were killed instantly.

When the concussions of the blasts reached Busik up in the gun director's deck, it produced a whiplike effect. Busik, already some sixty feet above the ship, was sent flying into the air. Sailors watching the drama unfold from nearby ships shouted and signaled man overboard—but in fact Busik's leg got caught in an antenna and mast guide wire. The wire wrapped around his right calf, and it left him dangling—unconscious—high above the ship. After a few moments he woke up, confused, upside down, amazed to still have breath in his lungs.

Dangling forty feet above the ship like a fish caught on a line, Busik thought of his wife. As he swayed through the air, he knew that if he fell he'd never see her again. "I gotta hold on," Busik said to himself. "I'm not letting go." Busik recalled all the football stories he had shared with the wounded soldiers just weeks ago, and he wondered what his life would be like if this war hadn't erupted and he'd been able to try out for Curly Lambeau's Packers. "I surely wouldn't be in this predicament now," he thought to himself.

After a few minutes, Busik took a personal inventory: Shrapnel had hit his ribs and legs, but other than that, he felt fine. Then he noticed that his naval academy class ring was no longer on his finger. It was snug on his left ring finger minutes ago—and all ten fingers were present and accounted for—but now his ring was gone.

Ten minutes after he was blasted into the air, a few shipmates reached Busik, untangling him and reeling him to safety. He was escorted below the deck where the ship doctor attended his wounds. "I guess the Japs are paying us back all that scrap iron we gave them before the war," Busik joked with the doctor. "By the way, doc, have you seen my ring?"

"Sorry, sir, I haven't," replied the doctor.

Some 5 hours later, two decks below the bridge, a sailor was emptying a garbage can when he noticed something shiny on the bottom. It was a naval academy ring from the Class of '43. On the top of the ring was a sapphire stone and engraved on the inside of it were the words: William S. Busik. The sailor walked to Busik's stateroom and knocked on his door.

"Sir, did you lose this?" the sailor asked.

"Good heavens," replied Busik. "It blew off my finger when the bombs went off. No matter what, I'm never taking this thing off again. I'm in your debt, sailor. Thank you."

Moments after Margaret Busik read that her husband was missing in action, she bolted from her seat at the kitchen table. She ran into her bedroom, fumbling to find a letter that she had received just days ago from her husband. She hastily yanked it out of the envelope and, with her hands trembling, looked for the date. There it was: January 2, 1944. Bill had sent it a week after he had reportedly gone overboard. Margaret then reached for the telephone, asking the operator to connect her to the *San Francisco Chronicle*.

"My husband is not missing," Margaret told an editor at the paper. "I got a letter from him just the other day that's dated after you said he was missing. This is going to upset a lot of people. Please run a retraction."

When Margaret wrote her husband and explained the mix-up, he laughed so hard it filled up the wardroom.

"I guess I'm on my second life," Busik joked to a few friends. "Who knows? If I'm lucky, maybe I've got a couple more in me."

16

EARLY JUNE 1944

WILLIAM LEAHY STOOD AS straight and still as a two-by-four, at full attention, as Dwight D. Eisenhower boarded the battleship U.S.S. *Texas* on May 19, 1944. Six months had passed since Leahy's friend and former teammate, Bill Busik, was nearly killed aboard the U.S.S. *Shaw*, and now Leahy stared into the blue eyes of the Supreme Commander of the Allied Forces with D-day just seventeen days away.

Eisenhower looked like an athlete. He had a powerful gait, his arms swaying confidently as he walked on board, and there was a bounce to his step. He had wide shoulders and a thick chest—a farmer's chest—and as Leahy looked at him he imagined that Eisenhower could still play football. Back in the fall of 1912, while at the military academy, Eisenhower was one of Army's top backs. After leading the Cadets to a victory over Rutgers, the *New York Times* called Eisenhower "one of the most promising backs in Eastern football." A few weeks later, however, Eisenhower severely injured his knee when he leapt off the back of a galloping horse. He never played football again.

But, at age fifty-three, he still possessed the graceful stride of a power player in his prime as he walked onto the *Texas*. Eisenhower had secretly flown to Belfast, Ireland, to inspect the gunfire support ships of the Western Naval Task Force that were anchored in Belfast Lough, near the city of Bangor. The U.S.S. *Texas* was the flagship of Battleship Division Five, and this was where Eisenhower came to deliver a message to the vast armada of Allied Ships amassed in the Lough. By most estimates, the total number of officers and sailors on these ships was probably around thirty thousand. One officer and one sailor from every ship in the fleet was on the *Texas* to hear the supreme commander speak; afterward they would return to their respective ships and report to their crews what Eisenhower had said.

A cool drizzle fell from a gray sky as Eisenhower prepared to make his remarks. The carpenters aboard the *Texas* had built a speaker's platform on the quarterdeck and Eisenhower's words were piped into the ship's loudspeaker system. Leahy, anxious like many young officers, leaned forward ever so slightly as the commander began speaking. "In the next battle we will have the greatest air coverage that has ever accompanied you and your forces in history," he said. "[Your superiors] provide for taking care of you when you are wounded, they see that you are disposed properly, that your guns are trained on the right targets, but, my God, men, you do the fighting! No general or other person in high capacity really fires that shot that knocks out enemy batteries and sinks ships. You are the people who do it. You are the men handling the guns and the turrets, the men handling the firing of the weapons, torpedoes, everything. You are the men who are winning the war."

As Eisenhower continued, his words stoked a fire inside Leahy. Ever since he learned of the attack on Pearl Harbor while he was sitting in Washington, D.C.'s Griffith Stadium on December 7, 1941, and watching the Washington Redskins play the Philadelphia Eagles, Leahy had been looking forward to combat. Though he never imagined he'd be stricken with it, he had caught war fever. He'd already lost many of his friends, former classmates, and former teammates. Just recently he'd heard that Bill Chewning, one of Navy's top tackles on the '41 team, had been aboard the submarine U.S.S. *Corvina* when it had been sunk on November 16, 1943, by a Japanese submarine near the Gilbert Islands. Leahy remembered that Chewning always seemed to be in the middle of the action. In the giddy aftermath of Navy's 14–6 win over Army in '41, it was Chewning in his smeared, bloody uniform, who had presented the game ball to coach Larson. That had been one of the best moments of Chewning's life. But now, like so many whom Leahy knew well, Chewning was gone forever.

As a first-division gunner officer aboard the *Texas*, Leahy, who had been stationed on the *Texas* since graduating from the naval academy, was assigned to what was called "Spot 1," located in the crow's nest 110 feet in the air. His job was to control the firing and aiming of the turrets. Looking through a large telescope, he'd determine if the shells were reaching their intended targets. After they had been fired, for example, Leahy might say "up one hundred." A shipmate standing next to Leahy would then relay the information via phone to the crew in charge of the turrets. As soon as they'd make the adjustment, they'd phone the crow's nest and then Leahy would give the order to fire. A lover of numbers, Leahy thought of his job as a problem-solving exercise. And now he knew he might soon be forced to give an order to fire that could kill hundreds of enemy soldiers with one command. "It's us or them," he thought to himself whenever he pondered this subject. "I have a job to do—and I intend to do it as best I can."

After Eisenhower finished his formal remarks on the *Texas*, he asked if there were any questions. A sailor, who Leahy thought couldn't have been older than eighteen, raised his hand and, in a cracking voice, asked, "I hear that in the upcoming invasion that we are going to land British troops and that the British Navy is going to land American troops. Is this true?"

Eisenhower smiled. "First of all, that is not true," he said calmly. "You're going to land the American troops. You're going to land your brothers, you're going to land your fathers, and you're going to land your sisters' boyfriends. And I will tell you right now that if we get to land I, by God, will keep us there. We are going to win this war!"

The answer caused the troops to clap and yell in approval. These were stirring words, and as Leahy listened, he knew he'd never forget them.

Twelve days later, on May 31, the ships were sealed; no more leave was granted. The sailors and officers were then told by their superiors that over five thousand vessels would participate in D-day. Now the wait began.

Robin Olds also was waiting. He'd arrived in England on a transport three weeks earlier, as primed as anyone to fight. After graduation from West Point he had joined the 434th Fighter Squadron of the 479th Fighter Group at Lomita, California, where he logged about 650 hours of flying time—far more than the average young pilot heading into combat for the first time. He also had spent some 250 hours in the P-38, the aircraft he'd be flying during the war. Called the Lightning, the P-38 had a top speed of 414 mph, making it a faster plane than any Olds would confront in combat. The Lightning handled well, but at low altitudes it sometimes wasn't as maneuverable as other aircraft.

Olds' first few weeks in the war were relatively quiet. His squadron mostly bombed bridges and railroads in France. Olds never encountered any enemy fighters during these runs, but one of his good friends from the Army football team, John Buckner, wasn't as fortunate. In mid-May of '44, Buckner, who had graduated fifth in his class in January of 1943, went on an early morning dive-bombing mission in northern France. His order was to take out a bridge. After crossing the English Channel Buckner spotted the bridge. Buckner dove down, released his bombs, and saw the bridge fall into the river it covered.

As Buckner climbed back into the sky, he felt satisfied, as if he'd just completed a five-course meal. Thinking all was clear, he allowed himself to relax as he guided his plane north toward the channel. But just as he started to think about what he was going to do when he got back to his base in England, enemy shells started exploding all around him. He continued to climb, gaining as much altitude as he could. But then a shell hit his engine. Before he could react, the engine stalled.

Buckner was now gliding at twelve thousand feet. He knew that if he attempted a belly landing—which he'd practiced many times—he could be taken prisoner, so instead he turned north and began gliding across the channel. When his plane dropped to one thousand feet, he knew it was time to bail. He could see the coast of England in the distance. Not thinking clearly, Buckner undid his parachute straps that were wrapped around his legs. Every time Buckner had gotten out of the plane, he always undid these straps. It was his routine. But now as he prepared to jump—this would be the first time he'd ever bailed—he paused just before leaping into the air. In the nick of time, he remembered a crucial bit of information: He needed his parachute now!

"Wait a minute, this is dumb," Buckner said to himself.

He then refastened his straps and jumped out of the plane and into the air, praying these would not be the last moments of his life. He was now at about eight hundred feet. Moments after his chute opened, he saw his plane plunge into the channel, crashing in a big splash. A strong breeze blew from the south, pushing Buckner closer and closer to the coast. After dropping from the sky for a few more minutes, Buckner landed safely on the beach. Knowing that the coast was heavily mined, he then sat in the sand and waited for someone to pick him up. Several hours later a few British soldiers arrived in a jeep and guided Buckner around the mines on the beach. Buckner had lost his plane, but not his life.

On June 5, 1944, a chilly midafternoon in southern England, Olds' commander called all the pilots in the squadron together for a briefing. "Our next mission is to escort some ships that are in southern England that will be heading south," the commander said. "Gentlemen, the invasion is on."

Finally it's here, Olds thought to himself. The moment he'd been training for since he arrived at the Point.

Henry Romanek was busy laying a live mine outside of Payton, England, when one of the forty-five men who was under his command finally spoke up. "Lieutenant, you're the bright one. Tell us where we're going."

Romanek wasn't surprised by the question. It was one that he'd been contemplating for weeks. Romanek had graduated number two in his class at West Point in military history. He knew the annals of strategy and tactics well, and after studying maps that depicted the shoreline of France, he knew exactly where the invasion was headed.

"We're going right here," Romanek told his soldier. He had grabbed a map and was pointing his finger to an exact location. A few soldiers leaned in close and read the words where his finger was resting: A beach the Allies called Omaha.

After the U.S.S. *Texas* had been locked down, the captain of the ship spoke to his crew. "The great events for which all of you have been working and preparing will shortly be launched," he said. "It also means that every possible effort must be made to prevent any leakage whatsoever of information from incoming operations, by whatever means—mail, personal contact, or signals. I consider that you are now at battle efficiency and the time has come to polish up all our weapons. From now until D-day only such drills as are necessary to maintain your present state will be conducted. But remember, the enemy we are going up against will tax our readiness to the utmost."

Leahy, like everyone else on the *Texas*, had been handed an order of the day when he filed onto the ship for the last time before D-day. It was from General Eisenhower, and Leahy read it with a high tide of pride in his heart.

> *Soldiers, Sailors, and Airmen of the Allied Expeditionary Force:*
>
> *You are about to embark on the Great Crusade, toward which we have striven these many months. The eyes of the world are upon you. The hopes and prayers of liberty-loving people everywhere march with you. . . . Your task will not be an easy one. Your enemy is well trained, well equipped and battle-hardened. He will fight savagely. But this is the year 1944! . . . The tide has turned! The free men of the world are marching together to victory! I have full confidence in your courage, devotion to duty and skill in battle. We will accept nothing less than full victory!*
>
> *Good luck! And let us all beseech the blessing of Almighty God upon this great and noble undertaking.*

After reading these words, Leahy had to take a deep breath. A seminal moment in history was rapidly approaching, he certainly understood that. Let the battle begin, Leahy thought to himself, as he folded the order carefully and put it in his pocket.

Hours after the *Texas* had been sealed, Leahy was handed the invasion battle plan. The *Texas*'s mission was to provide support of the troop landings on Omaha Beach. To prepare for the task, Leahy studied a detailed map of the area where the *Texas* would be providing cover to the invading troops. Analyzing the topography of Omaha Beach and the area behind it, Leahy noticed a church spire that rose about forty feet above the ground. The church sat on top of the cliffs that overlooked the beach. After examining the map for a few minutes, Leahy decided that he'd use the spire as his main marker. When he was up in the crow's nest and trying to figure out what directions he needed to give to his gunnery personnel, he'd locate the spire. From there, he would memorize how far all the main targets were located. "I just hope the Germans don't figure out what I'm doing and decide to take out that spire," Leahy told a friend on the ship. "It's a risk, but the spire is the best marker I can find."

On an early June afternoon in 1944, the *Texas* motored out of Belfast and began making her way toward the task force rendezvous point. The weather was poor, overcast with rain squalls, and there was a strong southwesterly wind. That evening, holed up in his quarters, Leahy studied the pictures and maps of Normandy with all the intensity he could muster. He laid all the material on the floor by his bunk and shined the yellow light of his gooseneck lamp onto the ground. He stayed up most of the night, imprinting every detail of the map into his memory. "I've got to know this better than I know my childhood neighborhood," Leahy told a few sailors on the *Texas*. "I'm not going to let anyone down."

The *Texas* and the column of ships from Belfast Lough were near the southwest corner of England when the postponement order was given. The invasion had been scheduled for June 5, but when Eisenhower received information that the weather forecast for the Normandy area called for overcast skies and a chance for thunderstorms, he decided to delay it. The only way the invasion would be a success, Eisenhower believed, was if it was performed under better conditions. Eisenhower hoped for clearer skies on June 6.

Leahy considered the delay a lucky break. It gave him more time to prepare.

A month earlier Romanek and his platoon moved out of the Payton area in England to meet the 29th Division in Dorchester. Leaving wasn't easy. For six months Romanek had lived in the St. Ann's Hotel in Payton, a place he'd grown to adore. Most of the local men were all off fighting in the war, and the women who were left behind showed open-armed hospitality to Romanek and all of his boys. Many of the soldiers in Romanek's platoon were quartered in the houses of locals, and Romanek would frequently stop in to see how everything was going. There, he'd play with kids and often was treated to a home-cooked meal. When Romanek and his platoon gathered up their gear for the last time and prepared to board a transport ship for Dorchester, the entire town of Payton turned out to say good-bye. For Romanek, it was like leaving family all over again.

Once Romanek and his platoon arrived in Dorchester, they drove on trucks into a massive camp that was enclosed with barbed wire. Soon after, the camp was locked down. On June 3, Romanek was summoned into a large tent. In it, a few sand tables were set up. On these tables every detail of the invasion was plotted. After being briefed on the invasion by superiors, Romanek called his men into the tent and explained exactly what they were going to do.

In the early morning of June 5, Romanek and his platoon were riding on the U.S.S. *Garfield*, an assault transport ship, when they were told that the invasion had been postponed. They were just hours away from going over the side of the ship and onto their landing craft, but now they were told to stand down for 24 hours. Romanek, like most of the young men he was with, enjoyed this extra day of peace. But this momentary reprieve also brought one hazard: it meant more time for reflection, more time to think about how June 5 might be his last full day of life.

Eisenhower awoke at about 3:30 in the morning on June 6. He drove from his trailer to Southwick House, located outside of Portsmouth on the south coast of England. This was the naval headquarters and Eisenhower first made his way to the mess hall. He was given a hot cup of coffee, but it did little to warm his spirits. Southwick House was shaking because of the stormy conditions outside. Eisenhower paced the room. Then Captain J. M. Stagg arrived with an updated weather forecast for Normandy. "I'll give you some good news," Stagg said. He then went on to tell the Supreme Commander that he was confident that the storm would break before dawn. All indications pointed to that, Stagg explained. For nearly a minute, Eisenhower silently considered the news as he paced around the room. Then he looked up and said quietly but firmly, "Okay, let's go."

17

OMAHA BEACH

HER BATTLE FLAGS FLAPPING in the wind, the U.S.S. *Texas* plowed through the rough seas, one of five thousand vessels motoring from England to the coast of France, pushing toward their date with destiny. The ships were ten lanes wide, stretching twenty miles across. Among these vessels were six battleships—three American, three British. The invasion planners expected to lose one or two of these battlewagons in the hours ahead, maybe more. The battleships would not only spray the beach with shells, but they would also draw the Germans' heavy firepower to them and away from the soldiers approaching the beach. Along with the U.S.S. *Arkansas*, the *Texas* was to unload her 14 inch guns about 10 miles off the shore of Omaha. The *Texas* was to fire on both Point du Hoc—where several German coastal batteries were located—and on enemy strong points defending the beach exits.

Now William Leahy stood on the deck of the *Texas*, a creaky ship that navy men called the Old Lady. Commissioned in 1914, the *Texas* was the oldest battleship in the U.S. fleet. Leahy started to walk along the deck and could see, splashing in the moonlight, the white tops of the waves smashing against the other ships as they pushed southward across the English Channel. As Leahy continued to walk, his mind raced. The ship boasted ten 14 inch guns, and Lehey, from his position in the crow's nest, would help direct the shore bombardment. Silently, he reviewed his orders: The *Texas* was not supposed to fire until 5:50 A.M. unless fired on. The first wave of infantry was scheduled to hit Omaha at 6:30. Just before that, the *Texas* would raise her guns and aim at targets farther inland.

Time ticked on. As the armada closed in on the coast of France, men on every ship wrote last-minute letters, frantically telling their loved ones how much they cared for them. Others played cards and tried to keep the mood light. Some huddled with chaplains, praying for strength and safety. The men who loved to read now tried to lose themselves in paperbacks that they carried in their back pocket. And many men just talked, confiding with each other. In many cases men who had just met began telling each other their most intimate secrets. But more than anything, all the men just waited . . . and waited . . . and waited for dawn.

Time continued to move. The *Texas* and the other ships came to a halt around two in the morning, about 10 miles off the five beaches of Normandy. Now the vessels bristled with activity. Chains clanked and rattled in the davits as assault boats were lowered into the water. Small patrol boats, their engines droning, zipped around from landing craft to landing craft. Announcements blared over the ships' PA systems: "Fight to get your troops ashore," one message roared. "Fight to save your ships and, if you've got any strength left, fight to save yourself!"

As men like Henry Romanek—who was aboard the U.S.S. *Garfield*—waited to climb down the nets and into the landing crafts that bobbed in the rolling sea, many exchanged home phone numbers and addresses, promising that they would contact each other's loved ones if they didn't survive the day. "Just in case," many of the men would say as they handed over a piece of paper with their information. Officers on every ship gave their final pep talks, imploring their men to be brave, telling them that the eyes of history were now focused on their every move.

Leahy climbed to his position in the U.S.S. *Texas*'s crow's nest, a perch about 150 feet above the ship's deck. As he looked down on all the action, it seemed as if an entire city was afloat in his field of view, humming with movement and bouncing up and down in the undulating waves. Leahy carefully watched the men load into their landing crafts, not knowing if he'd see any of them again.

The hands of the clock kept moving. At just after 5:20 in the morning, with the first waves of LCMs now headed for the beach, light started to rise, ever so faintly, over the eastern horizon. Minutes later, through his binoculars, Leahy could see the misty shores of Normandy. The beach appeared peaceful and quiet in the gray light of dawn, a place—Leahy thought—that would be perfect to take his girl on a romantic stroll. But at 5:35, as Leahy continued to inspect the beach with his binoculars, he saw movement at several shore batteries. "They're getting ready to fire," yelled Leahy. Realizing that he was under strict order not to fire unless fired upon, Leahy quickly phoned the captain. He explained that the Germans were about to attack the *Texas*, which was at anchor for fear of hitting a mine in the area. Leahy insisted that the *Texas* should fire first—the very first shot of this bloody day. "Hold your fire," the Captain told Leahy. "Repeat, hold your fire."

Just then, Leahy saw two shells whizzing toward the *Texas* out of the mist. "Brace yourself," Leahy yelled. The shells fell short of the *Texas* and exploded in the sea, causing a geyser of water to shoot upward. In seconds, Leahy then issued what he thought were the coordinates of the shore battery that had just targeted the *Texas* and gave the order to fire. Through his binoculars, Leahy tracked the shells as they streaked through the early-morning light. They exploded into the cliffs of Omaha Beach, causing chunks of the cliff to fall into the sea. A few Germans flew into the air as the shells dug a crater into the cliff.

Ernest Hemingway, a correspondent for *Colliers* magazine, was riding in a landing craft toward the beach when the *Texas* opened fire. He later wrote that the shells from the *Texas* "sounded as though they were throwing whole railway trains across the sky." He added, "Those of our troops who were not wax gray with seasickness were watching the *Texas* with looks of surprise and happiness. Under the steel helmets [the troops] looked like pikemen of the Middle Ages to whose aid in battle had suddenly come some strange and unbelievable monster."

By 5:50 A.M., fifteen minutes after the great battle had begun, enough light filled the sky that spotter planes began relaying information to Leahy on the accuracy of the *Texas*'s shelling. He was told that several of the pillboxes up on the cliffs had been hit, but were still operational. The shells had left indentations and pockmarks on the concrete pillboxes, exposing their steel reinforcing rods, but still the guns up on the hundred-foot high sheer cliffs thundered and continued to fire. The 14 inch shells weren't penetrating the pillboxes. They had rendered many of the Germans inside the pillboxes deaf, but they hadn't silenced the gunfire.

Every time the *Texas* was targeted, it appeared to Leahy and the other officers in the crow's nest that the enemy shells were headed directly at their perch. "Sir, we're going to take a hit any second now," one of the officers said to Leahy. "Sir, I, I, . . ."

"Don't worry," replied Leahy. "It's going to take an almost perfect shot to get us up here. And hey, it's better to be up here than down below. Down there it's a much wider target!"

Using the single spire of the church at Vierville as his main marker, Leahy continued to give the coordinates of where he thought the German machine gun fire was coming from. "I'm killing hundreds," Leahy thought to himself. "Better those bastards than us."

The guns of the *Texas* kept firing. Sailors watered down the hot barrels with hoses. Leahy stuffed cotton in his ears and shouted the command to fire over and over, hoping to take out as many shore batteries as possible and pave the way for the boys who were now closing in on the beach.

At 6:15 the Texas turned her 14 inch guns on the exit road D-1 on the western end of Omaha Beach. Fifteen minutes later, at H-hour (the hour the operation was to begin), the *Texas* lifted her guns and aimed at targets beyond the beach. The first wave of men from the free societies of the world was about to hit the beach. Minutes later, Leahy, still standing in the crow's nest, couldn't believe what he was seeing through his binoculars: The beach, which just moments earlier had seemed so tranquil, was now a slaughterhouse.

As the landing craft that Henry Romanek rode in started to slow about 50 yards off of Omaha Beach, German soldiers on the bluff pointed their machine guns in the LCM's direction. Bullets began clanking off the metal sides of craft—*ping, ping, ping*—as the square-faced ramp came down. Romanek stood in the back of the LCM with the rest of the engineers; the infantrymen were in front. When the ramp was lowered, men started to push forward, yelling, "Go, go, go." But the machine gunners on the bluff had drawn a bead on the LCM's exit ramp. Before the first American solider in the LCM even hit the water, dozens of men simply fell forward, instantly rendered limp and lifeless. Blood splattered and spit through the air. Suddenly, there was nowhere to hide.

Romanek kept pushing his men forward. He and his engineers were high—they joined about twenty other men, most of whom were wounded, some on their last breath. Romanek tried to stay alert and keep his eyes open, but then everything went dark. His body started rattling as if he were suffering from an internal earthquake. He slipped into shock.

From the cockpit of his P-38, Robin Olds could see that American boys were pinned underneath the shingle. All morning long he expected to engage German fighter planes, but they never appeared. In the previous months British and American fighters had driven the German Luftwaffe out of France. Olds and everyone else in his squadron believed the Luftwaffe would try to repel the D-day invasion and add to the congestion of the beach, but it never showed. (Of the 5,409 Allied fighter planes that participated in the D-day invasion, not a single one was shot down by the Luftwaffe.) So Olds just flew at 500 feet back and forth over the beach in a grid pattern.

Some ten hours earlier, on the eve of the D-day invasion, Olds and the other pilots of the 434th Fighter Squadron of the 479th Fighter Group were summoned to a briefing room at their base in Suffolk, England. "The invasion is on," the commander told the pilots. The commander then went over their orders, stressing that they were not to fire at anything on the ground. After the commander was finished, Olds approached him and volunteered to fly on the first mission in the morning. When a few other pilots also volunteered, Olds offered to fight them for it fist to fist. "Nobody wants this more than me and we can settle it outside if you want," Olds told his flyboy buddies.

But now that he was above Omaha Beach, Olds' frustration grew by the minute, unable to help his brothers on the beach. When he looked down through the smoke and dust that billowed up from the battle, he could see men jumping out of their landing craft and splashing into the water. Many landing craft had been capsized; others exploded right before Olds' eyes. When the German batteries thundered from the coastline, the vibrations of the blasts sometimes caused the wings of his P-38 to vibrate. Olds desperately wanted to strafe the beach—when he looked down, he had no problem discerning the Germans from the Americans—but because the Americans didn't have any air-to-ground communication, the invasion planners had decided that the P-38s wouldn't target anything on the beach. Yet now Olds could see that the action on the beach wasn't going well. He figured that Romanek was supposed to erect beach panel markers on Omaha exit D-3 that would act as guideposts for approach landing crafts. They had spent months training for these next few minutes, but now they couldn't even get off their landing craft. Romanek yelled to his men. "We gotta get outta here," he screamed. "Keep moving."

Soldiers in front of Romanek kept falling like tall blades of grass being mowed down. Still he told his men to storm the beach. "We're going to do this," he yelled. Finally Romanek reached the ramp exit. He handed a polelike casing that held a beach panel marker to one of men and then jumped into the water. Yet just as he splashed into the sea, a bullet sliced through his chest. As he floated in five feet of water, with his mind wandering back to those glorious days when he was a West Point football player, a medic on the beach saw him struggling to breath.

Wearing a Red Cross armband, the medic sprinted into the water and swam to Romanek. All the medics on Omaha were told that their main job was to pull the wounded to safety. In most cases once the medic reached the wounded he would conduct a brief examination, evaluate the wound, apply a tourniquet if necessary, clean the wound, sprinkle sulfa powder on the wound and bandage it. Then he would drag or carry the soldier out of harm's way.

The medic reached Romanek, pulled him out of the water, dragging him past bodies that washed back and forth in the surf, and moved him behind a metal beach obstacle that was the shape of an X. "I'm going to drag you on your back over the beach—help push with your feet," the media yelled to Romanek. Too weak to talk, Romanek nodded.

Keeping his head down, the corpsman grabbed Romanek by his right arm and dragged him from one beach obstacle to the next. When Romanek looked back at the water, he could see hulks from landing crafts now burning in the water. On the beach equipment was strewn everywhere. Radios, field telephones, helmets, canteens, gas masks, life preservers—they were washing up with the rising tide. In the distance Romanek could see tanks ablaze in the water, black smoke pouring out of them. And with every crashing wave, another bloody body seemed to turn up at the water line.

The corpsman kept pulling Romanek. He had no other choice, because staying on the beach meant signing your own death warrant. Romanek tried to push with his feet and move his body as the corpsman dragged him, but his strength was gone. When they reached the shingle—which was the first rise in the terrain on the beach and was about five feet down there somewhere; maybe he was even flying directly over him. Olds hoped to God that his buddy was okay.

Romanek opened his eyes. Everything was blurry, like he was underwater. The arms of the corpsman were wrapped tightly around him. The corpsman had warmed Romanek and now Romanek regained consciousness. Wiping his eyes, Romanek looked back at the beach. No, he hadn't been dreaming: Dead men littered the sand. The corpsman spoke to Romanek. "I'll give you some morphine and then I'll look at your wound," he said.

The corpsman carried a combat compressor. He peeled back Romanek's clothing and found a hole in his back. He cleaned the wound as best he could with water and sulfa powder, then put a compressor on both holes, temporarily stopping the bleeding.

The corpsman left and then returned moments later with a canteen full of water, which he handed to Romanek. He also gave Romanek twelve sulfa pills, which the corpsman hoped would stave off any infection. "Take one of these every four hours," the corpsman told Romanek.

"I don't know if I'm going to be around every four hours," replied Romanek. "Maybe I can fight off the infection if I take them all right now," which was what Romanek did.

Before the corpsman left to attend to other wounded men, Romanek asked, "Hey, what's your name?"

"Smitty," he replied.

"Where you from?"

"Raleigh."

"That's nice," replied Romanek. "My wife is from North Carolina and she . . ."

Before Romanek could finish, the corpsman was gone, headed back to the beach.

The tide continued to roll in. It was about 9:30 A.M. Fatigue washed over Romanek like a morning shower as he lay on the rough shingle rocks and looked back at the beach. The sight of the massacre, which was unfolding two hundred yards from Romanek's position, caused his heart to sink. As he watched soldiers drop and scream and cry for help, Romanek thought of General Omar Bradley, the head of the U.S. First Army, and the words he had delivered to the 29th Infantry Division a few days before D-day.

"You're going to go in there and this is what you're going to do," Bradley said firmly. "Nobody is going to surrender. If you're wounded and you have ammo, you will fight until you die. No one will need to surrender because you will not be deserted on the beach. I promise you, you will not be deserted on the beach."

As he looked out at the landing crafts continuing to roll ashore, Romanek realized that Bradley hadn't lied. Thousands were going to die, but Romanek knew he was not going to be deserted and forgotten on the beach.

In the moments when the Germans weren't firing from the positions up on the bluff, Romanek could often hear them talking. Their voices carried in the wind, traveling down the bluff to Romanek's ears. But then, just as quickly as the voices could be heard, they'd be drowned out by the noise of the battle. There was naval gunfire, artillery, small arms, mortor fire, aircraft overhead, the shouts and cries of the wounded—it was hard to think, there was so much noise.

For the rest of the morning and throughout the afternoon, Romanek watched the struggle to storm the beach through the smoke, dust, and mist that rose from the battlefield. Though he was as tired as he'd ever been and seriously injured, Romanek didn't allow himself to sleep. If he did, he figured he might not ever wake up. So he let his eyes focus on the destruction and devastation taking place just two hundred meters away. As he looked on with sadness, he guessed the life expectancy for most of the men hitting the beach was about two minutes.

When darkness started falling, the sounds of battle began to fade. Naval gunfire, tanks, and infantry had disabled most of the German pillboxes on the bluff. But many German snipers lurked on the cliffs, and nearly every time a shot rang out in the night a wounded man near Romanek would shriek in terror. As far as Romanek could tell, there were no able-bodied American soldiers in his vicinity. Many of the soldiers were despondent and babbling incoherently. Others sat in silence and smoked cigarettes, the red glow of the ash illuminating their tired faces, while others still talked bravely of how they were going to survive this bloody day and seek vengeance.

All around Romanek the beach was dotted with debris. Guns, canteens, helmets, packs, gas masks, packs of cigarettes, a guitar—they all rolled back and forth in the tide. And late in the evening, Romanek could once again hear German voices rising into the cool night air. He detected mess kits clanking as the Germans up on the bluff ate dinner. They were so close—too close.

Romanek didn't close his eyes for more than a few minutes during the night, still afraid that if he fell into a deep sleep he'd never wake up. And on this endless night, in the faint light of the rising moon, one boy after the next who lay near Romanek lost his life. Romanek dug into the sand as best he could and braced for the night.

Just after daybreak, the shingle became secure. Twenty-four hours had passed since Romanek had landed on the beach, and now, finally, it was under Allied control. Later in the morning Romanek's company commander was searching up and down the beach for his men when he found Romanek. "You're still alive," he told Romanek. "Excellent work, solider."

After being placed on a stretcher, Romanek was transported by jeep to an open beach area where landing craft were dropping off and loading troops. Romanek was taken out to an LST (Landing Ship Tank) that was unloading part of the 29th Infantry Division and an anti-tank company. As the soldiers exited the LST, they saw Romanek and hundreds of other half-living soldiers being hauled up the side onto the ship, which would carry the wounded back to England. As Romanek peered into the eyes of the men who were looking at his bloodied body, he saw that they were petrified. Yet Romanek didn't notice one man hesitate, even for a moment, to move forward with his mission. This was heroism, Romanek thought, because they knew exactly what kind of hell awaited them. Seeing these American boys brought tears to his eyes; after a few moments, his eyes started leaking like little waterfalls.

The next day, June 8, a navy medical corpsman named James C. Smith—serial number 08334787—was killed on Omaha Beach. The man who had saved so many unknown soldiers, including Romanek, could not be saved himself.

18

THE FIELD OF COMBAT

THE LINE OF AMBULANCES seemed to stretch for miles, deep into the drizzly English countryside. They were the first things Henry Romanek, through his groggy eyes, spotted late in the afternoon of June 7, 1944, when his transport ship reached the beach in England. When the ship's unloading ramp opened, Romanek, prone on a stretcher, noticed hundreds of ambulances preparing to ferry the wounded from Normandy to a train, which would carry the soldiers to a makeshift military hospital located outside Oxford in the fields of Cheltenham. Even in his sleep- and blood-deprived state, Romanek was stunned by the number of ambulances, all in a line that snaked for as far as he could see.

The trains to the hospital were full of mangled soldiers. They lay on stretchers, and the moaning and groaning of the wounded filled the cars. Men drifted in and out of sanity as quickly as a hiccup. Some boys thought they were back home with their buddies and sitting at the counter of a soda shop, while others believed that they were standing in the white light of heaven. It was a long train ride, over three hours, and midway through it Romanek was overcome with blinding pain. He quickly called for one of the white-uniformed nurses to come to his side. "Nurse, can you please give me some more morphine," he begged the nurse in his car. "I feel like I'm going to die."

"Of course," the nurse replied, as she left to get more medicine.

But that night, once Romanek had made it to the section of the hospital that housed those with head-and-chest wounds, the pain returned. It was unlike anything he'd ever experienced before, a sharp, stabbing pain. Though Romanek was an officer, he had been accidentally transported to an overcrowded enlisted ward and now his bed didn't even have a mattress. Instead, he laid on a covered box spring, and to Romanek it felt as if every spring was a knife being twisted into his back. "I'm dying," Romanek told a nurse in his hoarse voice. "Please give me some more morphine."

"You'll just have to grit your teeth, soldier," she replied. "If I give you any more morphine, you'll have the morphine habit."

The nurse then read Romanek's tags and realized that he had been placed in the wrong unit. He was transferred to an officers' ward and was given a bed that had a mattress. Romanek thought he had reached paradise. Later that night a doctor visited Romanek. His name was Major White.

"How long have you been in the Army, Doc?" Romanek asked.

"They drafted me in March," replied Major White. "Then they taught me to salute, gave me a uniform, put me on an airplane, and I got here in May."

"Where were you working before?" asked Romanek.

"In Boston General Hospital," he replied. "I was the chief chest surgeon there."

"Well, I guess I'm in good hands," said Romanek. "Go ahead and fix me up."

The bullet that hit Romanek didn't stay in his body; it had exited through his back, leaving a hole two-inches in diameter. "We're not going to operate," the doctor told Romanek. "We're going to patch you on your chest and back and we'll put a tube in your back to drain your lungs. You should be outta here in a few months."

It was the best news Romanek could have hoped for. Now he had to wait and heal. But as he convalesced, his mind wandered back to the battle. More than anything, he wanted to know if his boys were all right.

When the fighting was finally over on the shores of Normandy, William Leahy and several members of the U.S.S. *Texas* boarded small transports and went to inspect Omaha Beach on a clear mid-June morning. They wanted to determine how effective—and how accurate—their shelling had been during the invasion. But once Leahy hopped out of the transport and started walking on the sand, it was difficult to focus on anything other than the total destruction of the area. The beach and the bluff were still littered with dead Allied and German soldiers and with body parts that would never be matched to the soldier they belonged to. As Leahy walked around in the eerie quiet of the morning, with the soothing sound of waves crashing onto the shore, it was hard to fathom that so much death had taken place here, on this beautiful, once peaceful beach in France. Leahy couldn't even hazard a guess as to how many had died, or how many he had a hand in killing.

After two hours of examining the area, Leahy and his shipmates prepared to return to the U.S.S. *Texas*. They hadn't been as accurate with their shelling as they initially thought, but they all took solace in one simple fact: The invasion was over, and it was they—not the Germans—who had claimed this blood-stained beach.

19

THE UNFRIENDLY SKIES

THE VOICE BOOMED through the pilots' living quarters, imploring the men to wake up. Robin Olds popped his eyes open, suddenly awake and alert, his heart pounding. In the darkness he looked at his watch: 4:05 A.M. It was August 14, 1944. A little more than two months had passed since the landings at Normandy—the Allies were now marching toward Paris—and Olds was based in Suffolk, England with the 434th Fighter Squadron of the 479th Fighter Group. After wiping the sleep from his eyes, Olds dressed quickly and walked to the debriefing room, where he was promptly handed his order of the day: The 479th was to bomb a bridge at Chalons Sur Saons, in Eastern France. They were to leave immediately, even though the sun wouldn't be rising for two hours. "For Christ's sake," Olds said to a fellow pilot, "this'll be impossible to do in the dark."

Grabbing his flight gear, Olds walked out to his P-38 Lightning. As his plane sat in the moonlight, Olds couldn't help but marvel at it. The German Luftwaffe had taken to calling the P-38 the "Der Gabelschwanz Teufel," the Fork-Tailed Devil, the nickname stemming from the plane's twin-boom design. The Lightning represented a breakaway from conventional airframe design, power, and armament. The cockpit sat in the middle of the main wing. On each side of the cockpit were the engines in front of what looked like two missiles attached to the wing that were the booms. These were fixed together by the rudder in the rear. Not only did the plane have twice the power and almost twice the size of its predecessors, but it also had four .50 caliber machine guns plus a 20 mm cannon. The guns were concentrated in the central fuselage pod, which made it easier for the pilot to line up his targets. The concentration of firepower in the Lightning's nose was so effective that a one-second burst of shots could destroy an enemy plane.

Possessing droppable fuel tanks under its wings, the P-38 was used extensively as a long-range escort fighter. A versatile aircraft, the Lightning was also used for dive bombing, level bombing, ground strafing, and photo reconnaissance missions. It had a span of 52 feet, a length of 37 feet 10 inches, a height of 12 feet 10 inches, and a loaded weight of 17,500 pounds. Its maximum speed was 414 mph, its cruising speed was 275 mph, and it had a range of 1,100 miles. It was, to Olds, a beautiful aircraft, and as he climbed aboard in the still dark morning, he felt as comfortable in the Lightning as he did in his bed back home.

Olds eased into the cockpit and slipped on his aviator goggles. He taxied down the base runway, the last in line of the 434th to take off. As he waited for his turn, a pilot in another squadron, unable to see the runway clearly, had run off it and was stuck in mud. Only one full squadron and half of another—or about twenty-four planes—were airborne when Olds received word over the radio that his squadron was being called back, that they had been "scrubbed" from the mission. But Olds and his wingman were already taxiing down a different runway when this order came over the radio, and they decided to pretend that they didn't hear the directive to return to base. They made a split-second decision to go for it, to take off into the night and join the other P-38s already in the air.

Olds was desperate to see some action, and even though it appeared that this mission wouldn't involve any dogfights with the Germans, he still pressed forward, anxious to blow up the bridge. For weeks Olds had been studying intelligence maps that depicted key German targets. Olds was blessed with a photographic memory and these maps were etched into his mind so vividly that he felt he could find the target with his eyes closed. But now as he rolled down the runway, Olds noticed that another P-38 was disabled, this one about one thousand feet directly in front of him. Olds yelled over the radio to his wingman in another plane, "Pull up!" and they both did. Olds and his wingman cleared the P-38, but when

Olds had reached five hundred feet, he couldn't find his wingman anywhere. Olds quickly determined that he'd become disoriented in the darkness, and was hopelessly lost.

"To hell with it," thought Olds to himself. "I've got a couple five-hundred-pound bombs on me. I'm going for the damn bridge."

Without giving it a second thought, Olds set a course for his target. First he coasted out near Dover. Then on over Callais; then Soissons. Every so often Olds would hear chatter from the other squadron over his radio; they seemed confident that they knew exactly where they were going. But as Olds drew closer to the bridge, the tone of the chatter started to change. Eventually he heard one pilot utter, "Sir, we can't find the bridge"—a statement that Olds heard repeated several times. About 5 minutes before Olds thought he'd be over his target, he heard the pilots from the other squadron confess that they were lost. "Let's head back," Olds heard the pilots tell each other. Though he knew he'd be flying alone, Olds stayed the course, wanting to hit this bridge as much as Ahab wanted to bag Moby Dick.

Olds got closer. Dawn slowly began to break. There was just enough light in the sky that, down on the ground, Olds could see a river; it glistened silver-gold in the pale light. Seconds later, he could see the bridge clearly, sitting there like a cobweb waiting to be brushed aside. With a wicked smile on his face, Olds dove, his P-38 whistling through the air, and made his run over the bridge. He had a perfect view of the structure. "Could it really be *this* easy?" he thought to himself as he unleashed both of his five-hundred-pound bombs. Seconds later, he felt an explosion. Olds couldn't see it for himself, but the bridge had crumbled into the river. Mission accomplished.

As Olds cruised back across France, he enjoyed the sunrise. Purposely flying low at one hundred feet, Olds gazed down at the countryside. He saw poplar trees lining the dirt roads. He spotted old farmhouses that reminded him of a Van Gogh painting. And he noticed vineyards that were spread over rolling hills. It all seemed so peaceful, the scenery on this lazy flight home.

But then, suddenly, the tranquility of the moment was dashed. About a half mile in front of him, Olds noticed two specks, like flies on a windshield. His pulse quickened. "God, I hope they're Germans," Olds said to himself. Olds hadn't been engaged in any one-on-one combat yet, and the prospect of a fight excited him. He couldn't wait to test himself. He wanted to see for himself if all those hours that he spent flying up and down the Hudson River Valley would pay off.

The two German pilots didn't see Olds coming, so Olds was able to intercept them. When he got close enough to have a good look at the planes, he determined that they were a pair of German FW-190 fighters. When Olds jumped them from behind, he lined up the wingman in his sights, then pressed the trigger on the stick and fired his guns. As the bullets spit out of the P-38, Olds let out a primal roar, and the German wingman's plane burst into a ball of orange flames. Black smoke poured out of the engines. The pilot then bailed out, and Olds saw his parachute open in the blue morning sky as the pilot floated down into the countryside. He was still alive. "That's one," Olds said aloud.

The lead fighter, realizing that Olds was now hot on his tail, broke off. Minutes later, after some deft dogfight flying, Olds had a clean shot at the lead fighter. He plugged him as well, the shots causing a stream of smoke to shoot out from the German plane. His aircraft badly damaged, the Luftwaffe pilot bailed, and the plane crashed not more than 150 feet from the other downed plane.

After his second kill, Olds circled back over the area where the second plane had gone down. Flying slow at about one hundred feet, Olds could clearly see the smoldering wreckage in the distance as he approached. But as he neared the flaring fire of the crash, he spotted a surprising sight. The pilot had landed within two hundred yards of his aircraft in a ploughed field, and now was standing there looking up into the sky at Olds. Seeing Olds approaching, the pilot dove face down in the mud. Olds, with the slyest of grins on his face, pointed his P-38 in his direction. Just as he was about to pass over the pilot at an altitude of fifty feet, Olds pulled into a victory roll and wiggled his wings—his way of saying good-bye to his German counterpart; and serving him a dose of his dust.

Later that night at the base officers' club, as Cole Porter tunes floated up from the juke box, Olds told his flyboys about the morning's events. Knocking back a glass full of scotch, Olds' story held everyone's attention. Olds could always fill up a room just with his presence, and now his words captivated even the bartender. "This is just the beginning boys," Olds told his fellow pilots. "The biggest fights for us are yet to come."

Eleven days later, on the morning of August 25, Olds and his fighter group were once again summoned early in the morning and given their order of the day. For the first time, the 479th was told to perform a sweep to Berlin. This meant that they would sweep in front of Allied bombers. If any enemy planes got in their way, the 479th would take them out.

At the day's first light, Olds and his squadron took off from Suffolk, England, all the pilots excited at the possibility of an approaching dogfight. Once in the air, they assembled into a "spread" formation, meaning that the group covered more sky than usual. A captain now and a flight leader, Olds was flying in what was called Newcross Squadron, and he positioned his plane to the far left of the rest of the group and a thousand feet higher. For the first 30 minutes, the skies were clear. Then, a few miles south of Muritzee, Germany, Olds' number three man called him and said, "Bogies at the 10:30 level." Olds verified the enemy planes, flying at about 27,000 feet, with his own eyes and radioed Colonel Hub Zemke, the leader of the group, and said, "Highway (Zemke's call sign)—bogies, 1030, level. Headed north. Okay if I check them out?"

As Olds waited for a response, a few more enemy planes appeared in his field of view. They were headed for the bombers that the 479th was scheduled to pick up. Olds still couldn't see the Allied bombers in the distance, but he knew that they were out there, and that the Germans were going after them. Finally he heard back from Zemke.

"Newcross Blue Flight," Zemke called out to Olds. "Take it left, buster."

Olds didn't need to be told twice. He was already closing on the enemy gaggle. He and three other pilots poured the coal to their engines, pushing their throttles all the way down. But soon two of the planes experienced engine problems and had to break away. Olds' number one man, B. E. Hollister, sat on his wing, high to his right. They closed in on the enemy and soon they realized it was more than just a few bogies. Upon closer inspection, they counted fifty-five enemy aircraft, all heading for the bomber force. The bogies were several thousand feet higher than Olds and Hollister, and it appeared that not one of the Germans had spotted the Americans. In the distance, Olds could see the white contrails that streamed off the bombers' engines. Behind him he couldn't see any members of his Fighter Group; they had disappeared from eyeshot. It was two against fifty-five, but Olds and his number two man continued to close. Olds knew that the bombers wouldn't have a chance if he and Hollister retreated.

They got closer. Olds then remembered his droppable fuel tanks. To increase his speed, he released the two 165-gallon tanks that were located under his wings. As the tanks fell through the sky, Olds' P-38 leapt and accelerated. He rode up closer and closer behind the outside right member of the enemy V-formation. Olds and Hollister both prayed that the

Germans wouldn't look behind them under their bellies—they would have spotted the Americans clearly—as they prepared to fire. "Make the first shot count," Olds told Hollister, "because all hell will break loose right after that."

Olds lined up a bogie in his sight; he was so close that the wings of the enemy aircraft spanned the reticule. Olds began to squeeze the trigger on his right hand grip. But just as he did, both of his engines sputtered and quit. They coughed again, then quit a second time. "Holy shit," Olds yelled to himself. "I forgot to switch tanks!"

When Olds had jettisoned his drop tanks, he'd forgotten to switch the fuel line. Now his engines had run dry. He quickly switched the fuel line and, never taking his eye off his target, pulled the trigger and fired on the German Me 109 while in glide mode. The enemy plane quickly caught fire and dove off on his right wing. Olds saw the pilot bail.

Olds' plane was still gliding. In a matter of seconds, though, the engines started sputtering again, and caught. Olds and Hollister peeled back, unsure of how the other German 109s would react. But the Germans were at a disadvantage: They didn't know how many P-38s were attacking them or where they were coming from. This uncertainty caused them to break their formation and scuttle their plan of going after the Allied bombers.

But before the Germans turned back, several of the 109s spotted Olds and Hollister. After a few adept dives and twists and turns, Olds had another German plane lined up in his sights. He fired his 20 mm cannon and peppered the plane with .50 caliber bullets. The enemy fighter rolled, inverted, and with smoke pluming out of his cockpit, the pilot jumped just before the plane slammed into earth. It was kill number two for the day—and number four in Olds' brief World War II experience.

In the middle of this dogfight, which took place at about fifteen thousand feet, Olds had seen a German plane attacking an American P-51 Mustang thousands of feet below. The Mustang was chasing a German 109, but there was another German 109 right on his tail, firing on the American. After seeing the plane he'd just shot down crash to the ground, Olds rolled, inverted, and dove straight down to try to provide aid to the American Mustang as quickly as possible.

Seconds after Olds began to dive, however, he hit compressibility. His P-38 essentially became stuck in the dive. His controls locked and his plane shook so violently that his canopy blew off. A rush of frigid air hit Olds, taking his breath away. He was now at ten thousand feet. By five thousand feet he knew he couldn't bail out; he was going too fast. At twenty-five-hundred feet he pulled back on the control column as hard as he could, hoping that he could force the nose to come up. His plane was still shaking and the cold air continued to blast into his face. But still the nose didn't budge. Olds was plunging straight into the ground.

At one thousand feet, Olds could see that he was going to hit the ground near a farmhouse in the countryside. He continued to pull back on the throttle. At 750 feet a sign of hope: The wings began to creak. The nose slowly started to rise; the denser air was slowing the aircraft enough that it gave Olds a chance to perform a high-G pullout.

Olds was at five hundred feet, still hurtling toward the earth. He could clearly see the trees on the ground, and the leaves rustling in the wind. The nose, ever so slowly, continued to rise. Olds descended to four hundred feet. He could see, down on the ground, the field of wheat he was going to crash into. Still Olds kept pulling back on the controls, pulling so hard that he thought the controls might snap in two. At three hundred feet another sign of hope: The plane began to level off, but was it too late? Olds didn't know, but he kept pulling on the controls like he was trying to pull a lock off a safe. Finally, at an elevation of no more than fifty feet, the plane leveled, and Olds exhaled. He was lower than some of the treetops, but he was still alive.

"I could have been buried on that goddamn farm," Olds thought to himself as he made his way back to England.

With the wind blowing in his face, Olds set a course back to his air base, ready to call it a day. But minutes later, as he was still rehashing in his mind just how close he had come to crashing, gunfire flew over his right wing. "That dirty son of a bitch," Olds yelled. There was another German 109 behind him, his guns blazing. Olds immediately pulled up as hard as he could on his controls and broke left, causing his P-38 to stall, just as he'd hoped. The pilot in the Me 109 overshot Olds' plane. Olds then leveled his wings and fired, yelling as he squeezed the trigger. Almost instantly, the Me 109 burst into flames and rolled over. With black smoke spewing from its engine, the Me 109 hummed straight into the ground. And with that, Olds had five kills under his belt, officially making him an ace.

Olds still had some 450 miles to go to make it back to his base in England. The skies were now clear of Germans, and Olds, for the first time since he'd strapped himself into his cockpit this morning, let himself relax as he buzzed through the blue sky.

. . .

On his flight home, after coming so close to crashing, Olds recalled some of the good times from his life before the war. He thought about his Army teammates, and wondered where they were now. Was Romanek still alive? How about Hank Mazur, their splendid tailback? Or Ray Murphy, the captain of the '41 squad? Olds hadn't heard if any of his teammates had lost their lives in combat, but he feared some of them had.

As Olds got closer to his base in Suffolk, still flying through clear skies, Olds let himself slip into a reverie. On the grainy film of memory, he replayed the Army-Navy games of '41 and '42, recalling how special those afternoons were. Olds looked forward to the Army-Navy game of '44. Though kickoff of that game was still three months away, Olds was already thinking about how he'd listen to the game over the Armed Forces Network. For those two and a half hours, Olds figured the war would stop—at least for him.

In November of 1944 Army was ranked Number 1 in all the national polls, Navy Number 2. Unlike in '42 and '43, the issue of whether the Army-Navy game should even take place during wartime wasn't debated in the halls of Congress. But House Minority Leader William Martin did have an idea about how the game could help the war effort. He suggested that the purchase of game tickets be tied to the sale of war bonds. Weeks before kickoff President Roosevelt green-lighted the plan, and on December 2, 1944, the two teams squared off at Baltimore's Municipal Stadium.

The ticket prices for the game were the most expensive in the history of football—both college and pro. The prices ranged from $25 to more than $1,000, an unheard of amount for a ticket to any sporting event in the '40s. Before a fan would be handed a ticket, he had to show a war bond purchase receipt for each seat he was buying. Fifteen private boxes on the 50-yard line sold for $1 million apiece. When the gate was eventually tallied, the game wound up raising $58 million to repay the war debt.

The cadets traveled to Baltimore on a steamer that was escorted by five Navy destroyers, who protected the ship from German U-boats that lurked up and down the Atlantic Seaboard. They boarded the navy transport ship *Uruguay* on a Thursday morning, and they cruised into rough waters. Within an hour of leaving land most of the 2,300 cadets on board were seasick, many losing their breakfasts as they leaned over the rails and

vomited into the ocean. The Navy team, conversely, merely hopped on a bus in Annapolis and rode 30 minutes into Baltimore.

Never in the history of the Army-Navy game had the two service academies played each other with so much on the line. Army was 8–0; Navy was 6–2. The winner of the game would win the national championship. In three short years the war had helped transform the football teams at the academies into two of the nation's finest. The top high school players in the country were attracted to the academies for one of three reasons: They wanted to become commissioned officers before heading to war; they wanted to avoid the draft; or they just wanted to feel like they were playing for their country. As a result, Army and Navy were able to collect talent during the war as easily as little girls collected dolls. And by the time they faced off in 1944, it was like two all-star teams facing each other.

As in '43, Army was led by backs Felix "Doc" Blanchard and Glenn Davis, both of whom would win the Heisman Trophy (Davis in '44, Blanchard in '45) before their Army careers were done. Davis led the nation in scoring in '44 and had been on the cover of *Life*, *Time*, and *Look* magazines. With Mr. Outside and Mr. Inside paving the way, the Cadets steamrolled through their season, beating North Carolina, 46–0; Brown, 59–7; Pittsburgh, 69–7; and Villanova, 83–0. (Army lost so many footballs on extra-point kicks against Villanova that officials eventually forced the team to go for two-point conversions to conserve pigskins.)

Navy was almost as good. After starting the season slowly at 2–2, they rebounded to shut out three of four opponents and had risen to Number 2 in the AP poll. Two days before the game, Navy assistant coach Rip Miller—the man who had recruited Busik to come play for the Midshipmen five years prior—chatted with reporters as the Middies went through their final practice. "I wonder if people know what this game means to our ten million soldiers and sailors scattered all over the world," said Miller. "It means at least a short relief from the job of killing and being killed."

Indeed, as kickoff approached, soldiers and sailors all around the world huddled around shortwave radios to catch the Armed Forces Network broadcast. Busik and Kauffman, both aboard ships in the South Pacific, gathered with other officers and retold stories from their playing days. Olds was at his base in Suffolk, England, when he tuned in to the action from Baltimore. And Henry Romanek, who had recovered from his D-day injury, was preparing to kill Germans as he listened to the action in a farmhouse in France.

Before the game, wounded war veterans were escorted to seats at midfield. Many hobbled on crutches, some were pushed in wheelchairs. Ambulances filled with wounded soldiers drove along the stadium's cinder track. The ambulance would stop and then a half-dozen soldiers—some missing appendages—would struggle out and be escorted to their seats. Sitting not far from the wounded men was Anna Roosevelt, the daughter of the president, who munched on cold chicken and drank from a thermos filled with hot coffee. It was a cold, clear day in Baltimore—perfect football weather.

After the teams ran onto the field, Ted Gamble, national director of the War Finance Division of the Treasury Department, grabbed a microphone that was linked into the stadium's PA system. He first thanked everyone for coming and supporting the war effort, and then said, "Let's get on with the game—until the Navy goat and the Army mule march together into Tokyo and Berlin." The crowd screamed in approval.

On the other side of the Atlantic Ocean, sitting on a folding chair in the basement of a farmhouse in Normandy, Romanek gathered with a few other West Pointers around a short-wave radio. Five months after being shot on D-Day, Romanek was back in France. He had spent 90 days in a hospital in England recovering from his wound. Once he was healed and released, he rode into Omaha Beach in a landing craft—this time, not a single bullet was shot in his direction—and he assumed command of an engineering company in the 146th battalion. When he first walked on the sands of Omaha, Romanek still had trouble believing that so much horror had occurred right here, and that he had somehow managed to live through it. "I don't know if I'll understand why I'm still around in the world," Romanek told one of sergeants when he reached the beach. "I hope it's because God has something great in store for me."

Now sitting in a farmhouse just off the beach, Romanek regaled the other West Pointers with tales from his past, telling the men all he could remember from the '41 Army-Navy matchup. As kickoff of the '44 game neared, Romanek tuned the radio to the BBC, which was broadcasting the game in Europe. "Boy, if we had had Doc Blanchard on our team in '41, there's no way Navy would have beaten us," Romanek said to the men with excitement in his voice. "That kid is really something special." When the game kicked off, Romanek closed his eyes. He could see the action play out in his mind, in color, in three dimensions.

For the first 30 minutes of the '45 game, the action was back-and-forth. Though undermanned, Navy only trailed 7–0 at halftime. "This is

a little too close for me," Romanek said as he and the other men in the farmhouse sipped on scotch as they listened to the game. "Anything can happen when the score is this tight." Just as Romanek settled in to listen to the second half, the BBC interrupted the broadcast. "Ladies and gentlemen, we have inadvertently scheduled the wrong program," a voice said. "We now bring you a piano concerto."

"You gotta be kidding me!" Romanek yelled. "This is crazy."

Romanek wouldn't find out the score for a few days, but the Cadets did pull away late, winning 23–7. The victory gave Army its first-ever national championship. When the final whistle blew, the Cadets stormed onto the field and ripped down the goalposts. Army had lost five straight games to Navy, but now all the pent-up frustration and disappointment was washed away in one glorious victory.

Hours after the game Blaik and the Army players received a telegram from MacArthur, who was engaged in a bloody battle in the Philippines. It read:

"THE GREATEST OF ALL ARMY TEAMS—STOP—WE HAVE STOPPED THE WAR TO CELEBRATE YOUR MAGNIFICENT SUCCESS." — MACARTHUR.

20

THE END

EVERY TIME HE ROSE from his bunk, Jake Laboon rolled through hatches of the submarine like a blown-up balloon from the Macy's Thanksgiving Day parade. Aboard the U.S.S. *Peto*, he was known as the gentle giant who could blot out the sun, and he was constantly ducking and crouching whenever he rumbled from space to space. At 6' 4" and 220 pounds, Laboon had been a star blocker on the 1941 and '42 Navy football team; he mowed through opposing players like a machete through a wheat field. Against Penn in 1941, Laboon had punched a player in the face after the player had taken out Bill Busik with a cheap shot, and the sense of loyalty that drove him to take the swing was still with Laboon. He'd do anything for his brothers—a group that included everyone in the U.S. Army, Navy, and Marine Corps.

After graduating from the naval academy in June of 1943, Laboon was assigned to the *Peto*. Commissioned on November 22, 1941, in Lake Michigan, the *Peto* was the first naval submarine ever constructed on inland waters. In July of 1945 the *Peto* was on her tenth war patrol. She was eight miles off the island of Honshu, on lifeguard patrol; its mission was to pick up any downed Allied pilots. The Japanese had shore batteries set up on the beaches of Honshu, and they filled the sky with gunfire, trying to knock Allied planes out of the air. The batteries also targeted ships and submarines that got too close to the island.

At 2:39 on the afternoon of July 24, the *Peto* received a report from air cover that a "chicken"—a pilot—had gone down four miles off a beach of Honshu. No one on the *Peto* was alarmed by the report. They'd already picked up dozens of pilots without incident.

At first, the routine was like all the others. The *Peto*, which was already surfaced, motored toward the coordinates of the pilot, spotted him, then reeled him in. The entire affair took only seven minutes. But once the pilot, whose name was Lieutenant Clair, climbed aboard the sub, he urgently asked to speak with Captain Caldwell—on the double. "My wingman had to ditch closer to the beach," Clair told the captain. "Can you go after him?"

"What's his position?" asked the captain.

"I can show you exactly," replied Clair.

Grabbing a chart of the area, Clair pointed to the position of his wingman. He was only two miles off the island's coast, meaning that the *Peto* would be an enticing target to the shore batteries if she advanced to the downed pilot's position. The captain, fearing that the *Peto* would draw enemy gunfire, ordered all nonessential topside personnel to get below. The *Peto* then headed for Clair's wingman at full speed.

"He's in pretty shallow water and if those shore guns open up on us we won't be able to dive," the captain told Clair. "But we'll do our best."

When the *Peto* got within five hundred yards of the pilot, the shore batteries started hammering the water that *Peto* was now advancing into. As the submarine crawled forward, the captain told Laboon, who was standing with him on the bridge, "We can't get any closer. We'll have to put a man over the side. We'll have to pick this one up on the fly. I can't risk coming to a dead stop and making the *Peto* a sitting duck. Who's the best swimmer on board, Jake?"

"You don't have to ask for a volunteer, sir," replied Laboon. "You've already got one. I can do it."

Laboon was a transcendent athlete. Though he was known throughout the navy as a former Midshipman football player—in 1942 he earned All Big East honors as a tackle—Laboon had also excelled at lacrosse while in Annapolis. In 1943, his second year on the lacrosse team, he was a starting defenseman on Navy's national championship team and earned second-team

All-America honors. Laboon also was a deeply religious young man. He played the organ every Sunday at a local Catholic Church in Annapolis, and he was the president of the Catholic Midshipmen Organization. His friends often said he was too good to be true.

Laboon didn't hesitate to volunteer. He'd always been a strong swimmer and he was easily the strongest man on the submarine. Being so big made life difficult for Laboon on the *Peto*, but he chose to go into subs after graduating from the naval academy because he wanted to enter the war as quickly as possible. He'd considered becoming a pilot—that's what many of his buddies on the football team had done—but flight school required much more extensive training than submarine service. Like many in the naval academy, Laboon was afraid the war might end before he got a chance to fight, so he picked submarines as his specialty.

Up on the deck of the *Peto*, Laboon grabbed a rope, tied one end around his waist, and handed the other end to a sailor, telling him to hang onto it as if Laboon's life depended on it—which it did. As the *Peto* slowed, the shore batteries continued to fire in her direction. Shells splashed into the water all around him, exploding in loud thuds and sending sprays of water high into the warm South Pacific air. Before Laboon jumped into the mine-infested water, he looked up in the distance and noticed that on the shore of the island a passenger train had stopped on a bridge to let the civilians on board get a glimpse of the unfolding drama. Laboon, with the enemy shells still hurtling in his direction, then dove into the water.

He swam as quickly as he could, performing the breaststroke as he knifed through the cold and choppy water, covering a distance of about two hundred yards. When a shell landed near Laboon, he could feel the explosion thump in his chest. Laboon looked up. In the distance he could see the pilot bobbing up and down in the ocean swells. He put his head back down, and continued to plow through the water. On the submarine, the captain anxiously watched Laboon through binoculars, then looked up at the island, hoping that the Japanese wouldn't hit the sub—or Laboon.

Laboon reached the pilot. He had minor burns and wore a life jacket. He was so fatigued he could barely keep his eyes open, much less swim. As Laboon put his arms around the pilot, telling him that everything would be okay, he thought the pilot looked familiar. There was something about his face, his eyes, that he recognized. But Laboon kept that to himself—there were too many other things to think about right now. He told the pilot to wrap his hands around his waist; Laboon was going to drag him to safety.

Then he swam, paddling through the waters as furiously as he could, back to the submarine. The sailors on the other end of the rope helped reel them in, pulling on the rope fist over fist. The shore batteries continued to fire, each round sending sprays of water into the air. The shelling caused Laboon's adrenaline to surge, to rush through his blood like a stimulant, and he continued to swim, holding the pilot with one hand and pushing forward with the other.

When they finally reached the sub, Laboon was so winded he had trouble breathing. Still, he helped lift the pilot on deck, where a group of sailors grabbed the pilot's arms and carried him to safety. Laboon followed. But just as he struggled up onto the deck, another shell from the shore flew over the *Peto,* whizzing about ten yards over everyone's head. They scrambled below the deck and the sub dove.

As the *Peto* descended, Laboon caught his breath. Sitting on a chair in the wardroom, he took another long look at the pilot, who was being treated for his injuries. Laboon's thoughts traveled back in time—somewhere in his mental Rolodex, that face existed. He remembered being a kid in Pittsburgh. One morning when he was about fourteen he came to the kitchen for breakfast and saw his dad talking on the phone; he was furious. During the night the Laboon family car—it was a '31 Ford—had disappeared from their garage. The police had no idea who took it, but Laboon's father quickly figured out that their paperboy, E. P. Donnelly, had taken the car for a joy ride.

Laboon looked closely at the pilot, studying him up and down. He examined the nametag on his uniform. Improbably, it read: E. P. Donnelly.

Two weeks later, on August 15, Captain Caldwell spoke into the *Peto*'s loudspeaker. "This is the Captain. We have just received official word: The war is over."

The crew let out a collective roar. Men hugged and cried with joy. Soon the men would be going home to daughters, sons, mothers, and fathers. *The war is over.* To everyone on board, these were the four sweetest words they'd ever heard: *The war is over.*

Later that day Laboon cornered Captain Caldwell, saying he had some important news to share. "What would you say, Captain, if I told you that as soon as we get back home I am going to resign from the Navy?"

"You're kidding," replied the Captain.

"You know I'm a Catholic, don't you, Captain?"

"What's being a Catholic have to do with this?"

"Quite a lot, Captain. This patrol has made me realize something. I love the navy, but I want to become a priest."

"Are you sure this isn't a sudden impulse?"

"No, sir."

"Well, I'll be proud to approve your request."

Laboon and the captain then shook hands. The war may have been history, but Laboon was just getting started in the business of saving lives.

The morning of September 2, 1945, dawned overcast and gray in Tokyo Bay. It had been three years, eight months, and twenty-five days since Pearl Harbor had gone up in flames, a stretch of time in which 400,000 Americans had been killed in the world's second great war. But it was all coming to an end now, and Hal Kauffman had a front-row seat at the ceremony that would officially mark the conclusion of this global conflict. Kauffman was a commander now—he had been promoted from ensign shortly after the *Meredith* had sunk. And because of the courage and valor he had displayed during the *Meredith* disaster, he was invited to the U.S.S. *Missouri* to witness this final act of the war.

Less than a month earlier Kauffman had been standing aboard a destroyer as she was making her way toward Tokyo when he saw an enormous mushroom cloud swell high into the sky over the city of Hiroshima. The cloud kept expanding and expanding, growing impossibly big. The sky had been bright and clear over Hiroshima on that August morning, and it was as if a sudden storm raged over the city. Everyone on the destroyer guessed that a great bomb had blown thousands of people straight into eternity. "I'm sure glad I'm not there," Kauffman told a shipmate as they stood on the bridge and watched the cloud expand. "That must have been the biggest bomb in the world."

Forty-eight hours later a second atomic bomb was dropped on the city of Nagasaki. Now, as Kauffman waited on the deck of the U.S.S. *Missouri* for the Japanese delegation to arrive for the surrender ceremony on September 2, rage flowed into him. He couldn't stop thinking about his helpless *Meredith* shipmates; after the ship had gone down, many of his shipmates were killed by Japanese pilots strafing the sea. Kauffman imagined leaping out of his seat and breaking the Japanese foreign minister's neck as soon as he stepped on board. Like all of his Navy football teammates, the war had changed Kauffman. The gruesome reality of conflict had hardened him, making him question the inherent goodness of man. When he was at the academy, Kauffman was a daydreamer; now he only dreamed of going home. "I'd kill every goddamn Jap if I could," Kauffman told a friend a few days before the ceremony. "I know I can't, but it sure would make me feel good to get that much revenge."

Anchored about six miles offshore from the city of Yokosuka, the *Missouri* was chosen by Admiral Chester W. Nimitz as the location for the ceremony, a choice no doubt inspired by the fact that President Truman, who on April 12, 1945 was elevated from Vice President after Roosevelt died, was a Missouri native. More than one hundred ships from the Third Fleet surrounded the *Missouri*, their flags fluttering in the warm breeze. To the west, clouds obscured Mount Fujiyama. On the *Missouri*'s veranda deck an ordinary mess table had been covered with a green baize cloth, and on it rested two sets of surrender documents—one in English, one in Japanese. Two chairs stood on opposite sides of the table. Above the table, hanging on the quarterdeck bulkhead and encased in a black frame, was a tattered American flag with thirty-one stars. This was the very same flag that flew on Commodore Perry's flagship, the *Powhatan*, when he first sailed into Tokyo Bay in 1853, opening up the West's door to Japan. The flag had been at the naval academy's museum—Kauffman had seen it there frequently—but Fleet Admiral William F. Halsey had it flown in to the *Missouri* for this occasion.

Visitors began arriving on the *Missouri* at 7:00 A.M. Within an hour, all the Allied representatives, including Kauffman, were on board. At 8:00 the ship's band played the "Star Spangled Banner" while an American flag, the same one that flew over the Capitol in Washington, D.C., on December 7, 1941, was raised. The ship's superstructure was now jam-packed. More than 230 journalists from around the world were on board, and there was precious little space to stand.

At 8:43 General MacArthur arrived. Thirteen minutes later the Japanese delegation, led by Foreign Minister Mamoru Shigemitsu, walked up the gangway and was directed to the table. The ship grew silent. All eleven Japanese delegates squirmed in their uniforms and looked uncomfortable, a fact that pleased Kauffman as he watched the proceedings. Kauffman stood within a stone's throw of the Foreign Minister, so close that he could see the lines on his defeated face. Kauffman had come a long way to arrive at this moment. There was his train ride with Busik across the heart of the country when they were still teenagers. There were the football games, the grueling practices, the camaraderie of the team. It was his football experiences, Kauffman was sure, that had enabled him to survive the horrors of this war. The toughness he learned on the football field had made him a warrior on the battlefield.

At 8:59, MacArthur stepped up to several microphones a few feet from the table. One was hooked into the ship's loudspeaker system; another was piped into a worldwide radio network. MacArthur's voice was deep and serious. "It is my earnest hope, and, indeed, the hope of all mankind, that from this solemn occasion a better world shall emerge out of the blood and carnage of the past, a world dedicated to the dignity of man and the fulfillment of the most cherished wish—for freedom, tolerance, and justice."

MacArthur then motioned the Japanese delegates to step forward and sign the documents. Shigemitsu, fumbling with his silk hat, appeared confused, unsure where to sign. General Richard K. Sutherland then pointed to the appropriate line and, at 9:04, Shigemitsu signed the document and surrendered his country's sovereignty. After that MacArthur signed, carefully drawing out his signature, letter by letter, in a grand fashion. The sun was shining now, and in the bright morning light MacArthur said a few final words. "A way must now be found to preserve the peace, because science has given us war of utter destructiveness," he said. "We have had our last chance. If we do not devise some greater and more equitable system, Armageddon will be at our door."

That afternoon Kauffman went back to his ship. He was tired to the bone, and that night as he lay in his bunk he thought about his wife, of finally seeing her again. The madness was over; it was time to get back to normal life. If he was lucky, he'd make it back to the States in time to see a football game later in the fall, but not just any game: the 1945 Army-Navy clash. Maybe even some of his old buddies would be there—if they were still alive.

In his sleep that night, no ghosts rose to haunt Kauffman. On this night, for the first time in years, all of his ghosts were gone.

21

THE REUNION

THE PRESIDENT ROSE FROM his seat in his midfield box at Philadelphia's Municipal Stadium, and instantly thousands of cameras clicked and flashed to snap his photograph. He waved and smiled gloriously. It was halftime of the 1945 Army-Navy game, and President Harry S. Truman began to walk from the Army side of the stadium to Navy's. As he made his way down to the field, he shook the hands of service men and wounded war veterans who were seated along the sideline. Robin Olds and Henry Romanek were there, and they stretched out their hands like the rest. Olds and Romanek were back in the City of Brotherly Love for an Army-Navy game for the first time since November 29, 1941. It seemed like they were living in a dream, being here on this soft autumn afternoon, so far away from all the bloodshed they had witnessed in the last few years. It was like coming back to life again, being here on a football Saturday, back at this game, this town, this stadium.

On the other side of the field, also sitting on the sideline, was a smattering of navy officers, including Hal Kauffman. He was looking around for former teammates, and he realized that several were missing. Bill Busik hadn't come home yet. He was stationed on a ship just outside of

Sasebo, Japan, helping to clear the waters of mines. Busik listened to the first half of the game on the Armed Forces Network, and it made him think about his last Army-Navy game and all the guys he played with. Of the twenty-two players who started in the '41 Army-Navy game, three had been killed in war-related activities. Army's Tom Farrell, a tackle, was an infantryman who lost his life at Anzio, Italy, on February 25, 1944. One of Farrell's Cadet linemates that day in '41, guard Willard Wilson, was killed in an air training accident in Texas on July 29, 1943. And Navy tackle Bill Chewning still was listed as missing in action aboard the U.S.S. *Corvina*, a submarine that failed to return from patrol on November 30, 1943. He would never be found.

Swede Larson also was gone. Two months after the '41 Army-Navy game, Larson traveled to the Aleutians and led a regiment against the Japanese. He then stayed in the South Pacific and saw action at Tarawa, Kwajalein, and the Marshall Islands. While he was at sea, he wrote his two sons a letter. Dated May 17, 1943, the missive read, "On leaving home to join the Marines in 1917, Dad gave me the following written advice, which I have always carried with me. I pass it on to you as the best guide possible for your conduct and approach to a full life. Be cheerful. Be patient. Obey. Be a man. Trust in God and talk often."

In February of 1944 Larson was ordered to Marine Corps headquarters in Washington. He served there until the war was over. In early November of '45, after he'd already finalized his plans to attend the Army-Navy game in Philadelphia, Larson was watching a football game in Atlanta when he felt his chest tighten. He suffered a massive heart attack and died shortly after at the age of forty-six.

More than a dozen reserve players from that game in '41 also were gone—killed in action—and now, as Kauffman sat in his seat and watched the president slowly stroll toward him, he counted himself lucky that he wasn't listed among the dead. Kauffman felt that he couldn't be any further away from the war than he was at this moment. In front of him on the field a hundred police officers formed two lines, creating a lane of protection for the president as he walked across the field on this cool, sunny afternoon in Philadelphia. Army, the top-ranked team in the nation, led Navy 20–7 at halftime, but very few in the crowd of one hundred thousand cared a whit about the score. This game, more than any Army-Navy game before it, was a celebration of America. And more dignitaries turned out to see this athletic contest than any in the history of sport in the United States.

The stands were a virtual Who's Who of America. Nearly ever member of the president's cabinet was present. So were such giant figures as Generals George C. Marshall, Omar Bradley, Henry (Hap) Arnold, James Doolittle, Jacob L. Devers, and Carl Spaatz. From the Navy side in attendance were Admirals Chester W. Nimitz, William F. (Bull) Halsey, and Ernest J. King. British Air Chief Marshal Sir Arthur Tedder and Fleet Admiral Sir James F. Somerville also were in the stands, sitting in the same vicinity as hordes of senators, representatives, undersecretaries, governors, and even several mayors.

Television viewers in New York and Philadelphia were often shown shots of the dignitaries. For NBC, this was a historical game. For the first time ever, NBC televised a sporting event that took place in one city (Philadelphia) and broadcast it in another (New York). Also for the first time, NBC used its newly developed "image orthicon," a device that enabled NBC's cameras to provide viewers with close-up pictures. The cameras were frequently focused on the president, and viewers were shown several tight shots of the president's face, always caught in an ear-to-ear smile.

Though a biting wind blew around the old horseshoe stadium late in the game, very few left their seats. Led by backs Felix "Doc" Blanchard and Glenn Davis, Mr. Inside and Mr. Outside, Army won the game 32–13 to capture their second-straight national championship. Afterward Coach Blaik, with wet eyes, told reporters in the locker room, "This is the finest team we ever had at West Point, at least in my time. We've got a whale of a football team."

In five years since taking over the program, Blaik had built Army into the greatest football power in the country. The Cadets went 9–0 in '45. A few weeks after the Navy game, Doc Blanchard would win the Heisman Trophy.

Just how dominating were the Cadets? The Newspaper Enterprise Association named Army's entire starting eleven to its 1945 All-America team.

After the game, Olds and Romanek and hundreds of Army officers gathered at the Benjamin Franklin hotel for a party. Held in a ballroom that was decked out in the Army colors of black and gold, Olds and Romanek talked all night long, reliving their glory days as Cadet football players. Dressed in their sharp officer uniforms, they sipped scotch as they shared their stories. Though neither had reserved a room at the hotel, Olds and

Romanek stayed at the party until the sun rose over Philadelphia. They were just so happy to be here, and they didn't want the fun to end. For these men the Army-Navy game was a link to the old days, the prewar days, the last link that many of them had. Everyone in the room understood that today was a new day, and it was almost as if the rest of their lives began at this moment. "You know, I wouldn't have even really cared if we'd lost the game today," Romanek told Olds that night. "It just doesn't seem as important anymore."

That night a similar party was thrown for Navy officers at a ballroom in the Bellevue Stratford Hotel. There, Kauffman joined several former teammates and, like Olds and Romanek, they all reminisced about their time as Midshipmen football players. Late in the evening, after they had quit dancing the jitterbug and bebop and the music had stopped, the '41 game came alive in memory, its details rising again as the former players rehashed the events of November 29, 1941. That seemed so long ago, the teammates agreed. A war had come and gone since then, and the country had changed dramatically in those four years. But tonight, as the teammates toasted their memories and clinked their glasses, they didn't talk about the new America, or how the terrors of war had changed them. Right now all that mattered was that they were together again, safe, happy as schoolboys at recess, and able to do the one thing that each man loved almost as much as his country:

Talk about the game of their lives.

EPILOGUE

BILL BUSIK STEERED HIS CAR through the narrow streets of Annapolis, motoring closer to the spot where his college football career began. It was a brilliant Saturday afternoon in the spring of 2003, and Bill wanted to take me on a tour. We drove through the main gate at the Naval Academy, cruising past dozens of young Midshipmen dressed in their starched-white uniforms, and parked just outside of LeJeune Hall. "I think there's something inside of this building that will interest you," Bill said, winking.

Bill eased out of his car. At eighty-four years of age, his knees were aching, the result of all those hits he took years ago on the football field. He had out-lived his first wife and most of his contemporaries, but still Busik had a luminous, boyish smile. As we walked toward LeJeune Hall, he put one of his big hands on my shoulder and pointed into the distance with the other. "Right over here was where Thompson Stadium used to sit," said Bill. "They tore it down years ago. Boy, I sure had some great times there." Seeing the gleam in his eyes, I realized that Bill wasn't pointing at just any empty swath of land. This was his field of dreams.

We walked up a ramp and into LeJeune Hall. He picked up the pace.

"It's right over here," said Busik, excitedly. We stopped in front of a display case; inside was a black-and-white team photograph of the 1941 Navy squad. Bill examined the photograph like he'd just unearthed it from a time capsule, studying it closely, squinting his eyes. He told me a little bit about every young face captured in the photograph, about how this player had won a Purple Heart in World War II, how that one had died in Korea, how this one was living down the street from him in Annapolis. "This was an amazing group of guys," Bill said, his eyes moistening at all the memories. "They were some of the greatest men I ever knew."

After World War II, Busik served as Intelligence Officer on the Staff of the Commander Mine Force, Pacific Fleet, based at Sasebo, Japan, and took part in the minesweeping operations in the waters off Japan and China. In the summer of 1946 he returned to the Naval Academy to be an assistant football and basketball coach. He was then detached in February 1947 to serve as Executive Officer of the destroyer U.S.S. *Brinkley Bass*. Over the next fifteen years Busik would steadily climb the naval ranks. In June 1960 he assumed command of the U.S.S. *Mahan*. Two years later he was again called back to the Naval Academy, this time to be the school's Athletic Director, a position he held from July 1962 to August 1965. He retired from the Navy on April 1, 1971 after thirty years in the service. Today he lives with his wife in Annapolis, just a few miles from the Academy.

Over the course of several afternoons in 2003, Bill and I sat in his basement office and flipped through his old scrapbooks. The yellowed newspaper clippings would always light a fire in his mind, sparking long-forgotten tales from his time at the Academy. "You learn so many lessons in football that apply to war," said Busik as he sat in a chair with a dusty scrapbook splayed across his lap. "That's why I think everyone on my team and everyone on the Army team who played in that great game in 1941 all distinguished themselves in war. Not only were we the best athletes, which naturally makes you a good soldier, but we were also accustomed to facing adversity, accustomed to finding answers to problems that at first seem like they can't be solved.

"On the football field, you learn about hard work, perseverance, toughness, and so many other things that apply to your experience on the battlefield. We were officers in the war, but really, we were just kids in our early twenties. But most of us were put in charge of hundreds of soldiers. It's much easier to deal with that kind of responsibility once you've had the experience of playing football in front of 100,000 people. Now that's *real* pressure."

. . .

"YOU REALLY DON'T NEED TO COME HERE TODAY," said the gravelly voice over my cell phone in November 2002. "I'm nobody special. I was just a guy doing his job."

"I'll only take a few minutes of your time," I insisted. "Five minutes, Hal. That's all I need. I've driven from New York City."

"Okay, I'll buzz you through the gate when you get here," he wearily replied.

So began my introduction to Hal Kauffman in the autumn of 2002. Kauffman wasn't feeling well—he'd nearly died in a car accident a few years earlier—but he greeted me at the door of his Annapolis condominium with a friendly smile. Like Bill Busik, Hal was eighty-four years old now. His health was failing; he had trouble walking and his skin was sallow. After saying hello, we sat down in his living room. I turned on my tape recorder and nonchalantly asked, "So, what can you tell me about the war?" Five hours later, I asked my second question.

As Hal spoke, he leaned back in his chair, and, with a faraway look in his eyes, he gazed out a window at the fading afternoon light. The stories then spilled out of his mouth like water out of a hose, not in drips and drabs, but in a rapid, steady flow. The events he recalled—the cross-country train ride with Bill Busik in 1939, the Army-Navy game of 1941, the sinking of the U.S.S. *Meredith* in 1942—all happened over sixty years ago, but the most intricate details of each experience were still vividly lodged in his mind, as if it all happened five minutes ago.

When he talked about the horror of the *Meredith* sinking, his eyes began leaking tears. My heart sank. I suggested we take a break, but Kauffman kept talking through his tears, telling me how happy he was that somebody was finally asking him to tell the harrowing story of the *Meredith*. "We were helpless in the water and the Japanese still tried to kill us when they strafed the water," Hal told me as he grabbed my hand tightly and inched closer to me. "You don't ever forget something like that. Never. It's pure evil."

After the war Hal earned an advanced degree in electronic engineering at the Massachusetts Institute of Technology (MIT) in 1949. From 1954 to '58, he served in the Bureau of Ships at the Navy Department in Washington, D.C. There he was the Preliminary Design Assistant in charge of designing the U.S.S. *Enterprise*, the world's first nuclear-powered aircraft carrier. In June 1956, he was elevated to the Project Coordinator for the Contract Design work on the *Enterprise*. He retired from the Navy in

1969 and currently lives in Annapolis. His wife Lois—the girl he first saw in his 10th grade English class and was immediately enchanted by—died several years ago. Once in a while he'll see Busik, who lives just a few miles away, and they'll recall some of the good times they've spent together. Their friendship is going on sixty-five years now, and both men swear that the other one is the bravest man on the planet.

"I wasn't the biggest or the fastest or the strongest guy on the Navy football team, but I always figured I was more determined than anyone on the field," Hal says as he looks at his Naval Academy yearbook from 1941. "I basically never played, but what coach Swede Larson and all the other coaches taught me really helped me survive the *Meredith* sinking. They always demanded that you be disciplined, smart, and strong. There was always this expectation that you'd get the job done. Soon, all of us started to believe that we would get the job done, no matter what the circumstances.

"It was the same thing with the *Meredith*. I wasn't going to die. I just wasn't. I didn't even let myself think of that. I expected to get through it. So even when the sharks were attacking and men were getting eaten, I told myself that these sharks can go to hell, that I wasn't going to let them take me. I fought with all I had, and that's why I survived. I never gave in. Some guys lost it mentally. But I stayed mentally and physically strong. I think that all went back to my experience of playing football at Navy."

THE DOOR TO HIS STEAMBOAT, COLORADO, home swung open, and suddenly there he was, still big enough to cast an intimidating shadow. Robin Olds led me up a flight of stairs and into his living room, passing framed photographs that collaged the walls and told the story of his military career. Near the entry was a photograph of Olds in 1945 standing in front of a P-38, his young face looking at the camera with the intensity of a man about to do battle. Upstairs was a picture from 1967. In that black-and-white print Olds, a colonel by then, has a walrus mustache and is dressed in a flight suit. He was serving in Vietnam, where he would ultimately down four enemy MiGs, including two on May 20, 1967.

I visited Olds in July of 2002. He was eighty years old and still looked as if he was as tough as the hulking twenty-year-old Army football player he once was. Though his aching knees gave a twenty-one-gun salute of pops and creaks every time he sat down, he was in fine health. "I've had an incredibly interesting life," said Olds as he sat in a recliner in his living room, reviewing in his mind all that he had seen in his eighty years. "I wouldn't change a thing—except maybe beating Navy back in 1941. That loss still rubs me the wrong way."

After World War II ended, Olds began flying P-80 jets at March Field in California in February 1946 with the first squadron equipped to do so. Two years later he participated in the U.S. Air Force and Royal Air Force exchange program and served as Commander of the No. 1 Fighter Squadron at RAF Tangmere. When he moved to England, Olds took his new wife with him, a famous Hollywood actress named Ella Raines. Best known for her role as the heroine in the 1943 film noir *Phantom Lady*, Raines fell hard for Olds when they met on a double blind date—though they weren't set up with each other. "Ella was a movie star, a big celebrity," recalls Olds, smiling like he was just laying his eyes on Ella for the first time. "She made about twenty films and she even starred opposite John Wayne in *Tall in the Saddle*. We had a ball together in our early years. She'd join me in England and then she'd have to fly back to Hollywood for a few months to do another movie. But we parted company in 1975. It just didn't work out."

Though Olds didn't see any combat in the Korean War—from 1955 to '65 he commanded two wings in Europe—in September 1966 he assumed command of the 8th Tactical Fighter Wing at Ubon, Thailand. He was a forty-four-year-old colonel by then, but still flew with the determination of a young pilot. By the time he returned to the United States in December 1967 to become Commandant of Cadets at the U.S. Air Force Academy, Olds was credited with four confirmed kills in Vietnam. (For his career, Olds had sixteen confirmed kills—twelve in World War II and four in Vietnam.)

Olds retired from the Air Force on June 1, 1973—exactly thirty-two years and eleven months after he first reported to West Point. "It's funny how all the lessons that Earl Blaik taught us on the practice field had a real application to fighting in war," says Olds, as he steps out of his kitchen after making two peanut-butter-and-jelly sandwiches. "If I had to build an Army, I would start by selecting football players from West Point. There's no one in the world that's more prepared to fight and lead men than an Army football player. I really believe that."

THE WORDS ARE WRITTEN in a delicate, deliberate scrawl. They are dated April 5, 2004, and they came to me in a letter from Henry Romanek.

"Death has always been tough on me," wrote Romanek at age eighty-two from his home in Honolulu, Hawaii. "I've seen hundreds of our young men cut down by enemy fire—rifles, machine guns, artillery. I've listened to their cries for help; they always cry for their mothers, never for their fathers. There are rare displays of bravado before battle, but usually there is just quietness, reflection and fear of what's to come. . . . Football games can and have been very intense for me. I've witnessed many injuries on the football field, but never the death and destruction that I have seen on the battlefield."

One day in the spring of 2003, I phoned Henry Romanek, having no idea what his World War II experience had been like. After speaking to Romanek for just five minutes, I realized that I had just stumbled upon an historical treasure of a man—and a true American hero.

The next day we spoke for eight hours over the phone—the first of many conversations we would have. He detailed his childhood, his days at West Point, his interactions with Coach Red Blaik, his experiences in the Army-Navy games, and then we talked about D-day. His words and descriptions of what happened on that civilization-altering day—rehashing it moment by moment, second by second—painted such a vivid description it was as if I could see it all unfold in my mind. He broke down a few times as he spoke, but like Hal Kauffman when he talked to me about the U.S.S. *Meredith* disaster, Romanek insisted on continuing. He had a story to tell, and he wouldn't stop speaking until he was finished—simple as that.

After the war Romanek attended Cornell University and earned a master's degree in Engineering. Romanek then steadily rose through the ranks. Romanek was first assigned to the N.C. State College in Raleigh, N.C., where for three years he created and implemented a corps of engineering ROTC program. (Many of the men he trained were ultimately sent to Korea.) In 1951 he became the officer in charge of the Inter-American Geodetic Survey Project in Cuba, a position he held for three years. From 1960 to '61, he was the Battalion Commander, 307th Engineering Battalion, of the 82nd Airborne Division based in Fort Bragg, North Carolina. He retired from the Army in August 1971. His wife Betsy, the girl of his dreams that he met while in prep school, died on July 2, 1996.

"It's hard for me to dig up these old memories and talk about them, but I want to honor everyone I served with, so it's something I don't mind doing," says Romanek, sitting in his home in Honolulu with a copy of Stephen Ambrose's *D-Day* resting on his lap. "Some of the best experiences of my life involved playing football at Army. There's nothing like running onto a field and having 100,000 fans scream and cheer. The one bad thing is that I still have nightmares about how I failed to score a touchdown after I recovered a fumble in the 1941 Army-Navy game. It's amazing, but I still think about that one play all the time.

"There's no doubt that playing football under Blaik helped prepare me to fight in the war. I think the world of the American soldier. I saw more bravery on D-Day than I thought possible. Men kept charging forward even though they knew they'd likely be shot and killed. It was incredible. To this day, it makes me proud to be an American, what all of us did on that day."

SHE WAS DECKED IN RED, white, and blue bunting, and her signal flags flapped in the warm spring breeze. It was March 18, 1995, and a guided missile destroyer was being commissioned at Pier 12 at the Naval Station in Norfolk, Virginia. The ship was christened the U.S.S. *Laboon* in honor of the late Captain John Francis Laboon, known as "Father Jake" throughout the Navy. Cardinal John O'Conner of New York, one of Laboon's closest friends, told a crowd when the U.S.S. *Laboon* was launched two years earlier at Maine's Bath Iron Works, "He was both Mr. Navy and Mr. Church," the cardinal said. "He treated a seaman as respectfully as he treated an admiral. May you of the *Laboon* be assured that if Father Jake has the influence in heaven that he had in the Navy, you will always be blessed with fair winds and following seas."

Laboon, who was awarded the Silver Star for rescuing that downed pilot and pulling him safely aboard the submarine U.S.S. *Peto* in July 1945, left the Navy at the end of war and became a Jesuit Priest. In 1958, Father Laboon returned to the Navy and over the next twenty-one years he served in almost every branch of the Navy and Marine Corps. He was the first chaplain assigned to a ballistic missile submarine squadron and eventually became the first chaplain for the Polaris Submarine Program. Later he was named the Senior Catholic Chaplain at the Naval Academy. Today the Academy's Chaplain's Center is named in Laboon's honor. He passed away in 1988.

ALAN SHAPLEY RECOVERED QUICKLY from nearly being killed on the morning that the Japanese rained death down on Pearl Habor. Two days after the surprise attack, Shapley sailed to San Diego to become personnel officer to the Amphibious Corps, Pacific Fleet. During the war,

Shapley was awarded two Legion of Merits with Combat "V" for outstanding service. He went on to have a decorated career in the Marines, retiring at the rank of lieutenant general in 1962. He died May 13, 1973.

Throughout the years, Shapley stayed in contact with Earl Nightengale, the sailor who Shapley saved from drowning at Pearl Harbor—an act that earned Shapley one of the first Silver Star Medals awarded in World War II. After the war, Nightengale landed a job at the radio station KTAR in Phoenix. A few years later Nightengale went to work for CBS radio in Chicago, and he quickly became one of the most famous voices of his day. He was perhaps best known as the voice of Sky King, a radio hero that kids all around the country would tune in and listen to during the mid-50s. In 1985 Nightengale was inducted into The Radio Hall of Fame. He died in 1989.

THEY GATHERED AT THE WEST POINT cemetery on a sunny September morning in 1999, standing around a marble tombstone in the shape of a football. To pay respect to the man who remains the most successful coach in the history of Army football, forty-one of Earl "Red" Blaik's former players from the 1940s visited their old coach's grave just hours before the field at Army's Michie Stadium was renamed "Blaik Field." "Blaik was the most challenging and demanding person I ever met," said Doug Kenna, the quarterback of the '44 team, to the crowd that day in 1999. "But he was also the most caring person I ever knew."

From 1941 to 1958, Blaik led Army to a 121-33-10 record. He won two national championships, coached three Heisman Trophy winners, and to this day is Army's winningest coach, boasting a .768 winning percentage. In 1986 President Ronald Reagan awarded Blaik the Presidential Medal of Freedom. Three years later, Blaik died at the age of ninety-two.

ACKNOWLEDGMENTS

DURING THE THREE YEARS that I worked on this book, I frequently spoke to my dad over the phone, telling him the stories that I was uncovering in the course of my reporting. He was riveted by all these tales, and he told me repeatedly that he couldn't wait to read the final product. Then, on April 13, 2003, my dad passed away, unexpectedly, at age sixty-four. He served for forty-three years in the U.S. Navy, retiring at the rank of commander JAGC, and he loved his country dearly. This book is dedicated to him and all the brave Americans who lay by his side at Arlington National Cemetery in Arlington, Virginia.

Dozens of people assisted me in completing this project, but no one lent a more helpful hand than Sara Anderson, my dream of a wife. An editor at *Southern Living* magazine and a veteran of *Redbook*, Sara pored over two versions of the manuscript and her graceful, line-by-line edits improved the book immeasurably. Thanks again, SP. I also bow my head to my mother-in-law, Pat Peterson, who preaches—and practices—the gospel of proper grammar. Her keen eye caught several mistakes.

Along with thanking Bill Busik, Hal Kauffman, Robin Olds, and Henry Romanek for all the time they spent with me, I want to express my gratitude to the following former Army and Navy players who dredged their memories at my insistence: George Seip, John Stahle, John Buckner, Raymond Murphy, George Maxon, Robert Pearce, Charles Sampson, Fred Schnurr, William Leahy, Robert Day, Richard Fedon, Arthur Knox, John Hill, and Alexander Zechella. I also want to acknowledge Swede Larson Jr., Lynn Chewning, and Father Joseph Laboon for speaking with me and providing old scrapbooks and pictures of their loved ones who have passed away.

My agent, Scott Waxman, once again proved to be invaluable. Not only was he a 50-50 partner in developing the idea for this book, but he's also become a good friend. Neal Bascomb, a gifted writer and author, also helped me at the very beginning, offering insightful suggestions on structure and pace.

The enthusiasm of my editor at St. Martin's, Marc Resnick, kept this project moving along. This is the second book that I've collaborated on with Marc, and his big-picture suggestions are always right on the money. He's also become a trusted friend.

My colleagues at *Sports Illustrated* were all supportive of this project. I especially want to thank David Bauer, Sandy Rosenbush, Larry Burke, Rich O'Brien, Hank Hersch, Mark Mravic, David Sabino, and Richard Deitsch for all they've done for me over the years. Pete McEntegart, a loyal friend and fellow *SI* writer, deftly edited the manuscript; Pete's fingerprints are all over what you now hold in your hands.

Others who helped or inspired along the way are Paul Stillwell, a historian who is an expert on the U.S.S. *Arizona*; Russ McCurdy, a U.S.S. *Arizona* survivor; Keith Shirk, a World War II veteran; Sandy Padwe, an instructor at the Columbia University Graduate School of Journalism; Samantha Anderson, my nifty niece; and three people who all died too young: Captain Ray Heese of Lincoln, Nebraska; University of Nebraska Professor Theodore B. Wright of Lincoln, Nebraska; and my good friend who was also my-father-in-law, Bruce Peterson, of Holdredge, Nebraska.

My final thanks go to my mother, Rosanne Anderson. If there were a team that featured the great moms of the world, she'd be the captain.

Lars Anderson
Birmingham, Alabama
Spring 2004

BIBLIOGRAPHY

WHILE I CONSULTED hundreds of books, reference volumes, magazines, and newspaper articles, what follows is a list of sources that were most valuable.

BOOKS

Ambrose, Stephen E. *D-Day, June 6, 1944: The Climactic Battle of World War II*. New York: Touchstone Books, 1995.

Ambrose, Stephen E. *Eisenhower, Soldier and President*. New York: Simon & Schuster, 1990.

Bass, Richard T. *The Brigades of Neptunes: U.S. Army Engineer Special Brigades in Normandy*. Exeter, England: Lee Publishing, 1994.

Bealle, Morris Allison. *Gangway for Navy: The Story of Football at the United States Naval Academy, 1879 to 1950*. Washington, DC: Columbia Publishing Co., 1951.

Becton, F. Julian. *The Ship That Would Not Die*. Englewood Cliffs, NJ: Prentice-Hall Inc., 1980.

Bladwin, Hanson W. *Battles Lost and Won: Great Campaigns of World War II*. New York: Harper & Row, 1966.

Blaik, Earl "Red." *The Red Blaik Story*. New Rochelle, NY: Arlington House, 1960.

Boyne, Walter J. *Aces in Command: Fighter Pilots as Combat Leaders*. Washington, DC: Brassey's, 2001.

———. *Clash of Wings: World War II in the Air*. New York: Simon & Schuster, 1994.

Clary, Jack. *Army Vs. Navy: Seventy Years of Football Rivalry*. New York: The Ronald Press Company, 1965.

DeGregorio, William A. *The Complete Book of U.S. Presidents*. New York: Gramercy Books, 2002.

Desmond, Flower and James Reeves. *The War: 1939–1945*. London: Da Capo Press, 1960.

Glenn, Tom. *P-47 Pilots: The Fighter Bomber Boys*. Osceola, WI: MBI Publishing, 1998.

Greunke, Lowell R. *Football Rankings: College Teams in the Associated Press Poll, 1936–1984*. Jefferson, NC: McFarland, 1984.

Keegan, Jack. *The Second World War*. New York: Penguin Books, 1989.

King, Larry. *Love Stories of World War II*. New York: Crown Publishers, 2001.

Layton, Edwin, with Roger Pineau and John Costello. *And I Was There: Pearl Harbor and Midway: Breaking the Secrets*. New York: William Morrow, 1985.

McWilliams, Bill. *A Return to Glory*. Lynchburg, VA: Warwick House Publishers, 2000.

Morison, Samuel Eliot. *The Two Ocean War: A Short History of the United States Navy in the Second World War*. Boston: Little Brown, 1963.

Natkiel, Richard. *Atlas of 20th Century Warfare*. New York: W.H. Smith, 1982.

Prance, Gordon W. *At Dawn We Slept: The Untold Story of Pearl Harbor*. New York: Penguin Books, 1991.

Ryan, Cornelius. *The Longest Day: June 6, 1944*. New York: Touchstone, 1959.

Robinson, Robert. *Shipmates Forever: The Life, Death, and Men of the U.S.S.* Meredith. Self Published, 1990.

Schoor, Gene. *100 Years of Army-Navy Football*. New York: Henry Holt and Company, 1989.

Silverstone, Paul. *U.S. Warships of World War II*. Garden City: Doubleday, 1964.

Springer, Victor G., and Joy P. Gold. *Sharks in Question: The Smithsonian*

Answer Book. Washington, DC: The Smithsonian Institutue Press, 1989.

Stillwell, Paul. *Battleship* Arizona*: An Illustrated History*. Annapolis, MD: Naval Institue Press, 1991.

Van der Vat, Dan. *D-Day: The Greatest Invasion—A People's History*. London: Bloomsbury, 2003.

Wilson, Ian. *From Belfast Lough to D-Day: The U.S.S.* Texas. Bangor, Ireland: North Down Borough Council, 1994.

PERSONAL COLLECTIONS, which include scrapbooks, correspondence, newspaper articles, yearbooks, military documents, and military records.

Bob Adrian, former Navy player.
John Buckner, former Army player.
Bill Busik, former Navy player.
Lynn Chewning, brother of former Navy player Bill Chewning.
Robert Day, former Navy player.
Robert Evans, former Army player.
Richard Fedon, former Navy player.
Hal Kauffman, former Navy player.
Art Knox, former Navy player.
Joe Laboon, brother of former Navy player Jake Laboon.
Swede Larson, Jr., son of former Navy coach Swede Larson.
William Leahy, former Navy player.
Joe Maloy, nephew of former Navy player Jake Laboon.
Rip Miller, deceased Navy assistant coach, courtesy Bill Busik.
Raymond P. Murphy, former Army player.
Robin Olds, former Army player.
Henry Romanek, former Army player.
Charles Sampson, former Army player.
John Stahle, former Army player.
Fred Schnurr, former Navy player.
George Seip, former Army player.
Vito Vittucci, former Navy player.

MISCELLANEOUS

Ewing, William H. "High Dive Off the Mainmast: When the *Arizona* Blew Up, It Flung Major Alan Shapley in a Wild Arc into the Harbor." *The Honolulu Star-Bulletin*. December 12, 1961.

Videotape of 1941 Army-Navy Game, courtesy Nimitz Library Archives, United States Navel Academy.

A Guide to the United States Naval Academy. New York: The Devin-Adair Company, 1941.

Bell, Frederick J. *Condition Red: Destroyer Action in the South Pacific*. New York: Longmans, Green and Co., 1943.

Robinson, Robert. *The Life and Death of the U.S.S.* Meredith*: A Tribute to Those Who Died and A Search for Those Who Survived.* The Tin Can Sailor, January 1990.

Telander, Rick. "A Very Singular Way to Play." *Sports Illustrated*, September 20, 1982.

Tucker, Ajax. *Coral Sea Episode.* Self-published memoir concerning the sinking of the U.S.S. *Meredith*.

Time magazine, "The Long Grey Line," June 11, 1945.

Army-Navy Game Program, 1939.

Army-Navy Game Program, 1940.

Army-Navy Game Program, 1941.

Army-Navy Game Program, 1942.

Army-Navy Game Program, 1991.

The Log, Football Issue. October 3, 1941, United States Naval Academy.

Walters, John. "The Offense That Refuses to Die: Disciples of the Single Wing Loudly Sing its Praises and Seek Converts." *Sports Illustrated*, October 5, 1998.

The Dreadnought: Newsletter of the Battleship *Texas* Foundation. Volume 3, Number 2, Fall 2000. Feature article. "The *Texas* Crew Returns."

AUTHOR'S NOTE

I'LL NEVER FORGET the day I first watched an Army-Navy football game. I was only seven years old, and my father had been telling me for weeks about how special this game between the academies was. So on game day we plopped down on the couch in front of the television in our Lincoln, Nebraska, home. My dad explained to me how these young men would soon be defending our country, how they were giving the next years of their lives to America. His eyes welled up at the end of the game when the Army and Navy players met at midfield and embraced. This, he told me, was sport at its finest. Twenty-six years later, those words still ring true. This is why I wanted to write this book.

When I started working on this project in the spring of 2001, I had no idea what direction it would go. All I had in my hands were two pieces of paper—one from the sports information office at West Point, one from the sports information office at Annapolis—that listed all the telephone numbers of the surviving members of the 1941 Army and Navy football squads. But when I tracked down Bill Busik, Hal Kauffman, Robin Olds, and Henry Romanek, I knew I had stumbled upon a special story.

More than sixty years have passed since the main events of this book occurred. In the course of researching this project, I consulted hundreds of published works, conducted hours of personal interviews, and examined dozens of personal materials such as diaries and scrapbooks provided by all the main characters. But still, discrepancies did emerge. In these cases, I analyzed all the relevant material and went with what I believed to be the most accurate information. Nonetheless, if there are any errors in this book, they are solely my responsibility.

A word about Bill Busik, Hal Kauffman, Robin Olds, and Henry Romanek: I owe a great debt to these four American heroes. They spent countless hours with me—both in person and over the phone—reliving the good as well as the terrible times from their youth. Their generosity was heart warming, as all four of these men treated me like I was a curious grandson. Without their assistance, this book would not have been possible. So thank you, Bill, Hal, Robin, and Henry. This is not my book; this is your book.

AUTOMATION AND THE WORKER

A Study of Social Change in Power Plants

AUTOMATION AND THE WORKER

A Study of Social Change in Power Plants

FLOYD C. MANN and L. RICHARD HOFFMAN

*Survey Research Center
and Department of Psychology,
The University of Michigan*

A HOLT—DRYDEN BOOK

Henry Holt and Company, New York

Library of Congress Catalog Card Number: 60-7194

25451-0110

Printed in the United States of America

To John E. Sparling

PREFACE AND ACKNOWLEDGMENTS

This volume reports one of a series of studies in the broad area of organizational change. As a part of our research during the last ten years in the Organizational Behavior and Organizational Change Programs of the Survey Research Center of the Institute for Social Research, at the University of Michigan, we have studied the effects of various types of change in large-scale organizations. These include the effects of different procedures for increasing the utilization of research findings, of raising or lowering the level of autonomy within an organization, of executive succession, and of human relations training programs. In some of these studies we have both introduced the change ourselves and attempted to measure the effects of the change processes; in others the changes were introduced by the organization and we concentrated on determining their effects on the organization and its members. The present study—an investigation of the social and psychological effects of a new form of technology, automation—falls in the latter class. An examination of the impact of technological change on work systems extends the scope of our research on organizational change.

In an area where much speculation has been offered, this study was designed to provide some first systematically substantiated facts about the probable effects of automation on workers and organizations. When the research was initiated, it was just beginning to become clear that major technological changes were scheduled for our factories and offices of the near future. These reports about how new technologies were going to revolutionize the relationship between the worker and his job raised a number of questions for those of us who had already done intensive, quantitative studies of traditional assembly line manufacturing processes in plants making automobiles, tractors and earth-moving equipment, and washing machines. Recognizing that these assembly line processes were only intermediate between handicraft and automated production systems, we wanted to begin to collect facts about the impact of the new processes. We decided to obtain our first impressions about the character and the effect of these predicted changes by studying a type of continuous process plant which was already in existence and with which our society already had a good deal of experience—power plants. The introduction to the research proposal that was presented to the company and the union to obtain their support for the project states in broad terms the purpose we had in initiating it.

A Study of Power Plants

> In less than fifty years scientific and technological developments have transformed the industrial and social life of the United States. Machines have increased our productivity per man hour, created a higher level of living, and revolutionized the working environment of man. This environment of machines has demanded new methods of organizing men and work. Many of our new methods have a large number of unsolved human relations problems implicit within them. The mass production assembly line requiring little skill or ingenuity but a close adherence to a

> highly prescribed repetitive pattern of behavior is an illustration. On the other hand, highly automatic complex production processes probably make different requirements of men. We need to know a good deal more than we do today about the effect that such processes have on workers, and the effect that workers can have on these production processes.
>
> The patterns of man-machine relationships which are evolving in the most modern power plants today are indicative of things to come in American industry tomorrow. The number of men necessary to operate these intricate systems of machines is steadily decreasing, but the men who are needed must be more thoroughly trained technicians and engineers. Power plant operations appear to be a prototype of the fully automatic factory of tomorrow in terms of continuity of operation and the high percentage of maintenance, inspection, and "dial-watching" jobs. They probably contain the different types of human relations problems with which management and unions will have to learn to deal in future decades.

After the company and the union had accepted this proposal, we chose two of the company's power plants—one the most modern in the United States, the other a somewhat older one having an almost equally large electric output—as research sites for studying the possible effects of change in automated plants.

That the company was willing to support financially a project that had such long-range research implications and that the union was also willing to ask its membership to work with us toward this goal is indicative of the new type of relationship which was evolving between the company, the union, and our research group—that is, the use of the company as an organizational research laboratory. For many social scientists the laboratory is an organization itself. Many of the significant problems that our society faces today can be studied only in the setting of an on-going, functioning organization. When we first thought that power plants might serve as prototypes of auto-

mated plants, the idea of a mutually advantageous relationship between a social science group studying problems of organization and a company offering itself as a laboratory was just beginning to emerge. Since we had previously worked together for a number of years, there was a mutual respect for each other's problems and interests. It was on this firm foundation of tolerance for exploring each other's ideas that this project was finally accepted and launched.

It is scarcely necessary to state that the researchers are deeply indebted to the president, the principal executives, and managers of the company in which this study was done. Our policy of preserving the anonymity of the organizations in which we do research precludes us from indicating the support given us by each person from the president down through nine levels of organization to the men in the plants. While they must remain anonymous, each in his own way has contributed to the study by intellectual interest, actual participation, or encouragement. The book is dedicated to one of this group who early caught the excitement of trying to look ahead a bit to see what individual and organizational problems the future held, and who gave the project day-to-day support at crucial times, but who died before this written account of our findings was published.

The officers of the union, who must also remain anonymous, contributed to our work by helping us gain acceptance among the men and the stewards at the local plant level, and by meeting with us both individually and jointly with company personnel to discuss, first, specific study objectives and, later, the findings.

We are especially grateful to the men, the foremen, and the top management of the two plants studied. Without their willingness to talk with us about their aspirations and disappointments both in the plant and in their lives in general, and without their willingness to spend several hours filling out questionnaires, there could not, of course, have been a study. The support given us by the superintendent and the top organizational families in

each of the plants could not have been better—from the beginning of the study through to the interpretation and intensive reviews of the findings preparatory to their use in improving employee relations in the plants. We find that our friendships with a number of these men and their families have continued long past the completion of the study.

More recently both management and union officials have given of their time and energy to read an early draft of this book. Their suggestions for clarification and help in locating materials for the volume long after the study was complete are deeply appreciated.

Just as a number of people within the company and the union contributed to this study, so did a number of people within our research institute. In developing the study, analyzing the findings, and preparing them for publication we have probably drawn heavily, and sometimes unconsciously, upon the ideas of our colleagues in Ann Arbor and many other social scientists with whom we share a continuing interest in this field. Our friends and colleagues in the Institute and in the Psychology Department of the university not only contributed helpful suggestions and heard us out in many informal discussions, but also assisted by carrying the administrative load at times while we were writing.

Editors, secretaries, and families each in their own ways know the cost of a research project. Vera McWilliams worked closely with us to improve the draft of this book. Wanda Carroll not only typed and retyped the manuscript, but managed the work calendar so that we could find time to prepare more for her to type. Our wives arranged family calendars so that we could work together at times when we should have been performing other functions required by our family roles.

Finally, a word needs to be said about the way in which several different researchers have combined their talents and part of their professional lives to produce this book. The original con-

ception of the study, its design and continuing administrative direction have been the responsibility of Floyd Mann. The initial field work in the plants, the delineation of specific research objectives, and the formulation of questions to operationalize concepts were handled by James K. Dent (Study Director), Thomas Lough (Assistant Study Director), and Floyd Mann. The latter two pretested and personally collected the data.

With a change in personal academic plans of Dent and Lough, Richard Hoffman assumed responsibility for first processing the large quantity of material that had been collected and then directing the analysis of these data. He was assisted by Odile Benoit, now at the Institute des Sciences Sociales du Travail at the Université de Paris. His was the arduous task of fitting the pieces of the analyses together into a coherent, meaningful volume with text and tables. The work on the final drafts of the volume was shared by the two principal investigators, who now find that the working through of ideas and development of insights which have come from this collaboration was so complete that it is impossible to identify a particular idea as contributed by one or the other of us, or by other colleagues.

F. C. M.
L. R. H.

Ann Arbor, Michigan
January, 1960

CONTENTS

AUTOMATION AND THE WORKER

A Study of Social Change in Power Plants

Chapter 1

AN APPROACH TO AUTOMATION

Scientific and technological developments are transforming our industrial life at an ever-increasing pace. Scientific breakthroughs follow one another in rapid fashion, laying the basis for new and improved production processes. Applications of each technological innovation are no more than engineered and put into operation than they are made obsolescent by new developments of the same order. A wide range of forces in our society is maintaining and accelerating the pressures for such scientific and technical progress. These vary from the demand for military innovation to social pressures to increase the general standard of living. Changes in technology have basic effects on the institutions within a society, but particularly on the organization of the work and the life of the individual. As the rate of change increases, it becomes essential to be able to identify the effect of these changes in terms of their social benefit and social cost to society in general and to its individual members. Based on such knowledge, plans can be formulated, decisions can be made, and

new alternatives can be developed to enhance the positive features of technological advances and to forestall or mitigate the negative social consequences.

Automation—The Most Recent Technological Advance

There has been tremendous concern by businessmen, labor leaders, and congressmen about the most recent and dramatic advances in technology—those identified as automation.

The automobile and petroleum industries provide two good illustrations of the different forms that automation may take. Work-feeding and material-handling devices have been designed and installed in automobile plants. These mechanically move and position engine blocks before machine tools for the simultaneous boring of a large number of holes. Previously the holes had been drilled serially, with the block being transferred between stations by conveyers and being positioned at each station by a different worker. Petroleum refining is now a process in which there is a continuous flow from crude oil to marketable products. Feedback controls are used to control automatically the temperature and pressure of the crude oil as the proper amount and flow of powdered catalyst is introduced during the chemical cracking process to produce the desired kinds of products in the right amount. The present variety of petroleum products could not have been manufactured through the use of only the earlier thermal cracking methods.

It is clear from the multitude of articles in the literature, the proliferation of speeches at management conferences, and the hours of testimony before congressional committees that there is no agreement on a single manufacturing process or mechanical complex called automation. There is no doubt, however, that everyone recognizes that we are entering a new technological era, an era in which drastic changes are being made

in our world of work. To cope with these changes without being unduly fearful or optimistic, it is imperative to replace speculation with empirical research. The present study was designed to provide an initial empirical exploration into the social effects of automation on the worker in the plant.

Characteristics of Automation

The most careful descriptions of the new automated processes have stressed these basic characteristics: (1) more frequent use of automatic equipment; (2) greater mechanization of transfer operations and combination of work units; (3) the use of multiple, closed-loop feedback systems as controls to achieve greater unity of all parts of the production process. The last of these provides an example of an industrial application of a breakthrough in basic science. New discoveries in the fields of communication and self-regulating mechanisms have given impetus to the rethinking of entire production processes and have resulted in the development of the continuous, interconnected and self-regulating processes which have reached their most advanced form in the chemical and petroleum industries.[1]

It appears that each industry has progressed technologically in different ways according to the nature of the product, managements' willingness to commit capital, the size of the market, and any of a number of other considerations. In one "automated" plant, emphasis on transfer of material has resulted in the introduction of automatic, mechanized material-handling devices. In another "automated" plant, the continuous flow of the product requires the use of automatic feedback systems to control the quality of the final product. In still other plants we are likely to find different types and combinations of automatic equipment.

[1] Ayres, E., "An Automatic Chemical Plant," in *Automatic Control,* edited by the Editors of *Scientific American.* New York: Simon and Schuster, 1955.

While one characteristic of automation may predominate in a newly designed plant, it is probable that examples of the other characteristics will also be present.

The new plants incorporating these changes require a greater capital investment per employee—an increase in the proportion of fixed costs relative to labor costs. This heavy investment in equipment has two corollary effects. First of all, in order to spread the fixed costs over more units of production, automated manufacturing will tend to operate two and even three shifts per day. Around-the-clock operation means shift work for a greater proportion of the working population. Secondly, the almost complete unity of the production process under this new technology means that the incapacitation of one machine stops the entire system. Maintenance of this type of system thus becomes a more important problem. A preventive rather than a "crash-repair" basis of maintenance is required to avoid the tremendous cost of shutdowns.

Approaches to the Study of Automation

Automation as a pure form of technology can rarely be found at this time. The lack of pure cases makes it difficult to anticipate all the effects automation may have in this new technological era. It becomes necessary then to attempt to identify common aspects among various forms of the new technology, and to examine the effects which these common factors might be expected to produce.

Even after limiting the objectives of a study to the effects of common factors in technology the aim of our research is still not sufficiently circumscribed. We have noted the impact of previous technological changes on our entire society and on subsystems within society. Thus proper areas for study might be automation's effects on the geographical distribution of industry

or on the class structure or on the displacement of workers. There have been a few studies and a good deal of speculation in these areas. One authority states that automation should permit a greater decentralization of industry, a more effective utilization of space and human effort, and a "greater emphasis on service activities, recreation, education, welfare and other such activities.[2] Another contends automation will have rather drastic effects on the older workers in our population both by making the actual physical labor of work more possible through the reduction of physical effort and by changing the nature of the work so that a great deal of retraining will be necessary for which the older worker is ill suited.[3] Norbert Wiener, in an early book, had some rather dire predictions about the drastic displacement and unemployment effects of automation which would ultimately cause greater economic depression than existed in the 1930's.[4]

Another way of studying automation is to compare various situations in which automatic technology has been introduced and determine the similarities and differences in their operation. A notable effort in this direction was made in James Bright's survey of thirteen "automatic production systems" in a variety of industries.[5] He describes the changes and problems which occur in such areas of concern to management as maintenance cost, impact on the labor force, and personnel problems. Although the examination of a variety of situations is commendable, data presented on a qualitatively selected, rather than a systematic, basis denies the reader the opportunity to evaluate the extent to which the changes occurred. Bright also fails to help us

[2] Osborn, D. G., "Automation in Industry—A Geographical Consideration," *Journal of the American Institute of Planners,* Fall 1953.

[3] Stern, James, "Implications of Automation." Paper read at the American Association of Advancement of Science, Atlanta, Ga., December 1955.

[4] Wiener, Norbert, *The Human Use of Human Beings.* Boston: Houghton Mifflin Co., 1950.

[5] Bright, James, *Automation and Management.* Boston: Division of Research, Harvard Business School, 1958.

anticipate which effects we might expect to find in any new technological situation with which we might become familiar.

A third way to approach automation is in terms of its effect on the immediate work situation into which it is introduced and on the people employed there. In the last few years a number of case studies have been recorded describing the introduction of automation into a number of manufacturing and office settings. In this connection the work of the Bureau of Labor Statistics[6] is representative. Their studies in a bakery, an electronic equipment manufacturer, an oil refinery, and an airline ticket reservation system present quantitative data on the job and salary structures of these organizations. N. F. Craig observed the conversion of an office to an electronic accounting system and presented his findings as a case study.[7] He describes the various incidents which occurred during the conversion period and which he feels will probably occur in other attempts to introduce automation. Charles Walker describes the transition from an old to a new semiautomatic steel pipe mill.[8] The employees in this mill were asked systematically about such topics as the characteristics of the work, pay and incentives, and group relations. Each aspect of the job situation is contrasted at several points in the transition process to determine how the men's perceptions and feelings changed.

Although, as Craig says in his introduction, these case

[6] Studies of Automatic Technology: *The Introduction of an Electronic Computer in a Large Insurance Company*. Bureau of Labor Statistics, 1955, 19 pp.

Studies of Automatic Technology: *A Case Study of an Automatic Airline System*. Bureau of Labor Statistics, Report No. 137, 1958, 21 pp.

Studies of Automatic Technology: *A Case Study of a Company Manufacturing Electronic Equipment*. Bureau of Labor Statistics, 1955, 15 pp.

Studies of Automatic Technology: *A Case Study of a Large Mechanized Bakery*. Bureau of Labor Statistics, 1956, 26 pp.

Studies of Automatic Technology: *A Case Study of a Modernized Petroleum Refinery*. Bureau of Labor Statistics, 1958, 44 pp.

[7] Craig, N. F., *Administering a Conversion to Electronic Accounting*. Cambridge, Mass.: Riverside Press, 1955.

[8] Walker, C., *Toward the Automatic Factory*. New York: Harper and Brothers, 1958.

studies are useful in giving "some insights into the things which were important in the particular situation," they lack generalizability. Also, because they are selective in the events they report, in the people they interview, and in the data they quote, it is difficult to know how much credence to give to the facts described as important in these situations.

Our present study is within the third area. It deals with the impact of automation on the organization of work and on the work life of the people involved. The study, conducted in the latter part of 1954, was designed to explore one situation in a systematic, quantitative fashion to isolate a number of dimensions of technological change which might be useful in analyzing other, future, change situations. We attempted to identify and measure certain of the intraorganizational factors in the introduction of automation and to describe how these factors operated in one "automated" plant. In the succeeding chapters we shall describe the research site and the methods and limitations of the study, give an overall view of the changes which occurred, and discuss the data relevant to job changes, shift work, and supervisory attitudes and behaviors. In the concluding chapter we shall summarize the findings and offer suggestions for introducing and utilizing fully the advantages of automated technology, as well as point the direction for research needed to extend our knowledge of changes in industrial organizations.

Chapter 2

STUDY SETTING AND DESIGN

Automation in its fullest sense is only beginning to get underway in American industry. There are, however, a few continuous-process industries which have long employed some of the principal characteristics of this new development. One of these is the electric light and power industry, where automatic devices for both handling and controlling equipment have been increasingly adopted in recent years. Since early 1950 many recent innovations in the design of power producing equipment have been incorporated into a succession of newly built electric power plants. By introducing these latest innovations in its equipment, each new power plant exhibits more of the characteristics of automation—that is, increased mechanization, integration of function, and more frequent use of automatic equipment and feedback control devices.

One of these power plants became the primary research site for our exploratory investigation of certain effects of this type of technological change on an organization and its personnel. We undertook this study with the realization that it would provide few definitive results, but we hoped that it would sharpen our society's understanding of the shape of things to come and

give both management and labor a better insight into some of the possible effects of automation. We also expected that it would help point the direction for future research in other automated situations.

The new power plant in which we conducted this study was located in a small rural town about fifty miles from the company's general offices in a large city. It was built in response to an increasing demand for electric power. It and four other power plants of the company served one million customers over a wide geographical area through an interconnected electrical transmission system. One of these four older plants, one which is located in the heart of the city's most heavily industrialized section, was selected for comparison to investigate the ways in which the production technology of the new plant affected its organization and workers. We have called the new plant "Advance," in deference to its advanced design, while the older plant is referred to as "Stand," foretelling its increasing role as a standby plant in the company system.

The Technology of Advance and Stand

A brief description of the technology of the two power plants and of the major engineering changes in the new plant will provide the background for understanding the individual and organizational changes brought about by automation.

The process of electric power production was basically the same in the two plants—the continuous conversion of energy from coal into electric power through a system of boilers and turbine generators. A conveyer system carried coal from the yard into bunkers at the top of the plant. This coal was then fed into furnaces to be burned. Preheated water was pumped into boilers which surrounded these furnaces and converted into steam at extremely high pressures and superheated to high tem-

peratures. The steam thus produced drove turbine generators at tremendous speeds, producing electricity. This electricity was then passed through a complicated arrangement of relays, breakers, and transformers controlled by an electrical switchboard and tied into the transmission system of the utility.

By virtue of the engineering developments incorporated in the design of Advance, the new plant, its total capacity was 664,000 kilowatts at the time of our investigation. Its overall thermal efficiency—the conversion of energy from coal to electricity—was approximately 38 percent. In contrast, the capacity of Stand, the older plant, was 515,000 kilowatts, with an overall thermal efficiency of only 30 percent. The 20 percent greater capacity of Advance was produced, moreover, by only four boiler-turbine-generator "units," whereas the ouput of Stand was produced by a more complex system of fifteen boilers and nine turbine generators.

The greater capacity and efficiency of Advance were the result of changes in the design and capacity of boiler, turbine, and generator equipment, the relationships among machines, the pressure and temperature of steam used, and the kinds, number, and location of controls employed in the various parts of the system. The description of each of these two plants will illustrate the similarities and differences between them and emphasize those differences which affected the organization and the people of the new plant.

The Old Plant: Stand

In many respects, Stand was really quite new. It was originally built in 1915 but was modernized in 1936 and 1951. The addition in 1951 of equipment operating under high steam pressure made this plant one of the ten largest steam power plants in the country. Its fifteen boilers and nine turbine generators were located in two major sections of the main plant building. Four

boilers and two turbine generators with a combined capacity of 240,000 kilowatts comprised the "high pressure side," and eleven boilers and seven turbine generators with capacities ranging from 30,000 to 60,000 kilowatts made up the "low pressure side." The steam pressure used to operate the low pressure turbine generators ranged from 200 to 600 pounds per square inch (psi), and the high pressure side operated at 1350 psi. The temperature of the steam furnished by the low pressure boilers ranged from 640°F to 825°F, and the steam temperature from the high pressure boilers was 950°F. Photographically, the aerial view of Stand (follows p. 16) shows the coal yards in the foreground, the seven stacks of the low pressure side of the plant, and the new high pressure addition with two stacks; just behind the low pressure side is the electrical switching station. This plant was manned by 300 men at the time of our study: 246 nonsupervisory workers, 44 foremen, and 10 members of the top plant staff. These men worked in about 20 separate locations spread throughout the 60 acres of plant grounds. The greatest concentration of workers was in the low pressure side of the plant.

The major production operations at Stand—those involving the boilers, turbines, and electrical switching—were functionally separated, but there were common steam and water intakes and exhausts for the boiler and turbine equipment. It is this latter characteristic—common sources—that distinguishes this older, low pressure plant. The water which each boiler converted into steam was drawn from a common supply (a "ring header") for all the plant's boilers. The steam produced by each boiler was then routed into a common steam main (the "header") from which it was directed into specific turbine generators. The electricity produced by the turbine generators was handled similarly—that is, as a total plant product rather than as a product of individual turbine generators.

The use of the header system in Stand permitted maximum

flexibility in interconnecting boiler and turbine generator operations. When operating at less than full load, the common steam supply permitted the use of the most efficient of the twelve boilers to drive the most efficient turbines. This flexibility in production methods will be especially advantageous as the plant becomes more and more a standby rather than a straight production plant.

The principal locations and duties of the personnel in the major plant buildings can be visualized by following the production process from the coal in the yards to electricity in the company's transmission system. This step-by-step description will concentrate primarily on the low pressure side of Stand. The high pressure side represented an intermediate stage of technological progress between the low pressure side of Stand and the four units at Advance. We shall indicate any differences between the process on the high pressure side and that on the low pressure side.

The coal was carried from the coal piles in the yards by conveyer belts to bunkers at the top of the power plant, nine stories up. The personnel handling the coal (coal handlers) pushed the coal into reclaiming hoppers in the coal yards with bulldozers and large diesel coal scrapers. They also monitored the flow of coal from the hoppers through the coal breakers and transfer houses via elevating conveyer belt systems on up into the bunkers and the plant itself.

At this stage the firemen took over, and on the low pressure side the crushed coal was fed from the bunkers into the boiler furnaces by stoker rams. The firemen manually adjusted the speed of these stoker rams to compensate for changes in the quality and quantity of furnace fires. They were responsible for the operation of the forced- and induced-draft fans which respectively forced the air through the fire beds of the furnaces and eliminated the waste combustion gases. The firemen controlled by hand the operations of the stoker rams and the two

fans to produce efficient combustion and transfer of heat to the water, thus converting it into steam. They were also responsible for the maintenance of steam temperature, and through the use of dampers they could raise or lower the temperature of the steam to get the most efficient operation. Thus, in Stand the control of the steam temperature and steam pressure was a manual operation, its efficiency depending on the skill and judgment of the firemen. Helping them in these tasks were assistant firemen, water tenders, fan operators, and flue blower-ash handlers, in that order of descending skill. On the high pressure side, pulverized coal was automatically combined with air and injected into the furnaces to be burned. This was the same procedure as at Advance.

The steam from the boilers on the low pressure side entered a common supply at the top of the plant from which it plunged down to drive the turbines. The turbine generators were located on the third floor in a huge room which was separated from the boiler room by thick masonry walls. The turbine operators 1st worked in the turbine room. They were responsible for synchronizing the turbine generators going into production and for taking them off the line when they were no longer needed. Assisting them in this task and in checking the turbines to see that they were operating properly were the turbine room helpers.

After its energy had been used to drive the turbines, the steam was carried to the condenser room, two floors below, where it was converted to water once more. Before it reentered the boilers, where it was converted into steam again, the water passed through a series of stage heaters which raised its temperature. On the high pressure side, the spent steam from the high pressure turbines was redirected through the furnaces and reheated to drive a lower pressure turbine before it cooled to liquid form once more. Responsibility for the various heaters and pumps which recycled this heated water to the boilers be-

longed to the auxiliary operators. In addition, when a turbine was being taken off or put on the line, the auxiliary operators had to work in close coordination with the turbine operators 1st.

The total electric product of all the turbine generators was distributed by the men in Stand's electrical switchboard station, which was located in a building apart from the main plant. In this station the switchboard operators 1st and 2nd and the assistant switchboard operators coordinated the load produced by Stand's generators to the demands of the entire system. They were in constant telephone contact with both the systems supervisor in the downtown office and the operators in the boiler and turbine rooms. They were also responsible for the supervision of the "mat," the network of transmission lines, transformers, and circuit breakers located just outside the plant, from which the electric power was sent out through the surrounding area.

Groups of men in Stand were physically isolated from one another by the massive walls dividing the various production functions and by the location of the machine controls near the equipment they governed. Communication between the various control stations usually was by telephone, with informal contacts among the various operating groups occurring relatively infrequently. The physical separation of the three principal operating areas militated against the establishment of close social relationships among the men.

The New Plant: Advance

Advance was one of the most modern steam power plants in the United States at the time we were studying it. Each of its four boiler-turbine-generator units had a capacity of 166,000 kilowatts. The boilers were designed to operate under a steam pressure of 2050 psi at a temperature of 1000°F. The greater capacity, pressure, and temperature, and the lower heat rate of these units as compared with those in Stand resulted from major

advances in the design of production equipment since the relatively recent construction of the high pressure side of Stand. The overall increased capacity and efficiency of Advance derived not only from the ability of its equipment to operate at high steam pressures and temperatures but from the incorporation of many elaborate automatic feedback controls and other mechanical devices, and from the improved design of its production system.

The personnel complement of the new plant consisted of 171 men: 140 nonsupervisory workers, 21 foremen and general foremen, and 10 top plant management.

Advance operated on a unit system of production rather than the header system employed at Stand. A "unit" in Advance comprised a boiler and its furnace, a turbine generator, and the unit's own electrical switching system, with a direct one-to-one relationship between the boiler and its turbine generator. This unit system is one example of the integration of production functions which we previously identified as an important aspect of automation.

The substitution of the unit system for the header system resulted in a number of changes which directly affected the work of the employees in Advance. Inseparable from the effects of this integration of functions were those stemming from the introduction of another major characteristic of automation—feedback control systems. Four major feedback control systems had been incorporated into the design of Advance. These four systems were important to us because some of them performed functions that were previously the direct responsibility of operating personnel in the low pressure sides of older plants like Stand.

- One of these controls regulated the mixture of pulverized coal and air and the rate at which this mixture was fed into the boiler furnace. Variations in the pressure of the steam going from the boiler to the turbine automatically caused changes in the rate at which the coal mixture was being fed.

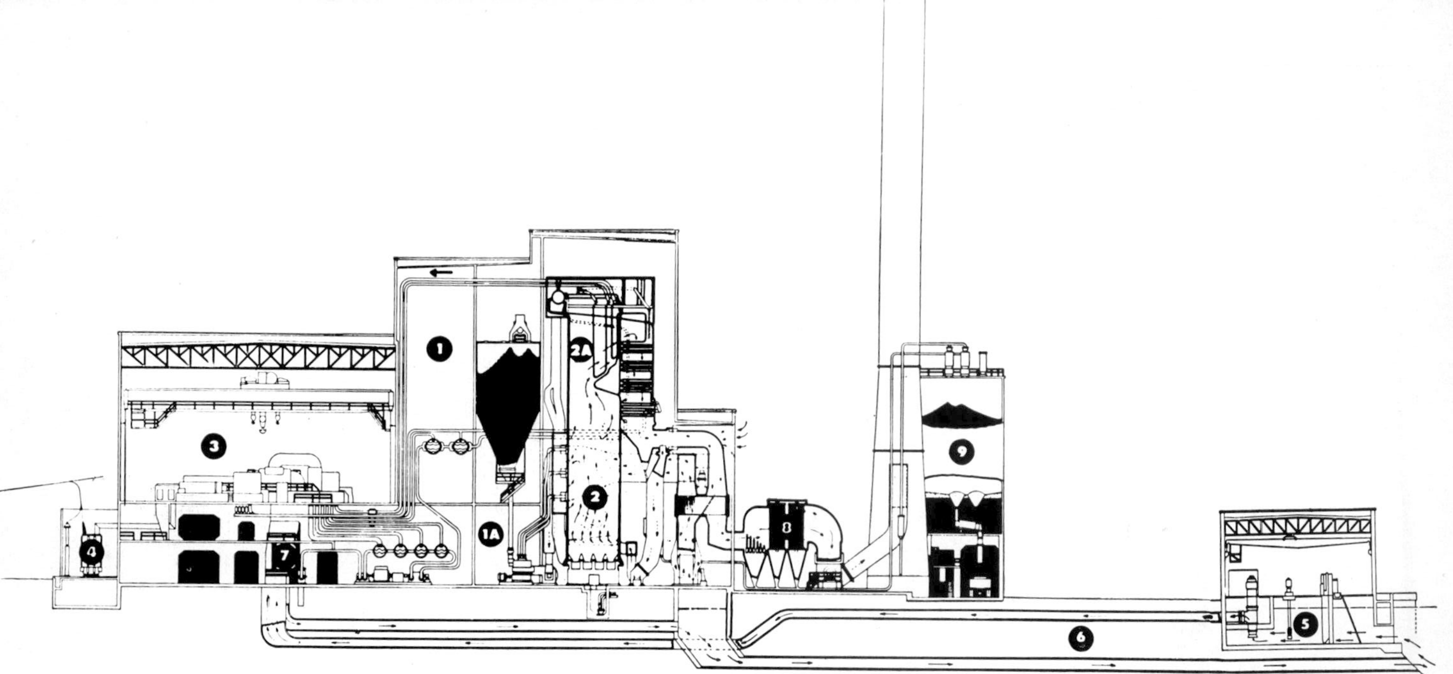

Coal to Kilowatts at Advance. Coal bunkers (**1**) receive coal by conveyor belt from breaker house. Ground to face-powder fineness in pulverizers (**1A**), the coal is blown into furnaces (**2**) and burned, turning water in the boiler tubes (**2A**) into steam at 1000°F and 2000 pounds pressure per square inch. The steam is piped to turbine generators (**3**) where it first passes through the high pressure unit and is sent back to the boiler for reheating. It then returns and spins the turbine in the associated low pressure unit. After use the steam is condensed and returned as water to the boiler to start the cycle over again. An Advance generator produces electricity at 15,500 volts, which is increased to 120,000 by transformers (**4**). Water to condense the steam enters from the river at pump-and-screen house (**5**) and is carried by steel and concrete tubes (**6**) to the condenser (**7**) where it cools the exhaust steam, turning it back into water for reuse in the boilers. The condenser water, its cooling job done, is returned to the river. Dust collectors (**8**) gather "fly ash" given off by burning coal. It is stored in silos (**9**) until disposed of by sale to concrete contractors and others or used to fill waste land.

Above, Stand and its industrial setting. **Below**, Advance and its rural setting.

Above, Stand and its coal-handling system. **Below,** the Advance power plant.

Above, electrical control console at Stand. **Below,** electrical control console for total plant at Advance.

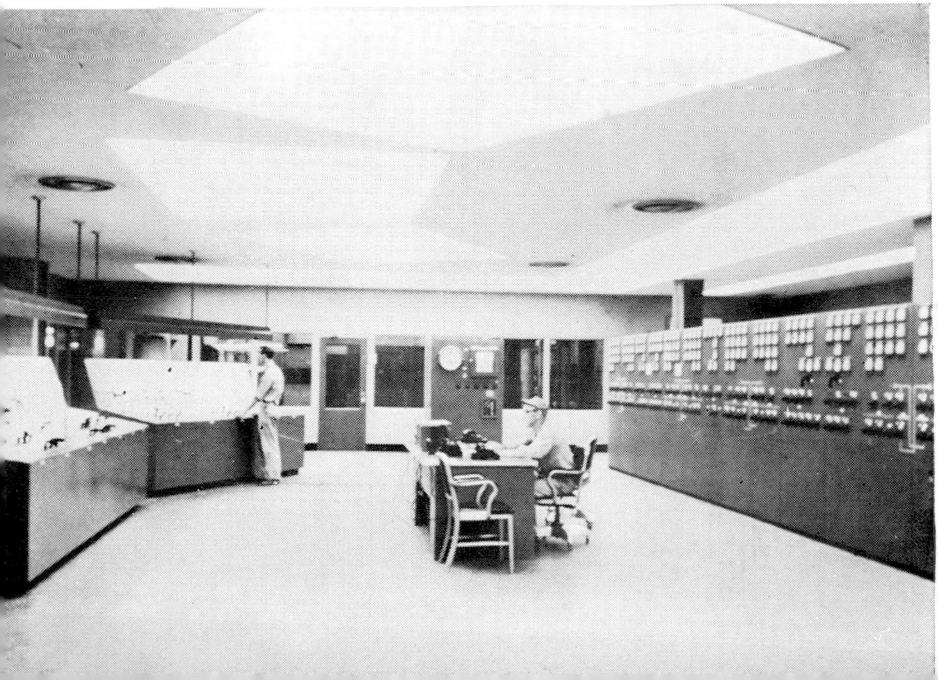

- A second feedback control system was also based on the pressure of the steam going from the boiler to the turbine. This control system regulated the functioning of two fans located in the boiler furnace. One of these was a forced-draft fan which forced combustion air into the pulverized coal burners in the walls of the furnace. The other was an induced-draft fan which removed combustion gases from the furnace. The proper ratio of air and pulverized coal had to be maintained for optimal combustion. Also, a slightly negative pressure had to be maintained within the furnace for the safety of personnel and the equipment. This second feedback system automatically coordinated the operation of the two fans while regulating their functioning. The firemen in the older plant manually performed the functions of both this control system and the previous one, but these tasks had been eliminated as elements of operating jobs in Advance.
- A third set of automatic devices controlled the steam temperature as it left the boilers on its way to the turbines. The production system operated most efficiently when the temperature of the steam was at approximately 1000°F. Major variations above or below this figure were costly. As in the older plant, dampers were used in Advance to regulate the steam temperature. However, two new methods had been added for temperature regulation: one to prevent the steam from overheating as it passed through the superheaters in the boilers on its way to the high pressure turbines; the other to reheat the steam as it passed from the high to the low pressure turbines. When the steam became too hot, water was automatically sprayed into it by means of an attemperator. On its way from the high pressure to the low pressure turbines, the steam was reheated by being circulated once again through combustion gases in the boiler furnaces. The feedback control system in this case regulated the dampers and the attemperator to provide an optimal steam temperature. In the older plant steam temperature could be controlled only by the manual adjustments of the fireman.

• A fourth control system was incorporated into the recirculating system that took the water from the turbine generators and brought it back into the boilers. This boiler feed system for supplying water to be converted into steam had been simplified by the rearrangement of several types of pumps used in Stand. This change had permitted the use of a feedback system to regulate the rate of flow of the recirculated water according to the level of water in the boiler drum. Too high a level of water in the drum might have allowed carry-over of water into the turbine generator, resulting in damage to equipment and costly repairs; too low a level might have resulted in overheating the boiler tubes and their subsequent rupture. Extreme variations of either type might have caused danger to personnel from the release of superheated water or a boiler explosion. This simplification and greater automaticity of the boiler feed control function had eliminated the jobs of the auxiliary operator and water tender, who were responsible for the more complicated system of pumps and valves in the older plant.

Another function had been mechanized in Advance, the result being that the work life of the operators was made a good deal less difficult. The continual burning of coal in the furnaces caused accumulations of slag and fly ash to form on the furnace walls, superheaters, and reheaters. These accumulations interfered with the transfer of heat from the fires to the water and steam, thus making the boiler operations less efficient. In the new plant the removal of this slag and fly ash had become an automatic job performed by an operator from a control station through a programed mechanical device. Rather than having to lance and hose manually to remove the slag and fly ash from the affected surfaces, as was done in most of the older plants, the operator now cleaned away the interfering accumulations by merely pushing a set of buttons which automatically activated deslaggers and soot blowers located in the walls of the furnace.

Each hose automatically sprayed its area of the furnace wall. The operators in Advance had thus been relieved of a dirty, tedious, and difficult job.

The integration of machinery which the unit system represented and the introduction of automatic feedback controls and other automatic mechanical devices had permitted the major part of the controls to be placed in a few centralized locations. There were, as a result, three main control rooms in Advance. Each of two of these controlled a pair of boiler turbine generators, and the third contained the electrical switchboard. All of these three rooms were located close to each other on the third floor of the plant. It is from these centralized control stations that most of the class A and class B power plant operators monitored the production of electricity. One class B operator and several power plant helpers were located two floors below, in the condensor room of the plant, to supervise the action of the equipment in that area.

A summary of the major characteristics distinguishing these two plants is presented in Table 2:1.

There was a marked difference between the physical condition and location of Stand and Advance. Stand not only had older equipment, but its buildings were soiled with forty years of smoke and soot from the plant and the surrounding heavily industrialized area. Advance had a new, modern structure, and its brand-new equipment housed in the clean, well-lit building provided a pleasant environment in which to work. While both plants were located on a river, the physical appearance of Advance was further enhanced by its location in a countryside away from any other industrial buildings. Instead of driving through stop-light mazes in the crowded industrial area surrounding Stand, the workers at Advance drove through small villages and farm land on their way to work. These differences undoubtedly affected the perceptions and attitudes of the men who worked in the two plants.

TABLE 2:1

Characteristics of New and Old Power Plants

	Advance	Stand
Dates Plant Built or Modernized	1954	Low pressure—1914 High pressure—1951
Location	Rural town	Large industrial city
Engineering Design	Unit system with greater feedback controls	Header system with manual controls
Operating Statistics		
Generating capacity	664,000 KW	515,000 KW
Overall net efficiency	37.9 percent	29.5 percent
Coal rate (lb/kw/hr)	0.75	0.91
Heat rate (BTU/kw/hr)	9240	11,590
Number of boilers	4	12
Steam temperature	1000°F	640 to 950°F
Number of turbine generators	4	9
Capacity of each	166,000 KW	30,000 to 100,000 KW
Steam pressure	1800 psi	200 to 1300 psi
Number of electrical switchboards	1	1
Coal-handling system	Modern conveyer system	Modern conveyer system
Total Complement	171	300
Nonsupervisory	140	246
Foremen and general foremen	21	44
Plant administration	10	10
Operating Complement per Shift		
Nonsupervisory	14	42
Foremen	1	6
Operating engineers	0	1
Location of Operating Personnel	Together in 4 locations	Spread out through the plant and in separate buildings

Study Design, Procedures, and Instruments

The optimal condition for studying the effects of any change is one that offers the opportunity to measure the state of the population before the change and again after the new situa-

tion has become stable. Unfortunately, in many real-life situations it is impossible to obtain access to the situation before the change takes place. In the present case, several units of Advance had already begun operation and nearly all the personnel were on the plant site by the time we were able to begin our study of the effects of the introduction of automation. Such circumstances obviously precluded obtaining measures from the men before they started working in the new plant. The study was therefore designed to compare the attitudes and perceptions of the men in Advance with those of a comparable group in one of the older plants in the company. Since a major part of the personnel in Advance had been transferred from older plants in the system, we thought it likely that their feelings before transferring to Advance probably had been about the same as the feelings of the men who were still in Stand, one of these older plants. Thus, any differences which we might find between the perceptions and attitudes of the men in Advance and Stand could probably be attributed to the changes brought about by the introduction of the new technology. We recognized that differences other than those in technology would also exist between the two plants. These differences include characteristics of the plant, of its operations, and of the personnel. A description of the differences actually found will be given later.

Stand was selected to be representative of the four older plants in the system. A review of the data from an attitude survey taken six years earlier showed Stand to be about average for these plants in employee attitudes toward their jobs, supervision, and the company. Relevant line managers felt that Stand was still typical of the older plants.

For about six months beginning in the summer of 1954 a team of researchers spent many days (and nights) in the two power plants.[1] They observed the workers and talked to them about their jobs and about the changes which had occurred in

[1] James K. Dent, Thomas Lough, and Floyd Mann were responsible for the exploratory interviewing and the development of the questionnaires.

their jobs. During this exploratory period of observation and interviewing, several major research areas were uncovered and the relevant variables within them identified.

Questions were developed to measure each of these variables, and the latter half of this initial phase was spent in pretesting the questionnaire on power plant personnel. Three drafts of the questionnaire were pretested, the questions on each draft being clarified and refined to ensure the measurement of the variables. The final questionnaire was cleared with the management and with the union officials concerned. Several questions regarding the relative effectiveness of work groups within each plant were eliminated at the request of the union.

Three questionnaires were ultimately developed: one for the nonsupervisory employees, a second for the foremen and general foremen, and a third for the top plant staff.[2] Because of the length of the nonsupervisory and foremen questionnaires, each of these was divided into two parts and administered at separate times. The first part of both of these questionnaires contained questions concerning working conditions and safety, job content and changes in the job, interdependence of work, wages and promotional opportunities, and shift work. The first part of the foremen's questionnaire also included questions concerning their own behavior toward their subordinates—that is, their perceptions of their own supervisory practices. The second parts of both the nonsupervisory and foremen's questionnaires included questions about the amount of information they received about the company and about the plant and about their attitudes toward training, job tension, supervision, management, and the company in general. The responses to these questions serve as the basic data for our study.

The questionnaires were administered in the two plants in December 1954 at separate sessions two weeks apart. Although

[2] A copy of the questionnaire administered to nonsupervisory employees is included in Appendix E.

all the foremen in both plants (15 in Advance and 44 in Stand) and 138 nonsupervisory employees in Advance completed both parts of their questionnaires, a much less than complete census was obtained from the nonsupervisory employees at Stand. Of the 246 employees at that plant only 203 completed the first part and 176 the second part of the questionnaire. The employees not returning questionnaires were fairly well scattered throughout the three principal units (operating, maintenance, coal handling), but resistance to answering the questionnaire was found within certain work groups within each of these units. In spite of thorough discussions about the purposes of this research with officials of the local plant and company and international union, some of the men did not want to record their feelings about their jobs and management. The effect of not having data from these employees was probably to raise the reported level of morale in Stand above what it "really" was.

Considerations Affecting the Comparison between the Plants

This study was designed to explore some of the direct and indirect effects which automation—as represented in the design of advanced power plants—had on an organization and on the people in it. As in any field situation, a number of differences existed between the two groups studied which were unrelated to the central question—in this case, automation. These differences set limits on the interpretation of our findings. To give the reader a basis for evaluating the relative effects of the technological changes within the framework of these other differences, a discussion of these factors follows.

Plant Conditions

Working conditions was one factor which contributed to the overall satisfaction of the workers in Advance. For a con-

siderable period in any new installation, the physical condition of the plant—the newness of equipment, the cleanliness of the building, the washrooms, the restaurant, and so forth—creates a particularly favorable environment in which to work. As time passes, the factor of newness probably ceases to be part of the worker's attitude and the ordinary feelings about his job situation predominate. At the time of this study, however, as can be seen in Table 2:2, the attitudes of the men at Advance toward their working conditions were significantly and substantially more positive than were the corresponding attitudes of the men at Stand. Sixty-one percent of the nonsupervisory Advance workers as against only 21 percent of the Stand workers said that their working conditions were very or quite satisfactory. Only 13 percent of the men at Advance indicated that their working conditions were unsatisfactory as against twice that percentage at Stand. Most of the dissatisfaction with working conditions at Advance came from the coal-handling group whose operations were still as dirty and dusty as they were in Stand. The major differences can be seen in the second question in Table 2:2, where the men were asked, "Which of the following things do you think can and should be improved?" A significantly greater percentage of the workers at Stand reported that the ventilation, the cleanliness of the plant, and the temperature of the place in which they worked could and should be improved. These three factors seemed to have received fairly careful attention in the design of the new plant.

Besides the increased satisfaction from working in a physically improved power plant, the prestige of working in the newest, most efficient power plant in the utility system was also a potential source of satisfaction for the workers in Advance. Although no direct measures of pride and prestige were obtained from the workers, the inference that the men at Advance were very proud of their plant and felt that it was an important plant in the system is easily gained from their responses to two ques-

TABLE 2:2

Working Conditions

(Nonsupervisory workers)

	In Percent Advance (N = 140)		In Percent Stand (N = 203)
1-1.[a] In general, how do you feel about your working conditions, things like lighting, heating, space, ventilation, noise, health conditions, equipment, etc.?			
Working conditions are very unsatisfactory	6	*	11
Working conditions are quite unsatisfactory	7		15
Working conditions are about average	25		49
Working conditions are quite satisfactory	43		18
Working conditions are very satisfactory	18		3
Not ascertained	1		4
	100		100
1-2. Which of the following things do you think can and should be improved?			
The cleanliness of the plant	16	†	44
The ventilation	29	†	48
The temperature of the place where you work	18	†	31

* The proportion of workers at Advance who felt that their working conditions were satisfactory was significantly higher at the .05 level of confidence than the proportion of workers at Stand. This difference was tested by chi-square. For a description of the statistical tests used in this book and their interpretation, see Appendix C.

In subsequent tables, as in this one, the .05 level of confidence will be used to determine statistical significance.

† Percentage differences significant using two-tail t-test.

[a] Refers to question numbers on Part 1 and 2 of questionnaire (see Appendix E). The first number refers to the Part of the questionnaire, and the second number to the question number within that Part. Questions quoted in subsequent tables will carry similar designations.

tions. We asked, "How important do you think each of the following plants will be to top management after Plant X (another plant the company was constructing which would be larger and even more efficient than Advance) goes into production?" Almost all (91 percent) of the men at Advance felt that their plant would still be "of great importance" at that time. Only 60 percent of the Stand workers thought that the high pres-

sure side of the plant would still be of great importance, and only 14 percent of them thought that the low pressure side would still be of great importance. Even the workers at Stand felt that Advance would be of greater importance than their own plant would be. Similarly, a significantly greater percentage of the workers at Advance than at Stand ranked their own plant

TABLE 2:3

Prestige of the Power Plants

(Nonsupervisory workers)

	Advance (N = 138)		Stand (N = 176)
2-27. How important do you think each of the following plants *will be* to top management after the [next new plant after Advance] goes into production?	*Percent responding "Of great importance"*		
Advance	91	*	69
Stand—high pressure side	53		60
Stand—low pressure side	3	*	14
2-25. How would you feel about working in each of the power plants in the company today?	*Percent ranking plant as the most preferred*		
Advance	91	†	15
Stand	9		74

* Percentage difference is significant.

† Difference in percentage of employees in the two plants who prefer *their own plant* is significant.

as the one within the company they would most prefer to work in. These differences are summarized in Table 2:3. From Tables 2:2 and 2:3 we find evidence that the workers at Advance were more satisfied with their physical surroundings and had greater feelings of pride in the plant in which they worked. Not only did Advance workers feel this way about the plant, but, judging from the responses of the men at Stand, the prestige and importance of Advance was recognized by the people in other parts of the company as well.

Wages and Advancement

The way in which the jobs were organized in the new plant required more knowledge and responsibility on the part of the nonsupervisory workers. This difference was reflected in the job grade structure of Advance. The top hourly rate for the combination of tasks performed by the A Operators of Advance was $3.07 per hour; the top rates for the principal operating jobs in the older plant were $2.88 for switchboard operator 1st, and $2.61 for turbine operator 1st and boiler fireman. Operations at Advance required that a higher proportion of its operators have the top job grade. This accounts, in part, for the proportionately higher number of workers at Advance who earned $105 or more per week (Table 2:4). The higher percentage of Advance workers in the below-$85-a-week category reflects the wages of new, unskilled workers recruited from the rural areas around the new plant.

Paralleling this difference in wages we found a somewhat greater degree of satisfaction with their wages among the workers at Advance than at Stand. Forty percent of the men at Advance were somewhat satisfied to completely satisfied with their wages; only 23 percent of the Stand workers were equally satisfied (Table 2:4).

Most (72 percent) of the men at Advance said that they had received promotions to better jobs within the last three years, while only slightly more than a third of the Stand workers reported similar promotions (Table 2:4). This differential promotion rate is reflected in the greater satisfaction with their progress in the company as expressed by workers at Advance than at Stand. Seventy-one percent of the men at Advance reported that they were very or fairly satisfied with their progress as against only 44 percent of those at Stand. At the time of our investigation, the men in the new plant saw their jobs for the most part as being promotions from older jobs and were more

TABLE 2:4

Wages and Promotional Opportunities

(Nonsupervisory workers)

	In Percent		
	Advance (N = 140)		Stand (N = 203)
1-58. Wage Level			
Less than $85.00 per week	44	*	29
$85.00 to $94.99 per week	14		22
$95.00 to $104.99 per week	11		30
$105.00 and over per week	31		11
Not ascertained	0		8
	100		100
1-60. Satisfaction with Wages			
Completely or very well or fairly well satisfied	40	*	23
Neither satisfied nor dissatisfied	12		16
A little dissatisfied	26		20
Very or quite dissatisfied	22		36
Not ascertained	0		5
	100		100
1-62. How long has it been since your last promotion to a better job?			
A year or less	37	*	11
Between one and three years	35		25
Between three and five years	6		15
Five years or more	2		25
Never had a promotion	14		17
Not ascertained	6		7
	100		100
1-64. How do you feel about the progress you have made in the company up to now?			
Very or fairly satisfied	71	*	44
Neither satisfied nor dissatisfied	10		17
Very or fairly dissatisfied	17		34
Not ascertained	2		5
	100		100

* This relationship is significant using the chi-square test.

satisfied than the men at Stand with their present wages and with the progress they had made in the company. Since satisfaction with wages and with past progress are usually found to be correlated with general work satisfaction,[3] we would expect that the higher satisfactions in this area would contribute to a higher level of general satisfaction among the workers at Advance than at Stand.

Management Philosophy and Practice

Another significant factor for understanding the different attitudes of the men in the two power plants was the "management philosophy" of the plant superintendents and their top administrative staffs. The major difference between the two plant philosophies seemed to lie in the attitudes toward the degree of administrative control which should exist in an organization. In Stand, there was considerable concern that control of all decision making should rest with the top plant management. The militaristic notions of strict lines of authority and conformity to superior commands seemed to characterize the thinking of the plant superintendent and his staff.

The top management of Advance, on the other hand, although retaining control of the plant and responsibility for it in their own hands, tended more often to delegate responsibility for decision making. The staff at Advance seemed to be more inclined to allow the foremen to make operating and administrative decisions appropriate to their level than they were to view these decisions as the prerogative of the plant staff.

These differences in the location of control and decision making can be seen clearly in the responses of the men and the foremen to questions concerning the amount of say and authority held by the foremen and plant staff. Both the men and foremen

[3] Morse, N. C., *Satisfactions in the White-Collar Job.* Ann Arbor, Mich.: Institute for Social Research, 1953.

were asked how much say respectively the men in the front office and the foremen had about how things were done in the plant. The men and foremen were also asked about the amount of authority the foremen had to make decisions and about changes which had occurred in the past few years in the amount of authority these men had. The responses to these sets of questions indicate that the front offices of the two plants were seen to have "quite a bit of say" or a "great deal of say in how things are done in the plant." In both plants, about nine out of ten of the men said that the men in the front office had a "great deal or quite a bit of say" (see Table 2:5). Eighty percent and 90 percent of the foremen in Advance and Stand respectively also said this. From these findings we see the usual pattern of administrative control resting at the top of the organizational unit.

The plants differed significantly, however, when it came to describing the amount of influence which the foremen had. In Advance, 52 percent of the men and 67 percent of the foremen said that the foremen had a great deal or quite a bit to say about how things were done in the plant. This was substantially and significantly higher than the 22 percent of the men and 36 percent of the foremen at Stand who made the same report. The foremen in Advance reported having, and the men in Advance saw them as having, a greater degree of influence in the affairs of the plant, than the foremen at Stand were seen as having.

These two sets of results indicate that both the men and the foremen at the two plants perceived the front office as having considerable control over the affairs of the plants. The men and the foremen in Advance felt that the foremen also had some say in the operations of that plant, but the foremen at Stand had substantially less influence in their plant. In both plants, however, the control exerted by the foremen appeared to be less than that exerted by the front office. A greater proportion of all four sets of respondents saw the men in the front office, rather than the foremen, as having a great deal or quite a bit to say about

the plant. Three of the four differences between the influence attributed to the men in the front office and to the foremen are statistically significant (see Table 2:5).

A similar picture is seen from responses to the question about the foremen's authority (see Table 2:5). Sixty percent of

TABLE 2:5

Location of Control and Authority

	In Percent					
	Men			*Foremen*		
	Advance (N = 138)		*Stand* (N = 176)	*Advance* (N = 15)		*Stand* (N = 44)
2-63. Men in front office have a great deal or quite a bit to say about how things are done in this plant	93		89	80		90
	*		*			*
2-52. Foremen have a great deal or quite a bit to say about how things are done in this plant.	52	*	22	67	*	36
2-46. Foreman has right amount of authority to decide things he should decide.	60	*	33	60		61
2-47. Foremen have a little or a lot *less* authority now than a few years ago.	12	*	44	27		33
2-48. Foremen feel much or somewhat *less* a part of management now than a few years ago.	4	*	39	0	*	38

* Difference in percentages is significant.

the men at Advance as against only 33 percent of the men at Stand said their foreman had the right amount of authority to decide the things he should decide. There was no difference between the foremen's responses to this question in the two plants. Similarly, a significantly larger percentage of the Stand workers reported that their foreman had a little or a lot less authority now than he had a few years ago. Although again the difference

in percentages between the Advance and Stand foremen is not statistically significant, it is in the same direction as the men's responses. In terms of the men's expectations about what the foremen ought to be able to decide, the foremen at Stand appeared to have less authority than the men felt they ought to have had. During our exploratory interviews, we heard the foremen repeatedly described as "messenger boys" between the nonsupervisory employees and the front office. The men felt they could never get immediate decisions from their foremen, since the supervisors always had to go back to the plant management for their answers. The responses to the questions about change in authority indicate that the foremen seemed to be losing authority. When we asked how much change there had been in the degree to which the foremen were a part of management, we found a substantial proportion of the men and the foremen at Stand feeling that the foremen were much or somewhat less a part of management now than they had been a few years carlier. Practically no one, neither the men nor the foremen, thought that the foremen felt any more a part of management now than they used to.

The greater concentration of administrative control in the front office at Stand was paralleled and probably to some extent caused by the greater concern for costs exhibited by management there in comparison to the concern by management in the new plant. A substantially higher proportion of both the men and the foremen at Stand than at Advance reported that the front office of the plant was "very concerned" with keeping costs down (see Table 2:6). Because of this overwhelming attention to the costs of running the plant, any change contemplated by a person in Stand had to be measured against the question, "Does it cost money?" If it cost anything, the men felt the superintendent was likely to veto it. In our exploratory interviews, we learned that there appeared to be no consistent set of standards which the foremen could use to decide whether an expenditure would or would not be approved. At certain times what appeared to the

TABLE 2:6

Attitudes toward Plant Management

	In Percent					
	Men			*Foremen*		
	Advance (N = 138)		*Stand* (N = 176)	*Advance* (N = 15)		*Stand* (N = 44)
2-61. Front office is "very concerned" with keeping costs down	39	*	72	40	*	74
2-67. Absence policy is handled "very or quite fairly" in this plant	79	*	36	not asked		not asked
2-62. Men in front office have "complete or considerable understanding of employee problems"	44	*	24	80		51
Men in front office do:						
The technical side of their job "extremely or very well"	not asked		not asked	87		74
2-58. The administrative side of their job "extremely or very well"	56	*	25	60		61
	*		*			*
2-59. The human relations side of their job "extremely or very well"	43	*	8	60		41
2-57. The plant is managed "very well"	42	*	14	60		38
2-60. Overall, I am "very or quite satisfied" with the men in the front office	71	*	22	87		64

* Difference in percentage is significant.

foremen to be absolutely necessary items were rejected and at other times "luxury" items were approved. The foremen soon became convinced that they were taking a risk if they failed to ask their superiors for approval of every expenditure. They refused to make any decisions or to answer their subordinates' questions without such consultation.

A specific example of the effects of the greater concentration of control and concern for costs in the top staff at Stand can be found in the differential administration of a company-wide paid-absence policy in the two plants.[4] Under this policy a person could be absent from his job and still be paid for the day if he had a legitimate reason—sickness, death in family—for being out. If he were out for any other reason, he was not paid for that day. Decisions as to whether a man should get paid for an absence and how to deal with frequent absentees were made in Advance by the first-line foreman. At Stand these decisions were made in the front office. A much larger proportion of Advance than Stand workers felt that the absence policy in their plant was handled fairly—79 percent of the men at Advance versus 36 percent at Stand (see Table 2:6).

The men in the front office at Advance were seen to be much more sensitive to the problems of their employees than were the staff men at Stand. Forty-four percent of the men and 80 percent of the foremen at Advance felt that the men in the front office had complete or considerable understanding of their employee's problems. Only 24 percent and 51 percent of the men and foremen, respectively, at Stand reported this. The percentage difference for the men is statistically significant. (The data for comparisons in this and the following two paragraphs appear in Table 2:6.)

Reinforcing this perception of the sensitivity of the staff at Advance are the differential evaluations given the administrative and human relations abilities of the plant officers by the men. A significantly higher proportion of the Advance than the Stand men reported that the men in the front office handled the administrative and human relations sides of their jobs "extremely or very well."

[4] A detailed account of the differential administration of the absence policy in the two plants is given in Mann, F. C., and Sparling, J., "Changing Absence Rates," *Personnel,* January 1956. Plant X and Plant Y in that article correspond respectively to Advance and Stand of this book.

In general, the men and the foremen at Stand saw their front office as doing a rather poor job of managing the plant. Only 14 percent of the men and 38 percent of the foremen at Stand saw their plant as being managed "very well." Forty-two percent of the men at Advance and 60 percent of the foremen saw their plant as being "very well" managed. The difference in percentages at the men's level is significant. Similarly, when asked to give an overall evaluation of the men in the plant staff, 71 percent of the men and 87 percent of the foremen at Advance as against only 22 percent of the men and 64 percent of the foremen at Stand reported being very or quite satisfied with them. Again, the percentage difference at the men's, but not at the foremen's, level is statistically significant.

Another factor probably contributing to the low level of satisfaction of the men in Stand was the way management treated the men after a strike in that plant. In 1952 a strike occurred in the power plants of this company and the foremen and plant management ran the plants. After a period of twenty days, during which the management men successfully maintained production, the union and the company settled their differences. To forestall any recriminations and to prevent continuing hard feelings between the men and the management, the president of the company, shortly after the return of the workers to their jobs, issued a statement of policy concerning management's attitudes toward the men. The policy came to be known as the "fair but firm policy," meaning that management would treat the men fairly within the strict letter of the new contract. Unfortunately from the point of view of management-labor relations in Stand, this policy was more frequently administered as the "firm but fair policy." This interpretation was seen as recriminatory by the men. In turn, the men maintained the gap, created by the strike, between themselves and the foremen. They did this by refusing to talk to their foreman in some cases and by refusing to allow the foreman to join again in their outside activities,

such as bowling. Even at the time of our study, two years later, the degree to which the foremen were considered separate from the work groups could be seen in the responses of the men to the question, "Do you feel that your foreman is really a part of your work group?" Seventy-four percent of the men at Advance said, "Yes, he really is a part or he is included in most ways in our work group"; only 47 percent of the men at Stand reported the same degree of relationship with their foremen.

As a new plant, Advance had no history of labor strife. Although most of the men in that plant had experienced the strike in some other plant, their attitudes toward the management at Advance were based principally on their experiences in the new location. The bitter antagonism of the men in Stand toward their plant management contrasts sharply with the more positive attitudes of the men in Advance. This contrasting attitude affected the nature of our research results in a way which cannot even be seen in the questionnaire data. It was impossible to overcome the suspiciousness of some groups at Stand about the nature and purpose of the study. The full cooperation of the men at Advance in completing our questionnaires contrasted sharply with the larger number of refusals at Stand. The loss of respondents in Stand from the first to the second administration of the questionnaire likewise can be partially attributed to this antagonistic attitude toward plant management.

On the whole, then, we find that the attitude toward the plant staff in Stand appears to have been quite poor and the assessment both by the men and by the foremen of the staff's ability to run the plant was low. This difference in the attitudes of the personnel in Advance and Stand toward the managements of their plants is another uncontrollable factor—a factor which is likely to have contributed to the differences in the general satisfaction of the men in these two plants and to have colored their perceptions of other aspects of their job environment.

Worker Characteristics

A final consideration to keep in mind in interpreting the findings to be presented in the subsequent chapters concerns the nature of the people who work in these two power houses. The combination of methods used to staff the new plant probably resulted in a work force different from that in the older plant.

In the first place, the men who finally transferred to the new plant were selected via a company-wide job posting procedure. That is, when a position opened up in the company a notice was placed on the bulletin boards with a description of the job and qualifications needed by the person to fill the job. Anyone who thought he met those qualifications and who wanted the job might then apply for it. This procedure was used to fill most of the jobs in Advance, especially the more highly skilled ones.

With respect to the final complement in Advance, then, a certain amount of self-selection presumably went on among those men who might have been eligible according to the qualifications. Such self-selection would be based on the man's ability and willingness to change his current residence, his desire to live in a small, rural town rather than in the large metropolis, his satisfaction with his current work situation, and his estimate of his likelihood of being chosen for the new job. Thus, the pool from which the company finally selected its workers for Advance was already a nonrepresentative group of power plant workers.

The company also established certain criteria for deciding which people would be transferred to the new plant. The factors considered most important were technical knowledge of their present jobs, capacity to be trained in new work methods, and good attendance records. This selection procedure probably made the work force at Advance even more different from the one at the old plant.

A further bias was introduced by the recruitment of personnel from the rural area surrounding Advance to fill jobs in

the coal-handling group and the low-skilled jobs in other parts of the plant. In most cases the recruits were young men taking their first jobs, this being their first experience in large-scale industry.

These methods of selection and recruitment resulted in the workers at the new plant being younger, having more formal education, and having had less service with the company than the men at Stand (see Table 2:7).

The major part of the technological changes with which our study is concerned occurred in the central operating functions of the new plant. Our attention in subsequent chapters will be focused primarily on *operating personnel.* It is particularly important, therefore, that no statistically significant differences were found when the age, education, and length of service with the company of the transferred operators are compared with those characteristics of the operators in the old plant. The comparisons of the distributions for these three factors for operators in the two plants are presented in Table 2:7.

Data were also obtained concerning three value orientations of the total nonsupervisory work forces in these two plants. These were related to political affiliation, mobility, and urban-rural living. We asked the men in both plants, "Do you think of yourself as being more of a Republican or a Democrat?" Forty-five percent of the men at Advance as compared to 24 percent of the men at Stand reported being "more of a Republican." Since 16 percent of the Advance workers did not answer this question, the 45 percent Republican figure represents more than half the respondents at that plant. As can be seen in Table 2:8, this proportion of Republicans is comparable to the proportion found among the supervisors in that plant, where we would expect such identifications. Thus, to the extent that identification as a Republican indicates a more conservative political philosophy, the workers at Advance were more conservative than were the men at Stand.

Evidence about the mobility orientation of the workers was

TABLE 2:7

Age, Education, and Length of Company Service in the Two Power Plants

(Nonsupervisory workers)

	In Percent				
	Total			Operators	
	Advance (N = 140)		Stand (N = 203)	Advance[a] (N = 35)	Stand (N = 109)
1-B-1.[b] *Age*					
Under 25 years	16		7	0	13
25 to 34.9 years	46		35	40	41
35 to 44.9 years	24		19	40	15
45 years or more	13		31	20	26
Not ascertained	1		8	0	5
	100		100	100	100
Mean age	33.4	*	39.5	38.2	36.7
Standard Deviation	9.37		11.56	8.46	11.21
1-B-2. *Education*					
Some high school or less	18	†	37	21	28
Completed high school	58		36	56	48
More than high school	23		15	23	18
Not ascertained	1		12	0	6
	100		100	100	100
1-B-8. *Length of Service with Company*					
Less than 2 years	37		7	0	6
2 to 4.9 years	16		18	14	30
5 to 9.9 years	25		27	40	21
10 to 14.9 years	9		8	20	7
15 years or more	13		31	26	32
Not ascertained	0		9	0	4
	100		100	100	100
Mean length of service	6.8	*	13.2	11.5	12.4
Standard Deviation	6.52		10.96	6.80	10.93

[a] These 35 Advance operators do not include the men who were recruited from the rural area surrounding the new plant. They all have had experience in other power plants in this utility.

[b] B refers to section of background questions at end of Part 1 of questionnaire.

* Difference in means is significant for the total plant groups, but not for the operators.

† Chi-square test of this relationship is significant for the total plant groups, but not for the operators.

TABLE 2:8
Political Orientation

	In Percent				
	Men			Foremen	
	Advance (N = 140)		Stand (N = 203)	Advance (N = 15)	Stand (N = 44)
1-B-17. Do you think of yourself as being more of a Republican or a Democrat?					
More of a Republican	45	*	24	40	56
More of a Democrat	39		60	53	26
Not ascertained	16		16	7	18
	100		100	100	100

* Differences in percentages between plants is significant.

derived from a set of three questions measuring the attitudes of each man about the kind of a company he would like to work for. These three questions were:

> In each of the groups below, check the statement that best fits your feelings.
>
> __I like a company that is growing very rapidly
> __I like a company that is growing gradually
> __I like a company that stays about the same
>
> __I like a company where there are always new kinds of jobs opening up
> __I like a company where you can stick to your kind of work and work up in it
>
> __I like a company that keeps up with the times and sets the pace for other companies
> __I like a company that doesn't worry about keeping ahead of other companies

An index was formed by combining responses to these three questions. The categories in this index define four points on a continuum from complete advocacy of a rapidly expanding, pro-

gressive company to advocacy of a rather stable, slowly growing company. The percentage of respondents from each plant in each of the four index categories are presented in Table 2:9. Sixty-two percent of the workers in Advance were in the first two categories as against only 39 percent of the men in Stand.

TABLE 2:9

Attitudes toward Company Growth and Preferred Place of Residence

(Nonsupervisory workers)

Index of Attitude toward Company Growth	*In Percent* Advance (N = 138)		Stand (N = 165)
Index Point 1. (I like company which grows rapidly, new kinds of jobs opening up, and sets the pace for other companies.)	23		18
2.	39		21
3.	30	*	43
4. (I like company which grows gradually, sticks to one work and works up in it, doesn't worry about keeping ahead of other companies.)	8		18
	100		100
1-B-26. Regardless of where you work, how would you feel about living in the following places? (Percent saying very good or fairly good)	*Advance* (N = 138)		*Stand* (N = 176)
Within [city] but away from center	7	†	48
Other towns in [part of state served by utility]	90		34

* Chi-square test shows significantly greater preference for growing company in Advance than in Stand.

† Difference in percentages between plants is significant.

A substantially and significantly greater percentage of Advance than Stand workers favored a company which grows rapidly, creates new jobs, and sets the pace for other companies.

Marked differences were also found in the preferences expressed by the men in the two plants as to where they would like to live. To the question, "Regardless of where you work, how would you feel about living in the following places . . . ,"

almost half of Stand employees said that they felt "very or fairly good" about living within the large metropolitan center in which they worked but away from the center of the city; only 7 percent of the workers at Advance felt this way. On the other hand, almost all (90 percent) of the Advance workers said that they would like to live in other towns in the part of the state where they worked, as against only a third (34 percent) of the Stand workers expressing such a preference. Since Advance is actually located in one of these other towns and since the men who work there are therefore required to live near the plant, the residential preferences of the overwhelming majority of the workers in that plant have thus been met.

The responses of the men at Advance differed from those at Stand in that the former were based on the men's experience of working in a highly changed work situation and of living in a relatively rural location. The men at Stand, on the other hand, had not experienced this change in work and residence and were responding in terms of the anticipated effects on them. We have no way of knowing whether the men at Advance would have responded similarly before they transferred, and we can only assume that their preferences existed before the transfer and may have contributed to their motivation in applying for positions at Advance.

These value orientations together with demographic characteristics of the workers, the management climate, recent advancements, wage differentials, and the better facilities of a new plant are probably related to the feelings of the men at Advance about being represented by a union. Attempts to organize the men in this new plant by the union which represents the men in the company's other power plants failed. Although the margin of rejection was small on the first election—only six votes—workers at Advance were not organized. This is one additional difference between Stand and the new plant, the effects of which are difficult to estimate.

In summary, then, although we had hoped to concentrate on the intraorganizational effects of introducing a change in technology in these two power plants, we found the plants differing on a number of other factors. The increased prestige, the higher wages and recent advancements, the improved working conditions, the rural location of the plant, and the lack of any history of management-labor conflict in Advance can predictably be expected to have resulted in a high level of general satisfaction among the employees in the new plant. In addition, the work force in Advance had different characteristics and values than the one in Stand—one manifestation of these differences being the rejection of union representation by the men at Advance.

While these factors probably contributed to a generally higher level of overall job satisfaction in Advance than in Stand, they did so by improving particularly those specific aspects of the job outlined above, namely wages and promotions, working conditions, plant management, etc. Previous studies of worker attitudes toward their jobs have shown that in reporting their job satisfactions they discriminate among the various facets of their job situation. The resulting intercorrelations among measures of satisfaction with these different facets of the job are therefore usually low though positive. The same low positive correlations among satisfaction items were found in the two power plants in our present study (see Table 2:10). We felt therefore that it would be worthwhile to study certain job areas which seemed to have been affected by or would give us insight into the characteristics of automation. We undertook these analyses on the assumption that the effects we observed would be relatively independent of the changes in wages, working conditions, or management philosophy in Advance. Quantitative findings regarding job demands, shift work, and supervision will be presented in subsequent chapters.

TAB

Intercorrelations amor

(Nonsuperviso

	1		2		3		4		5
Satisfaction in the Job Situation	A[b]	S	A	S	A	S	A	S	A
1. With working conditions	...		.10	.20	.11	.27	.26	.14	.16
2. 1-15 With job as a whole			...		.57	.44	.34	.24	.10
3. 1-48 With job, compared to several years ago					...		.46	.21	.06
Satisfaction with Supervisory Leadership									
4. 2-55 With immediate supervisor							...		.25
5. 2-60 With men in front office									..
6. 2-6 With amount of information on plant									
7. 2-1 With amount of information on company									
8. 2-9 With training									
Wage and Mobility									
9. 1-60 With present wages									
10. 1-61 With chances for promotion									
11. 1-64 With progress so far									
12. 2-79 With the retirement plan									
Overall Satisfaction									
13. 2-92 In continuing to work for company									
14. 2-93 With company and job as a whole									

[a] Product-moment correlations.

[b] A: abbreviation for Advance; S: abbreviation for Stand.

:10

atisfaction Questions[a]

orkers)

6	7		8		9		10		11		12		13		14	
S	A	S	A	S	A	S	A	S	A	S	A	S	A	S	A	S
.32	.25	.35	.22	.18	.02	.24	.18	.26	.05	.17	.06	.29	.21	.15	.15	.32
.26	.04	.28	.18	.21	.31	.17	.35	.42	.50	.40	.00	.14	.13	.38	.41	.43
.24	.03	.28	−.15	−.24	.33	.12	.32	.41	.57	.35	−.15	.16	.11	.42	.31	.46
.31	.17	.26	.49	.38	.13	.21	.38	.27	.27	.16	.14	.24	.24	.27	.46	.39
.42	.41	.56	.18	.42	.03	.33	.22	.39	.00	.30	.04	.36	.23	.49	.25	.69
..	.55	.67	.23	.38	.13	.31	.12	.33	.26	.27	.23	.32	.26	.24	.23	.45
	...		.27	.45	−.03	.35	.18	.34	.07	.32	.22	.32	.24	.31	.25	.47
			...		−.03	.20	.12	.36	.09	.22	.22	.32	.37	.27	.26	.39
					...		.28	.39	.44	.37	.02	.31	−.06	.23	.32	.33
							...		.47	.51	.21	.19	.25	.38	.38	.50
									...		.00	.15	.18	.37	.39	.33
											...		.22	.21	.22	.26
													...		.38	.62
															...	

Chapter 3

SOME OVERALL EFFECTS OF AUTOMATION

The technological changes incorporated in Advance brought about a number of changes in the company's organizational structure. The organizational structure within the older plants was modified; the relationship among the plants, and between the production department and several other closely related departments was completely reshaped.

Within the limited scope of this project it was impossible to assess these global organizational effects as intensively as they deserved. Using the restricted amount of relevant data collected, however, this chapter undertakes to describe some of the consequences on a total organization and its major subgroups when a new plant is introduced into the system.

Centralized Maintenance

While the maintenance of the equipment in power plants has long been on a preventive rather than a "crash" basis, the

installation of the unit system in Advance forced management to reconsider and, eventually, to redesign the organization of plant maintenance. This reorganization took place about a year before the construction of Advance, in anticipation of the changed requirements of that plant and of another proposed power plant.

Although the unit system of production in these new plants was designed for more efficient production than the header system provided, the costs of a breakdown, in terms of lost production, were disproportionately greater. In the header system, when a turbine generator broke down, its production alone was lost to the plant; in the unit system, the breakdown of a turbine generator meant the loss of the boiler capacity as well. The increased seriousness of an unscheduled loss of a unit in the new plants pointed to the even greater importance of preventing breakdowns and of handling the scheduled overhauling of equipment in the shortest time possible.

A centralized construction and maintenance group (C & M) was established to perform these functions. Its members were drawn for the most part from the maintenance crews in each of the power plants. This group's task was to perform all the construction work (except that done by contract through outside construction groups) and all of the major maintenance work in each of the power plants. The annual overhaul of equipment also became one of its principal functions. The group spent the greater part of its time going from one plant to the next, systematically examining and repairing equipment. Periodically the maintenance engineer in each plant called in the centralized group to do major repairs in his plant.

Prior to the reorganization, maintenance had been handled by a large force in each plant under the general supervision of the plant maintenance engineer. Such a group had been composed of the usual assortment of skilled craftsmen—electricians, pipefitters, welders, carpenters, painters, and so forth. These men

had been responsible for all repairs, both major and minor, and for the annual examinations and overhauls of the power plant equipment. Approximately 90 workers had been employed in the maintenance group of Stand before this reorganization reduced the group to 25.

Although under the new system the responsibility for maintaining the power plant remained with the plant's maintenance engineer, the reduced number of men under his direct supervision lessened his importance as a member of the plant's top staff. As a result of the loss of status and of direct control over the maintenance of the power plant, the men in the office of the maintenance engineer were antagonistic toward centralized maintenance. They tried in every possible way to show the company that they could do things more efficiently with their own group, and at times they resisted calling in the centralized group.

To provide increased flexibility in the small in-plant maintenance crews, the company abolished the usual craft specializations (carpenter, electrician, etc.) and proposed to make each worker a multiple-skilled maintenance man. Two job classifications, Mechanic A and Mechanic B, were established to replace the dozen or so specialized classifications which had previously existed. Men with the Mechanic A classification were expected to perform electrical repairs and the men with the Mechanic B classification pipefitting repairs.

The unions strongly resisted this elimination of craft specialities, but the case was brought to arbitration and settled in the company's favor. Despite this decision which established the new job classifications, most of the employees tried to maintain the old distinctions. There was also general resistance to the cross-training needed to develop the men for these jobs. Men who spent years acquiring proficiency in their particular specialities were reluctant to train others who had not served their apprenticeships in the trade. Status considerations also contributed to the resistance to change. Highly skilled artisans were being

asked to relinquish their expert positions and start training as beginners in new trades.

A large number of supervisors also contributed to the lack of acceptance of the new maintenance philosophy. Torn between the need to develop men and the need to do maintenance jobs efficiently and quickly, many supervisors took the easy way out

TABLE 3:1

Effect of Centralized Maintenance on the Jobs of Plant Service Groups

(Maintenance workers only)

	In Percent	
	Advance (N = 30)	*Stand* (N = 27)
2-22. Last year, the company set up the new Construction and Maintenance (C & M) department to do major repair jobs in the power plants. Has this change made any difference in your work?		
Centralized maintenance has made a *great deal* of difference in my work	17	36
Quite a lot of difference in my work	26	19
Some difference in my work	7	11
A little difference in my work	13	15
Centralized maintenance has made *no difference* in my work	37	19
	100	100

Percentage differences between Advance and Stand are not statistically significant.

by assigning men to maintenance jobs according to their expertness in the skill required. Thus, although the maintenance men carried titles of Mechanics A or B they were still treated as if they were primarily carpenters, electricians, etc., by many of the foremen.

About half the in-plant maintenance men in both plants (43 percent in Advance and 55 percent in Stand) felt that centralized maintenance had made "a great deal or quite a lot of

difference" in their work (Table 3:1). The resistance to the change in maintenance philosophy can be seen in their less than positive attitudes toward the new organizational setup (Table 3:2). When asked how well they thought centralized maintenance was working out for the men in the plant and how effi-

TABLE 3:2

Attitude toward Centralized Maintenance

(Maintenance workers only)

	In Percent		
	Advance		*Stand*
1-99. How well do you think centralized maintenance is working out for the men in this plant now? ("A" and "B" Mechanics only)	(N = 28)		(N = 22)
Working out very or fairly well	29		23
Well in some ways, not in others	36		50
Not so well or not at all well	21		5
Not ascertained	14		22
	100		100
2-23. How efficient is this new system of centralized maintenance (C & M) in handling large maintenance jobs?	(N = 30)		(N = 27)
Very or quite efficient	20		19
Efficient in some ways, inefficient in others	56		37
Very or quite inefficient	17		18
Don't know much about centralized maintenance	7		22
Not ascertained	0		4
	100		100
1-97. Would you prefer to work in the centralized maintenance group (C & M) or in the plant service group? ("A" and "B" Mechanics only)	(N = 28)		(N = 22)
Prefer to work in centralized maintenance	4		14
Makes little difference which group I work in	0		14
Prefer to work in plant service group	79	*	50
No interest in either group	7		0
Not ascertained	10		22
	100		100

* Percentage difference is significant using two-tailed t-tests at the .05 level of confidence. This level of confidence will be used in statistical tests in all subsequent tables.

cient the new system of centralized maintenance was, about a quarter of the maintenance people expressed fairly favorable attitudes. In most cases they saw some good and some bad things about the change. When asked whether they would prefer to work in the centralized maintenance group or to continue in the plant service group, more skilled maintenance people preferred to remain in their present group than to move into C & M. The fact that a significantly larger proportion of the Advance workers expressed this preference probably reflects the favorable working conditions of the new plant in addition to the unfavorable factors associated with working in C & M.

The attempt to solve the problem of holding production losses and "down time" to a minimum through the establishment of a centralized maintenance group created, then, a number of personnel problems, at least temporarily. These were caused by the reduced status of the jobs of certain workers and management men and by competition rather than cooperation between the in-plant maintenance and the centralized maintenance groups.

Reduction in Work Force

Visitors to Advance were impressed by the large amount of gigantic, expensive machinery and the few men apparently responsible for its operation. The change from the header to the unit system of production, the increased generating capacity, the design and integration of equipment, and the introduction of feedback controls permitted a substantial reduction in the personnel needed for the production operations. In fact, the personnel requirements of the new plant, relative to its production capacity, were a little less than half what they were in the older plants.

The reduction in personnel needs occurred principally in the operating groups. In contrast with the 42 operators, 6 foremen, and one operating engineer required on each shift in Stand, only 14 operators and a single shift foreman were used on each shift at Advance. The attitudes of the workers in Stand regarding the security of their jobs reflected this reduction of work force at Advance. The men in the older plants were made keenly aware of the growing obsolescence of their present skills and knowledge as they saw that fewer operating jobs existed in the new plant and that these required skills different from those they had.

Events at Stand stemming from the greater capacity and efficiency of the new plant further contributed to the job insecurity of the Stand workers. The company met all its power needs from Advance's production first, because of that plant's greater efficiency, using its other plants to fill the remaining requirements. Prior to the construction of the new plant, Stand had served this purpose, with men often working overtime to maintain the plant at full load. After the new plant went into production, however, the load at Stand had been reduced and, on several occasions, the furnace fires at the old plant were banked over the weekend. Overtime work had been virtually eliminated by the time of our study and, in anticipation of further reductions in the demands placed on Stand, a number of operators had been declared "surplus" and transferred to other jobs.

The impact of the new plant on the men in Stand was marked. They felt very strongly that the only thing saving their jobs was the continuing prosperity of the industrial area in which they worked. One-third of the men in Stand felt that if business conditions in the area worsened, the company would lay off "a good many people." Eighty-seven percent of the men at that plant felt that under such conditions Stand would "probably have

layoffs." The men at Advance had no such fears. The corresponding percentages on these same questions were only 11 percent and 14 percent, both significantly less than at Stand (Table 3:3). These data reinforce the perceived importance to the company of Advance and the decreased importance of Stand which was indicated in Chapter 2 (*cf.* Table 2:3).

TABLE 3:3

Feelings of Job Security

(Nonsupervisory workers)

	In Percent Advance (N = 138)		*In Percent* Stand (N = 176)
2-88. If there were a slump in business cond tions in [this area], and less demand for electricity, do you think [this company] might lay off some people?			
The company would lay off a good many people	11	*	33
The company would lay off a few people but not very many	65		48
No, the company would find something for everyone to do. No one would be laid off	20		14
Not ascertained	4		5
	100		100
2-89. If the company did lay off some people, would this plant be affected?			
Yes, this plant would probably have lay offs	14	*	87
No, this plant would probably not be affected	81		10
Not ascertained	5		3
	100		100

* Percentage difference between plants is significant.

These findings provide strong evidence for the importance of regarding the company as an entire social system with interrelated parts. What is done to one part of the system affects not only that part but the other parts of the organization as well.

From the point of view of the total organization, the increased feeling of importance given to the workers at Advance must be balanced against the feelings of insecurity and decreased importance engendered in the workers in Stand and presumably in the other older power plants in the company. It is not surprising that two-thirds of the employees in Stand said that top management was now less interested in its employees than it had been a few years ago, and that the company was much more interested in cutting costs than it was in the people who worked for it. It is apparent that management invested much more effort in thinking about and planning for the construction and staffing of Advance than it did in preparing for the effects which this new plant would have on the employees in older plants in the company.

Changes in the Organizational Structure of the New Plant

The reduced number of personnel and the fewer job classifications in the operating sections of the new plant resulted in a reduction in the size of the supervisory force as well. With the elimination of the separate operating classifications of boiler, turbine, and electrical, the company was able to eliminate one level of supervision from the new plant. Stand had a foreman for each of the production functions—boiler, turbine, electrical—as well as an operating engineer who was assigned to coordinate the activities of the three groups. The operating engineer on each shift reported directly to the plant operations engineer, a member of the plant's top staff. In Advance a single shift foreman was responsible for the entire operating force. He reported directly to the plant operations engineer.

What effect this elimination of levels of organization had on the operation of the new plant is difficult to say. The men at

Advance reported being significantly more satisfied with the amount of information they got about both the plant and the company than were the men at Stand (Table 3:4). Reducing the number of people between the top staff and the employees appears to have eliminated one of the communication barriers between these two groups and resulted in more men being satisfied with the amount of information transmitted from management to the employees.

TABLE 3:4

Satisfaction with Information

(Nonsupervisory workers)

	In Percent		
	Advance (N = 138)		*Stand* (N = 176)
2-6. How satisfied are you with the amount of information you get about what is going on in *your plant?*			
Very well satisfied	9		4
Fairly well satisfied	35		18
Somewhat satisfied but could get more	37	*	41
Not very well satisfied	14		32
Not ascertained	5		5
	100		100
2-1. How satisfied are you with the amount of information you get about what is going on in *the company?*			
Very well satisfied	13		9
Fairly well satisfied	42		20
Somewhat satisfied but could get more	31	*	40
Not very well satisfied	13		29
Not ascertained	1		2
	100		100

* The workers in Advance are significantly more satisfied with the amount of information they get about both the plant and the company by chi-square test.

Another phenomenon which may be a function of this change in the number of supervisory levels is illustrated in Chart 3:1. These graphs illustrate the perceptions of the men and the

CHART 3:1

Distribution of Perceived Influence

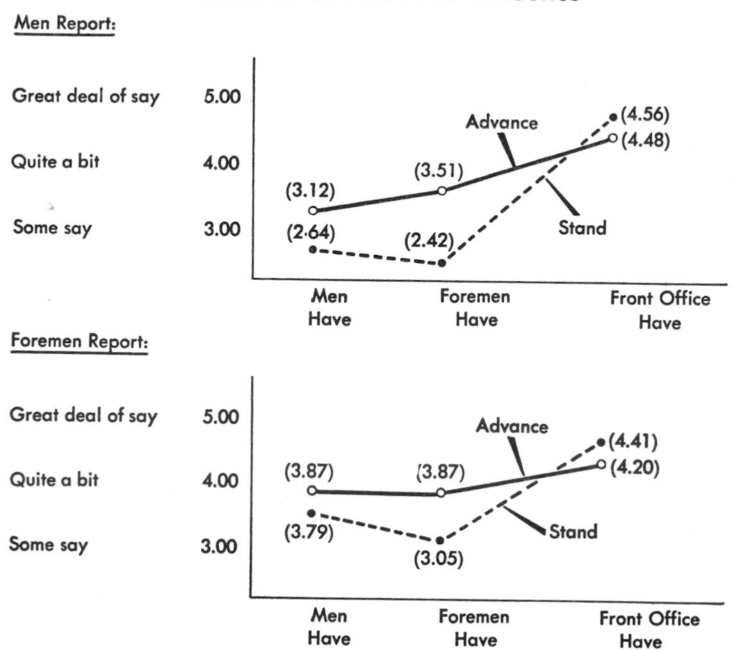

foremen, respectively, concerning the degree to which each of the major groups influenced the way things were done in the plant. The three questions from which the men's chart was derived were as follows:

> In general, how much do you and the other men of your work group have to say about how things are done?
>
> 5. Our foreman gives us a great deal to say in how things are done
> 4. Our foreman gives us quite a bit of say
> 3. Our foreman gives us some say
> 2. Our foreman gives us a little say
> 1. Our foreman gives us hardly any say at all in how things are done

In general, how much do you think the foremen have to say about how things are done in this plant?

5. They have a great deal of say
4. They have quite a bit of say
3. They have some say
2. They have a little say
1. They have very little or no say at all

In general, how much say do you think the men in the front office of this plant have in how things are done in this plant?

5. They have a great deal of say in how things are done in this plant
4. They have quite a bit of say
3. They have some say
2. They have a little say
1. They have very little or no say at all in how things are done in this plant

Parallel questions were asked of the foremen concerning these three groups:

In general, how much do the men of your work group have to say about how things are done?

5. I give them a great deal of say in how things are done
4. I give them quite a bit of say
3. I give them some say
2. I give them a little say
1. I give them hardly any say at all in how things are done

In general, how much do you think the foremen have to say about how things are done in this plant?

1. They have very little or no say at all
2. They have a little say
3. They have some say

4. They have quite a bit of say
5. They have a great deal of say

In general, how much say do you think the men in the front office of this plant have in how things are done in this plant?

5. They have a great deal of say in how things are done in this plant
4. They have quite a bit of say
3. They have some say
2. They have a little say
1. They have very little or no say in how things are done in this plant

Numerical values of one to five were assigned to the alternatives to each of these questions, 5 being assigned to the alternative "having a great deal of say" and 1 to the alternative "having very little or no say at all." For each question a mean value was computed indicating the degree of say which the respondents perceived each group as having about the way things were done in the plant. From the chart we see that the men in each plant reported that the front office group had the most say about what goes on in the plant, and that the amount of influence held by each front office group appears to be about the same.

The reduced number of supervisory levels in Advance seems to have increased the influence of the foremen in that plant. The foremen at Stand appear to have had relatively little influence both in the eyes of the men and in the eyes of the foremen over how things were done in the plant. The foremen at Stand had even less say than the men, according to both sets of respondents. In Advance, the foremen were seen as having as much or more say than the men.[1] Since the foremen at Advance

[1] The relatively higher influence accorded to the men in Stand is probably a function of the union in that plant through which the men influence the plant activities. Since the men at Advance were not organized, this means of influence was not available to them.

had proportionately greater responsibility for the activities of their subordinates than did the foremen at Stand, it is not surprising that they were seen as having more influence over these activities than did the foremen in the older plant. Another factor undoubtedly contributing to the greater perceived influence of the Advance foreman was the willingness of the top staff of that plant to allow their foremen to make important decisions. Extending the span of control over which these foremen were responsible may have had a democratizing effect on the distribution of influence over the plant activities. In the case of both the men's and the foremen's reports about the distribution of influence in the plant, the curves for Advance are flatter than are those at Stand. The amount of influence exerted by each level was seen as being more nearly equal at Advance than at Stand. In the latter plant, control of the activities appears to have been strongly concentrated at the top of the plant organization.[2]

Centralization of Equipment Controls

The placement on a single floor of the new plant of the major control boards for the operating units, as described in Chapter 2, appears to have had important effects on the attitudes of the men in the operating jobs. By centralizing the operating controls into two general areas of the main plant building, the design of Advance eliminated many of the isolated jobs which existed in the older plants. No longer was a man required to spend his eight-hour working day at the top of the plant separated from the main body of operators by several floors. Rather, the men usually spent the greater part of their time in the company of a large number of other operators.

[2] For a full description of the way in which control graph curves can be used to identify different types of organizations, see Tannenbaum, A. S., and Kahn, R. L., *Participation in Union Locals*. Evanston, Ill.: Row, Peterson and Co., 1958.

Although we were unable to ask direct questions about the relative effectiveness or cohesiveness of the various work groups, several questions were included in the questionnaire which appear to offer inferential evidence that the group feeling among the operators at Advance was more positive than that of the operators at Stand (see Table 3:5). On the question, "Do you feel that you are really a part of your work group?" 83 percent

TABLE 3:5

Attitudes about Work Groups

(Power plant operators)

	In Percent		
	Advance (N = 35)		*Stand* (N = 109)
1-34. Do you feel that you are really a part of your work group?			
Yes, I feel I really am a part of it	83		69
Yes, I feel I'm included in most ways but not all	17		14
Yes, I feel I'm included in some ways but not in others	0		16
No, I don't feel I really belong	0		0
Not ascertained	0		1
	100		100
1-20. When you have a problem on your job, how free do you feel to call on others in your work group to help you with it?			
I feel very free to call on them	71	*	48
Quite free	23		30
Fairly free	6		15
Not very or not at all free	0		7
	100		100
1-21. How important is your job as compared with the jobs of the rest of the men you work with?			
Much or a little more important than theirs	26		24
No more and no less important than theirs	71		58
Much or a little less important than theirs	3		14
Not ascertained	0		4
	100		100

* Percentage difference between plants is significant.

of the operators at Advance said, "Yes, I feel I really am a part of it," whereas only 69 percent of the Stand operators gave this response. Although this percentage difference is *not* statistically significant, it does offer evidence that there was a somewhat greater feeling of group membership among the Advance than the Stand workers. When one considers that the Advance groups had been in existence a much shorter time than had those of Stand and that the length of time that a group has been in existence is usually positively correlated with such feelings of group membership,[3] the difference in favor of the Advance workers takes on added importance.

More striking evidence of the extent to which the operators at Advance felt themselves to be associated in a common group endeavor is seen in the comparison of responses to the question, "When you have a problem on your job, how free do you feel to call on others in your work group to help you with it?" Seventy-one percent of the Advance operators, as against only 48 percent of those at Stand, reported that they felt "very free" to call on the other members of their work group. This difference in percentage is statistically significant and indicates a greater feeling of common goals among the Advance operators. The feeling that members of a group are willing to cooperate rather than to compete is characteristic of what has been defined as cohesive groups.

The unwillingness of the Advance operators to attribute any greater importance to their own jobs than to those of the other members of their group offers additional inferential support to their feeling of common group purpose. Seventy-one percent of the Advance versus only 58 percent of the Stand operators reported that their job was "no more and no less important" than the jobs of the other men they worked with. Although this percentage difference is *not* statistically significant, it does provide

[3] Seashore, S., *Group Cohesiveness in the Industrial Work Group.* Ann Arbor, Mich.: Institute for Social Research, December 1955.

some further evidence for the high degree of group unity among the Advance operators.

The responses to these three questions suggest that the centralization of the control functions forced substantial contact among the operators in the new plant. This enforced contact in turn created a high degree of psychological identification with the group and with the common objectives of its members. Despite the substantially shorter time the operators in the new plant had worked together, as compared with the men at Stand, the feelings of group attraction appear to be as strong or stronger there than in the older plant.

Summary

We have looked at the company as a total social system in this chapter. The introduction of automation into one part of the system had repercussions on other parts of the system, on the automated plant, and on the other units of the production department.

The high costs which would arise from losing the productive capacity of any of the units in the new plant caused the management of the company to expand its program of preventive maintenance by centralizing the maintenance operations. The impact of this reorganization was felt most strongly by the men in top maintenance positions in the various power plants and by the maintenance men who remained in the plant service groups. The construction of the automated power plant also reflected itself in the threat to worker job security in the older plants of the utility. Reduced operating loads and threats of skill obsolescence caused the operators in the older plant to be concerned about the security of their future in the company.

Within the new power plant the reduction in the number of levels of supervision was seen to have had effects on the rela-

tive influence of different groups and on the degree of communication achieved in that plant. There was an increase in the satisfaction with the amount of communication from the top of the plant organization to the nonsupervisory employees, and a greater sharing of the decision-making power by the top staff of the plant with the foremen and the workers. Structural changes in the plant design also seem to have had effects on the feelings of the workers about the other members of their work groups. The centralization of operating controls appears to have had positive effects in the creation of greater group unity among the Advance operators.

Chapter 4

JOB CHANGES ACCOMPANYING AUTOMATION

During the past half century two influences have caused American industrial managements to design the jobs of the workers in as simple a manner as possible. The first of these influences was the scientific management movement started by F. W. Taylor[1] and continued by industrial engineers to the present time. One of the objectives of this movement was to effect an "enormous saving of time and therefore increase the output . . . through eliminating unnecessary motions and substituting fast for slow and inefficient motions."[2] The theory behind this movement rested on the notion that "among the various methods and implements used in each element of each trade there is always one method and one implement which is quicker and better than

[1] Taylor, F. W., *The Principles of Scientific Management.* New York: Harper & Brothers, 1911.

[2] *Ibid.*, p. 24.

any of the rest."[3] This emphasis on the one best way resulted in the redesigning of jobs, based on time-and-motion studies, to require fewer motions.

The development by Henry Ford of the assembly line method for producing automobiles was the second strong influence toward the rationalization and fractionization of jobs. In assembly line procedure, as the product moves down the line each element is added or each small process is performed by a single worker; additionally, the fractionization of the product into its component elements is paralleled by a fractionization of jobs to correspond to these elements. The simple motions which are the objectives of the methods engineers found a natural setting in this procedure.[4] Thus, the typical assembly line job is a continuous repetition of the same small pattern of movements. For eight hours a day the worker tightens a few bolts, installs a gearshift, or swabs the cylinder holes in an engine block as a seemingly endless succession of identical parts is brought to him and taken from him by a moving conveyer belt.

The efficacy of these methods of designing jobs, both in the attainment of greater output and especially in their effects on the workers, has been questioned in many places.[5,6] The notion that the total pattern of the worker's activities during the day can be synthesized from an analysis of his elemental movements has been attacked as physically, physiologically, and psychologically unsound. This engineering approach to an analysis and resynthesis of the elemental movements loses sight of the wholeness of the person, the interdependence of all his movements.

[3] *Ibid.*, p. 25.

[4] The marriage of the scientific management movement to Ford's development of assembly line production methods resulted in the types of jobs caricatured in Charlie Chaplin's famous film, *Modern Times.*

[5] Ghiselli, E. E., and Brown, C. W., *Personnel and Industrial Psychology* (2d ed.). New York: McGraw-Hill, 1955, pp. 300–306.

[6] Gomberg, W., "The Use of Psychology in Industry," *Management Science,* 1957, Vol. 3, No. 4, pp. 348–370.

Another assumption of these procedures which lacks validity is the notion that there is one best way of doing the job for everybody. This idea neglects the obvious fact that there are individual differences in physical and mental ability from worker to worker. The best method for the ablest worker may not necessarily be the best one for a less able worker. A third fallacious assumption implicit in time-and-motion methods is that human performance in any given activity displays a high degree of consistency. Experimental evidence indicates that performance varies markedly from hour to hour. With the design of these jobs based on such invalid assumptions, it is questionable whether employers are benefiting from these innovations to the extent that they have been led to believe. It is possible that they are actually penalizing themselves by neglecting the physiological, psychological, and sociological realities of the work situation.

If greater efficiency and productivity are not being gained, then has this system at least benefited the worker by making the job more enjoyable, more interesting, *less* fatiguing? Walker and Guest,[7] of Yale University's Technology Project, in their study of work on the assembly line, have documented the dissatisfactions of these workers. The principal and almost universal complaint was, "I'd like to do more things. That's the trouble with the line. Monotony. You repeat the same thing day in, day out." Within these mass production industries the workers who were able to set their own pace and who had a variety of even these fractionalized tasks to do expressed greater satisfaction with their jobs than did the workers who had the more typical repetitive jobs. Interviews with workers in a meat packing house provide additional evidence for the monotony associated with assembly line jobs.[8] In this situation where the carcasses were car-

[7] Walker, C. R., and Guest, R. H., *The Man on the Assembly Line*. Cambridge, Mass.: Harvard University Press, 1952.

[8] Blum, F. H., *Toward A Democratic Work Process*. New York: Harper & Brothers, 1953.

ried past the workers on conveyor belts, the men indicated that the sameness of the work every day created feelings of fatigue and apathy, that they wished they could escape the repetitiveness of the work, and that the only reward for the worker from this kind of job was an adequate pay check at the end of the week. This lack of satisfaction, of interest, and of involvement in the work means that the worker looks upon his job as something he has to do forty hours or more a week to earn a living for himself and his family. Feelings of pride and enjoyment in the work, of task completion, of service to society, or even to the company, are missing for these workers.

Although the scientific management movement, with its concentration on the methods of work, has undoubtedly contributed significantly to the increased productivity of American industry, it has not taken into account the findings of biological and social sciences, and has therefore been less effective than it might have been. Increased productivity has been obtained at the expense of condemning workers to spend their working lives at repetitive, monotonous, and intellectually deadening jobs.

Apologists for the system of job rationalization have claimed that workers would rather have jobs which permit them to daydream and talk to the other men without having to concentrate on a continually changing job. They claim that the worker in our present society "wants a job in which he does not have to think." Although this statement may be true for a small minority of workers, the evidence available from the several systematic studies of repetitive work offers support for the claim by Professor Georges Friedmann of the Sorbonne that for most workers any expression of a preference for "mediocre, subdivided, segmentalized tasks [arises] simply because they *have never had experience in more responsible work*."[9] One of the consistent findings in studies done by the Organizational Be-

[9] Friedmann, G., *Industrial Society*. Glencoe, Ill.: Free Press, 1955, p. 154.

havior and Organizational Change Program of the Survey Research Center of The University of Michigan has been the strong positive relationship between the level of job grade—representing the skill requirements for the jobs—and the degree of intrinsic job satisfaction reported by the workers.[10,11] Walker and Guest found that those workers on the assembly line who expressed the least dissatisfaction with their jobs were the ones who had a variety of jobs to do or were occasionally shifted from one job to another. Job rotation has been suggested as a device for alleviating the monotony and fatigue of repeating the same pattern of movements hour after hour. Rotation permits the worker to use different sets of muscles, to make different movements, and to make different decisions.

As a result of his studies, Walker has advocated the "enlarging" of jobs by replacing the endless repetitiveness of the present jobs with a variety of challenging tasks. By having the chance to utilize his various skills and abilities, the worker would thus be provided a means of achieving job satisfaction.[12] This movement toward expanded responsibilities for the worker is only gradually gaining acceptance in American industry. Because the principle of job rationalization is so well ingrained in the minds of management, the idea that jobs must be designed to be as simple and unchallenging as possible is axiomatic and the possibility of job enlargement meets strong resistance. For this reason very few companies have redesigned their jobs along these lines and, in those that have, no systematic studies of the effects of such changes have been conducted.

[10] Morse, N. C., *Satisfactions in the White-Collar Job.* Ann Arbor, Mich.: Institute for Social Research, 1953.

[11] Mann, F. C., "A Study of Work Satisfaction as a Function of the Discrepancy between Inferred Aspirations and Achievements." Unpublished doctoral dissertation, The University of Michigan, 1953.

[12] Walker, C. R., "Work Methods, Working Conditions, and Morale." In Kornhauser, A., Dubin, R., and Ross, A. M. (eds.), *Industrial Conflict.* New York: McGraw-Hill, 1954.

Job Structure in Power Plants

In the new power plant, Advance, through the integration of the boiler and turbine operations, and the introduction of feedback and other automatic controls, the conversion to the unit system of production required management to reconsider the structure of the jobs. Since the division of labor used in the manning of the older plants could not be directly transferred to Advance, jobs in the new plant were designed by combining functions which had been performed by a single operator in the older plants. This made it possible to compare the attitudes and feelings of men with these enlarged jobs with those of the men in the older plant who worked at more fractionalized jobs.

In the older plant, three major operating groups performed the three production functions—boiler, turbine and condenser, and electrical operations. The electrical switchboard operators' status and pay were higher than either the boiler or turbine groups. The "top grade" wage rate for boiler and turbine men was three grades less—amounting to about twenty-five cents an hour less—than their counterpart in the electrical group. The men in the boiler and turbine rooms criticized this distinction as artificial and felt that it did not reflect true differences in either skill requirements or job responsibilities. Table 4:1 shows the point ratings assigned to each factor for each of the three jobs by a joint committee of representatives from the company and the union.

Within each of these operating groups there were a number of job gradations, especially in the boiler operations, where the simplest and dirtiest jobs existed. The following jobs were found in the boiler room, listed in the order of ascending skill requirements: flue blower-ash handler, fan operator, water tender, assistant fireman, and fireman. A similar division into more and less skilled jobs was made in the turbine and electrical groups.

Jobs in the low pressure boiler operations largely involved

the manual handling of equipment. The flue blower-ash handler had the assignment of directing the hoses inside the furnaces to clear the slag from the sides. He also operated the equipment for disposing of the ash at the bottom of the furnaces. The fan operator spent his working period in isolation at the top of the

TABLE 4:1
Job Evaluation Point Ratings

Factor	Switchboard Operator 1st	Turbine Operator 1st	Fireman
1. Work experience required	28	26	26
2. Specialized education required	5	3	1
3. Physical skill required	5	5	5
4. Physical effort required	3	3	3
5. Complexity of duties	47	40	40
6. Seriousness of errors	9	9	9
7. Hazards	9	3	7
8. Adverse working conditions	1	2	2
9. Contacts with people outside the company	1	0	0
10. Contacts within the company	6	4	3
11. Responsibility for safety of others	13	5	8
12. Responsibility for company property	2	1	1
13. Amount of supervision received	5	5	5
14. Responsibility for work of others	6	6	2
Total Points	140	112	112
Corresponding T-Grade	16	13	13

plant tending the operation of the induced-draft fans. The view of the production process, even by the highly skilled fireman, who was responsible for maintaining the proper boiler temperature, was restricted to the operation of his pair of boilers. The job responsibilities of the turbine and electrical operators were similarly limited to a small segment of the overall production process, although they included less manual work and more dial watching.

The operating jobs in the new plant were organized in an

entirely different manner. Part of this change was the direct result of the technological changes, but a major part stemmed from a decision by management to develop operating personnel qualified in all aspects of the production process. The integration of the boiler and turbine functions and their controls meant that only operators with knowledge of both turbines and boilers could be employed and that the distinction between the turbine and boiler operators could no longer be maintained. This requirement led the company to examine the possibility of further enlarging the operating jobs to include knowledge of the electrical switching operations as well as those of the boilers and turbines. As a result, the distinctions among operators in the older plant according to the type of equipment they operated were eliminated in the new plant. Only one class of operators was established for the new plant: power plant operators.

A skill hierarchy remained within the operating group, but it included only three skill classifications: power plant operator A, power plant operator B, and power plant helper. The A operator was the most highly skilled classification. The men in this category were expected to have most of the skills and, especially, the knowledge previously held separately by the skilled boiler, turbine, and electrical operators. Their jobs now encompassed responsibility for the entire production process. The A operators, all of whom had transferred from specialized jobs in the older plants in the system, experienced a tremendous job enlargement.

In parallel fashion but at a slightly lower skill level, those men who transferred to Advance as B operators also experienced an enlargement of their jobs. Each B operator was paired with an A operator in his work, learning and receiving informal work direction from him. At the time of the study these pairings were made to ensure complementarity of skills and knowledge. These men worked on all aspects of operations.

The operator helper was the lowest skill classification among the operating jobs. The men in this category performed

the few dirty and less desirable tasks which still remained in the new plant.

During each shift, pairs of A and B operators were assigned to the control stations and to a general utility position. One A-B pair was situated in each of the three control stations—the two boiler-turbine control rooms and the electrical switchboard. A fourth pair was split up, the A operator patrolling the various portions of the plant and the mat, and the B operator serving as the work leader for the helpers in the condenser room. The fifth pair served as additional personnel to be assigned to whatever special jobs had to be done during the shift.

Rotation among these jobs was also originally instituted as part of the training program to prepare the men for the new jobs. This practice was continued past the end of the formal training period, with the men changing positions weekly. Thus, differences between the perceptions and attitudes of the Advance operators about their new jobs and the Stand operators about theirs reflected both the differences between enlarged jobs and specialized jobs, and between job rotation and fixed, permanent assignments.

In the rest of this chapter we shall report comparisons of the questionnaire responses of the operators in the two plants concerning perceptions of changes in their jobs, the training they received for these jobs, and the changes in and present state of their feelings about their jobs.

Perceptions of Job Changes

These job changes had striking effects on the men in the new plant. They reported that their present jobs were bigger in many ways than the ones they held in the older plants (the following discussion is based on Table 4:2). Eighty-five percent of the operators who transferred from older plants reported that

they had "much more responsibility" on their jobs now than they had had several years ago.[13] Also, almost all of this group (97 percent) reported that their jobs required more training now than earlier. Their present jobs were perceived by the men to be ones with increased responsibility requiring a greater amount of training than did their older jobs.

Two aspects of this enlargement of the operating jobs—the use of present skills and the development of new skills—deserve attention. Although they occurred in combination in this job change, the evidence from the data in Stand suggests that their independent occurrence can have different effects on the workers' attitudes toward their jobs.

The first facet of this change was that the new jobs made greater demands on the abilities, skills, and knowledge which the men already had when they transferred to the new plant. Almost two-thirds (63 percent) of the men reported that they spent more time doing things they were skilled at than they had previously. There was a greater feeling that now their jobs really utilized their best abilities. More than three-quarters (77 per-

[13] In order to make the comparisons between the attitudes of the men in the two plants more valid, we included in this analysis only those men in Advance who had previously worked in the older plants of this company. By eliminating from consideration the operators who had been recruited from the surrounding area, it was felt that the remaining men in the new plant would have had previous work experiences comparable to the experiences of the men in the older plant. In fact, the distributions of the background and experiential characteristics of the selected group of Advance operators are very similar to the distributions of these characteristics in the Stand operators. On age, education, and length of service with the company, the two groups show little difference from each other. The only major difference between the groups was found in the number and kinds of licenses held by the men. All operators on the steam side of the older plants had to hold at least a high pressure boiler operator license. The turbine operators 1st had to have a higher level license—2nd class stationary engineer; and the foremen had to have 1st class stationary engineer licenses. Many more of the Advance operators than Stand operators had licenses higher than the minimal boiler operator license. Whether this difference represented a higher ability level in this group, greater motivation, or merely the different job requirements of the new plant cannot be ascertained from these data. The last is certainly an important factor since the jobs of all Advance operators included work with the turbines, and the men were therefore required to have the same licenses needed by the turbine operator 1st in the older plant.

cent) of the Advance operators said that their jobs gave them a "very good" or "fairly good chance to do the things [they are] best at." Of the operators in Stand, only 44 percent said that their jobs gave them a chance to do the things they were best at. The latter figure is characteristically found in most organizations where highly specialized, low-skilled jobs exist.

The second aspect of the change—and it was even more of a reversal of the trend toward job simplification—was the necessity for the operators to learn new things and acquire new knowledge and skills on the job. Seventy-seven percent of the Advance operators said that they were learning much more on their jobs now than they were several years ago, and 57 percent said they were spending more time now doing things they were not skilled at than they had previously. Thus, in addition to the jobs providing a greater opportunity to use the skills and knowledge which the operators already had, these new jobs also demanded that the men expand their capabilities by acquiring new knowledge and skills on parts of the operations with which they had had no previous experience or training. Note again that 77 percent of the Advance operators reported both that they had a "very" or "fairly good chance" to do the things they were best at and that they were learning "much" or "a little more" on their jobs now than they had before.

In addition to having the actual content of their jobs changed, the operators had the opportunity for greater physical mobility around the plant. The weekly rotation from position to position and the required patrol tours probably contributed to 66 percent of the operators saying they moved around the plant much or a little more now than before. These men were no longer restricted to one part of the plant and to a limited range of activities connected with a highly specialized job. Moreover, most (63 percent) of them said they made more contact with the other men now than they had done in the older plants.

Although these data show that a large proportion of the op-

erators in the new plant had experienced major changes in their jobs, the question may be raised as to the extent to which this proportion merely represents changes which occurred in the normal promotion process. In an attempt to answer this question partially, a comparison of the perceptions of the operators at

TABLE 4:2

Perceptions of Changes in Jobs

Men Who Report:	Percent of Men in Each Group Who Report: Advance Operators (N = 35)	Stand Operators (N = 109)	Advance Maintenance (N = 23)	Advance Coal Handling (N = 23)
General				
1-39. Much more responsibility on the job now	85	55*	26*	35*
1-47. Job requires much more training now	97	54*	57*	17*
Old Skills				
1-46. Much or a little more time spent doing things skilled at now	63	49	48	35*
1-9. Very or fairly good chance to do things best at	77	44*	70	48*
1-40. Much or a little less time doing dirty work now	74	41*	13*	0*
New Skills				
1-44. Learning much more on the job now	77	27*	61	13*
1-45. Much or a little more time spent doing things *not* skilled at	57	23*	48	39
Mobility				
1-42. Much or a little more moving around the plant	66	14*	48	25*
1-43. Many or a few more contacts with the men now	63	20*	52	13*

* Percentage is significantly different from the corresponding one for the Advance operators at the .05 level of confidence, the level of confidence used in all statistical tests in this chapter.

Advance with those at Stand is presented in Table 4:2. In columns 1 and 2 are shown the percent of operators in each plant who reported particular changes in their jobs in the two previous years. Only one of these percentage differences fails to reach statistical significance. This lack of significance represents more the changes accompanying the promotions of 44 percent of the Stand operators rather than a lack of change in Advance.

As an attempt to control for the possibility of a general positive "halo" effect being associated with working in a new plant, with better working conditions, and at higher pay, comparisons on these questions were also made between the operating group and the two other major work groups in Advance: maintenance and coal handling. The percent of men in these groups reporting recent changes in their jobs is presented in columns 3 and 4 of Table 4:2. On every question a greater percentage of operators than of either maintenance or coal-handling workers indicated that their jobs had been enlarged, that they had greater physical mobility around the plant, and that they were making many more contacts with other men.

Changes in Job Interest and Job Satisfaction

The combination of job enlargement and job rotation resulted in marked changes in the attitudes of the Advance operators toward their jobs. The variety of experiences and the greater opportunity for social interaction with their coworkers created a positive attitude toward job rotation in these men. Almost every one of the Advance operators reported that he liked doing the operating jobs in rotation. This attitude contrasted sharply with that of the Stand operators who were asked how they would feel about rotating on the operating jobs. Only a little over half of this group thought they would like to do the

other operating jobs in rotation with their own. Almost 25 percent of these operators actually anticipated disliking such a change in procedures. The distribution of responses to questions about job rotation appears in Table 4:3. Thus, although the data from Advance indicated overwhelming satisfaction with job rotation, a sizable proportion of the men in the older plant feared the effects of introducing such changes into their jobs.

TABLE 4:3

Feelings about Job Rotation

	In Percent		
	Advance (N = 35)		*Stand* (N = 109)
2-97. How would (do) you feel about doing these jobs in rotation with your own job?			
Like it very much	70	*	37
Like it fairly well	20		19
Don't care, don't like or dislike	5		14
Dislike it a little	2		6
Dislike it a lot	0		17
Not ascertained	3		7
	100		100

* Difference in percentages between the plants is significant.

All 35 of the new Advance operators said their jobs were "much more interesting now" than they were several years ago. In addition, 33 of the 35 said they were much or a little more satisfied with their jobs now than before. Forty-nine percent of the operators at Advance reported that they liked their jobs very much; another 31 percent said they liked their jobs fairly well. Thus, four out of five of the Advance operators said they liked their jobs, whereas only two out of five of the Stand men expressed similar feelings about their jobs (Table 4:4).

This high level of job satisfaction among the operators in the automated plant is obviously the result of a combination of

TABLE 4:4

Liking for the Job and Changes in Job Interest and in Job Satisfaction

(Comparisons of Operators in Advance and Stand)

	In Percent		
	Advance (N = 35)		*Stand* (N = 109)
1-41. Is your job *more or less interesting* now than it was several years ago?			
Job is much more interesting	100	*	33
A little more interesting	0		25
About as interesting now as then	0		16
A little less interesting	0		9
Much less interesting	0		13
Not ascertained	0		4
	100		100
1-48. Taking everything into consideration, how satisfied are you with your job now as compared to several years ago?			
Much more satisfied	71	*	16
A little more satisfied	23		11
About as satisfied now as I was	3		11
A little less satisfied	3		20
Much less satisfied	0		34
Not ascertained	0		8
	100		100
1-15. Considering your job as a whole, how well do you like it?			
Like it very much	49 } 80	*	21 } 40
Like it fairly well	31 }		19 }
Like some things about it, dislike others	20		47
Don't like it too well	0		7
Don't like it at all	0		6
	100		100

* Difference in percentages between the plants is significant.

all the various job changes which have been described above. As psychologists, however, we are more interested in the effects of the specific aspects of these changes than we are in their total

effect on job satisfaction. Were all of these changes of equal importance in creating these positive feelings? Or were some aspects of the job enlargement more crucial than others?

No definitive answer to these questions can be obtained from our data for several reasons. The principal difficulty is the lack of distribution in the responses of the Advance operators to the questions—they all perceived changes and liked them. This lack of variation probably resulted from the cumulative effects of job enlargement and the increased satisfaction with their recent promotions and with their improved wages and working conditions. Since there was no variation, it was not possible to correlate the degree of perceived job change with the level of job satisfaction among the Advance workers.

To obtain some estimate of the effects of the job changes on the workers' attitudes, we have investigated these relationships among the Stand workers, on the assumption that their attitudes were similar to those of the workers at Advance prior to their transfer. The responses of the men in this plant showed a wider range of attitudes than existed in Advance. Even in this older plant, because of the occurrence of promotions in the operating groups, a small proportion of the operators reported changes in their jobs in the direction of job enlargement. From the relative sizes of the correlations obtained between the perceptions of job changes and changes in job interest and satisfaction, it is possible to infer the relative importance of each aspect of the job changes in determining the satisfactions of the men with their jobs. If change in one part of the job is more highly correlated with changes in job satisfaction than is another change, then we can assume that the former change was more important than the latter at Advance.

The findings from both plants indicate that job interest, although a major component of job satisfaction, is not identical with it. Whereas all 35 of the Advance workers reported their job as being much more interesting, only 25 of them said they

were "much more satisfied" with their jobs. The correlation at Stand between change in job interest and change in job satisfaction was .43, which, although statistically significant, is by no means perfect.

Further support for the existence of a separation between job interest and job satisfaction in work attitudes comes from a consideration of the relationships of these two job characteristics with changes in Stand. Table 4:5 shows the correlations between

TABLE 4:5

Correlations between Perceptions of Changes in Operating Jobs and Changes in Job Interest and in Job Satisfaction

(Stand)

Job Change	*Change in:* *Job Interest*	*Job Satisfaction*
Increased job responsibility	.37*	.12
More training required by job	.32*	.33*
More time spent in skilled work	.43*	.26*
Less time doing dirty work	.60*	.15
Learning more on the job	.56*	.45*
More moving around the plant	.01	.16
More contacts with the other men	.15	.04

* Correlations are significantly different from zero.

each of the questions about job changes and changes in job interest and satisfaction in the old plant. (In every case except the question about change in the amount of dirty work, the positive end of the scale indicates more of the specific characteristic—for example, *more* learning on the job.)

There are two particularly interesting points in this table. First of all, it appears that several of the differences in perceptions of job changes between the operators in the two plants did not contribute much to changing the workers' job interests or satisfactions. This inference is based on the fact that whereas greater learning on the job, more training required, and more time spent in skilled work were significantly related to increased

job interest and satisfaction, greater physical mobility and more frequent contact with fellow workers did not show such a relationship. Thus, although a significantly greater proportion of Advance than Stand operators reported increased opportunity to move around and to meet with the other men, these changes appear to have had minimal effects in determining the men's total liking for the jobs themselves. Increased job interest derives, it would seem, from altering the job content rather than the more peripheral aspects of the job situation.

The other important point suggested by this table can be inferred from the differences in the size of the correlations between the perception of a job change and change in feelings of job interest and job satisfaction. Comparison of the two columns shows that most of the job changes which took place at Advance were more related to increased job interest than to increased job satisfaction. Giving a man much more responsibility made his job more interesting but not necessarily more satisfying. Decreasing the amount of dirty work to be done on the job was related to greater job interest, but not to greater job satisfaction. The generally stronger relationship of the job changes at Advance with increased interest may account for the unanimous expression there of greater job interest and the less than unanimous report of increased job satisfaction. This is not to say that job interest will not contribute to a worker's job satisfaction, but merely that this factor is not the only determinant of such satisfaction. The correlation between change in job interest and liking for the job was only .45, which, while statistically significant, indicates only a small proportion of common variance in the two measures.

Seemingly of much greater importance in creating a satisfactory job is the feeling by the worker that his skills are being utilized. Consistent with the findings in other studies of the Survey Research Center,[14] a strong positive relationship ($r = .68$)

[14] Morse, *op. cit.*

was found at Stand between the men's perception of having a "chance to do the things they are best at" and their liking for their jobs. This relationship emphasizes the importance which workers attached to being able to express themselves through their jobs. The feeling that the job they did eight hours a day required the use of their best knowledge and abilities made them more satisfied with their work.

The high degree of job satisfaction among the Advance operators reflected the strong feeling in most of the men there that their enlarged jobs had given them a chance to capitalize on their knowledge about power plant operations and to perform the tasks which they felt equipped to do. The importance of utilizing the skills of these workers in the design of the new operating jobs is even more dramatically underscored by a further analysis of the relationship between skill utilization and job satisfaction.

One of the major changes which occurred in the new plant (see Table 4:2) was that the men were generally given much more responsibility on their jobs. Increased responsibility has frequently been offered as a means of overcoming some of the defects of overspecialization of jobs. Our data suggest, however, that responsibility is a two-edged sword, and that merely increasing job responsibility may, in fact, diminish rather than augment job satisfaction. More than half the men in both plants reported that they had "much more job responsibility now than a few years ago." For some of these men this increased responsibility meant having a greater chance to use their talents, but for the others it did not. Table 4:6 compares the reported job satisfaction of these two groups in each plant. In both plants where the increased responsibility was accompanied by the chance to do the things the men felt they were best at, a significantly greater proportion of these men liked their jobs than did those who were given responsibility without this opportunity.

A similar but less strong relationship was also found from

an examination of the groups which reported that their jobs were now *much more interesting*. Again, in both plants, a higher proportion of workers who liked their jobs was found among those who felt their jobs gave them a good chance to do the things they were best at than among those who did not feel this

TABLE 4:6

Relationship between Chance to Do Things Best At and Liking for the Job

(Only those operators who reported having had much more responsibility)

	Don't like job or dislike some things, like others	*Like job very or fairly much*
Advance		
Very or fairly good chance	2	21
None, a little, or some chance to do things best at	3	* 3
Stand		
Very or fairly good chance	8	22
None, a little, or some chance to do things best at	23	* 6

* The chi-square tests of independence for each of these relationships were significant.

way (Table 4:7). Only the percentage difference in Stand was significant, however. This finding again supports the contention that making a job interesting is not sufficient to ensure worker satisfaction with the job. More crucial to ensuring intrinsic job satisfaction would appear to be the designing of jobs to utilize men's abilities.

The new design of the operating jobs at Advance was a major step in the direction of job enlargement. The new jobs increased the opportunity for the workers to learn new things about power plant operations while carrying greater job responsibilities. Relatively less effort was exerted to create jobs which

TABLE 4:7

Relationship between Chance to Do Things Best At and Liking for the Job

(Only those operators saying their job is much more interesting now)

	Don't like job or dislike some things, like others	*Like job very or fairly much*
Advance		
Very or fairly good chance	3	23
None, a little, or some chance to do things best at	3	4
Stand		
Very or fairly good chance	5	19
None, a little, or some chance to do things best at	9	* 3

* The chi-square test of independence was significant for Stand.

capitalized on the skills which were already present in the workers. This emphasis on the acquisition of new skills resulted in a more pronounced expression of increased interest than in increased satisfaction with the job. Presumably as these operators became more proficient at the parts of their jobs which were new at the time of this study, job satisfaction increased to an even higher level.

Worker Interdependence and Tension

Accompanying the considerable enlargement of the operating jobs in the new plant was a greater degree of interdependence among the operators. Even in the older plant the complex interrelationships among the various production functions required the men to coordinate their activities effectively and to rely on each other in order to get their jobs done. Coordination

may be required *among* different groups, as when changes in the electric power supply required changes in the boiler operations, or *within* operating groups, as when the turbine operators and the auxiliary operators had to cooperate in taking a turbine off the line. Interdependent activity among workers has long been a characteristic of the electric power industry.

The extent to which the men felt that the performance of other men in their work group and in the rest of the plant affected their own performance can be seen in Table 4:8. Even

TABLE 4:8

Perceived Effects of Others' Performances on Your Own Work

	In Percent	
	Advance (N = 35)	*Stand* (N = 109)
1-22. If the *other men in your work group* don't do their jobs well, does it make *your work* harder to do?		
Much or quite a bit harder	66	59
Somewhat harder	28	23
A little harder or makes little difference	6	17
Not ascertained	0	1
	100	100
1-23. If men in other groups in *this power plant* don't do their jobs well, does it make *your work* harder to do?		
Much or quite a bit harder	66	55
Somewhat harder	17	19
A little harder or makes little difference	17	24
Not ascertained	0	2
	100	100

in Stand, over half the operators reported that if other men in either their work group or the rest of the power plant did not do their jobs well it made their own work much or quite a bit harder to do. Only a slightly and not significantly larger propor-

tion of the operators at Advance reported that poor performance by their coworkers made their own jobs more difficult. These results indicate that there was no substantial change in the extent to which the men felt that their work could be influenced by the work of other people in the plant.

Although the degree to which the operators felt that they affected each other's work appears to have remained relatively unchanged in the new plant, the operators at Advance reported depending on each other and on the foreman to a somewhat greater extent than did the men at Stand. This dependence took the form of looking to the foreman and the other men for suggestions and advice about particular problems that came up on the job. The foremen at Advance, moreover, were seen as depending on the men more often than were the foremen at Stand. The responses to the three questions supporting these conclusions can be found in Table 4:9. Here we see that about the same proportion of operators in the two plants (about three out of ten) said that they depend on the other men or on the foreman a great deal or quite a lot, and were in turn depended upon by the foreman a great deal or quite a lot. It was in the "somewhat" category of dependence that the Advance operators were found proportionately more often than the Stand men. Very few of the Advance operators said that they depended or were depended upon "a little" or "not at all." Thus the operators at Advance more frequently found themselves depending on the other men or on their foreman for suggestions and advice than did the men at Stand.

The relatively frequent occasions on which the Advance operators have found themselves relying on the knowledge of other men in their groups appears to have created a feeling that their jobs were necessarily interrelated. In the eyes of these men it was not sufficient that they know only their own jobs; rather, they must know what is going on all around their area of

TABLE 4:9

Interdependence among Workers and Foremen

	In Percent		
	Advance (N = 35)		Stand (N = 109)
1-26. How much do you depend on the *other men in your work group* for suggestions and advice on particular problems *you* face on your job?			
A great deal or quite a lot	31		36
Somewhat	49	*	27
A little or not at all	20		37
	100		100
1-28. How much does *your foreman* depend on *you* for suggestions and advice on particular problems that come up?			
A great deal or quite a lot	29		25
Somewhat	51	*	22
A little or not at all	20		52
Not ascertained	0		1
	100		100
1-29. How much do *you* depend on *your foreman* for suggestions and advice on particular problems that come up?			
A great deal or quite a lot	29		26
Somewhat	60	*	27
A little or not at all	11		42
Not ascertained	0		5
	100		100
1-19. If each man knows his *own* job, how important is it to the running of the plant that they *know each other's jobs*?			
Very or quite important	94	*	76
Of no, little, or some importance	6		24
	100		100

* Difference in percentages between the plants is significant.

operations. When asked, "If each man knows his *own* job, how important is it to the running of the plant that they know each other's job?" all but two of the Advance operators reported that it was "very" or "quite" important. Only 76 percent of the Stand

operators expressed this same feeling of a need for mutual knowledge (Table 4:9).

The basis for the somewhat greater interdependence found among the Advance operators is suggested by the responses to questions concerning the way the men felt while on the job. When asked, "How often does your work make you feel 'jumpy' or nervous?" only about a quarter of the men in Advance indicated that they were "never" or "very seldom" jumpy or nervous on the job. The rest of the Advance operators expressed occasional or frequent feelings of nervousness in their work. Similarly, more Advance operators expressed a feeling of some tenseness and being on edge when important pieces of equipment were being started up or being shut down. Proportionately more of the Advance operators felt occasionally nervous or tense from their work than did the Stand operators (Table 4:10). Men who reported that they felt a "little" or "somewhat" tense or on edge when the equipment was being handled were also those who said that their work made them feel occasionally jumpy or nervous. These feelings of tension seemed to be very specific to those particular occasions when the major crises on the job occurred.

The specificity of the source of tension is attested to by the responses to other questions concerning the men's feelings about the general work situation. When asked how much danger or chance for danger there was in their work, a proportionately greater number of men at Advance reported that there was no danger or only occasional danger in their work. More Stand operators were concerned about the potential danger in their work. The distribution of responses to the question, "Do you ever worry that a problem will come up that you won't be able to handle?" was about the same for the operators in the two plants. Slightly less than half the men in each plant said they "never" or "very seldom" worried about such a problem (Table 4:10). These results indicate that the tension expressed by the Advance operators to the questions about their specific work

TABLE 4:10

Tension and Danger in the Operating Jobs

	In Percent		
	Advance		Stand
2-17. How often does your work make you feel "jumpy" or nervous?	(N = 35)		(N = 95)
Very frequently or fairly often	17		11
Occasionally	57		40
Never or very seldom	26	*	48
Not ascertained	0		1
	100		100
2-18. When some important piece of equipment (turbine, generator, boiler, etc.) is being started up or shut down, how does it affect you?	(N = 35)		(N = 95)
Makes me very or quite tense and "on edge"	17		9
Somewhat tense and "on edge"	14		6
A little tense and "on edge"	51		37
Not at all tense and "on edge"	18	*	45
Not ascertained	0		3
	100		100
1-12. How much danger or chance for danger is there in your work?	(N = 35)		(N = 109)
There is no danger or only occasional danger	37	*	12
Have to be careful constantly, but little danger if careful and alert	63		71
Work is very dangerous	0		11
Not ascertained	0		6
	100		100
2-20. Do you ever worry that a problem will come up that you won't be able to handle?	(N = 35)		(N = 95)
Worry a great deal or quite a bit of the time	14		18
Some of the time	43		33
Never or very seldom	43		48
Not ascertained	0		1
	100		100

* Difference in percentages between plants is significant.

situation derived primarily from their experiences with the equipment they operated rather than from a perception of general danger in their work situation or from any personal feelings of inadequacy.

This job-related tension probably accounted for much of the dependent behavior reported by the Advance operators. The relationship between their dependence on their fellow workers

TABLE 4:11

Dependence and Feelings of Nervousness and Tension on the Job

(Advance Operators)

1-26. Depend on the other men for suggestions and advice:	1-17. Feel "jumpy" or nervous:	
	Very frequently, fairly often, or occasionally	*Very seldom or never*
A great deal or quite a lot	11	0
	*	
Somewhat	11	6
Not at all or a little	4	3

1-26. Depend on the other men for suggestions and advice:	1-18. Handling of equipment makes me:	
	Very, quite, or somewhat tense	*A little or not at all tense*
A great deal or quite a lot	5	6
Somewhat	5	12
Not at all or a little	1	6

* 2 × 2 relationship is significant. (Exact chi-square test.)

for suggestions and advice on particular job problems and their feelings of nervousness and tension on the job are presented in Table 4:11. All eleven of the operators who said they depended a "great deal" or "quite a lot" on the other men expressed feelings of nervousness about their work occasionally or frequently. This is a significantly greater proportion than among those men who felt they depended only "somewhat," "a little," or "not at all." The same trend in relationship is seen in the proportions of men who said they were tense and on edge when equipment was

being started up. Proportionately more of the men who depended a "great deal" or "quite a lot" also felt "somewhat tense" than did the men who felt "somewhat," "a little," or "not at all" dependent. The difference, however, is not statistically significant.

Further insight into the possible reasons for the degree of dependence shown by the operators at Advance can be gained from another relationship, shown in Table 4:12. Here we see that the operators who reported depending on the other men "a great deal" or "quite a lot" were also somewhat dissatisfied

TABLE 4:12

Dependence and Satisfaction with Training

(Advance Operators)

1-26. Depend on the other men for suggestions and advice:	2-9. Satisfaction with training for job: *Less than fairly satisfied*		*Very or fairly satisfied*
A great deal or quite a lot	10	*	1
Somewhat	9		7
Not at all or a little	2		5

* 2 × 2 relationship is significant. (Exact chi-square test.)

with the training they received for their present jobs. By exact chi-square tests a significantly greater proportion of the men who felt more dependent were dissatisfied with their training than were the men who depended only "somewhat," "a little," or "not at all" on the other men in their group. The group that reported depending "somewhat" on the other men for suggestions and advice in turn reported proportionately less often that they were "very" or "fairly" satisfied with their training for the job than did the men who reported depending "a little" or "not at all" on the other men. This relationship indicates that the men at Advance depended on each other for solving job problems to the extent that they felt the training they received

failed to supply the kinds of information and knowledge needed to do the job on their own.

The relationships between dependent behavior, feelings of tension, and satisfaction with training for the new jobs offer some suggestion about the effects of the rate of transition for the operators from the older plants in the system to the new automated plant. At the time of our study one-third of the transferred Advance operators still felt that as a result of insufficiencies

TABLE 4:13

Dependence and Feelings about Dependence

(Advance Operators)

1-26. Depend on the other men for suggestions and advice:	1-27. How do you feel about depending on the other men for suggestions and advice? *Would like to depend much or a little less*		*Satisfied or like to depend more*
A great deal or quite a lot	8		3
		*	
Somewhat	3		14
Not at all or a little	2		5

* 2 × 2 relationship is significant. (Exact chi-square test.)

in the training they received, they must depend on the other men in their work group for suggestions and advice in solving the problems of the job. Presumably, these problems arose in the handling of major pieces of equipment which were being started up or taken down and about which the men felt they should have had more knowledge. After many years of power plant experience, they were again placed in a position of being dependent on other men for ideas about the operation of basic equipment. A man who over a period of years has acquired specialized skills can only find such a situation distasteful, for these dependence requirements diminish his feelings of adequacy and self-confidence. It is not surprising, then, to find that the men

who reported that they depended "a great deal" or "quite a lot" also said they would like to depend "much less" or "a little less" than they now had to (Table 4:13). A significantly greater proportion of the men who felt dependent desired less dependence on the other men than did the men who depended only "somewhat," "a little," or "not at all." Some dependence on the other men seemed to be tolerable (only one man of the 35 operators reported that he would like to depend "more" on the other men than he was now doing); but having to depend a great deal on others to get the job done was disturbing.

Training for the New Jobs

The inverse relationship between the degree of dependence reported by the Advance operators and their satisfaction with the training they received for these new jobs is indicative of how the men felt about the adequacy of their training program. A discussion of the training given these men and the men's attitudes toward this training is therefore appropriate.

The training efforts were concentrated in two programs: (1) a series of classes on the technical aspects of the new power plant, and (2) "cross-the-wall" training of men in the older plants.

When a man was selected for transfer from one of the older plants to Advance he was immediately relieved of his specific job responsibilities. He remained in that plant, however, for "cross-training"—training in parts of the power plant operations other than his own specialty. For example, a boiler fireman would be notified of his selection to go to Advance and would then report to a foreman in his plant who was also transferring to the new plant. The fireman would then be assigned by this foreman to the electrical switchboard to learn what he could about distributing the electric power produced by the plant. One

of the major complaints the men registered about this phase of the training program was that the operators who were doing the jobs generally refused to let the transferees try to do the job themselves. "Watch, but do not touch," they were told. The incumbent operators appeared to resent the assumption that these men could learn in a few weeks what it had taken them years to become skilled at. They were jealous of their equipment and did not want these "outsiders" tampering with it. Observation was fine; actual operating was not.

Thus, a potentially valuable source of on-the-job training was not exploited due to the resistance of the men who were expected to do the training. This resistance probably occurred because the task of training men from other groups for these jobs violated the norms of these men about such training. When asked how they felt about "teaching *men in other groups in the plant*" about their jobs, 36 percent of the Stand operators responded that they "would mind it or would not like to at all." About the same percentage (31 percent) of the operators at Advance, despite the general feeling there that cross-training could have helped, also reported that they would not like to teach men in other groups about their jobs (Table 4:14). With such a large proportion having negative feelings about cross-training, it is not surprising that resistance to training the transferees was met.

The evidence from a similar question suggested that this resistance was a reaction to the threat which cross-training offered to the established pattern of promotion and to the prevailing status system. It had been traditional that operators were promoted from within their own groups, going, for example, from electrical helper to switchboard operator 2nd and finally reaching switchboard operator 1st class. Having a man who had been in the boiler room come over to try to learn the electrical operations in a short time was resented by the men who had gone through this progression over a number of years. Whereas

only about 40 percent of the operators in each plant said they would like to teach men in other groups about their jobs, 80 percent of the Stand and 88 percent of the Advance operators expressed a willingness to teach the men in their own groups about their jobs (Table 4:14). This desire to maintain the system at Stand was understandable, since changing operating conditions had not occurred to create in them a need to change. It was surprising, however, to find the same feelings at Advance.

TABLE 4:14

Willingness to Train Other Men

(in percent)

2-15,16. How would you feel about teaching . . . about your job?

	Men in other groups		*Men in your work group*	
	Advance (N = 35)	*Stand* (N = 95)	*Advance* (N = 35)	*Stand* (N = 95)
Would not like to at all	11	20	3	0
Would mind it, but not too much	20	16	0	4
Would just as soon do it as not	23	22	9	16
Would like to do it fairly well	26	21	23	28
Would like to do it very much	17	19	65	52
Not ascertained	3	2	0	0
	100	100	100	100

The men there had learned through hard experience the importance of being adequately trained. Nevertheless they felt, for the most part, that the men who should receive the training should be men from their own work groups.

The six men who were selected for supervisory positions in the new plant were similarly relieved of specific responsibilities in the older plants and sent to other plants to learn about the operations they were going to have to supervise. They encountered some of the same problems. They felt they did not have enough time at these other plants to learn very much.

Shortly after the men were notified of their selection for the new plant and taken off their jobs at the old ones, a series of

classes was started (February 1952). These classes were intended to acquaint the operators with the equipment which was being installed in the new plant. A set of notes containing technical information about the boilers, turbine generators, fans, etc., was compiled by the Advance technical engineers with the assistance of the equipment manufacturers and distributed to the transferring operators. Approximately once every two weeks in each of the older plants a two-hour class was conducted for the transferring men and foremen on each of the "units" in the manual. The Advance technical engineers had major responsibility for these classes and taught most of them. Occasionally the foreman or a representative of the equipment manufacturer would lead the discussion of a particular unit. This series of classes lasted until May 1953, when the initial startups in the plant claimed all the energies of the technical group.

These were the two major parts of the formal training program established by the company. In addition the transferred men were encouraged to qualify for the licenses which the company required of men working with the boilers and turbines. Although the information necessary for passing the examinations for these licenses—that is, information about old equipment and steam principles—was not required for and was inappropriate to the equipment in the new plant, even men with previous training in only the electrical operations were encouraged to obtain these licenses. Classes were held regularly by the company to help all employees in all plants to pass the examinations and the new Advance operators were given time to attend these classes. Although many of the men actually did obtain licenses, this was largely an individual choice and the company had not forced them to meet the requirements. Thus not all the operators in Advance had this basic knowledge about the steam operations.

Before the first unit went into operation at the new plant the full operating force was on the site observing the construction and assisting in the testing of the new equipment. Here

again was an opportunity for these men to acquire some of the knowledge and skills necessary for their new jobs. Again, however, learning was primarily limited to observation and the skill training was left to chance.

The transferees also had an opportunity for on-the-job learning, although this aspect of the training was not systematized. As soon as the men moved to Advance the new shift rotation schedule[14] was put into effect. When the new equipment was being tested prior to putting it on the line, and when the unit was actually synchronized for production, the company management saw to it that the operators who were working at that time performed all the necessary operating functions. No conscious attempt was made, however, to distribute this kind of on-the-job equipment handling among all the operating groups so that everyone would have an opportunity to learn firsthand how to operate the machinery. This reliance on chance resulted in some operating groups receiving more of this practical exposure to the new operations than others received.

Handling machine failures was another type of experience which proved helpful in giving the operators a greater understanding of the new equipment. In the first months of operation, mechanical failures occurred quite frequently. These happened most frequently in the equipment which was unique to Advance and which did not exist in the older plants. When an accident occurred on any shift, the operators working at that time were responsible for adjusting the operations to minimize the effect of the machine failure. This learning under critical operating conditions gave the men a better understanding of the weaknesses and strengths of the new machinery as well as a feeling of mastery once the crisis had been overcome. This kind of learning, however, was also a matter of chance. If the failure of equipment occurred while the man was on shift, then he learned how to handle it; if he was not there, then he had to learn

[14] To be described in the next chapter.

secondhand. The importance of this kind of learning in the estimation of the men can be seen from the rather regular phenomenon of operators who were not on shift coming into the plant on their own time when some major event occurred to see how it was being handled.

The feelings of the men about the training they received for these jobs differed sharply from their attitudes about the jobs themselves. These feelings concerned both the content and the speed of the training program (Table 4:15). When asked how satisfied they were with the training they had had for their jobs, only 37 percent of the operators felt very or fairly satisfied. One in six was clearly dissatisfied with the preparation he had received for his job. Similarly, half (51 percent) of the transferred operators reported that they were not adequately trained for their jobs before being put on them. Thus, a large segment of this operating group felt that the company could have done a better job of preparing them for these enlarged jobs.

This feeling pertained not only to the content of the training but to the length of the training period as well. Twenty-eight percent of the new operators claimed the training was too fast, although another 23 percent reported that it was too slow (Table 4:15). Both these groups were less satisfied with their training than the men who thought the training was timed "just about right."

Although the men disagreed in their overall evaluation of the adequacy of the training program, there was a substantial amount of agreement in their evaluation of particular parts of it (Table 4:16). As far as the men were concerned, the most valuable source of learning—the people who taught them the most—was "the other men who were in training with me." Seventy-four percent of the operators said they learned "a great deal" or "quite a lot" from their colleagues in training. The next most frequently checked source of information was "the men who were already working on the job." Thus the men empha-

TABLE 4:15

Satisfaction with Training among Operators in Advance

	In Percent Advance Operators (N = 35)
Content of Training	
2-9. How satisfied are you with the training you have had for this job?	
Very satisfied	6
Fairly satisfied	31
Satisfied in some ways, dissatisfied in others	48
Fairly dissatisfied	6
Very dissatisfied	9
	100
2-11. Do you think you were adequately trained to perform this job before you were put on it?	
Yes	46
No	51
Not ascertained	3
	100
Speed of Training	
2-10. How long did it take you on this job before you really felt at ease doing this work?	
Less than a year	43
Between one and two years	37
More than two years	3
Still do not really feel at ease	17
	100
2-12. Do you think your training for this job was too fast or too slow?	
Much too fast	3
A little too fast	25
Just about right	40
A little too slow	17
Much too slow	6
Not ascertained	9
	100

TABLE 4:16

Perceptions of Effective Parts of Training Program and of Potential Sources of Information

	Percent saying "A great deal or quite a lot" (N = 35)	*Mean rating**
2-13. Who taught you the most when you were learning about your present job?		
Instructors in various classes	17	2.68
The men who put in this equipment	31	2.77
My supervisor	23	2.97
Technical engineers	43	3.14
The men who were already working on the job	51	3.21
The other men who were in training with me	74	4.00
2-14. Suppose you need to learn more about a job. How much can you learn in these ways?		
Attending classes on the theory of operation	43	3.40
Reading and studying on your own	71	3.94
Attending classes on the operation of equipment in this plant	88	4.34
Watching and talking with the men who are actually doing the job	91	4.37
Doing the job yourself under the guidance of other men	97	4.80

* There were five alternatives to these questions ranging from "none" (2-13) or "very little" (2-14) to "a great deal". "A great deal" was assigned a value of 5.

sized, in their responses to the questions, the importance of on-the-job experiences in preparing them to handle their new jobs.

Further support for the perceived effectiveness of on-the-job training is gained from the responses to the question, "Suppose you need to learn more about a job, how much can you learn in these ways?" The most preferred method indicated was "doing the job yourself under the guidance of other men." All

but one of the transferred operators felt they could learn "a great deal" or "quite a lot" in this way.

The men seemed to prefer the practical, pragmatic to the theoretical approach to learning. As seen in Table 4:16, the men reported having learned least from their "instructors in various classes" (not including the technical engineers) and from "the men who put in this equipment" and felt they could learn least by "attending classes on the theory of operation."

It is important to note that the preferences expressed here showed no relation to the degree of satisfaction an individual expressed toward the training he received. They showed substantially no relation, moreover, to such personal characteristics of the employee as age, education, length of service with the company, or the number of licenses held.

In light of the job enlargement which we have described earlier in this chapter, an interesting trend in an operator's perception of his training was the one that reflected the kind of experience he had brought with him to the new job. Although there was an insufficient number of men in each category to make any statistical analyses possible, there seemed to be differential satisfaction with the training received depending upon whether the man came from the steam or from the electrical sections of the older plants. The former electrical men seemed somewhat less satisfied with their training than did the former steam operators. This suggests that the training on electrical equipment had been somewhat better than that on the steam operations.

No objective criterion of the effectiveness of this training program was available to the investigators. Certainly the plant was running in a highly efficient manner and the operators had met several major crises in competent fashion. Nevertheless a goodly number of the men felt that the company could have done a better job of preparing them for the operating jobs at Advance. Both from the reports of the men and from our knowledge of methods for effective skill training, the importance of

on-the-job operating experience cannot be overemphasized. A greater concern for distributing such experience among all the men, in addition to the classroom sessions by the technical engineers, probably would have resulted in a training program more satisfactory to the transferred operators. In the long run, it might have been more efficient to have had the operators take down and start up equipment, even when it was unnecessary from the immediate production viewpoint, in order to be sure that all operators had direct experience with these operations.

Summary and Conclusions

In building the new power plant, technological changes and management decisions resulted in the redesigning of the operating jobs. This redesign consisted of enlarging the jobs of each operator by job rotation among different types of jobs and by increasing the scope of responsibility on each of these jobs. The results of transferring men from more specialized jobs in the older plants to the enlarged jobs in the new plant were for the most part positive. Expressions of increased job interest and job satisfaction were found in a large proportion of these transferred operators. The combination of job enlargement and of job rotation increased for many of these men—at least temporarily—the intrinsic satisfactions which could be derived from the work itself. Some negative effects in the form of somewhat increased tension were also found among these plant operators. To some extent, this tension was traced to the perceived speed and inadequacy of preparation for the transition from jobs in the older plants to jobs in Advance. An examination of the training program as it actually took place suggested that this tension could have been lessened if more attention had been devoted to ensuring on-the-job practical experience for the transferred operators in addition to the formal classroom training which they received.

Chapter 5

CONTINUOUS OPERATION: PATTERNS AND EFFECTS

With the introduction of automation, capital investment per employee increases markedly. Machinery and tools necessary for automated systems of production are costly; the labor force needed to man these systems is smaller. These economic facts will lead industrial management to consider the advisability of around-the-clock operations, since a company can spread its fixed costs over more units of production by extending operations from eight to sixteen or twenty-four hours a day. Similarly, the installation of expensive electronic data-processing equipment in many business offices will result in company consideration of instituting second and third shift operations. Such a change would introduce shift work to white-collar groups, traditionally a population of daytime workers.

For economic reasons, therefore, the introduction of automation into factories and offices is likely to increase the number of establishments engaged in continuous operation and enlarge the segment of our population presently doing shift work. The

problem of continuous operation cannot, however, be examined in terms of economics alone. If more people are to be asked to work shifts, the physical and social costs to workers must also be considered.

Among shift workers and others connected with shift operations, an extensive "folklore" has developed about the effects of working nights. There is widespread belief that shift work shortens workers' lives, that night workers have more illnesses, and that men age more rapidly doing shift work. Moreover, absenteeism, lateness, more accidents, and lower production are also thought to be associated with night-shift operations.

A number of investigators, especially in England and the Scandinavian countries, have provided empirical evidence on certain of these problems. Typically, however, these studies have been undertaken during wartime and have been concerned with the effects of night work on productivity and absences. The findings are inconsistent. Some studies showed poorer productivity and absence records for night workers; others showed no difference, or superior records. The one consistent major finding is that night work has a cumulative effect on the worker which results in lowered production and increased absences the longer he is on a night shift.[1]

European and American researchers have examined the physiological effects of shift work.[2,3] They all agree that when workers rotate shifts—that is, change from working nights to working afternoons—the natural rhythms of their bodies are disrupted and require some time to adjust to the new daily activity cycle. These disruptions have not been shown, however,

[1] Wyatt, S., and Marriott, R., "Night Work and Shift Changes," *British Journal of Industrial Medicine,* 1953, *10,* 164–172. And Kleitman, N., and Jackson, D. P., Variations in Body Temperature and in Performance Under Different Watch Schedules. Naval Medical Research Institute. Project NM-004–005.01.02, 1950.

[2] Kleitman, and Jackson, *op. cit.*

[3] Thiis-Evensen, E., "Shift Work and Health," *Industrial Medicine and Surgery,* 1958, *27,* No. 10.

to produce any greater incidences of sickness or death among shift workers than among day workers. One of the few pieces of published evidence on the attitudes of workers toward shift work states that shift workers complained about difficulties with their digestion and in obtaining enough sleep, especially when they rotated shifts.[4]

The lack of consistency in the findings of the various shift-work studies is probably due in part to the varied types of shift operations represented. Even with the restriction of an eight-hour working day and a forty-hour working week, there are many different ways of scheduling workers to staff a continuous operation. Fixed, rotating, and split shifts, and daily, weekly, and monthly rotation plans have been used in various combinations. Even the times of day at which shifts change differ from one situation to another. Each pattern can be expected to induce a different stress on the worker, and these stresses may in turn manifest themselves in different worker behaviors. Interpretations of the results of any study of shift work must be made in the context of the particular shift schedule employed.

The two power plants in our study of automation operated on an around-the-clock basis in order to provide the continuous flow of electricity required by customers. It was possible, therefore, to examine the social and psychological impact of shift work in two situations. This chapter will outline some of the factors affecting the men's attitudes toward working shifts, assess the effects of two different shift schedules on these attitudes, and relate the attitudes to the men's behavior on the job.

The Shift Schedules

Although in both plants there were three eight-hour shifts and the men rotated periodically from the day to the night to

[4] Wyatt and Marriott, *op. cit.*

the afternoon shift, the shift schedules for the two plants were quite different. Therefore, in order to place the attitudinal findings in the context of the appropriate shift patterns, descriptions of the shift schedules for each plant will be presented and the points of difference indicated. The fold-out chart at the front of this book shows the shift patterns at Advance and Stand. The blank areas indicate days on which the men worked "Days" (8 AM to 4 PM); the hatched areas, "Afternoons" (4 PM to 12 midnight); and the black areas, "Nights" (12 midnight to 8 AM). Off-days are noted by O, and Saturdays and Sundays off together are indicated by ●.

In the new plant the three shifts started at 8 AM, 4 PM, and 12 midnight; these three shifts were manned by four operating groups. The pattern of rotation, which permitted three working groups and one "off" group at any particular time, was essentially a weekly one. The week was a full seven days, however, not the usual five days. The top section on the chart shows the way in which the four groups are fitted into the three-shift schedule. The following points should be noted especially about the Advance schedule:

a. The men worked seven consecutive days between off-days.

b. They worked a different shift after each period of off-days, with rotation being essentially a weekly plan.

c. Weekends (Saturdays and Sundays) off occurred every fourth week.

d. The men and their supervisor always changed shifts at the same time.

In Stand, the three shifts started at 7 AM, 3 PM, and 11 PM, but only three groups of men operated them. The pattern of shift rotation in this plant was a monthly one, but each worker

and supervisor had his own individual schedule of rotation. In the bottom three sections on the chart are depicted the seven possible schedules of work within three typical work groups. The period shown is a complete cycle for worker number 1 in each work group. By looking at the three work groups together, it is possible to see how the three shifts were staffed at all times, and how, at times of shift change, the men worked for a short period with a work group other than their own. For this plant the following special points should be noted:

a. The men worked five (occasionally six) consecutive days before any off-days.

b. They worked the same shift for four (occasionally three) consecutive weeks before they changed shifts, with rotation being essentially a monthly plan.

c. Weekends (Saturdays and Sundays) off occurred for a man only once every six months.

d. Each man and supervisor in a work group had his own schedule of shift rotation.

From these descriptions the following important contrasts between the shift systems in the two plants can be made.

a. Shifts at Advance started at 12 midnight, 8 AM, and 4 PM; at Stand at 11 PM, 7 AM, and 3 PM. The latter schedule required the night crews to work a shift extending into the next calendar day. The inability to identify their working day was a minor annoyance which was felt by many of the men. A number of the Stand workers suggested "change shifts at 8, 4, and 12 so you start and finish the same day."

b. At Advance the "work week" was seven days long, at Stand only five. In the exploratory interviews and the write-in

comments on the questionnaires, a number of Advance workers expressed dissatisfaction with this deviation from the accepted five-day week. "There are too many days of work without days off."

c. The shift rotation occurred weekly at Advance but monthly at Stand. This difference in the frequency of rotation had advantages and disadvantages for both plants. Weekly rotation required more rapid adjustments to changes in living routines—meals, sleep—than did monthly rotation. On monthly rotation, the men worked the evening and night shifts for eight consecutive weeks, and were thus cut off from the usual daytime activities during that entire period.

d. At Advance the men and supervisors rotated together; at Stand the men and supervisors rotated individually, each on his own schedule. The simultaneous system kept the work groups intact, preventing disagreements between men and supervisors which can arise when things are done differently in different groups. However, it also prevented the cross-fertilization of ideas about jobs which occurs when men with different ways of doing things are forced to come to some agreement about how to do a job.

e. Advance shift workers had weekends off once every fourth week; Stand workers, once every twenty-five weeks. Since, for the usual day worker, weekends are periods of rest and relaxation from his work, they have become the common time for social gatherings. Although the shift worker on monthly rotation still had his two days off per week, the fact that the majority of these occurred when almost everyone else was working raises the question, "When is a day off not a day off?" The answer would seem to be, "When you have nobody to share it with."

Following a description of the shift-work population, quantitative data will be shown indicating the effects which these

different patterns of shift rotation had on the men's feelings about their jobs.

The Shift Workers

Two groups in each power plant, comprising about half of the total plant work force, were involved in shift work. These were the operators (electrical, turbine, and boiler, and their assistants) and the plant protection people, who were charged with maintaining the security of the plant.

In order to obtain a shift-work group from the new plant comparable in experience to the shift workers at Stand, only those operators at Advance who had transferred from the company's other power plants were included in the analysis. A comparison of the selected shift-work group at Advance with the shift workers at Stand showed no significant differences with respect to age, education, marital status, number of children less than six years old, length of service with the company, number of years at shift work, and number of years spent at non-shift work. A slightly greater proportion of Advance shift workers were in the age range from thirty to forty-five and a smaller proportion in the younger and older groups, but these differences were not statistically significant. (Tables showing these comparisons are presented in Appendix B.)

Because of the comparability of background and experience of the shift workers in the two plants, differences in their attitudes toward shift work can probably be attributed in large part to their experiences with different shift-work patterns.

Worker Attitudes toward Shift Work

A single question with five alternatives was used to measure the workers' attitudes toward shift work:

Taking everything into consideration, how do you feel about working afternoons and nights? (Check one)

__I like shift work very much
__I like it fairly well
__I don't mind it
__I dislike it somewhat
__I dislike shift work very much

The responses to this question by the shift workers in both plants evidenced an overwhelming dislike for shift work.[5] Almost three-quarters (73 percent) of the Stand and 35 percent of the Advance workers reported disliking shift work "very much or somewhat." About the most favorable attitude obtained was a tolerant "I don't mind it" from almost half (48 percent) the Advance men (Table 5:1).

Despite the generally negative attitude toward working shifts in the two plants, somewhat greater tolerance was reported by the Advance than the Stand shift workers. Whereas 65 percent of the men in the new plant said they liked shift work or did not mind it, only 27 percent of the men in the older plant

[5] Our main interest was in the attitudes of shift workers toward shift work. Within each plant the distributions of responses to the question, "Taking everything into consideration, how do you feel about working afternoons and nights?" were very similar for the operating and plant protection groups (table below). The responses of these two groups have been combined, therefore, in our analysis of the effects of shift work.

In Percent

	I like shift work very much	*I like it fairly well*	*I don't mind it*	*I dislike it somewhat*	*I dislike shift work very much*	Total Percent	N
Advance							
Operators	2	12	47	31	8	100	(55)
Plant protection	0	29	29	29	13	100	(7)
Stand							
Operators	4	2	20	34	40	100	(110)
Plant protection	9	0	27	37	27	100	(11)

Chi-square tests comparing "like" or "don't mind" and "dislike" categories for operators versus plant protection were *not* significant for either plant at the .05 level of confidence.

were of like opinion (Table 5:1). The gross evaluation of the two patterns of shift work is, then, that the rotation system at Stand was less tolerable than was the system at Advance.

We were interested also in the effects of more specific aspects of the two rotational patterns on the men and on their

TABLE 5:1

Satisfaction with Shift Work

Interplant comparison; shift workers only

(in percent)

1-73. Taking everything into consideration, how do you feel about working afternoons and nights?

	I like shift work very much	*I like it fairly well*	*I don't mind it*	*I dislike it somewhat*	*I dislike shift work very much*		*Total Percent*	*N*
Advance	2	14	45	31	8		100	(62)
Advance (experienced)[a]	0	17	48	26	9		100	(42)
						*		
Stand	4	2	21	34	39		100	(121)

	I like shift work very much, fairly well, or don't mind it	*I dislike shift work somewhat or very much*		*Total Percent*	*N*
Advance (experienced)[a]	65	35		100	(42)
			*		
Stand	27	73		100	(121)

[a] This is the Advance group of operators and plant protection people without the operators who had no experience in other power plants in the company. In the rest of the tables in this chapter, this group is referred to as Advance.

* The difference between Advance (experienced) and Stand is statistically significant by chi-square test at the .05 level of confidence, the level of confidence used in all statistical tests in this chapter.

The difference between Advance and Stand is also significant.

The difference between Advance and Advance (experienced) *is not* significant.

attitudes toward shift work. These aspects have been examined according to their effects on the physical well-being of the workers, on their family and social lives, and on their jobs and their attitudes toward their jobs. These will be discussed in sequence.

Physical Effects

Probably the most striking effect of shift work in the life of the worker is the necessary disruption of the normal rhythm of his life. Regardless of the pattern used to divide the day into work segments, for sixteen hours of that day the men who are working are "out of phase" with the normal sequence of activities. When the other people in the community are sleeping, they are working. When they want to eat, their family may be sleeping. The community's provision for eating at odd hours is usually minimal. Sleeping during the day, when activity is at a peak outside, is often very difficult.

When the workers are on any type of rotation plan, these disruptions are even further heightened. By the time the shift worker has established a pattern of eating and sleeping appropriate for one shift, he is rotated to a different shift and must start his adjustment anew. Since shift work at both power plants involved rotation, the effects of these disruptions were found among both groups of workers. The majority of shift workers in both plants complained that adjusting to eating and sleeping schedules was their principal difficulty with working shifts. Some representative comments were:

> Your whole system is upset, especially your stomach.

> I have a hard time to sleep when I work nights, and my stomach is always upset.

> The fact is that you have to change your living habits, mainly sleeping and eating.

> Improper sleep, poor appetite, poor digestion.

> Can't sleep and can't eat.

I can't sleep days. I have trouble keeping awake. I don't eat right.

These hours are just unnatural. I sleep light; noise breaks up sleep.

Never thoroughly get adjusted.

Other related complaints of being "tired most of the time" and of being unable to eat the "right kinds of meals at proper times" resulting in "upset stomach and poor digestion" indicated the physical pressures felt by the shift workers.

From the men's responses to the question, "What do you find gives you the most trouble in making these [shift] changes?" we found that difficulties with sleeping and eating were problems for a majority of the workers in both plants (Table 5:2). Although the percentages of respondents mentioning other problems of adjustment were small, they deserve mention for two reasons. First, the fact that this question required the men to write in a response, rather than only to check one of several alternatives, means that the difficulties mentioned were of major importance for the respondents. Second, the similarity in the percentages of respondents in each category in the two plants suggests that shift rotation, regardless of the pattern used, placed a burden on the worker's physical and social well-being.

The significantly greater proportion of Advance workers reporting sleeping difficulties can probably be explained by the speed of adjustment required by the weekly rotation of shifts at that plant. The frequent changes in routine required by the Advance system meant that many men never quite became adjusted to one routine before they were faced with a new one. Judging from the high percentage of Advance workers who complained about not getting enough sleep, the rapid rotation probably had its greatest disruptive effect in this area.

Although each change in shift required some measure of

TABLE 5:2

Complaints about Shift Work

1-76. What do you find gives you the most trouble in making these [shift] changes?

Area of Complaint	Percent[a] of shift workers mentioning this area Advance (N = 42)		Stand (N = 121)
Physical and Physiological			
1. Sleeping difficulties (getting enough rest, sleeping days, etc.)	84	*	67
2. Eating difficulties (scheduling meals, digestive problems, etc.)	45		47
3. Eliminative difficulties (irregular bowel movements, constipation, etc.)	6		5
4. Staying awake on the job (working at the time they had been sleeping)	3		8
Social			
5. Family life ("hardship on family," "making children understand I won't be home to play with them")	6		4
6. Social life and recreation ("letting friends know what shift I work," "no social life")	5		7
Miscellaneous			
7. General adjustment (routine of everyday life, "one hell of a lot of things," etc.)	0		7
8. Others (traffic problems, "too many days of work without days off," etc.)	5		2
Did not answer question	8		12

[a] Percents add up to more than 100 since some respondents mentioned more than one complaint area.

* Percentage difference between plants is significant

adjustment by the men, there was general agreement that the change from days to nights was the most difficult. Seventy-seven percent of the men in both plants reported this change to be the hardest one to make. "I have a hard time getting enough sleep in the daytime when working nights" was a typical worker's comment. The shock of abruptly reversing a "normal" daytime

schedule of activities by working at night and sleeping in the day was probably both psychologically and physically disturbing.

A majority of the men reported requiring several days to adjust to the shift change they found the most difficult (Table 5:3). Although there was considerable individual variation in

TABLE 5:3

Time Needed to Adjust to Hardest Shift Change and Satisfaction with Shift Work

(in percent)

	1-75. How long does it take you to adjust to the shift change you checked above (hardest change)?					
	A day or less	*2 to 3 days*	*4 days or more*		*Total Percent*	*N*[a]
Total						
Advance	31	50	19	*	100	(42)
Stand	5	25	70		100	(118)
Advance						
Like or don't mind shift work	92	57	38			
Dislike shift work	8	43	62			
Total	100	100	100			
N	(13)	(21)	(8)			
Stand						
Like or don't mind shift work	83	37	19	*		
Dislike shift work	17	63	81			
Total	100	100	100			
N	(6)	(30)	(82)			

[a] In this and subsequent tables, the number of respondents will vary due to a small number of nonrespondents to each question. An analysis of the people who did not respond showed no tendency for them to be the same ones on different questions.

* Chi-square test of this relationship, comparing three days or less with four days or more, is significant.

ability to adjust, the men at Advance, on the average, said they adjusted in a shorter time than did those at Stand. This difference paralleled the more tolerant attitude toward shift work found in Advance. Even in the new plant, however, one-fifth of the men said it took them four days or more to adjust. This

meant that they no sooner got used to a new schedule than it was time to change again.

Evidence supporting the extent to which the adjustment to shift change was related to a tolerant attitude toward working shifts appeared when the relationship was studied within each of the plants. In both plants, the longer the time required for becoming accustomed to the new shift, the greater the percentage of men who reported disliking shift work (Table 5:3). One of the important factors determining the worker's attitude toward shift work appeared to be, then, his ability to minimize its disruptive influence on his daily routine.

The fact that the men at Advance reported adjusting more rapidly than those at Stand accounted for only part of the picture. The question may still be raised whether psychological adjustment, represented in responses to the questionnaire, is really a reflection of physiological adjustment. Physiological investigations[6,7] have shown that after a certain period of time the bodily rhythms will conform to whatever activity cycle is maintained. Professor Nathaniel Kleitman of the University of Chicago has manipulated the hours of watch served on Navy submarines and found that the body temperature curve soon stabilized in conformity with the watch schedule. In all these studies, however, a substantial length of time, varying from several days to two weeks, was needed before a stable pattern emerged. If it takes several days after a shift rotation for the body temperature cycle to be restored, the readjustment of the functioning of the larger body organs probably takes even longer. The weekly rotational pattern at Advance seemingly made it impossible for a worker ever to become regulated to his living routine, since it was constantly changing. The monthly rotational pattern offered the worker a greater stability of body temperature and organic func-

[6] Kleitman and Jackson, *op. cit.*

[7] Bjerner, B., and Swensson, A., "Schichtarbert und Rhythms," *Acta Medica Scandinavica Supplementum,* 1953, *278,* 102–107.

tioning for at least three of the four weeks he spent on each shift. This stability should result in less difficulty with sleeping and eating schedules and thus contribute to better health.

In terms of the men's own reports, however, the physical condition of the workers in Advance was no better or worse

TABLE 5:4

Physical Condition and Satisfaction with Shift Work

(in percent)

	1-B-13. In general, how is your physical condition now?				
	Very good	Pretty good	Fair	Total Percent	Total N
Total					
Advance	55	40	5	100	(42)
Stand	46	40	14	100	(118)
Advance					
Like or don't mind shift work	52	82	50		
Dislike shift work	48	18	50		
Total	100	100	100		
N	(23)	(17)	(2)		
Stand					
Like or don't mind shift work	39	15	12	*	
Dislike shift work	61	85	88		
Total	100	100	100		
N	(54)	(47)	(17)		

* Chi-square test of this relationship, comparing "very good" with "pretty good" or "fair," is significant.

than in Stand (Table 5:4). About half the men in each plant said they were in "very good" physical condition and the rest were "pretty good" or "fair." In Stand, but not in Advance, the men's reported physical condition was significantly related to their attitude toward shift work. A significantly smaller proportion of men in "very good" condition disliked shift work than men in "pretty good" or "fair" condition. At Advance there was a slight tendency for the men in "very good" physical condition

to dislike shift work, though the relationship was not statistically significant.

It is conceivable that the physical manifestations of the constantly changing routine in Advance will show themselves only after several more years and will have to be ascertained more objectively than through the men's own perceptions of their overall physical condition. A study of the morbidity of shift workers in Norway indicated that the incidence of stomach disorders (gastric ulcer, gastritis, dyspepsia) is greater among shift than day workers,[8] although other diseases were equally frequent. The investigator concluded that, although shift work may not have caused the stomach disorders, the conditions of such work maintained and aggravated them.

For the Stand workers both their ability to adjust to the shift change and their reportedly good physical condition were related to a toleration of shift work. Among Advance workers, where the tolerance for shift work was greater and where the ability to adjust to shift changes was better, no relationship between good physical condition and tolerance for shift work was found. Nevertheless, the ability of the worker to adjust to the physical rigors of working shifts appeared to be an important determiner of his attitude toward shift work.

Social Effects

The disruptive effects of shift work also extend into the worker's relations with his family and friends. The family of a man on rotating shifts must constantly adjust to changes in his working, sleeping, eating, and recreating schedule. Any activities designed for the entire family must be planned in terms of the father's days off or hours of work at that time.

[8] Thiis-Evensen, E., "Shiftwork and Gastric Ulcer Disease," *Sartyrck ur Nordish Hygienish Tidskrift,* 1953, *3–4,* 69–77.

About 10 percent of the workers in both plants spontaneously complained of having difficulties with their social and family life. The younger children seemed to bear the major brunt of this disruption. As one worker put it, "[My major difficulty with shift work is] making the children understand I won't be home to play with them." Especially for children who are too young to understand explanations, the appearance of their father at different times provides little of the stable conditions necessary for establishing healthy and constructive parent-child relationships.

The pressures shift work places on family life were reflected strikingly in the men's responses to the question. "How does your family feel about you working shifts?" A majority of workers in both plants said, "They don't like me working shifts." The proportion reporting that their families disliked shift work (61 percent and 79 percent in Advance and Stand respectively) was greater than the proportion of the men who disliked shift work themselves (35 percent and 73 percent respectively). Thus, the men's own attitudes reflected only part of the negative feelings of their families.

In terms of the adjustments required of the family, the different shift schedules in the two plants had contrasting advantages and disadvantages. The frequent shift rotation at Advance raised the problem of keeping track of what shift the worker was on and when he was likely to be around the house. The monthly rotation at Stand made the worker's life more easily predictable over longer periods of time.

However, the social advantages of the weekly rotation probably far outweighed the disadvantages. On the Advance schedule the men had a "long weekend" off every fourth week and were never on a "poor" shift more than one week at a time (see fold-out). On this schedule, contact with the family was maintained more easily than on the monthly schedule employed

at Stand. On the latter schedule, the shift workers were "predictably" working afternoons or nights for two consecutive months, effectively isolating them from their families' activities.

As might be expected from the more frequent availability of the Advance workers to their families, a significantly smaller

TABLE 5:5

Family Attitude toward Shift Work

(in percent)

	1-85. How does your family feel about working shifts?				
	They like to have me working shifts	*They don't mind*	*They don't like me working shifts*	*Total* Percent	N
Advance	0	39	61	100	(41)
			*		
Stand	2	19	79	100	(120)

* Chi-square test of this relationship, comparing "don't like" with "like" or "don't mind," is significant.

TABLE 5:6

Strength of Negative Family Attitude toward Shift Work

(in percent)

	1-86. If your family doesn't like to have you working shifts, how strongly does your family feel about this?				
	Very strongly	*Fairly strongly*	*Not too strongly*	*Total* Percent	N[a]
Advance	12	12	76	100	(25)
			*		
Stand	26	28	46	100	(94)

[a] Includes only those men who reported that their families "don't like to have me working shifts."

* Chi-square test of this relationship, comparing "not too strongly" with "very or fairly strongly," is significant.

proportion of the men at the new plant than at Stand reported that their families disliked them working shifts (Table 5:5). Moreover, of those reporting that their families disliked shift work, significantly fewer of the Advance men reported they felt strongly about it (Table 5:6). Both the frequency and intensity

of antishift-work feeling were less among families of the new plant workers than among those in the older plant.

In both plants the men who reported their families didn't mind shift work were also more tolerant of shift work themselves (Table 5:7). The fact that the workers' reports of their families' attitudes toward shift work were less favorable than the worker's own attitudes suggests that the amount of family pres-

TABLE 5:7
Family Attitude toward Shift Work and Worker Attitude toward Shift Work
(in percent)

Worker Attitude toward Shift Work	1-85. How does your family feel about working shifts?		
	They like or don't mind me working shifts		*They don't like me working shifts*
Advance			
1-73. Like or don't mind shift work	81		56
Dislike shift work	19		44
Total	100		100
N	(16)		(25)
Stand			
1-73. Like or don't mind shift work	72		15
Dislike shift work	28	*	85
Total	100		100
N	(25)		(97)

* Chi-square test of this relationship is significant.

sure was a strong determinant of the worker's own attitude toward shift work.

Working shifts also deprives the worker of extensive friendship relations. Whereas social forces require the worker's family to adjust to his unusual working hours and days off, there are few such forces working to maintain friendships. The shift worker must keep his friends informed of his availability, and his friends must be tolerant, in turn, of his infrequent and erratic appearances. Since most day workers use the weekends for

their social activities, having to work these days regularly is an additional social hardship for the men working shifts.

To assess the degree of social deprivation suffered by the shift workers in these two plants, we asked three questions about their visiting habits:

> How often do you get together outside of work with any of the people you work with?
>
> How often do you get together with any other friends?
>
> How often do you get together with any of your relatives other than those living at home with you?

The men were asked to check a five-point scale ranging from "at least once a week" to "never or almost never."

Table 5:8 compares the responses of the shift workers and nonshift workers in each plant to each of the three questions. Shift workers did not differ from nonshift workers, in either of the two plants, in the frequency with which they got together with either their coworkers or their relatives. In both plants, however, the frequency of visiting friends was less among shift workers than among nonshift workers. Working odd hours cut down the opportunity for friendship activities. A member of the Stand staff, who had worked about twenty years on shifts, commented that shift workers are just like everybody else in the beginning, but in order to be able to live with shift work they gradually become more solitary people, enjoying individual activities.

Although the shift workers in both plants reported visiting friends less frequently than the nonshift workers, the weekly rotational plan of Advance seemed to permit more social activity than did the monthly plan at Stand. Table 5:9 indicates that the Advance shift workers got together with their friends more frequently than did the Stand shift workers. The long and

TABLE 5:8

Visiting Patterns and Shift Work

(Comparison of shift and nonshift workers)
(in percent)

How often do you get together:	At least once a week	A few times a month	Once a month or less		Total Percent	N
1-B-22. *With Friends?*						
Advance						
Shift workers	41	45	14	*	100	(42)
Nonshift workers	64	22	14		100	(77)
Stand						
Shift workers	34	30	36	*	100	(121)
Nonshift workers	48	35	17		100	(66)
1-B-23. *With Coworkers?*						
Advance						
Shift workers	12	17	71		100	(41)
Nonshift workers	18	20	62		100	(77)
Stand						
Shift workers	19	17	64		100	(121)
Nonshift workers	15	18	67		100	(64)
1-B-21. *With Relatives?*						
Advance						
Shift workers	29	26	45		100	(42)
Nonshift workers	39	35	26		100	(77)
Stand						
Shift workers	41	23	36		100	(120)
Nonshift workers	52	17	31		100	(64)

* Chi-square test of this relationship is significant.

continuous periods of working afternoon and evening shifts without weekends off, required by the Stand system, severely limited the outside social life of the shift worker in that plant.

Again we found that the friendship relations were the most sensitive to the deprivations of shift work. No significant differences in the frequency of getting together with coworkers or with relatives were found between the two plants. The lack

TABLE 5:9

Visiting Patterns and Shift Work

(Interplant comparisons of shift workers)
(in percent)

How often do you get together:	*At least once a week*	*A few times a month*	*Once a month or less*		*Total* Percent	N
1-B-22. *With Friends?*						
Advance	41	45	14		100	(42)
Stand	34	30	36	*	100	(121)
1-B-23. *With Coworkers?*						
Advance	12	17	71		100	(41)
Stand	19	17	64		100	(121)
1-B-23. *With Relatives?*						
Advance	29	26	45		100	(42)
Stand	41	23	36		100	(120)

* Chi-square test of this relationship is significant.

TABLE 5:10

Visiting Friends and Shift Work

(Comparison of nonshift workers only)
(in percent)

	1-B-22. How often do you get together with other friends?				
	At least once a week	*A few times a month*	*Once a month or less*	*Total* Percent	N
Advance	64	22	14	100	(77)
Stand	48	35	17	100	(66)

of difference in frequency of visiting friends between the nonshift workers in the two plants, shown in Table 5:10, adds further support for the disruptive character of Stand's monthly rotational system.

The importance to the worker of maintaining frequent relations with friends is implied in Table 5:11. In Stand a greater proportion of the workers who got together with their friends at

TABLE 5:11
Frequency of Visiting Friends and Attitude toward Shift Work
(in percent)

	1-B-22. How often do you get together with other friends?		
	At least once a week	*A few times a month*	*Once a month or less*
Advance			
1-73. Like or don't mind shift work	71	53	83
Dislike shift work	29	47	17
Total	100	100	100
N	(17)	(19)	(6)
Stand			
1-73. Like or don't mind shift work	37	33	14*
Dislike shift work	63	67	86
Total	100	100	100
N	(41)	(36)	(44)

* Chi-square test of this relationship, comparing "once a month or less" with "a few times a month or more," is significant.

least once a week was tolerant of shift work than was the proportion of the workers who saw their friends less frequently. The greater the social deprivation of shift work for the worker, the more intolerant he appeared to be of this kind of work.

Previous Shift Experience

Two measures of the workers' previous experience with shift work and with other types of work were included to assess the degree of tolerance which these workers had developed toward afternoon and night work. First we asked, "How much experience have you had working at a regular day shift job with weekends off?" No significant differences were found between the distributions of the two plants (Table 5:12). In Stand, however, a strong relationship was found between experience with regular day jobs—more than one year—and an intolerance for

shift work. A significantly smaller proportion of the men who had had more than a year's experience at day work was tolerant of shift work than the proportion of men with a year or less experience. This relationship did not hold for Advance.

TABLE 5:12

Experience At Nonshift Jobs and Satisfaction with Shift Work

(in percent)

	1-89. How much experience have you had working at a regular day shift job with weekends off?				
	A year or less	*Between one and five years*	*More than five years*	*Total Percent*	*N*
Total					
Advance	14	50	36	100	(42)
Stand	26	28	46	100	(116)
Advance					
1-73. Like or don't mind shift work	67	71	53		
Dislike shift work	33	29	47		
Total	100	100	100		
N	(6)	(21)	(15)		
Stand					
1-73. Like or don't mind shift work	42	19	21	*	
Dislike shift work	58	81	79		
Total	100	100	100		
N	(31)	(32)	(53)		

* Chi-square test of this relationship, comparing "a year or less" with "more than a year," is significant.

An even stronger relationship between tolerance for shift work and experience at shift-work jobs is shown in Table 5:13. Again no significant differences were found between the responses in the two plants to the question, "How many years have you worked at a job which required shift work?" Within Stand, however, a greater proportion of those with more than eleven years of service (the median length of shift-work service)

was tolerant of shift work than was the proportion with less than eleven years on shifts. Although the relationship at Advance is not statistically significant, the direction was the same as at Stand.

Although both Tables 5:12 and 5:13 would suggest that workers become inured to the rigors of shift work, there is an

TABLE 5:13

Experience at Jobs Requiring Shift Work and Satisfaction with Shift Work

(in percent)

	1-90. How many years have you worked at a job which required shift work?				
	Less than 3.5 years	*3.5 to 11 years*	*More than 11 years*	*Total Percent*	*N*
Total					
Advance	17	31	52	100	(42)
Stand	24	37	39	100	(114)
Advance					
1-73. Like or don't mind shift work	43	62	73		
Dislike shift work	57	38	27		
Total	100	100	100		
N	(7)	(13)	(22)		
Stand					
1-73. Like or don't mind shift work	19	21	40	*	
Dislike shift work	81	79	60		
Total	100	100	100		
N	(27)	(42)	(45)		

* Chi-square test of this relationship, comparing "more than" with "less than" 11 years, is significant.

alternative interpretation of these findings. It can be assumed that missing from the long-service shift group were those men who started working shifts, but who had transferred to jobs which were less demanding on their physical and social lives. Those who were left were more able, presumably, to cope with the demands of shift work. This could account for the higher

proportion of favorable attitudes toward shift work found in the long-service group. Even among those at Stand who had remained on shift work for more than eleven years, however, over half expressed a dislike for the system.

Job Adjustment

In the preceding pages the worker's satisfaction with shift work was shown to depend on his physical and psychological adjustment to change, on his family and social life, and on his previous work experience. We might now logically ask what

TABLE 5:14

Attitude toward Shift Work and Absence Rate

(Advance shift workers only)[a]

(in percent)

	Number of days absent, 1954						
	None	*One day*	*Two days*	*Three days*	*Four or more days*	*Total Percent*	*N*
Advance							
1-73. Like or don't mind shift work	31	31	15	15	8	100	(26)
Dislike shift work	13	34	27	13	13	100	(15)

[a] Individual absence data were not available for Stand.

effect the man's attitude had on his behavior on the job. Unfortunately, performance measures for this population have not been developed, and for neither of the groups—operating and plant protection—do good criteria of effectiveness exist.

Absence data were obtained for the men in both power plants, but since only the Advance workers had signed their questionnaires, the relationship between attitudes and absences could be studied only for the new plant. The rate for Advance was very low (90 percent of the shift workers had been absent three times or less for the entire year), hence very little relationship could be found between attitudes and absences. Table 5:14

compares the absence rates of those who "like or don't mind shift work" with those who "dislike shift work." No statistically significant difference was found between these two groups, although there is a tendency for the more dissatisfied men to have had higher absence rates.

Another measure of the job behavior of the workers was obtained in response to the question, "How often do you come in or stay at the plant *on your own time* to find out how to do a certain job?" We see in Table 5:15 that a majority of the Advance shift workers had been in the plant at least once in the previous year. The majority of the Stand workers had never been in the plant on their own time. Within Stand a greater proportion of those who "like or don't mind shift work" came into the plant on personal time than of those who "dislike shift

TABLE 5:15

Attitude toward Shift Work and Frequency of Coming into the Plant on Own Time

(in percent)

	1-72. How often do you come in or stay at the plant on *your own time* to find out how to do a certain job?					
	Once a month or more	*Once a year or more*	*Never*		*Total Percent*	*N*
Total						
Advance	12	61	27	*	100	(41)
Stand	18	22	60		100	(120)
Advance						
1-73. Like or don't mind shift work	11	63	26		100	(27)
Dislike shift work	14	57	29		100	(14)
Stand						
1-73. Like or don't mind shift work	21	36	43	*	100	(33)
Dislike shift work	16	17	67		100	(87)

* Chi-square test of this relationship, comparing "once a month" or "once a year or more" and "never," is significant.

work." Thus, one of the determinants of a worker's willingness to come into the plant on his own time appeared to be his tolerance for shift work.

Shift Problems in the Two Plants

Besides differences in the workers' attitudes toward shift work, the two contrasting rotational patterns produced differences in job relationships, unrelated to these attitudes. Because

TABLE 5:16

Pattern of Shift Rotation and Knowing Men on Other Shifts

(in percent)

	1-82. How well do you feel you know the men on the other shifts who do the same jobs you do on your shift?					
	Very or quite well	*Fairly well*	*Not too or not at all well*		*Total Percent*	*N*
Advance	36	14	50	*	100	(42)
Stand	68	25	7		100	(121)

* Chi-square test of this relationship is significant.

the shift groups in Advance rotated together simultaneously and the men never worked with groups other than their own, there appeared to be less interaction among men on different shifts in the new plant than in the old. A significantly greater proportion of the men in Stand said that they knew the men "on the other shifts who do the same job you do on your shift" very or quite well (Table 5:16). The individually staggered rotational schedules employed at Stand permitted the men to meet each other during the transition period of each shift change.

Despite this greater familiarity with the other men, more men at Stand said that they were left with problems which should have been handled during the previous shifts (Table

5:17). Similarly, a greater proportion of the Stand workers said that the different shifts worked together "not too smoothly" or "not at all smoothly" (Table 5:18).

Although these perceptions of problems between the different shifts were unrelated to the men's attitudes toward shift

TABLE 5:17
Pattern of Shift Rotation and Left with Work and Problems
(in percent)

1-81. How often do you feel that the men on the last shift left you with problems or work which they should have handled during their shift?

	Very or quite frequently	*Fairly often*	*Occasionally or very seldom*		*Total Percent*	*N*
Advance	5	14	81	*	100	(42)
Stand	24	8	68		100	(120)

* Chi-square test of this relationship is significant.

TABLE 5:18
Pattern of Shift Rotation and Smoothness of Shift Operations
(in percent)

1-83. How well do you feel the different shifts work together in this plant?

	Very or quite smoothly	*Fairly smoothly*	*Not too smoothly or not at all smoothly*		*Total Percent*	*N*
Advance	37	56	7	*	100	(41)
Stand	33	37	30		100	(119)

* Chi-square test of this relationship is significant.

work, they were certainly relevant to the effective operation of the plants. For a smoothly functioning organization it is obviously not enough for the workers on different shifts to know each other. They must also be willing to work together and not leave problems for subsequent shifts.

The Shift-work Problem

In this chapter we have examined some of the factors which are related to worker attitudes toward shift work. We found that a majority of workers actively and strongly disliked working afternoons and nights. The attitudes of workers in Advance, however, were less unfavorable than were those of the Stand workers. The workers in the new plant reported that they adjusted to shift changes more rapidly than did the workers in Stand, that their families less often disliked their working shifts and felt less strongly about it, and that they visited with their friends more frequently than did the workers at Stand. The more tolerant attitudes of the Advance shift workers can probably be attributed to the less disruptive effects of weekly rotation on their psychological adjustment and on their family and social lives.

In Stand the physical condition of the workers, the time they needed to adjust to shift changes, their families' attitudes toward shift work, and their ability to get together with friends were all related to their attitudes toward shift work. No significant correlations were found between responses to questions in these several areas. They represent separate and distinct areas, and the shift worker must adjust his life in each of them.

The degree of tolerance for shift work appeared to be related to the extent of adjustment to the physical and social demands of this type of work. Table 5:19 shows the increasing degree of tolerance expressed by men at Stand who reported adjustments in their families, their physical conditions, and in their adaptation to shift changes. The greater the reported adjustment in each of these areas, the greater the proportion of tolerant feelings toward shift work.

From a societal viewpoint, the unfortunate part about the results in Table 5:19 is that the majority of the men were in the group with two or more areas of maladjustment. The situation

among the Advance workers was not much better. Is it any wonder, then, that the majority of shift workers in the two plants responded "no" to the question, "If you were a young man starting out to get his first job again, would you take a job requiring you to work shifts?" We find in Table 5:20 that the Advance workers were somewhat more willing to work shifts again, one out of five saying "yes"; but there was generally

TABLE 5:19

Cumulative Determinants of Attitude toward Shift Work

(Stand shift workers only)

Family attitude	*Physical condition*	*Time for adjustment*	N	*Percent like or don't mind shift work*
+ (Like or don't mind)	+ (Very good)	+ (A day or less)	(7)	100
+	+	− (More than a day)	(4)	100
+	− (Worse than very good)	+	(5)	80
+	−	−	(5)	40
− (Dislike)	+	+	(13)	38
−	+	−	(26)	12
−	−	+	(12)	16
−	−	−	(39)	8

strong feeling against starting out to make a living this way again. Surprisingly, we found the responses to this question were unrelated to the length of shift-work service of the respondent. We have here the unhappy picture of a group of men doing something for their daily bread which they would prefer not to do if they had the opportunity to start over again. In both plants the unwillingness to work shifts again was more strongly expressed in the group which disliked shift work than among those who liked or did not mind shift work.

Despite the multitude of shift systems presently in operation in this country and abroad, the designers of these systems have employed only a limited perspective in the solution to shift

problems. Most shift systems are designed to minimize the disruption in one area of the worker's life, but tend to ignore all of the other areas.

In the past, shift work has represented employment security to many workers, particularly the men in these power plants.

TABLE 5:20
Attitude toward Shift Work and Willingness to Do Shift Work Again
(in percent)

	1-91. If you were a young man starting out to get his first job again, would you take a job requiring you to work shifts?				Total	
	Yes	Undecided	No		Percent	N
Total						
Advance	22	33	45	*	100	(42)
Stand	6	12	82		100	(118)
Advance						
1-73. Like or don't mind shift work	30	40	30	†	100	(27)
Dislike shift work	7	20	73		100	(15)
Stand						
1-73. Like or don't mind shift work	22	19	59	*	100	(32)
Dislike shift work	1	8	91		100	(86)

* Chi-square test of this relationship is significant.
† Chi-square test of this relationship, comparing "no" with "undecided" or "yes," is significant.

Now, with the supports provided by social legislation—unemployment insurance, government employment agencies—and the relatively full employment of recent years, the security provided by shift work is less of an inducement to workers. Consequently, management has found it increasingly more difficult to man afternoon and night shifts.

Both management and unions have turned to shift differentials—paying wage bonuses for working the less attractive shifts—as a "solution" to the problems of shift work. Shift dif-

ferentials of six cents or twelve cents per hour are deceptively attractive for the young man just beginning his career. For a man with a new family needing a house, furniture, and household appliances, the extra money is important. The added money does not solve, however, the physical, psychological, or social problems which shift work creates. The worker, therefore, probably gradually develops a dislike for the type of living required by this work. In most shift situations, by the time the worker questions whether the increased income adequately compensates for the deprivations of shift work, he can transfer to a day job only at a marked financial loss. Rather than solving the shift problem, paying a higher shift differential merely intensifies the difficulty for the worker in choosing between shift work and day work. The increased income means a greater ability to buy necessities and luxuries. Continued shift work, however, means a lack of time in which to enjoy such advantages. A company, by increasing the shift differential, may tend to hold employees to shift work for economic reasons long past the time when they should have transferred to day jobs for physical or social reasons.

The short-sighted solution of, "We will raise the shift differential until shift problems disappear" has not only been offered by management but enthusiastically sponsored by unions. Rather than being concerned with the real problems which shift workers face, both union and management bargain about the size of the shift differentials. Little effort is given to looking for new solutions.

The usual alternative to raising the shift premium is to alter the mechanics of the shift schedule. The variety of shift patterns found from one company to another indicates different attempts to ameliorate shiftwork difficulties. Unfortunately, differences in shift patterns usually represent historical circumstances rather than a consideration of the difficulties which might be overcome.

The origin of the weekly rotation at Advance provides a typical example of such a fortuitous basis for a shift schedule. Because the new plant was similar in design to a plant in another company, many of the operating procedures used in the latter plant were incorporated wholesale into Advance. Among these was the weekly shift rotation schedule. Thus, this change in shift pattern occurred more as a by-product of technological change than on the basis of the workers' needs.

There are no easy solutions to the problems of continuous operation. In the present study we found a number of problems common to both rotational systems. Although certain advantages appeared for the weekly over the monthly rotational system, the Advance workers still reported major adjustment difficulties. Even at Advance, more than three out of five of the workers reported that their families disliked their having to work shifts.

The men were asked, "How would you like to see the plant try out permanent shifts?" as an alternative to the rotational systems in the two plants. Table 5:21 shows that the men at Stand were much more favorable toward this suggestion than were the men at Advance. Even in the latter plant however, 30 percent of the men said that they would not mind or would like to try permanent shifts.

The relationships within each of the plants suggested that willingness to try permanent shifts was more an expression of the desire to escape from the current situation than a true preference for permanent shift operations. Proportionately more of the Stand workers who liked or did not mind shift work than of the workers who disliked it said they would not like to try permanent shifts. The same trend in relationship was found among the Advance workers. Permanent shifts as an escape from the problems of shift rotation trade one set of problems for another. The men who are to work on the afternoon or night shifts are destined to be out of phase with the rest of the community dur-

ing their entire working lives. Since schools, stores, and recreation facilities are all geared to a daytime routine, working permanent shifts requires the continual resolution of the conflict between the demands of shift work and normal society.

TABLE 5:21
Attitude toward Shift Work and Desire to Try Permanent Shifts
(in percent)

	1-92. How would you like to see the plant try out permanent shifts? (This would mean that the same group would always work days, another group always work afternoons, etc.)					
	Would like to try it	*Would not mind trying it*	*Would not like to try it*		*Total Percent*	*N*
Total						
Advance	14	24	62	*	100	(42)
Stand	53	20	27		100	(118)
Advance						
1-73. Like or don't mind shift work	11	19	70		100	(27)
Dislike shift work	20	33	47		100	(15)
Stand						
1-73. Like or don't mind shift work	29	19	52	*	100	(31)
Dislike shift work	61	21	18		100	(87)

* Chi-square test of the relationship is significant.

The traditional approaches to the problems of continuous operation are obviously of limited value in reducing the difficulties caused by shift work. Concern must be given to finding solutions to the physical, psychological, and social problems of the shift worker. The inadequacy of current fringe benefits was emphasized by this comment from a Stand worker:

> A large percent of the so-called benefits at [this company] which come to fifty some-odd cents an hour might be good for

> the day worker and the women in the general offices, but certainly cannot be realized by the shift worker. The gym, library, bowling alley, boat club, and others do most of us no good at all, when you work all night and have to sleep all day.

The new era of automation will increase the proportion of our population engaged in shift work. Industrial managements, government planners, and social and biological scientists should join forces to search for new solutions to the problems of continuous operations, based on workers' problems rather than on history. The following are some of the questions which must be answered.

> How can the physiological costs of working rotating shifts be reduced for the individual?
>
> What can be done to provide some stability in the sleeping schedules of shift workers?
>
> Can adequate eating arrangements be made to ensure night-shift workers of proper nourishment?
>
> What can be done to ensure family relationships from being overly disturbed?
>
> Can community or company facilities be expanded to provide recreational activities for the night worker?

Chapter 6

SUPERVISION IN POWER PLANTS

General Considerations

Management literature has recently contained a good deal of speculation on the nature of supervision in the automated factory of the future. It is clear that fewer men will be needed to supervise the activities of the smaller labor forces in these factories. The question may be raised, however, of what will be the most effective supervisory behaviors in the face of the increased complexity and drastic changes in the machinery and equipment for which supervisors will be responsible. Previous studies from the Survey Research Center of The University of Michigan[1]

[1] Katz, D., Maccoby, N., and Morse, N., *Productivity, Supervision and Morale in an Office Situation:* Part I. Ann Arbor, Mich.: Institute for Social Research, Monograph Series No. 2, 1950.

Katz, D., Maccoby, N., Gurin, G., and Floor, L. G., *Productivity, Supervision and Morale among Railroad Workers*. Ann Arbor, Mich.: Institute for Social Research, Monograph Series No. 5, 1951.

Kahn, R., and Katz, D., "Leadership Practices in Relation to Productivity and Morale," in D. Cartwright and A. Zander (eds.), *Group Dynamics: Research and Theory*. Evanston, Ill.: Row, Peterson, 1953.

and from other similar research groups[2,3] have indicated the importance of the human relations skills of the supervisor in the successful performance of his work. In one of these studies it was found that management appraisal of the supervisors' performances substantially agreed with the employees' evaluation of the supervisors' human relations abilities.[4] In other studies, productivity,[5] absences,[6,7] and employee satisfactions with the supervisor[8] showed significant relationships with the supervisor's human relations skills.

Although for many years company managements have been promoting their most technically competent people to supervisory positions, recently, with the increased emphasis on human relations, the technical side of the supervisory job has been accorded a subordinate role. Dealing with the complexities of human behavior has gradually been recognized as possibly the most important part of the supervisor's job. With the changes in technology represented by the introduction of automation, however, the technical requirements and skills of the supervisory job may assume greater importance. A number of writers have, in fact, indicated that training for the new supervisory positions should be principally of a technical nature. They have assumed that with the reduced number of people and the much heavier capital investment in machinery, the foreman's attention should be concentrated on the technical aspects

[2] Fleishman, E. A., Harris, E. F., and Burtt, H. E., *Leadership and Supervision in Industry*. Columbus, Ohio; Ohio State University, 1955.

[3] Comrey, A. L., Pfiffner, J. M., and Beem, H. P., "Factors Influencing Organizational Effectiveness: I—The U.S. Forest Service," *Personnel Psychology,* 1952, *5*, 307–328.

[4] Mann, F., and Dent, J., *Appraisals of Supervisors and Attitudes of Their Employees in an Electric Power Company*. Ann Arbor, Mich.: Institute for Social Research, 1954.

[5] Kahn and Katz, *op. cit.*

[6] Mann, F., and Baumgartel, H., *Absences and Employee Attitudes in an Electric Power Company*. Ann Arbor, Mich.: Institute for Social Research, 1953.

[7] Fleishman, *et al., op. cit.*

[8] *Ibid.*

of his job. Under these circumstances, the human relations aspect would become relatively much less important.[9]

Starting from the same basic fact—that the technology will be more complex—another group of writers has concluded that the supervisor should be even more concerned than formerly with the administrative and interpersonal aspects of his job. It is the contention of this second group that the knowledge and skills necessary for the handling of the new equipment will be held by technicians who are experts in particular specialties. Being experts, these men will require greater attention as individuals from the supervisor, and the job of coordinating their efforts will be even more crucial.[10]

In our investigations at Advance and Stand we attempted to provide first tentative answers to this controversy in the form of empirical data based on the perceptions of the workers in the two power plants. Were human relations behaviors still functional to supervisors faced with the new technology of the automated power plant? To what degree was technical proficiency required?

Among other questions concerning foremen practices, the power plant personnel evaluated their foremen on three dimensions of competence: technical, administrative, and human relations. Each of these areas was defined by specifying the kinds of knowledge or behavior considered, a priori, to belong in that area. The following questions were used to assess the competences of the foreman:

> How well does your foreman *know* the *technical side* of his job—the operation and maintenance of the equipment for which he is responsible?

[9] Drucker, P. F., *The Practice of Management*. New York: Harper & Brothers, 1954.

Department of Scientific and Industrial Research, *Automation*. London, England: Her Majesty's Stationery Office, 1956.

[10] Guest, Robert N., "The Impact of Changing Technology on Human Relations," *The Emerging Environment of Industrial Relations*. East Lansing, Mich.: Labor and Industrial Relations Center, Michigan State University, 1957.

How well does your foreman *do* the *administrative side* of his job—by this we mean planning and scheduling the work, indicating clearly when work is to be finished, assigning the right job to the right man, inspecting and following up on the work that is done, etc.?

How well does your foreman *do* the *human relations side* of his job—getting people to work well together, getting individuals to do the best they can, giving recognition for good work done, letting people know where they stand, etc.?

The distribution of responses to these three questions in each of the two power plants appears in Table 6:1. The proportions of men who perceived their foremen as having an adequate knowledge of the technical side of their jobs were approximately equal in the two plants, as were the proportions who saw their foremen doing the administrative side of their jobs adequately. A significantly greater proportion of the men in Advance than in Stand saw their foremen as performing their human relations functions extremely or very well (49 percent in Advance as compared to 32 percent in Stand).

Despite this difference in the level of human relations competence in the two plants, the intercorrelations among the three questions were similarly high for both plants (Table 6:2). These high correlations can be interpreted in two ways: (1) the supervisors who were doing an effective job were actually competent in all three areas; (2) the respondents were unable to differentiate among the three areas of competence and these correlations merely represented a general attitude—"halo effect"—about the supervisor. The data tend to support the first interpretation.

Partial correlations among these three questions (in each case holding the third question constant) are shown in the right-hand half of Table 6:2. Although five of the six partial correlations are significantly different from zero, the small size of the

TABLE 6:1

Employee Evaluations of Supervisors' Technical, Administrative, and Human Relations Competence

	In Percent	
	Advance (N = 138)	*Stand* (N = 176)
2-29. How well does your foreman *know* the *technical side* of his job—the operation and maintenance of the equipment for which he is responsible. (Check one)		
5. He knows the technical parts of his job extremely well	14	19
4. Very well	39	30
3. Fairly well	24	24
2. Some well, and others not so well	16	21
1. Does not know the technical parts of his job at all well	7	4
Not ascertained	0	2
	100	100
2-30. How well does your foreman *do* the *administrative side* of his job—by this we mean planning and scheduling the work, indicating clearly when work is to be finished, assigning the right job to the right man, inspecting and following up on the work that is done, etc. (Check one)		
5. He handles the administrative parts of his job extremely well	14	14
4. Very well	30	29
3. Fairly well	26	19
2. Some well	20	23
1. He does not handle the administrative parts of his job at all well	10	13
Not ascertained	0	2
	100	100

* The percentage difference between the plants is significant at the .05 level of confidence. This level of confidence will be used in statistical tests in all subsequent tables.

Table 6:1 (Continued)

	Advance		Stand
2-31. How well does your foreman *do* the *human relations side* of his job—getting people to work well together, getting individuals to do the best they can, giving recognition for good work done, letting people know where they stand, etc. (Check one)			
5. He handles the human relations parts of his job extremely well	17 } 49	*	32 { 13
4. Very well	32		19
3. Fairly well	21		26
2. Some well	14		15
1. He does not handle the human relations parts of job at all well	15		26
Not ascertained	1		1
	100		100

TABLE 6:2

Intercorrelations among the Evaluations of Technical, Administrative, and Human Relations Competence

First-order Correlations			Partial Correlations			
Correlation[a]	*Advance* (N = 137)	*Stand* (N = 172)	*Correlation*	*Advance* (N = 137)		*Stand* (N = 172)
r_{TA} =	.59*	.67*	$r_{TA \cdot H}$ =	.35*		.49*
r_{AH} =	.70*	.71*	$r_{AH \cdot T}$ =	.56*	†	.56*
r_{TH} =	.54*	.53*	$r_{TH \cdot A}$ =	.22*		.10

[a] T: Technical competence
A: Administrative competence
H: Human relations competence
* Coefficient is significantly different from zero.
† The partial correlations between technical and human relations competence for the two plants are significantly lower than the other two corresponding partial correlations.

correlations between the technical and human relations competences indicates that they are relatively independent of each other. Together they seem to have accounted for the administrative competence. The "halo effect" which is so apparent in the first-order correlations seems to have stemmed from the correlation of perceived administrative competence with the evaluation of technical and human relations competences.

Although the statistical independence of the technical and human relations characteristics of the supervisor's job is apparent from these data, the question, raised before, of the relative importance of these two aspects has not been answered. The criterion of supervisory effectiveness in this study was the satisfaction of employees with their supervisors. The subordinates were asked, "Taking all things into consideration, how satisfied

TABLE 6:3

Employee Satisfaction with Supervisors

	In Percent		
	Advance (N = 138)		Stand (N = 176)
2-55. Taking all things into consideration, how satisfied are you with your immediate supervisor? (Check one)			
5. Very satisfied	38	*	16
4. Quite satisfied	28		20
3. Fairly satisfied	20		34
2. Not too satisfied	6		16
1. Not at all satisfied	8		12
Not ascertained	0		2
	100		100

* Chi-square test of the difference in distributions is significant.

are you with your immediate supervisor?" The distribution of the responses to this question in the two plants appears in Table 6:3. A significantly greater proportion of the men at Advance than at Stand felt "very or quite satisfied" with their immediate supervisor (66 percent at Advance versus 36 percent at Stand). This difference paralleled the difference seen in Table 6:1 in the perceived human relations competences of the supervisors in the two plants. It is not surprising, then, to find in the left-hand side of Table 6:4 that the correlation of the employee's satisfaction with his supervisor to his evaluation of the supervisor's human relations competence was significantly positive and was some-

what higher than its correlation with the other supervisory competences.

The correlation between the worker's perception of his supervisor's human relations competence and his overall satisfaction with his supervisor was significantly higher at Advance than at Stand. This suggests that in terms of employee satisfaction, the human relations skills of the supervisor had assumed an even greater importance in the new plant—despite its more

TABLE 6:4

Employee Evaluation of Supervisory Competence and Satisfaction with Supervisor

First-order Correlations				*Partial Correlations*		
	Advance		*Stand*		*Advance*	*Stand*
Correlation[a]	(N = 137)		(N = 172)	*Correlation*	(N = 137)	(N = 172)
r_{TS} =	.58*		.60	$r_{TS \cdot AH}$ =	.24*	.23
r_{AS} =	.66		.64	$r_{AS \cdot TH}$ =	.19	.32
r_{HS} =	.76	†	.64	$r_{HS \cdot AT}$ =	.52	.44

[a] T: Technical competence
A: Administrative competence
H: Human relations competence
S: Satisfaction with supervisor

* All the coefficients in this table are significantly different from zero.

† The first-order correlation between human relations competence and satisfaction with the supervisor is significantly greater at Advance than at Stand. The partial correlations are not significantly different.

complex, automated technology—than in the old one. The substantial relationship between the perceived *technical* competence of the supervisor and employee satisfaction with him was *not* different in the two plants. The correlation at Advance between human relations competence and satisfaction, moreover, was significantly greater than the correlation between technical competence and satisfaction. This further reinforces the importance of the supervisor's human relations skills to his subordinates' satisfaction with him in the new plant.

In the first-order correlations all three questions of competence were significantly correlated with employee satisfaction

with their foreman. An analysis of the partial correlations, however, increases our understanding of the relative importance of the technical and human relations dimensions isolated earlier. In the right-hand half of Table 6:4 the relationships between each of the perceived competence questions and subordinate satisfaction have been purified of the effects of the relationship with each of the other two questions. For example, $r_{TS \cdot AH}$ represents the partial correlation between supervisor's technical competence (T) and employee satisfaction with the supervisor (S), holding constant both the supervisor's administrative (A) and human relations (H) competence. The results of this analysis clearly indicate the greater importance of the supervisor's human relations competence over his technical competence in determining the satisfactions of his subordinates. In both plants the partial correlation between perceived human relations competence and employee satisfaction with his supervisor was significantly greater than the partial correlation between the perceived technical competence and employee satisfaction. Using the criterion of employee satisfaction with supervision as the measure of effectiveness, the most important function of the supervisor was his ability to deal with his subordinates as human beings rather than his ability to handle the technical equipment. The relative importance of these two factors seems to have been the same for the supervisors in both the automated and the older plants.

The isolation of the technical and human relations factors in supervision and the determination of their relationship with employee satisfaction was done using individual employee perceptions of their supervisors, disregarding the fact that many of the men worked for the same supervisor. The next step in the analysis consisted of obtaining the mean rating of each supervisor on his technical and his human relations competence from the people who reported to him. Since both the technical and human relations competences of the supervisor were measured

on a five-point scale, the value of 3.50 was used as a cutting point for dividing each continuum into a high and low group. The high group on each dimension consisted of those supervisors who were on the average rated as doing that aspect of their job "extremely" or "very well."[11] Four groups of supervisors were formed: one group where the supervisors were rated high on both their technical and their human relations competence; a second group where they were rated high on human

TABLE 6:5

Employee Satisfaction with Supervisors of Differing Competences

	Supervisor Competence		*Number of*	*Number of*	*Employee Satisfaction with Supervisor*	
	Human relations	*Technical*	*supervisors*	*employees*	*Means*[a]	*S.D.*
(1)	high	high	5	39	4.10*	1.046
(2)	high	low	3	40	4.05	0.815
(3)	low	high	6	49	3.67	1.068
(4)	low	low	9	119	2.86	1.304

[a] The higher the score, the higher the satisfaction.

* One-tailed t-tests of the differences between pairs of means indicated that all of the differences are significant except that between (1) and (2).

relations competence but low on technical; a third group rated low on human relations and high on technical; and a fourth group rated low on both characteristics. In the extreme right portion of Table 6:5, the mean satisfactions of the employees with their supervisors are shown for each of the groups.

This table again emphasizes the importance of the human relations practices of the supervisor in determining employee satisfaction. The subordinates of foremen rated high on human relations, regardless of their rating on technical competence,

[11] For this analysis the supervisors from both plants were combined. This was done in order to have a more reliable number of respondents on which to base the analysis. In this analysis, as in all subsequent comparisons of supervisors, only data from employees of supervisors having five or more subordinates were analyzed.

were more satisfied than were the subordinates of supervisors who were rated low on human relations competence. Among the supervisors with a high human relations rating, the difference in their technical competence seemed to make little difference in their subordinates' satisfaction with them.

The technical ability of the supervisor appears to have been important among those supervisors who were rated lower in human relations competence. Among supervisors rated low on the human relations side, the employees of those who were seen as technically proficient were more satisfied than the employees of those who were seen as poor on the technical side as well. Unfortunately, in comparing these latter two groups, the difference in the employee evaluation of the supervisors' technical competence was paralleled by differences in the evaluations of their administrative and their human relations competence as well. It is probable that the difference in employee satisfaction between these groups was accounted for by both the technical and the slight human relations superiority of the supervisors in the high technical–low human relations group. An investigation of these factors on a larger population for which a greater range and variety of supervisory competence could be obtained would be a fruitful next step in this area. One might also expect somewhat different relationships of the patterns of supervisory competences with some other criterion measure such as management appraisal or productivity. In our study such criteria were not available.

The Human Relations Skills of the Supervisor

The previous section has shown the importance of the human relations competence of the supervisor in determining worker satisfaction with him. In the words "human relations," however, there are subsumed many specific foreman behaviors.

The employee questionnaire included a number of questions concerning some of these specific supervisory behaviors, and in this section the relationships between these supervisory behaviors and the perceived over-all human relations competence of the foremen will be examined. Behaviors which characterized the supervisor who was competent at *human relations* will be distinguished from those which characterized the person who was perceived to be *technically* competent.

Table 6:6 contains the correlations of the specific items of supervisory behavior and specific characteristics of foremen with the subordinates' perceptions of the foreman's human relations and technical competences. These pairs of correlations are shown for each plant. For each item, the more the behavior or characteristic was exhibited by the foreman, the higher the numerical value assigned to the response. Thus, the positive correlation between foremen being considerate of the men's feelings and human relations competence indicates that the more considerate a foreman was perceived to be, the higher the evaluation of his human relations abilities. Similarly, the negative correlation between a foreman being bossy and his human relations competence indicates that the more a foreman was seen to be bossy, the less competent his subordinates evaluated him. The items are listed in the approximate order of their appearance in the questionnaire.

There are two important points to be noted in Table 6:6. The first is that the magnitude of the relationship between each of these behaviors and subordinate's evaluation of the foreman's competence varies from item to item. The responses to these questions do not represent a general "halo effect" with respect to the supervisor being either "good" or "bad." Another interesting quality to these correlations is the consistency in direction and, to a large extent, in magnitude in the two plants. This consistency suggests that whatever was defined as technical or human relations competence in each of the two plants com-

TABLE 6:6

Correlations between Employee Perceptions of Specific Foremen Behaviors and Characteristics, and Foremen's Technical and Human Relations Competence

	Foreman Competence in			
	Advance		*Stand*	
Foreman Behaviors	*Technical*	*Human relations*	*Technical*	*Human relations*
2-38. Foreman recognizes good work by				
a. Recommending pay increases	.24	.42	.22	.33
b. Giving more responsibility	.35	.45	.07	.22
c. Giving a pat on the back	.33	.56	.33	.37
d. Telling his superiors	.35	.64	.27	.47
e. Training them for better jobs	.39	.64	.32	.40
f. Praising sincerely and thoroughly	.32	.57	.44	.59
2-32. Foreman concerned with costs	.13	.06	.30	.19
2-33. Foreman concerned for safety	.43	.53	.50	.62
2-34. Foreman supervises closely	−.06	−.19	.03	−.03
2-35. Help from foreman	.40	.65	.56	.52
2-36. Foreman goes to bat	.50	.61	.46	.56
2-37. Foreman reasonable expectations	.39	.54	.33	.42
2-42. Foreman understands men's problems	.50	.66	.49	.52
2-43. Sure of what foreman thinks of work	.13	.28	.16	.27
2-44. Free to discuss job with foreman	.46	.78	.52	.50
2-46. Foreman has authority	.06	−.05	.09	−.12
2-49. Foreman tells about changes in advance	.42	.56	.39	.28
2-50. Foreman gets ideas and opinions of group	.35	.56	.35	.45
2-53. Foreman lets superiors know how work group feels	.45	.60	.37	.34
2-40. Foreman characteristics				
a. Considerate of [men's] feelings	.50	.76	.52	.74
b. Unnecessarily strict with us	−.23	−.36	−.37	−.49
c. Is a "leader" of men	.63	.71	.60	.71
d. Bossy	−.40	−.50	−.41	−.53
e. Quick to criticize	−.35	−.59	−.42	−.50
f. Says one thing, does another	−.50	−.61	−.39	−.59
g. Is a "driver" of men	−.29	−.50	−.46	−.53
h. Can't keep confidences	−.39	−.49	−.46	−.45
i. Carries "weight" with his boss	−.03	−.04	.08	.04
j. Treats employees like inferiors	−.39	−.58	−.45	−.58
k. A warm and friendly person	.44	.60	.48	.65

Note: For all items except 2-38 (a–f) and 2-40 (a–k), *N* is equal to or greater than 132 in Advance, 164 in Stand; for these *N*'s correlations of .17 and .16, respectively, are significantly different from zero. For the remaining items, *N* is equal to or greater than 92 in Advance, 134 in Stand; for these *N*'s correlations of .21 and .17, respectively, are significantly different from zero.

prised, primarily, the same sets of supervisory behaviors. Where major differences occurred, they were usually the result of a restricted range on that behavior in one or the other plant.

The items that appear in Table 6:7 seem to be especially descriptive of human relations behaviors. The items showed a significant partial correlation between the behavior and human

TABLE 6:7

Behaviors and Characteristics of Foremen Correlated Only with Human Relations Competence

(Partial correlations partialling out the effects of human relations and technical competence respectively)

	Foreman Competence in			
	Advance		Stand	
Supervisory Behaviors and Characteristics	*Technical*	*Human relations*	*Technical*	*Human relations*
2-40a. Foreman is considerate of our feelings	.10	.67*	.05	.62*
2-40k. Foreman is a warm and friendly person	.13	.47	.08	.50
2-40j. Foreman treats employees like inferiors	−.07	−.47	−.10	−.42
2-38f. Foreman recognizes good work by praising sincerely and thoroughly	−.02	.50	.07	.44
2-40e. Foreman is quick to criticize	.00	−.51	−.13	−.32
2-38d. Foreman recognizes good work by telling his superiors	−.04	.57	−.07	.40
2-38e. Foreman recognizes good work by training workers for better jobs	.02	.55	.08	.26
2-37. Foreman is reasonable in what he expects	.11	.42	.07	.28
2-50. Foreman tries to get ideas of group in solving job problems	.03	.47	.07	.31
2-40g. Foreman is a "driver" of men	.00	−.41	−.17*	−.34
2-40d. Foreman is "bossy"	−.15*	−.36	−.09	−.38
2-40f. Foreman says one thing, does another	−.22*	−.45	−.01	−.48
2-36. Foreman goes to bat or stands up for employees	.22*	.45	.14	.38

* All correlations with human relations competence are significantly different from zero, as are the starred coefficients with technical competence.

relations competence, and a nonsignificant partial correlation between the item and perceived technical competence. Listed are the partial correlations between those foreman behaviors and the employee ratings of the foreman's technical and human relations competence, which partial out the human relations and technical competence respectively from each of the first-order correlations.

From this table we can see that a foreman who was considerate of his employee's feelings, was a warm and friendly person, and was reasonable in what he expected of his subordinates was considered to be competent in the human relations aspect of his job, whether he was in Advance or in Stand. This aspect of a foreman's human relations competence appears to be analogous to the Consideration scale developed at Ohio State University.[12] Employees who characterized their foreman as being competent in human relations also saw him as providing support for their job efforts through giving praise, assisting them in getting ahead in the organization by telling his superior about their good work, and training them for better jobs in the organization. Furthermore, these foremen were reported as generally trying to get the ideas and opinions of their men in solving job problems and as being willing "to go to bat or stand up for" their men. Taken as a whole, the foreman with whom employees were most satisfied was the man who considered them as individuals, both in his relations to them on the job and in seeing that they got ahead in the organization.

The items grouped together in Table 6:7A suggest additional functions of the foreman's job. Although in each instance the item was significantly correlated with the human relations competence of the foreman, the additionally significant correlation with technical competence would indicate that each of these behaviors serves a dual function, one which is more than purely consideration for the employee as an individual. There is a

[12] Fleishman, *et al., op. cit.*

suggestion in this set of correlations that these behaviors, which reflect the supervisor's technical as well as his human relations competence, help the subordinate do his job better. The specific behaviors include being concerned with getting the work done in a safe manner, showing an understanding of the problems the men have on their jobs, creating an atmosphere of freedom in

TABLE 6:7A

Behaviors and Characteristics of Foremen Correlated with Both Technical and Human Relations Competence

(Partial correlations partialling out the effects of human relations and technical competence respectively)

	Foreman Competence in			
	Advance		Stand	
Supervisory Behaviors and Characteristics	*Technical*	*Human relations*	*Technical*	*Human relations*
2-40c. Foreman is a "leader" of men	.37	.54	.24	.52
2-33. Foreman is concerned with getting work done safely	.17	.38	.15	.44
2-42. Foreman understands problems the men have	.18	.52	.22	.30
2-44. Men feel free to discuss important things about job with foreman	.00*	.71	.29	.24
2-35. Men get help from foreman when they need it	.03*	.56	.33	.24

* All correlations except these two are significantly different from zero.

which the men can discuss their job problems, and giving them help when they need it. Like those behaviors which are listed in Table 6:7, these also concern the supervisor's recognition of the subordinate as a fellow human being. Unlike those in Table 6:7, however, the behaviors in this table require the foreman to display a certain degree of technical competence in showing this concern for the worker. Thus we see, here, an implementing activity which seems to be appropriate for the supervisor to perform and which gives him high ratings on both the technical and human relations aspects of his job. It is very likely

that these are the supervisory behaviors which would be most highly related to a criterion of productivity. In this case, productivity would be gained by a foreman's consideration of his employees in the way he imparted his own technical knowledge to them. The foreman who was capable of this combination of skills was described as a "leader" of men by his subordinates.

Like the last two items in Table 6:7A, there was one final item concerning supervisory behavior whose partial correlations with the competence questions remained significant, but which was not listed in either Table 6:7 or 6:7A. The question asked, "How often does your foreman tell you in advance about any changes that affect you or your work?" The correlations were in opposite directions in the two plants. In Advance the partial correlations with technical and human relations competence were .01 and .43 respectively, whereas in Stand the correlations were .28 and .03. From these correlations it would seem that this item and the last two in Table 6:7A were interpreted differently in the two plants. In Advance they seem to have reflected entirely the human relations component of the supervisors' behaviors. In Stand, however, they reflected both the technical and human relations competence of the foreman.

Eight other items in Table 6:6 were significantly correlated with either the foreman's technical or human relations competence. These were:

- 2-38a. giving recognition by recommending pay increases
- 2-38b. giving recognition by giving more responsibility
- 2-38c. giving recognition by giving a pat on the back
- 2-32. being concerned with costs
- 2-43. making the men sure of what the foreman thinks of his work
- 2-53. letting superiors know how work group feels about things
- 2-40b. being unnecessarily strict with the men
- 2-40h. being unable to keep confidences

The partial correlations of these items with the foreman's technical and human relations competences are not significant.

Besides the items which showed significant relationships with the supervisors' technical and/or human relations competence, there were three items in Table 6:6 which showed essentially no relationship to the supervisors' competence. The first of these (2-34) referred to the closeness of supervision. In the two power plants the closeness with which he supervised seemed to have no bearing on the foreman's perceived abilities. Close or general supervision may be appropriate for varying situations, and a supervisor who uses close supervision may be seen as competent or incompetent, depending on the situational requirements.

The two remaining items showing no relationship with the supervisors' overall technical and human relations abilities are concerned with the power of the supervisor in the plant situation. The employees were asked whether they felt their foreman had enough authority to decide the things he should decide (2-46) and whether he carried "weight" with his boss (2-40i). In other words, the men were asked to evaluate their foreman's decision-making authority and his ability to influence his own boss in getting things done. Unlike the other items which have been discussed in this section, which are characteristics or behaviors of the foreman as a person, these two questions reflect his position in the structure of the organization. They place him in a setting where external forces are operating, in this case his superior. It appears that the employees in their evaluations of their foremen distinguished between situational and personal factors. Their ratings of the foreman's organizational position were not related to their evaluations of the personal competence of the foreman. We shall use this distinction in the next section to examine the effects of organizational factors on supervisory behaviors.

In this section we have isolated a dimension of supervisory behavior which pertained to the supervisor's concern for his subordinates as individuals. This concern seemed to take the form of consideration of his subordinates as individuals with feelings and with problems, and who were essentially his equals except for their position in the organization. He also provided a means for these people to get ahead in the organization by training them and by letting his superior know about their outstanding work. Another group of supervisory behaviors was also found which could be considered task facilitating. The supervisor provided the way for the employees to perform better the tasks of their everyday jobs, but in a way which considered their feelings. Finally, we have seen that the perceived competence of the supervisor was unrelated to the amount of authority or power he was seen to have in the organization.

Factors Related to Supervisory Behavior

Evidence from studies at the Survey Research Center of The University of Michigan[13] and at Ohio State University[14] suggests that the behavior of a supervisor is in some way determined by the way he perceives his position in the organizational hierarchy. Pelz found that the social distance between the supervisor and his subordinates, and the extent to which a supervisor pulled for the company versus his men were conditioned by the amount of power he exerted in the system. Supervisors with a high degree of influence were found more often to be close to their men and to side with their men instead of with

[13] Pelz, D. C., "The Influence of the Supervisor within His Department as a Conditioner of the Way Supervisory Practices Affect Employee Attitudes" (unpublished Ph.D. dissertation, University of Michigan, 1951).

[14] Fleishman, E. A., "Leadership Climate and Supervisory Behavior" (unpublished Ph.D. dissertation, Ohio State University, 1951).

management than were supervisors with low influence. Fleishman found that the "leadership climate" in which a supervisor operated influenced the amount of "consideration" he showed his subordinates. He concluded that foremen who reported that their bosses were "considerate" toward them also reported being considerate toward their own subordinates.

In addition to these variables of power and leadership climate, we were able to study in the power plants the effects of two others which we thought might affect supervisors' behaviors toward their subordinates. The first of these was the effects of the difference in management philosophies between the members of the top plant staff at Advance and those at Stand, which were discussed in Chapter 2. Management philosophy as a concept provides an extension of "leadership climate" to a larger organizational unit; it would manifest itself in within-plant consistencies of supervisory behavior in our study. The second added variable studied was the degree of management identification of the foreman—that is, the extent to which he is identified with the company and feels a part of its management. Does his identification with management interfere with his sensitivity to his men's feelings? Does it make him more concerned with attaining organizational objectives rather than his personal ones? In our study of power plants we have examined these four variables—management philosophy, leadership climate, power, and management identification of the foreman—for their influence on supervisor performance. We were especially concerned with their effects on those behaviors which were listed in Tables 6:7 and 6:7A as being related to the human relations and technical competence of the foremen.

Management Philosophy

As we indicated in the chapter describing the two power plants, one of the distinguishing characteristics between the

plants was the differing management philosophies represented by the plant superintendents and their respective staffs. Stand was characterized by a tight line organization in which the control of the plant rested almost exclusively in the hands of the plant superintendent. Relatively few decisions were made by the foremen and higher level supervisors in this plant; most decisions had to be referred to the top staff for approval or disapproval. At Advance, on the other hand, most of the control seemed to center in the first line supervisor. The plant superintendent and his staff served primarily a review function rather than a decision-making function with respect to the immediate problems of the nonsupervisory employees.

The effects of these differences in management philosophy can be seen in the comparisons presented in Table 6:8. Here are listed the mean ratings accorded to the supervisors by their subordinates in each plant on the items which have been shown to be significantly and consistently related to the human relations competence of the supervisor. (Again the higher the score, the more of the characteristic listed was exhibited by the foreman.)[15] As we would expect from the significant difference between the plants in the average human relations competence of the supervisors, the mean for Advance on all eighteen of these items was in a more favorable direction than was the mean for Stand. Moreover, on half of these items the difference between the plants was statistically significant. These findings suggest that there was a uniformity of behavior by which the supervision of each plant could be characterized. Whether in Advance this uniformity resulted from conformance to the management philosophy of the plant or was due to prior selection of the supervisors is a matter of speculation, since we had no data on the previous performance of these supervisors. From the

[15] In the analysis in this section, as in the initial one differentiating supervisors of high technical, administrative, and human relations competence, only the responses of subordinates of supervisors about whom five or more employees reported were used.

TABLE 6:8

Comparison of Foremen Behaviors Related to Human Relations Competence in the Two Plants as Perceived by Subordinates

	Foreman Behavior or Characteristic	Means (and Standard Deviations) of Foremen Behaviors as Reported by Men in: Advance			Stand	
	Items from Table 6:7					
2-40a.	Foreman is considerate of our feelings (+)[a]	2.85[b]	(0.938)		2.38	(0.970)
2-40k.	Foreman is a warm and friendly person (+)	3.00	(0.947)	*	2.52	(1.027)
2-40e.	Foreman is quick to criticize (—)	2.18	(1.093)		2.36	(1.025)
2-40j.	Foreman treats employees like inferiors (—)	1.50	(0.850)	*	1.96	(0.932)
2-38d.	Foreman gives recognition for good work by telling his superiors (+)	2.09	(0.860)		1.88	(0.907)
2-38e.	Foreman gives recognition for good work by training them for better jobs (+)	1.97	(0.878)		1.89	(0.975)
2-38f.	Foreman gives recognition for good work by praising sincerely and thoroughly (+)	1.86	(0.814)		1.78	(0.941)
2-50.	In solving job problems, foreman tries to get ideas of working group (+)	2.53[c]	(1.170)	*	2.08[c]	(0.900)
2-37.	Foreman is reasonable in what he expects (+)	3.60[c]	(1.344)	*	2.92[c]	(1.214)
2-40g.	Foreman is a "driver" of men (—)	1.64	(0.938)	*	1.94	(0.989)
2-40d.	Foreman is bossy (—)	1.75	(0.935)	*	2.25	(1.093)
2-40f.	Foreman says one thing, does another (—)	1.96	(1.033)	*	2.31	(1.015)
2-36.	Feel that foreman will go to bat or stand up for you (+)	3.85[c]	(1.237)	*	2.97[c]	(1.325)
	Items from Table 6:7A					
2-40c.	Foreman is a "leader" of men (+)	2.69	(0.872)	*	2.36	(0.979)
2-33.	Foreman concerned with getting the work done safely (+)	4.03[c]	(0.981)		3.78[c]	(1.129)
2-42.	Foreman understands problems you have (+)	3.11[c]	(1.084)		3.00[c]	(1.101)
2-44.	Feel free to discuss important things about job with foreman (+)	3.30	(0.918)		3.20	(0.891)
2-35.	Feel you get help from foreman when you really need it (+)	3.91[c]	(0.965)		3.72[c]	(1.105)

[a] The sign in parentheses is the sign of the correlation between the degree of behavior exhibited by and the human relations competence of the supervisor.

[b] The higher the number, the more of the behavior exhibited.

[c] These means were based on responses to a 5-point scale; all others were based on 4-point scales.

* t-test of difference between means is significant.

performance of the foremen at Stand, however, we believe that the former interpretation—that of conformity to the prevailing management philosophy—is probably the correct one for explaining the similarity of supervisory behavior at Advance.

Leadership Climate

Fleishman's study at Ohio State suggested that the behavior of the foreman paralleled the way he was treated by his own superior. In the present study a somewhat similar analysis to Fleishman's was conducted for certain specific supervisory behaviors. Questions which were included on the foremen's questionnaire concerning their bosses' supervisory practices paralleled the questions on the nonsupervisory employees' questionnaire concerning the foremen's own behaviors. For example, the foremen were asked, "From your dealings with your superior, how well would you say the following comment fits him? Treats people under him like inferiors." For the employees the equivalent question read, "From your dealings with your foreman, how well would you say the following comment fits him? Treats employees like inferiors." We were unable to use all of the pairs of questions which were asked for our analysis of the effects of leadership climate, since on a number of them there was practically no variation in the foremen's responses. The items used represent those items for which parallel questions were asked of foremen and employees *and* on which the foremen showed some variation in their reactions.

The use of the foremen's perceptions of their superiors' behaviors as the measure of leadership climate is conceptually and operationally equivalent to Fleishman's Supervisory Behavior Description. In both cases the superior's behavior was measured by the perception of his subordinate foremen. Similarly the measure of the foreman's own behavior was derived from the reports of his subordinates. Again this is equivalent

to the use by Fleishman of the Foreman Behavior Description in which the nonsupervisory employees described the behaviors of their supervisor. Thus the hypothesis that the foreman tends to translate his boss's behavior toward him into his own behavior toward his subordinates could be tested, since by this procedure we obtained measures both of the foreman's perceptions of how his superior treated him and of the parallel perceptions of the nonsupervisory employees about their foremen's behavior.

The results of this analysis are presented in Table 6:9. On each item the individual foreman's perception of his superior's behavior was used to determine whether the foreman was working under a positive or negative leadership climate. For example, four foremen at Stand said that when he gave recognition for good work their superior told his superiors very or fairly often (positive leadership climate); two foremen at Stand said that their superior practically never or only sometimes gave recognition this way (negative leadership climate). There were three reasons for using each foreman's perception of his superior's behavior to assign him to a leadership climate category rather than using some average perception of the superior's behavior by all his subordinate foremen. First, few of the superiors had more than one or two subordinate foremen, which would make such an average little better than an individual's report. Second, we assumed the foreman acts in terms of his perception of his superior's behavior. Third, the superior may, in fact, treat each of his subordinate foremen differently.

The mean responses of the 21 men under the four foremen at Stand in the positive leadership climate (Mean = 2.10) were compared with the mean responses of the 20 men under the two foremen in the negative leadership climate (Mean = 1.65). The difference between these means is significant. This indicates that for this behavior the employees of foremen in the positive leadership climate saw their foreman as more often giving recognition by telling his superiors than did the employees of fore-

men in the negative leadership climate. In Advance the effect of the leadership climate was in the opposite direction, but not to a significant degree. Similar analyses were performed for each of the ten items in this table.

The findings in Table 6:9 fail to offer consistent support for the notion that leadership climate forces a foreman to conform to the behavior of his superior. Only the item "feel free to discuss important things about the job with supervisor" showed significant effects of leadership climate in both plants.

The statistically significant differences between leadership climates offer a suggested modification for thinking about the effect of the climate on the foreman's behavior. Five of the eight significant differences appeared on items which failed to show significant between-plant differences. For example, while no difference between the plants was found on the item "the supervisor gives recognition for good work by telling his superiors," in Stand, foremen under superiors who used this method very or fairly often tended also to use it more often than did foremen under bosses who practically never or only sometimes used this method of recognition. The other items which were not different between the two plants, but which showed the effects of leadership climate, were receiving recognition through training, feeling free to discuss important things about the job with supervisor, and feeling of getting needed help from supervisor.

One of the limiting factors on the effectiveness of leadership climate may be, therefore, how this leadership climate relates to the overall management philosophy of the plant. Just as Fleishman showed that the foreman's behavior was affected by that of his immediate superior, these findings suggest that the superior, too, operates in a climate which may be set by somebody higher in the organization. This person may be the plant superintendent, as in the case of these power plants, or possibly someone even higher, at the divisional or even at the presidential level. One study of the effects of a human relations

TABLE 6:9

Comparisons of Employee Perceptions of the Behavior of Foremen Operating under Differing Leadership Climates

	Employees' Perception of Foremen at			
	Advance		Stand	
Foreman's Perception of His Superior's Behavior or Characteristic	Mean	N Fm, Men	Mean	N Fm, Men
Supervisor gives recognition for good work: Tells his superiors (+)[a]				
Superior does this very or fairly often	2.10[b]	(3, 20)	2.10	(4, 21)
			*	
Superior does this practically never or sometimes	2.17	(2, 23)	1.65	(2, 20)
Supervisor gives recognition for good work: Trains for better jobs (+)				
Superior does this very or fairly often	1.76	(3, 25)	1.53	(3, 19)
			*	
Superior does this practically never or sometimes	1.86	(4, 50)	2.01	(7, 69)
Supervisor gives recognition for good work: Praises sincerely and thoroughly (+)				
Superior does this very or fairly often	1.78	(2, 9)	1.89	(4, 35)
Superior does this practically never or sometimes	1.81	(5, 77)	1.82	(6, 57)
Supervisor treats subordinates like inferiors (—, P)				
Fits superior fairly well or not too well	1.41	(7, 82)	1.73	(7, 51)
			*	
Does not fit superior at all	1.54	(2, 34)	2.16	(3, 45)
In solving job problems, supervisor tries to get ideas of group (+, P)				
Superior always or almost always does this	2.75	(4, 32)	2.18	(7, 77)
Superior seldom, sometimes, or often does this	2.45	(5, 85)	1.91	(5, 44)
Supervisor is a "driver" of men (—, P)				
Does not fit superior too well	2.05	(3, 44)	1.92	(3, 26)
	*			
Does not fit superior at all	1.35	(4, 55)	1.99	(7, 73)
Supervisor is bossy (—, P)				
Fits superior fairly well or not too well	1.95	(5, 74)	2.18	(6, 62)
	*			
Does not fit superior at all	1.39	(4, 41)	2.28	(3, 32)

TABLE 6:9 (Continued)

Foreman's Perception of His Superior's Behavior or Characteristic	Employees' Perception of Foremen at Advance		Stand	
	Mean	N Fm, Men	Mean	N Fm, Men
Supervisor understands problems you have (+)				
Superior has complete or considerable understanding	3.21	(7, 81)	3.14	(5, 58)
Superior has no, a little, or some understanding	2.89	(2, 37)	2.87	(7, 60)
Feel free to discuss important things about job with supervisor (+)				
Feel very free to discuss with superior	3.43	(7, 81)	3.31	(9, 99)
Feel not at all, not very, or fairly free to discuss with superior	* 3.00	(2, 37)	* 2.68	(3, 22)
Feel you get help from supervisor when you really need it (+)				
Superior always or usually gives help	4.03	(7, 80)	3.90	(9, 94)
Superior never, hardly ever, or sometimes gives help	3.67	(2, 36)	* 2.81	(2, 16)

[a] In the parentheses after each item the sign of the correlation between that behavior and the human relations competence of the foreman is indicated by (+) or (−). P appears for those items for which there was a significant difference between the plants in Table 6:8.

[b] The higher the number, the more of the behavior exhibited.

* The difference between pairs of means is significant.

training course suggested that the prevailing supervisory philosophy even in as large a unit as an operating division may influence the behaviors of the foremen at the first line level.[16]

The other suggestion which will require further research for confirmation is that the leadership climate—that is, the behavior of the foreman's superior—may serve either as a positive model or as a negative model for the foreman. On the items, "the supervisor treats employees like inferiors" and "the super-

[16] Hariton, T., "Conditions Influencing the Effects of Training Foremen in New Human Relations Principles" (unpublished Ph.D. dissertation, University of Michigan, 1951).

visor gives recognition for good work by training his subordinates for better jobs," the behavior of the foreman was opposite to the behavior he received from his own superior. In the case of those foremen in Stand who reported that their superior did "not at all" treat his subordinates like inferiors, the subordinates of these men significantly more often reported that they were treated like inferiors than did the subordinates of foremen whose bosses actually treated them like inferiors. Similarly in Stand, the subordinates of those foremen who said that their boss trained them for better jobs significantly less often reported that they received this kind of training as a method of recognition from their foreman. Surprisingly enough, the direction of these findings was supported in Advance, although not to a significant degree. In both these cases then, the behaviors of the second line supervisor were not only not translated directly into the behaviors of the foremen, but were actually reversed.

Even between these two items a fruitful distinction may be made between the one which is beneficial to the subordinates and the one which is not beneficial to them. In the case of the behavior which was positively related to the human relations competence of the foreman—namely, training for better jobs—the foremen may have assumed that because they were receiving this kind of recognition, they were also giving it to their own subordinates. This explanation of the reversal is somewhat reinforced when we look at what the foremen said they were doing in this respect. In Stand, the foremen who said that their bosses trained them for better jobs "very or fairly often" reported that they also used this method of recognition "very or fairly often." The foremen whose superiors "practically never or only sometimes" used this method of recognition also reported using it less often themselves than did the foremen in the more favorable climate. The discrepancy between the foreman's report and the report of his subordinates about his behavior was much greater

among the foremen in the favorable leadership climate than among the group in the less favorable climate. The foremen who were receiving training for better jobs may have paid less attention to ensuring that their subordinates received this kind of training than did the foremen who were not receiving training. To a certain extent the latter may have been making sure that their employees were receiving training which they themselves were conscious of missing.

A similar explanation would appear to account for the differences on the foreman characteristic, "treats employees like inferiors." In this case, the foremen who reported that they were treated like inferiors by their bosses may have been especially careful that they did not treat their own suordinates in this way. We have no data to either support or refute this hypothesis since the foremen were not asked about their behavior in this respect.

These results suggest that the concept of a leadership climate having a unidirectional effect on a foreman's behavior is an oversimplification. The climate established by the foreman's immediate superior must be examined within the climate of the plant, the division, and possibly the company as a whole. In certain cases, moreover, the foreman may react negatively to the example set by his superior.

Power and Management Identification

In the previously mentioned study by Pelz,[17] the power of the supervisor seemed to be an important determiner of his relations with his men. In that study, the supervisor's influence was inferred from his responses in three areas: (1) the extent he participated in reaching decisions with his superior and how he felt about the amount of participation he had, (2) his frequency of contact with his superior—little contact meant high

[17] Pelz, *op. cit.*

power, and (3) salary—the higher the salary, the more influence. The assumption underlying the use of this index was that supervisors who have high salaries, who are brought in to participate in their bosses' decision making, and who are left alone most of the time to do their jobs are supervisors of high power.

TABLE 6:10

Foremen's Feelings about Authority and Influence

	In Percent	
	Responses of Foremen in:	
	Advance (N = 15)	*Stand* (N = 44)
Do you feel you have enough authority to decide the things you should decide?		
1. A lot less authority than I need	7	5
2. A little less authority than I need	33	25
3. About the right amount of authority	60	61
4. A little more authority than I need	0	3
5. A lot more authority than I need	0	3
Not ascertained	0	3
	100	100
Would you like to have more or less say about how things are done in this plant?		
1. I would like to have much more say	27 { 0	* 77 { 21
2. A little more say	27	56
3. I have enough say now	73	23
4. A little less say	0	0
5. I would like to have much less say	0	0
	100	100

* The percentage difference is significant.

The effect of the power of the supervisor on his behavior toward his subordinates was also investigated in our present study. The power of the supervisor was here conceived to be a combination of sufficient authority to make the decisions his job required and some say in how things were done generally in the plant. The two questions which appear in Table 6:10 were asked of the foremen concerning their authority in the

plant. These questions were used to identify foremen having different amounts of power. On the question, "Do you feel you have enough authority to decide the things you should decide?" a small percentage (6 percent) of the foremen who were working in Stand said they had more authority than they needed; none of the foremen in Advance said this. About 60 percent in each plant said they had about the right amount of authority; another third in each plant said they had a little less or a lot less authority than they needed. The question, "Would you like to have more or less say about how things are done in the plant?" however, differentiated between the foremen in the two plants. Seventy-seven percent in Stand indicated that they would have liked more say than they had, as against only 27 percent who said this in Advance. About three-quarters of the foremen in Advance indicated that they had enough say. The responses to this latter question probably reflected the concentration of control about most things in the hands of the top plant staff of Stand. One might also conjecture that "having enough authority to decide the things you should decide" may have meant different things to the foremen in the two plants. The predominant foreman satisfaction with the amount of authority in Stand may have reflected merely a restricted notion of the range of decisions which were appropriate for the foremen in that plant.

When the responses of supervisors in the two plants were combined and the relationship between the responses to these two questions was examined, it was found to be significant (Table 6:11). This relationship attained significance primarily because of the responses of people who said they had less authority than they needed. Of these sixteen supervisors, fourteen of them also said that they would have liked to have more say about how things were done in the plant. Of those supervisors who said they had about the right amount or more authority than they needed, half of them also said they had enough say; the other half said they would have liked to have more say than

they had. From the fourfold table in Table 6:11 we can identify a high power group—those twenty supervisors who said they had about the right amount of authority and who also said they had enough say about how things were done; a medium power group—those twenty-two supervisors who said they had about the right amount of authority but who would have liked to have more say; and a low power group—those fourteen who said they had less authority than they needed and would have liked to

TABLE 6:11

Relationship between Foremen's Perceptions of Their Authority and Influence

(Two Plants Combined)

	Feeling about Authority	
Feel about say	*Less than I need* (1–2)	*About right or more than I need* (3–5)
Enough say (3)	2	20[a] *
Like to have more (1–2)	14	22
	(58 supervisors)	

[a] This group of foremen constitutes the high power group in subsequent discussions.

* Chi-square tests showed this relationship to be significant.

have more say about how things were done in the plant. The high power group was a group of supervisors who felt that they had the authority to make decisions in their own situations and who had a feeling of being able to influence things that went on in the plant as a whole. The low power supervisors, on the other hand, would have liked to have more power to influence the way the plant as a whole operated and felt that they had insufficient authority to do the things they wanted to do in their daily activities.

The management identification of the foremen was another factor whose effect on the foreman's behavior toward his subordinates was investigated along with the foreman's power. Man-

agement identification as used here is the extent to which the foreman was made to feel a part of management and the extent to which he enforced company and departmental rules and regulations. The foreman who gave a great deal of attention to enforcing the rules and regulations and who felt very much a part

TABLE 6:12

The Foremen's Management Identification

	In Percent Responses of Foremen in:	
	Advance (N = 15)	*Stand* (N = 44)
How much attention do you give to enforcing company and departmental rules and regulations?		
1. I give very little attention to enforcing company and departmental rules and regulations	0	5
2. A little attention to doing this	0	0
3. Some attention to doing this	13	7
4. Considerable attention to doing this	60	44
5. I give a great deal of attention to enforcing company and departmental rules and regulations	27	44
	100	100
How much do you feel you are a part of management?		
1. I feel that I am hardly a part of management at all	0	8
2. I feel that I am not too much a part of management	13	15
3. I feel I am somewhat a part of management	54	41
4. I feel I am pretty much a part of management	33	23
5. I feel I am very much a part of management	0	13
	100	100

of management was considered to be identified primarily with the goals of management and the organization. Foremen with different degrees of management identification were grouped according to their replies to the questions in Table 6:12. On the question, "How much attention do you give to enforcing company and departmental rules and regulations?" only a

slightly greater proportion of the foremen at Stand than at Advance said they gave a great deal of attention to enforcing these rules and regulations. On the other question, "How much do you feel you are a part of management?" a slightly greater percentage of the Stand than the Advance foremen felt very much or pretty much a part of management. Neither of these percentage differences is, however, significant. Again, by combining the two groups of foremen and examining the relationship between

TABLE 6:13

Relationships between Foremen's Statements about Feeling a Part of Management and Attention to Enforcing Rules

(Two Plants Combined)

	Attention to Enforcing Rules	
Feel a Part of Management	*Less than a great deal* (1–4)	*A great deal* (5)
Very or pretty much (4–5)	9	14 *
Hardly, not too, or somewhat (1–3)	25[a]	11
	(59 supervisors)	

[a] This group of foremen constitutes the low management identification group for subsequent discussions.

* Chi-square test showed this relationship to be significant.

the responses to the two questions (Table 6:13), we isolated high, medium, and low management identification groups.

The effects of power and management identification will be discussed together even though initially we did not expect to find much relationship between the effects of these two factors. Because these factors seem to have had different effects according to the plant in which the foremen worked—thus possibly interacting with the management's philosophy within each of the plants—the interpretation of their effects becomes clearer when the results of the two analyses are presented together.

For purposes of reliability, in this analysis, as in the others, data were used only from supervisory groups in which at least five subordinates reported to a foreman. This requirement re-

duced the number of supervisors available and forced us to combine the remaining supervisors into two groups each on the power and management identification measures. This was done by forming high and low groups of approximately equal numbers of supervisors, without regard to the plant from which they came. Of the 21 foremen left by this elimination procedure for the management identification analysis, eleven were in the low identification group of Table 6:13—that is, they had reported that they paid less attention to enforcing rules and felt less a part of management; the other ten had been distributed among the other three cells in that table. Thus, on the management identification question we really have a group with relatively low identification to compare with a group being management identified, but not to a high degree.

On the power dimension, exactly the opposite phenomenon occurred. Nine of the twenty supervisors with five or more subordinates were classified in the high power group of Table 6:11. The other eleven were then combined to form a low power group. Thus, we had a group of supervisors who felt they had high authority and influence against a group with relatively less authority and influence. In Table 6:14, the distribution of these supervisors by plants, according to high and low management identification and power, is given. The total number of subordinates in each work group is also shown.

Two points should be noted in Table 6:14. First, the number of supervisors characterized as high management identification and high power was reversed in the two plants. More than half of the Stand supervisors were in the high management identification group, whereas only a third of the supervisors in the Advance group were in this high identification category. On the other hand, two-thirds of the Advance supervisors were in the high power category, whereas less than a third of the Stand supervisors were in this category. The second point to be noted is that there appeared to be relatively little relationship between

the amount of power a supervisor felt he had and his degree of management identification. Although there was some overlap in both plants, there were some foremen with high management identification and low power, and others with low management identification and high power.

The measures which we have used to classify supervisors into the different management identification and power groups

TABLE 6:14

Distribution of Supervisors into the High and Low Power and Management Identification Categories

(Supervisors Having Five or More Subordinates Only)

	Power		*Management Identification*	
	Number		*Number*	
	Foremen	*Men*	*Foremen*	*Men*
Advance				
High	6	68	3	40
Low	3	51	6	79
Stand				
High	3	34	7	80
Low	8	77	5	41
Total	20	230	21	240

were derived from the responses of foremen to their questionnaires. We also asked the subordinates of these foremen how much power and influence their foreman had and with which group he tended to identify. In Table 6:15, the responses of the subordinates of foremen in the high and low power groups in each plant are presented.

The employees were asked about the foreman's authority to make decisions and his ability to influence his boss. For each question the higher the score, the more authority and influence he was seen to have. The foremen at Advance were seen on the average (Mean = 2.55) as having more authority to decide the

things they should decide than were the foremen at Stand (Mean = 2.07). This difference in means was statistically significant. The difference between the plants in the "weight" the foreman carried with his boss, however, was not statistically significant.

Within each plant, on the other hand, the power classification of the supervisor seems to have made little difference in

TABLE 6:15

Foremen's Power and Employee Perceptions of Foremen's Authority and Influence

		Power		
		High		*Low*
2-46. Amount of foreman authority to decide the things he should decide				
Advance	(2.55)	2.62[a]		2.52
	*	*		
Stand	(2.07)	1.99		2.22
2-40i. Foreman carries "weight" with his boss				
Advance	(2.21)	2.78	*	1.93
		*		
Stand	(2.08)	2.23		1.83

[a] The higher the number, the more of the behavior exhibited.
* t-test of difference between means is significant.

the amount of authority he was perceived to have by his subordinates. At Stand, in fact, the high power supervisor was seen as having slightly less authority to make decisions (Mean = 1.99) than were the low power supervisors (Mean = 2.22). The power factor of the foreman seems to have made a difference, however, in the amount of "weight" he was perceived to carry with his boss. This appeared to be especially true for the high power group at Advance. The foremen in this group were seen as having more weight with their bosses (Mean = 2.78) than were those in both the low power group at Advance (Mean = 1.93) and the high power group at Stand (Mean =

2.23). The high power foremen at Advance were also seen as having more authority to decide the things they should decide than were the high power foremen at Stand. Thus, in subsequent analyses in this section we would expect to find the greatest effect of power being illustrated in the high power group of Advance foremen.

The question in Table 6:16 shows a similar comparison of the men's perceptions of their foremen's identifications "with the company," "with themselves," "with the men," or "with both the company and the men."[18] At Advance more than three-fourths of the men saw their foreman as pulling "both for the company and for the men." Only about a fifth of the men saw their foreman as pulling for the company alone, and only a small percentage saw their foreman as pulling for themselves. In Stand, however, almost half of the men saw their foreman as pulling for the company alone, a quarter as pulling for themselves, and only another quarter as pulling for both the company and the men. The difference between the distributions of responses in the two plants is statistically significant.

This difference between the plants maintains even when the management identification of the foremen is controlled, as at the bottom of Table 6:16. For both the high and the low management identification groups, the foremen at Advance were perceived as pulling both for the company and the men significantly more often than were the foremen at Stand.

At Advance there was no significant difference in the distributions of responses of subordinates of foremen in the high and the low management identification groups. In both groups the men saw their foreman as usually pulling both for the company and the men.

[18] The men were asked, "Does your foreman usually pull for the company, himself, the men, or both the company and the men?" Very few respondents (less than 3 percent) said their supervisor pulled only for the men. These responses were therefore combined with the response "company and men."

TABLE 6:16

Foremen's Management Identification and Employee Perceptions of Foremen's Identification

	In Percent Advance		Stand
2-41. Foreman pulls:			
for company	19		48
for self	4	*	24
for company and men[a]	77		28
	100		100
Management Identification of Foreman			
High identification			
Foreman pulls:			
for company	19		53
for self	6	*	13
for company and men[a]	75		34
	100		100
Low identification			†
Foreman pulls:			
for company	19		29
for self	4	*	47
for company and men[a]	77		24
	100		100

* Chi-square test of difference between plants is significant.
† Chi-square test of difference between high and low identification at Stand is significant.
[a] Includes respondents who answered "pulls for men only."

At Stand, on the other hand, a significant difference was found between the distributions of subordinates' responses in the high and low groups. Whereas 53 percent of the men under high identification foremen reported their foremen pulled for the company alone, only 29 percent of the men in the low group said this. In contrast, only 13 percent of subordinates of foremen in the high group, versus 47 percent in the low group, reported that their foreman pulled for himself. Only a slightly higher percentage of men in the high group (34 percent) than

in the low group (24 percent) reported that their foreman pulled both for the company and the men.

Foremen at Stand who had low management identifications were seen by most of their men as pulling for themselves, while those with high identifications were seen as pulling for the company alone. In other words, the low management identification foremen appear to have been concerned neither with the company nor with the men, but only with their own problems; they neither represented the men to the company nor enforced the company's rules and regulations for the men. The high management identification foremen at Stand were seen as performing only one half of their representational functions—namely, pulling only for the company. In Advance, on the other hand, the foremen in both groups were seen as being able to meet the dual demands in their role of representing both management and their men.

The behaviors which in Table 6:7 and 6:7A were shown to be related to the human relations and technical competences of the foremen have been listed again in Table 6:17, where the effects of the power and the management identification of the foremen on these behaviors are indicated. For each plant the mean of the men's responses about the behaviors of the foremen with high and low power and high and low management identification is shown. Again, the higher the mean score, the more the men saw their foremen acting in the way indicated.

From Table 6:17 we see that the foremen's power and management identification had different effects in the two plants. Neither factor had a consistent effect in both plants. Power of the supervisor appeared to be important in Advance, whereas management identification was important in Stand, although to a lesser extent. The high power supervisors at Advance were seen as practicing the appropriate human relations behaviors to a greater degree than were the low power supervisors. On 13 of the 18 behaviors listed, the high power foremen in Advance

TABLE 6:17

Power, Management Identification, and Foremen Behaviors and Characteristics

mean scores

Men's Perceptions of Foreman Behaviors and Characteristics Items from Table 6:7	*Plant*	*Power High*		*Power Low*	*Management Identification High*		*Management Identification Low*
2-40a. Foreman is considerate of our feelings	A	3.02[b]	*	2.63	2.89		2.83
(+)[a]							*
	S	2.43		2.29	2.59	*	2.00
2-40k. Foreman is a warm and friendly person	A	3.09		2.88	3.13		2.94
(+, P)		*		*	*		*
	S	2.43		2.47	2.69		2.21
2-40e. Foreman is quick to criticize (−)	A	1.83	*	2.64	1.97		2.29
		*					
	S	2.32		2.37	2.32		2.45
2-40j. Foreman treats employees like inferiors	A	1.34	*	1.71	1.47		1.51
(−, P)		*			*		*
	S	2.07		1.97	1.86		2.15
2-38d. Foreman gives recognition for good	A	2.32		1.81	2.26		2.02
work: Tells his superiors (+)		*					
	S	1.88		1.82	1.98		1.70
2-38e. Foreman gives recognition for good	A	2.17	*	1.71	2.21		1.86
work: Trains them for better jobs (+)	S	2.21	*	1.71	2.09	*	1.55
2-38f. Foreman gives recognition for good	A	1.93		1.93	1.93		1.83
work: Praises sincerely and thoroughly							*
(+)	S	1.78		1.67	2.00	*	1.37
2-50. Foreman tries to get ideas of group in	A	2.77	*	2.22	2.74		2.43
solving job problems (+, P)		*			*		*
	S	2.18		2.00	2.19		1.88
2-37. Foreman is reasonable in what he ex-	A	3.89	*	3.22	3.79		3.51
pects (+, P)		*			*		*
	S	2.86		2.82	2.97		2.83

[a] In the parentheses after each item the sign of the correlation between that behavior and the human relations competence of the foreman is indicated by (+) or (−). P appears for those items for which there was a significant difference between the plants in Table 6:8.

[b] The higher the number, the more of the behavior exhibited.

* t-test of difference between means is significant.

TABLE 6:17 (Continued)

Men's Perceptions of Foreman Behaviors and Characteristics	Plant	Power High		Power Low	Management Identification High		Management Identification Low
2-40g. Foreman is a "driver" of men (—, P)	A	1.44	*	1.90	1.43		1.74
		*					*
	S	1.87		2.04	1.70	*	2.38
2-40d. Foreman is bossy (—, P)	A	1.47	*	2.09	1.66		1.79
		*			*		*
	S	2.16		2.38	2.05	*	2.60
2-40f. Foreman says one thing, does another (—, P)	A	1.65	*	2.35	1.82		2.03
		*					*
	S	2.43		2.37	2.15		2.60
2-36. Feel that foreman will go to bat or stand up for you (+, P)	A	4.18	*	3.42	4.08		3.74
		*		*	*		*
	S	3.27		2.80	3.25		2.43
Items from Table 6:7A							
2-40c. Foreman is a "leader" of men (+, P)	A	2.82		2.52	2.74		2.66
		*					*
	S	2.38		2.30	2.53		2.05
2-33. Foreman concerned with getting the work done safely (+)	A	4.13		3.90	4.05		4.03
							*
	S	3.91		3.71	4.00	*	3.34
2-42. Foreman understands problems you have (+)	A	3.16		3.04	3.13		3.10
	S	2.88		2.97	3.12		2.78
2-44. Feel free to discuss important things about job with foreman (+)	A	3.46	*	3.08	3.38		3.25
							*
	S	3.26		3.10	3.42	*	2.79
2-35. Feel you get help from foreman when you really need it (+)	A	4.09	*	3.68	4.00		3.87
							*
	S	3.97		3.57	4.05	*	3.10

showed a significantly greater degree of human relations skill than did the low power foremen at that plant. Of the other five behaviors, the high power foremen had higher scores than the low power foremen on four items and equal scores on the fifth. The high power foreman treated his men with more respect by being considerate of the men's feelings, reasonable in what he expected, consistent, rarely quick to criticize, and seldom or never bossy. Furthermore he was more often seen as helping them get ahead in the organization by telling his superiors about their good work and training them for better jobs. The high power foremen were not significantly different, however, in the items from Table 6:7A (2-40c, 2-33, 2-42) which were correlated with both human relations and technical competence. In Stand, on the other hand, the only thing which distinguished the high from the low power foremen was that the highs were seen significantly more frequently as recognizing good work by subordinates by training them for better jobs. Thus, the power of the foremen at Advance was reflected in good human relations behaviors, but the foreman's power at Stand made little difference.

In contrast, the management identification of the foremen failed to be reflected in behavioral differences among the Advance foremen, while significantly discriminating among Stand foremen on 11 of the 18 items in Table 6:17. On all 18 items the Stand foremen with low management identification were seen as less competent in their human relations activities than foremen with higher management identification. Among the Advance foremen, on the other hand, the degree of their management identification failed to produce a single significant difference in their subordinates' perceptions of their behaviors. The low management identification foremen at Stand were seen as more often engaging in such negative behaviors as being bossy and saying one thing and doing another, and less often going to bat for their men or being considerate of their feelings. In addi-

tion they appeared to be especially poor in the items which were listed in Table 6:7A and in the bottom part of Table 6:17, behaviors correlated with technical and human relations competence. On four of these five items, the low management identification supervisors at Stand were substantially lower than any of the other three foremen groups.

On only one of the five items in the bottom part of Table 6:17, "The foreman is a leader of men," was there any significant difference between the plants on the average (see Table 6:8). The low management identification group at Stand was so seldom thus described that on this item it tended to account for almost the entire difference between the plants. On the other four items too, the high management identification foremen at Stand were almost indistinguishable from the foremen groups at Advance. It was the neglect of their men by the low management identification foremen that appears to have accounted for the differences found between the foremen in the two power plants.

When the data from both these analyses are considered together they present an interesting picture of the patterns of supervisory behavior in the two plants. There were two groups of supervisors, one group at each plant, who seem to have accounted for most of the differences between the plants in the average supervisory behavior exhibited. At Stand the greater part of the ineffective behaviors was found in five low power, low management identification supervisors. These five (see Table 6:15) were seen as having about an equal amount of authority and carrying an equal amount of weight with their bosses as the high identification group. They were also seen, however, as pulling for themselves for the most part, whereas the high management identification group was pulling for the company (see Table 6:16). Their men saw the low identification foremen as being less helpful on the job and to a large extent less "considerate" toward them than their colleagues in the high

management identification group. In Stand, where the foremen were seen as having much less authority than were the foremen in the new plant, and where few of the foremen were perceived as pulling for both the company and the men, it appears that the low power, low management identification foremen had virtually abdicated their responsibilities as supervisors.

In the new plant we found a group highly effective in their human relations practices. These were the high power—and low management identification—foremen at Advance. These foremen, as we saw in Table 6:15, had about the same amount of authority as the low power group at that plant, but had significantly more weight with their bosses according to their subordinates. These were the foremen who were seen as facilitating their men's mobility through training and recognition by people in the higher echelons of the organization.

Even among the two remaining groups—the low power group at Advance and the high management identification group at Stand—there were differences both in the authority they had to decide things on their jobs and in the perception of their subordinates as to their identifications. The low power group at Advance was seen to have more authority than the high management identification group at Stand, and to be pulling predominantly for the company and the men at the same time rather than for the company alone.

The overall satisfactions of the employees with the foremen in these groups were strikingly different (Table 6:18). The highest level of satisfaction with the foremen was reported by the men under the high power foremen at Advance (Mean = 3.99); the lowest level of satisfaction by the men under the low management identification foremen at Stand (Mean =2.48).

The interaction among the plant, the foreman's power and management identification, and satisfaction with the foreman can be seen clearly in the lower part of Table 6:18. In Advance the high power, low management identification group comprised

the foremen with whom the subordinates were most satisfied (Mean = 4.25). The men were a little more satisfied with these high power foremen who were only somewhat identified with management (Mean = 4.25) than with those foremen who were highly identified with management (Mean = 3.80). In Stand, on the other hand, the management identification of the foremen was more important than was his power. In this plant the

TABLE 6:18

Power, Management Identification, and Satisfaction with the Foreman

2-55. Taking all things into consideration, how satisfied are you with your immediate supervisor?		*Power*			*Management Identification*		
		High		*Low*	*High*		*Low*
Advance	(3.79)	3.99	*	3.53	3.80		3.78
	*	*		*	*		*
Stand	(3.03)	3.12		2.95	3.31	*	2.48

Plant	*Power*	*Management Identification*	*Number Foremen*	*Number Employees*	*Mean Satisfaction*
A	High	High	3	40	3.80
A	High	Low	3	28	4.25
A	Low	Low	3	51	3.53
S	High	High	3	34	3.12
S	Low	High	3	36	3.47
S	Low	Low	5	40	2.48

* t-test of difference between means is significant.

foremen with low power and high management identification were the ones with whom their subordinates were most satisfied (Mean = 3.47). In both plants the subordinates of foremen who had low power and were low in management identification were significantly less satisfied with their foremen than were those of either of the other groups in their plant.

The results of this section on the power and management identification of the foremen suggest the existence of an evolutionary sequence, or at least a hierarchy, of behaviors and attitudes on the part of supervisors, which are important to their

subordinates' satisfaction with them. Lowest in the respect of his subordinates is the foreman who is seen as pulling only for himself. Such a foreman is concerned only with his own need gratification and is insensitive to the needs of his subordinates. Somewhat higher is the foreman who is wholly identified with the company. He always takes management's side, never supports his men. Although the men feel such a foreman is unfair and biased, they respect him more than the foreman who is concerned only with himself. These two types of foremen were represented at Stand. It is interesting to note that the relative ability of these foremen to influence their superiors made no difference in their evaluations by their subordinates. We may assume that the men felt that this influence would never be used to aid them, and thus their foremen's influence did not affect their overall satisfaction with them.

At Advance virtually all the foremen had reached the next level of supervisory maturity, the stage in which they recognized the dual responsibility of their role.[19] Both they and the majority of their men reported that these foremen pulled both for the company and for the men. The foremen at Advance were attempting to integrate and reconcile the objectives of the organization and the needs of their men. Once this level of supervisory maturity has been reached and the men feel that the foreman will deal fairly with the daily difficulties which arise on the job, foremen are evaluated according to their power in the organization—that is, ability to influence their own superior. Thus it was among the Advance, and not the Stand, foremen that the high power of the foreman was related to the high satisfaction of his men with him. High power foremen were seen not only as being considerate of the men's feelings, as being reasonable in what they expected, and as giving recognition by training the men for better jobs, but probably even more importantly, they were

[19] Mann, F., and Dent, J., "The Supervisor: Member of Two Organizational Families," *Harvard Business Review,* 1954, *32*, 6, 103–112.

seen as telling their own superior about their men's good work and as being able to go to bat or stand up for their men.

The foremen in this study with whom the workers were most satisfied were the ones whom the men saw as representing both management and the men and who, in addition, had the power to influence their superiors to accomplish the goals of their subordinates. It is highly probable that had we asked management which foremen they were most satisfied with, they likewise would have chosen the ones whom they saw as representing both management and the men, and who, in addition, had the power to influence their subordinates to accomplish the objectives of the company. We would expect that the two groups would have chosen the same foremen.[20]

Summary and Conclusions

In this chapter the supervisory requirements of the automated plant were compared with those of the older plant. This was done on the basis of questions asked at the two plants concerning the foreman's technical, administrative, and human relations competence. When the two plants were compared, no differences were found in the subordinates' perceptions of the foremen's technical and administrative competences, but the foremen at Advance were seen to be significantly more competent on the human relations side than were the foremen at Stand.

In both plants the human relations competence of the foremen was found to be more highly correlated with employee satisfaction with his foreman than was the foreman's technical or administrative competence. There was even a suggestion that employee satisfaction with the foreman was more highly related to his human relations competence at Advance than at Stand.

[20] *Ibid.* Note especially the satisfaction of the employees with the supervisors evaluated as "immediately promotable" by higher management.

Since we found essentially no differences between the supervisory requirements of the automated and the old plant, further analyses were performed to identify more specific behaviors which were associated with the human relations competence of the foreman. In both plants the behaviors isolated were those which showed consideration of the employee as a person and which helped the employee to get ahead in the company. Another set of behaviors was related to both the technical and human relations competence of the foreman.

In an attempt to understand the conditions under which a foreman was likely to perform human relations behaviors, the effects of management philosophy, leadership climate, and power and management identification of the supervisor on these behaviors were examined and were found to have interacted in each plant. Large differences on certain items were found between plants, which were attributed to the contrasting management philosophies. In Advance, where decision making on the immediate problems of the men was delegated to the foremen by the plant superintendent, the atmosphere was conducive to the practice of certain good human relations behaviors. On the other items behavioral differences were seen within plants: between foremen under different leadership climates, with different amounts of authority and influence, and with different degrees of management identification. The effects of leadership climate on the foreman's behavior were not unidirectional but varied according to the plant and the particular behavior examined. Results of analyses of the effects of management identification and power emphasized the importance of the foreman's awareness of his dual responsibility to the company and the men. The more effective the foreman was in meeting both of these responsibilities, the more satisfied his men were with him.

Chapter 7

THE INTRODUCTION OF AUTOMATION: ADMINISTRATIVE AND RESEARCH IMPLICATIONS

Early in this exploratory study of some of the intraorganizational effects brought about by the introduction of automated technology it became evident to us that the term "automation" had almost as many definitions as authors writing about it. In the prolific literature on the anticipated consequences of the "Second Industrial Revolution" automation had become the name given to every form of technology introduced into American industry in the last few years. From this array of definitions we found it possible to define automation conceptually as the application of control devices of a feedback nature, such as servomechanisms, to provide self-regulating production processes. Whereas mechanization replaced man's muscles in the transport of materials, automation has replaced man's sensoria in monitoring production processes and has replaced his brain in certain regulatory decision-making functions.

Although automation can be conceptually distinguished as a form of technological advancement, in actual practice it is rarely, if ever, introduced in isolation from other technological changes. In the present study the introduction of automation was accompanied by other basic production changes, including the redesign of the power plant and the greater mechanization of certain aspects of the production process. Since this mixture of automation with other forms of technological advance will be the rule rather than the exception, it probably will be impossible to study automation in isolation from other forms of technological change.

Since we were unable to investigate the effects of automation per se, the goals of our study were enlarged to include the organizational and psychological dimensions of technological change, with special reference to the construction of a new plant with automated equipment. In which areas of an organization's functioning can one expect to find change when a new technology is employed? What are the important factors to be considered when changes in production methods are being contemplated? Because of the exploratory nature of this study, few definitive answers to these questions were found. The study has been productive, however, in isolating a number of factors which seem to have been relevant for the change described here. In the remainder of this chapter we shall discuss some of the characteristics of the change which we identified at both the total organizational level and within the automated power plant. We shall summarize the findings about each characteristic, discussing their implications for management and suggesting possible directions for future research.

Planning for Technological Change

Several traps await the planners of technological change—traps that are rarely side-stepped except by the thoroughly initi-

ated. The first is a preoccupation with the technical facet of the change—a failure to recognize the delicate interactive balance between technical and social systems. The second consists of attempting to devise at the outset a plan for the total program of change, rather than adopting a plan phased with check points for periodically evaluating progress and setting new objectives. The third amounts to overlooking the interrelatedness of a social system, forgetting that changes in one part will have consequences in another. Falling into these traps can be predicted to give both designers and implementors of plans the feeling that managing change is the most uncharted area of organizational theory and administrative practice.

A change in production methods leads management to think primarily in terms of the equipment to be introduced. Can we afford it? Will it perform as well as the designers claim? Can we fit it into the space we have available? How can we gain the maximum advantages of using the new equipment? After these questions have been answered, a new factory may be designed or part of an existing one redesigned. Frequently these new plans are based on the engineering requirements of the new process—the design which makes the most efficient use of the equipment; people are considered only as adjuncts to the machinery, where they are needed from an engineering standpoint. The social system is overlooked at this stage of planning.

People must be considered as being integral parts of the production process. Our present findings emphasize the profound effects which the design and location of equipment have both on the various jobs which workers perform in a plant and on the kind of organizational and group relationships which develop among them. In planning for automation, equipment and process design must be considered not only for its technical effects, but also in terms of its implications for the character of the workers' jobs, the subgroups which will form, and the total human organization which will evolve. It is essential to plan for all of these factors simultaneously rather than to rely upon

"patching up" the technical design to meet psychological and social requirements as they become problems.

That it is necessary to plan changes both at the technical and social system levels is not a new concept. It has been stressed by nearly every social scientist who has written about organizational and social change. Our data indicate, however, that while the point has been made again and again, planning continues to focus on the engineering design and to ignore the psychological and sociological factors in man-machine-organization systems. In the specific case of the automated plant, Advance, the plant structure and the design of jobs contributed to increased worker satisfaction, but this appears to have been an unanticipated by-product, and not the result of conscious design.

Typically, the plan for a new production process is developed by design engineers on the basis of the availability of plant facilities, technological advances, and certain economic factors. After this plan has been reviewed and approved by top management, the personnel staff is asked to develop procedures for selecting workers to do the jobs required by the new process and for preparing the organization for the transition to the new system. By this time, however, the possibility of designing the jobs to provide psychological satisfactions for the workers has been lost, and the effects of the new process on the total social system have been set. Thus, regardless of how much effort may be devoted at this point to planning for the administration of the change, the design of the production process—concentrating as it does on the technical factors to the exclusion of the social factors—places a heavy burden on the ingenuity of the personnel staff to develop the mechanics of a workable transition. Any major defects which may exist in the approved plant design are fixed and cannot be overcome. The best that can be done is to ameliorate the effects of these inadequacies and ensure that their full disruptive force will not interfere with the change-over.

Still typically, the human problems involved in a techno-

logical change are rarely recognized by management until the change procedure has been begun. While the new technology is being introduced and the usual initial technical difficulties are being encountered, certain groups and individuals begin to express misgivings about the new functions they will be expected to perform. They may even actively resist the implementation of the new process. Faced with this problem of human resistance, management, having accepted the new plan as the best of various alternatives examined, immediately assumes that the resistance arises from insufficient understanding of the plan. Management then shifts from a principal concern with technical problems to devising ways of increasing the flow of information to all those involved in the change. Or management may, on the recommendation of social scientists, recognize the resistance to change as a motivational problem. If seen in this light, the problem is alleviated by permitting personnel to suggest changes in their jobs—usually within the structure of the overall design of the production process—thus making them more committed and personally involved in the change and willing to carry it through to completion. With the personnel difficulties reduced through increased communication and participation, management once again turns its attention to technical problems for a time, only to find personnel problems emerging once more. Management thus finds itself pendulum swinging through the change process as it meets first the technical, then the social, then the technical problems which arise.

This cyclical process is often the result of a basic misconception in designing the new process—that is, the failure to consider at the start the psychological and social factors with the technological and economic ones. It is true that once a design for change has been agreed upon, increased communication can help employees understand better the way the new plan operates and the reasons for it, and that participation by employees in limited modifications of the new design can produce greater

involvement in and acceptance of the change. These are methods which recognize the importance of people's ideas and feelings, and they thus create an accommodation to the new work system and temporarily ease resistances. They do not, however, adequately compensate for the basic oversight of not considering both the social and technical systems simultaneously from the start. The use of engineering and social psychologists and sociologists as experts and the involvement of all relevant personnel working with the design engineers in developing a changed production function would permit this simultaneous consideration of the technical, psychological, and social facets of the new process and might materially reduce the magnitude of the entire problem. Such a procedure would provide a continual exchange of information among these people and thus relieve the need for special communications programs to inform employees of decisions made by others. For example, in the power plants of our study, the lack of communication to the rank-and-file employees concerning the purposes of the reorganization of maintenance was undoubtedly a major factor in the resistances to that change. Because the purposes and mechanics of the new system were unclear to the in-plant maintenance men, the system was seen by them as a threat to their job security. Much of the antagonism between management and the union might have been avoided had these objectives and the rationale of these procedures been planned with the men. Similarly the disturbing effects of the uncertainty and secrecy surrounding the criteria used for selecting people to transfer to the new plant—a lack of information which left the company vulnerable to circulated accusations of favoritism and of selecting men with antiunion attitudes—could have been avoided.

An overall plan which commits a company irrevocably to a particular form of change should be avoided as far as possible. Such a plan assumes the existence of adequate knowledge about the system and the impact of new demands on it. Optimally,

changes should be designed to proceed in stages. At the end of each stage an evaluation could be made, along with a forecast of the effectiveness of continued change in that direction, with the possibility of alternative actions being taken if the evaluations were poor. In our study, the company's early commitment to a particular system of centralized maintenance forced it to fight the union's resistance to the abolition of craft lines, rather than permitting it to consider alternative ways of achieving the objective of preventive maintenance. Understandably, the greater the capital investment involved in the machinery for a new method, the less flexibility possible in the introduction of change. With such reduced flexibility, however, comes an even greater necessity for considering the total technicosocial system in making judgments at the beginning of the planning process.

The problems of any new production process also tend to trap management into focusing its attention on the immediate demands of the new process to the exclusion of related areas of the organization. In the present situation, management was particularly concerned with the problems of Advance—of constructing the plant, of putting the new equipment into operation, of training the men to use the equipment—and little attention was given to the problems being created for the men in the older plants. Focusing on the point of innovation ignores the realities of the total organization into which the new unit is being introduced and fails to prevent the development of disturbing conditions which will have to be handled at a later date. The basis for such problems can be seen in the negative attitudes of the men at Stand.

As the greater efficiency and capacity of the new plant made it focal in power production for the entire system, we saw that the men in both plants recognized Advance's central importance to the company, and the concomitant decreasing importance of the older plants. The newness and the importance of the automated plant and its improved working conditions

combined to enhance the prestige of working at Advance, and the workers in the new plant showed considerable pride in having been selected to work there. The enhanced status of Advance decreased the prestige of working in any of the older plants, however, and this was undoubtedly especially critical for the men in Stand, which had previously been the key plant for the system. While automation thus increased the prestige of a handful of men working in the new plant, the vast majority of production employees felt they suffered some loss.

The perceived continuing importance of the new plant not only increased the prestige of the men working there but also gave them strong feelings of job security for the future. The workers knew that Advance was kept at peak capacity continuously to take advantage of its efficiency. They reported that reductions in demand would have little effect on their plant's level of production. For the men in the older plants, on the other hand, the elimination of overtime work, shutdowns over the weekends, and, for the operators, the perceived obsolescence of their operating skills created feelings of insecurity about their future with the company. The men felt that if business conditions worsened, reductions in personnel would follow in the older plants. Thus, whereas automation spelled job security and opportunity for personal growth for the men in the new plant, it created feelings of fear and job insecurity in the workers in the older power plant. Such feelings can be expected to result in mounting pressure by the unions for guarantees of job security, resistance to any changes in the older plants which might be interpreted in any way as threatening the security of jobs there, and increased rumors about any management activity which is perceived as eventually cutting costs at the expense of people.

A company which is planning to automate should be prepared to make explicit its policy on handling employees displaced by the new process. At the time of our study (1954) it

was easy and expedient for companies to announce as their policy that "nobody will lose his job as a result of automation." The demands of our expanding national economy allowed the production from the automated plant simply to be added to that of the existing production facilities to meet increasing demands. People displaced by Advance were reabsorbed into other parts of the company; hence there were no displaced employees to be added to the rosters of the unemployed, and the fact that the new process required considerably fewer workers was hidden from public view. Nevertheless, the men in Stand feared the effects of an economic downturn on their jobs despite company assurances that they would not be fired. Were they right in assuming that pressures on the company in the event of reduced business would cause some layoffs? If their fears were later justified, then the unemployment effects of automation were merely postponed, their impact being eventually felt when the displaced workers would find less opportunity for alternative employment.

Organizational Readiness for Change

The impact which a major technological innovation will have on an organization cannot be isolated from the history of employee relations within the company. A supportive atmosphere, in which the workers feel that management has previously considered their needs in any situation, provides more receptive ground for such change than one in which management is seen as being insensitive or hostile to the workers' needs. Although we were unable to measure the men's attitudes toward the company immediately prior to the construction of Advance, there were strong indications that the workers were quite dissatisfied with their treatment by the company in recent years. It appears that the strike and its aftermath had broken down much of the

strong company identification and loyalty which had previously existed among the employees. Many of the men perceived the construction of a new automated power plant with its reduced personnel requirements as another in a series of steps taken by the company's management to reduce operating costs at the expense of its employees. This perception was modified, we are sure, by the knowledge that the company had rarely laid off workers for other than most compelling reasons. The men remembered, for example, that during the depression of the 1930's the company had retained almost all of its employees. Nonetheless, concerning the construction of a new plant, the feelings of the men in the older plants may be presumed to have been mixed, and this ambivalence probably contributed to the negative attitudes of the men at Stand.

The readiness of an organization for change—the state of management-union relations, the level of employees' overall satisfaction with the company, the extent to which there is mutual trust and good will—is an important factor in the acceptance of innovations by its personnel. Subsequent research will need to develop operational measures of organizational readiness to assess properly the extent to which this class of variables conditions the success or failure of technological innovation. At present management must try to sense whether its company is ready for the disruptions involved in the introduction of entirely new production methods. If management has neglected its human relations functions in the past and has failed to create sufficient good will toward the company among the employees, it can expect a difficult period of transition. If the organization is not ready for change, it may be less expensive in the long run to forego the apparent advantages of an immediate conversion to automation until some attention has been paid to creating a more favorable climate.

A company with a history of little or only gradual change may find a sharp transition to automation quite difficult. Its

personnel will have established patterns of job activities and relatively long-term expectations of their future careers in the company, they will have developed confidence in their ability to handle the routine affairs of the company, and they will be ill prepared to accept the challenge of meeting more than minor deviations from this routine. Over the years a process of selection goes on, both by the workers and by the company, which results in the retention of employees whose personalities favor more stable situations and the rejection of people who prefer rapid change.[1]

In such a situation, the introduction of a new process and new procedures may be seen by the workers as a threat to the stability and security derived from the more stable prior conditions. The reduction of old skills to obsolescence, the breakup and re-formation of work groups and work relations, and the need to adjust to drastically new conditions could form the basis for considerable resistance to the change. When, on the other hand, a company has continually had to adjust to varying external demands and the workers have come to expect change, or when the workers' personalities make them eager for change, technological innovations can probably be made much more easily. It will be recalled that the men in Stand were ill prepared for change, as few of them wanted to be in a company that was growing rapidly and opening up new kinds of jobs. This preponderantly negative attitude toward change was probably related to the unwillingness of most of the men to cooperate in the program of "cross-the-wall" training (Chapter 4).

Management in a company with a history of stability is thus faced with a difficult task in adopting automated processes. At the extreme, such officials might consider constructing a new automated plant and hiring new personnel to staff it, as the Ford Motor Company did with its Cleveland engine plant. A much

[1] Argyris, C., "Human Relations in a Bank," *Harvard Business Review, 32,* 5, 63–67, September–October 1954.

less drastic move would be for such a company to remind its personnel periodically of the constant demand for organizations and individuals to adjust to change in our dynamic industrial society. In this way the groundwork can be laid for developing a readiness for change as well as for facilitating the actual transition. At the very least, the company needs to let its personnel know as soon as possible of its intentions to change—even as early as when the plans are only in the formulation stage.

Working Environment

Automation usually means a new plant and facilities in which to house enormous machines. The greater number of large pieces of equipment creates a complex environment of machines. The number of men is sharply reduced; the ratio of capital investment per worker is considerably higher. Within this mass of machinery, the men are usually found observing control panels, which record the activity of the automated system, and, occasionally, manually adjusting controls to restore the system to its normal self-regulating state. At Advance these control consoles were in immaculately clean, well-lighted, air-conditioned rooms, located several floors and several hundred feet away from the actual production processes. The improved physical conditions of the new plant—the bright lights, the fresh paint, the air conditioning—provided a pleasant working environment for the men.

Certain other features of automation, in addition to the improved working conditions common to most new facilities, can contribute to a worker's satisfaction with his job situation. One of these stems from the fact that automation has made work physically easier, even if it has made it mentally more demanding. With less heavy manual effort required, older workers may be able to fill jobs which, under the old system, they would have

been unable to hold. On the other hand, however, the great amount of new knowledge needed and the importance of being able to react quickly in critical situations may militate against hiring older workers and favor the hiring of younger ones. The ability to learn how new equipment operates and to appreciate how each piece of equipment fits into the total system, along with the ability to be continuously alert to the variations in operation which may produce inefficiencies and even dangerous situations, appears to be an essential requirement for workers in automated factories.

The newness of automated plants has its negative aspects as well. The more complex equipment of the automated system brings new tasks to be performed and new procedures and skills to be learned by the workers and supervisors. Mixed with the pride of working with advanced equipment is a fear of the unknown—a fear stemming from the inability to anticipate what might go wrong with the system and an uncertainty about what to do when something does go wrong. Both the men and the supervisors at Advance admitted that they were frequently, at the outset at least, quite apprehensive and occasionally actually afraid of their new environment. Adding to the strains of the uncertainties surrounding the new system was a tendency for management—a tendency which is probably not unique to this company—to demand that the advanced technology be exploited to its utmost. From the beginning, Advance was expected to produce at its maximum capacity. This meant running the machinery at peak load continuously. The high rate at which the machinery was driven meant, in turn, that the men had always to be alert for subtle changes on the dials and even in the hum of the machines generating electricity. Management frequently talked about the importance of taking calculated risks in keeping the system producing at full capacity. But it is one thing for executives in a downtown office to think in these terms and another for men to have to work under conditions of calculated risks.

The very size of the work force, moreover, may be anything but reassuring. For two of the three shifts at Advance, it will be remembered, only 15 men were responsible for the total operation of the plant. One of these was the shift foreman, newly transferred from a position in one of the older plants as supervisor of a specialized boiler, turbine, or electrical operation. On the evening and night shifts he was now responsible for the entire production operation. The five A- and five B-operators, although supposedly trained in their new enlarged jobs, were also only recently transferred from highly specialized positions in the older plants. Each of them looked to the others for the specialized competences which he lacked, but an objective appraisal of the situation indicated that nobody had the necessary understanding of the new total automated system. The remaining four men, finally, were relatively useless in this tension-ridden transition period. They were for the most part unskilled workers who, having been recently recruited from the surrounding rural area, had little or no experience with manufacturing equipment, to say nothing of the advanced technology of the new power plant.

Job Content

The effects which automation brought to the jobs of the individual operators in our study were striking. As we saw in Chapter 4, the combination of job enlargement and job rotation produced a high level of job satisfaction among the operators in the new plant. The unification of the previously separate boiler, turbine, and electrical functions into a single operating job gave the Advance operators greater opportunity to use their skills, to obtain variety in their work, and to learn new things about power plant production. The data suggest that more men were gaining intrinsic satisfaction from the work they were doing—

this in addition to their satisfactions from such extrinsic sources as their social relations and fringe benefits. It would appear that company managements through their design engineers are now in a position to restore to our working population some of the pride and satisfaction that stems from performing interesting and challenging jobs. Rather than making men adjuncts to machines, automation seems to be capable of utilizing workers as human beings with capacity for intellectual understanding.[2] Jobs designed in this way could provide part of the answer to developing more effective utilization of our shrinking supply of skilled manpower.

Training Personnel for Automation

In situations like the present one, where a company transfers employees from jobs in older parts of the company to jobs in the automated section, training the men for their new jobs is a major problem. The successful functioning of a new automated system will depend in a large part on the adequacy of the training given to the men, and this training must take into account the fact that the workers need to acquire new skills and knowledge as well as adapt to new types of jobs.

The principal inadequacies of the training program for the operators transferred to Advance resulted from management's failure to recognize that different methods are needed for the acquisition of intellectual as opposed to motor skills. The enlarged operating jobs required an understanding of the entire production system, and the program was designed to develop such understanding among the transferred operators. Thus the major formal training effort was directed toward teaching the men the characteristics of the new production system and of the

[2] Wiener, N., *The Human Use of Human Beings.* Boston: Houghton Mifflin, 1950.

individual units. In addition to the new cognitive elements of the job, however, many new motor behaviors were required as well. The lack of opportunity to perform the actual tasks they were to do in the new jobs was a severe defect in the operators' preparation. Although they were given extensive information about the various parts of the new production system, the operators were provided little opportunity to try out the new equipment. Unfortunately, understanding how to do a job is not the same thing as actually doing it. Laboratory research on the learning process has shown again and again that the acquisition of motor skills requires a constant repetition of the behaviors to be learned. Consistent with these laboratory findings, the men in the new plant reported that they learned the most about their jobs from actually doing the work.

To ensure that all personnel acquire the skills necessary for their new jobs, a successful training program may have to include an initial period of inefficiency in the operation of the new process. So that all trainees can "try their hand" at the new procedures, it may be necessary to repeat some of them before the new equipment is placed in full production. A well-trained work force manning the operation may, in the long run, be the most efficient and judicious guarantee for protecting a major capital investment. Although the economic pressures are very great to put the most efficient power-producing units "on the line" as soon as possible, they should be tempered with the recognition that having inexperienced personnel operating the machinery may result in economic losses which could far outweigh any initial advantages.

The pacing of the change is another factor which the designers of a training program should be aware of. Unlike new machinery which can be designed to be adapted into an existing production system almost immediately, the behaviors of workers cannot be altered so rapidly. Our data suggest that the speed of the transition from old to new jobs is important in determining

the men's future attitudes toward their work. There were wide individual variations among the new plant operators in their reports of the adequacy of the training they received and in the time they required to adjust to the new jobs. In contrast to their almost unanimous report of increased satisfaction with the enlarged jobs, a substantial number of the Advance operators expressed dissatisfaction with the preparation they had received. The moderate level of tension found among the workers in the new plant at the time of this study would probably have been even higher had the study been conducted somewhat earlier. By the time of the survey, the operators had confronted and overcome several crises, which gave them confidence in their ability to perform the required tasks. The rate of transition from old to new jobs, our data suggest, should probably be tailored to the abilities of each worker to absorb the requirements of his new position. The number of new ideas to be incorporated and the number of new skills to be learned at any one time are limited by the capacities of the people involved. A man who is placed in an entirely new situation without sufficient preparation may find it too demanding an experience, and the anxiety and insecurity resulting from such an experience may render him incapable of, or at least hinder him in, performing his functions effectively. The "sink or swim" method or even "book learning" alone provides obviously inefficient and inadequate preparation for the people responsible for the operation of new and expensive automated equipment.

Effects on Group Relations

Automation, as we have noted before, will vary in its form from one situation to another. These variations will produce different effects on an organization and its employees. We have seen in the present study how the design of the new power plant,

with its centralized control of the production units, increased the amount of contact among the operating personnel. Instead of finding men in separate stations physically isolated from each other, as many of the prognosticators led us to expect, we found the operators working more closely together in the new plant than in any of the older plants. A strong feeling of group identity and common purpose was present among the operators in the new plant.

The feeling of group identity was enhanced by the elimination of differences among the operating personnel that had been set up on the basis of the men's particular specialty. Wage rates at Advance reflected only differences in skill, not the particular part of the production process with which the worker was concerned. The differences among the boiler, turbine, and electrical functions, which the men perceived to be rather arbitrary, no longer interfered with the willingness of the operators to work together toward a common goal. A more positive attitude toward helping each other on job problems was found among the operators in the new plant than among the workers in the older plant, despite the greater length of time the latter groups had worked together. The results of this study suggest that proper care in the engineering design of a plant can bring workers together into cooperative relationships which may facilitate the accomplishment of the group's task.

Supervision

The complexity of automated technology will clearly require a certain degree of technical proficiency on the part of the production supervisors. It has even been conjectured that the supervisor will have to be more a technician than a supervisor. In the present study, however, we found that the men in the new plant looked to their supervisors for their interpersonal qualities

rather than for their technical skills. We found no evidence with our measures that the more complex equipment in the automated plant resulted in a higher evaluation of the technical competence of the supervisors there than in the older plants. The employees in both plants rated those supervisors as satisfactory who were considerate of them, who assisted them in getting ahead in the company, and who aided them in accomplishing their daily tasks. The human relations skills of the supervisors were even more related to their employees' satisfaction with them in the new plant than in the old plant.

It appears that since the automated production process is self-regulating under normal circumstances, employees have more time to be concerned with their own needs, and the supervisor must, therefore, be even more concerned with and skillful at the interpersonal aspects of his job. Our data suggest that since the technical complexities of automation may be handled adequately by the nonsupervisory operating force, the supervisor's job will be to concentrate more on the direction of employee activities and the meeting of their needs.

It should be emphasized that these conclusions are based on the reported *satisfactions* of employees. They may not represent supervisory practices necessary for the attainment of other organizational objectives. Studies comparing effective and ineffective supervisors according to other criteria are needed before one can completely accept these generalizations about the appropriate supervisory practices for automation.

Criteria of Organizational Effectiveness

Automation brings with it new problems in measuring individual and organizational performance. Traditional systems for the measurement of the work of an individual based on his productivity are inapplicable in automated systems since the

individual worker has little control over the quantity or quality of the system's production. Self-regulating mechanisms control the minute-to-minute operation of the machine complex by maintaining the rate at which manufacturing proceeds and by adjusting the various machines to meet specified tolerance limits. The operator has relatively nothing to do if the system is operating properly, and he cannot, by himself, either increase the amount or improve the quality of the product. There is, therefore, no way to evaluate his contribution to the organization's productivity; consequently incentive systems to improve his performance cannot be tied to his own productivity.

However, the worker's presence is needed, for his importance derives from his ability to react effectively to breakdowns in the system.[3] The extreme interconnectedness of automated processes means that the crippling of any part incapacitates the entire system. The worker must be able, then, to react to deviations in the operation by immediately identifying the difficulty, diagnosing its cause, and taking appropriate measures. His ability to limit the effects of breakdowns—to reduce the amount of "down-time" in production—is a measure of his effectiveness as an operator. The random occurrence of such breakdowns at Advance made even this an inadequate device for evaluating the operators in that plant. Many operators even at the time of our study had experienced only minor equipment difficulties, whereas others had been faced with major machine failures.

Down-time, especially where it is not scheduled for preventive maintenance, may provide one measure of total organizational effectiveness. It is already being used in a loose way as an index of the effectiveness of large computer installations. But even here one must be certain that operational efficiency can be controlled by the people involved and is not merely a function

[3] Appendix A shows how the attendance of workers has improved in the more highly automated plant.

of vagaries in the equipment. Since none of the other power plants in the company had equipment comparable to that in Advance and since the equipment they did have operated in a differently designed system, we had no direct basis for judging the efficiency of the new power plant's operation. If some acceptable standards of efficiency can be developed, it would appear that the use of unanticipated production loss as a measure of the effectiveness of these man-machine systems would provide management and researchers with a new and necessary criterion of how good a job the organization is doing.

Automation and the Worker's Relations with the Community

If we assume that the power plant worker is a prototype of workers in future automated production plants, we see a qualitative difference in the types of jobs he performs compared with those in the most important contemporary production system, the assembly line. Dial watching and reacting at sporadic intervals when the system breaks down will substitute for the constant and unvarying repetitiveness of the assembly line. Various studies of assembly line workers have suggested that the rhythm of the line is carried over into the leisure activities of the employees. Their authors have hypothesized that the popularity of mass forms of entertainment stems from their parallel with the mass production systems in which these workers are employed. If this hypothesis is true, the advent of automation should produce changes in the leisure modes of living of the workers in this new technology. What changes will occur is a matter for continuing investigation; examination of the leisure lives of the employees in the power plants was beyond the scope of the present study. We should not be surprised,

however, to find that the increased challenge of the new operating jobs would produce changes in the attitudes of the men toward other aspects of their lives.

One facet of the worker's relationship with the larger community formed an important area of our investigation. A seemingly inevitable social cost of the age of automation is the prospect of shift work for a larger proportion of our working population. In our study we found that shift work carries the possibility of maladjustments in the physical, psychological, and social aspects of the worker's life. It would be unfortunate indeed if shift work were imposed on new populations without a great deal of thought first being given to, and action taken on, the problem of reducing some of the associated ill effects. As presently administered, to quote two British investigators, "There is not the least doubt that night work is unpopular and, in the long run, is detrimental to health, efficiency, and the enjoyment of life."[4] They go on to recommend its abolition except in times of emergency and in certain continuous process industries. As a result of our own study we can only concur in recommending that, to minimize the unfavorable physical and social consequences of this type of employment, shift work be limited to those industries requiring continuous operation by virtue of their service functions or their manufacturing process.

Here is an area in which social inventions are clearly required. The demands of shift work sharpen mind-body conflicts: the physical nature of man tries to cope with the loss of sleep, appetite, and regularity of body functions, while his social nature requires that he meet his obligations to his family and the social order. Little is known about the positive and negative effects of different shift-work schedules on individual workers. The origins of shift patterns employed today are better understood as historical accidents than as the result of rationally

[4] Wyatt, S., and Marriott, R., "Night Work and Shift Changes," *British Journal of Industrial Medicine,* July 1953.

planned and tested procedures for handling a major societal requirement. If automation does bring shift work to a larger segment of our population, two needs are urgent: first, further research, to discover the basic effects of shift operations on workers' lives and, second, new inventions, based on the research findings, to make shift work less exacting for the worker and his family.

Conclusion

If the two electric power plants in our study can be taken as typical, the prospect of automation in the future seems to offer a tremendous potential for the workers and companies involved. There are, however, sizable obstacles to be overcome and numerous precautions which must be taken before these benefits can be achieved.

The greater efficiency of the new production units is substantial, and the continuing advances of science should make the efficiency gains even greater. Productivity per man hour and per any other cost can be expected to continue to augment the profits of companies employing the new equipment.

The reduction in size of the work force needed should simplify the organizational problems by eliminating supervisory levels and bringing the top and bottom of the organization closer together. Communication both from above and from below should prove easier.

The workers in the reduced labor force in the automated factory can have highly interesting jobs, in terms of the satisfactions arising both from the work itself and from the opportunity for freer association with working colleagues.

In presenting the results of our study, we have tried to point out the barriers which stand in the way of the successful introduction and functioning of automated production systems.

As an aid in overcoming these barriers the following conditions should exist prior to any change-over: The organization must be ready for change and unlikely to resist it actively. Complete thought should be given to the precise placement of the new process in the organization rather than considering the system as a mere replacement for older equipment and processes. Jobs should be designed to provide satisfaction for the workers. A workable plan of transition should be provided, and it should be effectively communicated to all concerned. There must be provision in the plan for the acquisition of the necessary knowledge and skills by the personnel who are to man the new operation.

These probably are not the only requisities and even these are not easy to meet, but the company which gives sufficient attention to them should be amply rewarded.

APPENDIXES

A. Absences in Automated Plants

B. Supplementary Tables

C. An Explanation of Statistics Used in the Book

D. Selected Bibliography of the Principal Writings and Empirical Research on Automation

E. Questionnaires

Appendix A

ABSENCES IN AUTOMATED PLANTS[1]

We have seen that automation means smaller work forces employed in around-the-clock operations. As crews decrease in size the presence of each worker at the appointed shift time becomes increasingly important. Adjustments in work assignments can be made relatively easily when a member of a large group in a factory or an office is absent, but when a worker on a small crew in an automated plant is absent, either another worker must be called in on one of his "off-days" or a worker from a preceding shift has to work a "double stint." Thus absences become a greater administrative problem for management and simultaneously a more sensitive index of individual and organizational effectiveness for both management and researchers. Does the quantitative evidence show that absence rates decrease when men go to work in new, more highly automated plants where jobs are more challenging and individually important?

[1] Most of the data and the computations for this analysis were prepared by Helen I. Tucker under the direction of John Sparling.

In our study of power plants the absence rates of the workers in the new plant were markedly lower in 1953 and 1954 than were those of either the workers in the old plant or the average for all the company's five plants, which includes both Advance and Stand. These figures indicate that for 1954[2] the absence rates for men at Advance were just less than half as large as those for the five-plant average, and 40 percent lower than those for Stand (Table A:1).

TABLE A:1

Absence Rates in Power Plants, 1953–1954

	1953	1954
Number of Times Absent		
Advance*	2.0	2.0
Stand	4.1	3.3
Five plants combined	4.1	3.6
Number of Days Absent		
Advance	3.5	4.3
Stand	8.8	7.2
Five plants combined	9.3	8.2

* Advance was just beginning operations in 1953. The average number of employees for that year was 106. The full complement for 1954 was 171, including management. The figures for Stand are based on 352 and 294 employees for 1953 and 1954, respectively. The corresponding figures for the five plants combined are 1555 and 1452.

To what can these differences be attributed? Are they due to factors in the work situation in the new plant—better working conditions, enlarged job content, different shift-work schedule, a different plant management philosophy—or to the type of employees who bid and were selected for transfer to the new plant? As a possible explanation, the latter is particularly important, for the selection of employees for Advance was based to some extent upon the employee's absence record.

In order to investigate this possibility, we obtained individual absence records of 72 Advance employees who had had at least two full years of employment at another plant before being transferred.

[2] The questionnaire data were collected in December, 1954.

Excluding the year in which the employee's transfer took place, the data were averaged for a two-year period before and after the transfer to obtain a more stable measure of each employee's earlier absence behavior. In Table A:2 below, the mean numbers of days

TABLE A:2

Absence Rates of Transferred Employees

	1951–1952 Before Transfer		1954–1955 After Transfer
Number of times absent (N = 72)	3.5	*	2.2
Number of days absent (N = 72)	6.1	*	4.2

* Mean absence rates before and after transfer are significantly different.

absent and times absent are shown both for the periods prior to and following the opening of the new plant. The average number of days absent for the company as a whole for the 1951–52 period was estimated to have been approximately nine days. The difference between this figure and the 6.1-days average for Advance gives quantitative support to the report that a man's previous absence record counted heavily in the selection process.

The differences in absence rates for the 72 men before and after transfer suggest, however, that Advance's low absence rates in 1954–55 were not due simply to selection of personnel with records of few absences. The decrease in both frequency and number of days absent for these 72 men from 1951–52 to 1954–55 is statistically significant. The fact that the men's attendance records at the new plant were much better than they had been in other plant locations before the transfer indicates that there were factors in the new plant situation which were conducive to still better attendance.

From our comparisons of Advance with Stand, it has become clear that important differences existed in working conditions, work schedules, job content, supervision and management philosophy, and a number of other variables. In the analyses of absences, as in those of overall satisfaction, it has not been possible to isolate or identify the effects of these factors individually. It is evident, however, that the combined effect of the improvements in the new automated plant resulted in a working climate conducive to good attendance.

While it is not possible to isolate the effects of these different factors, an analysis of the change in absence rates of certain groups of workers after their transfers provides an important clue for subsequent research. Of the 72 employees whose absence rates were computed for 1951–52 and 1954–55, three major classifications—operators, maintenance, and foremen and higher-level supervisors—accounted for all but six employees. Although for each of these groups there was a decrease in the absence rate after the men's transfer to Advance, the amount of decrease for the maintenance group was not large enough to be statistically significant (Table A:3).

TABLE A:3

Absence Rates of Transferred Employees by Major Work Classification

	1951–1952 *Before Transfer*		1954 *After Transfer*
Operators (N = 27)			
Average frequency absent	3.7	*	2.0
Average days absent	5.2	*	3.5
Maintenance (N = 19)			
Average frequency absent	4.1		2.6
Average days absent	6.2		5.7
Foremen and Higher Level Supervisors (N = 20)			
Average frequency absent	2.7	*	1.7
Average days absent	6.0	*	3.1

* Difference between means is significant.

Note the findings here: significant changes in the absence rates for foremen and key staff men whose new jobs carried a great deal more responsibility and for the operators for whom there was both job enlargement and job rotation, but not significant changes for the maintenance men. This pattern suggests that the change in the job content was the major variable affecting absence rates. It certainly provides a lead well worth investigating intensively in later research.

Appendix B

SUPPLEMENTARY TABLES

Background Characteristics of Shift Workers

(*in percent*)

Advance N = 42
Stand N = 121

Age	Advance	Stand
Under 20 years	0	0
20 to 24.9	0	11
25 to 29.9	21	17
30 to 34.9	17	19
35 to 39.9	19	7
40 to 44.9	24	10
45 to 49.9	12	10
50 to 54.9	5	11
55 to 59.9	0	7
60 and over	2	1
Not ascertained	0	4
	100	100
Mean age	38.2	37.6
Standard deviation	8.28	11.28

t-test between means was *not* significant.

Education	Advance	Stand
Some grammar school	0	4
Completed grammar	2	7
Some high school	10	15
Business or trade and some high school	10	4
Completed high school	57	48
Completed high and business school	0	2
Some college	19	14
Completed college	0	1
Not ascertained	2	5
	100	100

Chi-square for less than, equal to, or greater than high-school graduate was *not* significant.

Background Characteristics of Shift Workers (Continued)

Marital Status

	Advance	Stand
Single	2	8
Married	95	88
Divorced or separated	2	0
Not ascertained	1	4
	100	100

Chi-square for married-not married was *not* significant.

Number of Children Less than Six Years Old

	Advance	Stand
None	40	36
One	19	19
Two	19	20
Three	5	6
Four	5	2
Not ascertained	12	17
	100	100

Chi-square for none, one, two or more was *not* significant.

Length of Service with the Company

	Advance	Stand
Less than 1 year	0	0
1.0 to 1.9 years	12	8
2.0 to 4.9	17	27
5.0 to 9.9	33	22
10.0 to 14.9	17	11
15.0 to 19.9	12	12
20.0 to 24.9	2	3
25.0 to 29.9	7	6
30 years or more	0	8
Not ascertained	0	3
	100	100
Mean length of service	10.6	11.9
Standard Deviation	6.03	10.53

t-test of mean difference was *not* significant.

Experience at Nonshift Work

	Advance	Stand
None, always shifts	5	13
Less than six months	2	6
Six months to one year	7	6
One to five years	50	26
More than five years	36	45
Not ascertained	0	4
	100	100

Chi-square for less than a year, one to five years, more than five years was *not* significant

Background Characteristics of Shift Workers (Continued)

Number of Years Working Shifts	*Advance*	*Stand*
Less than 1.49 years	2	3
1.5 to 2.49	5	8
2.5 to 3.49	10	11
3.5 to 5.9	7	20
6.0 to 10.9	24	15
11.0 to 15.9	26	13
16.0 to 20.9	19	12
21.0 to 25.9	7	6
26 years or more	0	6
Not ascertained	0	6
	100	100
Mean	11.5	10.5
Standard deviation	6.29	7.91

t-test of mean difference was *not* significant.

Licenses and Papers (Operators only)	*Advance* (N = 35)	*Stand* (N = 109)
None	0	17
High pressure boiler operator	29	60
3rd class stationary engineer	37	7
2nd class stationary engineer	29	3
Not ascertained	5	13
	100	100

Chi-square for the four substantive categories *is* significant at the .05 level.

Appendix C

AN EXPLANATION OF STATISTICS USED IN THE BOOK

Statistics have been put to two principal uses in this book. One is in comparing people in the automated plant with those in the older plant to determine whether automation made a difference of some sort—for instance, in liking for the job. The other is in calculating the relationship between two variables, such as use of skills on the job and liking for the job, to determine whether and to what extent they occur together, usually with the implication that one variable causes the other—for instance, that high use of skills on the job creates liking for the job.

To compare the men in the two plants, one of two measures is computed to represent each plant: either the mean response to a question or series of questions, or the percentage of men responding in a certain way (for instance, "very" or "fairly satisfied"). The mean is an arithmetic average, calculated by summing the rated responses for all the men in a plant and dividing by the number of men. For example, the men were asked, "In general, how do you

feel about your working conditions, things like lighting, heating, space, ventilation, noise, health conditions, equipment, etc.?" One of five alternative responses, ranging from "Working conditions are very unsatisfactory" to "Working conditions are very satisfactory," was checked by each respondent. Values from 1 to 5 were assigned to the responses, indicating increasing levels of satisfaction. At Advance, 18 percent or 25 men rated their working conditions *5,* 43 percent or 60 men rated them *4,* 25 percent or 35 men rated them *3,* 7 percent or 10 rated them *2,* and 6 percent or 8 men rated them *1.* The mean satisfaction with working conditions at Advance was 3.6—498, the sum of the ratings, divided by 138, the number of men who responded to the question. Similarly calculated, the mean satisfaction with working conditions at Stand was only 2.8.

Another way of comparing the two plants is to calculate the percent of men in each plant who reported their working conditions were "very" or "quite satisfactory." At Advance this percentage was 61 percent, while at Stand it was only 21 percent. Comparing either the means or the percentages in this case showed that the men at Advance were more satisfied with their working conditions than were the men at Stand.

Two ways of calculating relationships between variables are also used: correlation coefficients and contingency tables represented by chi-square values. Because the mathematics involved in these two measures are more complicated and less familiar than those used to calculate the means and percentages, we shall not burden the readers with them here.[1] It is sufficient for the understanding of their use in this book to say that both measures indicate the extent to which people with high scores on one variable also have high scores on a second variable, *and* people with low scores on the first also have low scores on the second variable. When this occurs, we say there is a positive relationship or a positive correlation between the two variables. When the people who have high scores on the first variable have low scores on the second, and people with low scores on the first have high scores on the second variable, we say

[1] For the reader who wishes to pursue this topic further, an excellent discussion of statistical measures of relationship can be found in Walker, H. M., and Lev, J., *Statistical Inference.* New York: Holt, 1953.

there is a negative correlation between the two variables. When there is about an equal number of people with high scores on the first variable who have high and low scores on the second variable, and when low scorers on the first variable are also divided fairly equally between high and low scores on the second variable, we say there is no relationship or correlation between the variables. Examples of all three of these relationships are shown in Table 6:6, with items related to the question about the perceived human relations competence of the foreman. At Advance, a positive correlation of .76 was found between the men's rating of their supervisor's human relations competence and the extent to which they perceived him to be considerate of the men's feelings—that is, the men who saw their supervisors as considerate of the men's feelings generally gave them a higher rating on their human relations competence than did the men who saw them as inconsiderate. On the other hand, a negative correlation of —.59 was found at Advance between the foreman's rated human relations competence and his quickness to criticize—that is, the men who saw their foremen as quick to criticize rated them as less competent in human relations than did the men who saw their foremen as less quick to criticize. Finally, the foremen's human relations competence was correlated —.05 (which is practically zero) at Advance with the perceived authority he had to make decisions—that is, foremen who received high ratings on their human relations competence were no more or less often seen as having more authority than they needed than were foremen who were given low ratings and vice versa.

The major differences between the correlational and contingency measures of relationship lie in the degree of relationship which can be measured and in the way their statistical significance is determined. The correlation coefficient may have values from —1.00 to +1.00 (ordinarily the positive sign is omitted in reporting correlations) including all intermediate values, and these values indicate the strength of the relationship. As the numerical values increase from zero to 1.00, the relationship between the two variables becomes stronger (the sign of the correlation merely indicates whether the relationship is positive or negative). A correlation coefficient of 1.00 indicates a perfect relationship. If the people were

placed in two rank orders according to their scores on each variable, the rank orderings would either be identical (1.00) or exactly reversed (—1.00). Coefficients between 1.00 and —1.00 indicate differing degrees of deviation from these perfect orderings.

Chi-square values computed from contingency tables do not have such direct meaning as measures of the degree of relationship between two variables, since they increase with increasing numbers of categories and increasing numbers of people.

Statistical Significance

Even though the mean on some variable, such as satisfaction with supervisor, may be found to be somewhat larger at Advance than at Stand, or a positive correlation between two variables may be calculated—for example, between rated human relations competence of the foreman and his perceived consideration of feelings—the question may be raised as to whether this is a "true" difference or correlation, or whether it occurred by chance. We might ask whether we would be likely to find a difference or correlation as great if we were to give our measures a second time, a third time, and so on. We have assumed, for the exploratory purposes of our study, that if it is unlikely that a difference or a correlation as large or larger than the one obtained in our data would have occurred by chance alone less than five times in one hundred repetitions of our research (the .05 level of confidence referred to in our tables), then the obtained difference or correlation is a "true" one. (The reader should remember that in tossing coins he can expect to toss five heads in a row a little more than three times in a hundred tries.) Statisticians have developed methods (tests) by which the probability of differences between means or between percentages and of the existence of positive or negative relationships can be determined from obtained data. The tests used to determine the statistical significance of our results—whether the probability is less than five times in a hundred that the result could have occurred by chance—have been referred to in the text where they have been employed.

Differences between means and percentages were usually tested by t-tests, contingency tables by chi-square tests, and correlation coefficients by t-tests. The results were reported as being significant or not at the .05 level of confidence by the appropriate test. If they were statistically significant, we can be fairly confident that a true difference or relationship was found, one which warrants consideration as a fact in automation.

Appendix D

SELECTED BIBLIOGRAPHY OF THE PRINCIPAL WRITINGS AND EMPIRICAL RESEARCH ON AUTOMATION

Theory and Concepts

Automation and Technological Change. Hearings before the Joint Committee on the Economic Report, 84th Congress. Washington, D.C.: U.S. Government Printing Office, 1956, 644 pp.

Baldwin, G. B., and Shultz, G. P., "Automation: A New Dimension to Old Problems," *Proceedings of the Seventh Annual Meeting, Industrial Relations Research Association.* Madison, Wis.: The Association, 1955, pp. 114–28.

Diebold, J., *Automation: The Advent of the Automatic Factory.* Princeton, N.J.: D. Van Nostrand Co., 1952.

Editors of *Scientific American, Automatic Control.* New York: Simon and Schuster, 1955.

Friedmann, G., *Industrial Society.* Glencoe, Ill.: The Free Press, 1955, 399 pp.

Goodman, L. L., *Man and Automation.* London: Pelican Book, A401, 1957.

Jacobson, H. B., and Roucek, J. S., *Automation and Society.* New York: Philosophical Library, 1959.

MacMillan, R. H., *Automation: Friend or Foe?* Cambridge, England: Cambridge University, 1956.

Morse, D., *Automation and Other Technological Developments.* Report of the Director General, International Labor Conference, Geneva, 1957.

"Social Consequences of Automation," *International Social Science Bulletin, X,* No. 1, 1958.

Wiener, N., *The Human Use of Human Beings.* Boston: Houghton Mifflin, 1950, 241 pp.

Empirical Research

Bright, J. A., *Automation and Management.* Boston: Harvard University Graduate School of Business Administration, 1958.

Craig, H. F., *Administering a Conversion to Electronic Accounting.* Boston: Division of Research, Graduate School of Business Administration, Harvard University, 1955, 224 pp.

Faunce, W. F., "Automation in the Automobile Industry," *American Sociological Review, 23,* No. 4, 1958, pp. 401–7.

Man and Automation. Report of the Proceedings of a Conference sponsored by the Society for Applied Anthropology at Yale University. New Haven, Conn.: The Technology Project, Yale University, 1956, 117 pp.

Osborn, D. G., "Automation in Industry—A Geographical Consideration," *Journal of the American Institute of Planners,* Fall 1953.

Scott, W. H., Banks, J. A., Halsey, A. H., and Lupton, T., *Technical Change and Industrial Relations.* Liverpool, England: Liverpool University Press, 1956, 336 pp.

Studies of Automatic Technology: *A Case Study of an Automatic Airline System.* Washington, D.C.: Bureau of Labor Statistics, Report No. 137, 1958, 21 pp.

Studies in Automatic Technology: *A Case Study of a Company Manufacturing Electronic Equipment.* Washington, D.C.: Bureau of Labor Statistics, 1955, 15 pp.

Studies of Automatic Technology: *A Case Study of a Large Mechanized Bakery.* Washington, D.C.: Bureau of Labor Statistics, 1956, 26 pp.

Studies of Automatic Technology: *A Case Study of a Modernized Petroleum Refinery.* Washington, D.C.: Bureau of Labor Statistics, 1958, 44 pp.

Studies of Automatic Technology: *The Introduction of an Electronic Computer in a Large Insurance Company.* Washington, D.C.: Bureau of Labor Statistics, 1955, 19 pp.

Turner, A. N., "Automation: Revolution or Cliche?" *Man and Automation,* Report on the Proceedings of a Conference sponsored by the Society for Applied Anthropology at Yale University. New Haven, Conn.: The Technology Project, Yale University, 1956, pp. 3–15.

Walker, C., *Toward the Automatic Factory.* New York: Harper & Brothers, 1958.

Wallace, E., "Management Decisions and Automatic Data Processing" (unpublished Ph.D dissertation, University of Chicago, 1956).

Whyte, W. F., "Engineers and Workers: A Case Study," *Human Organization,* Winter 1956, pp. 3–12.

Zollitsch, H. G., "Maintenance Training Methodology for Automation" (unpublished Ph.D. dissertation, Cornell University, 1954).

Bibliographies

Automatic Technology and Its Implications. A Selected Annotated Bibliography. U.S. Department of Labor, Bureau of Labor Statistics, Bulletin No. 1198. Washington, D.C.: U.S. Government Printing Office, August 1956, 83 pp.

Economic and Social Implications of Automation: A Bibliographic Review. East Lansing, Mich.: Labor and Industrial Relations Center, Michigan State University, 1959, 125 pp.

Appendix E

QUESTIONNAIRES

Part 1

Part 2 (for nonsupervisory employees)

OWER PLANT STUDY
orm A — Part 1

University of Michigan
Survey Research Center
Ann Arbor, Michigan

This is a study of the attitudes and opinions of the men who work in the power plants of [redacted] It is being done by the Survey Research Center of the University of Michigan.

We want to learn how the men, their foremen, and plant supervisors see their jobs and working situations. 'e are especially interested in this study in the different types of human relations problems which are in-olved in operating different types of power plants. The study is being done in [redacted] 'his questionnaire was built from the attitudes and ideas which a number of you expressed during your in-erviews in August, September, and October. Jim Dent, Tom Lough, and I designed these questions to cover ıe major points you suggested might be looked into in this questionnaire for all employees.

The help you men have given us in constructing this questionnaire and in testing out the first wording of ıese questions has been tremendous. The final value of this study, however, will depend upon the frankness nd care with which you answer these questions. We would like to have your thoughtful consideration of all ıe questions. There are no right or wrong answers. This is not a test of any sort. It's your opinions and eelings that are important here.

As in the interviews, your individual responses are confidential. We will take the questionnaires back to ne University of Michigan and tabulate them there. No one in the company will ever see the questionnaire 'hich you fill out. The results will be tabulated by groups like they were in the 1948 study. The findings from hese tabulations of this questionnaire will be reported back to you. We will, of course, not violate any of the ledges of confidentiality we have made to you, the company, or the union in the way we handle these findings. Ve enjoy working with you fellows too much to make that kind of a mistake.

Sincerely,

Floyd C. Mann
Survey Research Center
University of Michigan

INSTRUCTIONS

1. Most of the questions can be answered by checking one of the answers (✓) listed under the question. Read each question carefully, then select the answer that best fits your case. If you do not find the exact answer that fits your case, check the one that comes closest to it. Or, if you wish, write your own answer.

2. Please feel free to use the space at the end of the questionnaire to make as many additional comments as you wish.

WORKING CONDITIONS AND SAFETY

1. In general, how do you feel about your working conditions; things like lighting, heating, space, ventilation, noise, health conditions, equipment, etc.? (Check one)

____ Working conditions are very unsatisfactory
____ Working conditions are quite unsatisfactory
____ Working conditions are about average
____ Working conditions are quite satisfactory
____ Working conditions are very satisfactory

2. Which of the following things do you think can and should be improved?

(You may check more than one answer)

____ None of the following things need to be improved
____ The space you have to work in
____ The tools and equipment you use on your job
____ The washrooms where you work
____ The temperature of the place where you work
____ The noise
____ The cleanliness of the plant
____ The lighting
____ The plant restaurant
____ The ventilation (dust, condition of the air, etc.)

Write in other things about working conditions that should be improved

____

____

____

3. How safe do you actually feel doing the kind of work you do? (Check one)

____ I feel very safe all of the time
____ I feel quite safe most of the time, but once in a great while I don't feel too safe
____ I feel fairly safe most of the time, but every now and then I don't feel too safe
____ I feel not too safe quite a bit of the time

4. How often do you feel safety is being sacrificed for economy? (Check one)

____ Never
____ Once in a great while
____ Occasionally
____ Quite often
____ Very often

5. How often do you feel that the men you work wi are not doing a job as safely as they might? (Check one)

____ Very often
____ Quite often
____ Occasionally
____ Once in a great while
____ Never

> Front office, in this questionnaire, will always refer to the top supervisory staff at your plant, not the foremen.

6. How willing is the front office of this plant to u the ideas and suggestions the men have about safety? (Check one)

____ The front office is very willing to use the men's ideas about safety
____ Quite willing
____ Willing to use some of the men's ideas about safety, not others
____ Not very willing
____ The front office is not at all willing to use the men's ideas about safety

> Top management, in this questionnaire, will always refer to the top, downtown management of [redacted] This will include the Head of the Production Department and on up to the President.

7. Do you think top management of [redacted] is interested in safety—safety precautions, safe working conditions, training in safe operation, etc.? (Check one)

____ Top management is very much interested i safety
____ Quite interested in safety
____ Fairly interested in safety
____ Interested a little in safety
____ Top management has very little interest in safety

8. Do you feel top management of [redacted] is more or less interested in safety than it was a few years ago? (Check one)

____ Top management is much more interested in safety now than it was a few years ago
____ Somewhat more interested
____ As interested now as it was a few years ag
____ Somewhat less interested
____ Top management is much less interested i safety now than it was a few years ago

BOUT THE JOB ITSELF

9. How much does your job give you a chance to do the things you are best at? (Check one)

____ A very good chance to do the things I'm best at
____ A fairly good chance
____ Some chance
____ Very little chance
____ No chance at all to do things I'm best at

0. How clearly do you understand the responsibilities of your job? (Check one)

____ I am not at all clear about the responsibilities of my job
____ I am not too clear
____ I am fairly clear
____ I am quite clear
____ I am very clear about the responsibilities of my job

1. How do you feel about the amount of responsibility you have on your job now? (Check one)

____ I would like a lot more responsibility than I have on my job right now
____ I would like a little more responsibility than I have now
____ I have about as much responsibility as I want right now
____ I would like a little less responsibility than I have now
____ I would like a lot less responsibility than I have on my job right now

2. What do the men you work with think about your job? (Check one)

____ The men I work with think I have an excellent job
____ A good job
____ A fair job
____ A poor job
____ The men I work with think I have a very poor job

3. What do your friends outside of the company think about your job? (Check one)

____ My friends think this is an excellent job
____ A good job
____ A fair job
____ A poor job
____ My friends think this is a very poor job

14. What do the members of your family think about your job? (Check one)

____ My family thinks that this is an excellent job
____ A good job
____ A fair job
____ A poor job
____ My family thinks that this is a very poor job

15. Considering your job as a whole, how well do you like it? (Check one)

____ Don't like it at all
____ Don't like it too well
____ Like some things about it, dislike others
____ Like it fairly well
____ I like it very much

ABOUT YOUR JOB AND THE JOBS OF OTHERS IN YOUR WORK GROUP

16. How well do the other men in your work group understand the problems you have on your job? (Check one)

____ They understand the problems I have on my job very well
____ Quite well
____ Fairly well
____ A little
____ They do not understand at all the problems I have on my job

17. How well do you understand the problems that the other men in your work group have on their jobs? (Check one)

____ I understand the problems they have in their work very well
____ Quite well
____ Fairly well
____ A little
____ I do not understand at all the problems they have in their work

18. How much does your immediate foreman know about the equipment you work with? (Check one)

____ He knows a great deal about the equipment I work with
____ Quite a bit
____ A little
____ He knows very little about the equipment I work with

19. If each man knows his own job, how important is it to the running of the plant if they know each other's jobs? (Check one)

____ Very important
____ Quite important
____ Some importance
____ Of little importance
____ Of no importance

20. When you have a problem on your job, how free do you feel to call on others in your work group to help you with it? (Check one)

____ I feel very free to call on them
____ I feel quite free to call on them
____ I feel fairly free to call on them
____ I don't feel very free to call on them
____ I don't feel at all free to call on them

21. How important is your job as compared with the jobs of the rest of the men you work with? (Check one)

____ Much more important than theirs
____ A little more important than theirs
____ No more and no less important than theirs; about the same
____ A little less important than theirs
____ Much less important than theirs

22. If the other men in your work group don't do their jobs well, does it make your work harder to do? (Check one)

____ If the other men in my work group don't do their jobs well, it makes my work much harder to do
____ Quite a bit harder for me
____ Somewhat harder for me
____ A little harder for me
____ If the other men in my work group don't do their jobs well, it makes little difference to my work

23. If men in other groups in this power plant don't do their jobs well, does it make your work harder to do? (Check one)

____ If men in other groups in this power plant don't do their jobs well, it makes my work much harder to do
____ Quite a bit harder for me
____ Somewhat harder for me
____ A little harder for me
____ If the other groups in this power plant don't do their jobs well, it makes little difference to my work

24. Do you think you have the right number of men in each classification in your work group?

____ Yes
____ No

25. Do you have more or less men in your group than you need? (Check one)

____ We have many more men than we need in our group
____ We have a few more men than we need in our group
____ We have enough men in our group, but no more than we need
____ We need a few more men in our group than we have now
____ We need many more men in our group than we have now

26. How much do you depend on the other men in your work group for suggestions and advice on particular problems you face on your job? (Check one)

____ I depend on them a great deal for suggestions and advice on particular problems I face on my job
____ I depend on them quite a lot
____ I depend on them somewhat
____ I depend on them a little
____ I don't depend on them at all for suggestions and advice on particular problems I face on my job

27. How do you feel about depending on the other men in your work group for suggestions and advice? (Check one)

____ I would like to depend on them much less
____ A little less
____ I am satisfied the way it is
____ A little more
____ I would like to depend on them much more

28. How much does your foreman depend on you for suggestions and advice on particular problems that come up? (Check one)

____ My foreman depends on me a great deal for suggestions and advice on particular problems
____ He depends on me quite a lot
____ He depends on me somewhat
____ He depends on me a little
____ He doesn't depend on me at all for suggestions and advice on particular problems

29. How much do you depend on your foreman for suggestions and advice on particular problems that come up? (Check one)

____ I depend on my foreman a great deal for suggestions and advice on particular problems
____ I depend on him quite a lot
____ I depend on him somewhat
____ I depend on him a little
____ I don't depend on him at all for suggestions and advice on particular problems

30. How do you feel about depending on your foreman for suggestions and advice on particular problems that come up? (Check one)

____ I would like to depend on him much more
____ A little more
____ I am satisfied the way it is
____ A little less
____ I would like to depend on him much less

31. How often do you feel you take on extra duties and responsibilities that your foreman asks you to take on? (Check one)

____ I always take on any extra duties and responsibilities that my foreman asks me to take on
____ I usually do
____ Sometimes I do, sometimes I don't
____ I usually don't
____ I never, or almost never take on any duties and responsibilities that my foreman asks me to take on

32. Every person does some things better than he does others. Some are able to work better with machinery than with people — others are able to work better with people than machinery. How does it work out for you? (Check one)

____ I am much better at working with machinery than I am at working with people
____ I am a little better at working with machinery than I am with people
____ I am a little better at working with people than I am with machinery
____ I am much better at working with people than I am at working with machinery

33. How do you feel about the amount of time during working hours, that you are able to get to talk to other men? (Check one)

____ I would like to be able to talk to the other men much more than I am able to now
____ I would like to be able to talk to other men a little more than I am able to now
____ I am able to talk to the other men as much as I want to now
____ I am able to talk to the men too much as it is now

34. Do you feel that you are really a part of your work group? (Check one)

____ Yes, I feel I really am a part of it
____ Yes, I feel I'm included in most ways but not in all
____ Yes, I feel I am included in some ways but not in others
____ No, I don't feel I really belong

35. Do you feel that your foreman is really a part of your work group? (Check one)

____ Yes, he really is a part of our work group
____ Yes, he is included in most ways but not in all
____ Yes, he is included in some ways but not in others
____ No, he is not really a part of our work group

36. How much do you feel you know about the technical operation of this plant? (Check one)

____ I know a great deal about the technical operation of this plant — more than most of the other men
____ Quite a bit about the technical operation of this plant — more than many of the other men do
____ Some — about as much as other men
____ Not too much — not as much as most of the men know
____ Not much at all — I don't know nearly so much as the rest of the men know about the technical operation of the plant

37. Which of the following have you ever worked at in the power plants for three months or longer?

(Check yes or no for each one)

Plant protection.	____ yes	____ no
Office and warehouse	____ yes	____ no
Coal handling	____ yes	____ no
Boiler operating	____ yes	____ no
Turbine and condenser operating	____ yes	____ no
Electrical and switchboard operating	____ yes	____ no
Building cleaner or janitor	____ yes	____ no
Electrical repair (electrician)	____ yes	____ no
Mechanical repair (pipe fitting, bricklayers, etc.) . . .	____ yes	____ no
Instrument repair	____ yes	____ no

38. How interested are you in learning more about the jobs in the following parts of the power plant? (Check one answer for each line)

	Very Interested	Fairly Interested	Would just as soon	Not very Interested	Not at all Interested
Plant protection					
Office and warehouse					
Coal handling					
Boiler operating					
Turbine and condenser operating					
Electrical and switchboard operating					
Building cleaner and janitor					
Mechanical repair					
Instrument repair					
Electrical repair					

65

CHANGES IN YOUR JOB IN RECENT YEARS

39. Do you have more or less responsibility on your job now than you did several years ago? (Check one)

____ I have much less responsibility now than I had several years ago
____ A little less responsibility now
____ About the same amount now
____ A little more responsibility now
____ I have much more responsibility now than I had several years ago

40. Do you have to do more or less dirty work on your job now than you did several years ago? (Check one)

____ I spend much more time doing dirty work now than I did several years ago
____ A little more time doing dirty work now
____ About the same amount of time now
____ A little less time doing dirty work now
____ I spend much less time doing dirty work now than I did several years ago

41. Is your job more or less interesting than it was several years ago? (Check one)

____ My job is much more interesting now than it was several years ago
____ A little more interesting now
____ About as interesting now as it was then
____ A little less interesting now
____ My job is much less interesting now than it was several years ago

27

42. Does your job allow you to move around the plant more or less than several years ago? (Check one)

____ My job allows me to move around the plant much less than several years ago
____ Move around a little less now
____ About the same now
____ Move around a little more now
____ My job allows me to move around the plant much more now than several years ago

43. Does your job allow you to make more or less contacts with men now than it did several years ago? (Check one)

____ I make many fewer contacts with the men now than I used to on the job
____ A few less contacts now than I used to
____ About the same amount of contact now as I used to
____ A few more contacts now than I used to
____ I make many more contacts with the men now than I used to on the job

44. Are you learning more or less on the job now than you did a few years ago? (Check one)

____ I'm learning much less on the job than I did a few years ago
____ A little less than I did
____ About the same amount now as I did
____ A little more now than I did
____ I'm learning much more on the job now than I did a few years ago

30

45. How much time do you spend doing things you are not skilled at now as compared to a few years ago? (Check one)

____ I spend much more time now doing things that I am not skilled at than I did a few years ago
____ A little more time now doing things that I am not skilled at
____ About the same amount of time now doing things that I am not skilled at as a few years ago
____ A little less time now doing things that I am not skilled at
____ I spend much less time now doing things that I am not skilled at than I did a few years ago

46. How much time do you spend doing things you are skilled at now as compared to a few years ago? (Check one)

____ I spend much more time now doing things that I am skilled at than I did a few years ago
____ A little more time now doing things that I am skilled at
____ About the same amount of time now doing things I am skilled at as a few years ago
____ A little less time now doing things that I am skilled at
____ I spend much less time now doing things that I am skilled at than I did a few years ago

47. Does your job require more or less training now than it used to several years ago? (Check one)

____ My job requires much less training now than it used to several years ago
____ A little less training now
____ About as much training now as it used to
____ A little more training now
____ My job requires much more training now than it used to several years ago

48. Taking everything into consideration, how satisfied are you with your job now as compared to several years ago? (Check one)

____ I am much less satisfied with my job now than I was several years ago
____ A little less satisfied with my job now
____ About as satisfied with my job now as I was
____ A little more satisfied with my job now
____ I am much more satisfied with my job now than I was several years ago

49. How much do you feel you have been "forgetting your trade" in the past few years? (Check one)

____ A great deal
____ Quite a bit
____ Somewhat
____ A little
____ Not at all

JOB POSTING AND TRANSFER

50. Several years ago a system of job posting was begun which makes it possible for employees to apply for jobs outside their own work unit. How well do you think that this system is working? (Check one)

____ Job posting works very well
____ Quite well
____ Fairly well
____ Not too well
____ Job posting doesn't work at all well
____ I don't know anything about how job posting is working

51. The following are a series of statements about job posting: please indicate whether you agree or disagree with them.

(Check one for each line)

Job posting is "phoney." Usually the new man has been selected before the job is posted	__ agree	__ don't know	__ disagree
Usually the new man is chosen because he knows the right people	__ agree	__ don't know	__ disagree
Jobs are not posted far enough in advance	__ agree	__ don't know	__ disagree
Applying for a job outside the work unit hurts a person's standing with the work unit and with his foreman. If he doesn't get the job, he is worse off.	__ agree	__ don't know	__ disagree
Some jobs are not posted on all bulletin boards at the same time	__ agree	__ don't know	__ disagree

52. Have you ever applied for a job as a result of job posting?

____ Yes
____ No

53. (If you applied) Do you feel that you were given a real opportunity to get the job?

____ Yes
____ No

54. When you think about taking a job in another plant in the company, what do you consider to be most important?

(Check one answer for every line)

	This is				
	Very Important	Quite Important	Fairly Important	Of little Importance	Of no Importance
Getting more money					
Getting a greater opportunity for training					
Getting a new plant management to work under					
Getting a chance to work on new equipment					
Getting off shift work					
Getting better opportunities for advancement					
Getting a new group of people to work with					
Getting a new supervisor under which to work					
Getting outside of [redacted]					

55. Would you transfer to the new [redacted] plant? (Check one)

____ I would go even if the job isn't quite as good as the one I have now
____ I would go if the job is as good as the one I have now
____ I would go if it were a little better job
____ I would go if it were a much better job
____ I wouldn't go under any circumstances

56. How do you feel about the way men were selected for the [redacted] power plant? (Check one)

____ Very satisfied
____ Quite satisfied
____ Fairly satisfied
____ Not very satisfied
____ Not satisfied at all
____ Don't know how they were selected

57. The following are a series of statements about the way men might have been selected for the [redacted] plant; please indicate whether you agree or disagree with them.

	(Check one)		
Men were given a chance to go if they had good attendance and good behavior records	__ agree	__ don't know	__ disagree
Men were selected if they were known to be anti-union or indifferent to the union	__ agree	__ don't know	__ disagree
Men were selected to go because they knew their jobs very well and could be trained for new jobs	__ agree	__ don't know	__ disagree
Anyone who really wanted to go could have gone	__ agree	__ don't know	__ disagree

ABOUT WAGES AND PROMOTIONS

58. What are your weekly wages on the average? (Before deductions)

$__________ per week

If you do not know how much money you make each week before deductions, indicate how much you make per hour.

$__________ per hour

59. About how much money do you think the company's "fringe benefits" amount to per hour for each employee?

$__________ per hour

60

60. How satisfied are you with your present wages? (Check one)

____ Very dissatisfied
____ Quite dissatisfied
____ Dissatisfied a little
____ Neither satisfied nor dissatisfied
____ Fairly well satisfied
____ Very well satisfied
____ Completely satisfied

> A promotion, in these questions, means a change in job classification. Going from B to A Mechanic would be a promotion. Going from a non-supervisory job to a foreman job would also be a promotion.

61. How do you feel about your own chances for promotion to a better job? (Check one)

____ Very dissatisfied
____ Quite dissatisfied
____ Neither satisfied nor dissatisfied
____ Quite satisfied
____ Very satisfied

62. How long has it been since your last promotion to a better job? (Check one)

____ Less than six months
____ About 1 year
____ Between 1 or 2 years
____ Between 2 and 3 years
____ Between 3 and 5 years
____ Between 5 and 10 years
____ More than 10 years
  ____ Never had a promotion

63. When do you expect to get a promotion? (Check one)

____ Less than six months
____ About 1 year
____ Within 1 to 2 years
____ Within 2 to 3 years
____ Within 3 to 5 years
____ Within 5 to 10 years
____ More than 10 years
  ____ I have no idea when I will get a promotion

64. How do you feel about the progress you have made in the Company up to now? (Check one)

____ Very dissatisfied
____ Fairly dissatisfied
____ Neither satisfied nor dissatisfied
____ Fairly satisfied
____ Very satisfied

65. What do you think counts the most today in getting a promotion to the job of foreman in this power plant?

Put the number 1 next to the item you think counts the most. Then, put the number 2 next to the item that counts second most.

____ How well a man does his job
____ Experience on the job
____ Education a man has
____ Seniority
____ How well a man stands with the foreman
____ How well a man stands with the front office
____ How well the man gets along with the men
____ Something else (Write in) ______________

____

66. What do you think should count most in getting a promotion to the job of foreman in this power plant?

Put the number 1 next to the item you think counts the most. Then, put the number 2 next to the item that counts the second most.

____ How well a man does his job
____ Experience on the job
____ Education a man has
____ Seniority
____ How well a man stands with the foreman
____ How well a man stands with the front office
____ How well the man gets along with the men
____ Something else (Write in) ______________

____

67. If you were offered the job of foreman, would you take it? (Check one)

____ Yes
____ No

68. If you would not take the job of foreman, please indicate why not

Put the number 1 next to the item which is the most important reason why you wouldn't want to be a foreman. Put the number 2 next to the the second most important reason

____ Do not feel qualified to handle the job
____ Requires licenses which I don't have
____ Haven't had enough experience
____ Foremen have to satisfy too many people; a foreman is always in the middle
____ I prefer the kind of work I am doing now
____ Too much grief for the pay

69. In general, do you think that the best men become foremen? (Check one)

____ All the time
____ Most of the time
____ Some of the time
____ Very little of the time
____ Never

73

ABOUT WORKING SCHEDULES AND SHIFTS

70. When you come to work (not after your days off), is it hard to find out what has been going on on the job? (Check one)

____ Very often it is hard to find out what has been going on on the job
____ Often it is hard to find out
____ About half the time
____ Occasionally it is hard to find out
____ Very rarely or never hard to find out what has been going on on the job

71. When you come onto your shift, how do you usually get most of your information about what's been happening on the last shift? (Check one)

____ The man I relieve tells me most of it
____ I get most of it from the "log"
____ Someone over me tells me most of it
____ None of these (Write in) ____________

____

72. How often do you come in or stay at the plant on your own time to find out how to do a certain job? (Check one)

____ Once a week or more
____ Once a month or more
____ Once a year or more
____ Less than once a year
____ Never

The questions in the following sections are for men doing certain jobs only. Check to see if the section concerns you; if not go on to the next.

For Operators and Plant Protection Only

The following questions are to be answered by operating personnel (Boiler, Turbine, and Electrical) and plant protection only:

Those not working afternoon and night shifts should skip to Question 95.

73. Taking everything into consideration, how do you feel about working afternoons and nights? (Check one)

____ I like shift work very much
____ I like it fairly well
____ I don't mind it
____ I dislike it somewhat
____ I dislike shift work very much

74. Which of these shift changes is it hardest for you to get used to? (Check one)

____ Going from nights to afternoons
____ Going from afternoons to days
____ Going from days to nights

75. How long does it take you to adjust to the shift change you checked above? (Check one)

____ Less than a day
____ About a day
____ Two or three days
____ Four days to a week
____ More than a week

76. What do you find gives you the most trouble in making these changes? Write your answer in

____

____

____

____

77. Put a 1 in front of the shift you like to work best; a 2 in front of the shift you like to work second best.

____ Day shift
____ Afternoon shift
____ Night shift

78. Put a 1 in front of the shift on which you work hardest; a 2 in front of the shift on which you work second hardest.

____ Day shift
____ Afternoon shift
____ Night shift

79. Put a 1 in front of the shift on which time passes the fastest; a 2 in front of the shift on which time passes the second fastest.

____ Day shift
____ Afternoon shift
____ Night shift

34

80. What two-hour period in each day do you find it the hardest to work? (Check one)

____ 7-9 AM	____ 7-9 PM
____ 9-11 AM	____ 9-11 PM
____ 11 AM-1 PM	____ 11 PM-1 AM
____ 1-3 PM	____ 1-3 AM
____ 3-5 PM	____ 3-5 AM
____ 5-7 PM	____ 5-7 AM

81. How often do you feel that the men on the last shift left you with problems or work which they should have handled during their shift? (Check one)

____ Very frequently
____ Quite frequently
____ Fairly often
____ Occasionally
____ Very seldom

82. How well do you feel you know the men on the other shifts who do the same jobs you do on your shift? (Check one)

____ Very well
____ Quite well
____ Fairly well
____ Not too well
____ Not well at all

83. How well do you feel the different shifts work together in this plant? (Check one)

____ The different shifts work together very smoothly; there is no friction
____ Quite smoothly
____ Fairly smoothly
____ Not too smoothly
____ The different shifts do not work together smoothly at all; there is quite a bit of friction

84. How much time do you usually take to let the man who is relieving you know what has been going on? (Check one)

____ Usually do not take any time to let my relief know what is going on
____ Less than 5 minutes
____ Between 5 and 10 minutes
____ Between 10 and 15 minutes
____ Between 15 and 20 minutes
____ Usually takes over 20 minutes to let my relief know what is going on

85. How does your family feel about working shifts? (Check one)

____ They like to have me working shifts
____ They don't mind whether I work shifts or not
____ They don't like to have me working snifts

86. If your family doesn't like to have you working shifts, how strongly does your family feel about this? (Check one)

____ They feel very strongly about this, and keep letting me know they don't like it
____ They feel fairly strongly
____ They don't feel too strongly about this, they mention it only once in a while

87. Have other members of your family ever worked shifts? (Check one)

____ No
____ Yes

88. How many children are there in your home who are under six years old?

______ children under 6 years old

89. How much experience have you working at a regular day shift job with weekends off? (Check one)

____ None; I have always worked shifts
____ Less than six months
____ Between six months and one year
____ Between one and five years
____ More than five years

90. How many years have you worked at a job which required shift work?

______ Number of years (approximately)

91. If you were a young man starting out to get his first job again, would you take a job that required you to work shifts? (Check one)

____ Yes, I definitely would
____ Yes, I probably would
____ Undecided, I might or might not
____ No, I probably would not
____ No, I definitely would not

92. How would you like to see the plant try out permanent shifts? (This would mean that the same group would always work days, another group would always work afternoons, and so on.) (Check one)

____ I would like to try it
____ I would not mind trying it
____ I would not like to try it

93. A power plant has to make electricity 24 hours a day, 7 days a week. Given this fact, do you have any suggestions for improving shift arrangements? (Check one)

____ None but what has been suggested above
____ Yes — (Please write in)

____

____

____

For Operators Only

94. How do you usually spend your time on the job when you are not actually operating the equipment—time when something does not have to be done?

Put a number 1 next to the answer that best describes how you usually spend your spare time on the job. Then, put a number 2 next to the second answer that describes what you do.

____ Talking to the other men
____ Walking around and looking at the equipment
____ Reading about the operation of the plant and equipment
____ Studying for licenses
____ Sitting and looking around

For Maintenance and Coal Handing Men Only

95. How would you feel about working afternoons and night shifts? (Check one)

____ I would like to work shifts very much
____ I would like it fairly well
____ I wouldn't mind it
____ I would dislike it somewhat
____ I would dislike working shifts very much

For "A" and "B" Mechanics Only

97. Would you prefer to work in the centralized maintenance (C & M) group or in the plant service group? (Check one)

____ I would prefer to work in centralized maintenance
____ It makes little difference which group I work in
____ I would prefer to work in the plant service group
____ I have no interest in working in either

98. Do you think the Company will extend centralized maintenance to include the work now done by the plant service work group in the power plants? (Check one)

____ The Company will probably extend it to include all maintenance
____ Probably extend it further, but not to all maintenance jobs
____ Probably not extend it any further than it is
____ The Company will probably cut down in the operations of centralized maintenance, and extend the maintenance responsibilities of the plant service group
____ I have no idea what the Company will do in this respect

99. How well do you think centralized maintenance is working out for the men in this plant now? (Check one)

____ Centralized maintenance is working out very well
____ Fairly well
____ Well in some ways, not others
____ Not so well
____ Centralized maintenance is not working out at all well

For "A" and "B" Mechanics Only

96. How well do you like these types of jobs?

(Check one answer for each line)

	Like it very much	Like it fairly well	Don't care, don't like or dislike	Dislike it a little	Dislike it a lot
Boiler and Stoker Repair					
Electrical Repair					
Machine Shop					
Pipe Repair					

100. When you come onto the job after your days off, is it hard to find out what has been going on, on the job? (Check one)

____ Very often it is hard to find out what has been going on on the job after I come in from my days off
____ Often it is hard to find out
____ About half the time
____ Occasionally it is hard to find out
____ Very seldom is it hard to find out what has been going on on the job after I come in from my days off

59

ABOUT YOURSELF AND YOUR EXPERIENCE WITH THE COMPANY

The way people feel and the ideas they have may be different because of the number of years they have worked, the amount of money they make, and the kind of a job they have. We, at the Survey Research Center, therefore, need to know a few basic facts about you. These facts will be used to combine your answers by groups. For example, we can find out whether employees who have been in the company for only a few years feel differently about things than employees who have been in the company a number of years. ALL THE INFORMATION IN THIS QUESTIONNAIRE WILL BE HELD STRICTLY CONFIDENTIAL.

1. What is your age?

_______ years

2. How much schooling have you had? (Check the highest completion)

____ Some grammar school
____ Completed grammar school
____ Some high school
____ Business or trade school plus some high school
____ Completed high school
____ Completed high school and business school
____ Some college
____ Completed college

3. What licenses or papers do you have? (Write in)

____

____

4. Are you—

____ Single
____ Married
____ Widow or widower
____ Divorced or separated

15

5. If you are married, does your wife have a steady paying job?

____ Full time
____ Part time
____ None
____ I am not married

6. How many persons (other than yourself) depend upon you for more than half of their support?

Number of persons over 18 years of age _____
Number of persons under 18 years of age _____

7. Do you have any other source of income than from [redacted]

____ Yes
____ No

8. About how long have you been with the company?

______ Years

9. How long have you worked under your present foreman?

______ Years

10. How long have you been in the work group you are now in?

______ Years

11. What is your present job title and grade? (Write in)

____

____

12. How much danger or chance for danger is there in your work? (Check only one answer)

____ There is no danger in my work
____ My work is occasionally dangerous, but only when something goes badly wrong
____ I work with things that I have to be careful of constantly, but there is little danger if you are careful and alert
____ My work is very dangerous

13. In general, how is your physical condition now? (Check one)

____ I am in very good physical condition
____ Pretty good physical condition
____ Fair physical condition
____ Poor physical condition
____ I am in very poor physical condition

26

14. Which of the following plants have you ever worked in? (Check as many as you need to)

____
____
____
____
____

15. Are you a member of the Union?

____ Yes
____ No

16. Have you ever been a steward?

____ Yes
____ No

17. Do you think of yourself as being more of a Republican or a Democrat?

____ More of a Republican
____ More of a Democrat

18. Do you have any hobbies (such as fishing, hunting, bowling, golf, woodcraft, metal working, etc.)?

____ No
____ Yes

If you answered "Yes" above, please answer the following:

Which of these statements best describe your hobby or hobbies?

18a. (Check one)
____ Outdoors
____ Indoors

18b. (Check one)
____ At home
____ Away from home

18c. (Check one)
____ With other people
____ Alone

19. What employee clubs do you belong to in the [redacted] now? [redacted]

1. ____________________
2. ____________________
3. ____________________
4. ____________________

20. Now go back and star (*) the ones you attend regularly and are most active in.

21. How often do you get together, outside of work, with any of the people you work with? (Check one)

____ At least once a week
____ A few times a month
____ About once a month
____ A few times a year
____ Never or almost never

22. How often do you get together with any other friends? (Check one)

____ At least once a week
____ A few times a month
____ About once a month
____ A few times a year
____ Never or almost never

23. How often do you get together with any of your relatives other than those living at home with you?

____ At least once a week
____ A few times a month
____ About once a month
____ A few times a year
____ Never or almost never

24. About how many minutes does it usually take you to get from your home to the plant gate on the day shift.

Usually about ______ minutes

25. Did you answer a questionnaire in the 1948 [redacted] (The first survey made in the Production Department by the Survey Research Center.)

____ Yes
____ No

26. Regardless of where you work, how would you feel about living in the following places? (Check one answer on each line.)

	Very good I would like it very much	Fairly good I would like it	Neither good nor bad I wouldn't care	Not very good I would dislike it	Not good at all I would dislike it very much
(1) Close to the center of downtown					
(2) Within but away from the center					
(3) The larger suburbs of					
(4) Other towns in					
(5) Rural areas in					

27. Number ____ above best describes where I live now. 47

PLEASE GO BACK OVER ALL OF THE PAGES TO BE SURE YOU DID NOT SKIP ANY OF THE QUESTIONS

POWER PLANT STUDY
Form A — Part 2

University of Michigan
Survey Research Center
Ann Arbor, Michigan

This is Part 2 of a study of the attitudes and opinions of the men who work in the power plants of [redacted] It is being done by the Survey Research Center of the University of Michigan.

In this section we want to learn how you feel about the way you are supervised by your foreman and the top supervisory staff of the plant. We will also ask questions about the top management of the Company, and the kind of a company you would like to work for.

Again there are no right and wrong answers. It's your opinions and feelings that are important here. Your answers to this questionnaire will be put with those from the other questionnaire when we analyze the study. Thanks again for your help.

Sincerely

Floyd Mann
Survey Research Center
University of Michigan

ABOUT INFORMATION

1. How satisfied are you with the amount of information you get about what is going on in the Company? (Check one)

____ Not very well satisfied
____ Somewhat satisfied but could get more
____ Fairly well satisfied
____ Very well satisfied

2. Do you feel you get more information about what is going on in the Company from your foreman, or from the "grapevine"? (Check one)

____ Always get more from my foreman than from the "grapevine"
____ Usually get more from my foreman
____ Get about an equal amount from both of these sources
____ Usually get less from my foreman
____ Always get less from my foreman than from the "grapevine"

3. How do you feel about Coal to Kilowatts, the Production Department magazine? (Check one)

____ I like it very much; I would miss it if they dropped it
____ I like it fairly well
____ I like some things about it, dislike others
____ I don't like it too well
____ I don't really like it at all; I wouldn't miss it if they dropped it

4. Where do you read it? (Check one)

____ On the job—during working hours when things aren't too rushed
____ At home

5. Do you keep your copies of Coal to Kilowatts? (Check one)

____ Yes, I try to keep all the copies
____ Yes, I keep some copies of particular interest
____ No, I don't keep them

6. How satisfied are you with the amount of information you get about what is going on in your plant? (Check one)

____ Not very well satisfied
____ Somewhat satisfied but could get more
____ Fairly well satisfied
____ Very well satisfied

7. How do you feel about your plant's weekly Newsletter? (Check one)

____ I don't really like it; I wouldn't miss it if they dropped it
____ I don't like it too well
____ I like some things about it, dislike others
____ I like it fairly well
____ I like it very much; I would miss it if they dropped it

8. How do you feel about the following in Coal to Kilowatts?

(There should be one answer for each line)

	Like Very Much	Like Fairly Well	Don't Really Care for This	Don't Know
The technical articles about plant and Production Department problems				
Statistical Summary Section indicating how each plant performed				
"Here and there" — giving news about men in the plant				
"Quiz and Tell" — question section				
On the job — giving information about recent changes in positions				
The pictures and drawings in magazine				

LEARNING ABOUT THE JOB

9. How satisfied are you with the training you have had for this job? (Check one)

____ Very satisfied
____ Fairly satisfied
____ Satisfied in some ways, dissatisfied in others
____ Fairly dissatisfied
____ Very dissatisfied

10. How long did it take you on this job before you really felt at ease doing this work? (Check one)

____ Less than 3 months
____ Between 3 months and a year
____ Between 1 and 2 years
____ Between 2 and 5 years
____ Between 5 and 10 years
____ Over 10 years
    ____ Still do not really feel at ease doing this work
    ____ Do not remember any more

11. Do you think you were adequately trained to perform this job before you were put on it? (Check one)

____ Yes
____ No

12. Do you think your training for this job was too fast or too slow? (Check one)

____ Much too fast
____ A little too fast
____ Just about right
____ A little too slow
____ Much too slow

13. Who taught you the most when you were learning about your present job?

(There should be one check on each line)

		Taught Me				
		A Great Deal	Quite A Lot	Some	A Little	None
a	Technical engineers					
b	My supervisor					
c	My instructors in various classes					
d	The other men who were in training with me					
e	The men who were already working on the job					
f	The men who put in this equipment					

14. Suppose you need to learn more about a job. How much can you learn in these ways?

(There should be one check on each line)

		A Great Deal	Quite A Lot	Some	A Little	Very Little
a	Attending classes on the theory of operation					
b	Attending classes on the operation of equipment in this plant					
c	Reading and studying on your own					
d	Watching and talking with the men who are actually doing the job					
e	Doing the job yourself under the guidance of other men					

15. How do you feel about teaching men in other groups in the plant about your job? (Check one)

____ I would not like to at all
____ I would mind it, but not too much
____ I would just as soon do it as not
____ I would like to do it fairly well
____ I would like to do it very much

16. How would you feel about teaching men in your work group about your job? (Check one)

____ I would not like it at all
____ I would mind it, but not too much
____ I would just as soon do it as not
____ I would like to do it fairly well
____ I would like to do it very much

THE EQUIPMENT

17. How often does your work make you feel "jumpy" or nervous? (Check one)

____ Very frequently
____ Fairly often
____ Occasionally
____ Very seldom
____ Never

18. When some important pieces of equipment (turbine, generator, boiler, etc.) is being started up or shut down, how does it affect you? (Check one)

____ It makes me very tense and "on edge"
____ Quite tense and "on edge"
____ Somewhat tense and "on edge"
____ A little tense and "on edge"
____ It does not make me at all tense and "on edge"

19. Suppose a piece of the equipment you work with breaks down on your shift, and it isn't your fault. How do you feel? (Check one)

____ I feel very concerned when some of the equipment I work with breaks down
____ Quite concerned
____ Somewhat concerned
____ A little concerned
____ I do not feel at all concerned when some of equipment I work with breaks down

20. Do you every worry that a problem will come up that you won't be able to handle? (Check one)

____ I worry a great deal that a problem might come up that I won't be able to handle
____ Quite a bit of the time
____ Some of the time
____ Very seldom
____ I never, or almost never, worry that a problem might come up that I won't be able to handle

21. How good do you feel you are on the technical side of your job? (Check one)

____ About average — as good technically as the next man
____ A little above average — technically a little above the other men
____ Quite a bit above average — quite a bit better technically than the rest of the men
____ A great deal above average — technically better than any of the other men

THE CHANGE TO CENTRALIZED MAINTENANCE

22. Last year, the Company set up the new Construction and Maintenance (C & M) Department to do major repair jobs in the power plants. Has this change made any difference in your work? (Check one)

____ Centralized maintenance has made no difference in my work
____ A little difference in my work
____ Some difference in my work
____ Quite a lot of difference in my work
____ Centralized maintenance has made a great deal of difference in my work

23. How efficient is this new system of centralized maintenance (C & M) in handling large maintenance jobs? (Check one)

____ It's very efficient
____ It's quite efficient
____ It's efficient in some ways, inefficient in others
____ It's quite inefficient
____ It's very inefficient
____ I don't know much about centralized maintenance

24. When the Company put in centralized maintenance, were you given a full explanation of the reasons for the new set up? (Check one)

____ We were given a full explanation of its reasons
____ Some explanation
____ We were given very little explanation of its reasons

ABOUT DIFFERENT POWER PLANTS

25. We would like to know how you would feel about working in each of the power plants in ████ ██████ system today.

Put a number 1 next to the plant you would most like to work in. Then, put a number 2 beside the plant you would next most like to work in, and so forth, until you have put a number next to each plant.

____ ██████ ____ ██████
____ ████ ____ ██████
____ ██████

. From what you hear, how good are the relations between the men and the plant management in each of the power plants?

(There should be one answer for each line)

Plants	Excellent	Good	Fair	Poor	Very Poor	Don't Know

. How important do you think each of the following plants will be to top management after the plant goes into production?

(There should be one answer for each line)

Plants	Of Great Importance	Of Some Importance	Of Less Importance
— High Pressure Side			
— Low Pressure Side			

BOUT IMMEDIATE SUPERVISION

. What is the name of your immediate foreman?

____

The following questions are about the man you named as your immediate foreman.

. How well does your foreman know the technical side of his job—the operation and maintenance of the equipment for which he is responsible? (Check one)

____ He knows the technical parts of his job extremely well
____ Very well
____ Fairly well
____ Some well, and others not so well
____ Does not know the technical parts of his job at all well

30. How well does your foreman do the administrative side of his job—by this we mean planning and scheduling the work, indicating clearly when work is to be finished, assigning the right job to the right man, inspecting and following up on the work that is done, etc. (Check one)

____ He handles the administrative parts of his job extremely well
____ Very well
____ Fairly well
____ Some well, and others not so well
____ He does not handle the administrative parts of his job at all well

31. How well does your foreman do the human relations side of his job—getting people to work well together, getting individuals to do the best they can, giving recognition for good work done, letting people know where they stand, etc. (Check one)

____ He handles the human relations parts of his job extremely well
____ Very well
____ Fairly well
____ Some well, and others not so well
____ He does not handle the human relations parts of his job at all well

32. In day-to-day operation, how concerned is your foreman with keeping costs down? (Check one)

____ Very concerned, he watches costs closely at all times
____ Quite concerned, he watches costs quite closely
____ Fairly concerned, he watches costs fairly closely
____ Not too concerned, he keeps an eye on costs, but he doesn't worry about them too much
____ Not concerned at all, he doesn't pay much attention to costs

33. In day-to-day operation, how concerned is your foreman with getting the work done safely? (Check one)

____ Very concerned that we do our work safely
____ Quite concerned
____ Fairly concerned
____ Not too concerned
____ Not concerned at all that we do our work safely

34. Does your foreman supervise you closely or does he put you on your own? (Check one)

____ He uses very little supervision; I am definitely on my own
____ A little supervision; I am pretty much on my own
____ A moderate amount of supervision
____ Fairly close supervision
____ He uses very close supervision; he doesn't put me on my own

35. How much help do you feel you get from your foreman when you really need it? (Check one)

____ Never gives me any help when I really need it
____ Hardly ever gives me any help when I really need it
____ Is sometimes helpful when I really need it
____ Is usually helpful when I really need it
____ Always gives me all the help I really need

36. Do you feel that your foreman will go to bat or stand up for you? (Check one)

____ No, he won't
____ Probably won't
____ May or may not
____ Probably will
____ Yes, definitely

37. How reasonable is your foreman in what he expects of you? (Check one)

____ Quite unreasonable
____ Not very reasonable
____ About average
____ Fairly reasonable
____ Very reasonable

38. How does your foreman give recognition for good work done by the employees in your work group?

(Check one answer on each item)

	ITEM	Very Often	Fairly Often	Sometimes	Practically Never
1.	Recommends pay increases				
2.	Gives more responsibility				
3.	Gives a pat on the back				
4.	Tells his superiors				
5.	Trains them for better jobs				
6.	Praises sincerely and thoroughly				

39. Which of these ways of giving recognition would you like him to use?

(Use the numbers above in the spaces below, numbering all three spaces)

( ) I would like the best
( ) I would like second best
( ) I would like third best

0. From your dealing with your foreman, how well would you say the following comments fit him? (Check one answer on each item)

ITEM	Fits Him Very Well	Fits Him Fairly Well	Doesn't Fit Him Too Well	Doesn't Fit Him At All
'onsiderate of our feelings				
'nnecessarily strict with us				
a "leader" of men				
ossy				
uick to criticize				
ays one thing, does another				
a "driver" of men				
an't keep confidences				
arries "weight" with his boss				
reats employees like inferiors				
warm and friendly person				

1. Does your foreman pull for the company or for the men? (Check one)

____ He is usually pulling for the company
____ He is usually pulling for himself
____ He is usually pulling for the men
____ He is usually pulling both for the company and the men

2. How well do you feel your foreman understands the problems which you have? (Check one)

____ He has a complete understanding of my problems
____ Considerable understanding of my problems
____ Some understanding of my problems
____ A little understanding of my problems
____ He has no understanding of my problems

3. How sure are you of what your foreman thinks of you and the work you do? (Check one)

____ I am very sure of what he thinks of me and the work I do
____ Quite sure of what he thinks of me and the work I do
____ Fairly sure of what he thinks of me and the work I do
____ Not too sure of what he thinks of me and the work I do
____ I am not at all sure of what he thinks of me and the work I do

. How free do you feel to discuss important things about your job with your foreman? (Check one)

____ Very free
____ Fairly free
____ Not very free
____ Not at all free

45. How well do you think you understand the problems that your foreman faces on his job? (Check one)

____ I understand the problems he faces on his job very well
____ Quite well
____ Fairly well
____ A little
____ I do not understand at all the problems he faces on his job

46. Do you feel your foreman has enough authority to decide the things he should decide? (Check one)

____ He has a lot more authority than he should have
____ He has a little more authority than he should have
____ He has about the right amount of authority
____ He has a little less authority than he should have
____ He has a lot less authority than he should have

47. Have there been any changes in the past few years in the amount of authority which the foremen have in the plants? (Check one)

____ Foremen have a lot more authority now than a few years ago
____ Foremen have a little more authority than a few years ago
____ Foremen have about the same amount of authority now
____ Foremen have a little less authority now
____ Foremen have a lot less authority now than a few years ago

48. Do you think there has been any change in the past few years in the extent to which the foremen in this plant feel they are a part of management? (Check one)

____ The foremen seem to feel that they are much more a part of management now than a few years ago
____ They seem to feel somewhat more a part of management now
____ They seem to feel about the same now
____ They seem to feel somewhat less a part of management now
____ The foremen seem to feel that they are much less a part of management now than a few years ago

49. How often does your foreman tell you in advance about any changes that affect you or your work? (Check one)

____ He always tells me in advance about any changes that affect me or my work
____ Nearly always tells me in advance
____ Tells me more often than not
____ Tells me occasionally in advance
____ He seldom tells me in advance about any changes that affect me or my work

50. In solving job problems, does your foreman generally try to get the ideas and opinions of you and others in his work group? (Check one)

____ He seldom gets the ideas and opinions of others
____ He sometimes does this
____ He often does this
____ He almost always does this
____ He always gets the ideas and opinions of others

51. In general, how much do you and the other men of your work group have to say about how things are done? (Check one)

____ Our foreman gives us a great deal of say in how things are done
____ Our foreman gives us quite a bit of say
____ Our foreman gives us some say
____ Our foreman gives us a little say
____ Our foreman gives us hardly any say at all in how things are done

52. In general how much do you think the foremen have to say about how things are done in this plant? (Check one)

____ They have a great deal of say
____ They have quite a bit of say
____ They have some say
____ They have a little say
____ They have very little or no say at all

53. Does your foreman let his superiors know how members of his work group feel? (Check one)

____ He lets his superiors know how his employees feel only when he feels his superiors will agree with him
____ He lets his superiors know how his employees feel about some things but not others
____ He lets his superiors know how his employees feel
____ He goes out of his way to let superiors know how his employees feel even when he knows his superiors will not like it

54. How many foremen do you feel you are directly responsible to? (Check one)

____ None
____ One
____ Two
____ Three
____ Four
____ Five
____ More than five

55. Taking all things into consideration, how satisfied are you with your immediate supervisor? (Check one)

____ Very satisfied
____ Quite satisfied
____ Fairly satisfied
____ Not too satisfied
____ Not at all satisfied

56. In general, do you feel your foreman is getting better or worse as a supervisor? (Check one)

____ Getting better as a supervisor
____ Staying about the same
____ Getting worse as a supervisor

ABOUT THE FRONT OFFICE OF THE PLANT

57. How well do you feel your plant is managed? (Check one)

____ Not managed well at all
____ Not managed very well
____ Fairly well managed
____ Very well managed

58. How well do the men in the front office do the administrative side of their jobs—by this we mean planning and scheduling the work, etc. (Check one)

____ They handle the administrative part of their jobs extremely well
____ Very well
____ Fairly well
____ Some of the administrative parts well, and others not so well
____ They do not handle the administrative part of their jobs at all well

59. How well do the men in the front office do the human relations side of their jobs—getting people to work well together, building a team, giving recognition for good work done, letting people know where they stand, etc. (Check one)

____ They handle the human relations part of their jobs extremely well
____ Very well
____ Fairly well
____ Handle some of the human relations parts well, and others not so well
____ They do not handle the human relations part of their jobs at all well

60. Taking all things into consideration, how satisfied are you with the men in the front office of this plant? (Check one)

____ Very satisfied
____ Quite satisfied
____ Fairly satisfied
____ Not too satisfied
____ Not at all satisfied

61. In the day-to-day operation of the plant, how concerned is the front office of this plant with keeping costs down? (Check one)

____ Very concerned; they watch costs closely at all times
____ Quite concerned; they watch costs quite closely
____ Fairly concerned; they watch costs fairly closely
____ Not too concerned; they keep an eye on costs, but they don't worry about them too much
____ Not concerned at all; they don't pay much attention to costs

62. How well do you feel the men in the front office of this plant understand the problems that the employees have? (Check one)

____ They have no understanding of our problems
____ Little understanding
____ Some understanding
____ Considerable understanding
____ They have complete understanding of our problems

63. In general, how much say do you think the men in the front office of this plant have in how things are done in this plant? (Check one)

____ They have a great deal of say in how things are done in this plant
____ They have quite a bit of say
____ They have some say
____ They have a little say
____ They have very little or no say at all in how things are done in this plant

64. In general, how much say do you think men in the front office of this plant have in how things are done in the Production Department? (Check one)

____ They have a great deal of say in how things are done in the Production Department
____ They have quite a bit of say
____ They have some say
____ They have a little say
____ They have very little or no say at all in how things are done in the Production Department

65. In your opinion, what kind of job do the supervisors do who are immediately over your foreman? (Check one)

____ They do a poor job of helping run the plant
____ They could do a better job in helping run the plant
____ They do a fair job of helping run the plant
____ They do a good job of helping run the plant
____ They really do a first rate job in helping run the plant

66. How do you feel about the way overtime is handled in this plant? (Check one)

____ Overtime is handled very fairly in this plant
____ Quite fairly
____ Fairly in some ways, not in others
____ Quite unfairly
____ Overtime is handled very unfairly in this plant

67. How do you feel about the way the absences are handled in this plant? (Check one)

____ The absence policy is handled very fairly in this plant
____ Quite fairly
____ Fairly in some ways, not in others
____ Quite unfairly
____ The absence policy is handled very unfairly in this plant

ABOUT TOP MANAGEMENT AND COMPANY POLICIES IN GENERAL

68. How well do you feel that ██████ ██████ is run? (Check one)

____ The company is not run well at all
____ Not run very well
____ Run well in some ways but not in others
____ Fairly well run
____ The company is very well run

69. How well do you feel the top management of the company understands the problems that the employees have? (Check one)

____ Top management of the company has no understanding of our problems
____ Little understanding of our problems
____ Some understanding of our problems
____ Considerable understanding of our problems
____ Top management has complete understanding of our problems

70. From your experience how much interest do you think the top management of the company has in the ideas and suggestions of its employees? (Check one)

____ Top management has no interest in employees' ideas and suggestions
____ A little interest
____ Some interest
____ Considerable interest
____ Top management has a great deal of interest in employees' ideas and suggestions

71. In the past few years, has there been a change in how interested top management is in its employees? (Check one)

____ Top management is much less interested in its employees now than it was a few years ago
____ Somewhat less interested now
____ There has been no change in top management interest in employees
____ Somewhat more interested now
____ Top management is much more interested now in its employees than it was a few years ago

72. In the past few years, has there been a change in how interested top management is in its Company's customers and the public? (Check one)

____ Top management is much more interested in its customers and the public now than it was a few years ago
____ Somewhat more interested now
____ There has been no change in top management's interest in its customers or the public
____ Somewhat less interested now
____ Top management is much less interested in its customers and the public now than it was a few years ago

73. In the past few years, has there been a change in how interested top management is in the Company's stockholders? (Check one)

____ Top management is much more interested in the Company's stockholders now than it was a few years ago
____ Somewhat more interested now
____ There has been no change in top management's interest in stockholders
____ Somewhat less interested now
____ Top management is much less interested in the Company's stockholders now than it was a few years ago

74. If you feel that there have been changes in the last few years, check those things below which you think caused these changes.

(Check as many as you think important)

____ Changes in economic conditions outside ██████
____ Changes in top management of ██████ ██████
____ Changes in the State Government at ██████
____ Changes in management at the Power Plan
____ Changes in Washington
____ Changes in management—union relations at ██████
____ Changes in the City of ██████
____ Changes in the size of the Company

75. Now go back and double check (✓✓) the change which you think was the most important cause of recent changes.

76. Do you feel that [redacted] is more interested in cutting costs than it is in the people who work for the Company? (Check one)

____ The Company is much more interested in cutting costs than in its people
____ Somewhat more interested in cutting costs than in its people
____ Equally interested in both
____ Somewhat more interested in its people than it is in cutting costs
____ The Company is much more interested in its people than it is in cutting costs

77. What do you think about the relations between labor and management in [redacted] (Check one)

____ The management-labor relations in [redacted] are very good
____ Fairly good
____ Not good
____ The management-labor relations in [redacted] are definitely bad

78. Do you think relations between labor and management are getting better or worse in [redacted] (Check one)

____ The labor-management relations are getting better in [redacted]
____ Staying about the same
____ The labor-management relations are getting worse in [redacted]

79. How satisfied are you with the retirement plan? (Check one)

____ I am very dissatisfied with the retirement plan
____ Somewhat dissatisfied
____ Satisfied in some ways, dissatisfied in others
____ Fairly satisfied
____ I am very satisfied with the retirement plan

80. How much effort does the company make to place people in jobs that they can do best? (Check one)

____ Everything possible is done to place people in jobs they can do best
____ Quite a bit of effort is made
____ Some effort is made
____ Very little is done
____ Nothing is done to place people in jobs they can do best

ABOUT THE KIND OF COMPANY YOU LIKE TO WORK FOR

In each of the groups of questions below, check the statement that best fits your feelings:

81. (Check one)

____ I like a company that is growing very rapidly
____ I like a company that is growing gradually
____ I like a company that stays about the same size

82. (Check one)

____ I like a company where there are always new kinds of jobs opening up
____ I like a company where you can stick to your kind of work and work up in it

83. (Check one)

____ A company should take care of all its men, regardless of what kind of a job they do
____ A company should take care of only those men who do a good job

84. (Check one)

____ I like a company that keeps up with the times and sets the pace for other companies
____ I like a company that doesn't worry about keeping ahead of other companies

85. Has there been any change in the past few years in the way your family feels about your working for [redacted] (Check one)

____ Yes, my family is more proud that I work for [redacted] now than formerly
____ No, they feel about the same now as they did earlier
____ Yes, my family is less proud that I work for [redacted] than formerly

ABOUT JOB SECURITY IN THIS COMPANY

86. Do you think that business in [redacted] will be better or worse in the next few years than it is now? (Check one)

____ Business will be a lot better
____ Somewhat better
____ About the same as now
____ Somewhat worse
____ Business will be a lot worse

87. How have the following things affected your future with [redacted]

(Check one answer for each item)

	Makes My Future Look				
	Much Better	Somewhat Better	About the Same	Somewhat Worse	Much Worse
The new [redacted] plant					
Centralized maintenance (C&M)					
Management's concern for costs					
Broadening and combining of jobs (Operators A, B, etc.)					
"Cross-the-wall" training					
Business conditions in [redacted]					
Job evaluation					
The Job Posting setup					

88. If there were a slump in business conditions in [redacted], and less demand for electricity, do you think [redacted] might lay off some people? (Check one)

____ No. The Company would find something for everyone to do. No one would be laid off
____ The Company would lay off a few people but not very many
____ The Company would lay off a good many people

89. If the Company did lay off some people, would this plant be affected?

____ Yes, this plant would probably have lay offs
____ No, this plant would probably not be affected

90. Taking all things into consideration, would you say your future in [redacted] looks better or worse than a few years ago? (Check one)

____ My future with [redacted] looks much better than a few years ago
____ Somewhat better
____ About the same as it did
____ Somewhat worse
____ My future with [redacted] looks much worse than a few years ago

91. How often do you feel you would rather stay away from the job than come in? (Check one)

____ Very frequently
____ Fairly frequently
____ Once in a while
____ Very seldom, but have felt that way
____ Never felt that way

92. How satisfied are you to continue working in [redacted]? (Check one)

____ Would leave company if I could find any other job
____ Would leave company for another job with the same pay and other benefits as I have here
____ Would leave company only if a particularly good opportunity came along
____ Would not leave under any conditions

93. Taking things as a whole, how satisfied are you the company and your job? (Check one)

____ I'm not satisfied and there are a great many things that could be changed
____ I'm not very satisfied but I can see no way things could be changed
____ I'm quite satisfied with the company but there are certainly many things that could be changed
____ I'm very satisfied but I know of some things that could be changed
____ I'm very satisfied with the company and my job and would not want to see them make any changes

For Men in the [redacted] Plant Only

94. How would you like to see the plant try out rotating shifts once a week or twice a month, instead of once a month?

____ I would like to try it
____ I wouldn't mind trying it
____ I would not like to try it

95. How would you like to see the plant try out the 4-Shift arrangement that they have at [redacted] (This means that the whole shift has its days off together.) (Check one)

____ I would like to try it
____ I wouldn't mind trying it
____ I would not like to try it

96. How would you like to see this plant try out some different schedules of working hours?

6 AM - 2 PM - 10 PM (Check one)

____ I would like the plant to try out a 6 to 2 to 10 schedule
____ I wouldn't mind it if the plant tried out a 6 to 2 to 10 schedule
____ I would not like to have the plant try a 6 to 2 to 10 schedule

7 AM - 2 PM - 10 PM (Check one)

____ I would like the plant to try out a 7 to 3 to 11 schedule
____ I wouldn't mind if the plant tried out a 7 to 3 to 11 schedule
____ I would not like to have the plant try a 7 to 3 to 11 schedule

8 AM - 4 PM - 12 PM (Check one)

____ I would like the plant to try out an 8 to 4 to 12 schedule
____ I wouldn't mind it if the plant tried out an 8 to 4 to 12 schedule
____ I would not like it if the plant tried out an 8 to 4 to 12 schedule

28

For [redacted] Operators Only

97. How would you feel about doing these jobs in rotation with your own job?

(Check one answer for each line)

	Like it very much	Like it fairly well	Don't care, don't like or dislike	Dislike it a little	Dislike it a lot
Boiler operating					
Turbine operating					
Electrical and switch-board operating					

98. The following are a series of statements about cross-training. Please indicate whether you agree or disagree with each statement.

(Check one on each line)

Everyone should have a choice of whether he wants to be cross-trained or not. . . . . ____ Agree ____ Undecided ____ Disagree

If one person in a group gets cross-trained the whole group should . . . . ____ Agree ____ Undecided ____ Disagree

If a person does not want to be cross-trained, he shouldn't have to. But those who do get this training should be given recognition for their extra effort. . . . . ____ Agree ____ Undecided ____ Disagree

Cross-training should start at the top and work down . . . ____ Agree ____ Undecided ____ Disagree

Cross-training should start at the bottom and work up . . ____ Agree ____ Undecided ____ Disagree

Cross-training should be given to all levels at once . . . . ____ Agree ____ Undecided ____ Disagree

Cross-training should start with the younger men, not with the older men . . . . ____ Agree ____ Undecided ____ Disagree

38

For [redacted] Operators Only

99. How do you feel about doing these jobs in rotation?

(Check one answer for each line)

	Like it very much	Like it fairly well	Don't care, don't like or dislike	Dislike it a little	Dislike it a lot
Boiler operating					
Turbine operating					
Electrical and switch-board operating					

39

The rest of this page and the following page is for any other points you would like to make. We woul appreciate knowing about any problem areas you think have not been adequately covered in this set of questions

Please go back over all the pages to be sure you did not skip any of the questions. Thank you for your help in filling out this questionnaire.

Sincerely yours,

Floyd C. Mann

INDEX

P9-CRP-434

A short history of Do-X-machines

9

A "Do-X-machine," as I told you, is somebody who suddenly appears in the middle of things-going-wrong to bring order, to right wrongs, to save the day. In Greek plays, it's a god; in *The Wizard of Oz,* it's the Good Witch Glinda. And in a play it's an actor playing God who gets lowered to the stage on a chair or swing controlled by ropes and pulleys.

I learned this from my brother Will and his best friend Brownmiller. They're always in the Big Garage, rehearsing one of their "productions," usually musical, as Mill is such a fabulous musician. They did me a favor recently, but in return they said I'd have to play a part in this production. I agreed. Little did I suspect they wanted me to be the Do-X-machine, sitting in a chair lowered from the rafters. I told them they were crazy and I wouldn't play their damned machine, not me.

My brother stared at me for a while as he slowly chewed gum. Will can look straight at a person, his dark eyes like ten-penny nails, but usually he's looking right through you. It's his "thinking" mode.

"You get to wear tulle," he said.

I was a little taken aback. I liked the picture of me in a tulle gown. But where would they ever get one? I said this.

Will and Mill flicked a conspirator's glance at each other; they do this like they're playing tiddledywinks with their eyes. They were artful in communicating this way. You could see they didn't want anyone in on the details of their precious production.

We'd had an argument before about Glinda, when they'd had her coming up through a trapdoor in the stage, instead of down, on pulleys. They had Paul, the dishwasher's boy, tossing a cloud of flour up to make it look like Glinda appeared out of nowhere. But they decided against that way of doing it in their present production because "it didn't look real."

"Real?" I said. "Whenever did you two bother with things looking *real?* Did it look real when you made Paul sit way up in that tree"—I pointed (we were in what we call the "cocktail garden" behind the hotel, surrounded by pines)—"eating a banana and trying to sound like a monkey?"

"He sounds like a monkey anyway," said Mill, pushing his glasses back on his thin nose.

I ignored that. "Did it look *real* when you did that Ku Klux Klan play and tied him to a pole with a lot of newspapers and kindling underneath?"

(I should say that there are no colored people in Spirit Lake or La Porte—or for miles and miles around. I think maybe the entire county steered clear of the Civil War.)

"That production," said Will, "was very educational."

"And we never lit the newspapers," added Mill.

I heaved a huge, trying-my-patience sigh. "Look, I refuse to *endanger my life* being lowered from the Big Garage rafters! How do I know you can work this pulley?"

"We're trying it out on Paul first to see," said Will.

Paul was everybody's guinea pig, including my mother's. If there was something in the refrigerator that had possibly been sitting awhile and you couldn't be sure from just sniffing it whether it was okay, she'd call for Paul to taste it. Then if he didn't fall over in a dead heap, she'd use it.

Paul's mother is the second dishwasher. She's tall and bony and bland looking, like vanilla junket. She has a deep voice like a man's but hardly ever says anything except to threaten Paul. So I see why Paul's strange; he gets it from his mother, unless he learned it from Walter. When the three of them are doing dishes, I like to hang around and listen to the talk, what little there is of it.

Poor Paul (not that I really feel sorry for him; I wouldn't have cared if they *had* lit the newspapers) gets into all kind of trouble. He hid under the pastry table once and when my mother walked away from the beautiful wedding cake she was icing, Paul reached up and just grabbed a chunk of cake in his fist. You can imagine. Once, his mother tied him to a chair to keep him out of trouble and he picked the stitching from his brand new shoes until they fell apart. It's not a good idea to leave his hands free, I told her.

You could say that Paul is the very *opposite* of a Do-X-machine. Things could be running smoothly until Paul comes on the scene, and then it all would go straight to hell.

I often come to the "cocktail garden" and swing on the big swing between two huge trees. It used to be exclusive, used only by the "in-crowd," meaning anyone with a bottle of gin. There used to be a white metal table with a big umbrella in the center and some white metal chairs. People also sat on the two green benches. It's really an elegant place to come and have cocktails in, and when the in-crowd came here, they were always dressed to the hilt in high heels or dark blazers. But like a lot of other things, it's no longer used. I don't know why; I think it's sad. Once it was on my list of Sorrowful Places, but something else more sorrowful beat it out. But you can't tell; it might be back on the list sometime.

I only wish it were harder for me to find Sorrowful Places.

Moses in the bullrushes

10

This bothered me a lot, and I thought about it for the two-mile walk into La Porte. I meant to go to the Rainbow Café, but as I was crossing the street near St. Michael's, I decided to go in and sit down.

I'm no church-goer; none of the family is, though my mother and Lola Davidow claim to be Episcopalians. I like St. Michael's because of all of its stained-glass windows and sculptures. Mostly, though, I think I just like to hang around and talk to Father Freeman, who is high up on my list of adults who don't talk down to children. Also, he's good-looking, very dark and elegant, although not as good-looking as the Sheriff.

Of course, Father Freeman wasn't around forty years ago, but I think he would still be interested in what I had to say about Mary-Evelyn. Probably, he'd at least have heard about the Devereaus and the old Devereau place, and certainly he knows about the shooting over at White's Bridge. I wonder with a kind of fearfulness if I'm the only person who thinks all of this is related. Does that make me more responsible for what might happen?

St. Michael's always strikes me as cool and dark and warm and light at the same time. This has to do with its silence and its windows and the way rays of sun weave color across the floor and the pews. I always stay on my feet and walk around and look at the windows. Even if I'm tired I try not to sit in a pew in case someone might think I'm praying.

Just as I knew he would, after ten or fifteen minutes, Father Freeman came out of one of the little doors near the altar, saw me, and smiled. He joined me in looking at one of the windows. We were pretty quiet. He is one of those people who don't have to be always talking and who are comfortable being around in silence.

I asked him if he was familiar with the case of Mary-Evelyn Devereau, and he said yes, a little. I told him all I knew, the details I'd written in my notebook, but not, of course, about Ben Queen. I did consider it for a moment; priests and lawyers cannot tell what you've told them. They are bound not to.

We fell silent again. And then he said, "That's one of the saddest stories I've ever heard." Sadly, he shook his head. "A little girl rowing herself out on a lake and drowning that way. Why do you think she did it?"

"They said it was an accident."

"Yes, but it was no accident, surely, that she was in the boat in the first place."

It was such a relief to have someone take my side in this. "I know. I've been trying to work it out. There are too many questions left unanswered. It doesn't make any sense the way it happened—" I felt myself rushing headlong into speech, the words tripping over one another. I was breathless.

"You've given this a lot of thought."

I nodded but kept looking up at the stained-glass window.

"Moses," he said.

"Huh?"

"The bullrushes," he said. "You know, when he was a baby."

I have hardly any acquaintance with the Bible, but I mumbled, yes, I knew. Which I didn't. All I knew about Moses was the Red Sea.

"To save him, his mother wrapped him in rushes and then put him in a little boat."

Then he fell silent again and seemed to be in a brown study (a phrase I adored, Maud Chadwick having told me what it meant) over

Moses. I didn't see really any similarity between Moses and Mary-Evelyn. It sort of irritated me he had to bring Moses into it. I said, "Well, but Moses got over it and came back and parted the Red Sea." I hoped Father Freeman was impressed with my grasp of Moses's life.

He nodded, and said, "I didn't mean they were literally alike."

"I guess *not.*" I said with real authority, although I didn't know what he meant.

I determined then to look up the story of Moses, but I didn't have time to go to the library now, and I'd have to allow myself some time after I got back to the hotel to talk to Aurora Paradise before dinner. Also, I wanted to stop at the Rainbow.

The Rainbow Café is owned by a bossy woman named Shirley. We call her Shirl. Like Lola Davidow, she is always complaining about her customers. Ordinarily, it's the customer who gets to complain about the management (the rude help, the cold room, the mile-long walk to the bathroom); for the Hotel Paradise and the Rainbow Café, it's the other way around. Shirl and Lola complain about the customers, as often as not to their faces. Once people get used to it, they don't pay any attention.

Shirl sits on a high stool behind the cash register, smoking and barking commands and selling her Heavenly Pie, which is an imitation of my mother's Angel Pie, the one with the meringue crust. Angel Pie is one of the hotel specialties—I guess Aurora would say its "signature pie." For Shirl, my mother threw in a couple of her extra ingredients, in this case a quarter teaspoon of cayenne pepper for the meringue crust and a tablespoon of mayonnaise ("Be sure it's Hellmann's") for the lemon chiffon filling. Who would be nitwit enough to believe this? you might ask. But you don't know my mother. She can lock eyes with you as if she's got a pistol at her temple and lie. Then you might say this is not a trait to want to imitate, but, again, you've never seen my mother do it. It's really not so much lying as *acting.* My mother has a great flair for it (and used to do it when she was young and put on amateur theatricals here at the Hotel Paradise), and she can change selves and accents like Lola Davidow can change martinis for mint juleps. I've heard my mother, among a group of guests from the Deep South, slather on the accent of the most solid Georgia peach-picker that ever lived.

This must be where my brother gets it; his dramatic flair, his ability to stare you down and lie—this must come from my mother.

So Shirl sits in the Rainbow smoking and complaining, her elbows on the glass case in which are housed her Heavenly Pies that no one buys twice. Her cakes and doughnuts, though, are quite popular.

One of the waitresses is Charlene, a pasty-faced girl whose big bust greets you before her eyes do and who's always getting pinched on the behind. The other waitress, one of my two all-time favorite people from anywhere, is Maud Chadwick. She's kind of tall and pretty with silky light brown hair and the clearest face I've ever seen. You can read Maud in her face. I don't know how old she is, maybe as old as thirty or thirty-five, I'd guess. But she has a way of sinking into herself and coming up seventeen, as if she's got all of these past selves right inside that she can call up whenever she wants to. Maybe that's why she seems to know how I feel: her twelve-year-old self is right there at her beck and call. It occurs to me that this is a real gift, almost to become the person you're talking to. In a way, it's my mother's ability to come on as a Southerner, except Maud isn't acting; she just *is.*

Shirl has imposed a ton of rules, tacked up on little signs; one of these is stuck up on the high-backed mahogany booths in the rear of the room warning that booths can only be used by two or more people. But Maud always sees to it I get to sit in a booth; she takes a break when I come in and sits there with me, at least until I get what I've ordered. Once "ensconced" (which is how Maud describes it) with my Coke and bowl of chili, she can go back to waiting tables. "Squatter's rights," she calls it.

The thing is that a lot of the time the booths are completely empty, as the people who come to the Rainbow are mostly by themselves and are regulars who sit at the counter—a lot of them on exactly the same stools, same time every weekday. There's Dodge Haines (who owns the Chevy dealership) and there's Mayor Sims. These are the two biggest fanny-pinchers, which I think in the mayor is disgusting; he should be setting a good example. Then there's Ubub and Ulub, the Wood boys, who do not seem to mind being called by the letters on their license plates. But then, the Wood boys have very even temperaments. I guess they'd have to, getting all the fun poked at them that they do, which I think is terrible.

Maud always waits on them because Charlene likes to make them order, just to hear them say things like "oat bee sanguid" for "roast beef sandwich." But Maud tells them the special and all they have to do is nod or shake their heads, and then she tells them something else until they nod, *Yes, I'll have that.*

One person who won't put up with anybody heckling Ulub and Ubub is the La Porte Sheriff. If he hears Dodge Haines or Bud Hemple or one of the others giving the Woods a hard time, he'll likely walk back out and put a ticket on the person's car. He knows everyone's vehicle and it's not hard to find a reason for a ticket, considering most of them (especially the mayor) park without any attention to signs. They know why they're getting a ticket, though, and when the Sheriff walks in, they shut up from teasing Ulub and Ubub and drink their coffee and talk about other things.

The Sheriff and Maud are good friends; you can sense their closeness even though he's always teasing her and she's always bickering with him. But still, you can tell. Maud's divorced, but has a son named Chad who's away at school. The Sheriff is married to a woman named Florence who I hardly ever see. I've heard my mother and Lola talking about her and how she goes with every man she sees. *Poor Sam,* they say and sigh.

If there's one person I can't imagine saying "poor Sam" about, it's the Sheriff. More than that I can't imagine any wife of his going with someone else. He's very handsome and though he might be a shade under six feet, he looks over it. There is a tallness to him that can't be measured in inches, and I don't think it's the holstered gun on his hip.

The Sheriff seems really glad to see me when I turn up, almost as if someone just shoved an unexpected present under his nose. For me, this is really something, as it is not a reaction I get from people most of the time. I have tried hard to live up to his idea of me. That I guess I failed is my biggest problem.

Moses and Aurora

11

Aurora Paradise is the only one I know who has a Bible. But, of course, she wouldn't let me see it until I made her a Cold Comfort. She called it my "signature drink." Not even Lola Davidow could make a Cold Comfort, for it took not only skill, but imagination. Well, imagination, anyway; skill didn't come into it much. As long as I started with Southern Comfort (from the Davidow supply), I could toss in anything else—brandy, Jack Daniel's, rye whiskey, crème de menthe—in addition to fruit juice. I perfected this concoction as I went along, adding an orange slice, a sprig of mint, or a cube of pineapple, and if I wanted her to really remember, to resurrect people and scenes from the past, I made a whole fruit kabob and tossed in more brandy. The Bible would not test my creativity in the drink department, as it made no demands on Aurora's mind. Just to get a look in her Bible, a maraschino cherry on the ice cubes would do.

She sipped her Cold Comfort and smacked her lips and squinched her eyes shut. "Umm-*hmm!*" she said and sipped some more, first making bubbles by blowing in the straw (which is so childish I hardly ever do it anymore).

"My Bible? Now what do you want that for?" She rocked in a satisfied way, her fingers in their dressy little net gloves, plying the soda straw.

"None of—" I was about to say "none of your beeswax" but caught myself. For Aurora might just know the whole story of Moses. I really didn't want to sift through all of those thin, tissue-y pages. Then I reminded myself that if Aurora Paradise didn't lie outright (as she did about the rules of cards and the find-the-pea trick), she liked to slyly insert a piece of *mis*information in an account, just to trip a person up. So I said, "I just want to read the Moses story."

"*Moses?* You suddenly get religion, girl? You been over there to the camp meeting with the Holy Rollers again?"

I had gone there once with Will and Mill, who only attended to hear songs they could make up new words for. I ignored that question. Then she asked, "Do you even know which part Moses is in? Old Testament or New?"

It was fifty-fifty so I took a chance. "Old Testament." As I've said, I'm on very shaky ground, Bible-wise. But she didn't contradict, so I went on. "I mean, how many chapters into it is Moses when he gets put in the bullrushes?" I certainly did not want to read any more about Moses than I had to.

Aurora blew down her straw again, but there was little liquid left. "Well, you don't have to read it. I can tell you the life of Moses." She said this while cutting me a sly glance.

"No! I want to read it myself."

She shrugged. "Please yourself, only you got to be careful. Some Bibles don't get the story right."

"What are you talking about? Bibles are Bibles, there's neither wrong nor right ones!"

Elaborately, she placed her glass on the little table beside her rocking chair and fiddled with her net gloves. I just knew she was trying to fill me with doubts and put obstacles in my path. And I stood (I was never invited to sit down) wondering what was the difference really between Aurora and someone like Ree-Jane? I answered myself. Easy. Ree-Jane has no imagination.

Aurora Paradise was much more like my mother giving out recipes with one wrong ingredient in them, like adding cold coffee grounds to the Chocolate Feather Cake. I think this is brilliant and very diplomatic. It makes her out to be generous and at the same time she holds onto her trade secrets.

"Yes, there are. Maybe I'd better tell you Moses's story."

"So which story would you tell me? The right or the wrong one?" I asked this in a put-on-sweet voice. When she cackled, I said, "For a woman ninety-one years old, you act really childish."

"Seventy-nine!" she snapped. "Not a day over, Miss!"

"Oh, well, that explains everything." I took the empty glass and left the room in what I thought was a grand fashion.

Falling out with the Sheriff

12

It wasn't until several days after she was shot and killed that the police were able to identify Fern Queen. There was no identification on her, like a driver's license. Finally, when Sheba and George Queen heard the description of the woman found shot over near White's Bridge, they called the police.

Cold Flat Junction doesn't have a police station or any "police presence" (as the Sheriff calls it), so the state troopers notified ours. Usually, the Sheriff is the one who goes when there's trouble in Cold Flat Junction, and this sure looked like trouble.

I could have told the police who the dead woman was, only I didn't. My trouble with the Sheriff started because I didn't tell him. But more important, I didn't tell him about Ben Queen. The police didn't seem to care too much as to *why* he'd shoot his and Rose's daughter. For if it wasn't Ben Queen, who else would have done it? I got the impression they did not linger over this question.

The Sheriff suspected I knew something; no, he *knew* I knew something when he sat down in my booth in the Rainbow and told me he was just back from Cold Flat Junction where he'd talked to Sheba and George Queen. They had told him, in passing, that Jen Graham's girl (that's me) had been to their house with an Elijah Root, who the Sheriff didn't know and wondered how I did: "I mean with Mr. Root being in his sixties, seventies, it was interesting that you'd be traveling around with him." The Sheriff could be sarcastic. As I'd seen the Sheriff every day since Fern Queen got shot, he wondered that I didn't mention this visit of mine to the Queens and also what else my personal (and unauthorized, he said) investigation had turned up.

All I said was "Nothing," which was hardly the gospel truth, seeing that it had turned up Ben Queen.

It was the night before I talked to the Sheriff in the Rainbow that Ben Queen had appeared at the Devereau house and been just as surprised to find me there as I was to find him. Because Rose had lived there, it didn't seem strange to me that he'd turn up there if he were looking for someone. Did he tell me why he was there? Did I ask him? No, because I thought I knew. I knew he was just out of prison. And someone had shot his daughter. But I knew, after we talked, it wasn't him.

We walked from the house to the spring, and that's when we talked about scapegoats. "There's people put on this earth to take the blame for others." Mary-Evelyn was one, he said; she was the scapegoat for the whole family, the person upon whose head was heaped the sins and misfortunes of the others, of all the Devereaus. It was an accident, he said, an awful accident that had happened to that child.

I believed him then about Mary-Evelyn. But after I'd had time to think about it, I changed my mind. In a way, I would rather not think Mary-Evelyn was so miserable she'd take the chance she did. A blind chance. I hate to think her head was so crowded with remembering things the Devereau sisters had done to her and would keep on doing, that she was driven to escape. The idea that someone our age could find life so hard it drove her to go out on that lake in the middle of the night—well, it hardly bears thinking about.

So the Sheriff and I had been sitting in the Rainbow that day after he visited the Queens. He was waiting me out, waiting for me to tell him what I'd seen and what I'd heard. What I knew. We sat in silence while his ice cream melted on top of his peach pie. I still remember the humming silence, as if everything had stopped except for the jukebox voice of Patsy Cline.

I was grateful for Patsy. I was grateful to hear someone knew how it felt. Keeping a secret like that from the Sheriff was hard. The reason I did it is not because Ben Queen told me to keep quiet about seeing him. No, he said the very opposite; he said: *If it goes too hard on you, turn me in.*

I couldn't do it; I couldn't turn in someone who put my welfare ahead of his. I would do it, too, the same thing, if it had been the Sheriff who'd said that to me.

But no one had ever said it to me.

It is not too late, I told myself as I stood in the rotunda of our courthouse, looking at the frosted glass of the door with SHERIFF painted on it in white block letters. It's one of several doors arranged in a half-moon arc around the rotunda. The other half is taken up by a wide marble staircase with columns on either side. It is an elaborate building for a town the size of La Porte. There are two dozen broad white steps leading up to its entrance, and stone lions flank its door. It also has a jail out back, where prisoners stand around with their hands gripping the bars of the windows, yelling comments whenever girls walk by, which I think is pretty disgusting and shouldn't be allowed. I asked the Sheriff once why he didn't crack down on the prisoners. I said it isn't very pleasant having a serial killer whistle and catcall when you passed. He could be memorizing your face for when he got out.

The Sheriff just shook his head. "I never heard anybody exaggerate the way you do."

Recalling this, I sighed. For that was back in the happy days when we were friends and walked all over the town, reading meters and giving out tickets.

Today, it was a little after two o'clock on a Saturday and the Orion was showing a matinee, as it always did on Saturdays and Sundays. It was in the back of my mind that if things didn't work out at the courthouse, I might just go along to the movies. I'm not sure what I meant by "work out." Probably, it meant that the Sheriff would ask me to go along with him on a meter check. But I didn't go into the Sheriff's office; I stood and watched shadows move back and forth behind the frosted glass. I didn't know whose shadows. The Sheriff might not even be in there.

I was carrying a white bag of Shirl's fresh doughnuts. There were two plain and two sugared and one iced. The Sheriff likes plain doughnuts and Maureen Kneff, the typist, likes sugar. Donny Mooma, the deputy, likes chocolate iced, so I got vanilla, just to let him know I was losing no sleep over his likes and dislikes. I do not like Donny; I can't stand the way he struts around and puts on when the Sheriff isn't there—sitting at the Sheriff's desk, pretending he's in charge of La Porte and everything else for a hundred miles around. I can't think why the Sheriff keeps him on, for Donny is really dumb. He's always tugging his wide black belt up to make sure you take notice he's got a gun in that holster.

I looked in the doughnut bag, then folded it closed twice over and went to the recessed fountain by one of the pillars. I tipped my head to drink, though I didn't like this water. It was nothing like Crystal Spring; it was flinty from all the chemicals they put in it. I wiped my hand across my mouth as I looked at the frosted glass door again. I was thinking up ways to introduce the subject of Ben Queen, like: *I got the biggest surprise when I was at the lake last week* or *Guess who I ran into?* How stupid. There seemed no way to get out from under not telling him before. I stood there for a while longer. Above me, the clock said two-twenty. It was set in the molding just below the dome that seemed to soar off into the slate gray sky.

I felt doomed. I turned and walked down the marble stairs. Outsidc, at thc top of more stairs I opened the bag and took out the white-iced doughnut. They were my favorite.

Uninvited

13

It was not until after my second helping of almost everything at dinner that I heard about the trip. And, of course, it had to be Ree-Jane I heard it from.

I was resting my stuffed self on the porch. Had I honestly needed that second helping of Mile-High Lemon Meringue Pie? It was so beautiful, the stacked clouds of meringue topping the sun-drenched yellow of the filling, that, yes, I had to have a second slice.

The evening light that seeped through the trees and lay across the porch railing was a paler note of the lemon pie, as if Nature, not feeling up to scratch, waited while my mother put the last meringue loop on the surface of her pie so it could settle down and copy the color. Only a person utterly immune to beauty and one with a leather tongue could have resisted another slice of that pie. . . .

And here was one, and here she came.

Groggy as I was with enough food in me to feed Cox's army (an army known only to my mother, who referred to it as a measure of size), I could still tell that Ree-Jane was going to tell me something that I wouldn't like but that she did. I watched her arrange herself on the porch railing in a dress that was noticeably new. I might as well ask.

"Where'd you get that?"

"Heather Gay Struther's, of course. I got this and four others and an evening gown and a swimsuit. Of course, I'll need more, so I'll buy them at the Beach House."

The Beach House was a shop in Hebrides that specialized in swimwear. "No kidding?" *No kidding* was not at all what I felt. What I felt was an urgent need to kill her. I refused to ask her why she was buying all of this.

So she told me. "I need a lot of new clothes for the trip."

She was watching me closely to gauge my curiosity level. I kept my face as expressionless as I could. "What trip?"

"Oh, didn't you *know?* We're going to Florida. To Miami."

I stilled my rocking. "What? When? Who's going?"

She was clearly pleased by my astonishment. "Three days from now. All of us—mother, me, and Miss Jen."

My mother? But my mother never got to go anywhere. She was always stuck with the Hotel Paradise.

"It's too bad you can't go along." The tone indicated she thought it anything but too bad.

So *I* was to get stuck with the Hotel Paradise. And Will and Mill, I supposed.

I said nothing because I was afraid I wouldn't be able to keep the disappointment out of my voice. I rocked back and forth in the green wicker chair.

"We'll be gone over a week. We want to spend four or five days there and it'll take us a couple of days to get there and back. We'll go down the west coast to the Tamiami Trail and cut over to Miami Beach along it."

Tamiami. For a brief moment I shut my eyes and said that word in my mind. *Tamiami. Tamiami Trail.* It was such a beautiful sound I could almost taste it.

". . . and we're staying at the Rony Plaza in Miami Beach."

Rony Plaza. Another one! I dropped my chin in my palm. Was Florida full of beautiful names? I should say that there is something in my nature that makes me adore certain names of things and places, almost as if the names were enough.

"It's quite luxurious," Ree-Jane went on. "It's right on the beach, so every morning I can roll out of bed and down to the ocean. I'll show you the swimsuit later. Perhaps I'll model it."

"Uh-huh."

"We'll go to the Keys, too."

"Like Key Largo? Did you see that? It had Humphrey Bogart in it." How I remembered the storm, the waves lashing the shore, the furious wind blowing the fronds of the palm trees like women's scarves. Howling winds in which I pictured Ree-Jane lifted off the beach in her Heather Gay swimsuit and hurled at the building. Then picked up and hurled back on the beach. This went on.

Ree-Jane gave a labored sigh. "This isn't a *film.*" That's what she called movies, thinking it much more sophisticated. "This is the real thing. Do you think life is like some film?"

"Yes."

"I suppose you would. You've never been anywhere. Too bad. We'll probably go to Key West, since that's the most famous one of the Keys. You can drive all the way down to it. It's the last one, I think. Those sunsets! I can hardly wait to see them, they're so famous! And that water! It's the color of turquoise. What colors! Like a *film!*"

"Told you." I snickered.

So that evening, after dinner was finished and my mother had changed into one of her good cotton dresses, we all sat on the porch around a green table, rocking. My mother had a glass of sherry and Lola had a tumbler of Dewar's Scotch. I was satisfied to listen as they talked about Florida because every once in a while the Tamiami Trail would come up and the Rony Plaza. And there were other names, like Biscayne Boulevard, and bougainvillea. Everything about Florida had this lush quality.

"Jane" (which is what her mother calls her) had left and gone up to her room to try on her new clothes which she said she'd model for us. From her room, which overlooks the porch, we heard strains of music, a little scratchy, coming from her old record player.

Mrs. Davidow, sitting back in one of the green rockers, leaned her arm on the railing, her hand extending over it to tap ash from her cigarette onto the shrubs. The world is her ashtray. But I shouldn't be so critical because she was in such a good humor. She called up to "Jane" with a musical request, a song named "Tangerine." This was a favorite song of hers, for she associated it with "my Florida years." I didn't know she'd had any Florida years before I'd heard that song, but she had, for she'd lived in Coral Gables for a while.

Coral Gables. That had a pleasant ring to it, although not as much as the other names did. It wasn't right up there with Tamiami Trail;

still, it was worth including. Including in what, I wasn't sure. Apparently, she'd thought up this trip in a sentimental wander through memories of her "Florida years."

"Tangerine" sifted down from Ree-Jane's room. I could not make out the words very well, though I did catch "lips . . . as bright . . . as flame." The melody was wonderful, something you could really do a slow dance to. Mrs. Davidow hummed the tune and sang a stray phrase here and there, such as "every bar . . . across . . . the Argentine." I wasn't surprised she liked the song.

So my mother (who had spent time there too, I was surprised to discover) and Mrs. Davidow talked about Florida—Miami Beach, Coral Gables, Hialeah, the pink flamingos in its center. *Seabiscuit. Whirlaway.* I was dizzy with names. And dizzier still to find out that Whirlaway was a *horse,* or used to be. Lola Davidow was regretting his loss. With a name like that, so did I.

The first night of driving, they could stay in Culpepper, Virginia, my mother said. With a word like "Culpepper" I knew we were not yet in Florida territory.

Perhaps recalling that I was alive, Mrs. Davidow said to me, "You won't mind keeping an eye on things here, will you?"

"Yes," I said.

For some reason they thought this answer was amusing and laughed.

"You'll be fine. There aren't any reservations for the next two weeks. There's only Miss Bertha and Serena Fulbright. And the Poor Soul might be coming back next week, but that's not sure."

Mr. Muggs. The ax murderer. I said this. That was howlingly funny. Didn't anyone ever worry about me? I rocked and drank my watery Coke and remembered the Sheriff had been really mad when they'd left me alone to watch the hotel once. I was thrilled when I found out he had *told off* Lola Davidow. Her face was beet red and her eyes were bloodshot when she reported this to my mother, as if some fire inside her were burning through to outside.

I shut my mind to this when Mrs. Davidow mentioned a street in Miami Beach lined with poincianas and royal palms. *Poinciana. Royal palm.* I'd heard of "coconut" palms and "date" palms and wondered how many different palm trees there were. "Royal" must be the handsomest of them all. I would have to research this at the Abigail Butte County Library. Mrs. Davidow called up to Ree-Jane to put on "Poinciana," another record. That it was a song was twice as good.

What did people remember of the past? When I was old, what would I remember of tonight? Would I see us sitting here rocking and talking, but with the actual talk itself vague (at best) or forgotten (at worst), or would I remember royal palm and Tamiami Trail? Would I care less that they hadn't taken me than I'd care about having heard these names?

And if the names were all I needed, I wondered what that meant.

Bunny and me

14

There were only two tables to be served breakfast and only Miss Bertha and Mrs. Fulbright for lunch, so my mother agreed, as long as I waited on tables this lunchtime, to let me off serving dinner, as Vera would be there to take care of a small dinner party, and she could easily wait on Miss Bertha too. I don't know about "easily," but that was fine with me. My plan for the day: to get a ride to White's Bridge and inspect the murder scene. I certainly was not going to take a cab and ride with nosey Delbert, and both the Woods' trucks were being repaired, so I thought of Bunny Caruso, who drove her pickup into La Porte most days to shop. I was supposed to stay away from Bunny Caruso, which made her that much more interesting. Like Toya Tidewater and June Sikes.

When I opened the dining room's double door, there was Miss Bertha in another of the gray dresses that matched her hair and eyes and made her look armored. She also looked as if she'd stepped out of one of those old pictures called "daguerreotypes," that make even little kids appear solemn and rained on. I'd seen several of my mother and her family when she was small: they were stiff and stern and unsmiling, as if in those long-ago days all pleasure and excitement were forbidden.

"Late again!" snapped Miss Bertha, consulting the silver watch she always wore pinned to her chest. I think she kept it running fast just so she could say this.

Mrs. Fulbright told her, no, it was they who were early, but Miss Bertha was already stumping across the dining room, back to their table for two. (I asked once why they couldn't have been put nearer the door, and Vera said they'd been coming for years and that was their table. They'd raise a fuss if they were moved.)

The other guests were a pleasant family of four, easy to serve, since they wanted to be gone to their exciting day just as much as I wanted them to go. Also, they all ordered the same thing: scrambled eggs, bacon, and toast, which had my mother pursing her lips and kissing heaven, for she always said breakfast was the hardest meal of all to prepare because of all the different things and combinations of things that could be ordered.

Miss Bertha would not give me an order until she'd inspected every single item on the menu, even though only one item had changed—corn cakes in place of yesterday's French toast. I stood and stood with my order book ready, wishing she'd sink in a vat of syrup, when she finally snapped out, "My three-minute egg and sausages."

I said, "But you didn't like the ones yesterday."

"I don't *want* the ones yesterday! I want today's."

"Yes, but that's the way my mother, I mean the cook, makes sausage."

"Tell her to make it another way."

Why was I bothering to argue? Probably because I wanted to. "The sausage patties are already *made;* they're already *seasoned.*"

"Well, for Lord's sake, girl, she doesn't have to slaughter a hog, does she?" She turned when Mrs. Fulbright put a hand on her arm. "Leave me be, Serena! All I'm doing is making my *point.*" She flung off Mrs. Fulbright's gentle hand. Turning back to me, she said, "Just make me a sausage without all that hot spice in it!"

"And what else?"

"What?" She still had some sausage-arguing left in her head and "what else" confused her. "Oh. Didn't I say? Didn't I say my three-minute egg? And see it's fresh!"

In the way of deaf old people, she barked all of this out so she herself could hear it, which meant the family of four heard it, too, and were enjoying it a lot. It was as good as one of Will's shows.

I told my mother all of this. The "slaughtering a hog" part had Walter laughing so hard he could have washed the dishes back there in his tears.

"And she wants her egg fresh so you better lay another one," I added. That broke my mother up and got Walter, hearing my mother laugh, laughing even harder until he was so overcome with it he had to sit on the floor.

I skimmed back into the dining room on the waves and swells of their laughter, my sails flying, and wondered if I was always on stage, too.

Bunny Caruso's truck wasn't hard to pick out, it was so banged up and rusted out. It was parked in front of the grassy slope leading up to the courthouse.

The Rainbow Café was directly across from the courthouse. I wondered if Bunny was in there because she told me once that she didn't want to run into men in town she sometimes saw "under previous circumstances." That sounded mysterious enough, but I didn't question it. Mayor Sims and Dodge Haines were regulars in the Rainbow, plus other men from the bank, the jewelry store, and the telephone company. They had lunch in the Rainbow on a regular basis. Ulub and Ubub usually did too, but now both of their trucks were in Abel Slaw's garage in Spirit Lake being fixed, so they were hanging out on the bench in front of Britten's store. They usually did that anyway, only now they did it more.

It was true that it was almost all men in the Rainbow, as if it were some kind of a clubhouse, like the Rotary. The only regular woman customers were Miss Ruth Porte (a descendant of the founders, supposedly) and Miss Isabel Barnett. People said Miss Isabel was filthy rich, but she never acted like it. She was as nice as could be and she was also a kleptomaniac, which made her more interesting than some. Most of what she stole came from the five-and-dime and hardly amounted to anything. Lipsticks, cheap costume jewelry, hair nets, and stuff. Nobody ever said anything to her about this, as there was an arrangement with the Sheriff that after she'd stolen a few things over a period, she'd go to the courthouse and give him the money and he would pay whatever she owed for the stolen items.

Maud loved that. She said that Sam should be in the United Nations, settling squabbles between countries. She was not being sarcastic, either, when she said it. But of course she didn't say it to him, only to me. Maud said Miss Isabel must really want to be punished. I said it didn't sound like punishment to me, just having the Sheriff go and square things with the store owners. Maud said maybe it's having to admit it to the Sheriff.

I thought about that and sympathized with Miss Isabel Barnett, thinking of what *I* didn't want to tell the Sheriff. "If Miss Isabel would just stop being a kleptomaniac, she wouldn't have to tell him."

How true, Maud had said, smiling. How easy.

Maud was there behind the lunch counter working the old milk-shake maker, the aluminum container stuttering in her hands. Charlene was hanging her big chest over the counter with her chin on her linked hands trying to be cute. She was an awful flirt.

Maud looked around, saw me, and smiled. Her smile really made you think that of all the people who might have walked through the café's door, you were the one she wanted most to see. It was the most honest smile I think I've ever seen, except, of course, for the Sheriff's.

I didn't know whether I did or didn't want to see the Sheriff. It was hard facing him, knowing I should be telling him about Ben Queen and yet not doing it. And he knew I was holding back. There were a lot of little giveaways like me not meeting his eyes, or not inviting him to have some of my bowl of chili, and being clearly flustered if he and Maud started talking about the murder. I wouldn't pass a lie detector test, that's for sure. Anyway, the Sheriff wasn't in the Rainbow, hadn't been in for a couple of days, Maud had told me. He was being kept busy looking for suspects. That probably meant Ben Queen.

Bunny wasn't in the Rainbow and I wondered if she was the real reason I'd come in or if it was because I hoped the Sheriff would be there, or if I would at least find out from Maud if any "progress" had been made in solving the murder of Fern Queen. They didn't know anything about the Girl, for they didn't even know such a person existed. Ben Queen and I knew, though. There were times I thought I would collapse under this knowledge, as if a house had fallen in. But I have to admit that at the same time, it was exciting. It was exciting to be the one who knew and could look at what was going on and see the folly in it. For they shouldn't have been looking for Ben Queen at all; they should have been looking for Her.

I finally found Bunny in Miller's Market where she does her shopping. I asked her if she'd do me this favor and explained what it was.

"I sure will, hon." She was over by the fruit stand, shaking a cantaloupe and holding it to her ear. "These darn things is hard as bowling balls. Just see." She handed me the cantaloupe, meaning me to shake it, which I did, though I didn't know why. "You'd know what's ripe and what's not, with all your hotel experience."

Whatever gave Bunny that idea, I can't say. But it was nice to be looked on as an authority. I shook it, but had no idea what was supposed to happen unless it was loose seeds sounding. I smelled it too. "It's not ripe *at all,*" I said, as if I knew. Disgruntled, I put it back and picked up another. I shook and sniffed this one and handed it to Bunny so she could, too. "This one's okay."

Finally, we were climbing into her truck. I asked her why she'd parked so many blocks away from Miller's, near the courthouse, and she said because she needed to see Sam. "Only he ain't there today." She sounded wistful, and I wondered if every woman in La Porte was in love with the Sheriff except for Maud and me. I told Bunny he was busy with all of this murder business.

"Oh, God, yes," she said. "I clean forgot that."

As we drove out of La Porte I told Bunny about my dinner date at the Silver Pear, a restaurant near White's Bridge Road. It was with my aunt, I said, from Miami, Florida. She was on her way to New York and was stopping to see us. I reported how this aunt had driven the Tamiami Trail and up the west coast of Florida. She lived every winter in the Rony Plaza Hotel. "Which is extremely luxurious," I added. Bunny exclaimed over all of this, about how my aunt must be real adventurous to do all that driving,

"And rich," I put in, to live at the Rony Plaza. "She also spends a lot of time at Hialeah, that racetrack? With all the flamingos in the middle?"

It was nice to be able to talk like this with no fear of any of it getting back to my mother, since my mother never talked to Bunny. My mother considers her not only common, but worse; even worse than Toya Tidewater or even June Sikes (who lives near the hotel and presents, I guess, a greater danger for that reason).

We drove past fields where cows grazed, lifting their square heads to chew in that dumb way of cows that makes you wonder if they know where they are and what they're doing. ("Is this grass? Do I eat it, or what?") We passed the Christmas tree farm that I thought really disillusioning and that I would never let any little kid see. Past the ramshackle trailer park and a rundown little shopping place.

It was comfortable driving along in silence and surprising, too, as I thought Bunny was more the chatterbox type, only she wasn't. When there was talk, I did most of it, tossing in details about my aunt's days in Miami—the beach just beyond the Rony Plaza, and the royal palms and poincianas. And did she ever hear of Whirlaway? Bunny would just shake her head in wonder, or click her tongue, words not sufficing. And of course that only encouraged me to fill in more awesome scenes such as the Key West sunset and how it would throw its pink and lavender lights across the water.

"My goodness, but it sounds like paradise!"

I agreed and wondered if either of us would ever see it.

Last of the Butternuts

15

The Silver Pear is an expensive restaurant on what the Lake Noir people call the Lake Road, but which is actually just an extension of White's Bridge Road. Maud says the Silver Pear's food isn't a patch on the Hotel Paradise's; she says my mother could cook better blindfolded. Still, the restaurant is in a huge and pretty Victorian house with a wide, wraparound porch, where customers can eat in warm weather. It is painted a soft gray-brown, much like the bark of the trees that surround it. It blends into its woodland setting in much the same way as the Devereau house blends with the trees on the other side of Spirit Lake.

Since Bunny's truck still sat in the driveway after I got out, I figured she wanted to see me safely up the stairs. So I climbed them and stopped on the porch to wave. Tables were set up on the porch and a few diners were observing Bunny and her truck, which looked out of place amidst all of the fancy foreign cars in the restaurant's parking area.

But still Bunny didn't leave, so, waving again, I walked through the open doorway. Was Bunny waiting to make sure my aunt was there? I disappeared from her view and stood by one of the side windows and watched her truck rattle down the gravel drive.

"May I help you?"

The voice made me jump. A man stood behind me with menus clutched to his chest. He was wearing a powder blue linen suit, and his hair was cut in a high silvery sort of pompadour.

I told him I was just watching for my aunt who was supposed to pick me up here. I didn't want to say I was to meet her here or he'd go check his list of reservations. I know enough about how a dining room runs to figure that out.

"I just saw someone driving away out there. Could that have been her in that old truck?" His nose twitched like a rabbit's.

"Of course not," I said, making my tone resentful. Would my aunt drive *that?*

"Oh," he said, and simply smiled and stayed.

If he was the headwaiter, why didn't he get back to his customers? You wouldn't catch Vera standing around in the dining room doorway gawking. And now here came another one. He was clutching menus, too, wearing a powder beige suit and his hair, similarly cut, was more ivory than silver. Then I remembered Maud had said their names were Ron and Gaby something. Something German, I seemed to remember. They did not look at all German. They looked more like the butterfly population out back of Dr. McComb's house. They simply looked fly-away, and I wished they would, but they didn't.

Why is it when you're up to no good, the world wants to visit. And how could they be so interested in a twelve-year-old with no money?

The first man explained to the second why I was there. I said I'd wait outside on the porch and thanked them. Did they watch me go as I'd watched Bunny? It was a peculiar feeling, imagining four eyes riveted on my back. But I couldn't hang around so I just walked down the steps and out the gravel drive.

It was barely a quarter of a mile to White's Bridge, which lay farther along the same dirt road, which I supposed to be White's Bridge Road, although I saw no sign. The walk was truly pleasant, with the smell of pine needles mixing with the fresh breeze off the lake. I couldn't see Lake Noir from here, but knew it was close by. It's the popular, rich people's lake.

Maud Chadwick lives in a small house on the lake, not far from Bunny. Maud's has a long wooden pier out over the lake. I've never been there, but I heard she has a chair and a lamp (with a really long extension cord) on the pier and she likes to sit there reading and drinking cocktails. The Sheriff is always complaining about that extension cord and the lamp being so close to the water, but she pays no attention to him. Or maybe she just likes the idea of the Sheriff worrying about what happens to her. She keeps vodka out on the pier in an ice bucket. Mrs. Davidow described it all to my mother, both of them laughing fit to kill. Yet, it wasn't unkind laughter; it was more appreciative. Anyway, Mrs. Davidow could hardly laugh unkindly at someone who spent her nights drinking martinis.

I thought about Maud as I pulled up a hayseed and chewed on it the way old-timers do. I pictured the lamp and the book and the bottle in the ice bucket, and wished I could go slowly by in a boat, for in my mind's eye it was such a pretty scene: the lamp shining on the pier and spilling over into the black water. But, then, I guess what your mind's eye sees is often better than the thing itself. I've never seen the Rony Plaza, after all. It probably looks nothing like what I imagine, nothing so grand. It may not be set among royal palms and poincianas, but still I see it that way.

I came to White's Bridge, a plank bridge that rumbles whenever a car crosses it. I was still thinking about Maud, the lamp being the only thing lit against the black night and black water, this image soon surrendering to the one of Mary-Evelyn, floating on the surface of Spirit Lake, her white dress lit like a big candle, floating in the darkness of night, woods, and water. What I felt was what I felt about Maud on the end of the pier, though I could never have said why. It made me stop on the other side of the bridge and ponder as I chewed my hayseed.

And then an image of the Girl came to me, how I'd first seen her at the railroad station in Cold Flat Junction in her dress of such a pale blue it seemed faded out to more a memory of blueness; her hair as pale as moonlight, her strange stillness, so that it was almost as if she was disappearing as I watched. Then how I'd seen her when I was trying to catch butterflies around Spirit Lake. I looked across the lake to the Devereau place and there she'd stood, where nobody should have been because nobody lived there. To me, she was just "the Girl"; she was one more thing I hadn't told the Sheriff about.

Two hours was how long I'd told Bunny I'd probably be (for she said she'd drive me back) and I'd frittered away nearly a half hour of it between the Silver Pear and stopping to think, so I put on a little speed for the last five minutes of my walk to Mirror Pond. It was a walk on soft marshy ground through leaves and branches that must have lain there since the year zero, so undisturbed did they look. But of course that was another illusion, for the area had been trammeled and sifted over by the police, and before that by Fern Queen and her killer two weeks ago.

The yellow tape that warned POLICE CRIME SCENE—DO NOT CROSS had been taken down. This made me feel sad, for it was as if the place was being returned to its long-gone-and-forgotten self, as if nothing had happened here. And I was sorry too because that canary-yellow tape was bright and cheerful, no matter what its message. It leant the place an air of habitation, of people and strolls and picnics.

This was plain silly; people hadn't picnicked here. I was wasting time. Yet, time, here, seemed meant to be wasted if it existed at all. It was the same sense I got about Cold Flat Junction.

Mirror Pond itself was not, as Suzie Whitelaw reported, clear and tranquil. It was overgrown with rush grass and weeds; you could barely see the water. It was the sort of place to sink a body in, though Fern Queen's had simply been lying at its edge.

Now the place looked returned to itself as if a page had fluttered backward in a book to what I'd read once and now read again. The pond was in a clearing, and two dirt roads came together here, though the one that went straight on was little more than a trail. White's Bridge Road, which I'd been walking on, turned to the right in the direction (at least I thought it was) of Spirit Lake. Going halfway round the lake is an old road no one uses anymore which passes the Devereau house and wanders off in this direction. It was this road Ben Queen must have driven his truck down when he went to the Devereau house that night, driving in on the other side of the lake, miles away.

I picked up a small, dry branch and drew lines in a patch of dirt at my feet, just to clarify this road business to myself. Where these two roads intersect, here, there's an ancient filling station with two bubble pumps and a clapboard building where they probably sold oil and soft drinks and things like that. The name of the place on the sign above the door, weathered nearly to invisibility, was FRAZEE. It's mostly faded out and hard to read, but there are a lot of Frazees around, so it's a safe guess. There were signs in the one window that still had glass in it for Clabber Girl Baking Powder and Mail Pouch Tobacco.

I wondered how long it had been since a car had stopped here. And how could there have been enough traffic to keep the filling station going? Sunlight, in a sudden sweep across the clearing, speckled the glass of the one remaining window. Looking at the pumps, I grew more and more heart-heavy. It was just so deserted. I have this feeling for abandoned places: it's as if they're more real than the ones where folks hang out and the ones people flock to. The bench, the building—Frazee's was like the ghost of Britten's Market.

I shook myself, wondering what I meant and knowing I should stop, for I felt the blue devils coming.

"Hey! Girlie!"

I turned so fast I nearly lost my balance. "You shouldn't sneak up behind a person like that!"

The old man—who I remembered from when Will and Mill and I came here—was standing less than ten feet away. He yelled—certainly louder than necessary—"Ain't you the one came with them police couple weeks ago?"

I nodded and walked over to him so that he'd lower his voice. "I was with them, yes."

"How come you're back here, then?"

"You know how police work is. We've got to go over and over an area where there's been a kill—, uh, a homicide."

He spat into a patch of leaves and fern. I guessed he was chewing some of that Mail Pouch Tobacco. As old as he was, he'd know all about the filling station.

As if arguing this point, he said, "Hell, I live right down there—" He shook his black walking stick off in a direction behind them. "I been here for near ninety years. My name's Butternut."

"I remember. There've been Butternuts around here for over a hundred years."

His eyes squeezed. "How'd you know that?"

"You told us."

Mr. Butternut looked up at the blank, cloudless sky. He seemed to be waiting for God to second what I'd said. "More'n a hunnert years, you're right. See down there?" Again, he took up his stick and pointed off down the road. "My house's down there. Lived in it all my life long. So did my daddy before me. My daddy's name was Lionel. Lionel Butternut lived to be a hunnert and one. I'm the last."

Mr. Butternut wasn't much taller than me. Age must've been shrinking him down and maybe instead of dying, he'd just disappear, blow off like puff ball filaments. Then I remembered Mr. Butternut had told Will (who'd said he and Mill were policemen) how he heard a car or a truck up here the night Fern Queen was murdered.

"Where was that truck when you heard it, Mr. Butternut. I mean exactly?"

"Ain't no 'exactly,' I just did. I was asleep and it woke me up." Impatiently, he said, "I done told all that to them lawmen. That there skinny po-liceman thinks he's God. He said I better tell 'em ev'rthing I seen and heard. Well, a 'course I did, why wouldn't I?" He spat another stream of tobacco against a rock. "They was out here and down the road lookin' for tire tracks, they said."

"Was it a car or a truck?"

"Truck. But there was more'n one ve-*hic*-le."

"You said one of them drove by your house."

"It did."

"What about the other one?" I remembered that Axel's taxi had driven Fern Queen here that night.

He was looking down at his feet, scraping mud off his shoe.

"Mr. Butternut?"

"Yeah?" He didn't look up.

"The *car.*"

"What car?"

I gritted my teeth. The Sheriff had to go through this all the time with witnesses. How did he stand it? I meant to ask him, whenever we were friends again. I was seized by a sudden and terrible breath of cold as if all around it had turned winter. Would there ever after be a rift, like the water between a drifting boat and the shore? Would there always be a distance in our friendship?

"You said there was another vehicle."

"Well, there was." He made it sound as if I'd been arguing the point.

"Did it go by your house too?"

For a long moment he said nothing, just looked off down the road to his house. Then he pointed that way with his briar stick. "Randalls lived down there further along from me. Bud Randall, he up and died like four, five years ago. Then there were the . . . what the jumpin' Jesus was their name? Lived here a long time."

I wanted to shake him hard. But then I recalled the Sheriff once telling me you should never hurry a witness, unless it meant someone might die because the witness was too slow giving up the information. *Witnesses have to find their own way,* he'd said. That if you try to yank back from the path they want to go on down, they'll forget something important. Happens all the time, the Sheriff had said.

Mr. Butternut wasn't giving two hoots for whatever I thought; he was still on that name he couldn't remember.

"Frazee!" he exclaimed. "That's the next house, about a half

mile down there. Frazees owned that fillin' station—" He pointed his stick in that direction now. "—but that was when there was lots of summer folks lived around here." He was lost again in thought. "There's a old summer cottage back in there, back from the road, but there ain't no path to it no more, it's been so long somebody ever lived in it. Calhouns did once. But you ain't goin' back in there, no ma'am."

"Why not?" It was an automatic reaction with me, that if someone said I wasn't to do a thing, I wanted to do it.

"They's things." He was looking off toward those woods. Now he was humming.

"What things?"

He shied me a glance like a flat stone skipped in water. Cunning, that's what it was. Then he said, "I'm makin' cocoa. Want some? Come on."

Whether I did or didn't, he turned and walked back down the road. I looked at my watch. More time gone and I still hadn't found any new information. I supposed he'd already told the Sheriff or Donny about the car and truck. Yet, Mr. Butternut might still be the most likely source of something new coming to light. If I could just remember to let him find his own way to it. Which I doubted.

For all the Butternuts who must have lived in it, his house was small. It was also cold. In the cold fireplace sat an old pot-bellied stove. Mr. Butternut opened the little metal door and looked in. "Thought so. Them coals is nearly ashes. But we'll get 'er goin' in a minute." He shoveled coal from the bucket through the opening and then took the bellows to it with a lot of enthusiasm. He must have been one of those people who get a kick out of fires. "There goes. Room'll heat up in no time." He stood and watched the black stove, looking satisfied. It was surprising how soon the coals started burning. I could see the flames' reflection on his face, turning it several shades of pink. It was almost sinister.

He rubbed his hands with enthusiasm and said, "Now for the Ovaltine."

"Cocoa, you said." He didn't answer. Pretended, probably, that he hadn't heard. I was sitting at a long wooden table that was probably where all the Butternuts had eaten for a hundred years. Mr. Butternut got a fire in the cast iron stove going; it was a coal or wood-burning one, the kind we had in the little kitchen. This was the kitchen we used when we stayed at the hotel in the cold months. I love that stove. You lift the four black tops off with a special handle. Sometimes I cook mushrooms right on the surface without a pan.

Mr. Butternut muttered as he got the Hershey's cocoa tin out of the cupboard and lined up the sugar and pan and other things he'd need. He was talking to himself as if no one were here at all, which I thought pretty much wasted the visitor experience. I doubted he had many of them. But, then, I don't know—maybe if you'd lived nearly all your life alone, just having someone there wandering around might make you less lonely. Talk wasn't even necessary.

I walked around the room that served as dining and living space—the kitchen was off to the right. There were two big easy chairs near the stove, gathered there for warmth and firelight. They were covered in a faded sprig-patterned muslin. The arms wore those separate little sleeves of the same material to keep the upholstery from rubbing too much. I took one off and the material underneath showed its little flower sprigs in blues, pinks and yellows so much brighter you'd think a garden might have bloomed there on the chair arm.

"Don't take nothin' now," said Mr. Butternut loud as a belfry bell and without turning from the milk pan he was watching on the stove.

"Of course, I won't." I got as much indignation into my tone as I could.

"You got to have a warrant to search the prem-ises, if that there's what you're figurin' on doing."

To his back, I said, "I told you I wasn't part of the police. Anyway, I'm not searching, I'm only looking." He said nothing to this, and I would have said he watched too many police shows, but I didn't see a television set anywhere. Around the walls were stacks and stacks of magazines, mostly *Time* and *National Geographic.* Probably he just looked at the pictures, like I did. I didn't see many books, only six or seven in a small green-painted bookcase. This stood at one end of a camp bed against the rear wall. A gooseneck lamp sat on top of the bookcase positioned for reading in bed. There were other rooms I could see through the door of this one; there must have been a bedroom back there, but maybe when it was cold, Mr. Butternut slept out here, to get the benefit of the pot-bellied stove.

The camp bed was covered with a light blue chenille bedspread, the kind that I've always loved. I sat down on it and ran my hand over the little tufts of cotton that crossed one another in a diamond design. I wondered what it would be like to be completely alone, like Mr. Butternut. I tried to picture myself here, lying at night on the bed with the lamp light falling over my shoulder onto the pages of a book. I looked in the bookcase: *Hiawatha* was there and a book

called *The Yellow Room* and some mysteries. I imagined myself reading and listening to night sounds—which I had to make up: whippoorwills, maybe; tiny branches scratching and tapping against the curtained window; a bark, a howl. . . . When the howl overtook my imagination, I snapped my eyes open.

"Whatcha doin'?" Mr. Butternut was standing there with the cocoa mugs.

"Nothing. Just thinking." I got up, took my mug, and followed him to the table. "I guess you don't have anything to eat, do you?"

"Crackers, maybe. There's that fancy restaurant you must've passed."

"I know; I was there. But I didn't eat."

He had risen to get a box of saltines, which he put on the table. We sipped in silence for a few moments. It was not unpleasant, but I was disappointed I hadn't found out more than I knew when I came. Except, of course, what cottages sat along this road and back in the woods.

Things. He had said there were "things" down the road. Probably, he was just making it up. I looked at my watch and saw less than an hour before Bunny was to return to the Silver Pear and pick me up. "What did you mean about 'things' happening in that house?" He better not ask "What things" again.

Mr. Butternut pursed his lips. "Brokedown House."

"What?"

"That there cottage. Brokedown House."

I considered the name. *Brokedown House.* It made a soft explosion in my mind, like a silent firework, showering sparks. *Wow.* "What about it?"

He sighed and ate a marshmallow. "Beats me. Except it's gone pretty much to rack and ruin. I seen lights out at the back." He ate his other marshmallow.

"There's nothing so strange about that. Maybe it was a flashlight or a lantern." I was pleased with myself for coming up with this reasonable view of a presence in the woods.

"You're doin' good considerin' you ain't never seen it."

This really irritated me in the way things do if there's truth in them. "It was probably just somebody hunting."

He cracked a smile at me. "Ain't hunting season. Ain't nothin' much to poach till fall, anyways."

"There's squirrel. There's rabbits. Raccoons."

He flapped his hand at me, impatient with my ignorance. "You don't know nothin' about it."

"Well, I'm *only* a schoolgirl." Here was a defense rarely uttered.

He sighed as if he'd had to put up too long with schoolgirls.

But why did I stray from the point just to defend myself? I'd make a terrible policeman. "When did you see it? This light?"

"Last time's couple days ago. Nights, I mean."

"But when did it start? How long ago?"

He pursed his lips as he set down his mug. "Some time ago, but I don't attend much to time. There's things happened yesterday that seems like they did a year ago. And vice-y vers-y." He chuckled.

"Then how about the truck or the cars you said you heard? Maybe you saw the truck go by and maybe you didn't?"

"Oh, I seen it all right. I'm just not exactly sure when. Gettin' old, I guess. But nothin' happens round here gets by me, no, ma'am."

It was then it occurred to me: Mr. Butternut had been in the road when Will and Mill and I came that first time. He'd been there this time, too. So why not nearby the night of the murder? But he'd already told Donny he neither saw nor heard anything suspicious, except for the vehicles. "Are you sure you weren't—?" No. "Do you think maybe something else happened, something you saw or heard and just forgot?"

"Well, now that's kinda dumb. Ain't you asking me do I remember something I forgot?" He dropped the spoon he'd been fooling with back in the mug. "I'm havin' more o' this cocoa. Want some? I've only got but one marshmallow, though."

Generously, I told him to have it, as I knew he would anyway. "What I meant was, maybe you saw something and didn't *know* it was important."

"Same difference. If a 'coon run by me and I didn't know it was important *then,* how would I know it was important *now,* 'less you told me a 'coon shot that woman?" He thought this was really rich and laughed the milk into the pan and the pan onto the stove.

I said, "Let's go over there."

He stopped stirring the milk. "Over where?"

What a pest. "To that house."

"Brokedown House? No indeed, we ain't."

"I will then." No, I wouldn't; you wouldn't catch me going into woods I didn't know. But I got up and pushed my chair back. My resolve must have been serious, to make me give up a second cup of cocoa. But I wasn't going there alone. "I'll go by myself, then."

"Now, girlie, that ain't smart." He was putting the one marshmallow into his cup, ready for the cocoa to be poured. "You got a gun?"

"Do I look like I have a gun?" I spread my arms wide.

He made a disagreeable noise in his throat. "Guess not. Well, okay, then." He pushed the pan away from the burner. His briar stick was leaning against the counter, and he took it up. "Guess I'm ready as I'll ever be."

Brokedown House

16

Down the road we walked, carrying flashlights he had supplied, and arguing who would go into the woods first.

We stopped to argue by a bed of dark nasturtiums looking almost black in the shadows cast by a mossy oak, and I wondered who had planted them, for they didn't appear to belong to any house here. Mr. Butternut said I should be the one to go in first, as it was my idea, and also he had a bad leg and needed his stick, which meant he had only one hand free if he had to shove something. I asked, Like what? He said, You never can tell. I said that he was the adult here, that I was just a kid, that he knew the woods and house a lot better, and even if he only had one hand free, still, he was bigger and stronger than I was. I actually didn't think this, as he wasn't much bigger than me, and probably no stronger. He wasn't as limber, that's for sure.

Like most arguments, this one was never settled; we just stopped talking about who'd go first when we got to a place where the end of a driveway headed off to the right. You could just make out the beginning of it because it was so overgrown with saw grass and moss and a wilderness of bushes. Felled limbs lay across its path; dead leaves were ankle thick. It seemed even denser than the woods surrounding the Devereau house, or maybe it was even part of it. I guess curiosity urged me on and I said all right, I'd go first.

"But you're to come directly behind me."

He agreed, but he didn't do it. I picked my way through what seemed like solid walls of bushes. Rhododendron and mountain laurel were heaped so high I couldn't see over the tops. It was as confusing as a maze. I had gone only thirty or forty feet when I looked back. Mr. Butternut was nowhere to be seen. I called several times, "Mr. Butternut! Mr. Butternut!" Finally he answered, but his voice was distant enough that I just knew he hadn't even started in yet.

To get back I had to pick my way through brambles and briars. Then I saw him; he'd taken no more than a half dozen steps inward, probably only because he knew I was coming back. I was ten feet away and really mad. "You're to stay *close.* You've hardly moved an inch. I can't do all the work!" Since whatever "the work" was wasn't clear, and since Mr. Butternut hadn't wanted to do it in the first place, my argument was pretty weak. But he couldn't remember anyway. He shone his flashlight in my face and I squinted and put my hand up to wave it off.

"It's this here ol' knee that's actin' up."

"Come *on.*"

He did, but he was grumbling.

It was dusk, but I could scarcely see light above the tangle of branches and the tops of the black pines. I could barely see the sky.

"Mr. Butternut?"

Rustle of bushes, cracking of twigs, what sounded like thrashing about with his stick. "I'm here! Never did see so many vines and stuff . . ."

I had to go back to where he was. I found him, sitting on a log. "What's wrong?"

"Ain't nothin' *wrong,* except we oughtn't t' be here anyways." He was poking the dark with his flashlight again, making me squint.

"I'm going on ahead," I said. "You're the backup, so come on. It's not that far, you said yourself."

He wobbled up. "Said lots o' things I wisht I didn't."

Brokedown House wasn't big, but still it seemed to loom. Whatever was left over from light outside did not penetrate inside. I switched on my flashlight. The place was still furnished with wicker chairs and tables and a love seat. If they hadn't been painted white I don't think I could have made out their shapes. Then I caught my foot on the corner of a heavy footstool and stumbled and dropped the flashlight. I straightened up. I thrust my arms out the way you do when you're going by touch. For a few moments I felt I knew what it was like to be blind. I passed through an archway that might have been to another part of the living room or parlor. I think there were bedroom doors on either side of this part of the house. I groped for my flashlight, although the sound it had made when it fell told me that it had rolled and was out of reach. Because there'd been light a moment ago, the lack of it made the darkness darker. All I wanted to do was leave.

Mr. Butternut must have shuffled in behind me. There was total darkness until he clicked on his flashlight and shined it right at me. "Get that out of my *face!*" But the light remained. I brushed at it as if it too were cobwebs.

"Girlie! Girlie!" His voice came from a distance.

From outside, from somewhere up the path. That moment looking into that white light must have contained every fright I ever felt. It held the nights when I was three or four and knew my bedroom at night was the most dangerous place on earth (I would have to go sit on the floor outside my mother's door); it held the day I got lost in a crowd of people doing their Christmas shopping, walking around me as if I were a rock in the middle of a stream; it contained the time Mrs. Davidow had gotten so furious with me she lay down on the floor and beat her heels; it held the doctors' needles, the dentists' chairs. The fright was all of that, it was acid, it was all of that distilled into that moment when the light was thrown, like liquid, full in my face.

My voice was a dry rasp in my throat. The air was choked with fear. My feet (which felt like they belonged to other legs than mine) were backing up. After that first lightning bolt of fear, I could think only of getting out. I turned and lurched toward the door. Once outside I moved as fast as the undergrowth would let me. I forced myself finally to stop and listen. There was nothing, no rustle of trees, no animal sounds, no sound to show I was being chased. There was no sound at all. How could there be no sound in such a place? A place where wild animals must hunt at night, where owls must roost in treetops. If a cone had dropped on velvet needles, if a star had laid a silver track across the sky, if the dead had turned in their graves—I swear I would have heard it, that's how silent it all was.

Breathing hard, I leaned against the thick trunk of an oak tree, wondering where Mr. Butternut's voice had come from. It seemed to me I should have reached him by now, or at least got closer to him. I knew I was closer to the road and I found my voice at last, cupping my hands around my mouth, I yelled: "Mr. Butternut! Mr. Butternut!"

He couldn't be that far away—unless he'd turned tail and gone home. But I didn't think he'd do that. At most, he'd just go back to the end of the driveway and wait for me. And then I heard it:

". . . lie, *Girl*— . . ."

It was a thread of sound. *Girlie, Girlie,* was what he'd been calling. But half of it was lost in the night air. If there'd been anything to stir up the woods at all—a wind, a falling branch—I'd never have heard him at all.

He was too far away.

I finally realized what had happened; I had left by way of a side door, mistaking it, in blind fear, for the front. Instead of running toward the road, I had run away from it. I had gone deeper and deeper into the woods. Which meant I'd have to go back. I wouldn't have to go *in* the house, but I'd have to go back; I'd have to pass by it, and me without a flashlight.

Go back there? No. I kept on going, slowly, deeper into the woods. I was too scared to have held onto any sense of direction. I looked upward to see if there was any break in this huge canopy of leaves and branches; light was gathering in, I was sure, and anyway the branches looked locked together in some kind of death dance. Because I'd lost direction, I wasn't sure I was going in a straight line away from the house; I could have gone off at an angle—several angles, maybe, a zigzag pattern.

Twigs snapped. I jerked around. It was one of those noises you think someone's trying hard not to make. My stomach seized up. I couldn't tell what direction the snapping came from in this dense place, or whether my ears magnified it, which wouldn't be surprising, what with every nerve and muscle, every cell and filament cocked to hear. I stood perfectly still, worrying over how my calling out for Mr. Butternut could have given away my position. How stupid that had been. But then I'd supposed I was safely near the road.

Carefully, I moved to a huge oak whose trunk and lower branches were so gnarled and deformed the tree looked blasted. The way the branches grew, the tree would be easy to climb, at least its lower branches would. I got easily to the second tier of branches, some of which swooped down so far their ends drooped heavily along the ground. I sat with my legs dangling on either side of a big knuckle of wood; it was like sitting in a saddle. Even though I was not all that far off the ground, I could be well hidden by the drapery of leaves I was now looking through. With some care, I could go even farther up the tree, but the branches directly above me reached upward as if they were beseeching heaven.

Here I was in a place as dense and damp as a rain forest, where there might have been bright birds and unfamiliar foreign flowers, but I saw nothing except my white socks sticking out below my jeans. They were as bright as the light had been in my face. I almost got my feet up on the branch and was taking off a shoe when I heard a shuffling nearby. I froze. Rabbit, 'coon, possum—it could have been anything. Fox, mouse. But it wasn't the startled movement of an animal; it was measured, like footsteps coming across the wet, black leaves and undergrowth.

I was so intent, so *listening,* that I knew every sound must have been magnified and distorted. I forced myself to move my hands and part the leaves. There was a flare of light that showed a man's face, or at least the part I could see from my perch in the branches looking down. He had a shotgun, broken, over his arm, and was smoking a cigarette. The light had come from a match.

Like a coal miner, he had a light attached to a cap. I could see this because he switched it on to bend down and look at something; then he straightened up and switched it off. He was wearing a wool jacket. He leaned against the tree and went on smoking. He did *not* have a flashlight, I was sure, as the light strapped around his forehead would serve that purpose and leave him free to handle the gun. This light was yellow and duller than the one that had shown in my face, but could I be sure he was not the person inside the house? Could I be sure of anything?

But why was he hanging about down there? Then I remembered arguing with Mr. Butternut about poachers. He was probably just a poacher! My body went slack with relief and I sighed and let my head fall against the bump of wood.

"Hey!" Suddenly, he'd stepped back and looked up. Then he snapped the shotgun up.

"Don't shoot me! Don't shoot me!" Quickly, I left the branch for another.

"What the *fuck*?"

I was scrambling down as fast as I could.

"Who in *hell*? . . . What're you doing up that tree, for Lord's sakes?"

Once on solid ground and picking scabs of bark from myself, I told him I'd got lost.

He was taller than he'd appeared, looking down on him. He was also strong-looking; even through the jacket I could see a slight bulge of muscle in his upper arm as he broke the shotgun again (which I appreciated) and leaned it against the tree. It wasn't a jacket he wore but a heavy shirt that did service as one. It was red or blue plaid. In the dull yellow light of his lamp, I couldn't tell colors. I couldn't tell the color of his eyes, either, but he had long eyelashes (the kind Ree-Jane claimed she had but didn't); in the downward reflection of the light, the lashes cast a little fretwork of lines under his eyes. The lamp lit the slant of his cheekbones and nose and the tilt of his chin, making dark slopes of the rest of his face. If he was ever in a lineup and I was the witness, he wouldn't stand a chance. Then he moved and the shadows shifted. He had crouched down and had his hand on a dead rabbit.

"What in the *fu*—?"

(I was hoping he'd say it again, but he caught himself.)

"—in the devil you doing out here in this place to *get* lost *in?* Ain't nobody comes out here, or never has been."

"There's you."

He stopped stuffing the rabbit in the sack (which already held others, I was sure) and just looked at me.

"All I was trying to do was to get to that road. Yonder." It was a word I'd always hoped to say. "Yonder somewhere." For it was the location of the road that had been causing me trouble.

He pointed at a slightly different angle, but not off mine by much. " 'Yonder' is that way."

"Maybe you could walk me there. I mean if you're through. What're you doing with those rabbits?"

"Never mind. I ain't going that way." He was really grumpy. I guess I'd butted into his poaching.

"But it's so dark. I'm only a kid." It was going against my principles, but I whined.

He just snorted. "Not too much of a one if you came in here in the first place."

I sighed. "How many rabbits you got in that bag, mister?"

He had slung the bag over his shoulder. The question made him a little uncertain. "None of your beeswax."

I couldn't help but smile. We used to say that in second or third grade. I always wondered what it meant, but this was no time to find out.

He must have thought my smiling meant something else. "What

do you care about rabbits? I shot a 'coon, too. In case you got any special feelings about 'coons."

"No. But hunting season's not until October. So you're poaching." This brought to mind the perfect circles of gold and white of my mother's poached eggs; I was hungry after being out here so long.

He just stood looking at me, trying to make me add up. "You don't know anything about it."

"Yes, I do. I'm friends with the Sheriff. He's told me about poaching."

"The sheriff."

It came out a statement, rather than a question. Now, he was sizing me up all over again. I smiled. "To get back to the road, I'd have to walk past that house," I pointed in its general direction, "and I'm afraid to."

He followed the line of my arm. "Brokedown House? There's nothing there."

"There is, too. There's *somebody*." As much as I didn't believe in hunting, I offered to carry the sack. "You've got that gun; you wouldn't want to trip."

"I ain't about to." He'd tossed his cigarette on the ground, pulverized it with his heel, and picked up the sack. "Okay, I'll walk you. Just remember: we never had this conversation."

"Right." Blackmail was a heady experience.

We started back in the direction of the house. Wanting him to have both hands free to handle the shotgun (if necessary), I offered again to carry the bag.

He said, "Never did tell me what you're doing here." The sack bounced on his back.

I tried to think, but it was hard, moving through the trees, getting closer to the house. "I lost my flashlight inside. It rolled away." I told him about the light in my face and Mr. Butternut.

He snorted: "That's one of the most damn fool stories I ever heard."

It wasn't, but it would be. "I'll tell you the truth: I've got this crazy old aunt lives out this way," I filled him in.

Shaking his head, he stopped. "I don't think even Billy Faulkner could come up with something like that."

"Who?"

He pulled the paperback book from the bag and held it up. *Light in August* was its title. "Oh, *him,*" I said, hoping I sounded well-read. "You mean *William* Faulkner."

"Yeah, well, I read so much of him, I figure we're on a nickname basis."

"*We* aren't. We don't even know each other's names."

He seemed to be thinking this over. Then he said, " 'A shape to fill a lack.' "

I screwed up my face. "What do you mean?" For a poacher, he sure had a way of talking.

"That's what Faulkner says about words. Or some words. Like 'love.' "

I squinted up at him. This talk didn't sound like his other talk.

He told me his name was Dwayne and I told him mine was Emma. He said that was a really nice name, but it didn't match up with me. I did not appreciate that, but didn't give him the satisfaction of asking what kind of girl it *would* match up with.

We were on White's Bridge Road now, and Dwayne said his truck was parked up there in the clearing, near the pond. He offered to drop me at the Silver Pear if I wanted. I'd said a friend was to pick me up there. It was by now nearly nine o'clock and Bunny would have come and gone, but that was all right, as I could always call Axel's Taxis. I didn't tell Dwayne it was past the time for my ride, as I didn't want him to feel guilty for leaving me at the Silver Pear, when, with his own vehicle, he could drive me the ten miles into La Porte. I pondered this, then decided it wouldn't be fair to blackmail him again. Besides we were by way of being pals by now. We were on a first name basis.

He wouldn't tell me his last name in case I forgot and "mentioned" it to "somebody." Why would anyone ever ask me? And even if they did, how many Dwaynes that looked like him and drove a truck were there around here? But I didn't say this so as not to insult his "power of deduction." The Sheriff talked about a person's "power of deduction" and that mine was extremely good. I don't want to compliment myself, but I think this is true, for I can almost always figure out who's guilty before the big courtroom scene on *Perry Mason*. So Dwayne's power of deduction was pretty bad if he couldn't see I knew enough on him to turn him in.

If it goes too hard on you, turn me in, came the voice of Ben Queen; it was the last thing he said to me. That got me thinking about Ben Queen's deductions. Because that's what it came down to; Ben Queen didn't *know* Mary-Evelyn Devereau's death was an accident. He was deducing it from what Rose said must've happened. Rose said it was an accident. And then a thought—more a hint than a thought—struck me almost like the white light flashed in my face in Brokedown House. Rose herself could easily be wrong. But you'd think from living in that house, she surely knew how awful the three sisters were to Mary-Evelyn. Unless—unless what? This was something I had to think about very clearly and I would have to wait until I was alone, back in the Pink Elephant, or on my corner of the porch.

Dwayne asked me what the matter was. He said I looked kind of pale. I told him because of a memory I had, and he said I was awful young to have memories that turned me pale. He said it as if he knew all about memories that turn you pale.

We picked up walking again, this time with me carrying the rabbits. I don't know why I insisted. The bag bounced against my back and I could feel their warm bodies. Or probably I was just imagining this, as I felt somehow guilty for their fate. I asked Dwayne if he'd read about the murder of this woman, Fern Queen, out here. Of course he had, he said, hadn't everyone? What about it? he said. You think I took a shotgun to her? he said. Of *course* I didn't think so. Of *course* not. I only wondered if he'd been out poaching that night—I could've put that better—and maybe saw something that he didn't want to tell the police because then they'd ask what took him over to that clearing that night.

To all of this, Dwayne grunted.

I asked him again if he was sure he'd never seen anybody in Brokedown House, or even seen anything at all, or heard anything. He told me no, and how many times did he have to say it? He was kind of crabby.

We were nearing Mr. Butternut's house and the clearing when we saw the cars and the lights, the domed red lights of three police cars. Several policemen were gathered around the cars. I could see one of the cars was La Porte's, the other two were state troopers. They were all angled in right in front of Mr. Butternut's. I was so surprised by this, I dropped the rabbit sack.

Dwayne grabbed it up and pulled me behind a moss-covered tree by a bed of nasturtiums so dark they looked black.

They were about forty or fifty feet ahead and I was trying to see if the Sheriff was there. I saw Donny standing with the troopers, his hand on his holster, as if he was going to draw at any moment and people better watch out.

Then the screen door opened and the policemen gathered on the road looked up at the porch. The Sheriff stood there and Mr. Butternut was holding the door open and they were talking. I couldn't hear anything except "Okay" and "I'll let you know." The Sheriff went down the steps then.

Dwayne whispered, "It's old man Butternut. What the hell's he been up to?"

"Do you know him?" I whispered back.

"Sure. He's lived around here forever."

What Mr. Butternut had been up to was (I was uncomfortably sure) not the point. What *I'd* been up to was.

The cars passed us and we watched them heading down the road we had just come up. We couldn't see them stop, but we heard them, heard car doors slam and voices raised. They were going to search the woods.

I should have told Dwayne we would have to stop by and tell Mr. Butternut I was okay, but it didn't mean as much to me to be nice to Mr. Butternut as it did to not get in bad with the Sheriff more than I already was.

Dwayne and I left our hiding placc and walked on a path he knew that paralleled the main road, passed Mr. Butternut's house, and ended up near Mirror Pond where his truck was parked. He seemed to be under the impression the cops had come for him until I asked why the La Porte police and the state police would get together just to look for poachers? Dwayne allowed as how that made sense. So they were here for some other reason, and maybe I was right; maybe there was somebody back there.

By the time we piled into Dwayne's beat-up truck, I wasn't so concerned any longer about the person in Brokedown House as I was with whether the Sheriff knew I was the one Mr. Butternut had called in about. (I guess I should have been more grateful.) But he didn't know who I was. I'd simply forgotten to introduce myself. All he could do was describe me, but there was nothing about me particularly describable. As the truck bumped over White's Bridge, I looked down at myself as if that might turn up something a person would remember about me and me alone, but I found I was perfectly ordinary. And my face looked like a lot of other faces so no one would recall anything particular. (Now, if it'd been Ree-Jane Mr. Butternut had met up with, I could hear him telling the Sheriff: *Pale blue eyes, look like they never had a thought behind 'em, and a real dumb expression, you know, emptylike, and this blond hair come out of a bottle. Skinny, too.*

We got to the Silver Pear, whose parking lot was crowded, for it was a fashionable hour for the Lake Noir people to eat, I supposed. All I needed to do was hop inside and call up Axel, and tell him to get here quick, since I was needed back at the hotel right away. For if the Sheriff *did* give it some thought, he might wonder what other child would be inspecting a crime scene (his powers of deduction being a lot more advanced than anybody else's). Well, I wanted to be home and in bed in case people came looking.

"Thanks a lot, Dwayne," I said, holding out my hand. "It was really interesting."

He turned in his seat to look at me, and I realized he was very good-looking. It was really my first opportunity to rate his looks. He was dark like Ben Queen, his hair and eyes much darker than the Sheriff's, and on the basis of looks alone, it would be hard to say who was the handsomest. I wondered how I came to be surrounded by handsome men—or was it just that they looked that way up against my plainness?

He said, "You sure do have a peculiar life for only being twelve years old."

"I'm actually nearer thirteen."

"Oh." He nodded. "Oh, well, that explains everything."

The silver-headed owner was very obliging about letting me use the restaurant's telephone, mostly, I figured, so he could listen in. For he was lavishly excited when he saw me, because hardly a half hour ago the sheriff's department had come in and asked if he'd seen a little girl in the vicinity. Well, of course he said yes, and asked what had happened.

"He—the sheriff—said you'd been reported as lost somewhere near here. Lost in the woods, he said."

I stood there frowning, holding my mouth open a little and breathing in an adenoidal way. At least I think I was; I've never been sure what an adenoid is, but I think it affects your breathing and makes you look sort of out of it. I shook my head in a wondering way, as good as asking, Are you stupid, or what?

I said, "Why do you think it was me? Do I look lost?"

He blustered. "No, no, not *now.* You don't look lost *now.*"

"Well, I didn't look lost before, did I?" I spread my arms out. "Do I look like I was *recently* lost?"

He sighed heavily and looked about to give up. It's interesting about adults, how little it takes to make them just roll over and refuse to deal with it. Talking to me, I can't say I blame them. "There are other kids around here, aren't there? I mean, I don't even *live* here. So it must be some kid who lives here and just wandered off into the woods."

He pursed his mouth and shoved the telephone toward me. We'd been standing by the wooden column with the little light where he kept the reservation book.

Lost girl

17

My eyelids flung themselves open like a blind snapping up, afraid I might have forgotten even now what I'd been thinking before I went to sleep. So I checked everything over: Mr. Butternut, Silver Pear, silver hair, Dwayne's shotgun, police, Donny swaggering around—check. Check. Check. Check. Yes, it was all there. (Of course, if there was something I *didn't* remember, how would I know?)

I would go into La Porte as soon as the breakfast chores were done, which would have been a lot sooner had Miss Bertha not sent back her three-minute egg, not once but twice, complaining it was overcooked. My mother was holding a heavy frying pan and hefting it, and I hoped she was going to brain Miss Bertha. But she set it down, removed her apron (which meant she was going into the dining room!), picked a fresh egg out of the bowl, and marched out of the kitchen, me dancing behind her.

She smiled in that dangerous way she has of smiling, greeted

I called Axel's Taxis and was told he'd be at the Silver Pear in a jiffy. I went out onto the porch, where diners sat at tables lit by candles, every once in a while flicking moths away. I rocked and munched a roll I'd taken from one of the breadbaskets lined up on a side table. The roll was cold and hard, a roll that would never have seen the inside of my mother's kitchen.

The cab pulled up in just twenty minutes, Delbert driving. I slammed the door and told him I'd like to get back to the hotel in a hurry. He took another road to Spirit Lake that was quicker than the highway to La Porte. Then I told him to go around by way of Britten's on the road that leads to the rear of the hotel so as not to wake anybody. He thought this was very considerate of me.

If the Sheriff had, for some reason, suspected the "lost girl" was me (and I don't know why he should, as far out of town as White's Bridge is), he apparently hadn't called to ask if I was here, since no one appeared to be up waiting for me. Probably, though, he was still out in the woods there searching; it made me feel guilty.

After I ate a bowl of potato salad in the kitchen (not turning on the lights), I went carefully up to my room. I lay in bed staring up at the ceiling, going over that night's events. So much had happened, these events seemed stretched out over nights and nights, over years of nights. I lay very quietly, my hands folded on top of the turned-down sheet, so as not to jar any part of the night loose into forgetfulness. Even this soon after it all happened, I had forgotten things like the exact color of the Silver Pear owner's hair, or the shadows of the leaves that had quilted Mr. Butternut's old face. And in time I would forget the way the light caught at Dwayne's eyelashes, or the smell of the rabbit bag.

Memory is slippery. I wondered, as I had wondered on the porch amidst all the talk of Florida: would the larger memories net the smaller ones and haul them back? Not just the memory of Mr. Butternut and his briar stick, but also the skin on his cup of cocoa? I read somewhere that we never completely forget a thing, that there are the imprints of everything we've ever seen or done, all of these tiny details at the bottoms of our minds, like pebbles and weeds that never surface from a river bottom.

Mrs. Fulbright kindly, then said, "Miss Bertha, this should be soft enough for you." Whereupon, she broke the egg onto Miss Bertha's plate, then turned and marched back into the kitchen, me pausing just long enough to catch Miss Bertha's reaction, then again dancing out to hear Walter's braying laughter back there in the shadows.

On that high note, my mother told me not to even bother with the damned old fool any more that morning and I almost sailed right out of the kitchen until I remembered my own breakfast. It was French toast and sausage and I ate it at the table with Walter, who was enjoying Miss Bertha's two rejected three-minute eggs. Walter said, "Tastes twice't as good, being the damned old fool's." Walter loves the way my mother puts things.

Delbert taxied me into La Porte and dropped me at the Rainbow Café. I had to find out about the police visit to Mr. Butternut and the woods. Since I wasn't supposed to have been there, I couldn't ask directly. The Sheriff generally stopped in the Rainbow midmornings to have coffee, so I would find out one way or another.

Maud was just taking her morning coffee break when I walked into the Rainbow and past Shirl, seated as always on her tall stool in front of the cash register. The morning coffee drinkers and early lunchers were there, including Ulub and Ubub (who must have walked to town, for their trucks were still in the garage). They gave me a cheery hello (though it came out "uh-o"). It was going on eleven A.M. Maud was just the person who would know about the White's Bridge incident, knowing the Sheriff as well as she did. Also, she was one of the few people in La Porte who had a lot of sense.

"Want some chili? It's just made."

My French toast breakfast was still crowding my stomach, so I said no thanks. But I needed something to do with myself in case the Sheriff walked in, so I said yes to the offer of a Coke. Maud stubbed out her cigarette and went to get it. It was nice being waited on for a change.

After she'd set the Coke before me, with a straw, she settled back into the booth and said, "There was something going on over near White's Bridge last night. In the woods there."

"Did someone else get murdered?" I asked that to let her know how far from a lost child I was thinking.

"No. Some man out there—named Butterfinger, I think—called up Sam and said this young girl had disappeared. Or got lost, he feared."

"No kidding? How did he know? I mean was she a relation of his or what?"

Maud shrugged. "I don't know. That was all Sam told me."

I wondered what Mr. Butternut had said to the police, whether he had played down his own role in this chapter of my life for fear he would be suspected himself of something awful. "Well, but did they find her?"

Again, Maud shrugged. "I guess we'll have to wait—Good! Here he is now."

She always sounded kind of joyful when the Sheriff appeared, no matter how she talked to him afterward. I kept my eyes down and sipped my Coke. My heart thudded, bumping around in my chest as if it only wanted a way out of its trouble. I still did not look up when I felt him standing by the booth.

"Emma."

He was just saying my name by way of hello. My eyes felt fastened to my glass, as if I couldn't raise them no matter what. I made a "hello" sound. Thank heaven Charlene was coming with his coffee and doughnut so that Maud didn't have to leave the booth. I did look up then to where Charlene simpered and managed to brush her chest against his arm when she set the cup down. He thanked her. She swayed off.

The Sheriff was looking straight across the table at me, smiling, but was the smile exactly what it used to be? I blinked. He raised his coffee cup.

Maud said, *"Well?"* in that tone that suggested he was holding out on her, being deliberately secretive, which he wasn't. She used that tone with the Sheriff a lot, and it was completely opposite of her earlier joy. I wondered a lot about Maud and the Sheriff.

"We didn't find her," he said, munching his doughnut. He liked plain doughnuts, not the iced ones or sugar ones. I didn't much see the point of a plain doughnut.

"What could have happened to her off White's Bridge Road?"

"Don't know." He sighed and took another bite out of his doughnut.

"You don't seem awfully *worried,* Sam!"

"If I worried about everything that came over my desk, I wouldn't have time to go out and search for people."

Maud was offended. "But you're the law!" There was that accusing tone again. You could almost see the words standing with their hands on their hips.

I was even *more* offended. After all, this poor girl could've been me. I almost said so, but thought better of it.

Maud asked, "How old was this girl? Did he say?"

" 'Bout Emma's age. He said around eleven, twelve, at most."

At that, my eyes snapped up from my empty glass. I don't look anywhere *near* eleven. My age has even been mistaken for fourteen by guests in the dining room.

The Sheriff regarded me with a bland expression as he polished off his second plain doughnut and picked up his coffee cup. "He said she could've been ten, even."

Ten! I had to wipe the indignation from my face and replace it with my dumb look, the one I'd copied from Walter: mouth slightly open, eyes partly closed. Walter would stand near the dishwasher shadows like this, thinking (or not thinking, seeing it was Walter).

"But what about the child's folks? Hasn't anyone reported her missing?" Maud asked.

The Sheriff shook his head. "Nope, not so far. This Mr. Buttercup who called—"

"Butter*n*—," I nearly corrected him.

He raised his eyebrows. "Yes, Emma?"

"It's just a funny name, that's all."

"Mr. Buttercup said he'd seen her near Mirror Pond, and that he'd talked to her and she wasn't from around where he lived."

"Then what on earth was she *doing* there?"

"I don't know, Maud. He said she seemed interested a lot in the murder of Fern Queen."

"Sam, this sounds *very* strange. It doesn't sound quite right."

"No, but it doesn't sound quite wrong either. Can I bum a cigarette?"

As she slid the pack toward him, I wondered what he meant.

"Are you sure this man's telling the truth?"

"No."

"Then he might have . . . done something to her himself and he's throwing you off the scent this way. I mean by calling the police himself."

"Possibly. But he sounded really worried."

I was glad *somebody* was.

"He seemed to blame himself for allowing her to go into the woods in the first place."

"Well, he damned well should!"

"He said she begged and *begged* just to see this derelict house."

I did *not!*

"But why would she want to see it?"

The Sheriff laughed. "Maud, you keep asking me why. I don't know. To me she sounded like one very curious kid." He pinched the match out he'd used to light his cigarette. "This Buttercup did tell me she said she'd been at the Silver Pear. He said it just didn't occur to him until they got separated in the woods that she must have been there with someone, her family or some adult. Little kids don't ordinarily eat out by themselves in restaurants. Like Emma, here."

"I'm not a little kid, anyway."

The Sheriff smiled. "Did I say you were? When I asked them, Ron and Gaby, they said, yes, a girl had been there but they didn't know her name."

I'd forgotten I'd told Mr. Butternut I'd come from the Silver Pear. It was the truth, too, which was even more annoying. "They should pay more attention to the customers instead of standing around."

"You've been there?" He sounded mildly surprised.

"Me? No." But then I thought, I might slip and say something that would show I'd been there, so I said, "I mean, not in a long time. Once I drove out to Lake Noir with Mrs. Davidow, and on the spur of the moment, she decided she'd like to have lunch there, and so I got to go too. The food is so—" What was Maud's word for it?

"Pretentious," she said.

"Pretentious, yes. Anyway, if this Mr. Butternu . . . Buttercup . . . murdered her and buried her, well, you'd have to get a lot more policemen out there searching than just four. I saw in an English movie where Scotland Yard got a whole long line of policemen—there must have been fifty or even a hundred—going over this field, and they all had to move forward at the same time. You'll have to get the dogs out too. They can sniff out the grave." I rather liked this scene as I was painting it, all of this trouble taken just to look for me.

"My God, Emma! Don't let your imagination run away with you!" said Maud.

"Always has before," said the Sheriff.

I didn't like the way he regarded me over the rim of his coffee cup. Just those blue eyes. And I didn't like some of the things he said; it was as if there was something underneath it, underneath the words he was saying. There was a phrase for this kind of thing, but I couldn't remember what.

"We did find some fresh footprints near that derelict house. There's been poaching going on in those woods."

Dwayne! Would the Sheriff find Dwayne if he really looked into this poaching? I don't think I was worried about Dwayne all that much, just how well he could describe me if the Sheriff talked to him. I must have groaned a little, for Maud asked me if something was wrong. I just shook my head.

"What are you going to do now?" Maud asked.

"There's hardly anything we can do, except maybe Emma's right. We could get up more men—get some from Cloverly if they can spare them. Trouble is, that would be pretty presumptuous when no one's reported a missing girl. I mean no family member. Without any evidence—" The Sheriff shrugged.

I was glad he wasn't going to bring anyone else in. For if he went to even more trouble to find out who the girl was, I hated to think how he'd react if he ever found out it was me and I let the police do all that for nothing.

"Wait," said Maud. "There's the owners of the Silver Pear. They must have described her, too, and at least if their description was like this Buttercup's, that at least would tell you he wasn't making it up."

The Sheriff had a studious look. "The description doesn't amount to much. She could've been a hundred girls. There was nothing to set her apart. Light hair, hazel eyes. But you're right, of course, they described the same person."

I looked down at my straw wrapper, ashamed there was nothing memorable about me. I was really disappointed. My eyes, that I liked to think were green, were only hazel. I rolled up bits of the wrapper and considered spitballs.

The Sheriff continued, "Now, one thing I did think might help is a composite drawing—you know, where the witness describes the subject and the artist draws him or her accordingly. Then show it around."

Well, I couldn't help myself; I looked up wide-eyed. But I quickly dissolved my fearful expression and looked down again.

Maud gave him a little punch on the arm. "That's brilliant. Only, you don't have a police artist, do you?"

"La Porte doesn't, no. But I'm sure I could find one if I want to proceed."

Imagine: my face, or near enough my face, shown all over kingdom come, maybe even pasted up on windows or tacked on poles, maybe in the Cold Flat Junction post office, next to the Drinkwater brothers who're still wanted for armed robbery.

HAVE YOU SEEN THIS PERSON?

Just imagine what Ree-Jane would do with *that!* It was then I remembered Bunny Caruso: why, she didn't even need a picture. She knew who I was and what if she just happened to mention in passing to the Sheriff (who I think she had a crush on) that she'd driven me to the Silver Pear? I kept my head down for I knew I was blushing furiously. I started tearing up the straw, having finished with the wrapper. All I seemed to be doing was getting in deeper and deeper; it was like a snowball rolling downhill that I didn't know how to stop, except by telling the truth, and I didn't want to do that, obviously. I heard the Sheriff say

". . . in the *Conservative*."

That made my eyes snap up. "What?"

Maud said, "Sam says they could run something in the paper about this girl—"

"Wait a minute!" I said, coming to my rescue. "Remember the Girl that I saw in La Porte?"

The Sheriff frowned. He was thoughtful. "I remember something about that but I never saw her."

I hated doing this; I hated "using" the Girl. I'm surprised I even brought her up, for I didn't want to let other people know anything about her. She was very mysterious and I was part of the mystery, I think. Not only that; I'd be endangering her, and Ben Queen too, which was unthinkable. I'd almost even rather tell the truth than that. "No, no. It couldn't be her. She's nearer . . . she's too old. But there's something, *someone* . . ." My hand gripped my forehead; my eyes were closed, and I must have looked like Mrs. Louderback over her tarot cards. "Listen: I remember now. I saw a girl walking the highway to Lake Noir. She was around my—she was eleven or twelve, I think. The only reason I noticed is she was alone. I mean, it's strange to see someone that age alone, isn't it? They're always with a gang of kids or a grown-up, at least. Someone." This made me wonder about myself. How must I appear to people? I saw her in my mind, walking along the highway by herself and she looked not so much lonely as left behind. Unclaimed, like a suitcase left in the Lost and Found. I set to wondering what her family was like. She had a family of sorts, it was just the wrong family. But I came to the conclusion family had little to do with her reason for walking out there by herself. No, it was something else.

I thought again of that day in Cold Flat Junction when I waited for the train back to Spirit Lake. I guess I was waiting for the Girl to turn up again. In that great stillness, I looked out over the flat empty land across the tracks, off to the line of dark trees where the woods began. I had seen this several times since, and it had never lost that look of land far away, unreachable, as far as imagination or the moon.

But all of Cold Flat Junction is like that. I remembered the small girl inside the empty schoolyard that I played Pick Up sticks with who had not said a word the whole time. On another day, there was a boy shooting a basketball by himself, and when he saw me, he stopped. Then there was the woman in black who I later learned must be Louise Landis, standing on the top step outside the rear door of the schoolhouse, shading her eyes with her hand and looking off toward that far horizon that surrounded Cold Flat Junction. What was she looking for? Ben Queen, perhaps. But way out there in the same emptiness I saw from my bench at the station. I had moved from that bench to the one directly across the tracks, for I was going in the opposite direction. Sitting there looking at the bench opposite, seeing myself still sitting there. I had felt either desolate or afraid, or perhaps they were in this case the same thing.

"Emma?"

I started, as if waking, surprised I was in a booth in the Rainbow Café. Both Maud and the Sheriff were looking at me.

"You seemed to be thinking so hard," said Maud.

"I guess I was in a brown study."

She smiled. "Well, I have to get back to the counter."

The Sheriff said to me, "Come on. Let's check the meters."

I was suddenly flooded with happiness. It was what we used to do before the Ben Queen business came up. I had arranged my spitballs on the table and now wiped them into my hand and dumped them on the empty doughnut plate.

But as I followed him to the front of the café I felt a little of this joy slip away. I thought it would never be exactly the same between us, me and the Sheriff, and this wasn't his doing, it was mine. It was the price I had to pay for keeping quiet about Ben Queen, and now maybe even for Dwayne.

I followed the Sheriff through the door, hardly bothering to do more than glance at the pastry display. But my eye did land on a Boston Cream Pie that I might come back for.

We walked down Second Street and had no sooner ticketed Dodge Haines's shiny new truck for parking in the loading zone of McCrory's, than I saw Bunny Caruso coming out of Rudy's clothing store right across the street. She was trying to balance one of the Rudy's bags with a load of dry cleaning from Whitelaw's, trying to hike one up with her knee to get a better grip.

No! I thought. As she was on the other side of Second Street, I might be able to get the Sheriff's attention so he wouldn't see her.

"Looks like Bunny needs some help," he said, making to cross the street when I caught his sleeve.

"Oh, she's a lot stronger than she looks and we've got nearly all the meters to do."

"I'll just give her a hand. You can go on ahead for a minute."

So, of course, I had to follow him to try and stop Bunny from saying anything about giving me a ride. This was all becoming such a load on me, a lot heavier than the cleaning bags. I guess when your conscience bothers you it's like bags filled with bricks.

"Well, hi, Sam! Hello, Emma. I swear, Sheriff Sam DeGheyn, you are the absolute last gentleman left on this planet."

I said, "He sure is. My mother and Mrs. Davidow always say so." Then I launched off on an account of Sam's changing a tire for Lola Davidow. Just taking up talking space. The Sheriff looked at me quizzically, as I was being pretty effusive.

Then, as I feared she would, Bunny smiled at me. "Did you have a nice dinner? I know the Silv—"

I jumped all over "Silver."

"Oh, yes. There's nothing like my mother's fried chick—."

Bunny jumped all over "chicken." "No, but I mean with your—aunt? Was it an aunt?"

The Sheriff was holding both the dry cleaning and the Rudy's bag. "You both seem to be talking at cross purposes."

Bunny squinted up at him; so did I. It's one aspect of our nature we have in common, Bunny and me: our squints.

"Maybe if you'd stop interrupting each other—" He smiled.

Bunny laughed, opening the door of her truck. "Oh, it ain't nothin', just small talk."

I agreed eagerly as the Sheriff stowed the bags and shut the door. "I just remembered, Bunny, you live out on Swain's Point. There's a young girl was reported disappeared in the White's Bridge area."

"How *terrible.*" It was not empty words of concern; Bunny sounded sincerely troubled. "When did that happen?"

"Last night, sometime around eight, nine o'clock."

"Well, who was she?"

"That's just it. We don't know."

I had stepped back into the shadow cast by Rudy's awning, creating the scene which I feared was coming: Bunny would say, *Why, last night's when I drove you out to the Silver Pear.* They both look at me. I put on my dumb expression; the Sheriff mightily surprised/angry/disappointed. He demands to know: "Why didn't you tell me you were near the scene of the crime?"

None of this happened, except I did put on my dumb expression, which turned to sheer amazement when nothing like this took place.

Then the Sheriff and Bunny said Good-bye, be seein' you, and we went back to walking our beat. My mouth still must have been open, for the Sheriff asked me what was wrong.

"Nothing, nothing," I said. I vowed to go immediately after the meter walk to St. Michael's and kneel down before whatever was there, and tell Father Freeman that now I believed in miracles. He might suggest I join a convent later on, and I'd probably agree, for joining would be many years away and by then he'd have forgotten I agreed. (It would certainly be preferable to making any promises to the camp-meeting Christians, for I'm sure they'd suck you right in and not give you a chance to change your mind.)

I said, "I guess it's going to be nearly impossible to find this girl. I can't imagine nobody missing her." Actually, I could. I could imagine it six ways from Sunday.

The Sheriff nodded thoughtfully. "It's sad, really."

"Why?"

He was slotting change into Miss Isabel Barnett's meter. He never ticketed her because I'm sure he realized how forgetful she was. "To think a girl could go through all of that, and no one ever know about it." Sadly, he shook his head.

It was easy for me to pick up on her trials and tribulations. "And she'd have been scared to death. There's hardly anyone lives out there excepting Mr. Butternut—"

"Buttercup."

"Buttercup. And those woods are really dark, I mean *really* dark. Not just your average night-dark, electric-out-dark, cave-dark, or even blind-dark—"

"You know a lot about the dark."

And suddenly, I remembered that I was *not* supposed to know a lot about the woods. "Will told me. Will and Mill, you know how they like to nose around whenever something happens. They went out to Mirror Pond after the murder."

"They shouldn't be doing things like that. Tell them."

"Uh-huh." That didn't interest me at all. "But getting back to this poor girl, why, a lot of things could have happened. She could have starved or died of exposure."

"Oh, I doubt she's dead. There's more than one way out of the woods. She sounded smart, the way Mr. Buttercup talked about her. He said she was as stubborn as Abel Slaw's mule."

I was *not!* I stopped and put my hands on my hips.

"Something wrong?"

"Well, *no!*" I shrugged and walked on. "But it doesn't make any difference. No family's reported any missing girl."

"Um. There is a good reason why they wouldn't have."

"What?"

"She's not missing anymore."

Once again, I stopped dead. "*Not* missing?"

He nodded. "She might by now be right back where she came from." He'd stopped and was writing out a ticket for Helene Baum's canary-yellow car. Above the law, she thought she was. He ripped it from the book and stuck it on the window, making a little rubbery twang with the windshield wiper.

"But—well, wouldn't you be furious if that's so?"

"No. No harm done." He smiled. "Would it be better if the poor girl was still missing?"

"But all the *trouble* she caused you! Getting the state police out there and having to talk to Mr. Buttern—, Buttercup, who's probably a hundred and talks a blue streak about his family—I mean he *sounds* as if he does." (*That* was close!) "I mean, you would have to be awfully disappointed after all of the trouble you went to."

The Sheriff stopped and adjusted his black glasses and looked skyward. "The only thing that disappoints me is I'll never know her. She sounds like a girl worth knowing." He sighed.

I gaped. I felt like a firecracker sent sparks of its hot self racing through my veins.

Then we walked on, left Second Street for Oak Street, walked and walked in our old friendly way, with me trying to figure out a way to let the Sheriff know the girl was me.

A new decor

18

The Abigail Butte County Library is a building of pale brown brick, and one of my favorite places. Miss Babbit doesn't talk down to kids the way most adults like to do, as if our puny brains could only take in information spoken very slowly and clearly. It's the same way adults talk to old people.

After serving lunch, I had gone down to the Pink Elephant to think about Florida. It was then that I decided to take my painting of flowers and water back to the library to exchange it. I handed over the Manet or Monet—I couldn't keep them straight. I think when they both discovered they were going to be painting pretty much the same things, one of them should have changed his name. But then they might have thought it was fun confusing people, like twins who let you think they're each other.

Miss Babbit asked if I'd enjoyed the painting and I said yes, I was going to look at some others, which I did. But none of them looked like Florida, except possibly one with a palm, some fruit, and two naked women. Miss Babbit came to stand beside me and said that the painting was a Gauguin. I was amazed she seemed not at all embarrassed for us to be staring at the naked women. I asked if it was supposed to be Florida and she said, no, the South Seas. She went on to tell me about Tahiti and Gauguin taking off—quitting his job, leaving his family in Paris to run off to Tahiti. Eyeing the naked women, I thought, no wonder.

Miss Babbit had to leave to take care of Helene Baum and Mabel Staines, who I would be surprised to hear ever read a book.

Under "Travel, U.S." I located two big Florida books, full of photographs, which I dragged over to a table to leaf through. I was searching for palm trees, mainly the royal palm. I wasn't disappointed; stately palm trees lined avenues and beaches, grew in profusion in parks, eclipsed the sun and moon with their black trunks and dark green fronds silhouetted against a sky full of melting crayon colors, so vivid the scene looked artificial, unreal. I found a royal palm in daylight, taking up the whole of one photograph, that was just perfect. I marked the place and looked for the Tamiami Trail. I found sections of it in the next book. Some bits of it were really not that pretty, so I ignored those and marked a picture which was, showing palms unreeling down a highway, into the blue distance.

I was suddenly very tired, as if a load of flour had just been dumped on me. I figured I was thinking about Paul and Do-X-machines again, so I rested my head on my outstretched arm on the table and looked at the pictures sidewise, lazily turning the pages. It was an interesting angle that gave the palm trees the appearance of moving when I slowly turned the page. And then there were pictures of beaches and buildings, and interior shots of rooms. One of a hotel lobby caught my eye. There were white pillars around which sat poincianas with flame-red blooms. They were truly beautiful, especially with the white backdrop of the pillars. This lobby was quite luxurious, with crystal chandeliers and bamboo furniture and a deep-looking dark green carpet. The photograph was not identified, but I decided this had to be the lobby of the Rony Plaza. I continued looking until I found the outside I wanted. This sat directly on the beach, surrounded by royal palms and coconut palms (and probably others I didn't know), a towering pink and white building that reminded me of one of my mother's birthday cakes.

I felt my time had been well spent and took both books over to the copy machine. Not only could you copy, but you could enlarge on the machine, which is what I did, first copying one-half of each image and enlarging as much as I could, then doing the other half. I read the message about how it was illegal to copy pages of a book without prior permission, but since I had no idea how to get that, I figured I could take my chances. The halves I could scotch tape together later.

Now all I had to do was buy poster board and crepe paper and take a taxi back to the hotel. I walked to the stationery store (which was really more of a jumble store that sold comic books and regular books besides typing paper, ink, pencils, and pens in addition to stationery) and bought these with tip money that I always had a supply of in spite of Vera's keeping the big tippers for herself.

I almost got weary again thinking of all the things I had to do: I had to wait tables, I had to go to Cold Flat Junction, I had to solve this mystery of Fern Queen and the Girl, I had to find a new decor for the Pink Elephant.

Life certainly wasn't about to leave me alone.

Back in the Pink Elephant I settled down to copy the two halves of the royal palm picture. I had green crayons and brown and gray with which I filled in the tree on the poster board. It was hard to draw, since the palm, even enlarged, was still smaller than what I wanted. But I finally got the outline right. I finished coloring the trunk and then cut up the green crepe paper and pasted wide strips to the top of the tree. I also colored and cut out a few coconuts to attach beneath the palm leaves. Finally, I cut around the tree as well as I could, leaving the extra at the bottom, which I then folded back as a support. It worked very well.

I had the missing coconut that my mother had been looking for, one of three brought back from town by Mrs. Davidow, and now took it up to the kitchen, which was empty except for Walter. I got a hammer and a screwdriver from the storeroom and asked Walter if he'd help me open up the coconut, and he was pleased to do it. Soon, he'd got it open and I poured the milk off into a cup. Then we each ate a piece and agreed it was "real good." Walter said come dinnertime, I should take a piece on a platter into "the old fool." Walter laughed his gasping laugh.

It was nice having the kitchen to ourselves with nobody to neb around and ask what we were doing. I sat on the stool my mother kept near the stove, and Walter leaned back against the serving counter. We ate another piece of the coconut. He asked where they came from and I told him coconut palms, as far as I knew.

"They're all along the Tamiami Trail, rows of coconut and royal palms." I didn't know this, of course, but it offered a chance to say "Tamiami."

"Where's that?"

"In Florida." I bit into my piece of coconut. It had the most wonderful cool and unsweet flavor. I could hardly wait to turn it into the drink my mother described. Probably I could do it in a blender.

"That's where Miss Jen and Mrs. Davidow are going." He made it sound like some huge coincidence.

I told him that was right. "Ree-Jane, too."

Walter shook and shook his head. "She's gonna drive that there white car straight to hell."

Knowing Walter, he meant literally.

"Wish't I could go to Florida." He sighed.

"Me, too." To keep him company, I sighed too.

I needed a number of other things, one being a fan and a bucket of sand. I decided to visit the Big Garage, even though Will and Mill didn't welcome visitors. On my way across the backyard, I stopped at the sandbox kept there for the small children of guests. The spade and sand bucket were a weathered blue, and rather small for my purposes, but they'd do. I filled the bucket and set it down on the walk to collect on my way back.

I knew Will and Mill had at least one fan in there, for I had seen them use it. As there was no electrical outlet in the Pink Elephant, I would just drop a long extension cord out of the dining room window above it.

As I walked up to the Big Garage, I took comfort in the knowledge that Will was being left behind, too. Still, I couldn't kid myself into believing they thought of Will and me in the same breath. Will was another thing altogether for most people. He was only there in spurts, when he'd appear to carry someone's bags or bus the dishes. Most of the time, he was either gone (with Mill, over to Greg's for Moon Pies and Orange Crush and to play the pinball machine) or they were both up in the Big Garage. Since Will didn't seem to be around, people had a chance to miss him. He'd come and go in an almost magical way. I'd guess you could say he was the pure performer. He was always on stage.

I heard the piano going, and they were singing some old gospel song, interrupting it now and then with hysterical laughter. When I knocked on the door that seemed bound shut from the ivy growing on it, the laughter stopped suddenly, as if I'd dreamed it. Then there came noises of the sort that went with whisking things out of sight.

I knew Will would come to the door and open it only a half inch to keep me from seeing in. It was all so melodramatic.

"What do you want?" he asked through the narrow opening. He spoke to me sometimes as if he couldn't remember who I was, or what I was doing on his planet.

I scratched my elbow. "I just wondered if I could borrow that fan."

"The rotating one?"

I wasn't sure, but I just said yes.

"You'll have to bring it back. We use it for special effects."

"Bring it back when?"

He shrugged. "Whenever. We're not using it right now."

I waited while he went to get the fan. When he returned, I asked him about Florida and how he felt about not being allowed to go.

"I could go."

That stunned me. What did he mean?

The door opened a bit wider as he shoved the fan through, and I could see him shrug. "I just didn't want to go. Why would I want to spend days in a car with Ree-Jane?"

I stood there, staring. When he asked what else, I shook my head. Then he closed the door.

The fan was taller than I was, but it didn't weigh much. Holding it up a little from the gravel road, I walked back around the rear of the kitchen to the Pink Elephant. I felt it was awful of my mother not to tell me that I wasn't going to Florida with them, and that Will had been asked, but said no. I knew my mother could hardly ever bring herself to talk about anything fraught. I felt I was of no account. Then I saw Walter on his way back from the mint field with a bouquet of it in his hand. It was a relief to see here was someone of even less account than I was. When we met up, I asked him to go and get the sand bucket.

Their Florida vacation

19

The next day they left. And what a leave-taking it was; it had started three days before they all piled into Lola's station wagon and actually went. My mother was, of course, too busy doing real chores to participate in the preparation. Ree-Jane modeled her new Heather Gay Struther clothes again, and that took quite a bit of time in itself, as she'd finally bought three dresses, a pale yellow linen suit, an evening gown, and three bathing suits.

Mrs. Davidow's preparations consisted mainly of getting in a new case of Bombay gin and one of Wild Turkey. Over the past three days, she consumed a lot of this as she discussed the route they would take and where they could stay over, while my mother fried chicken or made Angel Pie or slapped Paul away from her coconut cake. She had made the icing for this cake with real coconut, instead of Baker's canned, giving Walter the job of shaving and shredding the two coconuts that she still had. She had been quite surprised that Lola had found coconuts in La Porte, and so was I. My mother was also surprised that the third coconut had disappeared.

Lola Davidow would follow my mother around the kitchen with a martini in one hand and a map in the other, plotting their course through Maryland, Virginia, North Carolina, and South Carolina. She meant to do nearly all the driving, which I was sure the state police would like to hear in Maryland, Virginia, and the Carolinas.

I knew the route as well as they did. On my own map, bought at the stationery store in town, I had marked each place Lola had said they would stop at night, the first town being Culpepper, Virginia. I wanted to feel I had some control over the trip, especially over when they hit the Tamiami Trail. I'd marked it in red.

The day before they left, Ree-Jane had found me in my favorite spot on the porch where she modeled her evening gown. She said, "This is what I'm wearing to dances." She twirled, actually twirled, floating the light blue silk and chiffon in waves around her legs.

"Do they have them in Culpepper?" I refused to look up from my Key West sunset photo.

"Oh, for *God's sake,* no. In Miami *Beach.*"

Then she started doing a dance step and singing, "Palm trees . . . are gently swaying . . . They seem to hear me say-ing . . ." She swayed along, holding out the thin, tissue-y blue of her skirt, going back and forth, back and forth. As she was close to the top step of the porch, I was hoping she'd go over, but she didn't.

Ree-Jane never could carry a tune, but it made me remember her phonograph. "Would it be okay if I listened to your records while you're gone?"

Freed from the thrall of her invisible dancing partner and back on planet earth again, she asked (suspiciously), "Why?"

"Because I like your records. They're nice and old. Old songs are comforting." I don't know where that notion came from. Except maybe it was true. My mother liked to sing "Red Sails in the Sunset" sometimes, and I found that comforting.

She balanced herself and her long full skirt up on the porch railing, thinking it over. Then grudgingly she said, "Well. Seeing you have to stay here, well, I guess so. Only, *don't touch one single thing in my room!*"

"Uh," I grunted, meaning nothing.

"You can sit in my room and listen, but *nothing else.*"

To think I'd pay attention to that warning only showed her ignorance. Anyway, why would I want to mess with her stuff? I'd sooner go through Walter's belongings, which would be more interesting, I'm sure. Anyway, anything Ree-Jane owned that she thought would make me jealous she'd already shown me, so there wouldn't be much point in rummaging through her drawers. I had, of course, no intention of sitting in her room and listening. The phonograph was to go down with me to the Pink Elephant. I needed atmosphere.

While she posed there on the porch rail, I asked, "Are you going to model for Great-aunt Aurora?"

"What? Not after the last time I was up there. That crazy old bitch!"

The "last time," was, of course, the chicken-wing incident. But Ree-Jane clearly had forgotten she'd never admitted what had happened and had, instead, come back to the kitchen and said Aurora had complimented her on her beautiful self.

Then she added, with a slippery smile, "But I guess it figures, since she's a Paradise." Meaning all my back family was crazy.

Innocently, I asked, "Why? What did she do?" Ree-Jane wasn't about to tell me Aurora'd thrown a chicken wing at her and called her a "blond floozy."

"She's just crazy, that's all."

"Oh. Well, that's too bad. I mean she especially wants to see your Florida clothes."

Ree-Jane stopped pleating the chiffon of her skirt. "I don't believe it!"

Neither did I. "She does, though. She likes clothes, if you've noticed. And she's got those two steamer trunks. She still hangs her clothes in them. So she really likes travel, too."

Now, the trouble with vanity is you always want to believe something or someone so much that you'll believe it no matter how much it's against good sense or reason. But at this point, there was nobody left to model for. There were Will and Mill, but even Ree-Jane knew better than to try and get in the Big Garage. That place was like a fort. I was probably the only Zulu who dared even to knock on the door.

"Too bad," I said, sighing (as though I cared), "for she likes Heather Gay Struther's clothes a lot. She'd especially like to see this blue evening gown. Her favorite song is 'Alice Blue Gown.' " That was the only truth I'd told. Of course, Aurora only sings it when she's stinking drunk, but she still is really fond of it. "Listen: I'm taking her up her lunch in a little. Why don't you come with me?"

As I said, only a fool would have believed this, but of course, we're talking about Ree-Jane, who finally said, "Well, all right. When?"

"I'm going right now to get it and I'll bring the tray back through. So you can just wait."

My mother was dishing out creamed chicken over biscuits for two of Anna Paugh's customers and I said I could take up Aurora's lunch. "She wants a stuffed tomato."

My mother frowned so that her forehead took on the look of bean rows ready for planting. She pointed out that Aurora disliked stuffed tomatoes. "They're stuffed with tuna-fish salad, and she hates tuna fish as much as the tomatoes."

I was leaning against the countertop with my shoulders bunched, the heels of my hands pressing down as my feet did a little jig. "She changed her mind."

My mother just looked at me, almost as suspiciously as Ree-Jane had, but when I didn't look away, she set about getting the tomatoes from the ice box and arranging one on a little bed of salad. Then she added hot rolls and a small dish of peas. I transferred this to a tray and hotfooted it back to the front of the hotel, where Ree-Jane was waiting, flicking through one of her fashion magazines. Her blue evening gown was really very pretty. The hem was cut in a kind of zigzag, and fell over a silk underskirt. It was a beautiful shade of blue, a shade I imagined the ocean to look like, sweeping up on the Florida sands.

The last time she'd seen this tomato-stuffed-with-tuna-salad dish, Aurora had poked it around on the plate and said the Hotel Paradise was going to hell in a handbasket, serving these tomatoes. Why, if she, Aurora Paradise, were down there overseeing things, she'd have fried chicken and Angel Pie every night.

Anyway, the nice thing about the stuffed tomato was it fit your hand as good as a tennis ball. So up the stairs we went, Ree-Jane behind me, to the fourth floor.

The minute I walked into her room with the tray (I'd told Ree-Jane to wait outside) Aurora asked, "Where's my Cold Comfort?" She seemed to think I had twenty-four-hour access to the bar in the back office. The fact I'd brought Ree-Jane instead of her cocktail would not sit well at all.

"You hear, Miss? I want my Cold Comfort!"

"I'm sorry. I couldn't find the Southern Comfort."

"Don't be ridiculous. Lola Davidow wears a bottle on a chain around her neck. What's *this?*" She was wearing her gray net gloves, with the fingers cut out, and she poked at the tomato. "That's one of Jen Graham's goddamned stuffed tomatoes!" She waggled a mittened finger at me. "You know I can't stand these. I'm onto you, Missy!"

Aurora was a lot smarter than Ree-Jane (as Ree-Jane was about to see). I kind of fluted, "Somebody's come to *seeee youuu.*" Aurora wanted visitors about as much as Will and Mill did. "Come on in, *Jaaaane.*"

Here came Ree-Jane, waltzing through the door, her blue chiffon skirt held in thumb and finger, spread out like a fan. She hummed and pirouetted all around Aurora's chair—eyes closed, arms waving, as she'd done on the porch. It couldn't have been better (or worse, depending on your point of view).

Aurora followed these movements, gap-mouthed, speechless—but not for long. "You blond-headed *bimbo*!"

Ree-Jane's eyes snapped open and she quickly rose from a Cinderella curtsy she'd made, looking completely white.

"Floozy!" Aurora's mittened hand curled around the tomato, lifting it from the plate in that slow-motion way of awful things about to happen.

It was then my heart, which twenty-three hours out of the twenty-four yearned for Ree-Jane's ruination, turned tail on me and fled. Ree-Jane backed away, her hands in her blond hair like the heroine on the cover of a cheap detective novel. I grabbed Aurora's hand just as it was rearing back to let the tomato fly. It dropped from her hand, and the tuna salad plopped onto the tray as she yelled at Ree-Jane to get the hell out.

And I, really disgusted with myself, said something soppy to Ree-Jane, who had, of course, run out of the room, her face such a mottled pink above the sea-blue gown, it could have been the sun going down into the technicolor waters off Key West. Why had I stopped Aurora after all of my plotting and planning? I guess I'd felt sorry for Ree-Jane, or maybe for Ree-Jane's dress. I did not like confusing feelings or going back on myself. It could get to the point where I'd think *She's only a poor old lady* the next time Miss Bertha dumped her basket of rolls on the floor.

To shut up Aurora (who was heaving insults right and left at the Davidows) I told her I'd go down and make her a drink. On the way down the stairs—Ree-Jane had fairly flown down them and slammed the door to her room—I wondered why I felt that little drop of pity for her. I decided it wasn't all that much of a change of heart; I figured if the blue dress had wound up covered in tuna fish, there'd be hell to pay. And I knew who would pay it. My mother was no fool.

So I continued on my way to the kitchen to make the Cold Comfort with a cold conscience.

Will and Mill joined Walter and Vera and me to see the three travelers off. Will and Mill carted all of the luggage downstairs and out to the station wagon, but it was obvious none of this registered on them. Their minds were back in the Big Garage no matter where their feet were. This was especially true of Will, who Moses himself would have sworn was up on the mountain with him when Will wasn't even in the same country. I've never known anyone who could look you right in the eye and nod and not be hearing a single word. Mill wasn't much better. His fingers moved up and down his pants leg, so you could tell he was playing the piano in his mind.

But they both called good-bye, and have a nice time, as if they meant it, and waved until the car was down at the end of the drive. Then they turned and hotfooted it back to the Big Garage.

Sauerkraut

20

Roast veal and Salisbury steak were the entrees for dinner; before she left I'd heard my mother giving very specific instructions to Mrs. Eikleburger as to how the roast should be cooked. My mother's main fret in life is leaving the cooking to somebody else. I wonder if she isn't like Will—even though she'll be driving the Tamiami Trail, she'll still be back in the kitchen, overseeing the roast.

Miss Bertha knew that my mother was to go to Florida and she hadn't liked hearing that at breakfast, not one bit. The "other two" (meaning, of course, Ree-Jane and her mother) could "drive their car off Table Rock into a flaming pit" as far as she was concerned. This was one of the very few times I found myself in accord with Miss Bertha's feelings. But the absence of "Jen," well, that was a catastrophe. For who was this "Eikleburger" person? Miss Bertha was really hot under the collar and it took Mrs. Fulbright some convincing to get her to believe that she wouldn't be eating German food for several days. After she'd simmered down, I took the opportunity to un-convince her by saying that it wasn't *only* German cooking Mrs. Eikleburger did, for she sometimes cooked American dishes. But not often. Mrs. Fulbright winced, but still smiled at me.

"I'm of German extraction, myself," said Mrs. Fulbright. Mrs. Fulbright would have turned herself into an Eskimo if it would have helped me, she was that sweet.

So that afternoon when I'd finished putting up my pictures in the Pink Elephant, I got Walter to help me look through the cookbooks up on a shelf above the pastry table. He looked in *Foods of the World* and I looked in *International Cooking.* Walter was slow because he stopped so long to stare at the pictures. He said, "Here it says weiners, but it don't look like them. But it's from Germany, it says."

I looked over his shoulder. It was Wiener schnitzel and it was veal. I congratulated Walter on finding the very thing. We kept going to see if we could find German Salisbury steak, but the closest we could get was sauerbraten, which made my mouth pucker up to read about all the vinegar in the recipe. But sauerbraten was a piece of beef; it didn't look like hamburger. I scratched my elbows and considered this. The beef was covered with a lovely dark gravy, and Walter could probably make that from one of the ready-made packets. I could have, but I had entirely too much to do as it was.

I went to the stove to see what was bubbling away under the top. Sauerkraut! Probably that was to be one of the vegetables, and Mrs. Eikleburger, being, I now supposed, "of German extraction," would be cooking something like that. Now, my mother cooks sauerkraut like nobody else in the world. My mother can make sauerkraut haters (which most of us are) into sauerkraut lovers—nothing less than a cooking miracle, but that's my mother's cooking for you. Many people have tried to get that recipe out of her, but, again, I'm one of the few who know it. What she does is to wash and squeeze out canned sauerkraut, then spreads it on paper towels to absorb the moisture, *then* does the same thing all over, twice. After that she cooks it with white wine, and, I think, juniper berries.

Mrs. Eikleburger's sauerkraut was just cooking in water, the old sauerkraut everyone hates. Good. I went off to type the menus. I wanted to catch the afternoon train to Cold Flat Junction. I wanted to find Louise Landis.

Diner people

21

There are some words that can set up in me a kind of homesickness for a thing other than home. The feeling is such a close kin to fear, it could convince you that fear is what it is. The Florida words seem to have done this and made me homesick for a place I've never been and probably never will be.

I am easily haunted. If any spirit wanted to, it could take me over without any trouble at all, slipping in through the invisible cracks in my skin. We all have cracks but don't know it; we are all pretty windy.

Places, words . . . *A space to fill a lack.*

Cold Flat Junction is like that. It has something to do with the silence and the distances. The distances are all around me—north south east west. Wherever I look is endless; nothing stops my looking. Something should; you'd expect something to stop it, a wall or a mountain, but Cold Flat Junction land just seems to go on forever. There are houses, of course, though even these are kind of spread out. There are a few businesses, like the Esso station and Rudy's Bar and the Windy Run Diner. There are these, but it's the stretches beyond these that I'm talking about. From the railroad station, I look across the tracks and the land beyond and those dark blue trees that are its horizon and this homesick feeling comes over me.

Cold Flat Junction seldom sees passengers either coming or going. The reason the train makes the stop at all is because of the old railroad station, which I think is called by some "an architectural gem." I guess it is Victorian.

"The Junction," as people who live around here sometimes refer to it, was originally expected to be a bustling, busy place, with the two roads intersecting there—a junction through which much traffic was expected to move, but none ever did. I had been here three times, twice aboard the train, once with Mr. Root and the Woods boys. The train compartment was pleasantly stuffy, with worn, burgundy-colored and once flowered horsehair seats. When the conductor came, I handed him the ticket that I'd bought last time. It had never been collected and I expected him to refuse it, but he didn't.

I was the only person to step down to the Cold Flat Junction platform; I stood and looked at the imposing red brick station, which belonged in a much bigger, more interesting town. As always, it looked closed but wasn't, although the blind was once again pulled down over the ticket window. I waited for the train to pull out, and when it had gone, I looked out again over that cropped, empty land on the other side that stretched away to that far-off line of dark woods. Then I set my feet in the direction of the diner, which stood across from the Esso station and which was the place I always stopped for information, and of course, food.

Its interior was by now familiar to me; I could see it perfectly in my thoughts when I was somewhere else. The counter, where I always sat, was a kind of half-horseshoe design with four seats going around the end curve. There were tables with chrome legs and different-colored Formica tops; a few booths were installed in the corner nearest the door. The booths were dark red Naugahyde, and one torn seat back was bandaged with silver duct tape. It all gave the impression of being furnished with leftovers, not enough of any one thing to fit the place out correctly. Skimpy flowered curtains too short to reach the sill hung at the small windows. I took my usual seat at the curved end of the counter and pulled out a menu. It was the same.

So were the customers. I recognized all of them, including the married couple in a booth. There was Billy, the one who looked like a truck driver but probably wasn't, as he spent so much time in Cold

Flat Junction, at least in the diner. Down the counter were the two whiskered men wearing the same blue caps that looked like those old railroad caps you see in pictures. One was named Don Joe; I think the other was named Evren. There was a heavy-set, chain-smoking woman in thick glasses who sat at the counter. And of course, the one waitress, "Louise Snell, Prop." (This was on the badge she wore on her uniform.)

Now, here I came, blowing in like the dry wind that carries grit and sand across the railroad tracks, and no one seemed to think it peculiar that this was the fourth time I'd been here, unaccompanied, as usual, by any adult. The first time, Louise Snell had asked, in a friendly and not nosy way, where I was from, or what I was doing here in her Windy Run Diner. My reason had been that my dad's car had broken down and it was being fixed over at the Esso place. The times I had come before today had been information-gathering events. Once for Toya Tidewater (who I never found) and again for Jude Stemple (who I did).

"That car done been fixed yet?" asked Billy.

This question was not asked in a joking manner, but in a small-talk way. Would that car still be at the Esso station after nearly three weeks? But this didn't faze them one bit. Nothing much did. Things just didn't seem to change here, at least that's my impression. It accounts, I guess, for the mysterious quality of Time, as if Time had been misplaced and we all had to get along as best we could without it. I remembered one of our hotel guests who explored a lot, talking about his travels in Tibet: the farther up he went into the mountains and the villages in them, the more time rolled back until he got to one so far up he felt completely outside of time.

I'd finished looking at the menu, still making up my mind as I waited for Louise Snell to come for my order, and she did.

"What'll it be today, hon?"

Thinking of the ham pinwheels with cheese sauce my mother had left for our lunch, I had to check with my stomach to see how it felt about the hot roast beef sandwich. It told me the roast beef would be too much, and I had better just settle for pie and a Coke. The pies were displayed in a cupboard behind glass. The chocolate cream looked really good so I ordered that.

Instead of starting right off with asking Louise Landis's whereabouts, I decided that mentioning Ben Queen would be the best route to take to her. After all, it'd been all over the papers that police were looking for him "to assist in their inquiries" into the shooting death of Fern. Since Ben Queen came from here, they'd regard the place itself as more or less famous and would be glad to talk about it. I smiled at everybody to get them feeling friendly toward me, but it was a wasted smile, as they were always glad to see a stranger here, even if the stranger was a kid.

I asked, "Doesn't that man police are looking for live in Cold Flat Junction?" I mustered up my dumb look. But as soon as the words were out of my mouth, I knew it really *was* dumb, for the question set off a spate of reactions that would go on and on until doomsday and would never get to Louise Landis.

"Those policemen got it all wrong," said Billy, who, as usual, led off. "Ben Queen never killed nobody, and that's a fact."

The woman in the booth put in, "Ben'd never kill anyone and sure not his own *child*."

Everyone nodded and muttered words of agreement.

Louise Snell said, "There's just some folks in this life that've got to be scapegoats."

Scapegoats. It's exactly what Ben Queen and I were talking about that night by the spring.

The husband part of the couple in the booth turned around and said, "Well, but Ben *was* kind of wild."

His wife slapped the hand holding his spoon of soup and all the others more or less turned on him. It was not a popular opinion.

"Where you goin' with this, Mervin?" Billy turned on his stool as if meaning to make something of it.

"He ain't going nowhere, Billy." Mervin's wife whispered something to him and gave his hand another crack.

"I was only *sayin'*—"

Billy waved a dismissive hand at the two and turned back to the counter. Just as Louise Snell passed him with my pie, he said, "Don't know his ass from a hole in the ground."

Louise Snell stopped and leveled a look at him as she pointed her head in my direction.

Billy slid a look off me and said, "Oh. Sorry, ma'am."

Ma'am? *Me?* Mervin sticking his nose in had kind of calmed things down, so I stirred them up. "Maybe he's hiding out here somewhere—some*wheres*." (I thought it would make them take to me more if I adopted a few little habits of speech.)

"Round here? You mean in Cold Flat Junction?" Don Joe's voice slid up on a rising scale of notes, ending in a kind of astonished squeak.

Up and down the counter they regarded one another as if this was crazy but interesting. "I just thought if he came—*come*—from here, well, it'd be where he'd want to hole up." "Hole up" was good, I thought.

Don Joe frowned. "It'd be the first place police'd look."

How naive, I thought.

Don Joe went on: "If I was Ben Queen, I'd've hotfooted it right to the border." He slid one hand off another in imitation of the speed he'd fly off with.

"What border?" asked the woman in the thick glasses.

"Who cares? Alaska. That's where I'd go. Yes, sirree. To get me back to the U.S. of A. they'd have to exterdite me."

Louise Snell was leaning against the pie cupboard. "That's part of the United States, Don Joe."

"Since when, woman?"

"I don't know *when.* It just is. Has been for a long time."

"Twenty-one years," I put in, thinking if I appeared knowledgeable, they'd be more inclined to pay attention. I didn't know how long Alaska had been a state. I'm not even sure I knew it was. I knew there were two states added on to the forty-eight, but they could have been Nova Scotia and the Florida Keys for all I knew. For all any of us knew. They turned to me with something like respect. I looked around at their softly blinking eyes. What they reminded me of was the forest creatures' eyes peeping into the dark where Snow White lay asleep. But I felt more like Cinderella than Snow White, for Cinderella had those evil stepsisters. It would take two to make up one Ree-Jane.

I told myself to stop thinking about fairy tales and get back to the real world and its problems. But then I wondered, looking into the sleepy-seeming ring of eyes: were the seven dwarfs any more of a fairy tale than what we'd got going here in Cold Flat Junction? I shook myself a little, for I felt spellbound, or about to be.

They seemed to be waiting—Billy and Don Joe and the others—for further historical revelations. I remembered Hawaii. "Number fifty's Hawaii. That's been a state for, oh, ten or eleven years, at least." We were way off the subject. I squinted my eyes up and said, "Now, what were we talking about? Oh, this Ben Queen. But if he's from here, he must have . . . kin (a good word) around here."

Evren entered the conversation. "Well, now, I dunno whether he's still got kin or not in the Junction."

How could anyone not know everyone who lived in Cold Flat Junction? Especially the Queens?

"Of course he does, Evren," said Billy. "Queens has lived here long as we have. That big house over on Dubois Road. Ben's brother and sister-in-law, that Sheba, live there. Ben lived there with Rose and Fern when their house was gettin' built."

"Who was Rose?" As if I didn't know.

"Pretty girl from over Spirit Lake way. Yeah, ol' Ben, he really give us a surprise there." Billy was fingering a cigarette from the pack in his shirt pocket.

I was hoping someone would nose in with "What surprise?" but all they did was nod and murmer, so it was left to me. I imagine I knew as much as they did about Rose Devereau Queen.

But my purpose in coming here hadn't yet been served. "I'll bet this Ben Queen's got some kind of good friend here who'd help him out."

They pursed their lips and looked thoughtful. For heaven's sakes, why was it so hard to remember Louise Landis had been Ben's steady girl before Rose?

Louise Snell, who had lit another cigarette, leaned her weight against the glass-enclosed cupboard again and said, "Well, if Ben wanted help, there's always Lou Landis."

At last!

"Yeah, Lou, she was always sweet on him," said Billy.

"Hard to think," said the chain-smoking woman in glasses, "she'd be living all these years in the Junction."

Don Joe leaned so he could look past Billy and down the counter. "Why's that? The Junction ain't a bad place. I growed up right here all my life!" He slapped his small hand on the counter.

She turned to him. "I never said it wasn't a nice place. But Louise Landis, shoot, she's too smart and educated to spend her life here teaching in that little no-account school. She graduated college. *Then* she went to some big university and got herself a—whaddayacallit?—an Advanced Degree."

I could hear the capitals she gave those words and wondered what kind of degree.

The husband in the booth put in his second contribution. "Master of Arts, that's what."

Wow! I thought. What was Louise Landis doing in Cold Flat Junction? "Is Ben Queen? Educated, I mean?" I knew he wasn't, but I wanted to hear more about the two of them.

Billy snorted. "Hell, no—'scuse my French—Ben, he couldn't hardly sit still for stuff like that. He was one wild kid," he added, obviously forgetting he'd laid into the man in the booth for saying just that.

I waited for more on Ben's "wildness," but Billy just clammed up, not giving thought to Ben Queen, but merely to the fact everyone here knew him. I drew little but air and ice through my straw and said, "I hate school." They all smiled and nodded because that was what a kid should do. Hate school. But they didn't say anything more about Louise Landis. "This Miss Landis, she must be a good teacher."

"Absolutely," said Louise Snell. "Of course she's wasted here because she's oversmart, even though she's the principal. And the school only goes up to fifth grade. Then they have to go to Cloverly to the big school."

"Real nice person," said Billy. "Ev'ry year she has a treat for them orphans that live up to that institution outside Cloverly, takes 'em out to lunch and stuff. Real nice woman."

There was I guess you'd say a "respectful silence." Then Don Joe asked Louise Snell, "Does Lou Landis still live over there in the Holler?"

I could have *clapped.* Here's the information I wanted. At the same time, I felt just a trifle irritated because I myself hadn't wormed it out of them.

Louise Snell nodded. "Surely does. Same house her folks lived in all along. They're dead," she said to me, as if it was information I might need. "It's an awful big house just for one person."

"That's over where Jude Stemple lives," said the woman with the thick glasses. "You got to go on a ways from his house."

I stayed looking down the length of my straw and hoped it wouldn't jog their memory that I'd been here not long ago asking about an Abel Stemple. But they didn't remark on that.

"There's some really big houses here," I said. "I guess hers is one of them." But it would be no problem at all to find out which it was, as all I'd have to do is ask Jude Stemple. We were by this time by way of being friends.

"Kind of pretty. Sort of a leaf-green," said Louise Snell as she began to polish glasses with a tea towel.

With a final clatter, I set down my Coke glass. "Well, it's real nice talking to you. I guess I better be on my way." I smiled brightly and slid from the stool, then looked up at the big clock, gasped, "Oh, I'm late," and rushed to the cash register with my check before they could ask where I was off to.

Flyback Hollow

22

I walked along Windy Run, which meant passing Rudy's Bar and Grill on one side and the Esso station on the other, sitting in its own couple of acres of sandy ground. There were no cars in sight being fixed or filled up with gas. A wind tunneled down the road (which is where the road got its name, I guess), and blew a Milky Way wrapper against my foot.

As I looked across at the Esso station and wondered how business was, I asked myself why I hadn't just gone there to find out where Louise Landis lived. Gas station attendants always know everything. Why had I gone to the diner and more or less created a lot of confusion? For I knew they'd all disagree about any topic, including the whereabouts of some villager. I suppose Lola Davidow would put it down to just being "troublesome" (which she'd told me I was on many occasions).

But this was my roundabout way. I think it had to do with what the answer came out of, how it came about. Yet, what difference does it make if the answer comes out of a long, out-of-the-way conversation, or just comes out as a simple answer? I don't know; it just does.

It's said the older you get the more philosophical you become. I'll be thirteen in a couple of months. I have always looked forward to my teens, but now I'm not sure. I really don't want to get more philosophical than I already am.

As I passed Rudy's Bar, I stopped to look in the window. I couldn't see much but my own reflected self right above a blue neon sign that said BEER—EATS. I would have liked to cup my hands around my face and peer through the window—it was really dark in there—and see if anybody was "drunk and disorderly." (I enjoy police terms, when the Sheriff says them: "drunk and disorderly" sounds almost poetic.) But I didn't stare in. I told myself it was because I respected people's privacy, but it was more because I didn't want Rudy coming out and yelling at me to get away from the window. I am not a risk taker.

Walking on, slowly, I kicked up leaves that skittered along the pebbly ground. Why were there dead leaves on the path in this early summer? The land all around looked as if it were between seasons. Or you'd think the place had only a single season that had to make do for all four. I had this sinking feeling as I always did in Cold Flat Junction when I was alone, just looking around. Often, there was no one else around, and when I did see others, they were few and far away. There was something collapsible about all of this, as if it were a plan of a village, a mock village, or a replica, a village cut from cardboard and put up as an experiment in lastingness. And everyone was surprised it had indeed lasted, the way that tall, thin people outlive dumpy, fat ones (or at least that's what Ree-Jane keeps telling me).

I had come to Schoolhouse Road. The school always looked to me more like a church than a school, with its white clapboard and steeple bell. The playground was empty even of the girl I'd played Pick Up sticks with the first time I'd been here. That was scarcely three weeks ago, yet it seemed like months, years even. Time, here, stretched to breaking.

I knew exactly where Flyback Hollow was and where the Queens lived on Dubois Road, and the post office, too—a square, gray, cinderblock building. I went in and found no one about, as there hadn't been before—no one at the window selling stamps or anything. I stopped at the bulletin board where I was glad to see there was no "Wanted" poster for Ben Queen. The Drinkwater brothers were still up there looking mean, and I wondered if the FBI had forgotten about them. I also wondered how effective the FBI was, as the Drinkwaters had been "at large" for nearly a year now. They might be up in Alaska.

"At large." I supposed it meant being all over, being out there in some helter-skelter way, hardly visible, anonymous. I left the post office and walked on, wondering if this was a good description of me.

On Dubois Road, I stopped out in front of the Queen house. I wound my hands round the white and peeling fence pickets, and leaned back and wondered if they were home and could see me. Would they remember me from being here with Mr. Root? Of course they would, for hadn't they told the Sheriff about me? It felt as if months had passed since I'd seen them, and I wondered if Time were like a glass of water or a Cold Comfort: if you poured too much into it, it would spill over onto any available surface. If Time has to contain too much—too many murders or lost people found or chicken wings thrown—does it have to expand to take care of it all?

I walked on, thinking about this, until I got to Flyback Hollow.

If Cold Flat Junction was a place where Time worked in strange ways, Flyback Hollow was its midnight. Dubois Road ended here, where the name "Flyback Hollow" was painted in whitewashed letters on a large rock. Trees and foliage grew around the place where it began. It had got nearly all of the trees in Cold Flat, as if they'd got together as saplings and decided to stick together and Flyback Hollow was where they stuck.

The branches above me lapped across the narrow road and created a tunnel of coolness and partial dark. It was like a little park in here, almost, the road dividing and arcing around a couple of acres where Jude Stemple's house sat. There were other houses, little ones, square and uninteresting and dropped about as if Aurora Paradise had tossed playing cards on the floor, which she sometimes did.

I slowed down and picked a black-eyed Susan, humming and pulling its petals. It was so nice not having to be anywhere, not having anyone to serve at dinner except for Miss Bertha and Mrs. Fulbright. I turned around and around in quick circles like a skater, my arms thrown out and my head back. I did this until I was too dizzy to stand and had to go and lean against an oak. Then I did it again, this time moving the circles forward down the road. I suddenly stopped, wondering why I was dawdling this way and making myself dizzy when I had important things to do, like talking to Louise Landis. I hadn't even given thought to what I was going to say.

Jude Stemple had been building the wooden fence around his house, sawing wood, when I first came across him. The fence was finished and I opened the gate. I didn't see him outside, or hear any sawing noises coming from the shed behind the house, nor did I hear noises coming from inside, either. His hound dog was lying on the porch as usual. I walked the path up to the porch and the dog beat its tail, though it did not rise. There was a screen door and behind it the front door was open. I knocked on the doorjamb and called out, "Mr. Stemple!" I knew the open door didn't necessarily mean anyone was home; people didn't bother locking their doors around here.

Wearily, I sat myself down on the step beside the dog. He was really old and tired. I scratched his ears, knowing how he felt, though moments ago I'd been dancing crazy circles down the road. Again, I had that strange feeling of Time lying heavy and gathering itself together, as at a formal dance a woman might stop to scoop up the train of her gown. Time wasn't passing, it was bunching. Bunching before me and this old hound.

What I really wanted to do was lie down on the porch and go to sleep, too. I can't recall ever feeling so tired. Maybe once I did before in the Rainbow with the Sheriff sitting across from me, waiting for me to tell him what I knew. I saw again Ben Queen walking away that night from Crystal Spring and heard him say, *If it goes too hard on you, turn me in.* It wasn't dog-tiredness I felt now, it was a tiredness all my own. I leaned over and put my chin on my knees and studied the gray porch step.

"I don't have to do any more. I didn't *have* to do all this," I said to the dog, who beat his tail against the porch. I guess he understood.

I did not understand the reluctance I felt as I left Jude Stemple's place and got farther back into Flyback Hollow. The road had come together again and continued on its way. Masses of trees divided this part of the Hollow from the part I'd just left. I thought of Brokedown House and that white light in my eyes, and I stopped dead amid the unfamiliar, glad it wasn't night. Even so, the trees seemed to have drunk in last night's darkness and were throwing it off in blue shadows along my path.

"You got to go on a ways," the lady in the diner had said, and I wondered just how far. I looked back, anxious that the road might be closing up behind me. It was ridiculous. Still, I surely did wish Dwayne were here, even if it meant I'd have to carry a sack of rabbits.

Then I saw the house, up on the right; it had to be the Landis place, as there was no other, and it did—as they had said—melt in. Its dull olive-green paint and dark green roof separated themselves from their surroundings like the figures finally seen in one of those cloud puzzles. You have to look hard. If I hadn't been looking for it, I would have passed the house right by.

Now there was another road, narrower than the one I was leaving, a driveway, I guessed, for I was sure an educated person like Louise Landis would drive a car. I did not take to this road very quickly. I stopped to pick some more black-eyed Susans and tiger lilies and thought as I did it (though this had not been my clear intention) that Louise Landis might appreciate a bouquet. Then I realized they were her flowers in the first place and dropped them by a tree.

I told myself to stop acting like I was the Gretel part of Hansel and Gretel and that Louise Landis was a perfectly normal person, not someone to stuff little kids in an oven, and that she wouldn't have changed over the years, despite yearning after and maybe even waiting for the man she had always loved (except it hadn't done the Phantom of the Opera any good, all that waiting around). With a firmer step I walked on, recalling I'd seen her three weeks ago, the woman in black who'd stepped out of the school to look off into the dense beige distance of Cold Flat Junction.

But wait: I stopped again, feeling I'd walked miles and the house was receding before me. How did I know that woman was Louise Landis? It could have been just another teacher. But I didn't think so. The woman I saw standing on the top step and shading her eyes against the sun had an air of certainty about her that went along with being a school principal.

I still hadn't decided what to say and thought I'd better hurry up about it. My brain paraded several choices before my eyes: one, I was lost, or two, I used to live here (which she'd know was a lie, since *she'd* lived here all her life). Three, I just moved here and was walking around—only, that would lead to being lost again; four, I was visiting—

The door opened before I'd settled on something and it was the lady in black I'd seen, just as I knew it must be, only now she was wearing blue. Her skin was like mine: no matter what color we put on, it looked good.

Five, I was selling subscriptions; six, I lost not me but my dog . . .

She looked down at me with one of the pleasantest smiles I'd ever seen and said, "Hello." It might even have been her second hello, offered in a warm and friendly tone, but my mind was still busy: *seven, I was collecting for the First Tabernacle Church; eight, I was helping the Humane Society and did she have a pet?* She was a person you just knew you could put your trust in, and so I did: "Hello. Jude Stemple sent me."

"He did? Well, you'd better come in then, and tell me all about it."

My mouth was open to deliver whatever the next part of this lie was, but when she said that, I was completely stumped. I mean that she seemed to be so accepting in advance of the queer people who turned up on her porch. After I entered, she closed the door and I watched her back as she led me from the hallway, scented by furniture polish and roses, into the living room. Her hair was coiled into an elaborate scroll at her neck. It was shiny, pale brown, almost blond, maybe that color called ash-blond. I thought it was very nearly the color of mine, but hers certainly wasn't mouse-brown or dishwater-blond, as Ree-Jay said mine was. Just before I sat down in the armchair she indicated, I pulled a lock of hair around and looked at it out of the corner of my eye and thought, yes, we did have similar hair. Skin and hair, two ways we were alike. I wondered if she ever had a hankering to go to Florida.

We were in her "parlor"—a word I preferred to "living room" but one which my mother thought to be "common." "Parlor" suited this room better, as it was so comfortably old-fashioned, like the hotel music-parlor. (I would have to ask my mother why "music-parlor" was okay.) Hers contained a piano, upright against the far wall, and velvet upholstery on a settee and several side chairs in a red so deeply touched with blue it was almost purple. A fireplace with orange flames that seemed on the verge of going out, licking around and turning to ashes a few blue coals. There were pictures and portraits on one wall, and more books than I'd ever seen outside of a library on the other. They covered an entire wall and looked, as books always do to me, warm and colorful and inviting.

The whole room was that, really. The walls were papered with village scenes—little people walking in little streets past tiny houses on tiny squares. Wide mahogany moldings shone with that same polish that scented the hallway.

We were sitting in armchairs covered with a brown, flowered chintz that didn't match but didn't clash with the velvet and the wallpaper. There was a little ball of yarn between the cushion and the arm of my chair and I pulled it out. Maybe she had a cat. My eyes traveled back to the books. We sat in silence and listened to coals sifting and sputtering; somewhere, a clock chimed, and for once I didn't have to count the chimes.

The silence surprised me. Here was an adult person who just sat, her elbow on the arm of her chair, chin supported by her hand, waiting for . . . well, whatever I had to offer, I guess. All of this, you would think, would edge me closer to telling the truth of why I was here, but, strangely, it didn't. Maybe the room seemed so overwrought with imagination—all of those writers hidden in all of those books, all of those villagers in the wallpaper—that I moved instead toward greater foolhardiness. That was the danger of imagination; you could so easily fall right on your face. But it was like, well, writing a play, the way Will and Mill were always doing. Writing it *and* performing it, so for once I had the lead.

I said, "I've got—kin around here." This was not a good start on why Jude Stemple sent me. I frowned and picked at a loose thread on the chair arm.

Surprisingly, she picked up on this. "Are the Stemples—Jude—relations?"

"The Stemples?" Now I was looking up at the ceiling, thinking that I might not want to be related to Mr. Stemple, as he was definitely what my mother would call "common." I didn't want to be unkind to Mr. Stemple, but I didn't want to be related to him, either. "No, not directly. He's more by way of being a cousin of a cousin." She had not asked me my name or where I'd trucked on in from, or where I went to school, or how old I was.

In her just waiting there, seeming fully prepared to wait if she had to forever, and not making any judgments, I knew who she put me in mind of: Ben Queen.

"My name's Emma," I said, surprised at this little bit of truth escaping me, just as it had with Ben Queen.

Orphans

23

As I looked around, I felt mired in the past, lost in something old I couldn't identify, other than in the photos on the wall, the stiffened collars imprisoning necks, the cameos pinned to shoulders, the hair skinned back. Her question hadn't quite gotten through to me. "Pardon me?"

"Jude Stemple," she said. "He sent you here?"

"Oh, I nearly forgot!" I scratched my head, thinking hard.

But Louise Landis rose and asked me if I'd like tea, that she was going to have a cup. Except Miss Flagler, who has the gift shop, and Mr. Butternut giving me cocoa in their kitchens, no one had ever offered me a cup of tea like that. "Do you want me to help?" I asked, remembering my training.

"No. You just sit there and relax. Or look at the books, if you want. I'll only be ten minutes."

After she left, I sat for a moment, my mind empty. Beside my chair was a knitting bag with some orange yarn lying loosely across it. I picked up a loose piece and wound it around my finger. I should have sat there and worked on my Jude Stemple story, but instead, I looked at the bookshelves. Besides, I had already managed to get inside the house. I was tired of thinking; it seemed to me I had to do so much of it. Not easy thinking, either, like what to have for breakfast—French toast with sifted maple sugar and fresh berry compote or walnut pancakes. (I'd had both that morning, so that wasn't much of a decision.)

What was it about food? I liked it so much, mostly my mother's, of course. But there were also Dr. McComb's brownies, and there was the chili at the Rainbow Café, and the hot roast beef sandwich at the Windy Run Diner. So this liking must be connected to something else, or someone.

I had been standing before the wall of books, reading the spines. I had taken down and returned *Huckleberry Finn* to the shelf, promising Mark Twain that I would read his book one day soon. I bounced on the balls of my feet to get more eye level with the shelf above. My eye fell on the dark spine of a book by Wilkie Collins called *The Woman in White.* I remember trying to read this book when I was a child, but it was too hard for me. I do recall the woman, who appeared suddenly on the road, her face as white as her gown, frightening the hero (and me).

I took the book down and stood looking at the cover, which pictured the woman in white. Suddenly, I drew in breath and thought of the Girl. Her dress was such a pale color that it might as well have been white. I saw her again, standing in the rain at the edge of the woods just beyond the Devereau house. I'd just put a record on the old phonograph of a French song, the singer's voice hollow and reedy, but the words, soft and elegant. The Girl watched the house for a moment. Maybe the music had drawn her; more likely she had wanted to go into the house, but, seeing me, she stopped. She had this *waiting* air about her. Then she'd turned and walked away.

The only person I had ever told about the Girl was Ben Queen. I seemed to be keeping her to myself; I don't know why. Except for that one excited time in La Porte, when I had seen her and followed her and fairly flown into the Sheriff, I had never mentioned her. And even with the Sheriff, I caught myself before I'd really told him much.

I was sure the Devereau family was cursed. If I ever told that to anyone I would be laughed at. I don't care. Rose was murdered;

her daughter Fern was murdered. And Rose's little sister, Mary-Evelyn? In my mind's eye I see the three Devereau sisters, moving through the woods by lantern light. The sisters had told the police they were looking for Mary-Evelyn. Were they? Only Ulub had seen this strange procession and he didn't know what it meant. It is too heavy, too weighted, to have been an accident. It is—really—too mysterious.

A tray rattled and I shook myself, drawn back from that scene by the sound of clinking china. Miss Landis was carrying the tea tray in and setting it down on a small table. She said, "I was hungry and thought you might be, too."

"I am, a little." I didn't see how I could possibly eat anything else—not after the walnut pancakes, French toast, ham pinwheels, and chocolate cream pie—but since she'd gone to the trouble, I couldn't refuse. I said yes to both milk and sugar in my tea, since that was what she was taking, and I wanted to be thought accomplished at tea drinking, which I wasn't. I took my cup and picked up a sandwich half. It was chicken, and all white meat. I almost expected Mrs. Davidow to come by and snatch it out of my hand. With my tea and sandwich, I sat down again.

"I like that book," she said, nodding toward the chair where I'd left it. "Have you read it?"

I wanted to say a plain "yes." But I didn't want to be caught out if she asked me something about the ending. "Some of it I have."

"Did you think she was a ghost?"

For one frightening moment, I thought she was talking about the Girl. But then I realized she meant the woman in the book.

"The woman in white," she said, nodding toward the arm of the chair where the book lay.

"Maybe. I don't know."

"I did. That white face." She shook her head, as at something hard to accept.

During the brief silence that followed, I wondered again why she wasn't asking me why I was here. She was certainly polite not to. But after all, it *was* her house. Perhaps, I thought, it was because she'd been a teacher for so many years and had gotten to know the ways of children pretty well and how they didn't like being questioned. Adults did, nearly all the time, because they never seemed to know what else to do.

She sat, looking into the blue firelight, peacefully eating her sandwich. I couldn't get over this October feeling, the fire, the glazed look of the windowpanes. Asking me nothing, she treated my visit as if it was what she'd planned to do for today. I studied her. She had the kind of smooth good face that makes you think either nothing had ever ruffled her or if it had she knew so well what to do that any disturbance left her face untouched. It put me in mind of lake water, the placid center of Spirit Lake.

And to think she must be sixty! I hoped I could be that way when I got older. She had a calming effect, like the Sheriff, like Maud. Even when people like that go against themselves and get angry or fearful, there's still that part of them at their center which remains untouched.

Drowsily I watched the fire and almost forgot the second half of my sandwich, which was not like me at all, especially where the white meat of chicken was concerned. I wound the yarn, trying to make a cat's cradle, and thought about Jude Stemple and came up with, "I didn't mean Mr. Stemple actually sent me here; no, I should have said he gave me directions."

Louise Landis nodded and waited.

"See, it's really—" I stopped to pick up my tea cup and had this choking fit and spilled it. On myself, not on the chair or the rug. I was careful. I finished coughing and said I was really sorry. Miss Landis went to get a kitchen towel.

In her brief absence, I remembered Billy talking about the orphans. I wiped at my shirt and said, "It's really my mother who sent me." Since she was driving through the Carolinas about now, Louise Landis couldn't very well check on what I said. "She wonders if you'd like to have your annual lunch—the one for the orphan children—at Hotel Paradise." Well, it must've seemed to Miss Landis an awfully roundabout way (which, of course, it was) of getting to this lunch business. My mother could easily have phoned her instead of sending me along. "We could even supply entertainment."

She smiled. "What a wonderful suggestion. What kind of entertainment? Like a magic act?"

"More like part of a show that's going to be put on. Or maybe music. Piano playing, maybe."

"That's a fine idea. How much would all of this cost?"

"Oh, don't worry about that." I waved cost away as I finished my sandwich.

"I'm sure they'd love that. They have, well, as you can imagine, not a very happy sort of life."

Wide-eyed, I hoped with concern, I said, "It must be hard for them." I wondered who they were, but that was only my general nebbiness. I was much more concerned about how hard things were for me. I was a little ashamed at this reaction; I felt I should be better able to identify with the less fortunate. My mother was always telling me this when I complained about things like having to eat the dark meat of chicken: "You should remember those less fortunate than you." I pointed out to her that Ree-Jane wasn't one of the "less fortunate," and my mother said, "Oh, really?" I hate it when my mother is quicker than I am.

So whenever I see newspaper pictures of floods or hurricanes wrecking things and killing people, I sometimes bow my head and say a brief prayer, usually for the dog sailing atop some sinking building, moving downstream. I have a particular feeling for animals.

My mind had been so busy with false reasons for coming here that I nearly forgot the true one. Now I was trying to figure out how to work Ben Queen and White's Bridge into the conversation. So I just plunged. "We had a murder not far from La Porte, I guess you know."

"Yes. That must have been an awful shock to you. The woman who was murdered was from here."

"It was really horrible," I said enthusiastically. "Everybody's still talking about it. She was somebody's daughter from here. What was his name . . . ?" I pondered.

"Ben Queen." She looked around the room, as if the name might call him up.

It was strange the way she said it, unadorned, you could say, the name without any other words around it explaining. It was as if the name itself had the power to acquit him.

"But she was his daughter. A person wouldn't kill their own *child,* would they?" As the chain-smoking lady in the diner had said.

She hesitated, as if familiar with child killings and not wanting to tell me. "I imagine it's possible, but not for him." She looked at me, abashed. "I shouldn't have brought this up. I'm sorry."

No, no. "Well, but you didn't. *I* did. Anyway, it's all right; it doesn't scare *me."*

Her smile was quick, gone in an instant, like a bird lighting and flying off. "Oh, I bet it would take quite a bit to scare you."

I took this as a compliment, as they were few and far between for me. "And wasn't he the man that went to prison? For killing his wife?" For someone who didn't even know his name, it struck me I was being pretty quick handing out details about him. I put on my dumb look.

"Yes." She nodded.

"I guess everybody in Cold Flat Junction must know him. I guess you do too?"

"Nearly all my life."

I shook my head in a wondering way. It was sincere wonder, too. To think you could stay friends all these years! I wondered if the Sheriff would still be friends with me when I was sixty, though I didn't see how I'd ever get there. Not to mention how *he* would. He'd be ninety or around there. And what if Ree-Jane was still here? The two of us hanging around like Miss Bertha and Mrs. Fulbright? The few friends I had now, like Hazel Mooma (a distant cousin of Donny and just as swaggering), I couldn't imagine being that old. Especially when Hazel, passing Miss Ruth Porte on the street, said she'd kill herself if she ever got that old. We were all afraid of it, I guess, age and the loss of our looks and charm (what little there was). Hazel would be staggered by Louise Landis, I bet, and refuse to believe she was as old as she was. Hazel would probably say Miss Landis had been turned into a mummy ages ago and all the wrappings had preserved her. Hazel would believe this too, as she could believe anything better than that she was ever wrong, including about mummies.

I cast about for a way to bring up Fern Queen. "Mr. Stemple says Ben Queen's wife was a Devereau from Spirit Lake." I held my hand up toward a shaft of sunlight to see its transparency and the blood in it.

"Rose Devereau was her name. She was a beautiful girl, certainly beautiful by our standards around here, where there isn't much of it."

I watched her look around the room and then out of the window, as if she were trying to find even a trace of that vanished beauty, and had to report back: Gone.

"And Fern was her daughter? Hers and Mr. Queen's?"

"That's right."

Then I came to the part which always made my heart lurch; it was one of those dreadful, full-of-dread things. Anything could bring it back—a black twig snapping, the yowl of a dog. It was the image of Brokedown House and that bright white light. If it wasn't for Dwayne being there and the rabbits, I think I'd have had a harder time believing in it than in mummies. I chewed at the inside of my lip and said, "That was out near White's Bridge where she got murdered."

"That's right."

"There's a family of Butternuts who've lived there for a hundred years, at least that's what Mr. Butternut says." But what could I say or ask to set her feet on that road or in those woods? What really *was* I asking? I had to admit it: I was asking for help. I could feel a welling up of my unhelped and helpless life. It took me by terrible surprise, the threat of tears.

"Are you all right, Emma? You look a little—peaked." She did not wait for a reply, but got up and said, "I'll get you a glass of water."

I took this to be her way of not embarrassing me, in case I wanted to be left alone. Water. What good would that do? For once I could see the advantage of a Cold Comfort or a plain old glass of gin.

Louise Landis was back in a minute, handing me the water. I took a drink and set it on the table and then sort of scooted down in the chair, making a plane of my body. This position looks uncomfortable but isn't; it's mainly an unconcerned position. Anyone sitting this way could hardly be on the verge of tears or haunted by something in her mind. I twined some more yarn around my fingers and listened to Miss Landis carry on with the talk of White's Bridge.

"I've been to Lake Noir a few times, when I went to dinner at a restaurant out there. The Pear Tree?"

"The Silver Pear. I was there too. A man with silvery hair owns it. Well, two men with silvery hair. Do you know somebody that lives out that way? There's this Mr. Butternut, but he's the only one I know." I finished fashioning a cat's cradle. My heart was pounding as if I were coming too close to a thing I didn't want to see.

"No." She shook her head. "One time I did go for a walk along White's Bridge Road. It's quite beautiful. It seems pristine, almost. You know, untouched and uninhabited."

I just looked at her over my fingers. Untouched? She sure didn't know Dwayne. Uninhabited? She *really* didn't know Mr. Butternut. He was inhabiting all over the place. He was born nebby. "How far down that road did you walk?"

"Not far. Why?"

I pulled my fingers apart to tauten the yarn. "Did you see that old, falling-down, worn-out house back in the woods to the right? They call it Brokedown House?"

"No, I didn't," she said, frowning slightly, as if worried she'd missed something important. "Why? What's there?"

"Oh, nothing. I just noticed it, is all. Mr. Butternut and I went there, but he doesn't know who owns it. Nobody lives there; it would make a good haunted house." Again the image of that blinding light rose up before me. The more I thought of it, the more strange and mysterious it became, until I was almost ready to believe the house was a figment of my imagination. But Mr. Butternut and Dwayne, they weren't figments, that's for sure.

She smiled. "You weren't frightened, though."

I wasn't? Tell that to my feet that felt like two cement blocks, as in a dream when you want to run. "Me? Oh, no." I held my hands before me again and pulled at the cat's cradle.

"Whose house is it? Or was it?"

"Mr. Butternut says some people named Calhoun lived there once. But what was Fern Queen doing in that place? That's what the police wonder."

"You seem to wonder, too."

I shrugged, which was kind of hard to do in that position, but I managed. We were silent for a moment. "Did you know Rose Devereau's sisters?"

"I knew of them. I know the little one drowned. That was terrible."

I was glad she brought it up instead of me trying to work my way around to the subject. It was like digging with a shovel; it was hard work. "Mary-Evelyn." And as usual when I spoke it, I felt that weighted sadness. I kept my eyes on the cat's cradle for fear of giving more away than I wanted to.

"I remember, now. She apparently went out in a rowboat and the boat capsized. But it sounds strange, doesn't it? Why was she out at all and dressed the way she was?"

I stared at Louise Landis. Here was another person who had really thought on the matter. "She didn't have any shoes on, either. And the Devereau sisters left it until morning to report it. But Ben Queen—" I stopped.

Now it was her turn to stare at me. "Ben Queen?"

"I . . . nothing." *But Ben Queen* (I'd been going to say) *said it was an accident, too. The boat had a leak in it.* But of course there's no way I could know that unless he'd told me.

It was in my mind to say it would make a good hideout, and I sat up and dropped my hands. The cat's cradle went limp. I was thinking again about who'd been in Brokedown House. It was the Girl or Ben Queen and I couldn't see him shining a light in my face, since he knew me. But she might have wanted something from me, or maybe she wanted to scare me away.

I stood up. "I didn't know it was so late. I've got to get back to the hotel and wait tables. I really, really enjoyed talking to you, Miss Landis."

She rose too and walked with me to the door. "So did I, Emma. I wish you'd come again."

I think she meant it, too. "Well, I'll tell my brother that the orphans would like to see the show." Will would kill me.

"And some piano playing, too," she said.

I nodded. Mill would kill me.

"Both," she said.

"Both."

They'd both kill me.

Tracking poachers

24

At seven-thirty the next morning I was in the big kitchen heating up sausage patties and pouring buckwheat pancake batter on the griddle. I had punched it down and let it rise again. (Most people don't know this about buckwheat: to get that wonderful sour taste, first you've got to use real buckwheat flour, and second, the batter has to rise, like bread dough.)

Walter wasn't in yet, so there was nothing to do but eat, which was fine with me. Mostly when I eat, I eat, preferring not to talk so I can enjoy the food without distraction. I'm not sure why the sour taste of real buckwheat cakes appeals to people who know their pancakes; maybe it's that the syrup supplies a little pool of sweetness for the sour taste to rest in.

As I ate my highly spiced sausage patty, I thought about my new freedom. Freedom can make a person lightheaded. But freedom brings a lot of anxiety with it, for to spend my time doing whatever I wanted made me feel responsible for myself. If I frittered my time away I would have only myself to blame. I reminded myself I didn't have *complete* freedom, for there was always Miss Bertha three times a day to attend to, so I could still blame her if things went wrong, which was a relief.

Still, in a way it was good having guests in the place, for without any, there'd be just me and Aurora Paradise, who I don't think would be handy at getting rid of an intruder. Will and Mill are just as useless, as they wouldn't know there ever was an intruder unless he went up to the Big Garage to audition.

Walter isn't live-in help. He lives in a big un-Walterish house, a big blue-and-white-painted Victorian with a wraparound porch and a lot of gingerbread detail around the roof over the porch. It looks as costly as any of the important houses in Spirit Lake, and I wonder if Walter is secretly wealthy. I like the idea of Walter having suitcases full of money. I like thinking he isn't beholden to the Hotel Paradise for his living (though I can't understand why anyone would work here if he weren't).

Halfway through my pancake stack (which was pretty high), my thoughts turned to White's Bridge. I wondered if Mr. Butternut knew Dwayne. Dwayne was around there a lot, but as he was poaching, he wouldn't be dropping in on people to pass the time. He must live somewhere near there, though. The Sheriff would know, as I suppose Dwayne might have had one or two encounters with the law. How could I ask the Sheriff, though, without him suspecting anything?

I tried to make short work of Miss Bertha and Mrs. Fulbright's breakfast, but I didn't get very far at it, with Miss Bertha complaining about that rude man who waited on them the night before, and why was it my mother was taking off for exotic places when she had guests to feed, and how could I cook her eggs the way she liked them if I couldn't do anything else right?

I stood my ground and tried not to yawn (the buckwheat cakes having made me drowsy) as every so often Mrs. Fulbright put in, "Now, Bertha," making me wonder again how Mrs. Fulbright had stood it all of these summers they'd been coming here. I put their breakfasts together—boiled eggs and toast and sausage (which Miss Bertha had said she'd never eat again, after the sausage had nearly poisoned her) and the thanks I got was that Miss Bertha poked the egg all over her plate, saying it was tough.

Well, I took it for as long as I could, and finally told them Walter would be bringing more coffee, as I would be late for Bible class if I didn't leave right then. Even though Miss Bertha is a church person (for all the good it does her), she still managed to slow down my leaving by complaining about the camp meeting grounds over across the highway and its members, "a bunch of heathen dimwits."

I went back to the kitchen and asked Walter to please take more coffee in and pay no attention to her, and Walter just said, "the old fool," and picked up the coffeepot.

Delbert drove me into La Porte, thinking he was funny saying things like, "You oughta have your own cab, number of times you go back and forth." Ha ha ha ha. I answered, "I'd put Axel out of business." Ha ha ha ha. I asked to be dropped off at St. Michael's Catholic Church.

Although I seem to do a lot of it, I really do hate to lie when it comes to religious matters. I don't think this is because I'm so respectful of religion; it's more that offending God makes me nervous. Also, Father Freeman might be around. He's another adult I really like, though I keep forgetting about him since I'm not Catholic or a church-goer. I wondered if my mother could be blamed for being lax in my religious training.

What I intended to do was just sit in a pew for a minute and apologize for not coming here right away after Bunny didn't tell the Sheriff about our trip to the Silver Pear, which was a miracle if there ever was one. I also apologized for giving Bible class as an excuse to get away from Miss Bertha. I could have stopped on a street corner and delivered up this apology, of course, but there is a lot more to look at here in the church. The stained-glass windows are beautiful.

Finished with apologizing, I exercised my face muscles by pulling my mouth back and trying to move things around in a kind of circle. I had heard a woman guest at the hotel telling another one that your face will fall if you don't exercise the muscles. Think of women singers, she said—Lena Horne, for example. You won't catch her face falling, not with all the singing she does.

Since my eyes were tight shut, I didn't see Father Freeman standing there until he said hello. Then I jumped and said hello to him. I hoped he hadn't seen me exercising. He was smiling and leaning on the pew in front of me. Father Freeman always gives the impression of having all the time in the world, which makes him very relaxing to be around.

"Mind if I sit down a minute?"

I told him of course not, and he sat down in front of me, twisting around to face me, his chin on his fist, the way I do in the Pink Elephant when I feel too tired to hold my head up on its own.

"How's your mother, Emma? I wish I saw her more."

"Fine." Then, surprising myself, I said, "My mother and Mrs. Davidow and Jane have all gone to Florida." I said this in a rush, as if I were admitting to something awful, maybe the kind of thing people admit to in confession. It was almost as if I were ashamed I hadn't been invited.

Father Freeman looked at me and (as he always does) thought for a few moments before he said anything. I like that; it makes me feel I've said something deep, something deserving of thought. Finally, he said, "You know, it's my experience vacations never turn out to be as good as you expect. It's really thinking about the places you want to go, reading about them, imagining them that's the great thing. You don't actually have to go. Really, you could be better off *not* going."

To this I listened openmouthed. He seemed to have read my mind. He seemed to have been looking over my shoulder, down there in the Pink Elephant. "No kidding? Do you believe that?"

"Absolutely. At least, that's how I am."

I thanked him sincerely and left, feeling lighter than I had when I got there.

When I walked into the Rainbow Café, Shirl was perched on her cash-register stool, smoking. Through a puff of smoke she leveled a look at me that said she couldn't place me but hardly cared. I said hello to her, and she nodded, uncertainty shading off into suspicion. Then Charlene called to her for a couple of Danish and Shirl slipped from her stool to reach into the pastry case and slide two apple Danish onto a plate. I offered to carry the plate to Charlene to save Shirl from exertion and she was glad not to have to walk the six steps to take it herself.

There was never much talk in the Rainbow on mornings except for ordering breakfast, and even that was very subdued. Throat clearing, cigarette smoking, and checking themselves in the long mirror to see what bad humor looked like took the place of wisecracking and giving Charlene a pat on the behind. Everyone seemed sore at morning for making them go through it all over again. As the day wore on, the customers would loosen up and by lunch be downright jolly, kidding around and telling bad jokes. It was kind of like the progress Mrs. Davidow made through her martini pitcher.

Maud, though, was always the same; she didn't have a morning person who differed from her afternoon one. You could always depend

on Maud. Right now she was taking orders in the rear booths while Charlene worked the counter.

The Sheriff would have been in probably by seven A.M. What I was hoping was that he'd come back, and I'd no sooner thought it than he walked in the door. More than anyone else I know, the Sheriff walks with authority written all over him. He placed his visored cap on the pole between the booths, sat down, and asked how I was.

I felt something beneath the innocent question and decided to jump right in. "Did you find her? That poor girl who was lost?"

"Nope. No one's notified us."

He was obviously not worried, but I'd rather he'd move his not-worried blue eyes from mine. I had to look away. I shrugged and said, "I guess she must've been found." I crinkled up my forehead to show the difficulty I had working my way to this conclusion. But when I looked up again, the blue eyes were still with me. It probably was not wise, but the only other thing I could think of was Ben Queen. Casually, I said, "I guess you don't know any more about the man you think shot that woman? The one out near White's Bridge?" I added, as if there were so many shot women around he might have trouble identifying this one.

"Ben Queen."

"You know, maybe it's better just imagining you caught him than to actually do it." I realized as soon as I'd said it that vacations and catching killers didn't exactly go by the same rules of imagination.

"Whatever that's supposed to mean."

He just went on looking at me and I sighed and buried myself in the menu, which I never did because it never changed. Once I flicked a look his way to find the blue eyes hadn't faltered. I felt like a snowman melting under a hard blue sky. I suddenly realized I might work on his sympathy. "Guess what? My mother and Mrs. Davidow and Ree-Jane have all gone to Florida. I bet it's really nice there." I looked really sad. He would have to sympathize.

"They left you and Will behind?"

I slowly nodded and wished I had an onion. I batted my eyelashes as if I was holding back a current of tears. Funny, but this was different from the way I'd felt giving this news to Father Freeman.

The Sheriff still looked at me as he took out a cigarette (this being the smoking booth), lit it, and clicked his lighter closed. He inhaled, then exhaled, as if he weren't at all pressed for time. "I can understand why you'd stay behind."

That sounded odd. I frowned. "Why?"

"You're too busy to go to Florida."

I sat back, *thump,* as my mouth fell open. This was my *involuntary* dumb look. I thanked my lucky stars that Maud came back. She sat beside me and his blue gaze shifted to her.

"I've just been out to the Silver Pear."

"Oh? Having lunch on your expense account?" Maud said.

"No. Showing the owners some pictures." He took three snapshots from his shirt pocket, buttoned the pocket again, and set them down on the table, side by side.

Maud squinted. "How sweet. You were showing pictures of me around."

His finger tapped the second one.

Maud smiled. "Look there, that's all three of us. Did they recognize you from the picture?"

"Very funny." He turned it so I could see it. I squinted, suggesting the snapshot was so bad the people in it were scarcely recognizable.

The Sheriff said, "That's the three of us one day checking the meters."

"Interesting," said Maud, "how other people get their pictures taken at weddings, or strolling in Rome, or even just having drinks by the pool. But us? We get ours snapped by a parking meter."

I'm glad she kept talking, even though he didn't much care to hear her, for it gave me time to frown in a huge bout of failing to understand this picture. I frowned not only as if I failed to understand *this* snapshot, but as if I would never understand any snapshot ever again.

He said, "Both Gaby and Ron agreed this little girl was the one they saw the night we got called out by Asa Butternut." Pause. "How about that?" He looked at me as if he were some sculptor chipping away. His eyes chiseled my forehead into a frown. So, I guess he knew what was behind it, in there behind my forehead. But I was not going to give in just because some dumb, blurry snapshot supposedly proved things.

I said, after a lot of careful thought, "Wait a minute!" I snapped my fingers. "That was the day Mrs. Davidow and I went to the Silver Pear for lunch!"

The Sheriff leaned halfway across the table and said, "Emma, knowing your relationship with Lola, I doubt she'd be taking you to the Silver Pear."

I'd started shaking my head and kept on shaking it through this little speech. "I just happened to be with her. She had to go out to see a person who lives on the lake. Then she decided she'd give herself

a treat—and me, as I happened to be with her—at the Silver Pear. That's why they saw me." I smiled, but not too widely.

"According to them, this girl was alone."

Now I sighed heavily, as if explaining something to a mongoose. "Well, they just didn't *see* Mrs. Davidow. We sat out on the porch, around the corner. They saw me because I went in to use the ladies room."

His eyes burrowed into mine. "The girl asked them for the use of the telephone."

"I didn't *say* I didn't use the *phone.* Mrs. Davidow wanted me to call my mother to tell her she'd be back a little late. By then she'd already drunk three martinis and was telling me what a pain Ree-Jane is. I could have told her that without drinking even one."

My hands were clasped on the table and the Sheriff leaned over and put his own hand around them, as if he were cuffing me. His hand was nice and warm. "Now, you listen to me, Emma Graham. You are not, I repeat *not,* to mount your own investigation here. You are *not* to go around to these places, especially the White's Bridge Road area, asking questions. This is a murder investigation and there's a killer still out there and I don't want to find you lying in a damned pool of blood—"

"*Sam!*" Maud exclaimed. "You don't have to scare her to death!"

He sat back. "Scare *her*? You're kidding."

Maybe he was being sarcastic, but it helped answer the courage question I was always putting to myself.

I had taken all of the Sheriff's remarks in, of course, and it made me feel good that he was worried about me. But it just wasn't getting me any further along and I didn't have time to waste. And now, with him being suspicious, the method I was going to use to find out about Dwayne would never work. And that left Donny. I asked the Sheriff if he was going back to the courthouse when he left here.

"No. I'm going out to the lake."

In La Porte, that meant Lake Noir, not Spirit Lake, where nobody goes except me. I felt suddenly very sad. "I'm sorry, but I have to leave."

"Just remember what I said, now."

"Sure." I thanked Maud and stopped on the way out for doughnuts.

"Interview a *what?*" said Donny. He looked like a squirrel when he squinted.

"A poacher."

Donny threw his arms wide as if to present this unbelievable request to everyone in the room. It wasn't very effective, as there was only Maureen Kneff, the typist, and she was cracking gum, resting her chin on her overlapped arms, which were positioned on her typewriter. Maureen's eyes were washed-out blue, the only eyes I'd seen to compete with Ree-Jane's for pure absence of thought.

I really can't stand Donny Mooma. He likes to make people think he's dangerous when all he does is hide behind the Sheriff if they run into trouble out on a call. I made sure he would not be going back to the courthouse right away, then bought three vanilla-iced doughnuts (my favorite, not Donny's), and crossed the street.

Donny was sitting with his feet up on the Sheriff's desk, looking belligerent. He thawed out a little when I handed over the doughnuts, taking one for myself first. I told him I had this school project: "I'm writing this paper on poaching. There's a lot of it going on around here, especially over around the lake. Bunny Caruso told me."

"Bunny Caruso? Your mom know you're talking to Bunny Caruso?"

I realized too late Bunny wasn't the best source to bring up. I sighed. "I'm not really talking to her. I mean we're not sitting around jawing at each other over a couple of beers."

Donny's look was clouded. "Yeah, well, you best be careful."

"Anyway, why shouldn't I talk to Bunny? She's nice."

Donny would be too embarrassed to tell me what was wrong with being around Bunny and we could go back to poaching.

"You know, places like White's Bridge, around there. There's a lot of rabbit hunting going on."

"*Poaching* ain't exactly what me and Sam would call a major event. It ain't what this office would have at the top of its list. Top pri-*or*-i-ty, if you want to know." He'd polished off one doughnut and reached into the bag for the other. "Hey, Maureen! How's about some *coffee?* You ain't too *busy*?"

Like a sleepwalker, Maureen rose from her typist's chair and swayed out of the room to wherever the coffee machine was.

Donny brushed a bit of icing from his shirt, sat back with his free hand behind his head, and started on the doughnut. He had no intention of offering them around. After munching half of it down, he said, "And what poacher would do an *interview,* God's sakes? It's against the *law,* little lady—"

(I gritted my teeth. I hated being called that.)

"—so who'd ever *admit* to it?"

"Well, of course, I wouldn't *name* the poacher. I have to respect my sources."

"*Sources?* Who d'you think you are, Suzie Whitelaw?" I got treated to that wheezy laugh of his, which if anybody else did it you'd think they were strangling to death.

"It's not my fault, is it? I'm not the . . . social science teacher." I wasn't at all sure what subject poaching would come under.

"Go to the library and bone up."

"I have. That's not going to help with poaching around *here.*" I considered for a moment. "I need a human interest part. See, the best report is to be printed in the paper. I don't mean the school paper, I mean the *real* one—the *Conservative.* So I need one poacher interview and one police interview." That should get him going.

"Oh?" The way he wrinkled up his nose pulled on his upper lip so he looked like a pig. "That right?"

I nodded. "The Sheriff says you're really good at nabbing poachers."

Donny looked astonished. "No kidding. Well."

"The Sheriff says 'If Donny can't nab 'em, they can't be nabbed.' " I pretended to be reading this out of my notebook. "I'd like to use that quote, if you don't mind."

"Nah—that's okay. But put in my last name." He shook his finger up and down toward my notebook. "And make sure it's spelt right." His doughnut now forgotten, he leaned back again with his fingers laced behind his head. He pursed his lips and blew out air. "Well, I guess it don't matter if I give you a name or two. It ain't no secret, as these've been reported anyway in the paper. One's named Billy Kneff." Here he looked over his shoulder to see if Maureen was still absent. He whispered. "Maureen's cousin, but he don't mean no harm, I guess. Let's see . . ."

Patiently, I waited to be done with Billy Kneff.

"Billy lives out your way, across the tracks. We had him in three times for out-of-season deer hunting. Then there's a fella named Dwayne Hayden—"

Without moving a muscle, I came immediately to full life.

"—lives in the White's Bridge area. We—I—nabbed him, like Sam says, twice."

My pencil was poised. "Where does he live?"

Donny just flapped his arm around. "I never seen his house, but it's in that area. Not far from that fancy restaurant."

"The Silver Pear?"

"Yeah, that's it. Dwayne works over at Abel Slaw's garage. He's what you call a master mechanic. You don't really think these guys is gonna talk to *you?* Hell, girl, they'd tell Suzie Whitelaw to get lost, and she's a *real* reporter." He leaned forward suddenly. "And for God's sakes, don't go tellin' 'em where you got their names."

"I promise. Thanks."

As I turned to go, Donny was sniffing the air, like a dog sensing danger.

Master mechanic

25

I wondered how much more a "master" knew than a regular mechanic. Pondering this alternated in my mind with the Florida trip. Walter and I had calculated they'd be driving the Tamiami Trail by now. So naturally I wanted to keep my eye on the clock.

I was sitting on the bench outside Britten's store. It was the one I always sat on when conferring with the Wood boys and Mr. Root, and right now I was waiting for them to come along, for they always did about this time, after the Woods got back from La Porte and their hot roast beef and mashed potatoes lunch at the Rainbow.

Lunch in the dining room had been fairly quiet. Only once did Miss Bertha raise a rumpus and that was because I'd put a tomato slice in her grilled cheese sandwich. I told her I was just trying to make it more interesting (which I wasn't; I just wanted to see how she'd react), and she said grilled cheese wasn't supposed to be interesting.

I heard something like a shout behind me and turned. Ulub and Ubub were coming along the path that ran by Britten's. They waved and so did I. Mr. Root was limping across the highway and I could see he was hurrying, seeing me and them, and probably was afraid he'd miss something important. He waved too with his free hand. The other was carrying a brown bag which looked like one of Greg's hamburger bags.

Ubub and Mr. Root got to the bench about the same time, Ulub having gone into Britten's for soft drinks. We sat down as if we met here every day and were pretty much used to one another's complaints and comments. Mr. Root went on about the rheumatism in his knees and Ubub and I made noises of sympathy.

Ulub came across the sandy gravel with Cokes for them and a Nehi grape for me. I told him thanks and I'd pay him back. He just waved that away as he did Mr. Root's outstretched hand holding money for the soda. The Woods are really generous. They always shared, even if it was just one Hershey bar among us.

We were quiet awhile, sipping our sodas. Mr. Root examined the pickle on his hamburger and asked if anyone wanted it. No one did. Then I told them, in detail, the story of my night on White's Bridge Road, and Mr. Butternut, and Brokedown House. I must say I had them more enthralled than Will's and Mill's audiences ever were. Mr. Root even forgot to eat all of his hamburger, saying "I'll be," and "B'jeezus" every once in a while. Ulub or Ubub would echo it. They were really awed when I told them about the Sheriff coming, together with the state troopers.

Round-eyed, Ulub said, "Nay er nookin er *ou?"*

I was getting more used to Wood-speech, and figured Ulub had said, "They were lookin' for you?" I answered, "Yes. They were looking for me. Only they didn't *know* it. Then the Sheriff for some reason got suspicious—" (I stopped short of that "stubborn as a mule" bit) "—and he went back to the Silver Pear with a picture of him and me and Maud and, of course, the Silver Pear owner, Gaby, recognized me. I had to make up a story about being there with Lola Davidow."

Mr. Root had his railroad cap raised and was scratching his head and shaking it, sorely astonished.

"And he told me I was *not* to investigate on my own."

Well, at this, Mr. Root just looked away and made a blubbery sound with his lips, waving the Sheriff away, as if to say, "Damn fool." Ulub and Ubub watched him and they did the same thing, their blubbery lip sounds saying the same thing and somehow I was pleased that they thought I wasn't going to pay any attention to the Sheriff's order, and he could like it or lump it. I was not quite that sure of myself, and, not that the Sheriff wasn't worth paying attention to, but I was glad they thought I was doing a good job.

Finally, I got to my point. "This Dwayne Hayden works over at Slaw's Garage."

Ulub and Ubub started talking a mile a minute to each other and to us. "E fenz eye ruck!" said Ulub.

Ubub nodded quickly and said, "Eye'n oo. On ut eye'nm ill air."

Mr. Root worked this out fast, snapping his fingers. "This Dwayne's fixing their trucks—right, fellows?"

They both nodded.

"Well," I said, sliding off the bench, "I think we should go see how they're doing."

Abel Slaw was a wiry little man who'd had this garage since time began. Lola Davidow brought her station wagon in here and had nothing to say against Abel Slaw. This alone was a huge recommendation. Ree-Jane took her convertible in even if there was nothing wrong with it, and now I knew why.

Whether the master mechanic worked on their cars, I don't know. There were two other ordinary mechanics walking around with tools in their hands and grease and oil-spattered coveralls. One of them I think was named Rod and I never did know the other one's name, for all they called him was You-boy, as that's what his mother had called him all his life ("You-boy, come on away from that!"). They both stopped when they saw us and pulled grimy rags from their back pockets and wiped their hands. Abel Slaw came over to us, also wiping his hands on a rag, though I didn't see he was working on any cars. Maybe there's something special about wiping your hands on a rag pulled from your back pocket that sets you apart as a mechanic.

"Evenin,' Ulub, Elijah. You too, young lady."

I managed a smile.

"S'pect you're here about your ve-hic-le." He turned to look at the truck. Dwayne Hayden must have been the pair of legs under Ulub's truck; the license plate read ULB, so it was definitely Ulub's. "Hey, Dwayne," Abel called as if they were on two sides of a huge canyon. "That truck 'bout done?"

Whatever Dwayne answered was lost on the far side of the canyon. It was being underneath a truck that garbled the sound of his reply. But Abel Slaw understood it, maybe in the same way Mr. Root understood Ulub and Ubub. Master mechanics didn't have to make smart conversation. Abel said, "Not quite, but he will be mebbe in a hour? Or thereabouts."

It sounded like a question, which only made the amount of time even more vague. "Sure, we can wait, can't we?"

Abel kind of raised his eyebrows at this coming from me, but he just shrugged and said, "You want to set down, you k'n go into the office."

Mr. Root said, "Thank you kindly, but we'll just hang around."

"Folks ain't supposed t'be out here, what with all the equipment and stuff lyin' around. But suit yourself." He retreated as if at the end of a long argument.

I hadn't worked out exactly what I was going to say to Dwayne; all I knew was, I needed someone there when I went back to Broke-down House. I mean, someone with a gun.

For a while I chewed the inside of my mouth, then I walked over to the side of the car, closer to where Dwayne's head should be. I was wearing a skirt today and made sure to knife it down between my legs when I squatted, in case he looked up it.

"Hey, Dwayne," I said. "I just want to talk to you for a minute."

"Who're you?" There was more clanging underneath.

"Emma Graham."

"Don't know anyone of that particular name."

"Yes, you do. We never got properly introduced," I whispered. "I wanted to talk to you about where we were—you know—a few nights ago, and the rabbits?"

The pallet he was lying on rolled out from under the truck pretty fast. For a minute he looked at me and frowned, and then, apparently deciding there was no thrill in it, he eased himself back under the truck. Maybe he still didn't recognize me. (According to Ree-Jane, mine was the most forgettable face in the universe.)

But Dwayne's face wasn't forgettable; you'd have thought I was telling—or living in—a fairy tale the way the handsome men lined up: the Sheriff, Ben Queen, Dwayne Hayden. Any one of them could have stood in for the prince who saves the girl (me)—that is, if you go just by looks alone. I, of course, do not. I tried to get down as far as the running board to look under it and see his face. "I only wanted to ask you something."

The pallet slid out again. He just looked at me.

"Can't you at least get off that for a minute?"

I didn't think he'd pay any attention to that, but he surprised me and stood.

"I gotta look under the hood, anyway."

He said this as if he wanted to be clear he wasn't coming out just to see me. Then he pulled a cloth out of his rear pocket—confirming my impression that mechanics always have to do this—and began wiping his fingers with it.

"The way things went, I'd think you'd remember me. How many kids do you meet up with out there?"

He didn't smile; I should say he gave me the impression of someone trying not to smile.

"I was just wondering if you go around there much on a regular basis? Where I saw you night before last?" When I get nervous I sometimes stand on the sides of my feet the way little kids do. I'm embarrassed when I catch myself doing it. I stood up straight.

Still wiping his hands free of oil, he said, "Uh-huh. And just what do you want to know that for? You planning on turning me in?"

I thought of Ben Queen and felt a sudden bleakness. "I don't turn people in. Anyway—" I lowered my voice. "—I carried the rabbits, so that makes me a . . . accessory co-conspirator." I frowned. Was that the word?

"So why do you want to know?"

"I've got a really good reason." I made myself look as earnest as possible.

"Yeah. You keep saying."

I looked around at where I'd left the Woods and Mr. Root. They were all taking to Abel Slaw as if they'd been in some car graveyard for years and were just now surfacing.

Again, I lowered my voice. "I can't tell you *here;* it's too public."

"Well, better you come over to my place later on and we'll split a beer."

I frowned. "I don't drink."

Now, he stuffed the rag back in his pocket. His hands didn't look much cleaner.

"I'm surprised."

I guess he was making fun of me, but I would ignore that. "Listen: I could meet you out there at Brokedown House. But you'd have to *promise* that you'd come."

He screwed his face up in the most utter surprise I'd ever seen, except when Will was playing innocent. "Promise? You're talking like you're doin' *me* a favor."

I shook my hands in impatience. "Well, but *will* you?"

He paused for some moments, watching me and probably thinking I was crazy. A crazy kid.

"Hey, Dwayne!" Abel Slaw was calling him. "Ulub wonders will he get his truck back this year?"

That, of course, was ridiculous. Ulub wouldn't have strained himself putting that into words.

"Yeah, Abe. Won't be but another few minutes."

And he went around to look under the hood. I followed. "Will you do it? Meet me at where we were before?"

"My Lord, girl, you are crazy to go around asking strange men to meet you in some deserted place at night."

I laced and unlaced my fingers, another nervous habit. "That's just it. It's not deserted."

Tamiami Trail

26

We set the meeting for seven-thirty that evening, which would allow time for serving dinner at six. It was an annoyance to have to stop my life just to wait on Miss Bertha, but I couldn't make Walter do all the work. Also, I didn't want Miss Bertha reporting back to my mother that he was doing it.

When I got back to the hotel I checked my Florida map again with Walter looking over my shoulder as he wiped a big oblong pan. (I wondered where he found all these dirty dishes and utensils that had him washing and drying all day.)

"Where do you think they are on the Tamiami Trail?"

"Along in here, mebbe." Walter poked a finger in the middle of the red line I'd drawn.

I told Walter my vacation plans and that if he wanted, he could share them. He'd be sharing by waiting on me, but I didn't exactly put it that way. He said he always wanted to go to Florida, which I doubted, for I didn't think he was even aware of it until everyone decided to go there. Right now, I asked him to mix up some of the coconut drink and I'd be back as soon as I changed clothes.

My swimsuit was over a year old and too little by now and flouncy, with its gathered skirt, which I thought was babyish, and its bright daisy design, which I disliked also. But I wasn't about to go to the expense of buying a new swimsuit. I forced myself into the daisy design and wrapped a big towel around me, which I'd taken from a guest room. I stuck my feet in sandals, gathered up my reading matter, went down to the kitchen to pick up my drink, and made my way to the Pink Elephant.

I imagined the Tamiami Trail. It was straight and white and lined with royal palms stretching away into the blue distance. We were too far inland to catch sight of the ocean yet, but I still thought I could make out the sigh of the waves coming from the invisible sea, as well as the rustle of the palm fronds. Cooling breezes holding the smell of the sea washed through the open car windows and stirred up little eddies of sand by the road. The day was as soft as a feather bed; it was a day you could lie down in and be comforted.

The car sped along, passing shacks and stores that didn't come clear in my mind until we passed a petting zoo and Ree-Jane chimed in that we weren't going to stop, thinking I wanted to. I didn't because the animals I glimpsed looked awfully sad. I had enough sadness going on without adding more to it. We went through a little town that I didn't want to bother with. On the other side, though, was a coconut grove and a stand where a girl was opening coconuts and carving up pieces from the shell. She also had a big pitcher of the coconut drink sitting in ice. I said we should stop, and we did stop. (This was clearly one of the benefits Father Freeman was talking about.)

Ree-Jane howled with impatience and my mother told her to shut up, a thing she would never do if left to her own devices. But these were now my devices. We got out and all had a glass of the coconut drink. (I picked mine up from the picnic table before me.) I told them all it was excellent. Mrs. Davidow said a little rum would liven it up and we all laughed, except for Ree-Jane, of course, who was in a mood. The coconut milk was really good. We piled back into the station wagon and Mrs. Davidow said we should look out for a place to eat lunch.

I thought it was really too bad that the graceful palm tree landscape had to be broken up here and there by clapboard buildings selling souvenirs, surfboards, and conch sandwiches. Boys in shorts and sneakers were milling about in front of one, and Ree-Jane, of course, wanted to stop there, and got into a real snit when her mother said No, she had no intention of eating a conch sandwich.

A little farther along, I spied a hamburger place. It was impossible to miss, for a giant hamburger atop iron legs stood outside like a water tower. There was something about this hamburger that awoke in me a rush of nostalgia, but I couldn't grasp for what. And I think it was the bun instead of the hamburger itself that did this. It was silky smooth, a light brown running into copper at the edges. Where had I eaten such a hamburger? How was it I could still taste it in my mind?

But Ree-Jane didn't want to stop at a "kids' place" and her mother was on the lookout for somewhere that served cocktails, so I was out-voted, even though my mother would have been willing to have hamburgers. It was not really a tie, though, as my mother's agreeing with me was pretty weak.

Not too much farther along we passed—well, nearly passed—a place called Trader Bob's. The sign outlined in neon sported a martini glass, also in neon and winking on and off. Lola Davidow slammed her foot on the brake so hard it nearly sent me through the front window. It was a little way off the Tamiami Trail, and we drove up a rutted road to its fake island-cottage front.

Inside, it was dark, dark even after my eyes adjusted from the brightness outside. The shadowy interior made it hard to report on what I saw, except for Mrs. Davidow's drink when it arrived. It looked stronger even than one of Aurora Paradise's Cold Comforts. It seemed to sit in rainbow layers of liquor and was as tall as her forearm. My mother had something with a splash of rum in it and Ree-Jane hautily asked for a wine spritzer. I had a Trader Bob's Special, which left out the alcohol but put in everything else. All the drinks were decorated with tiny paper umbrellas in turquoise and pink.

The six-piece band started in playing.

(Here, I left my chair and put "Tangerine" on Ree-Jane's phonograph.)

The band in Trader Bob's didn't have a female singer and I offered my services. They were delighted when I sang:

Tan-ger-eeen,
She is all they claim,
With her eyes of night and lips as bright as flaaaame . . .
Taaaan-ger-eeen . . .

I was up now singing and swaying to the music, a little in the way of a palm tree, I hoped. The customers (who I couldn't see clearly and it was just as well) applauded many times. They didn't want me to sit down but I explained we were driving the Tamiami Trail and couldn't stay. I returned to the table where Ree-Jane was laughing in that dark and soundless way of hers that was more like charades than an actual laugh. My mother told me I was good, and Mrs. Davidow ordered another drink and shrimp salad.

There was a knock at the door of the Pink Elephant and I called, "Come in!"

Walter entered carrying a plate of grass I had told him to cut and set it on the table. "Here's your seagrass salad, ma'am." I thanked him, and he left. I did not eat it, of course.

My mother and Ree-Jane were now arguing about which one would drive as we more or less had to support Lola Davidow out to the car and slide her in the passenger seat while she sang "Tangerine" at the top of her lungs. My mother won, naturally. She might have entrusted a plate of fried chicken to Ree-Jane, but she wasn't about to entrust our lives to her.

So eastward we drove on the Tamiami Trail into a deep coral sky, the sun going down behind us, darkening into a grainy blue dusk with the black silhouettes of the royal palms vanishing into the distance. It was just like the picture I had tacked up on the wall of the Pink Elephant. It was just like it, down to the faintest bluish-pink line of the horizon.

It was a relief to know that some things are real, that some things don't lie.

My real life

27

My real life is what I thought about, standing at the stove watching Miss Bertha's dinner heat up.

My mother had cooked a lot of food (having no faith in Mrs. Eikleburger) and put it in the freezer, clearly marked. She had left oven temperatures and cooking times for me, too. Tonight it was to be meat loaf with mushroom gravy. I had told her Miss Bertha's favorite, or one of them, was meat loaf, which it wasn't. Mrs. Fulbright liked it a lot. As for the mushroom gravy, Miss Bertha really hated it because she was sure all mushrooms were dangerous and called them toadstools. She was certain she'd get a poisonous one, which she probably would if I knew where they were. Since she wouldn't eat the mushroom gravy, I cut her square of meat loaf open, scooped out some, and stuffed the sauteed mushrooms inside. I sealed it back up. You really couldn't tell.

Now I stood before the stove, watching the peas warming in

one pot and the mashed potatoes in the other, thinking about my real life. Was it now, waiting for the food to heat up? It made me uncomfortable to think my real life was watching over Miss Bertha's dinner.

I walked over to the tin-lined counter at the end of the draining board, where Walter was washing dishes, and set down some dirty utensils and the frying pan in which I'd resauteed the mushrooms. I asked, "Walter, do you ever wonder what your real life is?"

"Uh-uh." He shook his head.

He could be so annoying. "Well, wonder *now.* Wonder what your real life is."

"Okay." He went around and around a glass platter with a dishrag.

There was this exasperating silence. I didn't know whether he was wondering or not. Probably not. I was scraping bits of blackened onion grit from the frying pan, waiting.

"Well?"

"I guess it's washin' this here dish."

Deesh, he said. Walter was *so* practical about life.

"Not just your *life.* Your *real* life. What you're *meant* to do."

He was silent for a moment, then he said, "Washin' these here pots and pans, looks like. Looks like the same thing to me."

I heard Miss Bertha's cane smarting the wood floor of the dining room and picked up their basket of rolls from the serving counter. I took them in with the water pitcher.

As she looped her cane around a third chair at the table, Miss Bertha complained again that the "two of them" had no business going off both at the same time, and what was for dinner?

Meat loaf with mushroom gravy.

There came a sound of satisfaction from Mrs. Fulbright and a big grunt from Miss Bertha. She complained that my mother wasn't there to cook her something else, and wasn't that part-time German cook here?

No, not tonight.

I let Walter dish up the food, as he really enjoyed doing that and was very neat about it. After taking in their plates, the steam rising from the potatoes, I went back to the kitchen and waited.

There came a yell and a chair overturning and I started for the back door, asking Walter to go see what was wrong.

Then I ran across the grass to the other back door and up the stairs to my room.

As I changed my skirt for my jeans, I wondered again what my real life was. Or what it should be. I stared in the mirror, pressing my fingers into my cheeks, and watched as the skin whitened and the color returned when I took my fingers away. Then I pressed my finger tips against my forehead. I was seeing how solid I was. I felt ghostly, as if the inside of me had been scooped out and replaced with nothing, not even mushrooms.

I was told to keep Aurora happy and that meant Cold Comforts. And that meant getting another bottle of Southern Comfort out of the storage room. I knew Mrs. Davidow kept the key way back in a cubbyhole in the rolltop desk in the back office (which would have been the first place I'd look if I'd been a thief). After I knuckled it out, I stuck my head into the dumbwaiter opening in the wall beside the desk to listen to what might be going on. Aurora could make more noise for her single self than any human being I have ever encountered. It often sounded like she had a party going on.

I went up to the third floor and got the bottle, stopping among the clothes and blankets to admire some of Ree-Jane's clothes. I always had a secret hankering after one of her evening dresses (she had several): it was the one my mother had made for her for her Sweet Sixteen party. It was white tulle and chiffon, the skirt spangled all over with sequins, very small ones that seemed to show not themselves but their reflected light. It was white and silver. I took the dress down and put it over my arm and carried it, along with the Southern Comfort, to the kitchen.

After I poured the Southern Comfort and brandy, I mixed in the usual ingredients of fruit juice, some gin, and my secret ingredient, which changed every time I made it. I took the glass back to the office and called up the dumbwaiter shaft: "Aurora Paradise, I'm sending up your Cold Comfort!"

Then came a scuffling and a creaking and her voice bellowing down the shaft: " 'Bout time you did!" She gave two knocks with her cane, the all-clear signal, though why it wouldn't be clear was more than I could say. I set the glass—which reminded me of Lola's drink at Trader Bob's—in the box and pulled on the cord. Up it went.

"You got it?" I called, half of me in the shaft, looking up at semidarkness. She yelled back that she had. "I'll have Walter bring up your dinner." Silence. I guess now that she had her Cold Comfort she saw no need to put herself out by answering. "I have to go out," I called up.

Then I heard her whine: "Go out? You? Wherever would you have to go to? It's evening."

"I do have a life of my own."

"No, you don't."

That really irritated me. But the irritation only masked something else. A cold center gathered inside me. I was afraid she might be right.

Brokedown House, revisited

28

The Woods and Mr. Root were already at Britten's when I got there a half-hour later. They were gathered by the truck, talking at a great rate as if they'd just discovered a common language in a country of foreigners. Maybe they had.

As it was Ulub's truck, he drove and I insisted Ubub sit in front as he was the brother and they could talk (which would save me from trying to talk to them). Mr. Root and I argued briefly over the jump seat; he said his rheumatism was really acting up, and I had nothing to go up against that, so I sat on a blanket on the floor.

"Dwayne must not have gotten around to fixing this truck," I said, after we'd driven through La Porte and were bumping down the highway. My voice was as bumpy as the ride. Then I was sorry I'd commented, as both Ulub and Ubub went into the details of the repairs, none of which I understood, and Mr. Root was chawing at tobacco and seemed miles away. I never realized before how much Ulub and Ubub talked to each other. Their speech kind of fitted in with the choppy ride.

"Turn off!" I said. Nobody was paying attention.

Ulub swung the truck right to the narrower road, and soon I saw the Silver Pear, its big silver sign turning everything in its surroundings an eerie, ashy shade, flashing in and out among the trees like a knife that might at any moment bury itself in the ground, and I wondered if it would draw forth silver blood.

I was hanging over the front seat giving directions that the pond was just over the bridge. The bridge rumbled beneath us as if every plank was loose. It was just the truck, though. We braked to a stop beside Mirror Pond and got out and stood looking at the muddy, weed-choked pond.

"Ain't much of a pond," said Mr. Root. After delivering a stream of tobacco off to one side, he wiped his mouth with the back of his hand and added, "Ain't much of a place."

"I never said it was." I was secretly offended but didn't want to show it. "It doesn't have to be fascinating to have somebody killed near it."

Mr. Root warmed his hands beneath his armpits and didn't comment.

"Ar eh aunt'd owz?" Ubub said.

I scratched my elbow, frowning. It was "Where" something.

Scarcely hesitating, Mr. Root repeated, " 'Where's the house?' That it, Bub?"

"Aun'd, aun'd!"

I frowned. "Awning?"

"You sayin' 'haunted,' ain't ya?"

Ubub nodded enthusiastically and it kind of irritated me that Mr. Root could always figure it out. But then I reminded myself I'd never have gotten this far without his ability to do that. "It's not exactly haunted, Ubub."

"Uhn abow neh ite?" This was Ulub this time. It was hard to tell between them, although Mr. Root thought Ulub spoke more clearly.

" 'Tonight'?"

"That ain't it," Mr. Root said again, with more authority than I liked. "He's askin' about the light. You know, you told us some sissy showed a flashlight right in your face."

"Oh, but that was no ghost, Ulub."

I stood looking down White's Bridge Road, looking for something familiar, but there was nothing familiar. With all that had happened that night, with all of the people and commotion, I expected things to be burned into my eyes—the mossy tree, the spot in the road where I'd dropped the rabbits, the oil drum, the bed of black nasturtiums, the ruts the police cars had angled into the dirt—why, this place had been *crowded.* Tonight it was empty, as if all the life had been sucked out of it.

Mr. Root must have seen me as being uncertain and said, "Maybe we ought to stop and get this Butternut feller to show us—"

"No!" I said. "He was the one reported me missing, don't you remember? Anyway, Mr. Butternut would only spend all the time talking. Come on, it's just right down here." I'd say I led thc way except there wasn't more than one way to lead.

As dusk seemed about to cave into dark, the road and the things along it grew more familiar, as if they would only make themselves known at night, like the stars, one or two of which were showing faintly, near the vague moon. "Some of those stars are a billion—a lot more than a billion—miles away. It would take us thirty years to get to them. Shooting stars are bits and pieces of broken-up planets." We had stopped while I delivered this information and now we picked up walking (Ulub and Ubub still with their eyes clamped on the sky). Then I told them there were many more universes than just ours, and planets that had more than one moon going around them. "Every planet has moons. Some a few, some many." I thought a bit. "That's where that expression 'many moons' comes from, from planetary language." This was most of what I knew of star lore, and some of what I didn't.

Mr. Root stopped. "Now, that ain't so. 'Many moons'—that's some old Indian sayin'."

"I *know* it's Indian; it's what the Indians said about moons."

We walked on.

"Hey!"

We all turned.

"Wait up, now!"

I groaned. It was Mr. Butternut. If he was the spirit of the place, I might as well go home.

Hobbling up to us, he didn't look in too good shape. "Mr. Butternut!" I tried to make it sound like there was no more pleasant a surprise for me than seeing him.

After I'd introduced him around, he started in asking questions. "Where you been? I had to call the *po*-lice on you."

I looked really concerned, though puzzled. "Why's that? Did something happen?"

"Well, a'*course,* girl! You was missing! You sayin' you don't recall?" He took out his tobacco and bit off a plug. Remembering his manners, he offered it around. The Woods shook their heads, but Mr. Root accepted, having run out of his own.

These few seconds gave me time to think, all the while keeping the puzzled expression on my face, which was still there when I answered: "Missing? I was never missing or lost."

Mr. Butternut heaved a sigh: "Girl, we was both down there—" He pointed with his cane down the road. "—near to Brokedown House and you went on that path to it and just disappeared."

I sighed myself, meaning to register as much impatience as he had. "Well, of course I know *that.* I dropped my flashlight and couldn't find my way, so I wound up back on this road and just walked back to the Silver Pear. I never saw you so I figured you'd gone on home to bed." I smiled more at myself than anyone else for it was really a plausible story. Was my life becoming a pack of lies?

He looked at me in a squinty way and chewed. Mr. Root looked at me squinty-eyed too, as if he knew Mr. Butternut better than he did me. I guess they'd forged a tobacco bond between them. Ulub and Ubub weren't paying much attention but were looking up at the darker sky and the handfuls of stars now scattered there, probably thinking of the long trip to get to them.

"And I went and called the *po*-lice. I thought that *Deg*-un fellow—"

"It's not '*Deg*-un,' it's 'De-*geen.*' "

"I thought he was goin' to throw a fit."

My eyes widened, really interested, now. "Why? What'd he say?"

"Well, it ain't so much what he *said* as the way he *looked.* I was tryin' to describe you and I couldn't recall too much how you looked. I did tell him you was real headstrong. Then *he* described you. Light-haired, blue-green eyes, freckles across your nose, and real pretty." Mr. Butternut frowned, looking at me as if testing that description.

My mouth fell open. *Pretty. Real* pretty! It was worth a trip to White's Bridge Road to hear that. It was worth a trip to a brokedown planet to hear that. I tucked this away in my mind to look at later. And it made me feel kindly toward Mr. Butternut. I apologized for causing him so much trouble and he said never mind, only he hoped I let it be known to that Sheriff I was okay.

I said I would, and now we were all looking up at a black sky where the stars were a drift of white that made me think of that tulle dress of Ree-Jane's that hung now over a chair in the Pink Elephant.

But it was all so far away it was hard to say which was drifting, the stars or us.

"Ah i'ky 'ay," Ubub said.

Mr. Root gave him a pretend punch on the shoulder. "Milky Way; you got it, Bub."

And in the next moment I knew what was meant by night falling. For it did. I think it's the sort of dark that waits in all our closets, mine being a wardrobe that I hardly ever had to look in any more to see if anything's there.

We got to the overgrown path that led to the house and Mr. Root stopped us with a fierce whisper: "Lookie there!"

A dim light moved through the trees. It was probably a flashlight or maybe a lantern and reminded me of those lanterns Ulub said the Devereau sisters carried as they made their way through the woods beyond their house. We were all quiet, even me, and watching in a wondering kind of way. I said, "Maybe it's Dwayne."

"Dwayne?" said Mr. Root. "What the hell's—pardon my French—Dwayne doing here?"

"Let's go see." I pointed to the path. "You can be first if you want."

"Me?" Mr. Root clapped his hands to his chest. "It's *your* expe-di-tion."

"I don't want always to be hogging first place." I turned to Ulub and Ubub. "You can lead the way." I smiled brightly.

But Mr. Butternut stuck his cane in the ground. "Don't you do it, Bub. Nor you neither," he said to Ulub.

Now, I was getting really irritated with Mr. Root and Mr. Butternut. Mr. Butternut, of course, didn't want to go anywhere; he just wanted to link up with us so he could talk.

"Oh, for heaven's sake," I said, and in what I thought was a high-born, queenly manner, lifted my chin and walked the path to the cottage. I thought surely they'd be following on my heels, but when I looked back, the four of them just stood there as if struck in stone.

I gestured for them to follow and finally they did, single file, coming up the path. I said, "What we should do is, each one of you should take up different positions around the house in case whoever was here comes back."

Mr. Butternut didn't like that, but the other three were perfectly agreeable. Mr. Root asked if I was really going in the house.

I wasn't. "Yes," I said. "In a minute. Right now I'm going around back."

Which I did, and found Dwayne. *"Dwayne!"* I tried to breathe the name, but in this silence I might just as well have yelled.

He turned, looked first one way then the other, then at the rhododendron bush I was peeking over. "Oh, Christ a'mighty! You near scared me to death."

I couldn't make out whether he was glad to see me or wished he never had. "Shush!" I said, coming around the bush. "Keep your voice down. Listen: was that you?"

"Was that me what?" He was lighting a cigarette, hands cupped around a match. It had a good effect on his face, the light and the shadow.

"We saw a light, a flashlight, probably, over there—" I pointed off to the stand of maples.

"Who's 'we'?"

"Me and and Mr. Root and so forth."

"Brought your goons this time, did you? So what'd you want with me?"

I didn't answer. Instead, I asked, "Was that your *flashlight* we saw?" There was a big square one sitting on the ground beside his sack. "Is that rabbits?" Tentatively I touched the sack with my toe. "I didn't hear any gun go off."

He didn't comment. I supposed he didn't want to bother. I sat down on a nearby stump, regardless of the others who were waiting at their appointed places. Dwayne had opened the bag. There was only one rabbit.

"Defenseless little creature," I said.

"More'n I can say for you."

I was impatient. "Well, did you? See it?"

"You mean that light? Well, we're not the only poachers here. Ever think of that? Easiest answer is the right one, usually."

No, it isn't, I thought. Still, I felt deflated, thinking in this case he might be right. But that still didn't explain whoever had been in the house. I said so.

"Why not? I've been inside that place and maybe I'd've shined a light in your face too, stop you jabberin'."

Here he did just that, and I threw up my arm to shade my eyes. "Stop that! This isn't funny."

But the light had also hit something else, judging by Dwayne's reaction. "What the hell?"

The others had appeared out of the bushes and come around the house, and even though I knew they were around, it seemed creepy even to me, as if the familiar could change in the seconds it took to shine a light in your face.

"Looks like I should've brought a keg," said Dwayne, smiling a little. " 'lo, fellas."

"Dwayne," said Mr. Root, nodding. The Woods both said hello, too.

"Now, I just got this feelin," Dwayne said to me, "that whatever spook you're after, he or she ain't about to come out to greet a group of six."

He was really annoying me. "Who said 'spook'? It's not a ghost or the Headless Horseman. It's not Creepy Hollow."

"*Sleepy* Hollow, you mean. Ichabod Crane."

I ignored this. "It's a *person. Somebody* shone that light in my face." Suddenly, I was near to tears, tired of not being understood.

They were silent and almost respectful, even Dwayne, who I bet was always just one step away from a joke. They looked almost ashamed. Which suited me fine. "You're supposed to be surrounding the house in case someone comes. They'll have to pass near enough that one of us sees who it is. And everyone's talking too loud—"

"And too much," said Dwayne, going back to his other self.

"So split up and surround the house. Dwayne can stay here."

Dwayne wasn't about to move, anyway. He was flicking his flashlight on and off at the ground.

"Du-*wayne*," I said, the way Vera liked to say, "*Emmm*-a," as if no one could be slower on the uptake than me. "This isn't a *game*."

"It ain't nothin, far as I can see, but okay, let's do it so I can get back to killing rabbits. What about yourself? What are you going to be doing while we're surrounding?"

Astounding myself, I said, "I'm going to be inside—" I looked over my shoulder at the cottage. "—looking around."

As far as I was concerned, now was the time to argue with me. But no one did. I wasn't going in that house again, alone. Of course, I wasn't going to admit this, so what could I say? After some thought, I said, "Well, I like that. Here's five grown men who'd let a little kid just walk right into danger!" I shook and shook my head in disbelief and only stopped shaking it (my legs were rubbery and hardly good for walking with) when Dwayne heaved a great sigh.

"Come on then," he said, looking around at the others. "You fellas are safer outside with whatever than inside with you-know-who."

I told the others as they went to take up places not to make so much noise and watch where they walked. To be truthful, I was probably making more noise than any of them. Yet it was odd how the silence out here could be shattered so easily by a twig's snap or dead leaves crisping underfoot, or the creak of a high-up branch moving in the slight wind. Each sound was distinct and seemed carved out of the night, like those profiles carved in ivory, raised against a dark setting. It was the way I think I'd feel if I'd never heard these sounds before. Was it like the world waking up and hearing itself for the first time?

"Well, come on," said Dwayne, as I was bending down to tie my shoelace, which I did so he could get in front of me.

"You don't have your gun," I said, following at what looked to be a safe distance.

"What the Sam Hill you think we're gonna run into?"

"I don't know. Snakes, maybe?"

He picked up the gun and looked at me, shaking his head. "Snakes. So I just load up my gun and draw a bead on old man milk snake and blast him to kingdom come?" He started walking again, ahead of me. "Girl, that is not how you kill a snake. You wouldn't last five minutes out in the real world."

I *have* lasted, I wanted to say. But I settled for sticking my tongue out at his back.

The back door was off its top hinge and listing to one side. "Doesn't look like this door's been used for a long time." He tried to open it, but it was warped shut.

"There's a side door," I said, pointing. "Go on," I said, urging him in. He just gave me a look, shook his head, and went in through the door. I had not meant, of course, I would go in right away. Rounding the corner I bumped into Mr. Butternut, standing stock still on the path. "You're supposed to be off there," I motioned to an off-there place, "hiding."

"I done. I hid by that old mulberry bush and didn't see nor hear a thing."

I was so exasperated. It was as if "hiding" was an activity you did in a predetermined time period, like school lunch hour. "So go back."

"Aw right, aw right. Don't be so damn tetchy." Grumbling, he went off.

I could see the spread of Dwayne's light through the side window. Since I was supposed to be inside too, I had the strange feeling I was watching myself. I walked through the door that Dwayne had left open. Inside it was black as sin and I tried to blink up shapes. It was the front room where I'd been before when that light turned on my face.

"Dwayne!" Forget about quiet. I yelled it.

"Yeah?" He yelled back.

Then I heard a tapping on the glass pane behind me, whirled around, and felt my heart fall into my shoes at the sight of a face.

It was only Ulub, but Ulub's face isn't the best-looking even at high noon in the Rainbow Café. With that lantern of his below it making pits of his eyes, well, it's not the best thing to see when you're already scared. I was surprised the window opened, but it did. Was this evidence the house was occupied?

"Ulub! You scared me nearly to death!"

"Ah een nun ah nun owin—"

"Uh-huh. Okay," I said, not understanding a word except "I." He trotted off. I wanted only to be where the gun was and hurried into the next room.

Dwayne was standing by a chiffonier, inspecting an old tin box on its high top. This room was a bedroom, and it was hard to tell whether someone was using it or not, for the disarray could be new or could be old. I'm sure the Sheriff could have told in ten seconds by observing dents in the cushions, dust on the bedside table, the warmth of the sheets. But these told me nothing. The daybed was roughly covered by a patchwork quilt. I felt to see if the bedclothes were warm, but of course they were neither warm nor cold. In one corner of the room was a chair with stuffed animals and dolls on it. I went over and looked at them: two bisque dolls that appeared to be very old, their dresses stiffened and yellow; a rag doll with one button eye missing; another doll with a pretty white dress. I thought it was peculiar they wouldn't have been removed in the course of moving. I picked up the rag doll with one eye missing. Was it a child's room?

Probably not. The room reminded me, when I looked around again, of the one up on the fourth floor, the one kitty-cornered to Aurora's room. In that room, my mother stored her own things. But it was not nearly so neat as Mrs. Davidow's storage room. My mother's jewelry and clothes lay here and there, as if she'd recently been either examining them or wearing them. There were scarves and shoes about, again as if my mother had just thrown them off. The guests' kids sometimes snuck up there, and if Aurora didn't kill them first, they crept into this room and played with all the stuff. It was never locked. It upset me, this careless disregard for family treasures and mementos. For if that's not worth standing watch over, then what is?

Dwayne held up a ring, a deep blue stone, oval and set among tiny diamonds. Or at least the bits looked like diamonds; they were probably rhinestones. "There's jewelry in here, there's even money. Other stuff too: pictures and letters."

The tin box was a more elaborate version of my Whitman's candy box. It reminded me of other things too: the box that Mrs. Louderback sorted through to get her tarot cards, and the cigar box in the back office where Lola Davidow kept small things like erasers and lipsticks. I wondered if everyone had such a box at least once in her lifetime.

"Some of it's old, some looks new."

For evidence of this he showed me an old photograph, speckled brown with age, of a young man. He recalled to me someone I thought I knew, but who? "Let me see. Hold your lantern up." He did and in the dark room it cast a sickly, bleached light across the contents of the box. There were all sorts of things: a twenty-dollar bill, coins, costume jewelry. Besides the blue stone, there was an amethyst ring surrounded by seed pearls. There were letters and cards, a valentine, its lacy doily stiff with age.

"Maybe they're love letters," I said, excited and breathless.

"Could be." Dwayne picked one up and held it close to the light. " 'Darlin', I slaughtered a hog this morning . . .' " He shook his head. "I hope no lady ever writes me that."

"It does not say that! You're making it all up." I yanked the page from his hand and read: " 'Wonderful to see you; I can scarcely wait until the summer.' See? He's writing how much he misses her."

Dwayne grunted. "How'd you know it's a he?"

As he turned away to put the tin box back atop the chiffonier, I made a face at him by pulling back the corners of my mouth. Making faces was something I'd pretty much given up as I got older, but he deserved it, being such a smart aleck.

"While you're getting all teary over that mail," he said, "whoever's living here might come back. And I don't want to be here when she does."

"How do you know it's a she?" I asked, smartly.

In answer, Dwayne held out a bottle he'd picked up from a cluttered piecrust table and held it out to me.

I sniffed it. It was a pleasant, green scent, the scent of grass and new leaves. "That could've been here from long ago."

"It's a half-full bottle. It would have dried up by now. The top's not even on tight."

"Should we take it for fingerprints?"

He gave me a lopsided look. "Whose fingerprints? Mine or yours?

Anybody else's, what the hell would they match 'em up with? Unless whoever it is has a record."

That made me think again of Ben Queen.

I heard a haunting cooing sound like the hoot of an owl. I took a few steps toward the other room, as it seemed to come from that direction, but then just stood where I was. I was overcome with such a feeling of oppression that I hadn't the heart to move farther. A memory came back to me of ice and snow and a sloping bank somewhere, and me going down it on my sled, whooping. Then the landscape broadened and, except it was winter, it looked just like the view across the tracks from the railroad station in Cold Flat Junction that had left me feeling empty like this—a far horizon studded with trees that looked like a solid line of navy blue, and the blue trees became that white line of trees, snow-shrouded, branches packed with snow so that they made, like the dark blue trees of Cold Flat Junction, a solid line. And above both landscapes, that sky hung, grayish-white, blank, and heavy as slate.

How had I got to that slope with my sled? No one else was about and no trail led to or away from it—no tracks, no footprints. I seemed to be whooping with joy in this memory, but I knew I wasn't happy. The truth was, I didn't feel anything. I think I must have been like the indifferent landscape. I fit right in.

"Emma."

Dwayne's voice jarred me out of my thoughts. I was still holding the doll with the buttonless eye.

"You're standing there like you're hypnotized or something."

"I was thinking."

"God help us all."

Then he picked up his gun, which had been leaning against the chiffonier. Suddenly, as he did this, the hairs on the back of my neck felt electric, and tiny currents of alarm traveled over them to my insides. "What's wrong?"

"Hear that noise?"

"You mean that owl sound?" Had it only just sounded? Did all of that landscape happen in my mind in only a second or two?

"Ain't no owl."

"What then?"

He was already walking out, taking the rifle and the light with him. Only the candle kept me from a plunge into darkness. Then came a light outside in the window. Ulub's and Mr. Root's faces showed on the other side.

" 'Ru ne'r, 'ru ne'r!" Ulub said, when I went to the window. He was motioning wildly to the woods on one side of the house. I left through the side door to see what the trouble was.

Mr. Root and Mr. Butternut had come around from the rear of the house. " 'Hell's he saying?" Mr. Butternut frowned at Ulub.

Mr. Root said, "You just mind your own talk." Then to Ulub, he directed, "Now, Bub, say that again."

" 'Ru ne'r. A ent 'ru ne'r." But poor Ulub sounded like all the starch had gone out of him, just trying to get this across.

Mr. Root said, "You're saying 'They went through there'?"

Ulub nodded, starchy again and pointing off to that part of the woods.

"More'n one person, Ulub?" asked Dwayne.

Ulub shook his head. "O'ney un. U ub en af er um."

"Only one," said Mr. Root. "You're sayin Ubub took off after them?"

Ulub nodded again.

There was that beaten path through the trees which came out on White's Bridge Road, the path we had taken when the police were outside Mr. Butternut's. So my story to Mr. Butternut before as to how I had missed him was perfectly plausible. It's nice to have a lie confirmed.

"Never mind," I said. "You were really brave to run after him in the first place. You don't even have a gun or any weapon at all." I hoped Dwayne would not take this personally—that I thought he should have gone after this person himself.

He didn't. He probably was not even paying attention to what I said. He was squinting off into the dark as if taking the night's measure. His jaw was quietly working; he was chewing gum and concentrating.

Mr. Butternut decided to build on my compliment to Ulub, saying, "That's absolutely right—what'd you say your name was?"

" 'On-no."

"Alonzo," said Mr. Root. "Nickname's 'Ulub.' "

Dwayne said, "I'm having a look." Off he went, on the narrow path into the trees, and I felt something like what I'd felt when Ben Queen walked away from Crystal Spring. We all stood around silently, waiting for him to come back. I think we were all really tired. Yet, it was pleasant in its way, this waiting sleepily among friends.

But Dwayne came back in a couple of minutes with nothing to report, "Except I picked this off the ground."

He held out a small tube. Atop it was the little painted head of

My Florida vacation II

29

If anyone ever needed a vacation it was me.

The next morning, I was checking into the Rony Plaza, wishing I'd brought more than one suitcase, as there were plenty of bellhops.

I gave my name to the desk clerk, informing him I was one of a party of four, and gave their names, too: Davidow and Graham. He asked where they were, and I was vague. "Held up," "Around," "They'll be here."

I was annoyed with myself for not having planned where they'd be, but last night I was too tired, and this morning I'd had to deal with Miss Bertha, who was trying to make an egg sandwich with her soft-boiled egg. She threw her toast on the floor after she'd got the egg all over everything. I told her for an egg sandwich she needed a fried egg, and I would fry her one. I helped Mrs. Fulbright clean the front of Miss Bertha's gray silk dress and then went out to the kitchen.

As he dried a roasting pan, Walter watched the egg fry. I stood

Niece Rhoda. I caught my breath. "Mr. Ree," I said. "Where'd you find it?"

"On the path." He hitched his thumb back over his shoulder. "Who's Mr. Ree?"

"A detective. It's a game." I was rapt. It was a game and someone was playing it with me.

with the spatula, waiting to turn it over. "That there egg's tough as shoe leather, it looks like." Walter smiled as he said this.

"After it fries on the other side, we can take it to the roof and use it for a shingle."

Walter laughed his gasping, braying laugh.

I did not wait around to see Miss Bertha's reaction to her shingle sandwich but instead whipped up to my room and got my bathing suit on again.

Down in the Pink Elephant, the first thing I did was turn on the fan aimed at my palm tree, and once I got the crepe paper fronds fluttering in the wind, I sat down and (as I said) walked into the Rony Plaza.

It really made me gasp, the lobby, as it was even more opulent than I had imagined. The ceiling was domed and inlaid with bits of gold and lapis lazuli and other semiprecious stones and looked something like the ceiling of St. Michael's in La Porte. I didn't want to linger on the ceiling as I didn't want to add any kind of religious stamp to the lobby. Between the high windows on either side of the long, long lobby were frescoes of flowers and fruit, sand and sea. Potted palms sat everywhere. Their fronds made lacy patterns on the faces of some of the guests who sat around on champagne- and cocoa-colored leather sofas and chairs, sipping vodka martinis or pastel-colored drinks from fluted glasses. I noticed (for Lola Davidow's sake) that the martini glasses were as big as skating rinks.

The desk person handed over my key to the bellhop—or he might have been the bell captain, as he was rather snooty—and inquired again about "the others." Oh, they'll be along, they'll be along, I said breezily, deciding as it was my vacation I didn't see why I should take up mental space figuring out what they were doing. (Though I would, of course, reserve plenty of space for Ree-Jane later on, as she nearly drowned, got bitten by a coral snake, or drank too many of those pastel-colored drinks and got arrested for being drunk and disorderly.)

Yes, my mother and Mrs. Davidow might remain vague presences at the Rony Plaza, wispy figures swirling here and there, but Ree-Jane would be rock solid in every detail of her soon-to-be-exposed modeless-ness. Ree-Jane was in for it.

But right now I was more interested in my room, and its balcony, and the filmy white curtains billowing in the open casement window, and the sea air coming through, and the wonderful view of the wrinkled sea. I stood on the balcony astonished by a blue that I had never seen before except in stained-glass windows. It was a blue that farther out turned to amethyst and purple. Royal palms lined the beach for what must have been a mile, for I could not, even leaning over the balcony balustrade, come to the end of them. They had no end, at least not in my Miami Beach.

I came in from the balcony. While I was unpacking my suitcase, I noticed a square envelope leaning against the mirror of the bureau. It was addressed in an elegant hand to me: *Miss Emma Graham.* I slipped the card from the envelope. There was to be a private dance, by invitation only, in the ballroom the next evening. How wonderful! I turned and regarded the closet with a sigh of relief. I was so glad I'd brought my white tulle dress with the sequins. From somewhere in the distance, the sounds of "Tangerine" came floating toward me—(Here, I jumped up and put the record on and poured my bucket of sand across the floor.)—and I practiced my dance steps, sliding across my room's champagne-colored carpet until it was time to change and go to the beach. I collected my suntan lotion, my big towel, and a copy of *Vogue.* I was wearing my wraparound sunglasses. Downstairs, I sailed out the door (a bellhop behind me, lugging my beach chair) onto the hot, white, Florida sand.

At this point my mind was too tired to actually go swimming, but I gave myself a kind of preview—like the "coming attractions" before the feature movie—hitting the high spots I'd see later, like when Ree-Jane goes in swimming (in her old black bathing suit), and the people on the beach see a big fin cutting through the water. I think it's called a "dorsal fin"; anyway, it's the one in movies you always see knifing the water and aimed right at you or, in this case, at Ree-Jane. But it was time to stop for the day. Ree-Jane's fate could be decided later. I planned also on giving my mother many new colorful dresses. Lola Davidow would wear nothing but brown.

Rainbow

30

I told Walter I had to go into town and would he please give Miss Bertha and Mrs. Fulbright and Aurora their Welsh rarebit for lunch. He said he sure would, and asked me how my vacation was going. I said I was going to a dance tomorrow evening and he said that was nice, and would I like him to wait tables at that hotel in Miami Beach? Or did they have enough help? Walter could really fall right into things.

Forgetting I was still in my bathing suit, I called Axel's Taxis and ordered up a cab. His dispatcher said Axel was right there. Then she must have turned around, for her voice got farther away. "Ain't doing nothing, are ya, Axel?" There was laughter. He'd be to the hotel right away.

I rushed up to get into my jeans and T-shirt.

When Delbert showed up, I told him to drive me to the Rainbow. I sat in the back and chewed my thumbnail, wondering how I could talk to the Sheriff without actually talking to him. My life was too complicated, and I was glad in between times I could rest up in Miami Beach.

The Rainbow was full as usual during lunchtime. Maud was in the act of setting their hot roast beef sandwiches before Ulub and Ubub. But I was surprised to see Mr. Root, who generally took his meals up at Greg's, which was across the highway from Britten's. The Woods must have brought him to the Rainbow; I was pleased to see his social life was expanding. Mr. Root was having a hot roast beef sandwich, too, and calling Maud "young lady," which made Maud smile.

They all said hello to me with real enthusiasm. Others at the counter also greeted me—Dodge Haines and Mayor Sims and Dr. Baum. It was nice to have all of these people happy to see me around.

Maud motioned me to the back booth as she filled a Coke glass. I sat down and she came along with my Coke and her cup of coffee. "Sam says your mother and Lola Davidow went off to Florida." She took out her cigarettes.

"And Ree-Jane, don't forget her." I told her they'd all gone to Miami and Will and I were supposed to take care of things at the hotel. I blushed; I felt oddly ashamed, but did not know why. Did I feel it was a judgment on me, having to stay behind? Did I feel I wasn't worthy of this trip?

"Well, that's—too bad that you couldn't go."

But her look was angry, and her clipped tone suggested she'd been going to say something else entirely.

Maud lived in a little cottage on Lake Noir. I thought she must know the White's Bridge area. "You wouldn't happen to know Dwayne Hayden?" I asked her. "The master mechanic?"

"Sounds like a magic act to me."

"He lives out your way is all."

She frowned in concentration. "The name sounds kind of familiar. Where's he mechanic at?"

"Slaw's Garage."

"Ah! Yes. I think he worked on my car once."

"But you don't have a car."

"Once I did. It was really old, but he did get it going for me. Told me it needed a new—something—and I couldn't afford it, so ever since it's been sitting at my house up on blocks. I kind of miss the poor thing."

Maud could even sympathize with inanimate things. She was really sensitive. But we were off the subject. "He lives somewhere near White's Bridge."

"Dwayne does? I didn't know that."

"No reason you should." I thought for a moment. "Mrs. Davidow and I stopped and ate at the Silver Pear once. It's really fancy, I mean the way they decorate their dishes, especially desserts."

"That's for sure. Decoration is most of the dinner. Leaves me hungry. Your mom's a better cook."

I didn't respond to that because I could see us getting off the subject again. "Well, while Mrs. Davidow was talking to some friends out on the porch there, I kind of wandered on across the bridge to have a look at Mirror Pond."

"You did?"

"I recall there was this old man there, and I wonder if it's the one the Sheriff was talking about. Anyway, he said he'd lived in this same house all his life, and his parents before him. His name's—" I pretended to be searching my memory.

"Butternut."

The Sheriff was standing right there. I hadn't heard him come up to the booth. Nor had we seen him approach because we were both sitting facing the wall and he'd come up behind us. "Asa Butternut. He's the one who called in about that lost girl," the Sheriff said, still wearing his black sunglasses, so I couldn't read meaning in his eyes.

"Oh, *yes,*" I said. "I forgot he was the one."

"But you didn't know him when I asked before. You'd never heard of him."

He removed his sunglasses and the blue of his eyes scorched me like the hot sands of Miami Beach. "So what about this Butternut?"

"Nobody but him, he says, lives along White's Bridge Road anymore, at least not up at his end. But of course it goes for miles, I think all the way to Spirit Lake. So he was telling me all about his family and how long they'd lived there, and of course we started in talking about the murder. This Mr. Butternut doesn't have a lot to do with his time, I guess, and so the murder was all he talked about. He talked to the police he said, but he didn't know anything much; I mean he'd never seen this Fern Queen before in his life."

The Sheriff only looked at me. I bet this was his way of dealing with suspects. You just look at them glassily and it makes them so nervous they finally give up information they want to keep. I wondered if his dark glasses were some protection for him. It was hard to think of the Sheriff needing any, but maybe we all did. I went on:

"Mr. Butternut told me about this house you were talking about: Brokedown House, I think. And he wondered if maybe someone might be—" Here a dilemma presented itself: I wanted the Sheriff's help, but if the person who might be using Brokedown House was Ben Queen, I sure didn't want to go leading the law to the door.

The Sheriff leaned toward me and broke the silence. "Someone might be what?"

I shrugged. "Using it, maybe?"

"Butternut didn't mention that to me. And that's where he took me. That's where he'd last seen this girl he called us about."

I should have known we'd get around to that again.

He said, "I doubt she was ever lost, not really."

"Brokedown House," I said, ignoring the lost girl. "Did it look to you like somebody might be living there?"

"We weren't looking for that. What makes you think somebody is?"

"I'm not saying it. Mr. Butternut was saying it." I certainly couldn't tell the Sheriff about someone shining a light in my face. But if Ben Queen were hiding out anywhere around here, I'd think he'd use the Devereau house, where I'd seen him. He might have gone to Louise Landis's. Her house was about the most private I'd ever seen. She'd have to be a pretty good actress, though, not to give anything away when I was there.

It was Maud who said, looking at the Sheriff, "Maybe you should take a ride over there, Sam. Maybe *we* should. Then you could drop me off at my house."

He looked at me. "You know, you ought to get together with this lost girl—if she ever gets herself found. You're two of a kind."

Lazy days at the Rony Plaza

31

***Two** of a kind.* Those words stayed with me. The Sheriff was kidding, but still it set me to wondering. I thought again about that day in Cold Flat Junction when I'd looked across the railroad tracks at the bench where I'd been sitting and thought I could make out myself on the bench, or maybe a ghost of myself. Could we have ghosts of ourselves before we're even dead? And if we can, are those ghosts like the ghosts of others who are dead? Not that I believe in ghosts; I was only wondering.

Fingerprints, footprints; the scent of perfume left behind; or charred paper, ashes of letters burned in a fireplace; a light moving in an empty house. Could the ghosts of us leave behind, like suspects in a crime, evidence we'd been there? Evidence for someone extremely smart in the ways of ghosts and suspects to decipher and track us down? Like the Sheriff or Father Freeman.

This would be a good question to ask Father Freeman, whose ability to see ghosts and spirits is a lot better than mine, his mind having been brought up, you could say, in the ways of the invisible.

All of this was making me hungry as I lounged in the Pink Elephant, so I ate the chicken-breast sandwich the beach waiter (Walter) had brought me as I studied the pop-up book of palm trees while I sunned myself on the Rony Plaza's beach that afternoon. I had found this book in the children's section of the Abigail Butte County Library. I was amazed to learn there were over four hundred varieties of palms. Comparing the pop-ups with my tree (its fronds moving gently in the sea wind), I decided mine might be more of a coconut than a royal palm, but if it was, it should have coconuts under the fronds and it didn't. So I decided I'd been right in the first place.

The book also had a pop-up of a hotel surrounded by palms but the hotel didn't resemble the Rony Plaza, for it didn't have the same kind of entrance and looked like it was farther back from the beach. I compared it with the big picture on my wall. Still, I thought the pop-ups were quite clever, even though they weren't realistic, and that children would probably like the book.

I watched the sun go down behind the Rony Plaza. It was after eight o'clock and all the sun and swimming and sea air had made me sleepy. I was glad the dance was tomorrow night as I honestly don't know how I'd have stayed awake for it tonight.

As I waited for Walter to get down here with my cocoa, I could hear Ree-Jane throwing a tantrum because she hadn't been invited to the dance by the hotel management. I did not know why (not yet, anyway). I thought about the dance minus Ree-Jane. Although anything minus Ree-Jane made me happy, in this case I wanted her to attend. I know that seems very generous of me, but it is not. If she doesn't go, I won't have the pleasure of dressing her in mud brown or watching her do numerous foolish things that will certainly not add to her popularity. I was too tired tonight to discover what she'd do, but it wouldn't be pretty, I was sure. So I saw myself leaving the beach where the floodlights had just come on and going to locate the manager—who had silver hair—and saying to him, "Look, it's the hotel's dance and all, but would you mind inviting the others in my party to it? I kind of hate to be the only one." The manager said he understood "absolutely," and the other members of my party would be welcome, although they couldn't "stay after midnight." I found that a peculiar rule and asked why. All he said was that only a very select group could stay beyond midnight. He did not tell me why.

At least my mother would get a new dress out of it. Lola would, of course, have to wear one of her old ones.

Scent of grass

32

As the next day wore on, I grew more and more excited, waiting for evening. Maud had called me to find out if I could drive with Sam and her out to White's Bridge Road, as she had suggested the day before. I was really astonished that the Sheriff would do this; on the other hand, as Maud had said, what did he have to lose? It was the crime scene, after all, and he'd found out precious little about who shot Fern Queen (which is what Maud had said to him, and which I didn't think was the most diplomatic way of getting him to agree to what she wanted).

Anyway, we were to meet up at the Rainbow that evening at seven o'clock. That was when Maud finished her stint. The Sheriff never seemed to finish his. He could be up until all hours on police business, as he had been when Mr. Butternut called in about the lost girl.

That brought me skidding to a stop in the dining room as I was going to Miss Bertha's table to put out the butter. If Mr. Butternut showed up when we were there—and didn't he always?—he'd certainly say something to the Sheriff about me being the girl he'd walked to Brokedown House with, the one who'd "disappeared." I pondered: could the Sheriff have guessed it was me? His description of the girl it might have been fit me, except for the "stubborn" part.

I found a rock-hard butter patty in the bottom of the bowl of ice and plopped that on Miss Bertha's bread-and-butter plate. Then I searched the butter on top until I found the softest one and dropped that on Mrs. Fulbright's.

I had made arrangements with Walter to serve them their dinner that evening and he said he thought he could manage. There was something put-upon in his reply and I figured he was just imitating my mother, who was always pressed for time but who also just "managed" whatever it was she was called upon to do. I said to Walter I was sure he could, as he had been smart enough to make my chicken sandwich out of white meat. Sometimes it's best to butter people up; in some instances I've never known the truth to help.

Maud and the Sheriff were standing on the sidewalk outside the Rainbow Café as the taxi rounded the corner. She was wearing her old brown coat, flared in a feminine fashion and buttoned at the neck with one big tiger-eye button. The Sheriff had one stem of his dark glasses hooked in his shirt pocket and I hoped that meant his mind was off duty. Not off duty in the sense he wouldn't be as smart as usual, just that he wouldn't be as suspicious as usual.

I caught this glimpse of Maud and the Sheriff through the window as Delbert slowed the taxi down and before they knew it was me. It jarred me, the way they were turned slightly to each other and how deeply involved they were in their talk. Even if the talk was just their usual banter, and though they stood in the wide, bright main street, the meeting still looked secret.

As I said, it jarred me. I hardly ever saw the Sheriff's wife; in fact, I had almost forgotten she existed until I saw her a little while ago in the Rainbow, buying pastry. He had been there too, coming in for his regular cup of coffee, and when I remembered that now, I thought it strange. For their meeting had looked accidental, like acquaintances who hadn't seen each other for some time. Florence was dark and stormy looking, her face shut down as a house would be in a storm, windows closed, doors bolted. But Maud's face was as clear and placid as lake water, so open you could have slipped right in.

We all piled into the police car, Maud remarking it was the first time she'd ever got a ride in one, and the Sheriff responding by saying it wasn't a taxi, after all, and me responding to his response that not even Axel's was a "taxi" as I never saw anybody in it.

"Fern Queen was in it," said the Sheriff.

Yes, and that made Axel's movements all the more mysterious. I reflected on this as the countryside flew by, as the same cows near the same fence looked at us curiously. It was rare being with peoplc who didn't have to talk all the time to feel comfortable with one another. For there were stretches of silence as we drove the highway to the lake. It was rare and I liked being part of that rarity.

I saw the sign of the Silver Pear right after we turned off the highway and felt I'd spent a large part of my life by now at White's Bridge. Inside of another five minutes we had crossed the bridge and were bumping along past Mirror Pond.

There was no sign of Mr. Butternut. The windows of his house were daubs of gold in the dusk. He liked having the lights on. This road had grown so familiar to me that I felt more than just a visitor; it was as if I'd been away and now was on the road home. No, not home exactly, but I think it's how *much* you feel when you're in a place that puts your personal stamp on it. Why Brokedown House should make me feel this, I honestly don't know.

The front door was stiffer than I remembered and I wanted to creep back when the Sheriff pushed at it. I said we could use the side door and he asked me how often I'd been here; I seemed to know it pretty well. As we three filed in, I saw how unlived-in and run-down it looked, with its possessions strewn about. The light coming through the fly-specked windows now was ashy and gave the walls and floorboard a gloomy look.

The small fireplace mantel had pulled out from the wall. It was some sort of marble, but after years of its bathing in fire and smoke, I couldn't tell whether the veins in the marble were green or black.

"It's cold," said Maud, drawing her coat closer about her. "It's the kind of cold a furnace wouldn't warm up."

I nodded. "I know just what you mean."

"It's the kind of cold you hear about that's on the sills of doors you walk through."

"The cold ghosts make."

"Oh, for God's sake," said the Sheriff, sighing. He was running a finger across the spines of a row of books. There were built-in bookshelves on both sides of the fireplace. Looking at one of the dusty books, he said, "The cold's different because the place hasn't seeped up any human warmth for a long time; the warmth has leaked out."

"Oh, sure," said Maud, disbelievingly.

"It has," he said. "Probably there isn't any heating except for space heaters. It used to be a nice summer cottage."

On the way here, the Sheriff had told us he had the county clerk look up the deeding of the property. The earliest information she had found showed the house had belonged to a Marshall Thring, had passed on to his heirs, then gone through the hands of several owners—Reckard, Bosun, Wheat—bought and sold, sold and bought, the last people being named Calhoun. I was familiar with none of these names, except for Calhoun, which is the name Mr. Butternut had said. The other names were useless to me in the solving of this mystery, would be soon forgotten. I think I wished the house itself had been plunged in mystery, that the Sheriff, for all of his searching through titles and deeds and documents, had found nothing, and that the owners were nowhere. Or that it had never changed hands after the original owner, a tall, black-bearded man named Crow, who, it was reported, had murdered his wife and put a curse on the house . . . well, something like that.

The furniture was wicker, similar to our own green wicker on the front porch but here a dirty white. The cushions were covered in cretonne, my mother's favorite material. The rose and lilac pattern was faded now, and dusty.

There were three bedrooms, one of them the one Dwayne and I had investigated, still with a trace of that green scent in the air from the half-full bottle of cologne. I only noticed it probably because I knew about it. The scent was very faint.

The Sheriff was looking over the letters on the bureau and had picked up one of them when he looked around and asked, "You wearing perfume, Maud?"

"Me? No, I hardly ever do. I forget to put it on." She was sitting on a footstool, looking at the stuffed animals and dolls. She was holding one, studying it.

I picked up the bottle of toilet water from the dressing table and waved it under his nose. "This?"

He sniffed. He nodded. "Yeah, that's it." He took the bottle from me, held it out to the quickly fading light of the window.

I said, "It hasn't been sitting around long. At least not all these years. It would have evaporated."

"You want to join the force? I could use a crime scene expert."

I had, as they say, the grace to blush. I wasn't about to tell him the idea had come from somebody else. So I just shrugged, as if such crime-scene-expert powers of mine were for me an everyday occurrence. If I kept up the way I had been lately, maybe they soon would be.

The room was dimly lit, as if only a vapor of light hung in the air and, like the trace of that grassy scent, evaporated as the minutes passed. Outside the light grew dimmer. Maud said, looking at the window, "I hope we have a flashlight. All I've got is this little penlight thing." She was searching in her canvas shopping bag.

He pulled a flashlight from the inside pocket of his jacket and held it up wordlessly. He appeared to be as interested as Dwayne had been in the collection of stuff on top of the bureau. He was looking at the ring with the dark blue stone set among tiny diamonds. "Lapis lazuli."

"What?" Maud turned from the doll collection.

"This ring. It's beautiful. Semiprecious, not valuable, still . . ."

I said, "Are those diamonds around it?" I could hardly see the ring from across the room, but he didn't seem to notice.

"I doubt it. Pretty, but not diamonds." He picked up one of the letters.

Do men with guns all go woozy over a few pieces of jewelry and somebody else's old love letters? If they were love letters. I never got the chance to read them, which was very annoying; I was the one, after all, who'd started investigating this place. "Do you think you should be reading other people's mail?"

He had rested a forearm on the bureau and angled his flashlight down on the paper. "In the line of duty," he said, without taking his eyes from the page. It might even be the same letter that had fascinated Dwayne.

"Well? What's it say?"

"Here—" He held it out. "You want to read it?"

"No. I don't read other people's mail." If I could ever get my hands on the hotel mail before Ree-Jane got it, that would change.

"Someone's very unhappy about leaving. I don't know if it's the leaver or the left." He had resumed his reading posture.

In spite of the cold, the growing dark, and my irritation that the Sheriff, and maybe Maud, too, were getting so much enjoyment out of this visit when I was gaining next to nothing, despite this, a warmth stole over me, stealthily, as if fearing rejection by my stiffer, glassy-eyed self. I did not know what the reason for this was.

Maybe there was a similar feeling when I was around Dwayne and the Woods and Mr. Root. The thing is, I did not have to bow and scrape to these people. Not that I'm much of a bower-and-scraper anyway, but I know I'm expected to be for Mrs. Davidow, Ree-Jane, the hotel guests, and people in La Porte like Helene Baum and the mayor. I could divide up everyone into the people who expect me to bow and scrape and the ones who don't. Most adults don't realize my feelings are just as important to me as theirs are to them. So maybe it's not so much not being taken to Florida, it's that no one wanted to listen to my feelings about not being taken—

The dance! The dance! It was to be tonight. But it didn't start until ten P.M. It couldn't have been more than eight, so I had plenty of time.

"What dance?" asked Maud.

I had said it aloud. That was so embarrassing. "What? Nothing, nothing. I was only thinking."

She just looked at me a moment longer and smiled.

Now, that's another thing about people who aren't like Maud, the ones you have to bow and scrape to. They don't really want to know how you're feeling, they want to know you're feeling the way they think you should be feeling. That's what they want to know.

I got annoyed with myself. Here the Sheriff is investigating—well, he's reading, so I guess it's investigating—and Maud is helping, in her way, and all I'm doing is going on to myself about myself. Can't I think of other people sometimes? But that question doesn't sound like me. What sounds more like me is wishing Shirl would slip on one of her banana cream pie banana peels and land on her butt right in front of everybody in the Rainbow. My wish list is long and murderous and I can only square that with my better self (I guess I have one) by saying, "They deserve it."

Maud was holding the doll on her lap when I saw her glance stray over my shoulder and heard her draw in a sharp breath. *"Sam!"* He turned to her; her finger pointed at the window. "There was a man out there, looking in."

Dwayne. I bet it was. Was he that stupid to be out there poaching with the Sheriff's car, clearly marked POLICE sitting right on the road? I positioned myself at Maud's side (for my sake, not hers).

The Sheriff went to the window and raised it. Now came sounds of a loud thrashing, like an elephant hurtling through the bushes. The Sheriff picked up his flashlight, slid his gun from its holster, and went into the front room. We followed close behind.

As he opened the front door, he said, "Stay here."

Sure. With only Maud's penlight between us? It was dark out. We waited until he was out the door and had rounded the side of the house before we followed him.

His arm was crooked, gun pointing at the sky. In the other hand he held the flashlight, fanning out light over the shrubbery, which was dark and dense. The rhododendron and mountain laurel were big enough to conceal a person; the dew-wet grass was tall enough in spots to wet my shins.

Behind him, Maud whispered, "It's probably just raccoons."

Or rabbits, I didn't add.

"Making that much noise? I don't think so. . . . Here comes—"

The dark shape coming through the weeds and bushes lightened steadily in the path of the Sheriff's flashlight and showed up as Dwayne. It didn't surprise me, of course, and I hadn't been scared, really. And Dwayne didn't seem in the least bit abashed at being caught red-handed. Well, he hadn't been *caught,* exactly, as there were no rabbits in evidence. Still, there was his rifle, which didn't look especially innocent.

"Sheriff," Dwayne said and nodded.

"Dwayne Hayden? What're you doing out here, Dwayne?" The Sheriff reholstered his gun and, strangely, I felt a rush of sadness. I was beginning to think that nothing in the world could make a person feel safer—not a parent's arms, not a million dollars, not a lifetime supply of ham pinwheels—than a man with a gun, cocked, ready to fire. Maybe I was entering my violent years.

"Nothin', really. Just walkin'," said Dwayne.

"You usually take that Winchester on your walks?"

"This?" As if he'd forgotten he had it. "Yeah, matter of fact, I do. Never can tell who you might meet up with."

"What was all that noise we heard? Maud here—"

"Maud." Dwayne dipped his head slightly in a greeting.

"Dwayne." She smiled. Dwayne had a way of making you smile even when he wasn't.

"—saw a face at the window," the Sheriff ended.

"T'wasn't me. Someone's around though, I know that. That's what the noise was, to answer your question." He turned and looked back through the undergrowth. "I was coming along from just through there—there's a sort of path through the brush that goes along more or less parallel to the road—and someone slipped past me. I don't mean on the same path; I was a little deeper in."

The Sheriff said, "Come on." They went back the way Dwayne had come, disappearing into the trees and thicket. I didn't like it, the way the woods could just swallow you up, the way the woods around Spirit Lake had swallowed up Ben Queen that night. It was black and thick with undergrowth. I heard them talking and wondered what they had found, but not enough to go into those bushes. Maud was holding my hand and I could tell she was not budging either. Their voices got farther away. Then there was silence. I looked at Maud, alarmed. She was straining to hear, too. Why was I so afraid now, when I hadn't been as much as ten minutes ago?

They came back. The Sheriff was asking Dwayne, "Did you get any sort of look at him?"

"Not really. And I wouldn't say it was a 'him,' neither. I think it was a woman. Woman or girl."

The Girl. I hope not. I hope she left this place. But she didn't strike me as a person who thought much about her own safety. Or anyone's safety, for that matter. There are some people who have a purpose, one purpose and only one, and disregard anything that's outside of that purpose. I think hers was getting rid of Fern Queen.

There was a silence as Dwayne lit a cigarette, then, remembering his manners, I guess, offered them around, including to me. At times, I thought everything was pretty much of a joke to Dwayne, probably including being arrested for poaching.

The Sheriff asked Maud, "Could it have been female, that face you saw?"

Maud seemed to be trying to bring the sight back to mind. "I don't think so, I don't . . . This face was so *heavy,* so . . . Russian."

Well, we all frowned at that. The Sheriff opened his mouth, then closed it, shaking his head. " 'Russian.' So you're saying it was a man?"

After more frowning, she said, "Look, I wouldn't want to die in a ditch on it, but, yes, I think it was a man's face."

He flicked his flashlight on and off, on and off, then said, as he started walking, "I want to have a look at that window. It was this one, right?" He pointed toward the side of the house around the corner.

"That's right," said Maud. We all followed him.

The Sheriff handed Dwyane his flashlight and knelt down, looking at the ground beneath the window. He told Dwayne to shine the light on the ground as he held his hand above the faint impression of a footprint. He rose. "I'll have Donny come tomorrow morning and go over this ground."

Oh, hell! I thought. Donny. If there's anyone I didn't want messing around in my mystery, it was Donny Mooma.

"You should've brought your murder bag," said Maud. She asked Dwayne for a cigarette.

The Sheriff stared at her. So did we. "My what?"

"Your murder bag. They all use them at Scotland Yard." She thanked Dwayne for the light and blew out a stream of smoke.

The Sheriff reclaimed his flashlight. "Now, just how do you know that?"

"Books, of course. Many books."

We had started walking now toward the car, Dwayne too. It was wonderful the way he just sort of fell in with whatever the crowd was doing.

"You like William Faulkner?" asked Dwayne, who was playing his own flashlight across the ground.

"Faulkner?" Maud seemed surprised. "Well, I tried reading him, but he's awful hard."

I walked with them, not wanting to be left out of the literary discussion.

"Some are," Dwayne said. "I agree. *Sound and the Fury,* that's hell on wheels, ain't it? But *Light in August,* that's not too tough. You should try that next time."

As if Maud were always picking up and tossing away one Billy Faulkner after another.

The Sheriff offered to give Dwayne a lift home, since he was dropping Maud off.

That meant I'd have him all to myself on the trip back to town. For that I'd read *The Sound and the Fury, Light in August,* and anything else Billy Faulkner ever wrote, hell on wheels or not.

End of the pier

33

Maud's house was really nice; it looked just like where Maud would live. It was a cottage, small and unfussy, and it backed onto Lake Noir, which was huge, black, and gleaming with the moon's reflection. Some time ago I'd heard this name was not the lake's real name, that some show-offy summer people had renamed it "Noir," and that hardly anyone could pronounce it right ("hardly anyone" being the uneducated people who lived here full time). Most people called it "Nor." Ree-Jane, naturally, went to great pains to give the word its French pronunciation. Mrs. Davidow tried to and sometimes did and sometimes didn't. My mother pronounced it correctly, as she felt it was a mark of "good breeding" to do so. I called it "Black Lake" because this really irritated Ree-Jane.

In the car, Dwayne had said that he'd get out at Maud's and walk from there, that the walk wasn't very far. Probably, he didn't want the Sheriff to see all the dead rabbits. But when we got to Maud's place, we all got out; that is, the Sheriff got out when the other two did, and when I saw that, of course I got out too. This surprised me, as we were to go back to La Porte after dropping them off.

Maud started down the sloping lawn and called back that we should all go down to the pier and that she'd bring us out something to drink. Apparently, we were really going to make a night of it. Being included in this made me feel very adult.

The Sheriff was the only one of us who had actually been out on the pier, though I remembered seeing it from a distance when driving to the lake with Mrs. Davidow. From what Dwayne said about the pier and the view, I could tell he'd never been here before. Maud went inside and we followed the Sheriff. I heard him mumble something about the "damned pier." He seemed not to be in a very good mood.

I thought the pier was wonderful. It was a little rickety, smelled of damp cedar or pine (I do not really know my woods), and stretched out into the lake. Most docks are kind of stubby, but this one sort of meandered out for forty or fifty feet. At the end of it, there was the rocking chair, table, and floor lamp.

"It's like an outdoor living room," I said.

"One of these days that damned lamp's going right over," said the Sheriff.

"Great for reading," said Dwayne, looking seriously as if he wished he'd brought Billy Faulkner along.

Maud came out with a tray rattling with beer bottles and glasses. For me I knew there'd be a Coke, which there was. Maud set the tray on the little table and handed the beer around.

The Sheriff said, "You got a half dozen extension cords running up to that house and some day you're going to set the place on fire if you don't electrocute yourself first."

By the way he shook his head and the look on Maud's face, I knew they must have had this argument more than once. Out on the lake, a speedboat carved the water and the moon's reflection folded and stretched and folded again.

Dwayne was sitting on the end of the pier with his legs dangling. I sat down beside him, and we both gulped from our bottles at the same time. Maud sat in her chair and switched on the lamp, most likely to annoy the Sheriff, more than from a need for light, as the moon was casting plenty of that, its surface so hard and white-bright it looked like a stage moon. The Sheriff stood behind Maud's chair, still looking in a bad mood, especially when Dwayne spoke to her.

"I wouldn't mind coming out here to sit and read." He twisted around to see her. "What kind of stuff do you read, Maud?"

She sounded pleased as punch to talk about her chair and lamp and reading with someone who approved and with the Sheriff listening. "I like poetry."

"You're ahead of me there," said Dwayne.

It occurred to me that Dwayne's manner of speaking—I mean his words and phrases—was sometimes as good as my own. I mean, Dwayne sounded like a hayseed a lot of the time, such as in Abel Slaw's garage, with his "don'ts" and "ain'ts," but around Maud he sounded well educated. I wondered if he was. William Faulkner sounded like the sort of writer that most people around here wouldn't touch with a ten-foot pole. Maud thought it was hard reading, and she was certainly intelligent.

"Well, I guess I better be getting back," said the Sheriff, drinking off the last of his bottled beer. "Emma?"

I didn't want to leave yet, for I was enjoying sitting here on the end of the pier, swinging my legs over the edge and with that marble platter of a moon shining down. But I got up, sighing, and we said our goodnights. The Sheriff offered again to drive Dwayne to his place and again Dwayne declined.

The Sheriff was quiet driving, and I had an idea he was wondering about Dwayne Hayden and Maud. I looked over at him while I pretended to be really fascinated by the police radio, putting my ear close to it, which allowed me to look at his face. I thought I saw something I hadn't seen before in it, but wasn't sure what it was. It looked like sorrow.

I sat back, trying to think of some way to bring up Maud without it seeming I was bringing up Maud. I asked, "When's Maud's son coming home from school?" Maud had a son who was four years older than me, but who I didn't see much because he was away at school. He always seems to be away, which is too bad because he's really good-looking. I recalled the times I'd seen him in the Rainbow. His name is Chad. He looks just like Maud, except, I don't know—"brighter" maybe. As if he were carrying a high-wattage light around inside him. At the same time, he isn't one of those people in constant high spirits who are always smiling and backslapping, like Dodge Haines, whom I can't stand.

"He lives part-time with his dad. It's his dad that pays for the fancy school. Then he and his wife take Chad on fancy vacations, too. I think right now he's in the Seychelles. Some exclusive trip."

It was exclusive all right. I'd never even heard of it. "What's the Seychelles?"

"Islands off—Madagascar? I think that's what she said."

"That's nearly all the way on the other side of the globe! It sounds like his dad just wants to keep him as far away as he can. That's really mean." As if to ward off such meanness, I turned to the window and crossed my arms across my chest. It really did make me mad.

The Sheriff was quiet. But I could sense he thought it was mean, too.

"And all Maud's got is her job at the Rainbow." I considered this unfair distribution of wealth. It was a little like me and Vera and the tips from guests. Vera saw she got most of it. "She can't afford exclusive vacations."

"Well, she lives on the lake. He can always swim and go boating and so forth. I mean, he *could* refuse."

I couldn't *believe* the Sheriff said that; he was usually so smart about people. "Refuse? Re*fuse* to go to the Seychelles? Refuse an exclusive *trip*? They wouldn't even take me along to *Florida*. Do you think *I'd* refuse a trip to the Seychelles?"

The Sheriff coughed and cleared his throat. "Well, I don't know, Emma. You never even heard about them till a minute ago."

"You know what I *mean*. You'd have to be nuts to think somebody our age—" I was glad to link myself with Maud's son that way. "—would turn down some fancy trip because we thought our mother wanted us to stay home with her. How nice do you think we *are?*" I don't think I put that right.

"Not very, I guess."

I punched his arm, lightly. "Anyway, it's different if you *live* in a vacation spot; you can't hardly think of it as a real vacation. Look at the Hotel Paradise. Do you imagine Aurora Paradise stands out on that stupid balcony on the fourth floor thinking what a wonderful vacation she's having in this great summer resort?"

"Aurora better not stand out on that balcony period unless she wants the fire marshal shutting down the hotel."

Really irritated with him, I slid down in the seat and shut my eyes. "That's so ridiculous. That's such an exaggeration." I was amazed to see out the side window the Dreamland Motel and sat up. "We're in *La Porte.*"

"Yep. I missed the Seychelles turnoff again."

Again I punched him and he laughed, really laughed, as if he'd forgotten all about Maud.

Good.

The Sheriff dropped me off, pulling right up under the porte cochere, saying goodnight and he'd see me tomorrow. He waited until I was inside the screen door and had turned and waved.

Waiting like that was the polite thing to do, I had learned from a series of lectures delivered by Ree-Jane on boys' manners: "Anyone boorish enough not to make sure you're inside the house should not be gone out with again," she'd said.

"You must know a lot of boorish, then."

"You mean *boors,* for God's sakes!"

"You're the one goes out with them, not me."

"What are you saying?"

"Just you haven't gone out with them again. I've never seen them around."

"You're *so* stupid."

I smiled. I always like it when she can't come up with anything better than *You're so stupid.*

As the Sheriff circled in front of the entrance, he tapped the horn, saying goodbye, and I watched the car down the long driveway to the highway. And then it hit me, as if the taps were on my heart: I'd wasted it. I'd wasted the time we'd been in the car together. There I had been, alone with the Sheriff, and could have talked about anything on earth that I wanted to and got his opinions and his advice. I could have talked about how awful waiting on tables was, and how I felt like the runt of the litter around Mrs. Davidow; I could have gone on about the stars, or love, or the Tamiami Trail. I could have told him about being left all alone, and not been invited to go to Florida—

The dance! I'd gone and forgotten it again! Mad as burnt cinders, I stomped up the stairs, making as much noise as I could, hoping to wake up Miss Bertha and Aurora. That was really dumb, as Miss Bertha was deaf as a doorpost and Aurora was probably drunk, and I'd just manage to bother nice old Mrs. Fulbright. (Nothing would bother Will and Mill except the Big Garage in flames.)

But all was quiet as I took off my jeans and shrugged into my nightshirt. Then I plopped down on the bed, pushing aside the teddy bear that sat against the cushions. I thought some more, and was annoyed some more, about having wasted all that time in the car arguing with the Sheriff, and play-punching him, after all the incredible things that had happened at Brokedown House. I had just frittered the time away, when I could have discussed anything.

Yet, I also realized you can never talk to anyone about anything you want to. You can only talk more to certain people (like the Sheriff, or Maud, or Father Freeman) than you can to others (like you-know-who). No, talks-about-anything are the talks you carry on with yourself; that's the only person you feel absolutely free to say whatever you want to.

I lay with my hands beneath my head and thought about the Rony Plaza. I found out the dance had been postponed: it was to be tomorrow night. I found another envelope emblazoned with the hotel crest, leaning against the mirror. The manager (who'd written it in a flowing script) apologized for this postponement, and assured me that one of the "hotel personnel" would make certain I got to my room safely afterward. *The Rony Plaza is well-known for its exquisite manners.*

I'm sure it is, I said to the bear, who I had picked up to see about its stuffing. He was a really old bear. He seemed not to have lost any more stuffing, so I held him against my chest and thought about the events of the night. I wondered if Dwayne was telling the truth about somebody running by him. There was absolutely no reason he wouldn't have; why wouldn't he be truthful? It was just that I knew the truth was hard to come by (especially if you were face-to-face with the Sheriff), but I decided, no, of course it was the truth.

I yawned and could barely keep my eyes open to think. I put the bear back against its pillow. I had stopped playing with him some time ago, but I kept him around, just as I kept a photo album to remind myself of what I used to look like and what I used to do.

Bartending

34

Miss Bertha threw her buttered toast on the floor at breakfast the next morning, much to Mrs. Fulbright's "mortification." Mrs. Fulbright had lived in the days when young ladies grew "deeply mortified" instead of just getting embarrassed. I think "mortify" is a nice word and does seem to suggest an embarrassment of the soul instead of the face (in other words, blushing), as if the mortified person has a lot more at stake. I did not pick up the toast.

Aurora usually didn't eat breakfast, but as I wanted more information from her, I decided she wouldn't say no to one of the "brunch" drinks listed in Mrs. Davidow's drink encyclopedia. The brunch drinks all had names meant to suggest flowers and summery flowery smells, like "Mimosa," and used a lot of champagne, all this to make you think you weren't really drinking at this early hour, at the same time knowing that champagne is just as good as anything else to get drunk on if you drink enough of it.

I knew I would need some fruit juice and knew we had orange and apple, but I had to look at the liquor supply before deciding. I made my way through the dining room, ignoring Miss Bertha's shouts for raspberry jam. I was making for the back office, where Lola Davidow kept her select bottles, the ones she liked to keep by her side in case of an earthquake. When she goes on a trip anyplace, she locks these bottles up in the black safe; I know the combination because she was out on the porch one evening and didn't want to get up herself and told me the combination. I made a note of it for future use.

Besides the Smirnoff and the Gordon's gin, there were bottles of Myers's Jamaican rum and Dewar's Scotch. I took these two out, figuring they'd be a nice change from vodka and gin. I closed the safe and marched back through the dining room with the rum and Scotch, again ignoring the howl Miss Bertha set up when she saw a slave walking by. As I slapped through the swinging door to the kitchen she was saying something about telling my mother on me. If Miss Bertha only knew how little my mother depended on her word to mete out punishments.

Orange juice and rum were probably good together, but then what wouldn't be if it was tossed in with Scotch and a thimble of brandy? I had out the orange and apple juice and was trying to think up a name. "Jamaica Juice" might do. I studied the bottle of Scotch. I had it! "Appledew"! Now that sounded like a beautiful morning-after drink! I jumped up and down a couple of times, cheering myself on for originality. Walter (back in the dishwashing shadows) called over to ask if I was on my vacation up here. I called back Not yet, but I would be after I took this Dewar's and apple juice up to Aurora.

"Appledew," I said to her, as she was turning it this way and that, inspecting it as if it were a precious gem. "It's a morning drink, a brunch drink."

She *hmpf'*d and said, "You know and I know only reason people eat brunch is so's they can vacuum up the Bloody Marys."

I found it interesting that she was beginning to think of me as the hotel bartender who'd heard it all. I watched her sipping and tasting, sipping and tasting. That was just for show, to let me know she wasn't a guzzler.

"Pretty good, pretty good. What'd you say its name is?"

"Appledew. It's mainly Dewar's Scotch and apple juice. Then there's the secret ingredient, too." Aurora loved secret ingredients. I stood as always with the small tin tray under my arm. She never asked me to sit down. She was playing solitaire and cheating as she always did. A queen of clubs sat atop a king of spades. It just exasperated me, but I told myself not to say anything. I think I got drawn in because her reasons for cheating were so ridiculous.

"You can't put black on black." I couldn't help myself.

"You can if it's the queen of spades."

"That's the queen of clubs you've got there."

"I meant the queen of clubs."

"It's no fun if you cheat."

"It ain't no fun if you *don't.*"

"You admit it! You admit you're cheating!"

"I never did; I never said I was having fun."

I gritted my teeth. This could go on for hours if I let it. "Okay, never mind the cards. I have a question."

"And I have an empty *glass.*"

When had she drunk it all? But I was sly. "Well, I'm not making you any more Appledew until you answer my question."

She, of course, was slyer. "Well, I ain't answering your question till you bring me another Appledew. How you like them apples, Missy?"

She thought that was *so* funny. Slapping her leg, she laughed and laughed, but it wasn't real laughter. It was put on for me. "Okay, I'll go ask Walter. He knows as much about Spirit Lake as you do."

"That man? He don't know—"

"Walter's lived here all his life."

"So've you and you don't know squat." Leaning forward in her rocking chair, she slid a ten of diamonds on a jack of hearts and looked up at me from under her stubs of gray eyelashes.

But I was sticking to my guns. I turned on my heel and marched out.

"Just you come back here, Miss! Ain't you got no manners? You don't walk away from your elders unless you're excused."

My back to her, I stuck my tongue out at the stair railing. I didn't want to push my luck; anyway, sticking your tongue out is something little kids do when they can't think of a good comeback, like Ree-Jane saying *You're so stupid!* I never wanted to get that desperate. Then I put on my blank expression, which is similar to but not exactly like my dumb look and turned back into the room.

"Oh, all right, all right, ask your question. One question." She held up a bony forefinger.

"Do you know a house over near White's Bridge called Broke-down House?" One question, she'd said, so I hurried on ". . . *and* whoever lived there? And the house might not have been called Brokedown years ago, as it probably wasn't broke down until—"

"Oh, stop runnin' at the mouth! Yes, I know that place. Long as I can think back that's what people called it. They was Calhouns lived there."

Calhoun. That was one of the names the Sheriff had listed.

"Last ones were Ethelbert Calhoun and his family. Had five or six kids. Kids is hard on a place as I am sure Jen Graham knows." She made shooing gestures with her fingers. "Get goin'. I'm parched."

"Well, but did this Calhoun family have—"

"*One* question, Miss Smartypants. I already answered two. You cheated and stuck an extra question onto the first one, don't think I didn't notice."

"Oh, all right." My tone was a bit too pouty for my tastes, and I turned and left and made my noisy way down the three flights of steps, running down them as I wanted to get back with the Appledew as fast as I could to hear more about Brokedown House.

Out in the kitchen where Walter was still polishing up the same serving platter, it looked like, I carelessly tossed rum and apple juice into the glass (not terribly concerned about proportions, not with all of my bartending experience) and thought about the Calhouns as I poured in the Dewar's. Calhoun: another name I'd never even known forty-eight hours ago, which now would attach itself to all of the other names, a cat's cradle of names that loosened or tightened depending how you pulled. Why is it, when you've got a mystery to solve, instead of getting answers along the way, you get still more questions? But maybe that's the way mystery goes—something like a painting, where the artist fills in more and more brush strokes, details, but the filling in makes the painting wider and wider.

I poured in orange juice, some more Dewar's, added a couple of maraschino cherries, and was off again up to the fourth floor.

"Ah!" said Aurora, whether to the Appledew or slapping a red king on a red ace, I don't know. She took the drink in her mittened hand.

"So, go on," I said.

"With what? This is better'n the last one. Did you add anything different?"

Only a quart more scotch, I didn't say. "Go on about the Calhouns."

"What about them?"

I squeezed my eyes shut, as if the effort would keep me from bonging her over the head with my tray. My sigh could have blown her off her balcony. "I thought you might just remember something useful about the Calhouns."

"No'm, I cannot think of a useful thing." She slurped her drink.

I would have to plod. "First off, did you know them?"

"Knew him, knew Ethelbert Calhoun, the daddy. He used to work around here doing odd jobs and such. Bert had a crush on me."

I nearly dropped my tray, I was so astonished. "The Calhouns were connected with the Hotel *Paradise?*"

"He was, so was his oldest girl, Rebecca. She waited tables sometimes. Brought her little sister with her to baby-sit."

I shook my head, so stunned by this bit of news I could hardly get off another question. "Well . . . *when*? When was all this?"

Aurora was busy poking her straw at the melting ice cubes. "Oh, forty, fifty years ago." She glanced up from her glass with that cunning look. "When I was just a girl."

Forty years ago, Aurora would have been middle-aged. But I thought it wise to let that go.

"My, yes. That was back in the days when every man from miles around was after me." She sat back and looked up at the ceiling, its plaster swimming with fine cracks. "Let me tell you the story of my youth."

Oh, no, I thought. We'd never get back to the Calhouns now. When Aurora got on herself, it meant we'd be here till the cows came home. Besides which, you couldn't tell what was truth and what was lies. But I would have to humor her if I ever wanted to find out more about Ethelbert Calhoun and his family.

She pointed behind her with her stick, too lazy to actually turn and look. "See that steamer trunk there? Got all them labels on it? I been everywhere, Miss Priss, and I mean *everywhere.*"

The old trunk, with its drawers open and spilling out silk scarves and underclothes and its small hangers holding beautiful, elaborately decorated gowns, looked to me as if it were on display, a stage setting. I groaned inwardly to think I might have to travel with Aurora to Rome and Hong Kong and India before I could get back to Brokedown House.

"It was in Sydney, Australia, when we all went to the opera house . . ." Again, she motioned behind her. "Go over to that old Victrola and put a record on. Put on the one on the top. That's Maria Callas, who invited us to supper after the performance."

Still carrying my tray, I went to the phonograph by the window and set the tray on the floor so I could wipe dust from the record with my arm. There were arias, it said, from different operas. I dropped it on the turntable.

"We traveled to the outback of Australia, then after Australia . . ."

I was prepared to be bored, not only by Aurora, but by opera. Instead, I was transfixed. As the music and Maria's voice swelled, I looked at the ceiling as if this heavenly sound were leaking through the honeycomb of cracks up there. Aurora talked and I listened. Every few seconds, Aurora's voice lapped over Maria's.

". . . Copenhagen's just full of prostitutes."

But her voice only registered for a moment, then it was gone. I dropped my head and closed my eyes, the better to hear Maria, and wondered why everything in the universe didn't sound like this record, I mean, if there was a God.

". . . then skinny-dipped in Lake Como."

Aurora cackled so hard she choked.

My thoughts seemed to turn liquid: the White's Bridge Road running into Maud's house and the end of the pier where Dwayne and I sat; light coming from the lamp moving across the Sheriff's face; the empty fields on the way back melting into the Tamiami Trail. It was all as if it was endless, seamless, with no starts and stops, no beginning and no end.

Something pointy dug at my shoulder. I lurched to find Aurora waving her stick in the air. "Ain't you payin' attention, Miss? That record's done. Put on . . . hmm . . . Patience and Prudence." Her drink finished, she licked the straw and smacked her lips.

Wearily, I got to my feet. I might have been as old as Aurora at that moment, what with the weight I felt on my back. I took Maria off the turntable, then looked through the dusty stack for the Patience and Prudence song. When I found it, I wiped it and put it on.

At the opening bars, Aurora said, "Good! We can have a sing-along!" She pounded the floor with her stick and started in:

I knoooow that you-hoo-hoo-hoo-hoooo
Have fow-ow-ow-ow-ound
Someone new-hoo-hoo-hoo-hoo,
*But to-*night *you be-*loong *to meeee.*

I just shook my head. I ought to have been more careful with that second drink. At this point I knew the Calhouns would have to wait; it was no good trying to get anything out of Aurora now. So I turned on my heel and left, saying goodbye, goodbye to her and Patience and Prudence.

I knooow with the daw-aw-aw-aw-awn
That you-hoo-hoo-hoo-hoo
Will be gah-ah-ah-ah-one
But to-night—

It followed me down the stairs.

—you be-loong *to meeee.*

Deaf

35

Walter had one of the kitchen aprons on and was stirring a pot. I apologized for being late and he said, as always, "Oh, that's all right," in his lumbering, uncomplicated voice. He said he was stirring cheese sauce for the "rabbit" (the Welsh rarebit, but I didn't correct him) and he could wait on Miss Bertha if I wanted, but I was feeling guilty for asking him to do so many things.

He stirred slowly; he did everything slowly. I stood next to him, watching. "We had this yesterday, didn't we?"

"Yeah. She don't like it, neither."

I watched the spoon smoothing out the sauce. "Leave some lumps in, she hates lumps."

He laughed his wheezy laugh.

It wasn't too bad at all being here without the usual kitchen drama supplied by my mother and Vera and Mrs. Davidow, who liked to sit on the edge of the white-enamel middle table where I did salads. No, it was kind of relaxing and left a lot of time and space to think in. (Also, it was nice being able to tell someone else what to do.)

I thought of what Aurora had told me. I was sure there was more. "Walter, do you know any Calhouns?"

"Prob'ly. Which ones? There's Calhouns all over."

"This one's an Ethelbert and he lived on White's Bridge Road."

"Ethelbert," said Walter, in his thinking voice.

"See, he once worked here. Before your time, of course. Forty years ago. You'd only have been a baby then. He's dead, I imagine, but some of his kids might still be around. The Calhouns is what Aurora told me; she says the daughter Rebecca waited tables here."

Walter frowned thoughtfully and tapped the wooden spoon slowly on the pot to dislodge the oatmeal.

"Rebecca. There's a Becky Calhoun I think married a Spiker."

I was excited. "Where do they live?"

Walter paused for a long thought. Then he said, "I think Cold Flat Junction. There's lots of Spikers around, too. I think she married Bewley Spiker. I ain't sure, now," he said, warning me not to put my complete faith in what he said and then be disappointed.

Cold Flat Junction! This was Fate.

I figured if Rebecca waited tables here, she must have been at least seventeen or eighteen (although the management here never seemed much bothered by child labor). That would make her in her midfifties now.

There was noise coming from the dining room, though how two old ladies could make so much I couldn't imagine. One old lady, I mean. I wasn't going to fool around with her this lunchtime. I had things to do. Walter put the bacon he'd fried onto a paper towel to absorb the grease, before putting it atop the toast and cheese sauce. (I was going to tell my mother how Walter had a real eye for detail.)

"You can dish up, Walter." He loved to do this.

"What about the old fool? You just know she's gonna want an omelette or somethin'."

"She'll want anything we're not serving."

Walter tittered and got the warm plates from the shelf above the stove.

I heard laughter and talk choked with it coming from outside the kitchen screen door. "That's Will and Mill," I said, surprised. I wasn't used to seeing them in the kitchen during the day.

It was laughter that could scarcely contain itself, doubled-up laughter. But the laughter ended the minute they walked through the door, as if God had cut through it with a cleaver. They were always like that; it astonished me how Will and Mill wanted everything they did to be a secret, and thus did not want to be caught out doing anything, including laughing.

"What's so funny?" I asked.

"Huh?" said Will. " 'Lo, Walter."

"Hey, Will."

Then I said to Mill, "You both were laughing fit to kill."

Mill adjusted the glasses perched on his blade-thin nose as if that would tell him who this person was who was speaking to him. "Laughing?"

Walter had spooned cheese sauce over the toast triangles, which he then decorated with the bacon strips. I picked up my tray and headed for the dining room. When I reached the swing door, I got an idea and turned. "Will, come and do your hearing-aid thing so I can get out of the dining room quick."

Will looked at me and said, "I'm too tired."

"No, you're *not.* I'll do something for you later." It was dangerous making an open-ended bargain like this with him, but I didn't have time to think up anything better.

"Okay. Come on," he said to Mill.

Wreathed in smiles, Will said *good afternoon good afternoon* to the two old ladies. Miss Bertha started in complaining when I put the rarebit in front of her.

"Where's the menu? We had this yesterday."

Will worked his mouth as if he were talking to her but no sound came out.

Miss Bertha tapped at her hearing aid and said, "What's wrong? I can't hear."

Will kept working his mouth, saying something to Mill, who worked his mouth back. They carried on a silent conversation for a few seconds.

Now, I really think this routine amused Mrs. Fulbright no end, but she did nothing except cut up her toast.

"Serena!" cried Miss Bertha. "What's wrong with this fool thing?"

Mrs. Fulbright just smiled and went for the pepper.

"Say that again!" she demanded of Will.

Will mouthed silent syllables.

Miss Bertha took the hearing aid out and shook it, even hit it several times on the edge of the table. "Damned contraption!"

Will smilingly took it from her, looked as if he were messing with it, then handed it back. She screwed it into her ear. Will spoke to her in his normal voice, “It’s okay now.” Mill echoed this sentiment.

Then we scattered.

Diner life

36

There are times I think all mysteries begin and end in Cold Flat Junction. Spirit Lake itself might seem the more mysterious, what with the Devereau house there and Mary-Evelyn drowning there, and Ulub's story of the lights in the woods. Or White's Bridge Road where the murder occurred. Yes, you might think either of these places held the greater mystery.

But whenever I get off the train at Cold Flat Junction, and it pulls away, and I'm left looking across the tracks at that empty land that seems to go on forever, Cold Flat Junction seems to me the real mystery. My gaze is stopped only by that dark line of trees on the horizon, the only thing that keeps my eye from falling off the face of the earth. I don't know what word to use to describe it—"unreal," or "unearthly," maybe—but that doesn't say it, for if ever a place were "earthly," it's here. It's raw land, forgotten land, land you wouldn't give a second thought to, so why do I? Even the milky sky, colored the gray-tinged white of an opal, seems to suffer under a blight of indifference. So I sat on the platform bench and looked over there, and even grew weary with looking.

I sat there for some minutes, then walked the worn path from the station to the Windy Run Diner.

They were all there today, again, either sitting at the counter on the same stools, or in the same booth. I had the eerie impression of stopped time, the diner frozen in time and its customers turned to ice sculptures. The only person missing was the wife of the man who occupied the booth. He seemed pleased by her absence. I took my same stool at the counter, the end that butted against the wall.

Don Joe and Evren both nodded to me at the same time and the heavyset woman in dark glasses smiled at me and smoked her cigarette. They actually seemed glad to see me, but I didn't put that down to my likeability. I just figured there was so little happening in Cold Flat Junction that any news was good news.

Louise Snell said, "Well, hello, darlin', nice to see you again."

It wasn't really a question, but I said, "I'm on my vacation." This was partly true, for I really was on vacation, except it wasn't here; it was in Florida. But hadn't I told them I was from La Porte? So why would I be vacationing around here unless I was insane?

Billy was the first to comment on this: "Vacation? Thought you said you was from La Porte." He acted like he'd told a good joke, for he laughed and slapped Don Joe beside him.

"What happened is, our car broke down again over in Spirit Lake so we took it over to Slaw's Garage. It's been there now for nearly four days. We've been staying at the Hotel Paradise, which is really nice, so things could be worse."

They were all listening intently, Louise Snell going so far as to get out her cigarettes and light one up as she leaned back against the cupboard that held shelves of pie wedges. (I was planning on having the banana cream.) Maybe I liked the Windy Run because I was paid such close attention to.

"And Mr. Slaw," I went on, "employs a master mechanic, so I guess he'll spot the problem."

The heavyset woman in the dark glasses beside Billy said, "Better than Toots's trying." Everyone laughed.

Toots was the owner of the Cold Flat Junction filling station and garage where the car was supposed to have been fixed the first time I was in the Windy Run Diner. I was almost beginning to believe there was such a car, it having caused such trouble.

The woman said, "Well, Toots could sure use a mechanic like

that, so maybe you could go by and drop off this mechanic's phone number." Everyone laughed.

Billy was irritated because someone else was leading things and asked, "If your folks is over in La Porte, what you doin' here? Not that we ain't glad to see you, now."

"My ma wants me to look up an old friend of hers, name of Rebecca—?" I squinched my face as if trying to recall the last name, then pulled a scrap of paper from my pocket and pretended to read it. "Rebecca Calhoun, at least that's what her name was when Ma went to school with her. She lives on—" I consulted the paper again. "—Sweetmeadow Road." I knew there was no such road. There was a Lonemeadow and a Sweet-something, but I could get them arguing over which road it was and where the Calhoun house was.

And of course they did; they fought over the right to set me straight. Billy, Don Joe, the lady in the dark glasses, and even Louise Snell said all at once: "Sweet*meadow?*"

Billy took over. "Ain't no such a road, little lady. Now, there's *Lone*meadow, and there's Sweet*water,* so your ma must of just mixed 'em up."

"Oh," I said, in my disappointed tone.

"Ab-so-tive-ly," said Billy, as if I weren't believing him.

Don Joe and Evren nodded in agreement.

Don Joe said, "This Rebecca person, she'd be living on one or the other?"

While they were all deep in this problem I requested of Louise Snell a piece of the banana cream pie.

"Sure, hon." As she pulled a wedge from the shelf, she said to the diner at large, "Well, for the Lord's sake, help her out, whoever knows where this Rebecca Calhoun lives."

They all seemed to be putting on their thinking caps, consulting one another in whispers, when a voice said, "Red Coon Rock." It was the small man in the booth. "That's where." He held his white coffee mug with his thumb on the rim. His other hand held a cigarette and he was flicking ash from it with his little finger.

Billy turned on his stool. "Now how'n H you know that, Mervin? There's no Calhouns round here. Calhouns, they live over in the La Porte area. I never heard tell of one in Cold Flat."

Mervin answered, "Her name ain't Calhoun no more, that's why. She was a Calhoun, only she married a Spiker, Bewley Spiker that was, only he's dead now."

That all of this useful information came from someone in a booth seemed to aggravate the counter-sitters.

Mervin went on: "Then Rebecca, she passed away, too."

My heart sank. I couldn't believe that my fresh lead had dead-ended.

"It's only Imogene lives there now. That's Rebecca's sister."

Sister! I was too excited by this news to stay quiet. "Which sister's that, Mr. Mervin?" I had no idea what his last name was.

Their heads all swiveled to look at me. They were not used to me taking part in the discussion, even if I was the whole reason for it.

"Rebecca's sister?" Mervin scraped the heel of his hand across his whiskers. I could hear the rasping noise even halfway across the room. "Well, I don't rightly think she had more than one. This Imogene, she'd be younger than Rebecca by a good ten, fifteen years."

Imogene must be the little sister Aurora mentioned, the one Rebecca took with her all the time when she had to work; she'd have been ten or eleven when she went to the Devereau house, almost the same age as Mary-Evelyn.

Louise Snell said, "But you was looking for Rebecca, right?"

I tried to look disappointed, and in a way I was, thinking of how Rebecca was waitress at the Hotel Paradise and I'd've really liked to hear her talk about it. "My ma will be disappointed as she was such a good friend." I looked down at the plate my pie had rested on and mashed my fork against the crumbs. When had I eaten it? "But Imogene, maybe she'd be worth talking to, for she might remember my ma. Where does she live?"

"Red Coon Rock over past Flyback Holler," Mervin said. "Where Jude Stemple lives."

Don Joe said, "Why, you was asking about Jude, too. Did you find him?"

"I did, yes."

"Huh," said Don Joe. " 'Fore that, it was somebody else."

"The Tidewaters," said Louise Snell.

"No, ma'am. I never did find the Tidewaters."

"And there was somebody else you was lookin for—"

I broke in before he could remember about Louise Landis. "See, my ma's very best friend, besides Rebecca, used to live in these parts."

"She did? What's her name?" asked Louise Snell.

It took me only a couple of seconds to say, "Henrietta Simple. Her maiden name, of course." Where that name came from I have no idea. Names just pop into my mind. Maybe because I spend so much time making things up, my mind is really greased. Well, I could see them putting on their thinking caps all up and down the counter, for here was a name to contend with, one they could try to lay claim to.

Billy shook his head. “Ain’t no Simples in Cold Flat Junction. You ever hear of a Simple?” he asked the others.

And it was kind of like one of those relay races where you hand off a stick to a team member. Even Mervin got it before handing it back to me.

“I never *said* the Simples lived in Cold Flat Junction. I said *Ma* used to live in these parts.”

They had no choice but to accept there were Simples somewhere, or had been, that were outside their kin. They looked pretty defeated over this name they weren’t familiar with, so I thought I should do some explaining. A cool breeze blew through the diner’s louvered blinds, and I sat thinking for a moment.

“The Simples, you wouldn’t know of them because they lived and maybe still do on a farm. It’s really huge. They were what you’d call—or at least my ma says so—recluses. Hardly ever left the farm except for George—Henrietta’s father—and he’d go into town once a week for supplies. They allowed only a few people to come to their house who they had business dealings with. My ma for years went to the Simple farm for eggs. That’s how she got to be friends with Henrietta and how she found out her little brother—Miller was his name—was touched.”

Well, their eyes really opened at that, and a couple more cigarettes got lit. They had perked up a lot listening to the story of the Simples. For if they didn’t know the Simples, at least the Simples might be discredited and so not worth knowing.

“Touched how?” asked Evren, who sat beside Don Joe and never said much.

“Miller got kicked by a mule when he was hardly more than an infant and it did something to his brain.”

“Like what?” Evren asked, and I wondered if he could be touched himself and was eager to know someone else in that condition.

“Well, he could turn really bad—violent, you know—and attack a person. He did my moth—, my ma one time. He just picked up a chair and went after her like a lion tamer. George saw and saved her. You can see how they’d be recluses. They couldn’t afford to have Miller in an institution, so they kept him, like I said, at home. But they had to be really careful about visitors.”

I saw all of this in my mind’s eye—Miller charging my mother, Henrietta yelling, George hurrying to the rescue. The farm came clearer and clearer, the vast acres, the chickens scratching in the dust, my mother getting a basket of eggs. I blinked and looked around and for a moment wondered where I was. It was like when I come out of the Orion, wondering what world I had entered. But in a flash the diner came back and I was on firm ground. Or at least as firm as ground could be in Cold Flat Junction.

"So, you see, Imogene Calhoun might know what happened to Henrietta Simple. You said she lives at Red Coon Rock? And that's past Flyback Hollow?" I figured even if any of them ran into Imogene Calhoun and mentioned the story of the Simples, and Imogene said she'd never heard of such a family, it wouldn't matter as the whole story was so complicated they'd think they remembered it wrong or Imogene was touched too.

"It ain't far past, though," put in Mervin. "Not more'n three, four blocks."

Billy was mad at having his directions questioned. "For God's sakes, Mervin, ain't no blocks out there. You just have to measure off a length of road. I'd say a quarter mile if I'm any judge."

I asked, and was sorry I did, "What's her house look like?"

"White, with a big porch around it," said Don Joe.

Billy sighed. "It ain't white; it's this beige color."

"It's blue," said Mervin. "Spiker painted it this sky-blue."

Mervin, I thought, could really talk when his wife wasn't around. He must have lived for these occasions. "We all agreed it was the dumbest color to paint a house."

Billy swiveled around on his stool. "That ain't the Calhoun house, for the Lord's sakes! That's Wanda Leroy's. And it ain't anywhere near Red Coon Rock."

The woman in the dark glasses shoved her mug toward Louise Snell and Louise went to get the coffeepot.

Don Joe said, "It's olive green's what it is, that sour-green color." When Billy went to contradict him, Don Joe held his hand out. "I guess I oughta know, Billy, all the deliveries I made to that place."

I wondered what he delivered, though I didn't really want to know, for that would take Don Joe outside his diner life and onto that great flat uninhabited land across the railroad tracks. He could wander there forever. It was strange I should think this, when I was making it all up anyway. Or making up a lot out of whole cloth (as my mother said), spreading a little truth a long way.

"Hey, sugar."

I felt Louise Snell's hand on my arm and I shook myself.

"You all right? You had your eyes closed."

"I was just wandering in my mind."

Mervin was giving directions. “All you do’s go up past the schoolhouse and then left on Dubois and that there’ll take you past Flyback Holler and then it’s an easy scoot—” Here he scraped one hand off the other to mean scooting “—to Red Coon Rock.”

I thanked them and took my check to the cash register by the door. The pimply-faced boy cashier who’d been there when I first came to the diner hadn’t been there the last several times. I wondered if he got fired. Louise Snell came to take my money and give me change.

“Hey, girl,” said Don Joe. “If you been in La Porte and Spirit Lake a while, maybe you heard some about Fern Queen getting herself shot. We don’t get the news here; all we get’s that *Conservative* every week.”

Evren gave a tittery little laugh that shook his narrow shoulders. “ ‘Don’t get the news here’; that’s funny, Don Joe. Nothin’ ever happens here. There ain’t no news.”

I wondered at this strange notion of Cold Flat Junction and just looked at Evren. Then I answered Don Joe. “Sheriff’s still looking; I guess they don’t make anything public until they’re pretty sure of what’s going on.”

“Well, if that DeGheyn fella’s still thinkin’ it’s Ben Queen, he’s not ever goin’ to get nowhere.”

I would have asked why he was so sure of this, but I knew it wouldn’t tell me more than I already knew.

Louise Snell wished me good luck.

Good luck. It was as if I was setting off on a trip that might be harder to make than Mervin allowed it was. This didn’t bother me one whit; I figured if I could get all the way to the Rony Plaza, I could surely find my way to Red Coon Rock.

As the diner’s screen door banged shut behind me and I had to shade my eyes against the glare of the sun in that white sky without mercy, I wished I had a diner life to anchor me to something, a place like rock in a riverbed where water just flowed around you but never moved you, a place where they didn’t get the news.

Lemonade

37

By this time I was so familiar with Cold Flat Junction I was tempted to stop off and see people. Off Schoolhouse Road was the house where they kept hens and where Mrs. Davidow came to get eggs (a lot different from the Simples's farm). I passed the Queen house on Dubois Road. I followed it to its end, to the whitewashed rock with "Flyback Hollow" written in large white letters. I would have liked to talk to Louise Landis again, but decided I had too much to do.

Past Flyback Hollow the road narrowed and what showed signs of having been a hard-surfaced road had pretty much gone back to its old rutted-earth self. A distance ahead, I made out a girl who appeared to be sitting at a table, which struck me as no-end peculiar; when I got closer I saw it was a lemonade stand. A sign taped to the rim of a card table said "Lemonade 10¢" On this lonely road, business couldn't be all that good.

"Hello," I said.

"Hello."

At first I thought she was the Pick Up sticks champion, as her wide-eyed and sorrowful look was like that girl's. Maybe it was just the Cold Flat Junction look.

I had plenty of money, most of which I was going to pay whoever might be a source of information, and it looked like it would be Imogene Calhoun. That still left enough for a stop at the Windy Run Diner and for lemonade. "I'll have two cups," I said, taking twenty cents from my change purse. It wasn't lemonade, either; it was Kool-Aid and I asked about this: why had she put lemonade on her sign?

"Because it's a lemonade *stand.*" She crossed her arms over her chest and scratched her elbows, which I sometimes do myself, so I guess we had something in common, except she was more stubborn than I was. I drank my Kool-Aid, a yellow color but tasting nothing like lemons. It was warm, too, but I didn't complain; I thought it kind of brave of her to set up here where she had so little chance of success. I pondered this. Or was it just dumb?

As she filled my paper cup again, I asked, "Do you get much business on this road?" She shook her head in a defeated way. "You might do better if you moved your stand back there," I pointed toward the way I'd come, "at an intersection." That was a stupid way of putting it; did Cold Flat Junction have intersections? "You could get the traffic from Flyback Hollow and the Dubois Road, too."

She nodded. "My ma doesn't like me to go all the way down there."

"Oh." I squinted skyward. Was that a reason?

I thought, if she lived here she must know the Calhoun house. "I'm looking for Imogene Calhoun's place. Do you know it?"

She pointed up the road. "It's that next house."

I made out a dark green roof, poking above the trees. The houses here, what few there were, were hard to see because of the densely leafed trees. Here and Flyback Hollow seemed to have got all of the trees in the region. I set down my half-drunk cup—I hated Kool-Aid—thanked her, and started walking again.

It was not very far. The house was set into the wood around it as if it had grown there like another tree. It was part fake brick and part real wood and the whole was painted a seasick green, as tan as it was green, and it just sort of melted into its surroundings, which I actually found rather nice.

The lady who came to the door looked a little like the lemonade girl, only older, and with the Cold Flat Junction look, unhappy and unsurprised, worn, like the long print skirt and brown sweater she was wearing. Her hair and her eyes were coffee-colored, and she was holding a can of Schlitz and a cigarette.

"Miss Calhoun? Are you Imogene Calhoun?"

She nodded behind the screen door. "You want something?"

I couldn't tell if her tone was belligerent or just bored. "My name's Emma Graham, and I live in Spirit Lake? I'm writing this history paper? It's what my teacher calls a 'project'? He wants us to *delve* (a word I really liked) into something around these parts—you know, where we live—and to write it up. I understand you once lived around White's Bridge and your sister—"

"My sister is deceased."

"Yes, ma'am. I heard she was." I dredged up what the Sheriff always said in these sad circumstances. "I'm sorry for your loss."

"Chrissakes, she's been dead nearly ten years. Come on, you best come on in."

The screen door slapped shut behind me. The living room was dark, not simply because it got only slanted light, but because everything in it was dark—walls, woodwork, furniture. She sank back into her slipcovered rocking chair and told me to sit down in one of the armchairs. The upholstery was a burnt biscuit color and kind of scratchy. Dust shimmered up from it, caught in a slant of light when I sat down.

I went on, opening my purse and taking out a five-dollar bill. "Also, our teacher told us if we interviewed anyone we should pay them for their time. So I'll be glad to pay five dollars an hour, or of course for less than an hour." I put the bill on the coffee table.

That surprised her. "Well." She smiled and the smile made her look younger than fifty, for she'd have to be in her fifties. Maybe it was the way she was dressed in that flowered skirt and sneakers, or maybe it was her long hair. I didn't know. I would have mistaken her for thirty if I passed her on the street. "It's sure okay with me, but what I could talk about for an hour that you'd want to hear beats me."

"Did your sister wait tables at the Hotel Paradise sometimes?"

"Yeah. Becky worked there part-time for two or three summers. She used to take me with her places she went to work so I wouldn't have to stay home by myself. And partly because I could do some work too and help her out." She pushed her light brown hair back off her forehead. "Lord, but that must've been forty, forty-five years ago." She sipped her beer in quite a ladylike fashion, considering she was drinking it out of a can. She tapped ash from her cigarette into a tin ashtray she kept on her lap.

I thought back too and wished I had a rocking chair to do it in, for with her leg pulled up and the foot resting on the cushion, and the smoke clouding the air around her, Imogene seemed honestly to be back there with Rebecca. I myself settled into the dark, rough armchair and listened to her talk in her dreamy way about the kitchen and the help and my mother, who she called "Miss Jen." I reminded myself that these were pre–Ree-Jane days, pre–Lola Davidow days and my scattered thoughts flew to those days I hadn't lived as if the past were a magnet.

"There were those trees up behind the kitchen, near that big garage, where I'd sneak off with the dishwasher's kid and smoke cigarettes behind one of those trees."

She went on about the hotel, the people who worked there, and the guests she sometimes ran across when she was making up their beds. Yes, she was definitely worth the five dollars I was paying. The atmosphere seemed so heavy with memories, my eyelids drooped. She might have been talking about me and Paul, our dishwasher's son, who I could get to steal brownies from where they were cooling on the pastry table, and to bring them up to the woods where we ate them, and Paul got blamed.

It was getting so I was living not only my regular life, but other little lives. It was almost as if I were everywhere. I wondered if I was going crazy to the point where I would be like Miss Ruth Porte, making candlelight suppers for myself, or being a kleptomaniac like Miss Isabel Barnett.

". . . Devereau house."

My heavy eyelids snapped up. She was talking about the Devereaus and I hadn't been listening!

"They were awful hard to work for. That Isabel should have been in the slave trade."

"Wasn't that the house where—" No, I was being too direct. You have to sneak up on what you want to know; you have to peek through windows at the facts so they won't run off and hide. You cannot go smashing through doors.

"My mother says some sisters lived there. Maiden ladies, she calls them."

"I guess you heard about what happened?" said Imogene.

"What?"

"That little girl that drowned? She was their niece, I think."

I squinted up my eyes as if memory were refusing to budge. "Drowned . . . yes, I guess somebody said . . . But go on." I tried not to sound overeager.

Imogene lit another cigarette from the butt of the old one and threw the butt into the empty grate. The way the sun stole through the venetian blind and lay in stripes across her face lent her a shadowy prettiness. "It was early one morning, I think. Those sisters called the police and said this little girl Mary was missing—" She stopped to take a swig of beer. "Now, this is what Rebecca told me as best I can recall. They found the little girl in the lake, that one over near the Hotel Paradise?"

I nodded and tried to be careful about believing everything I was told, for a lot of what I heard was secondhand, and the person doing the telling had heard it from somebody else. Either that, or the teller couldn't really know because they hadn't been there. Jude Stemple was certainly an example of this when he said, *Fern never had no kids*. Fern could have and he not know, which is what I was sure was the truth of it.

So far, of course, Imogene was right; the things she was saying had been part of the newspaper report.

"She was supposed to have taken out a rowboat in the night and then couldn't get back; the boat was old and leaky. Does that make any sense? Why didn't those police look into it more? One thing that clinched it for sure in my mind was—"

I knew what it meant to be on the edge of your chair. "What?"

She stopped talking, as if she were holding on to a surprise, a gift she opened layer by layer—ribbon, paper, box, tissue. She stopped and started picking at the red polish on her fingernail. It was dark red and chipped.

"What?"

She blinked. "Oh . . . sorry. I guess I just got—you know—carried back there to the Devereau house and those sisters." Deeply, she frowned. "Those *sisters*. I keep thinking of three sisters, but wasn't it four?"

She was asking not me—even though she looked at me—but the air around me, as if knowledge hovered in the room like light, like air, hovered but couldn't settle.

"Rose Devereau was the fourth sister, and nothing like those other three. She married Ben Queen from here in Cold Flat, but I won't go into all that. Rose was younger than the other three by a good fifteen, twenty years. She was real pretty, real alive. Those three, though, always seemed to me more dead than alive. There was no prettiness there." Again she stopped to drink and smoke. "There was this kitten that was so scrawny it wasn't much bigger than a pencil. Rebecca said there was always a water dish but no food."

This actually scared me. I knew about the starving kitten, for Ulub had told us, but I never heard its fate. I never wanted to.

"It was the little girl's—Mary's. They wouldn't allow her to feed it. It would've died, of course, but what Becky did was, she put the kitten under her coat and took it home with her and fed it for the week, then brought it back just so the sisters would see it and know that she hadn't stole it. Then she'd take it away again. She brought in a little box of cat food for it, but she was afraid to leave it with Mary; it just seemed too dangerous, for what if the sisters found it?"

"It was like prison. She was in prison."

Imogene laughed, but it wasn't a carefree laugh. "That's for sure. They didn't like me coming there, either. But if they wanted Becky, they had to take me in the bargain."

I was so relieved about the kitten. "Your sister Rebecca must have been a really nice person."

"Yes, she really was. This little girl Mary, she was so pale. It's funny, I can't call back her face, the features of it, I mean, but I do recall the paleness of her." Imogene frowned. "Why did they hate Mary so much? It was as if she'd been visited upon them as a punishment."

Then Imogene stopped talking and just smoked and drank. I wondered if she'd forgotten I was there, even. But I didn't want to say anything for fear of interrupting her chain of thought.

"She had these beautiful dresses, like party dresses. It's what she always wore—a dress. Never shorts or jeans like me. What we used to do was stay in her room and play with the stuff in her toy chest."

I thought about the Mr. Ree game and how Mary-Evelyn had cut faces from snapshots and pasted them over some of the character cards that stood for the people in the game: Mrs. White, Niece Rhoda, Colonel Mustard. I knew I'd have to go back to the Devereau house and look at things in the light of what I knew now. Yet, what did I know?

"You said there was something that clinched it for Rebecca. Clinched what?"

"How she died. That it wasn't an accident. What accident could befall a child in that way? Police called it a 'suspicious death.' No damn kidding. Why in God's name would that child take out a boat at night, anyway?"

These had been my questions, the ones I'd made a list of after I read the forty-year-old report on the death in the *Conservative* offices a while back. How I wished Imogene's sister, Rebecca, was still alive! For she had got her information direct. Of course, Imogene had too, but being only ten years old, her memory of all of this would be colored by her older sister's comments.

Imogene went on: "No shoes. Now, that always got me. Or it did Becky. How was that child supposed to walk through that thick wood without shoes? And no coat, don't forget. Here it was October and the child had no coat."

"Then you think—maybe her shoes were never on? Like, maybe they carried her?"

Imogene took a sip of beer. "Maybe she was already dead, that's what I think."

My heart really leaped into my throat. This had never occurred to me. I thought of what Ulub had seen at a distance: those lights, either flashlights or lanterns, moving through the woods, a kind of silent procession. How could Mary-Evelyn not have cried, or yelled, putting up some kind of resistance with no shoes and no coat on? She was already dead—that would explain it.

Imogene was talking about the kitten again. "He was almost white but with a faint blue or gray tinge to him. Poor thing didn't even have a name. Mary-Evelyn really loved him. She told me she'd gone down at night sometimes and stolen bits of food and that's what kept it alive. But the sisters caught her at it and put a padlock on the refrigerator. And of course they punished her."

"How?"

"They had her pick up leaves. This was October, remember."

"What?" My mind, used to Mary-Evelyn's mistreatment, still could not take this in.

"From the yard. It was in October, so they kept falling. The leaves, I mean. One by one, she was to pick them up and put them in this potato sack. And when it got full she was to dump it and start again."

Here Imogene turned her head to look out the window, as if maybe she could see it out there beyond the side of the house. And I did too. Mary-Evelyn, in one of her party dresses, stooping to pick up a leaf and put it in the potato sack.

There wasn't a sound, both of us gazing out the window. By now I had moved without even knowing it and was standing by Imogene's chair, my hand on its arm, as if I could draw comfort from it.

In my mind I saw Mary-Evelyn look up at me and even though I knew it was my own imagining, I could feel her telling me or us that we had to find out what happened, get to the bottom of it, that though I might have figured out Fern Queen's death, that it might have avenged some part of Mary-Evelyn's awful life and death, it still wasn't enough. And that if I didn't do this, she couldn't be released from her terrible punishment and would be picking up leaves throughout eternity. It was like one of the fairy tales I read years ago when I was little, how in a lot of them the princess was under a spell, and the prince had to figure out what had happened before the princess could be released. So it was like Mary-Evelyn was under a spell. Or I was.

"What was Mary-Evelyn like?"

"Like I said. Quiet."

"What was she like when she wasn't quiet?"

"Oh . . . she was real sweet."

That pained me. It made thinking about her that much harder.

The clock chimed. It was four-fifteen. More than an hour had passed. I realized that Imogene was an ally, and I had the perfect reason for coming back: my history project. I also realized I owed Imogene another five dollars and took it out of my change purse.

"Honey, you don't have to give me any more money. I liked talking. It brought back a lot of things about me and Becky."

I put the bill on the chair arm. "Just say it's for feeding the kitten."

I walked back down the road. There was a terrible feeling in me, a heaviness. I felt I was dragging myself along, that my feet didn't want to move, but since they didn't have any better idea where to go, they had no choice.

The lemonade stand was where I'd suggested the girl move it to, where this road met Dubois Road, but she was gone. I guess she meant to return, for the Kool-Aid pitcher was there. It was a different color, orange instead of yellow, and I saw where she'd crossed out "Lemonade" and written in "Orangeade," which sounded like my sort of truthfulness. Anyway, that might mean she'd been doing some business. I poured a little into one of the plastic cups and put down ten cents. It might encourage her to see business was going on even while she was away. I used to do things like selling lemonade myself, when I was young, only mine was real lemonade which my mother helped me make. It tasted as fresh as if it had dripped from a lemon tree.

Flyback Hollow was off to my right and for a minute I stood by the stand and thought about Louise Landis. She knew everyone in Cold Flat Junction. She certainly knew Rose Devereau and Fern Queen. I couldn't think of a good enough reason for stopping in to see her. I guess I had made up so much of my life that it didn't occur to me to tell the truth. Even if anyone wanted to hear it.

I poured the Kool-Aid out and stood there with my paper cup, afraid I was emptying out like the cup. Looking around me I had this vision of Cold Flat Junction that I never could have explained: there did not seem to be anything in it. It was like the card table and the pitcher and the missing girl; like the lone girl in the school playground and her Pick Up sticks; the lone boy there on a different day with a basketball he wasn't playing with; like the empty train platform where I had first seen the Girl.

I knew what was both restful and fearful about Cold Flat Junction: it had all stopped. As in those old *Twilight Zone* episodes, where the street was always empty, leaves and blown paper being the only movement, and what people you finally met seemed made out of clay and in a different time and space. But such words as I could use were husks, empty of true meaning. I could put no words to it. You had to find words for it to get a handle on it. I didn't even know what "it" was.

I walked Dubois Road, passing the Queens's big house, wondering. Not that I expected to find Ben Queen sitting in the front parlor. It would be the last place he'd choose to hide out.

I heard the whistle of the 4:32 as I was walking down Windy Run Road and I broke into a run. It was moving right past me as I ran the open stretch, the beaten path there, between the diner and the station. I saw it stop up there and knew I'd never make it, so I slowed down as I came to the steps leading up to the platform.

I was down at the far end of the platform when I saw someone boarding. With one foot on the top step and one on the bottom, she turned, and, only for a moment, looked at me. If I had run fast, I might have made it. The engineer might even have waited, seeing a poor kid running for all she was worth (one of the few advantages of being a kid), only I couldn't. I was frozen in place.

It was the Girl.

I sat in the silent landscape, thinking about her, wondering what her business was in Cold Flat Junction. This was where I'd first seen her, on this railroad platform, nearly a month ago.

I think she's Ben Queen's granddaughter. Ben's and Rose's. Anyone who saw her and knew Rose would think so, for Rose was who she looked like: she could have been Rose when Rose had been about the age to run off with Ben Queen. The trouble was, no one else I knew had seen her. But I admit I hadn't been very forthcoming in any description of her. She looked nothing like her mother, Fern—at least nothing I could tell from the pictures of Fern in the paper. I bet Jude Stemple would see it, for he had been really taken with Rose Queen, had described her pale hair and her skin and eyes so vividly

I could almost see her. Jude Stemple would have known he was wrong about Fern being childless.

I sat on the platform, on the brown-varnished bench, waiting for the six o'clock train, hardly thawed from my state of frozen stupification. I was that close to finding out who she was for sure. Only a few yards of station platform between us. That close.

I was almost certain the Girl had shot Fern Queen. And one of the reasons was that I knew Ben Queen *hadn't* shot Fern that night when he'd dropped the gun on the sofa in the old Devereau house.

But if he had a gun—? I imagined someone arguing.

It wasn't his gun (I answered in my mind). *He dropped that gun like it was a snake could have bit him.*

A girl shooting her own mother? This was Lola Davidow's voice, and no wonder she might have cause for concern.

It's no less likely—the Sheriff said, who knew the score—*than a man shooting his own daughter.*

No, no, no, no, just about anybody would say, for it was, I agree, a fearful thing to have happen.

Hell! Donny was saying from his seat behind the Sheriff's desk. *Sam's right. It was him shot Fern. How in hell you know it wasn't his gun? Man walks in, drops a gun on a chair, you say it wasn't his. That don't make no sense at all!*

Maybe.

I sat there and looked across the tracks at that empty, blistered land that drew me. Why would a place so barren and exposed pull at me this way? Dry earth the color of sand, sunbleached saw grass, some scattered rocks. And far off, that line of dark trees like a distant horizon. Not a single building, not a soul.

Yet, for some reason, it gave me a sense of ease, made me less tired. Indeed, looking at it, I realized how tired I was and how much things weighed on me. It was as if over there was the place where you could stop worrying things to death, where you could finally stop caring about Ree-Jane's taunts, where you could set down the tray of dishes, where you could stop the lies and the connivery, where you could finally own up. Where you could drop the gun on the chair.

Solitary blue

38

The train ride was only fifteen minutes long, three minutes shorter because I was getting off in La Porte instead of Spirit Lake. I was going to call on Dr. McComb.

I spent the short train ride wondering about the Girl and why she was traveling between Cold Flat Junction and Spirit Lake. Maybe I'd have been better off figuring out what reason I was going to give Dr. McComb for visiting him. The last time I used the excuse that I wanted to ask him if there were any White Lace butterflies around this area, for I thought I might have seen one.

Butterflies were a speciality of Dr. McComb's. We had spent some time out behind his house in grass up to my chin swishing nets around. At Spirit Lake, I had certainly seen a white butterfly, and it might have been a White Lace, but it looked so peaceful, swaying on a stalk of Queen Anne's lace, that I couldn't net it and stick it in the box I had taken for that purpose. I couldn't stand the idea of carrying it to its death.

I stepped down from the train, loving that little yellow metal stool and the way the conductor placed his hand beneath my elbow. I walked up and down the platform, looked in the station waiting room. There was no sign of her; I guess I didn't really think there would be.

One of Axel's taxis was standing by the station, its motor running as if it were a getaway car. Delbert was driving, as usual. I wondered how Axel had ever started his taxi business with only the one ghost cab he himself drove. I walked over and asked Delbert if he was waiting for someone and he said, no, just sometimes he parked here in case anyone getting off might need a cab.

"I do," I said, and got in. I told him I wanted to go to Dr. McComb's house.

"Dr. McComb, Dr. McComb. Now whereabouts does he live?"

"You're supposed to know where people live. You drive a taxi." I sighed. "You go to Red Bird Road and along it until you come to Valley Road. You go along that and his house is at the end."

"Hokey-dokey," said Delbert, and turned the car toward the street.

I settled down in back, biting the bit of calloused skin near my thumbnail. I did this sometimes when I was thinking hard. I pictured the butterfly I had seen, clinging to the Queen Anne's lace, when I had looked across the lake and seen the Girl. She and the butterfly seemed to occupy the same space.

Full of itself, the First National Bank rolled by. Banks always strike me as so self-important. Then we were coming up on the corner where the Abigail Butte County Library sat, and as it came into view, I yelled to Delbert to stop.

Delbert acted like he was having a heart attack, and I only hoped he'd get the car to the curb before it happened.

"I need to go in for just a minute," I said, poking my head through his window. "Wait for me."

Delbert said, "It'll cost you waiting time."

"That's okay." I darted across the road wondering how he figured "waiting time." I skipped up the wheelchair ramp. I knew I was too old to skip, but I wanted to see if I still remembered how. I went into the library.

The butterfly books were on the "Nature" shelves, but I had found Dr. McComb's book before in with "Local Authors and Authoresses." These books were gathered on a table prominently stationed near the oval information desk. There were any number of local authors; I'd read scraps from different books when I was on my butterfly search two weeks ago. I thought none of these authors could write except for Dr. McComb (whose writing name was L. W. McComb). His descriptions of the various butterflies he'd seen and studied were, I thought, poetic.

Since I already had nine books out that were overdue, I didn't want to try and check this book out because I didn't want Miss Babbit looking up my record. I would just copy a page or two of Dr. McComb's illustrations and comments. I carried the book to the copier, which children weren't supposed to use without supervision. It was more or less hidden at the end of the stacks. I put the page facedown and dropped in my money.

From the tiny bit I'd read just standing there, I knew I would like to check the book out, for it was very pleasant—dreamy, almost, as several of his passages mentioned he had to stay still so long he sometimes fell asleep. I thought it very brave of him to admit to this weakness in his scientific procedure. I then stuck the book back with the local authors and hurried out and back to the car.

"That's going to be extra," said Delbert, starting up the engine.

"I know. You already told me."

"Well. Just so's you know."

I gritted my teeth and made some kind of throat noise.

"You say something?"

"No."

"Cause Axel, he says waiting takes time up just as good as driving does, so we got to charge for it."

He was looking worriedly at me in the rearview mirror. I could see the mirror over the top of my copied page, which I raised to blot out his eyes. Delbert would go on and on about the "waiting" charge for days if a person encouraged him. I held the page so he couldn't see my eyes and read Dr. McComb's account of a blue butterfly that was really beautiful. Here, he'd climbed to the crest of a hill called "Hatter's Hill," a place I didn't know about. Dr. McComb had gone there purely to try and see this blue butterfly. On this page, he described the scene before him:

> I wondered to whom this land belonged, for it looked unfarmed, untenanted. I gazed out over the fields which seemed as nothing, as endless. And I sat for over twenty minutes, nearly dropping off (a bad habit of mine, as I've said) when my peripheral vision caught a movement near the base of a yew. Carefully I turned my head downward and there in a patch of some weedy nectar plant swayed what appeared to be the Reakirt's Blue, very rare

in these Northern parts. Of unprecedented hue, it was no shade of blue that I had ever seen before. Perhaps I was partial to this butterfly, also called a Solitary Blue, because it tends to be a loner.

"Here's Valley Road!"

Delbert's voice snapped me back to my surroundings, only mine—the trailer home with its pink flamingos on the left, the falling-down barn on the right—were far less seeable than the words on the page. A blue "of unprecedented hue," no blue I had ever seen, and I guess never would unless I saw his butterfly.

"Well, go *on*. Didn't I say it was at the *end?*"

Delbert sighed, the world on his shoulders. "Yeah, I guess."

Finally he stopped where the road ended, outside of the square stone house. This time I told Delbert not to wait, as I knew I'd be gone long enough for him to have a conniption fit over the "waiting time" charge. As it was, he only charged me another fifty cents for waiting outside of the library.

I hoped Dr. McComb's housekeeper or sister or whoever she was would not answer the door, as she had made me feel really uncomfortable the last time. But the door was open and I just went in and called Dr. McComb's name into the silence. The room looked just the same, and why shouldn't it? I'd been gone from it for only a few days, not ten years. Yet, life had lately taken on a ten-years-gone tinge. Lately, my sense of time was stretching out to accommodate all of the trips, talks, plans, ideas that I'd had going—not to mention that I was still in Florida, which about doubled everything.

The silence was nice, though, broken only by a grandfather clock ticking away. It was a place where I didn't feel crowded the way I did in other places, as if there were room here to think, to lay things out in your mind and take your own good time examining each one. But I didn't stop; I went through to the kitchen where another clock ticked quietly. I looked under a napkin covering a plate of what I hoped were brownies like the ones we had eaten before but were sugar cookies, which would do in a pinch. I did not take one. And something was in the oven, for the air was heavily scented with something sweet, a cake or brownies. I did not open the oven door.

I went out the kitchen door into the rear garden, though it could hardly be called a garden now, for it was overgrown with weeds, ivy, and bramble. Weeds stretched back to woodland. There was blue grass and buffalo grass; black-eyed Susans and Queen Anne's lace; butterfly

A drowning

39

At last the butterfly grew tired of being looked at (which seemed to be its chief occupation) and flew off. I reminded Dr. McComb that there was something in the oven that might burn up. We wended our weary way back to the house.

Overseeing the pan he took out of the oven—brownies!—I asked him what kind of butterfly it was. A Dogface, he said. I objected to that name for something so pretty. Then he told me a lot more about it than I needed to know, as he shook powdered sugar over the pan of brownies. I said my mother does that with cakes, only she places a doily on top and then the powdered sugar makes a perfect design. I went on in some detail about my mother's cakes, which was probably more than he needed to know, so I guess we were even.

But Dr. McComb didn't seem to mind at all, probably from a lifetime of listening to patients go on about their ills. (Imagine having

Aurora Paradise as a patient!) He said my mother was the best cook he'd ever come across and was I one, too?

The question kind of staggered me because it was, after all, a reasonable question. Yet I can't remember ever having asked it of myself, maybe because of the hint in it of death. I don't think I really believe that my mother will die and I will then have to carry on. Me taking my mother's place in the kitchen is the most harebrained notion I can imagine.

"I can't cook worth a lick," I said, I suppose to lay that notion to rest. I sat chin in hands watching the brownie pan while Dr. McComb went about the coffee. "I'm pretty good at bartending, though," I added.

"Are you now? I like martinis, myself. Vodka."

"That's Mrs. Davidow's favorite drink. But martinis are easy; they don't take any imagination." I watched him cut the brownies into squares.

"Martinis aren't supposed to. They're supposed to make you drunk."

The brownies were now on the Blue Willow plate. I looked them over. "Well, you can get drunk with imagination as well as without it, can't you? I'm talking about drinks that take two or three kinds of liquor. Among other things, of course. They're my inventions. Cold Comfort's one of them. That's made with Southern Comfort."

We both took the two largest brownies. He said, "That sounds imaginative all right. What else goes in it?"

"I'm sorry. The recipe's a secret." The recipe changed every time I made one, which was why it was a secret.

"Maybe you can make one for me sometime."

"I'd be pleased."

I drew from my pocket the page I had copied from his book, unfolded it, and slid it across the table.

"That looks familiar." He seemed pleased.

"I got it from the library. I didn't want to check the book out because other readers wouldn't see it then. There was only the one copy."

He sat down and studied it, nodding. "I remember this day well."

"Where's Hatter's Hill?"

"Mile or two the other side of Hebrides."

Hebrides was the nearest big town. I loved it, for it had department stores and bookstores and candy shops. Stores that we didn't have in La Porte. I liked to do my Christmas shopping there.

"I liked what you wrote there."

He smiled. "Well, thank you."

"You said you looked out over fields that seemed endless and 'bereft of adornment.' That's very pretty. There's a piece of land I look at sometimes and I get that same feeling. Only I can't explain the feeling."

"Where's that?"

"Cold Flat Junction."

"I haven't been over there in a long while. It always struck me as deserted. A strange place. A sad place."

Sad wasn't really the right word, but I didn't want to waste time thinking up the right word, as I wanted to get around to Mary-Evelyn's death. The coffee tasted surprisingly good with the brownie. Dr. McComb is the only person who has ever offered me coffee. "It must take a lot of patience to watch butterflies."

"Does. It takes a lot of patience to watch anything. I mean really see it." He had polished off one brownie and was now studying the plate for another. "Most people aren't really very observant." He took the brownie I had my eye on. I guess we were both ultraobservant.

"But if you're a doctor, you really have to be. I mean, you've got to be able to tell things—oh, like about death. What people die from. Don't you always have to fill out those certificates?"

"Death certificates? Yes. Not any more, though." He sighed. I couldn't tell from the sigh whether he did or didn't miss writing out death certificates.

"It's probably not easy, a lot of the time. I mean some deaths can look like they're caused by more than one thing."

"True."

I smiled. What I liked about Dr. McComb (and the Sheriff, and Maud) was that he didn't tell me I was being morbid, or I should be out playing ball. And he didn't look fearful. I've noticed how easily adults become fearful when children say something they don't expect.

I went on: "Like, you can't tell that somebody's died of a particular poison unless you go looking for that particular poison."

"You been reading up, I'd say." He poured us some more coffee. "I'm glad I made the brownies and not you." He laughed.

Eating my second brownie, I said, "Oh, it's just interesting. Especially about poisons." I was getting good at this. "I guess arsenic is the most common to murder someone, right?"

He munched and frowned. "I can't say with any certainty. I haven't come upon such cases. I've come on *accidental* poisonings, of course. But poison in that case is pretty obvious. Kids getting into things, stuff like that. Or sedatives, taking too many, which of course might not be accidental at all."

I brought up shootings.

"You've been hanging around Sam DeGheyn too much. What about them?"

"Didn't you ever have someone get shot you had to pronounce dead?"

"Yeah, sure. Hunting season's full of 'em."

"But that's accidental. I mean deliberate."

He shook his head. I thought it was safe now to bring up drowning, drowning as just one way of dying among others. "How about drowning? Can you always tell that?"

"You mean tell if someone did or didn't? Oh, sure. Your lungs fill up with water, you drown. No way I'd mistake that."

I paused, frowning, as if thinking hard. "Remember Mary-Evelyn Devereau?"

"How could I forget? How could anyone forget that poor little girl?"

I stopped eating. That expression, *tears sprung to my eyes,* actually described it. It was the surprise at finding Mary-Evelyn's death was important to somebody else, and after all this time.

Dr. McComb pushed the Blue Willow plate toward me and then took out one of his cigars.

"I know she drowned—"

He sighed. "Indeed she did. No two ways about that."

"But can you be sure—" I should have led up to this question more, but I was getting impatient. "—where she drowned?"

Dr. McComb stopped in the act of lighting his cigar. "What? She drowned in Spirit Lake." He looked at me for quite a time. "You getting at something?"

I shrugged. "Oh, I was just thinking. Here's an example: what if I shoved Jane Davidow's head (it hadn't taken long to scare up an example) down in a bucket of water until she drowned. Then I dragged her dead body (I can't deny I was enjoying this) to Spirit Lake or Lake Noir and dumped her in. How would you know she didn't drown there?"

"How? Well, it'd look pretty damned suspicious for one thing." He dragged in on his cigar, hollowing out his cheeks.

"Why? What if everyone knew she wasn't a good swimmer?" Which she wasn't. "Okay, so it looks suspicious, say. What would you do?"

"Analyze the water. See if it was lake water. See if it was *that* lake water." He rolled his cigar around in pouty lips and gazed at me. "What you're talking about is the Devereau girl, isn't it? You're saying maybe that girl didn't drown in Spirit Lake, but elsewhere."

There wasn't much use beating around the bush, I guessed. "I'm saying—" I chomped my brownie "—they killed her."

Dr. McComb finished lighting his cigar as he stared at me. He seemed unable to say a word. He did not make fun of me or try to dismiss the idea. I knew he wouldn't.

"You thought it was strange too, you said so."

He nodded.

I went on: "Of course, they could still have done it in the lake, only probably on the other side, the side their house was on, for it would have been nearly impossible to take her through the woods and get her into a boat without her yelling or crying. If she was alive, I mean. Ulub would've heard her if she'd yelled. You know he was there because he came with Ubub to tell you." Carefully, I cut the last brownie on the plate in half. I took one half and pushed the plate across to him. But he didn't seem to notice. He sucked in on his cigar. I ate my brownie, trying not to swing my legs under the table the way I did when I was little. He was looking around the kitchen as if it weren't his and he couldn't make out whose it was. Then he studied the ash end of his cigar as if he wasn't sure whose that was either. I suppose because I wasn't used to being taken so seriously, or giving any adult something worth thinking about, I was surprised by his silence. I wanted to ask him if he felt guilty about Mary-Evelyn, but I didn't. It wasn't my place to.

By now what was left of my coffee was cold, but I drank it just the same, not wanting him to think I didn't appreciate his trouble.

He said then, "I should have done something."

He knew. That was probably why I'd told him. I knew he knew. "I should have done something," he said again.

I was quick to disagree. "The *police* should have done something. It was their job, not yours."

He blew out a thread of smoke. "It's the job of anybody who thinks there's a wrong been done to try and right it, I'd say. It being your job makes it only one more reason." He said, "I remember that sheriff. He wasn't like Sam DeGheyn."

Who was? I wanted to say.

"He was just a toady, spent most of his time at the pool hall or licking the mayor's boots. He wasn't about to mount an investigation."

"Wasn't he even suspicious?"

Dr. McComb shrugged. "Beats me. He didn't let on if he was."

He held his cigar over an ashtray and flicked the long ash from it. "No one I knew of knew the Devereau sisters very well. They were considered very odd. They left Spirit Lake right after. I heard later one of them died, don't know which one. But I guess they're all dead by now." He frowned. "Maybe not. At least one of 'em was probably my age, and I'm still alive. Seventy-six, I am." He sighed.

Seventy-six. But of course Aurora Paradise was a lot older still, and it'd be some years before he caught up to her. Somehow, as he sat back, he looked older, his eyes now not bright as they had been out there chasing butterflies. He asked, and it seemed more of himself than of me: "Why would three grown women do such violence to a little girl?"

I looked up from the Blue Willow plate. And the word locked in my brain as if it were a puzzle piece that I'd been looking at sidewise out and upside down and every which way but the right one. But now it locked in perfectly.

"Revenge."

A word, a space to fill a lack.

Waiting time

40

"Again?" Delbert whined when I told him I wanted to stop at the library. "There's waiting time—"

"I *know*."

He pulled out, saying, "It's your money."

"Well, then, stop acting like it's yours."

I watched the same scenes go by in reverse outside the window on the other side of the cab. The trailer, the plastic flamingos—

Flamingos! I pounded my head with the heels of my hands, picturing them out there in the center of Hialeah racetrack, where I hadn't gone as I'd planned this afternoon. I sat back, sighing. I'd just get Walter to call the bookie.

Inside the library I said hello to Miss Babbit and made my way to the history shelves. I looked for Greek history. I cannot say why I was going about solving the mystery this way, when what I should be doing was gathering evidence. But what evidence was there to gather in Mary-Evelyn's story?

Yet, I knew it wasn't only Mary-Evelyn's story; it was also Rose Devereau's and Fern Queen's; it was Ben Queen's and Lou Landis's; it was Rebecca and Imogene Calhoun's story. It was also mine.

I dragged book after book off the history shelf, but I couldn't find Do-X-machine. One reason was because I couldn't spell it. I couldn't look it up for that reason. I really hated asking Miss Babbit because you should be able to do your own research and also (mostly) because I was embarrassed to.

I leaned back against the stacks. Mill had said it was a Greek idea and I thought: if Will and Mill are using it in a play, then maybe I should look under Greek plays. I went to the drama shelves, where I found an anthology of Greek plays and ran my finger down the index under "D." I couldn't find it, again, because I couldn't spell it, so I went back to the top and started looking much more slowly.

Here it was, or must be: *deux ex machina.* Wow. Seeing it that way, it looked even more important. Mill certainly hadn't pronounced it right, though he did know what it was. Here it was explained as "God-from-a-machine" and Mill was right about this character (God) coming down in some contraption to set things right. But it didn't tell you how to pronounce it. I guess the book figured if you were smart enough to know what it was, you must know how to say it. I took the book to Miss Babbit.

She adjusted her glasses and smiled down at the page. Miss Babbit always seems in a lovely temper, never harsh or saying things to make you feel dumb. "I *believe* you pronounce it 'day-*uus ex* mack-*in-ah*.' "

My eyebrows slid upward in wonder. Wow, I thought again. I tried it out: "Dayus-ex-MACKinah."

"That's right. Only the first word is more of a 'day-u.' Think of two syllables."

" 'Day-you.' "

"That's about right. It's very difficult, I know."

She only said that so I wouldn't feel dumb. I smiled. "Thank you, Miss Babbit." I knew I had to get back to the taxi or Delbert might just take it upon himself to leave. "Now, would you happen to have a picture of Hialeah racetrack?"

All the while we drove through town, past Miller's and the Prime Cut and Souder's Drugs, up Second Street and past the Rainbow Café, I watched out for the Girl. She could have gone on to Spirit Lake as easily as alighting in La Porte, or she could still be traveling to some stop up the line, some stop she knew but I didn't.

I could have danced all night

41

Walter told me when I came in the kitchen that he didn't call my bookie because I never told him how much or what horse. I said that was okay, and I might have time to go to Hialeah tomorrow and place my own bets. He then said that Miss Bertha was mad as hops she never got her dinner at the usual time. "They was settin' down in there," he nodded toward the dining room, "and I just went in and told 'em you got called away on an emergency."

I tied on my apron. I hadn't bothered changing my clothes as it was nearly seven-thirty.

As I filled a water pitcher, Walter said, "I set the rolls to warm and put them butter patties on the bread plates."

The rolls were in a basket on the ledge above the stove. My mother never served cold bread. I thanked Walter and asked him if he'd take

Aurora Paradise her dinner. I'd make her a drink, but if I started fooling around with her I'd never be done. He said sure he would.

"I don't want to be late again for the dance," I said, and pushed the swing door through to the dining room where Miss Bertha waited like a big gray spider.

Ree-Jane came to the dance (as my guest), wearing a mustard-colored long dress with puffed sleeves and a sweetheart neckline. The style was more that of a ten-year-old, which it was, as it had been my first long dress. If I do say so myself, I had looked pretty cute. Ree-Jane didn't.

My mother wore a black linen dress with a string of (real) pearls. This plain but perfectly cut dress shot from shoulder to floor and looked grand. She looked free and unburdened for once.

Lola Davidow wore a dark brown satin two-piece dress, the top straining across her bosom and the bottom straining across her stomach.

I, of course, wore my white tulle with the sequins and the moment we all stepped through the door, I was asked to dance by the son of the Rony Plaza's owner. My mother twirled off with the owner himself. I asked the son (whose first name I hadn't caught, but what do names matter at times like these?) to dance me by Mrs. Davidow and Ree-Jane so I could wave to them, which he did and I did. Ree-Jane was as red as fire from falling asleep in the sun (again) and her face was peeling. The mustard color against her hair and skin made her look like a big hot dog. Mrs. Davidow stood at the rim of the dance floor pursing her mouth in and out like a fish, wanting either a dance or a drink.

The ballroom was immense. The twenty-foot ceilings had vaulted marble arches. The chandeliers turned the sequins of my dress into tiny stars and I looked like the Milky Way. The orchestra sat on a platform at one end of the room, all of them dressed in black pants and flamingo-pink jackets. In the very center of the ballroom was a circular pool planted with royal palms and poincianas. In this pool flamingos waded up and down and around, more graceful than anyone on the dance floor (except for me and the son).

The band was playing "Poinciana" as Ree-Jane, who had finally been asked to dance by a short bald man, stumbled by. Her partner was not more than five feet five or six. Ree-Jane sported a phony smile on her empty face as she looked over his head, pretending she enjoyed all this. He stepped on her foot. She gritted her teeth as the son and I floated on by. I called out, asking her if she was having a good time.

Lola was. By now she'd had three or four martinis, and she'd found herself a drinking buddy. They were doing some dance that wasn't a jitterbug but also wasn't anything else, that involved dancing in place and shoving the index fingers of each hand up and down and up and down. They were both laughing. That was fine with me.

On several occasions, new dancing partners had cut in on us, and each new partner twirled me away. The son looked disappointed when this happened, but we always got back together again.

The bandleader brought a fast number to a close and then announced a special treat for the dancers. They were now to hear a rendition of "Tangerine" sung by Miss Emma Graham.

Imagine! It seemed my fame had spread all the way from Trader Bob's to South Florida!

Breathless, I moved up to the stage, passing Ree-Jane and the bald man. You could tell she was just beside herself, seeing me get all of this attention.

At this point I got out of my beach chair and put the needle on the record and swayed to the music.

And down in the Pink Elephant, while my royal palm fluttered in the breeze stirred up by the fan, and the waves lapped the beach of the Rony Plaza, and the flamingos bunched among the poincianas, I belted out—

Taaaan-ger-ene,
She is all they claim,
With her eyes of night,
And lips as bright as flame;

Taaaan-ger-ene,
(Here I was joined by three backup singers.)
Da du de da
When she dances by
[I trucked along the stage]
Do do de do do
Senoritas stare and caballeros siiiiiigh!
And I've seeeen—
(Boo be boo be boo)
Toasts to Tangerine
Raised in every port across the Ar-gen-teeeeen—

Here all of the dancers raised their champagne and martini glasses in a toast. I was a tremendous success.

And the night, as they say, was still young.

Psssst! from overhead

42

The next morning I lay in bed an extra few minutes casting my mind back to Brokedown House, to Maud and the Sheriff and me in that fusty old bedroom, and something I was trying to remember. I saw the room, Maud, the Sheriff reading, the ring he'd held out. My mind's eye roved that room, but I couldn't discover what I needed to remember.

I got out of bed and padded down the hall to the bathroom. The stairs to the fourth floor are near the bathroom and I could hear Aurora banging around up there and talking to herself. I sat down on the toilet with my head in my hands, still seeing us in Brokedown House. I tossed cold water on my face and swiped my toothbrush across my teeth a few times. I studied my face in the mirror for signs of dis . . . another "dis" word, dis, dis, *dissipation!* I left the bathroom.

"Pssst! Psssst!"

I looked up. Aurora was hanging over the fourth-floor bannister. I honestly couldn't remember ever seeing her out of her chair before.

"Psssssst!"

"Why are you going 'pssssst'? There's no one else around."

"Don't you get fresh with me, Miss! I want an Appledew."

"But it's hardly more than seven A.M.!"

She responded to that by saying—fluting, more—"I have something you'd like to see."

I hadn't noticed she was holding a book, or journal, until she patted it and looked really smug.

I'd been standing at the bottom of this last flight of stairs up, and as I started up them, she yanked the book back. "Oh, no you don't! You don't get to see it till I get my Appledew!"

Stopping on the third step, I said, "What is it? You can at least tell me that." More than likely, what she had was of no interest to me. But then I thought, no, if she tried tricking me with it, then I'd never know whether to believe her; I'd always think she was tricking me and wouldn't fall for it.

"It's a picture album." She patted it again.

Now, photographs have a lot of promise in them as far as information goes. I said, "I've got to serve Miss Bertha and Mrs. Fulbright their breakfast before I can make any drinks."

"You mean that Bertha is still coming here? Crazy as a bedbug, that old lady. Okay, then bring it after, but don't make me wait too long. These pictures might just waltz away if you don't come back soon."

And here, Aurora began to waltz around, reminding me of the dance last night. Maybe I should have invited her.

Miss Bertha wanted pecan waffles with orange syrup and I said I was sorry (which I was, but not for her sake), we didn't have any, that we did have grits and hot biscuits (one of Mrs. Fulbright's favorites), and eggs, of course. "Any way you want them," I generously added, knowing how she'd get them.

After much grumbling and tomfoolery and moving things around on the table—her silver, the water pitcher, the vase of wildflowers—and stabbing her butter patty with her butter knife, she said, "I'll have eggs over easy, since you can't boil an egg. Mind you get the grease off."

I put my pencil behind my ear and minded I wouldn't and returned to the kitchen.

Walter was standing at the stove stirring the grits in the top of a double boiler. That's what my mother always used to keep things hot. The biscuits were in the oven heating up. He was wearing one of my mother's aprons. He turned to me and said, "What's the old fool want?"

I laughed because he sounded just like my mother and almost looked like her too, as he stood with arms splayed and hands resting on the long counter.

"Eggs over easy, no grits. Can you do it without breaking the yokes?"

"Sure can, I watched Miss Jen do it."

"Well, don't. At least break one."

"Got it," he said, just as my mother would have.

"I've got to make Aurora Paradise an Appledew."

"Ain't no more apple juice, but there's pineapple. You could make a pineapple dew." Walter broke two eggs into a small bowl. They both ran. Calmly, he picked up another egg and broke that and the yoke stayed whole. He heated up the frying pan.

I considered a Pineappledew, leaning on the counter as Walter had done and as my mother did. It was her thinking position. Vera would march in and rattle off four totally different orders and my mother would stand arms akimbo, her head bowed a little, eyes shut, nodding. When Vera was finally done, she'd say, "Got it."

A feeling wrenched me, almost as if someone had literally grabbed me around my waist. It was a terrible feeling, no doubt caused by her absence, that there would come a time when my mother would not stand so, arms splayed and eyes tight shut. Vera would come no more to bark out her food orders nor would Mrs. Davidow come to sit on the center table, to smoke a cigarette and gossip. It was the same feeling that had washed over me in the upstairs storeroom where cobwebs floated in the thin light that slanted through the grimy windows, the same feeling as I had got when I remembered the Waitresses. In this lingering absence, it was as if something knocked loose within me to roll across a green baize table, like the one in the poolroom next to the *Conservative* offices—to roll away and out of control. I could not find words for it, or maybe I did not want to find words for it, for they might give it a shape (as William Faulkner says) and I did not want to see the shape. Then I wondered if not wanting to see it was just my cowardly way. I hung my head and wondered if anything could set all of this to rights.

"Is this broke enough?"

Walter's voice snatched me back from this hard place and I'd half forgotten what we were doing. I looked at Miss Bertha's fried eggs.

"Yes." One yolk had spread flat and hard and the white was tough and stringy. Just the egg my mother would never have allowed into the dining room, not if they tortured her for a spy.

"Sorry," I said to Miss Bertha, when I'd set the breakfasts before them. "We used the last egg on that." But somehow I didn't feel as gleeful as I usually did nor think the joke as jokey.

An album

43

Whatever had knocked loose from me had rolled out of sight by the time I'd finished making a Bombay Breakfast for Aurora. What inspired this new drink was the bottle of gin in the back office safe called Bombay. The finished drink, I thought, surpassed the Appledew. Besides the rum, the Jack Daniel's, and the Curaçao (which I discovered had an orange flavor), I put in orange juice, pineapple juice, and half a mashed banana, which I whisked together with one of the broken eggs Walter had saved. (This also felt thrifty.) The whole thing struck me as a very healthful drink. The egg especially gave it an honorary breakfast standing.

"This ain't an Appledew," said Aurora Paradise, complaining right off.

Still, she looked at the tall glass with an air of expectation. For had I ever let her down? I had also found among Mrs. Davidow's souvenir swizzle sticks one with a camel sitting atop it. It made, I thought, a nice Bombay-ish touch.

She sipped and smacked her lips. "This is a *good* drink, Missy." She took another, longer swallow and said it again.

"I'm glad you like it, but don't expect it every morning. It takes a lot of trouble."

She flicked her fingers at me. Today her crocheted mittens were pale olive green with tiny darker green leaves done in satin. I wondered if she had made all of these mittens herself. I couldn't imagine her having the patience. "Oh, you're just so all-fired lazy."

"No, I'm not. Listen: I can't be making you drinks every time you get a mind for one, remember. Mrs. Davidow will be back soon and I can't be getting stuff out of her safe all the time."

"Well, I'll give you some money and you can go to the liquor store."

I rolled my eyes at this crazy suggestion. "I'm *twelve,* remember?"

"Then send that man."

"Look, we had a bargain you'd show me that photo album, there." It sat on the side table at her elbow.

She slid a glance that way, then gave me a sly look. "How about doing the pea-trick first?"

"No! It's not even a trick because you hide the walnut shells right from the start."

She sighed. "Oh, all right, if you're going to be contrary." She set aside the drink and picked up the album. It was covered in an olive-green silk the color of her mittens. It was water stained and a little threadbare. She turned a few pages quickly as if she knew exactly which one she wanted, and said, "There!" Her finger tapped one of the snapshots.

A young pale-haired woman sat on the top rung of a wooden fence; the dark-haired young man leaned against it. They were both smiling happily.

I gasped. They were Rose Devereau and Ben Queen.

"Couldn't've been more'n twenty when that was took."

Questions tumbled in my mind. I picked one. "Where are they?"

"Spirit Lake, looks like."

"There's no sign of the lake."

Aurora looked again. "Could be Paradise Valley or Cold Flat Junction." She shrugged. "Could be anywhere, I guess."

Most places seemed to be so hard to pin down they did seem "anywhere." It was important to anchor the two to a particular place. While I was studying the snapshot for clues, she whipped the album out of my hands.

"That ain't all!" Now she flipped to another page and turned the album so I could see it. Here was another couple, and this snapshot was older than the one of Rose and Ben. They were posing, she awkwardly, he easily, as if used to the camera's attention. He was dressed in a dark blazer and light trousers and was very good-looking. She was wearing an embroidered white dress. His smile was brilliant. He was the young man in the old photograph Dwayne had shown me.

"That there is Isabel Devereau."

I couldn't help it; I snatched the album from her. Isabel Devereau! Younger than in the snapshot my mother had of the sisters, and almost pretty—at least, not as grim. Her expression was softer. "Who's *he?*"

"Jamie Makepiece is what I believe his name is. I *thought* she had a beau. That's him right there. I remembered when I found this album. I thought it was lost and I found it over there where Jen Graham keeps her stuff. *Someone* had removed it from amongst my possessions."

"Well, don't look at me." She sounded so self-righteous, but I didn't want to get her off on another subject.

"When I saw this picture, it all came back. Isabel Devereau and Jamie Makepiece. Why, that was fifty years ago. When I myself was eighteen—" She slid me a glance to see if I bought this point, which I didn't, but again I didn't want to argue.

"There was talk of marrying. But then they didn't. He was from New York and you can see by how he dresses he's a city boy. A sharpie and a ladies' man. This was taken," here she tapped the snapshot again, "when he come to visit one summer, visited some relation in Spirit Lake, I don't know who. "Actu'ly—" She primped her hair with her bony, mittened hand. "—he was sweet on me, I could tell."

I kept from pointing out that Jamie was a good twenty years younger than she was, like Ben Queen (who, she'd said, also had a crush on her).

"But that ain't the reason he left before any marrying could take place. No sirree!"

I waited. She was silent. "Well, why did he?" I shifted my small tray from under one arm to the other. I must admit I was on pins and needles for I was sure there was more to come. But her thin mouth had swung shut like a letter box. I should have known.

She snatched up her empty glass and moved it back and forth. "I'll just have another Bombay Brunch before I continue my story."

" 'Breakfast,' " I corrected her. "It's too early even for brunch. How could you drink another when it's hardly nine A.M."

"I'll push myself." She raised the glass.

This was *so* maddening. I went through some pretantrum motions of whining and stomping my foot, knowing it would do no good but not being able to help myself. It might be surprising to hear that when I was little I had a leaning toward temper tantrums, though not any more of course. It got to be all I wanted to do was throw my physical self around, even while knowing this wouldn't get the outcome I desired. But here I was so irritated the tale of Jamie and Isabel was being interrupted I could hardly keep myself from doing something physical. My feet seemed to have a mind of their own, like Frankenstein feet. They stomped several times. Aurora just sat with her album clamped to her chest, her lips sealed.

"Oh, all right!" I grabbed the glass and left with my tray and stomped downstairs until I was out of earshot. Then I ran.

Walter had gone up to Britten's store, so I was alone in the kitchen watching the liquor, a banana, and a fresh egg I'd broken sweep around in the blender. I decided to pour in everything and let the blender whirl it all together.

Jamie Makepiece. Another character added to the story, an even older story; another player to add to the Mr. Ree game. Jamie Makepiece and Isabel Devereau. It was hard imagining one of the Devereau sisters having a romance, especially with a good-looking New York society ladies' man. If Aurora remembered all of this right. Back then she would have been in her thirties, I figured, and fifty years ago—why, Rose Devereau would have been only ten years old. Younger than I was now. And the same went for Ben Queen. And my mother would have been just a girl. It was so hard to imagine these people as children. It was hard to imagine one of the dour Devereau sisters in a party dress, to tell the truth.

I was pouring the frothy drink into Aurora's glass and nearly dropped the pitcher. I saw the awkward Isabel in her white dress, embroidered with dark little flowers whose color didn't show in the picture but which I'd bet several years' worth of tips was blue.

The same material as Mary-Evelyn's dress, the same blue silk flowers, only a different design. I remember how Miss Flagler, who owns the gift shop, had talked about one of the Devereau sisters as being an accomplished seamstress, and how a Devereau dress was to be coveted then much more than anything Heather Gay Struther could come up with now. Miss Flagler had said whenever she saw Mary-Evelyn, the child was beautifully dressed. And I'd seen those dresses, for they were still hanging in the closet of Mary-Evelyn's room. Still in mint condition forty years later. I had tried them on, so I knew.

Floating in the thick water growth of lily pads and grass, Mary-Evelyn had been wearing her white ruffled dress, made from the same material Isabel Devereau must have kept for ten years. But it was not this which had caught my attention—the two dresses made of like material. No, what kept me standing and staring out of the window by the icebox was what I'd been trying to remember when I woke up. It was the doll Maud had been holding in that bedroom of the house on White's Bridge Road, dressed in white organdy with little blue flowers sewn onto it. What was that doll doing in Brokedown House?

The picture, the photograph. Was *that* where I'd seen Jamie Makepiece?

It was in a kind of stupor that I walked the Bombay Breakfast up to the fourth floor. I think I might have walked it all the way to Bombay and hardly noticed. It kept going through my mind: the doll, the photograph—what were they doing in the Calhoun house? For I have no doubt the doll was Mary-Evelyn's. Miss Flyte hadn't said the Devereau sister made doll clothes to sell. And the Calhouns were a whole different society from the Devereaus. They wouldn't have mingled. It appalled me to think I would have to go back even further in time and consider things done then, fifty years ago, but I recollected the story of Agamemnon and his family and realized fifty years of revenge was just an eye blink for the Greeks.

"You in a coma?"

I had got to Aurora's room and handed her the drink (at least I guess I had, since she was drinking it) and must not have been wearing my usual know-it-all expression. I wondered how much the album had shaken loose in her memory. If nothing else, there was still more of the Jamie Makepiece story. "You agreed to tell me why Jamie left," I said testily, to let her know I was out of my coma.

Slowly she sipped her drink, then set it aside and made a few small movements, such as resting her hands in her lap, as if gathering herself together. She looked pleased to death with herself, as she usually does when she has information I want. "There was talk."

"About Jamie and Isabel?"

"About Jamie and *Iris.*" She delivered up this name with a little hiss as if the name were dangerous.

Wide-eyed, I jumped back. "*Iris?* But you said Isabel before. Isabel was Jamie's girl."

She nodded. "Um-hmm."

It was almost as bad sometimes as talking to Ree-Jane, the way she held on to information I wanted, but was quick to give me information I didn't want, like what was on my X-rays, if I'd had any taken. "Are you saying he was *both* of theirs?"

"That was the talk, that Iris got him away from Isabel. Now, I can't say if he broke off with Isabel and picked up with Iris, or if he started seeing Iris on the sly behind Isabel's back. But then he left real quick, that's what was said. Talk was, all the girls were after him. Well, as you can see, he's right handsome. I didn't have time for him; I had other fish to fry."

"How long was he here?"

"All that summer, if memory serves."

Memory wasn't serving very well if she couldn't recall this when I first asked about the Devereaus several weeks ago.

"That was one fine summer, indeed. We went swimming almost daily in Lake Noir—" (Surprisingly, she was one of the few people around who could say it right.) "—and had weenie roasts nearly every night beside the lake. That water was cold as ice and clear as glass. And we'd take boats out on Spirit Lake, too. At night when the moon was up, we'd just drift and drift around."

It sounded more like some movie about high school kids than something that really happened. Why would she be attending weenie roasts at her age? That was the trouble with her stories; you never knew what part to believe in. But something told me it was true about Isabel, Iris, and Jamie Makepiece.

"Then Elizabeth stepped in; Elizabeth took over like always."

This detail surprised me. "What did she do?"

"Why, she sent him packing's what I heard. Elizabeth was pretty much boss, being the oldest. I guess he went back to New York and his New York ways. Elizabeth sent Iris off to relatives. That was her punishment. I can believe it." Here she slewed a look around at me as a relative, then picked up her drink and sipped it.

I stood looking at her intently, as if my look were a kind of hypodermic syringe that could siphon more of the Iris and Jamie story out of her. Imagine Iris going back finally to the Devereau house and that grim fate.

"Did anyone ever see him again?" I was getting concerned for Jamie for some reason. Isabel, of course, would blame Iris and hardly attach any blame at all to Jamie, as she would want to think it was her, Isabel, he truly loved and had just slipped for a moment. At least that's the way I'd do it if it were me.

Aurora held up a mittened hand, palm out, as if to push my questions back. "That is all I recall."

I was frowning in simple frustration at not getting more details. "Why didn't you tell me this when I first asked about the Devereaus."

Complacent, she was shuffling her tattered deck of cards. "When you get old you start remembering things that happened long, long ago."

"You're hardly three weeks older than you were when I asked."

She didn't reply, just started laying out the cards. I couldn't stop here forever hoping for more of the story, and I had no desire to watch her cheat at solitaire, so I left.

My mind ran down names of people who were old enough to have been here and heard this "talk." There weren't many. Miss Flyte and Miss Flagler, in their sixties and seventies, respectively, would have been young, back then. Miss Flagler owns a gift shop in La Porte, and Miss Flyte has a candle store next to it. The two of them would sometimes invite me to their morning coffee breaks. It was more often cocoa for me and coffee for them. I knew Miss Flagler recalled something of the Devereau sisters, certainly of the one who was the seamstress, for she gave me a description of an ice-green organdy and silk dress sewn by one. So she seemed to remember that time pretty clearly.

Miss Flyte, though, was the one with the greater imagination, so even if she'd only been in her teens, things might have impressed her more. I'm only twelve, and things impress me, though I tend to be more literal and go by evidence more (somewhat in the way of the Sheriff). Miss Flyte (for instance) could probably take a trip on the Tamiami Trail and to the Rony Plaza without even having to tape up pictures or make a palm tree, or bring in a fan or play records on a phonograph. Her imagination is such that she doesn't need props.

What other seventy- to ninety-year-olds did I know? There was Dr. McComb, of course, but he would have mentioned it if he knew about Isabel and Iris and Jamie. It would have been a bit of a scandal, I would guess. There were probably dozens of people still around who might have heard about Jamie, but they were probably all in Weeks's Nursing Home. No, I could think of no one more likely than Miss Flagler, so I called Axel's Taxis to come and pick me up just before ten.

The Oak Tree Gift Shoppe is the next shop up from the Candlewick, separated by a narrow alley. Inside, it appears not to have changed in a hundred years, though I know Miss Flagler changes her window display every week. I studied it now. That thing that makes it look always the same is that what Miss Flagler puts in looks like what she takes away. The little silver fox that sat beside the porcelain bowl looks like the silver pig she had moved somewhere else. The blue-flowered bowl sat in the same place as had a pink-scrolled china bowl; a gold bracelet had taken the place of last week's silver; amethyst earrings had replaced emerald; a single strand of pearls replaced a double. I loved to look in this window because I found it restful.

No, a better word is "comfortable." It was the comfort of seeing small changes occurring within a background that never does, that was dependably always the same. This was the opposite feeling to what I'd felt yesterday, leaning on the kitchen counter—the feeling that enormous changes would come. I placed my palms and my forehead on the gift shop window, willing the fox to come back if the pig left, the amethyst to replace the emerald earrings—anything like that except to find the window barren, swept clean.

I saw Miss Flagler coming through the curtained alcove behind the counter and I suspected it was time for her to change the OPEN clock-sign to the one that said BACK IN. She always moves the hands to show "15 minutes," which was never enough time, for her tea and coffee breaks always took a half an hour to forty-five minutes. But she explained that she did not want to discourage trade, and any customer happening along would go off and do something else for an hour or so, and then return.

She was surprised to see me at the window and gave a little wave, which I returned. She opened the door and told me that Miss Flyte was in the kitchen and invited me to join them. She turned the clock hands to "Back in 15 minutes."

Miss Flagler is tall and thin and Miss Flyte is short and thin, but aside from that, age seems to have made them sisters. I've noticed this age thing the few times I've been to Weeks's Nursing Home to deliver cakes and pies my mother donates. The old people all look strangely alike, as if age is another country, a country of relations, and anyone not a relative (such as me) stands out like a sore thumb.

Both Miss Flagler and Miss Flyte have gray hair, worn similarly in a bun, and filmy blue eyes, like one of those rainy-day skies where the blue is glazed over. They dress differently, though. Miss Flyte likes wool sweaters and skirts and Miss Flagler always wears gray dresses and cashmere cardigans. (Her dress indicates family money, or money from another source than her gift shop, whose profits wouldn't run, probably, to silk and cashmere.)

Hello, hello, hello, I said, the third hello being directed to Albertine, Miss Flagler's queenly white cat, who also joins us during coffee breaks. Albertine likes to sit on a painted shelf right above my chair, sometimes lightly chewing at the crown of my hair. Miss Flagler busied herself at the big cast iron stove, having offered me, as she always does, a choice of tea or cocoa. (Dr. McComb is the only one who has me down as a coffee drinker.) I chose cocoa, as always. Miss Flyte must have started the percolator, for it was perking away.

"Emma," said Miss Flagler, "has something to ask us. Some business."

It seemed to please both of them that I was there on business and not simply in my cocoa-drinking capacity. Even Albertine sat alert instead of lying down on the shelf.

"Really?" said Miss Flyte, with enthusiasm. She made it sound like my "business" was important (which shows how uneventful life can be around here, aside from the ongoing recent mystery). She laced her fingers on the table as Miss Flagler set down her coffee. The cocoa had been made earlier and had only to heat. My cup was served with two marshmallows and I was glad Mr. Butternut wasn't here to compete for them. I quickly stirred the cocoa to keep a skin from forming.

We three settled now, I began: "It's those Devereau sisters. You remember, we were talking about the Devereaus. They were Elizabeth, Isabel, and Iris—"

"Iris!" said Miss Flagler. "That was her name; Iris was the one who sewed so wonderfully. Do you remember her?" Miss Flagler had turned to Miss Flyte.

Miss Flyte pursed her lips. "Vaguely. I'd have to think." Her brow furrowed.

"Iris Devereau made me a dress. I believe I told you that?" said Miss Flagler.

I nodded. "You said it was ice-green silk or organdy. It was a garden party and Mary-Evelyn Devereau was there, handing sandwiches around."

"Indeed, she was. Such a solemn child. But such pretty clothes. Her Aunt Iris must have sewn them too. Iris was quite famous for her dresses. Everyone wanted a Devereau dress. She wouldn't sew for just anyone, either. I remember Helene Baum—well, she wasn't Baum back then, of course; she was Helene Smith—anyway, Helene, who was only a teenager then, nearly had a fit when Iris Devereau wouldn't make her a gown to wear to some dance. I myself felt quite flattered that she made one for me."

"What was she like except being a great dressmaker?"

Miss Flyte said, "What I remember is I thought it just a shame she lived with the other two. Elizabeth and—?"

"Isabel," I said.

"Yes. Well, Iris was the youngest and pretty, while the others were plain—grim, really—and I imagined they resented Iris. All three of them living together like that, and with that little niece to take care of, I'll bet they were rife with resentment."

It was strange to me that again Rose had been left out. "Four of them."

The two looked at me, quizzically, at first. Then Miss Flyte said, "You mean Rose? Yes, that's right. But Rose was a Souder, only a half sister, and she looked so different. She was blond and quite beautiful. You recall her, Eustacia?"

This was Miss Flagler's first name. I thought it suited her.

"Now, didn't she run off and get married?"

Neither recalled this so I told them.

"Queen?" said Miss Flagler. "But that's the name of the woman who was shot over near White's Bridge, isn't it?"

I didn't want to get off on that as it would keep us sitting here all day. "Yes. But I was wondering about Iris. Going back, going back ten years before, do either of you recollect a man from New York City. His name was Jamie Makepiece. He might have been engaged to one of them." I didn't want to put memories in their mouths.

"You know, I always wondered why those girls never married," said Miss Flagler. "I mean none of them. Especially Iris. But now you mention this Makepiece fellow . . . Yes, I do recollect something. There was a row—now, where was this? I honestly think it was at the Hotel Paradise. Yes, it was. Fifty years ago, how it does take me back."

Her voice was sad now, whether at what was there fifty years ago, or what isn't here now, I don't know.

"Your own mother was just a child, back then. It's hard to believe, isn't it?"

Miss Flyte said, "Jamie Makepiece. At the time, I could only have been, oh, thirteen. But I remember him. He cut an elegant figure, let me tell you, and I think all us girls were a little silly about him, flighty. Tipsy." She smiled. "Even me, young as I was."

In my mind's eye I pictured that old photograph on the wall in the Devereaus' parlor. It was hard to imagine those women in their high-necked dresses and pulled-back hair and serious, reproachful faces as ever having been flighty or tipsy. Except, that is, for the fourth one, Rose.

Miss Flagler had stopped, back there fifty years ago. I wanted her to go on. "What about this row you overheard. Was he—Jamie—fighting with someone?"

She had started to raise her coffee cup, and, perhaps realizing it was cold, put it down again. "Yes, with one of the Devereau women."

"Did you hear them?" My cocoa almost forgotten (I was letting the marshmallows melt), I scrunched forward on my chair.

"Well . . . no . . . I honestly can't remember. My goodness, I'm amazed at any of this coming back after fifty years."

"My great-aunt Aurora Paradise says that as you get older you remember more from the far past." I hastened to add, "Of course she's a lot older than you."

"Elizabeth." Miss Flagler's look was vacant, as if her mind were seeing, not her eyes.

We both looked at her. "Elizabeth?" I said.

"It was she, the one who was arguing with Jamie Makepiece."

I waited, but it seemed her mind wasn't going to turn up any more of this scene. I thought for a moment. "What happened to them? To the Devereaus?"

Miss Flyte answered: "They just left, didn't they, Eustacia?"

Miss Flagler nodded. "After the drowning death of poor Mary-Evelyn, yes." She added, "No, but wait: one of them died, remember? I think Iris. Yes, it was the youngest one. I recall that because people commented that it was a pity it should be the youngest. The most talented. Mind you, the other two weren't all that much older—five or ten years, perhaps. They just acted so old, so set in their ways. As I said—grim. Even Iris soured, later in her life, like milk gone off." Miss Flyte picked up the snapshot and gazed at it. "Can you imagine the life that poor child would have led in that house? With those dour old maids?"

Miss Flagler poured more coffee, which had been sitting forgotten on the table between them. "I suppose people say the same of us."

Miss Flyte laughed. "Not 'dour,' not 'grim,' I hope."

"Nobody ever says anything about you that's not complimentary," I said. It was true, except for Lola Davidow, who got mad because the McIntyre wedding party wanted Miss Flyte to light the reception for them. I said, "The Devereaus left nearly everything behind. They even left Mary-Evelyn's dresses."

"How do you know that, Emma?"

"I've been there."

"Really? It's sad to think, but perhaps they wanted no reminders with them."

I was suddenly overtaken by a surge of loneliness. There were pictures in the house of the three sisters and even of the black sheep, Rose. But none of Mary-Evelyn. This hadn't occurred to me before. All we had to remind us of her was this snapshot under the porte cochere, this and memory. And the sisters even wanted to wipe out memory.

Light in August

44

My life had become crowded with people I hardly knew existed a month ago; I counted them up and it came to twenty-one new people. This was even leaving out Rose, since my list had to be people I had actually talked to. For that reason, too, it left out the Girl, even though she might have been the most important of all.

Twenty-one new people! It was staggering, since these are not people I met and only said hello and goodbye to; these are people I am *involved* with, such as Dwayne and Louise Landis and the folks in the Windy Run Diner. Yes, I was staggered by this. The next time Ree-Jane makes a comment about my lack of social life, I will tell her this.

After I left the Oak Tree Gift Shoppe, I decided I needed to think for a little before I talked to Dwayne later on, so I walked down to Second Street to McCrory's, which was usually a relaxing place to be, especially the makeup counter. I liked to look at the lipsticks and powder and eyeliners, deciding what I'd wear if I wore makeup. Ree-Jane said that makeup wouldn't do you any good if you didn't have the bones to begin with.

None of this was getting me closer to how I would convince Dwayne to go to Brokedown House again, so I left. But then I got some notion of what I might do and hurried to the Abigail Butte County Library, a couple of blocks up Second Street.

Inside the library (where I should have gone in the first place), I headed for the literature shelves, where I started looking for William Faulkner. I was amazed to find he wrote so many books. Where did he ever find the time? For one thing, he didn't have to wait tables. I had decided I would take down just one instead of piling a bunch of his books on my library table and thus confuse myself. Also, it was working its way around to noon and I had to get back to the hotel. It was irritating to have to get back and serve lunch to Miss Bertha, but I couldn't keep putting this off on Walter. After lunch I would go to Slaw's Garage.

I ran my finger along the spines of William Faulkner's books, reading the titles. *As I Lay Dying* (no thanks, unless it's being told by Ree-Jane); *Python,* which I didn't know what it was; *The Sound and the Fury,* which I read the opening paragraph of and put back; *Sanctuary,* a title I really liked, for it sounded peaceful. I leafed through it and found one of the characters was named Flem Snopes and put it back, too. *Light in August.* This title I thought was the prettiest, and wasn't that the book Dwayne carried around? I took this book to my favorite reading table, which sat by a sunny window. I liked the way the sunshine made a latticework of light coming through the little square panes. It must be fate, for here I was, reading *Light in August.*

On the very first page, the woman named Lena is remembering when she was *twelve years old.* I could scarcely believe it. Talk about fate! Here's a double dose of it! She thinks about her mother and father, who died when she was my age. William Faulkner described her house and rooms lit by a "bugswirled kerosene lamp."

Bugswirled. What a wonderful word. I looked up and I could see above me the thick whiteness of our porch light and small moths circling and fluttering around it as if its whiteness were some sort of moth landing, like a landing on the moon. I read on. "Stumppocked." Here was another wonderful word. Since he was describing where the trees had been cut, I suppose it means stumps that look diseased. Then there's "hookwormridden." I did not want to linger too long over Lena's condition. I guessed she must be going to have a baby.

I suppose all writers get around to sex sooner or later, only Faulkner got around to it on page two.

It was noon and I had to get back. Holding the book, I went up to Miss Babbit where she was working behind the checkout desk and asked if I could please have a sheet of paper and borrow a pen or pencil. Of course, she said, and reached to a shelf and brought up the paper and handed me a pen. She noticed the book I was carrying. My, my, she said, Mr. Faulkner. Faulkner-country is not an easy place to be, she said. Neither is Graham-country, I said, surprising myself with this comeback.

I thanked her and went back to my desk, where I started going through my book, just looking anywhere, quickly running my eye down a page here, a page there, stopping if I found something and copied it down. After I'd taken down three different things, I went back to "hookwormridden" and wrote that down too. Then my eye fell on the paragraph that followed:

> *There was a track and a station, and once a day a mixed train fled shrieking through it.*

This was Emma-country. Wow!

In Slaw's Garage, the mechanics were all wiping their hands on oily rags, so I guess they must have seen someone coming.

They weren't very impressed seeing the someone was me. Especially Dwayne, who made a huge production out of getting down on the flat board and sliding under a gray car. I said hi to Abel Slaw and the rest and walked over to the gray car. "Dwayne?"

"Yeah?" His voice sounded miles away. There was a lot of metal clanging on metal, the sounds of being busy.

"Come on out from there, will you?" I sat down on the running board of an old Ford pickup that looked like Ubub's but wasn't, for the license plate didn't read UBB. You-boy was whistling, searching under the hood of an ancient convertible up front.

"Why? I got work to do."

"I can see that. Come on out anyway. It's important."

"You think everything you want's important."

"That's kind of dumb, Dwayne. Everybody does."

He didn't answer. I pulled out the sheet of paper with my three quotes to see which one best fit the situation. None of them really did, but I decided on:

There were words that never even stood for anything, were not even us, while all the time what was us was going on and going on without even missing the lack of words.

I knew Dwayne favored words. So did I.

As he shot out from under the car, I quickly folded the paper and shoved it in my pocket. I wanted him to think I knew it, and had recited, not read, it. I sat with my chin on my updrawn knees and tried to look heartfelt.

"What'd you just say?" Prone on the board, he bent his head back as if he thought maybe Billy Faulkner were under the car with him.

I wasn't at all sure what I'd said. "You heard."

Dwayne got up off the wood flat as if he were rising from Lake Noir, buoyant. The oily rag came out and he stood wiping his hands.

"Don't you recognize it?"

He grunted, but he was near to smiling. His eyes already were. "Recognize the writing. I have not memorized everything Billy Faulkner wrote."

"I thought you'd like that, as it's about words. You remember what you said about words being 'a shape to fill a lack.' "

"So do you know what all that means? What you just said?"

I couldn't even remember what I'd read, much less what it might mean. "No, but it sounds good. It's from *Light in August.*"

Dwayne stopped wiping his hands and shoved the rag in his back pocket. It hung limply over the edge and was a dull rose color.

"I decided I really like him. Billy Faulkner, I mean. William." I hadn't yet read enough to be on a nickname basis with him.

"He'd be pleased."

"When do you get off work?"

" 'Round seven this evening. I still got a truck to do. Why?"

"We need to go to Brokedown House."

" 'We' do, do 'we'? And why's that?"

"I need to go in that room again to see some things. You're going home anyway. White's Bridge is hardly any detour at all."

"So where's all your buddies? Night before last, it looked like a Fraternal Order of the Owls meeting."

"There's too many of them. They get in the way."

"What about your good friend Butternut?"

I sighed. "Du-*wayne.* You know Mr. Butternut wouldn't have any idea what to do in an emergency."

"And just what emergency might announce itself?"

"I don't know. But you do recall the police came that time."

"From what I gather, a missing girl was that particular emergency."

I ignored that.

"What's in this house that's so all-fired important?"

Abel Slaw shouted from the door of his tiny office, "Dwayne, you better come on and finish up Teets's truck. I promised he could pick it up before we close."

I said, "So I'll come back at seven, okay?"

"Emma!" called Abel Slaw. "Now you shouldn't be hanging 'round the cars."

Dwayne said, "Okay, come ahead."

I answered Abel Slaw: "I'm leaving, Mr. Slaw."

"Yeah, well, it ain't I don't want you around, but it's dangerous out there where all the machinery and stuff is."

Some idea of danger he had.

Miss Bertha found another reason to complain, with having to come into dinner at six instead of her preferred time of six-thirty. It was as if she had a schedule of events on her social calendar that would be completely thrown out of kilter by this earlier time. She demanded to know why as she and Mrs. Fulbright sat down at their table.

Pouring the water, I knew if I said it was because I had certain plans for the evening, she would do everything in her power to make me at least a half-hour late, so that I would gain nothing from the change. I had to make it worth her while. When I'd set their menus before them, I told her that our candy supplier (for the display case at the desk) had called up and said they just got in the York peppermint patties—which was Miss Bertha's favorite—that we'd been out of for so long and that he'd be there till seven this evening if I wanted to pick them up. It was a special trip I'd have to make but seeing how much she liked them I would make the effort.

I love going to the candy wholesaler when Mrs. Davidow goes to pick up boxes of Hershey bars, Butterfingers, Snickers, Mounds, and Three Musketeers, my favorite. It's because the bar is in three sections of chocolate, vanilla, and strawberry. Candy boxes, each containing one or two dozen bars, are stacked in the warehouse ten feet high, row after row. I often wonder how they sold all of that candy. To Miller's and the five-and-dime and the drug stores, I guessed—all around.

When I'd told her this, she didn't know how to respond. She was on what is called the "horns of a dilemma" (a state I myself am often faced with), as she wouldn't want me to miss delivery of her York peppermint patties, but then she'd have to go along with this time change. The York patties won out, for she told me to get their first course (fruit cup) and be quick about it.

I smiled and told her "Coming up!" and made for the kitchen. Miss Bertha would not be happy when she saw the display case tomorrow, but I'd worry about that tomorrow. As Scarlett O'Hara liked to say, tomorrow is another day.

I looked out my window and thought those were the exact same cows standing and looking at us over the rail fence. I wondered what they thought. I wondered *if* they thought. For a moment I shut my eyes and put myself in cow-mode, me behind the fence looking as the truck passed. But nothing came to mind and Dwayne was talking.

"It means I'm good."

"Well, You-boy is *good.* I guess so is Abel Slaw." When he didn't bother answering, I said, "I bet you could easily do something to a car so it couldn't run." Naturally I was thinking of you-know-whose. Then I realized the Dewey's Do-Nuts hut wasn't far off. I said, "Suppose we were being chased and we all stopped for doughnuts. I'll bet you could just nip out to the chaser's car and put it out of commission." I could see the blue neon Dewey's sign ahead. "Couldn't you?"

At the doughnut hut, he pulled his truck over. "I always stop here. Got nothing to do with you dropping big hints."

We piled out and piled into Dewey's Do-Nuts. I was starved. I had sacrificed my own dinner for this.

On our way again—I had insisted on paying for the doughnuts and coffee and was glad he didn't make some remark about me drinking coffee—I ate my vanilla-iced doughnut and decided Dwayne was mysterious. I didn't actually know anything much about him, I mean about his life so far. He didn't talk about himself, which was awfully unusual in a person. I inspected my powdered-sugar doughnut; I've always loved powdered sugar from watching my mother make designs with it on cakes. I like to watch the powdered sugar drift down from the sieve like sweet snow.

We were just a short distance from the turnoff. I wondered if Dwayne was running from the law and that was the reason for his secrecy. But he hadn't been at all bothered when he'd met up with the Sheriff that night.

We turned off and I saw the Silver Pear sign casting its moonish glow on the branches, turning them pale and unearthly looking. The restaurant's parking lot was crowded as usual.

Dwayne said, "You can buy me dinner there some night by way of repaying this favor."

"Oh, sure. Listen, maybe you shouldn't park by the pond."

"Why's that?"

We were trundling over White's Bridge now. "Because Mr. Butternut will see the truck and come to Brokedown House and we'd never get anything done."

"Just what are we trying to get done?"

"It's a long story." Mirror Pond came up ahead and Dwayne

Master mechanic II

45

It really bothers me sometimes, this life of lies, but more times it doesn't. I thought this while bumping along in Dwayne's pickup. It was noisier than either Ubub's or Ulub's trucks. It sounded like every little pipe and wire was getting jostled loose.

"How come with you being a master mechanic your own truck's falling apart?"

He shifted gears and they ground as if they were hammering into the highway. "Don't have time."

"I don't want to be rude, Dwayne, but it's not a very good advertisement for a master mechanic to have a car like this." We had passed what city limits there were and were rumbling along the highway.

"Yeah, well, of course, I don't often get the extreme pleasure of a customer driving around with me listening."

What childish sarcasm. "What is a master mechanic, anyway?"

stopped and braked in the same spot as the first night. So much for my advice.

"I like long stories. Come on." He opened his door and I opened mine and both of us climbed down.

He went around to the back of the truck and pulled out his shotgun. It looked absolutely lethal. Well, it was, wasn't it? Just ask a rabbit. He broke it over his arm and jerked his head at me in a "come on" gesture. We crossed the road and went up a small embankment. We were taking the way through the woods instead of the road.

It was dusk, the same part of the day as when I'd been here before. Dwayne was carrying his square flashlight with the handle and switched it on. I love the woods but not if I'm walking through them. With Dwayne there I felt considerably more comfortable, even more than with the Woods and Mr. Root. Every scraped rock, every snapped twig, brittle leaf, wind rustle sent a chill down my spine. It was dark activity of such a level I really thought God ought to be notified. (When I said to Father Freeman I didn't hold with the belief that God knows everything, he said back, Maybe that's just wishful thinking.)

There was this beaten path that we kept to. I wondered how a path had ever gotten trampled out here, with so few people in the place, and no one living in the houses farther along than Mr. Butternut's.

"How come you brought your gun, Dwayne? I mean, you're not going rabbit hunting, are you?" Frankly, I wished he'd say yes, he was, for I didn't like to think he'd want to carry it for protection.

"Always do, going in here."

I didn't care for the sound of that, so I kept quiet. Matted leaves, rotted and wet, squished unpleasantly beneath my feet. Narrow ribbons of water ran down the bark of an oak we passed as if the trees were raining after the sky had stopped. Every so often a shower of drops lighted on my head. Dwayne played his flashlight on either side of the path.

"What are you doing?"

"Just lookin' to see."

"See what?"

"You might recall I saw someone the other night."

I certainly did recall it. I edged closer to him. The path was really too narrow for two people walking abreast, but I wasn't going to hang around behind him. "You're not the only person that comes out here hunting, I guess. Maybe it was another poacher you saw. Or heard."

"This ain't hunting season, as you were quick to remind me. No, it wasn't another poacher."

I heard running water. We must have been near a stream. I asked him.

"That's the creek, one that runs under White's Bridge. It runs into the lake. So if you ever get lost, just follow this creek, you'll get out okay."

Lost? I had no intention of getting lost.

He left the path and I was right beside him. In another forty or fifty feet we'd come on the creek. Dwayne looked up at the sky. "Full dark in another fifteen minutes." He leaned his gun against a tree and set his flashlight on a stump.

"Stumppocked, this place is," I said.

"Where'd you hear that word?"

"Light in August."

"You're one for details, aren't you?"

Beneath the tree was a wide flat stone, its surface as fine as pewter. He fingered a cigarette from the pack in his shirt pocket. He sat down on the slab of rock and motioned for me to sit, too. "I always stop here, take a cigarette break, and think."

I sat down. The rock was worn perfectly smooth and was big enough to hold us both.

"Cigarette?" He reached into his pocket.

I just gave him a look, ha ha ha.

"You gave it up? Wish I could. Here." He held out his hand.

It was a piece of candy, a Caramellow, that I love just as much as Miss Bertha does her York peppermint patties. Caramellows are hard to find. I felt less anxious when I bit down into its softness. "Thank you."

"You're welcome. Now, what the devil is it inside that house you want to see?"

"You know that letter that you read and the picture of the man?"

"I remember the letter. Yeah, so?"

"It's just possible it was written by the man in the photo. *Just* possible." I made it sound as if I didn't want Dwayne to build his hopes up.

He frowned and sucked in on his cigarette. "So what you're saying is you think you know him."

"Know who he is. *Maybe.*" It amazed me that Dwayne didn't ask the next question: who? He must have figured he wouldn't know him anyway, so why ask the name? He was leaning forward, one arm across his knees, chin in the other hand. I kind of copied how he sat, my legs drawn up, my skirt pulled down over my knees. It occurred to me if anyone (my mother, for instance) knew I was out here in the woods with a strange man, she'd be totally horrified. (But what would she do about it?) I could hardly be afraid of Dwayne since I was the one who talked him into coming. Maybe if his mother knew he was out here with me, she'd be horrified too. I felt I should say something else. "It's just a hunch." But it was more than that.

"Most things are."

I had no idea what he meant. Dwayne said strange things a lot of the time that seemed unrelated to what was happening. I would like to talk to him sometime when we hadn't so much to do.

"You finished your smoke break?"

"Yep. You finished your marshmallow break?"

"*Cara*-mallow."

He smiled and crushed his cigarette on the stone, then brushed the bits away.

I couldn't say if the wood was darker than before since whatever light had filtered through the trees had stopped before it hit the ground. Upward it was dark. Except for the squelch of our feet, sounds were blanketed so that the *too-whit* of a barn owl or the scraping of branches or the snap of a twig seemed awfully insubstantial in all of this creaking darkness. He was still checking the undergrowth beside the path.

"How much farther?" I whispered for no reason. I had hold of the hem of Dwayne's bulky wool shirt. When he stopped and knelt down, I did too. He pulled something from a thick bush of mountain laurel, dwarfed I guessed from a lack of light. It was a piece of cloth I saw when he shone the light on it. In this light it was hard to tell the color, though I could see it was dark—dark red or blue, or a kind of plum color. The material was heavy, probably wool. It had been torn off by the small sharp branches; threads had unraveled from one end.

"So what do you think, looking at that?"

I felt complimented that he was asking my opinion—seriously, too, for his expression bore no sign of the usual Dwayne-mockery.

"It's from clothes," I said, "somebody's shirt or dress, maybe."

"Uh-huh. Last month, last year, when?"

I frowned. "When was it caught here, you mean?" He nodded. "Can you tell?"

"Sure, whether it's old or recent. Look at the tear. The threads haven't stiffened up with cold or anything. You can tell that even without a magnifying glass."

"So it's just been torn recently?"

"Recent as a couple of nights ago, maybe."

I handed the bit of cloth back. "Dwayne, that's really jumping to conclusions."

"Sometimes conclusions can't be got at any other way."

It was then I realized that Dwayne was taking this whole thing seriously, that he wasn't seeing it as just some crazy twelve-year-old's notion. He pushed the cloth into his shirt pocket and we walked on, me clutching his shirt again. It wasn't long before I could make out the roots of the big oak, where I'd hidden that first visit, just coming into the edge of the flashlight's light. It seemed months ago, years even.

"You've got to be realistic, Dwayne." This coming from *me?* "It probably doesn't mean a thing."

"Sound and fury is all. That's what Billy Faulkner said about life. Or what Shakespeare said; I believe those were his words, originally."

I was having enough trouble with Faulkner. I didn't want Shakespeare adding to it.

Dwayne stopped and stopped me, too. He put on a listening face, the two of us standing a few feet from the rear door. He shone the flashlight carefully, seeming to walk the light from right to left and back again. Nothing moved, nothing sounded. I wished for some sign of life, even a rabbit scurrying (though I guessed what its fate might be). Both the screen door and the back door protested when Dwayne creaked them open and we went in.

What I noticed first was the scent of grass, the toilet water that first Dwayne and then the Sheriff had opened. This faint scent had escaped the bottle and stayed.

"Dwayne, you smell that?"

He nodded. "Probably from the other night."

I stopped as he had and listened.

"There's no one," he said.

"How do you *know?*"

"Used to be a cat burglar. Come on."

I looked at his back, openmouthed. He was kidding. Wasn't he?

There were two bedrooms we had not paid any attention to before. Dwayne swung the light across the bed, dresser, and bureau. The surfaces were empty of what small items they might have held before: jewelry, brush, comb, mirror, stuffed animals, a doll. There were no bedclothes except for a blanket folded at the bottom of the bed. The second bedroom was much the same, except here there were curtains at the window and a closet on the side of the dresser. I stayed in the doorway while Dwayne went to the closet and opened it.

Anxiously, I asked. "Are there clothes and stuff in there?"

He shook his head. "Nothin' except a couple worn-out suitcases." He pulled them out; they were cheap plastic or the cardboard that suitcases used to be made of a hundred years ago.

"Come on," I said, "into the other room."

Still looking at the cases, one of which he'd opened—it was empty—he grunted and rose up.

The third bedroom was as we'd left it. The bottle of grass-scented toilet water stood in the same spot, tightly stoppered. The dolls and animals sat back in the same corner. While Dwayne lighted the two thick candles, I headed for the doll Maud had been holding. It was true: the doll was dressed in the white organdy, a little yellowed and stiffened by time, that had made both Iris's and Mary-Evelyn's dresses. The tiny, faded, blue satin flowers were the same ornaments as on the dress that had been Mary-Evelyn's shroud. The fact of this doll was dizzying. I turned away from the night beyond the window full of woe, woeful. I was making way for the blue devils, misery's misery. It was never going to go away. It was the return of the feeling I'd had in the kitchen the day before, and again tonight. I felt the end of something.

"This is it, here." Dwayne was holding the letter he'd read to me, the same letter the Sheriff had read. "You want to read it?"

I shook my head. "You read it."

He read:

> *"My dear, I have faith that we will be together again and soon. It has become too much for me and, I'm sure, too much for you. It's better I leave for a little while until this fury quiets down. I suppose a century ago, my faithlessness would have been shouted in all the newspapers!"*

"It's signed, 'Your, J.' "

He handed it to me, that and the photograph. "Now here's a guy more interested in saving his own skin than being true to her."

I studied the man in the photograph. There were differences between this picture and the snapshot Aurora had shown me—the color of his hair and the shape of his eyes. The snapshot had been taken in bright sunlight, the hair lighter, the eyes squinting against the sun. In Aurora's picture, he had a hand raised, covering his eyes. But I still was sure that this was Jamie Makepiece, this was he. I think I had found out more than I expected, more even than I wanted to know.

My dear I Have faith that we will be together again and soon.

I didn't make the mistake Dwayne did, only because the "I" meant something to me.

"Dwayne, it's not 'I have faith.' The 'H' is a capital. He's saying to her, 'Have faith.' See?" I handed it back.

Dwayne looked at the script, frowning. "Who's 'I'?"

"Iris or Isabel, and I'd say Iris because I don't think he felt that way about Isabel."

"Who the hell are Iris and Isabel?"

"They were sisters. They were both in love with the same man, him." I held out the picture.

He took it and sat down in the rose slipcovered rocker. His gun was leaning against the side of the chest of drawers. "Which one did he take to?"

"Both."

"Well, hell, there's trouble right there comin' down the road."

"First he was engaged to Isabel, then Iris came along."

He smiled a little. "That sounds romantic: the real thing came along. There's a song goes like that. So he broke off with Isabel and got engaged to Iris."

This butting in annoyed me. "Dwayne, will you let me tell it? This is *my* story." With that momentary irritation I was once again overcome with that feeling of woe. The woe, the sorrow I know was part of the fear. What was coming to an end was my story.

"Sounds like something out of Faulkner." He fingered another cigarette from his pack.

I thought about *Light in August.* "Maybe it does, except they hadn't got in this Lena's, you know, condition."

"What?"

I shrugged. "Her 'condition.' "

"Oh, you mean she was fixing to have a baby. Sometimes I think every woman Faulkner writes about is in that condition." He struck a match, inhaled. "How do you know?"

I frowned. "Huh?"

"How do you know they weren't—or one of them wasn't—in that 'condition'? This Jamie would have to be a hell of a fella if they both were." Dwayne got up. "I'm going out to have a look-see round the house." He picked up the rifle. "I'll be right outside, don't worry."

He left. I followed, all the time thinking.

Was that what it was? Was it only a story?

For what did I really have—as the Sheriff would say—as evidence that they had killed Mary-Evelyn? She drowned in strange circumstances. Things were left unexplained, such as the party dress and her not wearing shoes. But all of Mary-Evelyn's dresses were beautiful; any one of them could have been a dress for a party. As for the shoes, she could simply have removed them because it seemed the natural thing to do if she was going out on the lake in a boat.

It all might be just as Elizabeth Devereau had told the police: they didn't realize until late that Mary-Evelyn wasn't in her bed and had then gone looking for her. It could have happened that way. And did they actually hate her so much? Could Ulub and Imogene have misunderstood what they saw?

And then there was Rose. As beautiful as people say she was, there must've been more than one man to make Ben Queen jealous. But that didn't make any sense if Ben Queen was innocent of her murder. And he was; I was sure of that. It was Fern who had the motive. In this light it made sense: Rose was going to send Fern off to an institution and Fern got in a rage and stabbed her. Over and over, if the accounts were true. Stabbed her the way someone worked up into a crazy frenzy might have done. It made horrible sense. I would have to go back and talk to Louise Landis, who struck me as the person with the most sense in Cold Flat Junction. Only it was tiring, making up reasons for talking to people. Oh, of course I *could* tell the truth about what I was doing. But imagine how they'd react: *Hello, I'm inquiring into a forty-year-old murder of a little girl. And two other murders besides.* Yes, I can just imagine the folks in the Windy Run Diner hearing that.

About Fern's murder. I asked myself if she couldn't just've been going to the Silver Pear; she was all dressed up. Maybe going to the restaurant to meet someone. But there was nothing to show that; the Sheriff had asked everyone in the area around White's Bridge (not that there were many to ask) and no one had seen her. So what made another kind of awful sense was that she was going to meet her daughter and wanted to look her best. After twenty years, her daughter might not have been too impressed. I mean, if Fern just left her child somewhere twenty or so years ago. If she just abandoned her, left her in an orphanage, or worse. I didn't want to think too much about worse. Of course, there were a lot of orphans around and they didn't end up killing their natural parent, if they could even find the parent. There were a lot of blind places in this theory, but all I know is Ben Queen didn't do it, and if he didn't who did? No, it all made awful sense if I was watching a Greek tragedy.

As for the beginning of this, as for Mary-Evelyn Devereau's death: there *was* this doll, this letter, this photograph—and all in a house where there was no reason for them to be. Unless Mary-Evelyn had given Imogene the doll. I didn't think so, but I could always go back and ask Imogene. That still didn't account for the photograph of Jamie Makepiece, or the letter.

What were they doing in Brokedown House?

Dwayne came back. "Ain't nothing around I could see. You find anything else? You're good at finding things, that's for sure."

"No."

"It's about time I took you home."

"Oh." I was surprised at myself that it hadn't occurred to me Dwayne would have to do this. "You don't have to, Dwayne. I can just get a taxi to come to the Silver Pear."

He shook his head. "I'll take you. I figure you been at large enough in the world for one night."

"I'm going to take these things." I picked up the doll, the letter, the picture. "I'm taking these to the Sheriff. It's evidence."

Dwayne considered this as he folded a stick of Doublemint in his mouth and offered a stick to me. "It's some interesting story you cooked up, that's sure."

I felt complimented until I reminded myself I only just told it; I didn't "cook it up." But it *is* my story. I looked at the letter again. "I guess *you* wouldn't do that, I mean save your own skin instead of being true to a girl?"

"I should hope not. 'Course, it'd depend pretty much on the girl, wouldn't it?"

"Now, that doesn't make any sense, Dwayne." He could be so irritating. "If you were *already* involved with this girl."

He picked up his gun. "Boy, you sure are a stickler. Sometimes you're worse than Billy Faulkner, I'd say."

I took that as a compliment, though I didn't know what he was getting at.

I didn't mind the walk through the woods going back as much, but then I guess you wouldn't mind having danger behind you instead of before you. On the ride back I said, "What if it was true?"

"What if what was?"

"About Jamie and Iris having a baby."

"You thinking of that little girl that drowned being theirs?"

I nodded. "Maybe."

"For one thing, it'd be one of the most awful things I ever heard of outside of Faulkner."

"I wonder if his stories were true."

"Depends what's meant by 'truth' I guess."

Irritated again, I slid down in my seat. Why did adults have to make so much of a simple question. "You know what I mean. Whether it actually happened to *Lena.*"

He thought this over, then said, "Do you read much?"

"Well, of *course.* I'm reading *Light in August,* aren't I?" Actually, I wasn't, not after those first ten or a dozen pages.

"Haven't you come across characters in books so real they just wander off the page and around town, so to speak?"

I had saved my stick of gum and now unwrapped it. I had to admit Lena seemed to have stepped off the page and onto that dusty country road she meandered along, not unlike the road to Spirit Lake. I could walk along with her, hoping she didn't have that baby then and there with only me around. "Yes. I guess," I answered Dwayne. I thought of what Father Freeman told me about trips in the mind being better, maybe, than trips actually taken. They must have been talking about the same thing. I didn't know whether I believed it, though.

I looked at the doll and imagined Mary-Evelyn holding it while she stared out of her window at the rain-pocked lake and the boat dock on the other shore and imagined escaping. I wondered if Maud, sitting out there on the end of the pier, watching the boats and the water, imagined escaping, too.

I could ask Maud. Mary-Evelyn, I couldn't.

Out of the clouds

46

It did not help my state of mind much to find a note pushed under my door from Will and Mill telling me to come to the Big Garage right after breakfast the next morning. They were like that—or at least Will was—issuing orders when one of their productions was in process ("in rehearsal," Will liked to say). Despite the annoyance of being ordered around and maybe delaying my trip into town, I had to admit I was curious to know what they'd been doing in the garage.

Did they know this note read like a blackmail demand? Like, COME TO BIG GARAGE WITH $10,000 IN SMALL BILLS OR YOU WILL NEVER SEE REE-JANE AGAIN.

Oh, if only it *had* said that! To think I wouldn't have to hand over the ten thousand *and* get what I've always wanted! So I might as well do it, and quick, so I could take my evidence—photo, letter, doll—in to the Sheriff. Not that I expected him to actually do anything;

I just wanted some clear thinking brought to bear. I wanted to know if someone agreed with me or thought I was plain crazy.

Walter was at the stove "aproned up" (as he liked to say) when I walked into the kitchen yawning at seven-thirty. He was frying himself eggs and offered to drop one or two in the pan for me.

"But I guess you'll want them buckwheat cakes."

I frowned. "It can't be buckwheat cakes, Walter, as it's too early in the year. You can't get the flour till the fall."

"Don't ask me; someone must've, for there she sets." He pointed his spatula at one of my mother's mixing bowls. It was covered with a damp cloth, which meant the flour was rising, or had already.

I removed the tea towel, and I'd say my eyes lit up, but it was really my stomach that did.

"Miss Jen showed me what to do before she left. It's easy." Walter transferred his eggs to a plate, scooped three pieces of Wonder Bread from the wrapper, and sat down at the serving counter to butter his bread. "I greased up that skillet for you. It's heatin'." He hooked a thumb over his shoulder. The cast-iron pancake skillet sat atop two burners, it was so big.

I looked at the risen dough as if it were Christ himself (and quickly told myself not to make that comparison when Father Freeman was around). When I try to draw up a list of my favorite foods, it never runs up and down, but kind of travels across the page:

Buckwheat cakes Ham pinwheels and cheese sauce Angel Pie Chocolate Feather Cake

and so on.

Miss Bertha and Mrs. Fulbright completely forgotten (I heard the cane doggedly *tap tap tapping* across the dining room floor), I shook droplets of water on the skillet and watched them dance as if they were happy about the buckwheat cakes too; I then dropped a large dollop of batter in the center and watched it slowly spread. Even in that movement there was something delicious. In a moment the outer edges crisped and shrank and tiny bubbles erupted on the surface of the batter. I waited while more bubbles appeared, until the surface was coated with them before I turned the cake over. The cooked side had that fine-line crazing that you get only on buckwheat cakes, a honey-brown crackle that always reminds me of pottery glaze.

As I slid this cake onto a plate, Walter said, "I warmed up the maple syrup."

The little pan sat on the ledge above the stove, staying warm. I thanked Walter and poured syrup in thin ribbons across the cake. It was real maple syrup, caught in a bucket tied to a tree (or however they caught it), just as this was real buckwheat. Whenever I took my first taste of a buckwheat cake—that incredible mix of sour-sweet—I could almost hear them in the Tabernacle way over across the highway shouting "Hallelujah!" I could also understand why Mrs. Davidow had to have her pitcher of martinis every evening. There are certain things that make you crave more of what you've just had, as if your taste buds suddenly woke up and said, "Gimme!"

By this time, Miss Bertha's non-Hallelujah shouts were coming from the dining room, but I went right on eating. Nothing could get between me and a buckwheat cake.

Walter got up from his stool, said "I'll take the old fool her orange juice," and went on in the dining room with the juice pitcher and two small glasses.

Even though I had been told to appear at the Big Garage, I still had to wait through three knockings until the door opened its usual two or three inches, enough for Will's eye to appear at the crack.

"It's me," I said.

"What?" Will's tone was, as usual, suspicious.

"What do you mean, 'what'? *You're* the one who ordered me to come here." This was really irritating. "You wrote that note."

He still hesitated before closing the door enough to remove the chain, then opened it so that I could pass through. I still thought the space he allowed was very stingy. Who in heaven's name were they afraid would see what they were doing?

The Big Garage was like a huge cave with artificial lighting. They loved to fool around with lighting and they had managed to get their hands on some lights from the playhouse on Lake Noir. It was some dumb summer theater with a lot of bad acting. They covered the lights with different colors of crepe paper, today's being blue and green. The effect was eerie and it almost made some of the rafters look like stalactites. At one end of this huge cave was a stage, part of it hidden by several tarpaulins, tented across it. A piano sat near the stage. Mill came out from the tarpaulin tent, hauling a thick rope behind him. I couldn't tell what it was, or what for, which wasn't unusual. He uncoiled it as he walked.

"What's under there?" I asked.

"You don't have to know," said Will. "All you have to do is rehearse your part."

It was my turn to be suspicious. "What part?"

"You know what part. We've already discussed it."

I started to reply when a high voice came from somewhere around the rafters: "Hi, missus!" It was Paul's voice. (Paul called all females "missus," from my mother on down, except for his own mother.)

Paul seemed to be straddling the rafters twenty feet above us. It was hard to see exactly what he was doing, but what difference did that make since I couldn't imagine him up there in the first place. "What's Paul doing up there?"

"He's going to work the clouds."

"The *what?* For God's sakes, are you crazy? He could fall and break his neck! Look how high up that is!"

Will—who had never had any particular interest in Paul's welfare—just shrugged. "We tied him."

"You *tied* him up there?"

"Well, we had to. Otherwise he'd fall off, probably."

Why bother objecting? I shaded my eyes with my hand—as if that would do any good. I could see the pale skin of Paul's legs, the legs swinging away as if he were on a hobby horse. But the rest of him was bathed in this weird green light and his towhead disappeared into the dark shadows. I could also see a few white objects. These, I guessed, must be the "clouds." For a moment, Paul looked like pictures I remembered from an old book about ships. He was the sailor up in the crow's nest. "Clouds," I said. "Clouds."

Mill sniggered and ran down the few steps from the stage and plopped down at the piano. He thumped off a bunch of chords that sounded like an accompaniment through the gates of Hell, which I guessed was appropriate.

Will said, "What he does is, he lets out the string the clouds are attached to so they move along, down in front of you, so when you appear it's just like you came out of the clouds. Pretty neat."

It was not a question. Will was not asking me to attest to the "neatness" of this harebrained idea. If Will said it was neat, it was neat. Then, as my eyes got a little more used to the dark green-blueness of this cave, I repeated, "When I appear? When I appear *where?*"

"See up there? Near Paul?"

I made out a swing—an old-fashioned board-notched-in-rope swing, the sort you see tied to a high tree branch. It was dangling near Paul, up where he was. "So what's that?" As if I had to ask.

"It's the 'machine,' you know, the one God comes down in. Or Zeus, or whoever."

Mill had stopped playing his death march and come over to stand beside us. He said, "The *deus ex machina.*"

Of course he pronounced it wrong—"Do-X-machine"—as we all had been doing. "You mean 'DAY-*us ex* mack-*in-ah*.' " I must admit I simpered a little when they both looked at me, and repeated the phrase in the labored way one must do with fools and babies. "DAY-us *ex MACK-in-ah*."

They were both chewing gum, Will slowly, Mill, fast, and they stopped. "Nah," said Will.

I continued laboriously, "Well, go look it up in a Greek dictionary." I did wonder why the proper pronunciation of this seemed to be more important to me than what the *deus* did. "If you think I'm getting on that swing, you're crazy."

"You're going back on our bargain?" said Will. "You swore you'd play a role in this production and we took Jane's car and drove you to White's Bridge. You *promised.* You gave your *word.*"

Will liked to make it sound as if a person's entire value in life was honor, was his word, when actually a person's value was measured in how useful the person was to Will. If Will ever made a promise (which I can't remember if he ever did), he would break it as fast as my mother breaks eggs if it served his purpose.

"I said I'd play a role; I didn't say I'd be willing to go up there in a swing." I looked rafter-ward.

"Hi, missus!" Paul called down again.

"Okay, okay, we'll show you how safe it is. Let the swing down, Mill."

At that, Mill whistled himself off to some sort of pulley he'd rigged up out of rope, rope cranked around what might have been an old car wheel, and in a minute the swing descended. With a disconcerting tilt and knock when it hit the stage.

"See how simple it is?"

"Sure, without me in it."

"Christ!" said Will, walking over to where Mill and the swing were. I could hear them talking about all of this in low voices. Will got on the swing, then. Mill started cranking away and Will and the swing swayed upward. He shouted to me, "I can't believe you're such a coward."

This insult was, of course, to appeal to my vanity. It didn't. "Well, now you can!"

I could have just turned around and left, but that would be a bad idea because I never knew when I would need their help, and if I didn't do what I promised, they'd never do anything for me again.

Will must have been telling Paul to start moving the clouds around, for as the swing descended, so did two of the clouds. For the clouds it was a much jerkier descent than the swing. The swing didn't look all that dangerous, I told myself. But the idea that Paul—probably the most homicidal person I had ever come in contact with and one who'd grow up to be a serial killer if it was possible to serial-kill people by accident—was up there (tied on or not) manipulating the clouds or anything else having to do with my descent really made me nervous.

The swing tilted when it hit the stage and Will got out. "You see! Would I do it if it wasn't safe?"

"You'd do anything. Both of you are like mad scientists. Paul's one of your experiments."

A huge, dramatic sigh from Will, as he turned, hands on hips and paced back and forth shaking his head. He has always been *so* dramatic.

"I'll go up halfway to see how it feels," I said.

"Good, good!" said Will. "She's going up!" he called over to Mill.

"Good!" said Mill. They were always echoing each other.

Gingerly, I sat myself on the swing, then told Mill to pull it up just clear of the stage, which he did. I bounced on it to see how sturdy, how firmly the plank fit into the rope that curved around it, and decided it was pretty good. Anyway, I guess if the plank fell off I could still cling to the ropes. "Okay," I said. "Slow!" The swing started its ascent and I reminded him to stop in the middle to see how I felt. So he cranked and cranked and didn't stop in the middle (why did I think my orders carried any weight?) although I yelled and yelled, Stop! No one paid any attention. I finally got all the way up to Paul and the clouds, which I think he was trying to slice the top off with a razor. Oh, that was wonderful! Paul was up here with a *razor.*

"I want to go back down. Back down! Right now!"

"Okay, okay!" called Will. "Paul, start lowering the clouds!"

"Hello, missus!" he yelled, as if I were still thirty feet down.

I looked to see if the rope was tight enough around his chest to keep him from leaning any closer to me. "Paul! Don't you *dare* do that!" He was whittling at the rafter with the razor, or maybe it was a pocket knife; it was too green-dim up here to tell. Between his legs sat a brown grocery bag.

"What's he doing?" yelled Will.

"Only cutting up the clouds with his razor!" I was happy to shout back.

Mill yelled at Paul. "Any of those clouds damaged you won't leave here alive, Paul!"

Paul stopped and he laughed.

"I'm lowering the swing, Paul. Understand? *Understand?*"

I heard paper rustle. It must have been the grocery bag. Then as I slowly descended I felt something light falling on my head. I shook myself. Then it was falling all around me, falling thicker. I saw a flurry, what going through a cloud might actually look like.

Flour. I looked back up at Paul just as he was dumping it and got a blast in my face. I was fuming, I was furious. I yelled down, "Damn it! You didn't say anything about flour."

"Yes, I did," Will yelled back. "We had to experiment to see if it added anything, what with the clouds, too."

"Experiment with yourselves!" I said this as the swing dumped me on the stage.

"I don't want to get flour all over me. Boy, do you look funny."

"What's this stupid production *about* that you need to go to these lengths?" I wiped some of the flour from my face. The top of me was pretty much covered in it.

Ordinarily, they wouldn't have answered this question, but perhaps because they'd made a guinea pig of me, they felt they owed me something.

Will said, "It a Greek story. It's about Medea. She got jealous of Jason and killed their kids to get back at him. That's just like the Greeks," he added, with a sniff.

"Well, if she murdered them, what's the purpose of the Do-X—I mean *deus ex machina?*"

"We'll think of something."

Now I was really beside myself. "Think of something? You're just going to tack it on at the end? It's because you like it, that's all, even though it serves no purpose. I just went through all of that for no reason *at all.*"

Mill pushed his glasses up his nose with a fingertip. "The Greeks always had a Do-X-machine."

(I noticed he made no attempt whatsoever to pronounce it correctly.)

"It wouldn't be a true Greek tragedy without one. What we really wanted to do was that story about Agamemnon's father and one of his enemies' fathers. See, Agamemnon's father did something, I forget what, so of course the friend's father had to exact revenge. He killed his kids and served them up in a pie."

Will said, "That's a great story. The Greeks were always killing off their kids right and left."

Mill said, "And other family members. They were a really bloodthirsty bunch."

They both sounded as if this was the best news they'd ever heard. I shook my head in disbelief. "So who's playing Medea?"

"June."

My mouth dropped open. "June *Sikes?* You know we're neither of us to have anything to do with her! She's worse than Toya Tidewater."

"No one will recognize her, not in the weird clothes and all that makeup. And the long hair. June's pretty good, actually, the way she handles a knife."

Mill said, "She slits their throats. The kids', I mean."

Will chewed his gum faster, as if the thought excited him. "We've got a lot of fake blood. A lot."

"Who plays the children? How many are there?"

"Two. Paul plays one. But we've got to train him to stay still. We kicked his butt several times."

"Who else?"

They both looked at me and slowly chewed their gum.

My eyes widened and I stepped back. "Oh, no you don't. If you think I'm going to appear on stage with June holding a knife and Paul with a razor—*forget it!*"

As if I'd said nothing at all, Will said, "We got to double up some roles, actors have to be in more than one part. I'm playing Jason and also a Greek messenger."

"Well, you can play the other kid, too." I turned and stomped out. It's hard to look indignant when you're covered with flour.

"You musta been up in the Big Garage," said Walter as I fumed into the kitchen.

"How'd you know *that?* Is that towel clean?" I pointed to one in a pile Walter kept near the dishwasher.

"Uh-huh. I know because they ax'd me to do it, come down in that swing thing."

I glared. So I wasn't even the first choice. I rubbed the flour from my face.

Walter went on: "They got Paul up there tied to the roof some way. I ain't seen him for nearly three days and his ma come lookin' for him, but I never said nothin' about where he was."

"You think he's been tied up for *three days?*"

Walter picked a big serving platter from the rinse rack and began drying. “They might of let him down nights. I seen a cot back in a corner I expect they got for Paul to sleep on. Maybe they lock him in.”

I shook my head. “They wouldn’t do that. Not, mind you, because they’re so nice. It’s because they’d be afraid to have him around their scenery. He’d ransack the place. You know Paul. He’s like Wile E. Coyote only without the brains.”

Walter placed the platter with the other dry dishes and said maybe I was right. I asked if I’d got all the flour off and Walter said yes, and I went to call a taxi.

Deputy Dawg

47

With the evidence on the seat beside me in a gym bag, I leaned back and closed my eyes and hoped Delbert wouldn't talk all the way into town.

"You fixin' to see Sam?"

I had told him to drop me at the courthouse. "Yes."

"I think maybe he ain't there."

I didn't comment.

"Thing is, he got his hands tied with all that's been happening. That murder you know."

I clinched my eyes shut. "I know. Well, if he's not there, I'll wait."

" 'Course he might just've stepped across to the Rainbow, him and Donny. Donny loves Shirl's doughnuts."

I sat silently, willing him to shut up.

"On the other hand, Donny'd more'n likely know where Sam's at."

Sliding down in my seat, I plugged my ears with my fingers. I wondered if there was ever a cab driver in any Greek tragic play. Probably not, but there must have been an equivalent. If it were China, it might have been a rickshaw operator. I could hear Delbert even over my stopped-up ears.

"There's the Teets's place, so we're almost there." He nodded toward a big yellow house behind us now. What was he saying all this for, talking as if I were a stranger to La Porte? Finally, finally, he pulled up in front of our grand white courthouse and I gave him the fare, hauled myself out of the cab, and fled. He was still talking.

Donny sat at the Sheriff's desk, leaning back in the creaking, leather-cushioned swivel chair. He always did this when the Sheriff wasn't around, as if he, Donny, were the law in La Porte. "Sam ain't here, he's out at Lake Noir. He pronounced it 'Nor,' as did most people. Having myself learned *deus ex machina,* I could certainly say "N'wah."

"I'll wait."

"For God's sakes, girl, he could be out there for hours."

"Then I'll wait for hours." It was now a point of pride that I not move from this chair. I knew it would be really hard not to go across to the Rainbow for some chili. It was way after lunchtime and I didn't know how long I could hold out. I had never been tested in this way, what with my mother's cooking always available. That made me wonder if they had started back from Florida. Which day was it? I hoped I could get to the Pink Elephant in time to say goodbye to my dancing partner and the staff of the Rony Plaza. These thoughts held me for a while—dreaming on palm trees—and I didn't bother commenting when Donny said "Suit yourself."

He didn't want me waiting because he didn't want me to know how little there was for him to do. For a while he stayed in the swivel chair, opening and closing drawers with a yank and a shove, as if whatever he was looking for better give itself up. Then he got up and swaggered around, his thumbs hooked into his Sam Brown belt, one close to his holster to impress on me how dangerous he could be. This all went on for a good ten minutes.

It's best, I've found, to remain silent with someone you can't stand so that they just fizzle out or give up. But it's so hard to follow my own advice. "Don't you have anything to do?" I just couldn't resist it.

At that he swung around from where he'd been messing with Maureen's In and Out boxes. "I got puh-*lenty* I ought to be doing but Sam wants somebody here, in the office, case he needs backup." He adjusted the holster looped over his belt, adjusted his gun, adjusted his height. He managed to stretch himself an inch taller by leaning over slightly backwards.

"Backup for what? Has he gone after the killer?"

Donny paused. "Could be." He narrowed his eyes in a threatening manner, or at least what he thought was such a manner.

"No, it couldn't. He doesn't know who killed her. Fern Queen," I added, as if he might have forgotten.

His eyes got even more squinty looking. "And just how do you know *that?*"

"I know."

Donny half sat his butt on the Sheriff's desk and fake-laughed. "You know somethin', Emma, you always have been too big for your britches. Think you know everything. Hell, you're but twelve years old, chrissakes."

Maybe I'd tell the Sheriff Donny worked the Devil and Jesus Christ into the same sentence that he said to a twelve-year-old. I stuck my tongue in my cheek.

"You don't know *nothin'!*" he said.

It all sounded so much like Ree-Jane, just the kind of thing she'd say. How pathetic that an officer of the law couldn't come up with better put-downs. "Well, I know more than you do."

Now he was up and stalking about, as if that would give his reply more weight Only, he couldn't think of anything to say. He sat down again and pushed a few of the items on the desk around and started talking about their search for Ben Queen.

"We catch him and put him away, you got a dead man walking." Donny looked at me, looked pleased with himself that he'd come up with something that might scare me.

I made my face expressionless and didn't comment.

"You know what that means, I guess. Dead man walking?"

I could tell he was irritated I didn't ask.

"Means when a killer's going to his execution," he said. "When he's walking that last mile, so to speak. Guards call out 'Dead man walking!' Yep, that's what's comin' down the pike for ol' Ben Queen!" He smiled, showing a bottom row of crooked teeth.

He had sensed something—I guess the word is "intuited" something—of the way I felt about Ben Queen. It was then I realized that Donny was like Ree-Jane in this respect: he had a way of ferreting out the beliefs that kept a person going—like Ree-Jane knew I did not want to know the report in the newspaper about the death of Fern

Queen, and so proceeded to read it to me. It was this uncanny grasp of what was important to me that had her figuring out ways to get at me; it had nothing to do with being clever. No, it was like they'd both received the same blessing from Hell.

Had this been Ree-Jane talking, I would have thought up rejoinders that would really get her goat. But Donny wasn't worth the thinking up. Donny was not a constant thorn in my side; he was by way of being an occasional mosquito bite. Still, he got to me. It was important not to let it show in my face or voice, but I felt I had at least to stick up for Ben Queen. "How do you know he did it?"

Donny had risen again to go to Maureen's desk for nothing in particular and now he swaggered back to the Sheriff's swivel chair and resat himself, fake-laughing as he did this. "How do I *know?* Plain as the nose on your face. Right after he gets free of prison, another family member gets murdered, which is exactly what got him twenty years in jail That time it was the wife he murdered. Now, don't that strike you as just too much of a coincidence?"

"No. It's a coincidence, but not too much of one. You think maybe it's just a habit Ben Queen got into—killing off family?"

This irritated Donny no end. "What're you talkin' about? You don't know one damn thing about it."

"Sure I do." I still kept my face and voice expressionless. Your expression and your voice, those are the dead giveaways to a person who's trying to undermine you. I'd had lots of practice at this sort of thing; I pretty much had to know it to survive.

Well, Donny just didn't know how to handle my being so cocksure. He stared at me, then he pointed his finger at me. "I can't hardly wait to tell Sam he's been barking up the wrong tree."

"What tree's that?"

Donny snatched up this question, which betrayed my ignorance, finding in it an opportunity for sarcasm: "With you and him being such friends and all? You don't know what Sam thinks about all this?"

Again, it was the brand of sarcasm Ree-Jane stooped to. Then it suddenly struck me—it was the strangest sensation—that Donny was jealous of my friendship with the Sheriff. So I said that: "You're jealous."

Well, at that he looked like he'd turned to wax (his natural coloring, only not usually hardened into immobility). He couldn't think of a response weighted enough to do justice to what I'd said. Finally, after a few moments of pursed-mouthed movements, he blurted out, "Of you? I'm jealous of *you?*"

He made sounds, blubbered his lips, shook his head. Finally, he came up with, "Okay, you just take care of things here while I go across the street and get me a cup of coffee and a doughnut. Anyone stumbles in here bleeding or shot, you just take care of him. If the mayor calls about the budget, you can fill him in, too." Donny grabbed up his black-visored cap and snapped it on his head.

"Sure," I said. "If the Sheriff comes back I'll just tell him you left me in charge while you went for coffee."

For a flicker of time he looked frightened, his water-colored irises freezing up, congealing. But all he did was give me a flip of the hand, as if he were done with answering fools. He walked out.

I moved over to one of the windows that looked out on the street and across to the Rainbow Café and watched. Donny was in the middle of the street stopping the one approaching car. He just thrust his arm out, palm flat against space, as if he were a comic-strip hero like Superman. He strutted on. There was only this single car, and he couldn't even wait for it to go by. Why did the Sheriff keep him on? Maybe because no one wanted the job of "deputy." Was he good at anything? Paperwork? Organizing?

I turned and looked across the room at the banks of file cabinets. Did Donny realize he'd left me alone with all of their reports?

The drawers were arranged first according to the violation; second, alphabetically. There were a lot of drawers, the cabinets stacked with a row on the bottom and one on top. Two of the bottom drawers, the ones at the end, were devoted to old cases. They went decades back, back to the 1920s. These files were pretty scruffy and stuffed in without much care taken and little arrangement. On the tabs were written what I guessed was the key word in each case, or the key name. I went through them quickly. Towards the back was a file marked "Devereau." I yanked it out.

I was not prepared for the pictures; it hadn't occurred to me there would be any, but of course it was logical that there would be. Two of Mary-Evelyn's face, two of her face and torso, one of her whole waterlogged body.

And then I realized that I had never seen her except in the snapshot taken of the sisters in the shadowy vicinity of the porte cochere. I had made her up in my mind, building on what I could see of her in the snapshot. In some ways I had caught her, in other ways, missed her completely. But then the girl in these pictures was dead.

I took the doll out of my gym bag, smoothed its dress and held it next to the picture that showed Mary-Evelyn's dress most clearly. Though the wetness of it had turned it dark in places, there was no mistaking the clothes were the same. The same dark little handsewn flowers marched down the front.

Statements made by the Devereau sisters: that's what I wanted to read. Elizabeth, the oldest, told the sheriff (a man named Win Whittle, back then): "We dined at the usual time—seven—after which Mary-Evelyn went to her room and, we supposed, to bed."

I frowned over the 'we supposed.' Was Mary-Evelyn allowed to drift around like a little pile of leaves, with no one knowing what she did or where she blew? And besides, how could she have gone to bed so early? For they couldn't have spent more than a half-hour or forty-five minutes eating dinner. (With me, ten minutes would do it.)

I set aside Elizabeth's statement temporarily and went to Isabel's. Her statement matched Elizabeth's, and added a little more. Neither did she know how Mary-Evelyn had slipped out at some point in the night. "After dinner, Elizabeth played the piano and I sang; we often do this in the evening. Iris was in her room, sewing. We have no idea why the child walked to the other side of the lake and took out that rowboat. Why on earth would she do that? She never liked to swim or have much to do with water sports. But she did, and that was that," Isabel's statement read. "Iris woke us sometime much later, around midnight, I think. She told us Mary-Evelyn wasn't in her bed."

I turned to Iris's statement: "I sleep poorly. That night I was up late sewing. I'm a dressmaker. I found I needed some material that I'd shown to Mary-Evelyn for a new dress I was making her, and remembered I'd left it with her. So I went across to her room."

If she went "across" that meant the room exactly opposite was Iris's. I remembered the rooms, how the second floor was laid out.

"That's when I discovered she was gone," Iris continued. "Her bedspread wasn't turned down and her pajamas were under her pillow. She was gone."

Elizabeth: "We dressed and we went looking for her. We searched the grounds around the house and when we didn't find her, we searched the woods. It was a black night and we had only hurricane lamps and a flashlight."

Isabel: "When we went up to bed, about nine it was, Mary-Evelyn was in her room, lying on the bed, reading. The door was open; we always insisted she keep the door open."

(Imagine. *Imagine.* Never to have any privacy, always to have to be public. That might have killed her if the water hadn't. It certainly would kill me.)

What I wondered was, if Mary-Evelyn's room was across the hall from Iris's and both doors were open, then how could Mary-Evelyn have sneaked out without being seen? I remembered the room that was Iris's; I closed my eyes and pictured the furniture. Besides a bed and dresser, hadn't there been an easy chair near the door of the room? And a sewing machine? I had concentrated on Mary-Evelyn's room and hadn't paid much attention to the other bedrooms, other than to just give them a quick look. The easy chair, I thought, could be seen through the open door, which must mean Iris would be able to look into Mary-Evelyn's room. I would have to go back there and look. For if this were true, there is no way Iris would have failed to see Mary-Evelyn leaving her room.

I was disgusted with this Sheriff Whittle. You could only believe the sisters' accounts if it was too much trouble *not* to believe them. The Sheriff—my Sheriff, that is—would have punched the living daylights out of the Devereau sisters' statements. Their story made me wonder, too, why they hadn't gone to more trouble over the details of Mary-Evelyn leaving the house. And why hadn't they questioned Mary-Evelyn's getting in that boat, if she was afraid of water? After all, she wouldn't be around to contradict them. She wouldn't be around for anything anymore.

The answer, I guess, is that they didn't think their version of events would be questioned, no matter how fickle it sounded, and they were right. They were right. It all made me feel like crying.

I looked at the photographs again, wishing I could see Mary-Evelyn's eyes, the eyes that were lost in shadow on the snapshot. But the eyes were closed. Her face was kind of heart-shaped, a valentine face. She had freckles across the bridge of her nose, not going wild over her whole face, as if even the freckling had been kept within strict boundaries. I rolled up the photograph and walked over to Maureen's desk to get a rubber band to hold it. It fit into my gym bag easily. That I shouldn't be stealing police documents was perfectly clear to me and perfectly meaningless. I stopped short of taking the entire file, settling for using the copy-maker in the room. I copied the sisters' statements and also the doctor's report, Dr. McComb's. There wasn't anything in it that would throw light on the case; he had already told me pretty much what was in his report. But I thought I would show it to him and see if it jogged something loose in his memory. I stared at the copier as it *whicked* away. It was very slow. When I had all of the sheets I wanted, I put the originals back into the folder and the folder back into the file cabinet, where it had been before.

Where was Donny? I'd had the file open for forty-five minutes or so. Not that I wanted to see him; I wondered if the Sheriff knew he left the office for long periods of time. Or that he left the office in the hands of someone who might want to go over police reports.

I sat down again to wait for the Sheriff. The office was strange with no one in it. Hanging on the opposite wall were framed pictures of the police forces in neighboring towns. These consisted of two policeman in Hebrides, eight in Cloverly (where the Davidows went for their clothes). The pictures must have been turn-of-the-century, for the unsmiling men were dressed in heavy, old-fashioned uniforms and several of them had handlebar mustaches. (This was a fad I was very glad had gone out of fashion.) The Sam Brown belts across the dark, heavy material seemed wider than the ones today.

In the room were four desks, the fourth minus anyone to sit at it. I guessed this desk was for the extra deputy that the Sheriff hadn't acquired because the mayor wouldn't allocate the money.

My head felt leaden. I must have dozed off. Was it dusk already? The light at the window had turned as gray as granite, and seemed heavy, too. Then I must have slept a second time, but surely not for more than a minute. What dragged me awake was the advancing voices. What time was it? I looked wildly around. Was it dinnertime?

Inadmissible evidence

48

The door to the office opened and the Sheriff walked in, followed by Donny, who was in the middle of bragging about how he'd "cuffed" the Snavely boys that morning.

"Emma?" The Sheriff was taken aback. It was hard to take him by surprise, but my being there certainly did.

"You still here, for God's sake?" Donny said. A look from the Sheriff cut him short. "She's been here all afternoon. I told her you were over White's Bridge way."

"I was just waiting. There's something important I need to talk to you about," I said, holding up my gym bag.

The Sheriff turned on Donny. "You left her *alone*? Now, listen up, Donny: you don't leave this office when somebody's in it, and for God's sake, you don't leave *Emma* alone in it."

I considered. There were two ways of taking what the Sheriff just said: one way was that he was concerned for my safety. I might be here alone when there was a jail break (the jail being on the opposite side of the building) and the escaping prisoners would find me here and hold me hostage. The other way of taking the Sheriff's order was that he didn't trust me around the filing cabinets. I guess I'd have to go for the second interpretation, since he was right.

He had by now removed his cap and uniform jacket and had sat down. He motioned me over to the chair beside his desk. "Must be *really* important if you waited all this time."

I looked over to see what Donny was doing. He was at his own much smaller desk and was pretending to be busy pulling out drawers and taking files out. What he was really doing was listening. I shifted around so my back was to him and whispered to the Sheriff, "In here—" I unzipped my gym bag. "—is evidence." I pulled out the letter, the photo, the doll.

Frowning, the Sheriff picked up each in turn. "I've seen these things before, haven't I? In that old Calhoun cottage?"

"Brokedown House," I said, nodding.

Donny just couldn't resist getting in on things. "You talking about that old falling-down place near Butternut's?" Now he was out of his chair, moving toward the Sheriff. "Ain't nobody lived there for years, not since old man Calhoun moved out. You recall him, Sam—"

"Donny. You were supposed to check out that fracas at the Red Barn. And that complaint from Asa Ledbetter about someone messing with his stock. Have you done it?"

"Well, I was just about to when—"

The Sheriff tossed him the keys to the cruiser. "Good. So do it."

"It's almost six—"

"We don't keep regular hours, Donny. You want a nine-to-five, get a job at the Second National."

It was so much a point for my side, I didn't even bother gloating.

"I'll say one thing," said Donny. "She tells you anything that trans-pired here before I left, you better take it with a grain of salt, hear?"

How stupid of him. He'd just let the Sheriff know, just with that comment, that something had "trans-pired" which would put Donny in a bad light.

"See you later, Donny."

Donny, unhappy, left.

"Okay. Now what were you doing in that Calhoun house? You aren't going over there alone?"

"No, of *course* not. I was with—Mr. Butternut." Something kept me from saying Dwayne Hayden.

"Same thing. What about these things?"

"The doll is wearing a dress like Mary-Evelyn Devereau's the night she drowned. I mean—what's that word the police and papers use when they can't come right out and accuse someone?"

" 'Allegedly'?"

"That's right. Allegedly drowned."

The Sheriff looked surprised. "You're saying she didn't?"

"I'm saying she didn't." I weighted the words.

"A doctor has to sign a death certificate," said the Sheriff, "and drowning is pretty easy to identify. Especially when you take the body out of a lake."

I wasn't in the mood for his smile (for once). "It shows she drowned, but not where."

Puzzled, he said, "You're saying she drowned somewhere *else?*" He leaned forward, as if getting closer to me might explain me.

"If somebody held your head under water, it could look like you drowned, couldn't it?"

Leaning back in his swivel chair, he nodded, but his eyes widened.

"When they put her in that boat she was already dead."

Never had I seen the Sheriff appear so astonished. His chair crashed forward. "*What?* You think the Devereau women killed that little girl?"

Since I had just said it, I sat there.

"*Why?* Why would they do such a thing?"

I shrugged. "I don't know, yet. I know they hated her, is all. I know from what Ulub said. He used to do odd jobs for them." From his expression, I could tell the Sheriff might be just as suspicious of Ulub's brainpower as most other people around here. "Ulub said he was looking through a window one night when he'd been raking leaves and saw Mary-Evelyn playing the piano and crying. The sisters were eating dinner. She wasn't allowed to eat dinner with them that night. She was being punished. If nothing else, I think playing the piano is a funny way to punish somebody, don't you?" But I could tell the Sheriff wasn't putting much stock in what Ulub might say, and that made me angry. But I tried not to let it show. I tried not to get emotional, since emotions weren't convincing. "You probably don't think you can believe what Ulub and Ubub say; but I know them better than you. They're perfectly sensible and sane. Then there's Imogene Calhoun."

The Sheriff sat back. I must be switching topics too fast for him. He said, "You mean the ones who lived in that cottage?"

I nodded. "Imogene lives in Cold Flat Junction. When she was ten or eleven, she'd go with her sister Rebecca to the Devereau house. She told me how they mistreated Mary-Evelyn. Things like they wouldn't let her feed her kitten. And other things."

Instead of being shocked, he pondered. "But if this Imogene was only a little girl then, could she have misunderstood—?"

I shot out of my chair. "You don't know anything about all of this and you're already arguing *against* it! Why? It's not as if you'd given Mary-Evelyn Devereau any thought because you haven't. I pointed at the filing cabinets. "There's old cases in there. I'll bet, I'll *bet* one of them's Mary-Evelyn's. You don't have any *history.* For you, they were just born yesterday. They came and went in an eye blink. But you're wrong. *They'll be around forever.* You're wrong about Ben Queen, too. He never killed his daughter Fern."

As if he'd only been waiting for this topic to arise, the Sheriff said, "What do you know about Ben Queen? What haven't you told me?"

I was still standing. "You haven't heard a thing I've said. All you want to know is stuff that you think will be more evidence for what *you* believe. As for *my* evidence, I'm taking it with me." I picked up what I'd brought and shoved it back in my gym bag and walked to the door. But before leaving, I said, "You're wrong about Ben Queen; you're wrong about him killing Rose. And you're dead wrong about him murdering Fern Queen. I know who killed her." I yanked the door open.

The Sheriff had risen when I left his desk. "Who did, then?"

I turned. "Her daughter." I added, "If you ever read a Greek play, you'd understand. Good-bye."

Hell-bent

49

Her daughter.

Saying it out loud made me shiver in the icy light that looked more moon than sun. But who else could she be but Fern's daughter? The Girl looked exactly like Rose Devereau, to go by Jude Stemple's description of Rose. Fern, the mother, was a plain woman, and this was a case of what I guess is called beauty skipping a generation. It had skipped out on Fern altogether.

And Ben Queen was protecting the Girl, just as he'd protected Fern and kept her from the jail sentence he then had to serve. I remembered what he'd said when I told him that night I'd seen this Girl:

"Maybe this girl you saw, or thought you saw, maybe she was just a figment of your imagination."

He was pretending not to believe the Girl was his own granddaughter; I was pretending to believe he was right, when both of us knew who she was or, at least, *that* she was. He knew either that she'd shot Fern Queen or that she could be blamed for it. But *why* the Girl had shot Fern—it must've been revenge for being abandoned.

I thought all of this as I was making for the Rainbow Café, for I wanted to talk to a sympathetic person. My anger at the Sheriff had not lessened one whit, but what added to it, or was maybe a feeling riding sidesaddle with it, was the misery at being let down. He had *really* let me down. Ben Queen had made me feel just the opposite when he'd said, *If it goes too hard on you, turn me in.*

The Sheriff, I thought, as I walked through the door of the Rainbow, had done just that—had ratted on me, had told the enemy where I was, had broken faith, had let me down. Had turned me in.

I sat down in the back booth. In a couple of minutes, Maud came back carrying a cherry Coke to where I sat with my head in my hands. She sat down and placed her cigarettes on the table, as usual. When I said nothing but a mumble she tapped the pack and slid out a cigarette, lit it, and gave me time.

When the squall of tears started I dug the heels of my palms into my eyes to stop their flow, but of course, I couldn't. Tears have a life of their own and pay no attention to whether you want them or not, or whether they'd embarrass you or not.

Maud went off; when she came back, she set something before me. I looked through my fingers to see if it was a bowl of chili, but it was only a glass of water, so I dug my hands into my eyes again. Finally, I raised my head and shook and shook it and the tears weren't so much falling as flying off my face.

Maud handed me a handkerchief that looked so fresh and new I didn't want to dirty it, though I did dab at my eyes with it; for nose-blowing I yanked a paper napkin from the stainless-steel holder on the table.

She put an arm around my shoulders and said—as if it would be a real comfort to me—"Sam just walked in."

What? I looked up to see him nodding to friends along the counter as he passed it. Then I grabbed up the glass of undrunk water and tossed half of it on my eyes, and, no longer caring about the new handkerchief, I wiped it all over my face. I yanked out a menu and was studying it hard when the Sheriff came up to the booth and said hello. I did not return this greeting, as I had to begin not speaking to him sometime and it might as well be now. I read the menu.

He sat down opposite me. "Emma," was all he said and he said it very nicely.

With my eyes still on the menu and aware that my T-shirt was sopping wet, and also aware that it was nearly six-thirty and Miss Bertha might be banging her cane on the dining room floor at any minute, I said, "I believe I'll have a bowl of chili."

"Sure," said Maud, who got up before I could stop her. The chili hadn't been a good idea, as it would mean I'd be left alone with the Sheriff. I looked up at the slow-circling ceiling fan.

"I'm sorry, Emma, sorry I hurt your feelings."

My *feelings*? I just sat looking at him, mouth agape. He thought all that I had said was nothing at all; his concern was not for what I'd told him, but only for my feelings about what I'd told him. He didn't care about what I knew (for he probably didn't think I knew anything), but for what I felt. Unused to having my feelings considered, I suppose I should have been grateful. Only I wasn't.

"It's not my *feelings,*" I finally said. "My *feelings* were only because you didn't even take in what I was telling you." I pulled my gym bag up from the seat beside me and set it on the table. "You didn't give a thought to this."

"Look, Emma—"

I heard him dismissing it all over again.

"Look: this half-a-century-old Devereau business that for some reason you're hell-bent on solving surely can't have anything to do with the murder of Fern Queen."

It was just too much. "How do you *know* that? You haven't talked to people like I have."

"This is important, Emma. This isn't a game. Where did you see Ben Queen?"

I just stared. He was doing exactly the same thing again. On top of that, he was accusing me of thinking it was all a game. A *game!* If Ben Queen had been the shadow on the wall behind him, I wouldn't have pointed it out.

Maud returned with my chili. "Good Lord but you two look grim. What's going on?"

I would not be so babyish as to "tell" on the Sheriff. I was not even going to produce the doll, which Maud had held and would remember, for what good would it do unless I produced one of the police photos to show her it was the same dress? Even then, what conclusions would she draw from it, knowing as little as she did about the Devereaus and Mary-Evelyn. No, it was my story and I was stuck with it. "Is it six-thirty yet?" I asked.

"Not quite. Have you got dinner guests?"

"Yes. I'm sorry, but I won't have time to eat the chili."

"Don't worry about it. You go on. What's in the gym bag?"

I didn't answer; I looked at the Sheriff.

He said, "This child is hell-bent on getting into big trouble. You might even call it obstruction of justice."

I slid across the seat of the booth, hauling my bag with me. "Obstruction of something, maybe, but not justice."

I was enormously pleased that this was my exit line. My head up, I walked out of the Rainbow, haughty and hell-bent.

She's Medea

50

I apologized to Walter, who was set to take in Miss Bertha's V8 cocktail (into which I usually shook a few drops of Tabasco sauce because I liked the way her mouth pursed up when it hit). Tonight was meat loaf again, and I couldn't think of anything I could do to Miss Bertha's portion. I had overworked my mind today and I guess it balked. Standing at the serving counter, looking at the harmless meat loaf and pan of gravy, I asked Walter could he come up with anything?

He was silent, thinking. Most people have no patience with Walter but I do, as I think he makes a good accomplice. Also, he can share the blame, or even take the whole of it. He never rats on a person.

"Well," he finally said, "there's them mushrooms still. You could put them in that gravy. Miss Bertha hates mushrooms."

"Except I used the mushrooms once, don't you remember?"

"How about I make her an omelette and you use some of that Spanish sauce (tomato sauce with diced up vegetables) and cut up one of them hot peppers—" Walter had left his dishwashing station to root in the refrigerator. He drew out a small can. "These is hot as blazes. I know because Will tricked Paul into eating one. Paul run around like a house on fire."

"Paul does that anyway. Walter, that's a great idea. I'll just dice one up if you make the omelette. I'll take in their V8 juice and tell her."

Walter reached in for the eggs and I went to the dining room, set down the juice, and said to Miss Bertha that as tonight was meat loaf and she didn't like it, we were making her an omelette. Mrs. Fulbright heartily approved of this idea when Miss Bertha didn't do anything but go *"umpf."* Mrs. Fulbright, of course, preferred the meat loaf; it was a favorite of hers.

"I want a *Spanish* omelette," said Miss Bertha.

Oh, how wonderful! I told her absolutely, she'd get a Spanish omelette.

Returning to the kitchen, I told Walter. He gave his choking kind of laugh and drew his spatula carefully through the eggs, just as my mother does. As the omelette cooked, I chopped up a hot pepper and tossed it in the sauce Walter had heated. Then I fixed Mrs. Fulbright's plate, tossing a plump morsel of parsley on the meat loaf. Walter whisked the omelette onto a plate. I poured the doctored Spanish sauce over it.

"You make a beautiful omelette, Walter," I said.

"I watched Miss Jen do it enough times I got it memorized. You ought to tell Miss Bertha not to drink any water to try and cool things down as that only makes it worse. I read that somewheres."

So dinner went off without a hitch. I mean, from Walter's and my point of view. Miss Bertha nearly fell out of her chair when she got her first taste of that jazzed up sauce and I enjoyed patting her back (or her hump, I guess) and saying I had no *idea* Spaniards liked things so hot. She was shouting she was on fire. I shoved her water glass closer to her.

There was nothing else I could do, so I let Mrs. Fulbright handle things. She was waving her lacy handkerchief uselessly in front of Miss Bertha's mouth when I returned to the kitchen.

Because I was upset with the Sheriff, I didn't have much of an appetite and ate only one helping of everything, except of course the Spanish sauce. Dessert was Peach Blossom Pie, one of my mother's cloudlike confections the color of the sun coming up over the Rony Plaza's stretch of beach, just that first flush of rosy-gold fast disappearing. Tiny bits of peach and pecans were scattered through the meringue crust.

Walter, who'd been standing with an ear against the dining-room swinging door, now joined me at the kitchen table for the pie. *"Um-umm!"* he said, taking a bite of the pie.

"Unbelievable," I said, taking one too.

There was another note under my door:

Rehearsal after dinner

Not *again!* I groaned. Why did I need a rehearsal, anyway? I didn't have words to say. All I was supposed to do after I got down to the stage was get off the swing and bop Medea with my silver wand. This sounded a lot more like Cinderella's fairy godmother than a *deus ex machina.* I told Will. He replied that they were taking certain "liberties" with the original. I could imagine. I didn't bother asking him if they'd even read it.

I had agreed I'd play a role. In return for them driving me to White's Bridge, I had to do this. Considering how much I'd learned as a result of that first visit, I guess getting flour thrown on me wasn't too much to ask. I tied a scarf around my head and pulled it forward a bit over my eyes to keep as much off me as possible.

Tonight in the cave of the Big Garage, instead of blue and green lights slicing the darkness there were pink and gold cones passing back and forth across the garage, something like pictures you see of Hollywood premieres. There had to be someone making them move. "Who's up there?"

"Chuck."

Chuck was a boy maybe a year older than me and really dumb. He was good at following directions and that made him useful to Will and Mill, more useful than he ever was to his family. Will and Mill loved nothing more than giving directions.

"Hi, missus," yelled Paul.

Will called up to Chuck: "Try the blue and green . . . let's put them all on just to see." He turned to me. "Go up there and stand." He gestured toward the stage.

"Why?"

"Do you have to question everything?"

"Yes, if it comes from you. And where's Medea? If this is a rehearsal, why isn't she here?"

"She's coming. Go *on.*" He gave me a little shove.

I clambered up to the stage and turned and saw watery reaches of pink and gold, blue and turquoise, their paths crossing and in combination creating even more color. It was probably very pretty from out there, but with these colors crossing and recrossing my face, I felt a little seasick. Will called up to douse the blue and green for a while. I wondered what I looked like in this eerie light.

June Sikes was, I guess, what you'd call hard-pretty, the kind of prettiness you'd find in a woman whose past was a little too full. She wore so much makeup it was difficult to tell just how much was her and how much was added color. She had walked in a moment ago and was stopped now by Will's side.

"Where's my costume?"

Changing her clothes (Marge Byrd once told me) was pretty much all June Sikes was good at.

Will had gone off and was back now with June's "costume." This Medea-gown looked familiar to me, though I couldn't for the life of me think where I'd seen it. It was really pretty—a flow of dark blue tulle shot through with silver and a satin top.

Then, suddenly, I recognized it. It had belonged to one of the Waitresses and had been, when they'd worked here, my favorite article of clothing. They must have left it in a storage room over the kitchen, and I couldn't understand why I'd never seen it. June Sikes wearing it! I wanted to fall on her and rip her eyes out, even though it hadn't been her choice.

That the Waitresses had years ago left this gown behind and I hadn't seen it, hadn't known it was there in that storage room where I go far more often than Will and Mill—that this dance dress should hang now on the back of June Sikes—was too much after all of the disappointments of the day. *No!* June was *not* going to wear this particular memory! But I would have to pretend this wasn't important to me. I thought for a moment and frowned at Will and said, "Medea wouldn't wear that."

Will, who was not as sure of things as he appeared to be, asked, "Why?"

"It's too dark. The Greeks almost always wore *white.* You ought to know that if you're putting on a Greek *play.*" My mind was outracing my words. I tried to be casual. "I know just the thing. Give me that dark dress and I'll go get it." I held out my arm.

"No," said Will. "Get it first."

How stupid! "Okay." I walked out of the Big Garage and ran all the way to the Pink Elephant, pulled Ree-Jane's white gown off the hanger, and ran back to the Big Garage. I slowed down for the last little way, not wanting to appear hurried.

Will looked at the white dress and shrugged. "It's okay with me. But where'd you get it?"

"Nowhere in particular," I answered, as I exchanged the white dress for the midnight blue one.

June went off to a dark corner and changed clothes. She came back. Ree-Jane's white gown was too long for her and too tight across the top, making her look mummified. But I guess she was so pleased to have a fancy dress to wear on stage she didn't much care. "Where's a mirror? Have I got this on right?"

I assured her she did. There wasn't a mirror.

She went traipsing around holding the skirt bunched so she wouldn't trip. I did not make the point that she couldn't do this the night of the performance because she might insist on having the blue dress back again. I decided to take the blue dress out of harm's way and rushed back to the Pink Elephant, where I put it on the hanger and the hanger on a hook in the wall. I stood back and looked at it. Oncc, they had dressed me up in it and danced me around the room. The Waitresses. They flashed in and out of memory like sunlight striking the turquoise ocean along the shore of the Rony Plaza, for what I recall mostly about them is their color: their bright clothes, their glossy red and blond and dark hair. I closed my eyes.

Once I had asked my mother whether they were good waitresses. "Oh, they were all good waitresses, I expect, but silly girls."

Silly girls. I do remember they were always laughing. They put on records and danced me around. My mother didn't know how much time I spent with them, since she would have stopped it. She did not care for our befriending the "help."

If my days now are mostly black and white, the days of the Waitresses were technicolor. For before they left, everything, I sense, was different: my father was still alive, my mother did not have to work so hard, the Davidows were unknown. Imagine! Imagine a time without Ree-Jane. It was almost impossible to, for Ree-Jane is one of those people you must have around to test yourself on. I sometimes wonder: without her, would I have been up to a challenge?

June was up onstage, and Will was calling for Paul to come down and to be careful doing it. I could see him up there maneuvering from rafter to swing, the rope around his middle in case he fell. Thank goodness for that. I think his foot slipped once on the rafter. But he managed to get into the swing, and Mill told him to untie the rope so the swing could be lowered onto the stage.

Will said, "You go stand beside June."

"Hi, missus," Paul said to June. She didn't answer.

I asked, "What's he going to do?"

"Nothing. It's not a speaking part."

"Well, what's he going to be, then?"

"He's one of Medea's kids."

I looked around. "Where are the others? Because I'm not going—"

Will crinkled up his forehead in exasperation. "Oh, relax, will you? Since you were so testy about playing one of them, we rewrote. In our rewrite, the other kids are dead, she's already bumped them off. Paul's the only kid we can make do what we want." Will's head was bent over his "script," chewing gum.

Mill was at the piano, standing before it, barking orders. "Okay, Medea, sing after me: 'I'm Med-e-a—' Go on."

June, still holding up the white tulle, sang:

"I'm Med-eee-ah."

This, I thought, was crazy; it was crazy even for Will and Mill. "What *is* this?"

"Be quiet," said Will.

Now Mill was pointing at Paul. "Now, after June sings that line, you're supposed to echo it—"

" 'Echo it?' I'm sure that's crystal clear to Paul. Echo—"

"Oh, be quiet," said Will.

Mill went on: "Echo it and sing, 'Sheee's Med-e-ah.' " Mill brought his arm down, slicing up air and saying, "GO!"

"Hi, missus," said Paul. He had the tune down right; it was just the words.

"No!"

Mill rarely yelled; he left that up to Will. "You're supposed to sing, dammit! Mill sang, " 'She's Med-e-ah.' Will, go up and take care of him. We'll be here all night."

Will marched up onstage and got behind Paul and placed both hands on Paul's shoulders. He shook him. "Sing it right."

Mill came down on the piano again, and sang, "She's Med-e-ah."

Paul nearly turned his head upside down to gather in Will's face and got himself a good shaking. Then he sang—shouted, rather—"Sheee's Mud-a-uh."

Will shook him. "Med, Med, not Mud."

Paul sang it again, correctly this time.

Mill ordered, "Okay, now from the top—first June, next Paul. Paul you just have to sing what June sings."

You'd think he had the Gospel choir up there.

Mill played the chords and pointed. June sang (with feeling) "I-I-I'm Medea."

Paul sang (as my brother's thumbs dug into his shoulders) "Sheeee's Mah-de-a."

"Great!" Mill yelled. "Terrific!" Mill was a much more positive person than Will. Mill believed in getting people to do things by encouraging them. Will believed in hitting them. He left Paul to his singing and returned to stand beside me.

"Now!" Mill brought his hands down on the piano again. "Here's the second line: "Mama mia!"

June sang, "Mama mee-ah."

Paul sang, "She's Medea."

Mill ordered him to stop. "No, no, Paul. You sing 'Mama mia' for the second line."

I gaped. "That's crazy! That's Italian!"

Will was tapping his foot in time to what music there was and didn't answer.

I grabbed Will by the arm. "You can't have Greeks singing that. 'Mama mia'—that's an Italian saying!"

Will chewed his gum and thought. "It's . . . international."

Mill was still playing and baton-ing the air like a symphony conductor and the two were still singing. Then I said to Will, "If you think God is going to come down in any machine to save *this* mess, forget it!" I turned and marched toward the door.

Will called after me, "God works in mysterious ways!"

"Not this mysterious!" I slammed the door behind me.

Golden girl

51

Back in the Pink Elephant, I took everything out of my gym bag and lined it all up. From my Whitman's candy box I took the Niece Rhoda tube Dwayne had found, and the snapshot of the sisters and Mary-Evelyn. I balanced the photo of Jamie Makepiece against one of the fat bottles that served as a candleholder, the hardened wax dripping down its side. My hands crossed on the table, my chin lowered to them, I ran my eyes over this little collection. I got down to eye level with Jamie Makepiece. Where was he now? He'd be in his seventies if he was still alive. How I'd love to talk to him! Not just for the things he could tell me about Iris and Isabel, but because he inhabited a period of time from which I was excluded.

I read again the statements of the Devereau sisters to see if there were any other clues. I looked at the photo of Mary-Evelyn, her closed eyes, her water-scattered hair, water-darkened. Darkened. I frowned. What had Imogene said about Mary-Evelyn? *I thought she was so lucky, having that pale hair and the bluest eyes, and having all those dresses.* Pale hair. Only Rose had that kind of hair. The other Devereau sisters had dark hair. I thought of the photograph hanging on the wall in the parlor. The three sisters grouped around light-haired Rose when she was only a child. Their hair was almost black.

Sitting back, I tried to recall something Dwayne had said when we were talking about Lena from *Light in August* and her "condition." Dwayne had joked about nearly every woman in Faulkner being in some kind of "condition." I looked at the photo of Jamie again, saw how handsome he was, saw his golden hair. And I thought of Lena, walking along that dusty road in Tennessee, hoping to find the baby's father.

I looked up and stared at what was in my head. Mary-Evelyn couldn't have been Rose's child because Rose was only a child herself back then. But she could have been Iris's. Iris's and this golden-haired Jamie Makepiece's child. It made sense of all the attention Iris had lavished on Mary-Evelyn's clothes, since she wouldn't dare lavish it on the girl herself, even if she'd wanted to, not living as she did with Isabel and Elizabeth watching.

Mary-Evelyn was their scapegoat. That was why they hated her, especially Isabel. Imagine every day having to be reminded you'd been thrown over for your own sister. Worse, that Iris's and Jamie's child made sure she'd never forget.

That was why they wanted her dead, at least why Isabel did.

I picked up Jamie's letter and read it over again.

> *My dear I Have faith that we will be together again and soon. It has become too much for me and, I'm sure, too much for you. It's better for me to leave for a little while until this fury quiets down. I suppose a century ago, my faithlessness would have been shouted in all the newspapers!*
>
> *Your, J.*

Did he ever know about Mary-Evelyn? I doubted it. But what happened to him?

He had not come back.

I lay in bed that night, weary with thinking, and still thought. Where was Ben Queen? He was around; I felt it. If the Girl was still here—and I'd seen her boarding the train just two days ago—if she was still here, so would he be. Ben Queen was not the sort to leave on account of trouble. He was not a Jamie Makepiece. Ben Queen would never desert a person.

I think he really did believe that what happened to Mary-Evelyn was an accident. He believed it because Rose believed it. Even though she had lived in that house for years, still Rose believed it was an accident because she couldn't bear not to. You do that sometimes; you slam the door on the truth because you don't want it inside overturning tables and knocking photos off shelves.

That's what I felt the Sheriff was doing—shutting out the truth. He was seeing my gym bag as nothing more than a bag of tricks. Or maybe he was angry with me because he thought I knew something and had refused to tell him what it was. That was true. I had let him down. Maybe our way of seeing this was that we'd let each other down.

I suddenly felt very old and reached over for the teddy bear that was always on the bed. I had to check to see if the stuffing was still in place.

We remember it well

52

"Well, my goodness," said Louise Snell as I took my place at the counter in the Windy Run Diner, "a person'd think you moved to Cold Flat Junction, hon. You want the roast beef sandwich? It's real good today."

"It's always good. Yes." I had become a regular; I had my own stool and my own story. Maybe I'd tell them another chapter about my mother's friend Henrietta Simple and the Simple family, if I could recall what I'd told them before.

Billy asked if I had found "that Calhoun gal," and I told him I had and thanked them for such good directions.

Don Joe gave me a wide smile that showed a lot of broken and nicotine-stained teeth. "So who you lookin' to find this time? Seems to me you spend half your life lookin' for people."

Everybody laughed. I smiled back displaying my own perfect,

white teeth. "Seems like it. Well, today I'm not looking for anybody." Saying that, I almost felt I was here under false pretenses.

"What's goin' on over in La Porte about Fern Queen? They any nearer to finding who done it?" asked Mervin from his booth bench. He was here without his wife again; I'm sure he was happy about that.

I had been trying to think of a way to bring this up, so I was grateful Mervin had done it. "I don't think so, at least I haven't heard. But I do know the Sheriff's looking for Ben Queen. That's who he thinks is guilty."

"With Fern being his own child?" said Louise Snell, indignant. She had given the cook my order and was waiting for it, leaning up against the Plexiglas pie shelves. "Your sheriff mustn't have kids of his own to think a man could shoot his own child."

"The Greeks did it all the time," I informed them. "Killing off kinfolk (a word I loved)—kids, mothers, dads, all sorts. It was like a way of life with them. Didn't think a thing of it." The little window barrier shot up and the roast beef sandwich appeared. Louise set it before me and I got my nose right into the steam coming off the mashed potatoes. I wished my mother would make it, but it was a dish she thought "common."

"Greeks? You sayin' like that fellow outside La Porte has that restaurant—?"

"It's Arturo-something," said Don Joe.

"Yeah. That Arturo fella."

"He's Italian," I said, eating instead of thinking.

Don Joe, wanting to broadcast his superior knowledge said, "Hell, yes, Billy. He's one of them I-ties. Arturo ain't no Greek name."

Billy was irked. "He sure *looks* Greek."

Why did I have to open my big mouth? We were getting miles away from Ben Queen.

"Looks?" said Don Joe. "How come?"

"That real dark hair and what's called 'swarthy' skin. And his eyes looks like black olives. Yessir, Greek to the core, far as looks go. Just because his name's Italian-sounding don't mean he is."

It was like being back in the Big Garage.

"Well, why in hell would he have an I-tie name if he wasn't an I-tie?"

I stepped in. "I think you're both right. He's half Greek and half Italian. His mother was Greek. I think his middle name is something that ends in -opolis. You know, like so many Greek names. 'Acropolis,' that's Greek. And so on." I shoveled a forkful of mashed potatoes in my mouth, feeling quite proud of my mastery of nationalities.

"Well," said Billy.

"Well," said Don Joe.

Frankly, I think they were both glad I'd put an end to that discussion. Now, I would have to work the talk around to Ben Queen again, so I picked up where I'd left off. "All I meant when I brought up the Greeks was pointing out that their plays often have characters killing off their kinfolk." (I managed to work that in again.) "Kinfolk (again) being children sometimes."

"That's horrible, hon. Why, you ought not to be seeing things like that! Where's it at? They got this summer theater in La Porte, I know."

When she looked away, I rolled my eyes. Then I said, "No, they don't put on the Greek tragedies at the summer theater." Maybe I should invite them all over to the Big Garage. "All I'm saying is it's perfectly possible for a mom or a dad to kill their own child. I'm not saying Ben Queen did it, though." I decided to ask a jackpot question. "Were any of you here then?"

You'd think this was a perfectly simple question, but they had to argue about whether they were or not. It was Mervin who said, "I can tell you everybody who *was* here acted like they'd been hit by a truck. Yessir."

Don Joe agreed and tried to get in on the telling of it, but Mervin just ran right over his words. "First person they thought of—the sheriff's people, I mean—was the husband, Ben, for as we know, it's most often the husband or wife." Here Mervin got out of his booth and came to the counter to sit beside Billy on the stool that was usually occupied by the woman in dark glasses. Billy didn't like this one whit, Mervin moving to the counter. He went on: "When Ben Queen come in, there wasn't a spot of blood on him. Yet the crime scene was covered in it; there was like a lake of blood and it was ev'erwhere. So that told me right there it could not of been him."

Just to argue, probably, Billy said, "So? He coulda just changed his clothes. Mind you, I ain't saying Ben done it, for I definitely *don't* believe he did."

Mervin said, "How's he goin' to change his clothes without the Queens seein' him? He'd have to come in from the barn and get past Sheba and his brother George. That's when Ben and Rose was livin' with them that time. When their house was bein' built."

Louise Snell interrupted. "That's all beside the point. The point is Ben Queen never would've harmed Rose. Never."

Evren said, "Except they was fighting, him and Rose. There was this big row they had the night before."

Billy flapped his hand at Evren. "Be quiet, Evren. You wasn't even here, so you don't know."

"I'm only goin' by what Toots said, over to the Esso, that's all. Toots was here, wasn't he?"

"Where was Ben Queen when Rose was killed?" I asked, feeling something significant was being left out. They all looked at me as if this question had never come up.

Mervin, now back in his booth, answered me. "Hebrides. That's where he was at."

"But then somebody in Hebrides must've seen him."

Billy held up his cup for a refill. He said, "Nobody come forth to say."

I frowned. If the Sheriff waited for somebody to "come forth" he'd never be arresting anyone. "But didn't the police investigate?"

Mervin was up and over to the counter again, this time on the empty stool nearest me. "That's just the thing," he said to me. "That's what's so damned fishy. There was hardly any questions asked, and after they took in Ben Queen, then there was none. So as you see there was precious little investigatin' going on." He slapped the Formica countertop.

Louise was pouring refills and said, "That's because Ben never put up any resistance. He hardly even said a word, according to Boyd Spiker."

Don Joe said, "Oh, hell, Boyd Spiker's an injit."

What I was thinking now was that I should have paid more attention to the details of the police investigation of Rose's murder. I knew Ben Queen didn't do it and so did people like Louise Snell, but the law didn't. "Who's Boyd Spiker?"

Mervin answered, "He's a trooper. Troopers got there first. When Ben come back, they took him in. First thing."

"But if he was *gone* from Cold Flat Junction, then how could he have killed her?"

"That was my point," said Louise.

"Cops just figured Ben was fixin' to alibi hisself," said Don Joe.

For me, this was just like Aurora and her find-the-pea so-called trick. She just told you you were wrong no matter what walnut shell you chose. She wouldn't lift the shells, either. That's what all of this sounded like. The *obvious* conclusion for the police to draw was Ben Queen *didn't* do it. One, he was in Hebrides, two, his truck was being worked on, so how did he get back? And, three, he adored his wife. It was crazy, and I said so.

"I'm with you, hon," said Louise, giving me a fresh Coke.

I asked, "Didn't the Sheriff from La Porte investigate?"

"Not really. Come around, asked a few questions. But like I said, Ben never put up any fight."

Louise asked, "Who'd have the gumption after finding the wife you dearly loved had been knifed to death?"

That wasn't exactly logical, but it was a point. "Did he confess?"

" 'Cording to Boyd, he just said, 'Let's get it over with,' " said Billy.

Mervin was still determined to get his first point in. "Witnesses said him and Rose'd been fightin' somethin' awful."

"What were they fighting about?" I asked.

"Their girl, Fern. You know, the one that was killed out your way. They went round and round about her, Rose and Ben did. She wasn't playin' with a full deck—" Here Billy made circles near his ear.

Louise was annoyed. "No need to make fun, Billy; the woman was just retarded, and you shouldn't be speaking ill of the dead, anyhow."

"Anyway, they fought a lot about Fern. Rose wanted to ship her off to an institution but Ben didn't. That girl was a handful."

Louise wiped the counter, absently. "It was a real shame. They'd only the one child and she turned out that way. Didn't seem to get nothing from Rose and Ben, certainly not looks."

Don Joe said, "I think you had a crush on him."

"Oh, don't be ridiculous. I wasn't more'n eight or nine years old then."

"Still, every woman around was sweet on Ben."

"Like every man was sweet on Rose," said Billy, tapping ash from his cigarette with his little finger.

Billy must have been older than he looked, for he said this as if he remembered. Remembered it well.

An alibi

53

I left the Windy Run Diner minutes later. Now I had something else to discover and that was what else Ben Queen was doing in Hebrides besides getting his truck fixed. People who would know this would be his brother and sister-in-law, the ones who lived in the big yellow house I had visited once. I had taken Mr. Root along as a reason to go, for Bathsheba Queen had once been his "girl," he said.

Today I stood outside their house trying to make up what I would give as the reason this time for visiting. My mind was as blank and smooth as an eggshell. It was still blank five minutes later when George Queen, Ben's older brother, came out on the porch with a newspaper, meaning, I guessed, to sit and read. I thought about the newspaper.

"Hello, Mr. Queen!" I called, as if I had just then been passing by. I didn't want him to find me skulking outside his house. I waved as he got up from his chair and kind of squinted down the path between fence and steps. "It's just me, Mr. Queen, Emma Graham. I guess you don't remember me." I'd found that the elderly don't like it if you suggest their memories are slipping, so that comment might get him up and going. Mr. Queen came right down the path and unhooked the garden gate.

"I sure do remember you. Come on up to the porch. I bet Sheba will rustle up some lemonade and cookies. You just sit yourself down and I'll be back in a flash."

I hoped Sheba would produce store-bought cookies, as her own were so bad. I settled into an old wooden rocking chair and waited for him to come back. I saw he was reading the Cloverly paper, which was a daily. Our own *Conservative* was a weekly, out every Thursday. I don't know how much was in it now about the White's Bridge murder, but I didn't need to read the paper to find out, as I knew more than the paper did. I looked through the first two pages of his paper but saw nothing about the murder or about Ben Queen. I folded the paper back carefully and returned it to the seat of his chair.

Mr. Queen came out then with a pitcher of lemonade on a little tray with three glasses, which meant his wife would be joining us. "Sheba'll be out in a minute. She's taking the cookies out of the oven." I winced as he drew over a round table and set the tray down. "Nothing like fresh-baked cookies, I'm sure you'll agree."

Depends who baked them, I didn't say. "I surely do, Mr. Queen."

He poured out lemonade and handed me a glass and sat down with his own.

"This is really good," I said, which it was. Then for some reason I remembered the girl with the Kool-Aid stand. It was only two streets up and over from here. I pictured her there with a drink nobody much wanted and with nobody much passing her way. I wished she had some of this lemonade to sell. I looked at the paper and asked, in an offhand way, if there was anything in it of interest.

"Not much. I was looking for mention of Fern—you know. The city paper thinks it's old news."

Cloverly hardly rated as a "city." I said, "I'm really sorry about her, Mr. Queen. And I'm sorry about your brother, too."

Just then Sheba Queen came out carrying a plate of the same kind of cookies she'd served before. "Well, hello, Em'ly. How are you? How's your mother? You came just at the right time. Here I was baking cookies and only us to eat 'em."

"Thank you, ma'am." "Ma'am" was a word I was never to use, as my mother considered it common; so in her honor I corrected myself. "Thank you, Mrs. Queen." I took a cookie, the smallest I could find, wondering why Sheba Queen seemed so much more friendly than the last time. But I guess people can have on-Em'ly-days and off-Em'ly-days. I wondered where I could slip the cookie.

Sheba Queen sat down in the third rocker and munched her own cookie. I bit into mine and gave her a big smile back.

"We were talkin' about there not being any news." George fluttered the paper a little.

Sheba put on her *hrr-umph* look as she resettled her shoulders. "Police ain't done a lick. That sheriff of yours is just dragging his feet."

"I think he's really trying, Mrs. Queen." Even though the Sheriff and I were on the outs, I would still defend him. I made a note to tell him what we said here to show how objective I could be.

"Well . . . maybe," said George Queen. "Depends how hard he's looking for anybody *besides* Ben."

That was a good point. I would add this to my defending him. "Yes, sir. I know what you mean." I did, too. I could have kissed him for bringing Ben up, but settled on another bite of the cookie to express my gratitude. There was a silence into which I dropped Rose's name.

Sheba stiffened, for she had always disliked Rose Devereau; I had learned that plain enough from my visit here with Mr. Root.

George just shook his head in a woebegone way. "That poor poor girl. Ben never did that, and I'll say it with my dying breath."

" 'Course he never did it." Sheba looked away, out over the garden.

I took the opportunity to break my cookie into little pieces as I pursued my point. "I was overhearing some people talk about it in the Windy Run Diner—"

Sheba had to butt in and comment about the customers there. "That Billy and Mervin and Don Joe. All's they do is sit around and talk silliness."

I winced. "Anyway, they were saying your Ben went to Hebrides that day."

"He was in Hebrides, that's right," said George. "He always went on Thursdays."

I waited. *To do what?* I silently urged. I was afraid to get too technical on them, as that might make them wonder about my reasons for coming. "They said in the diner he had to go to get his truck fixed." George set down his lemonade glass as I dropped some cookie bits between the slats of the chair.

"Not exactly. His truck got something wrong with it while he was there in Hebrides. So he took it into the shop."

I frowned. "But if he was in Hebrides, how could he have been in Cold Flat Junction and killed Rose?"

"They said at the trial there was time after he picked up the truck to get to the house here and after he killed Rose to go back to Hebrides. They claimed Ben had used the truck as an alibi, but the alibi didn't work, as it turned out. Those police doctors can figure times pretty good. Anyway, they didn't have to do much figuring out because Sheba saw Rose go out to the barn to feed the chickens and after an hour or more when she never came back, I went looking for her." As if the vision were rising up before him, he closed his eyes against it. "Blood everywhere. Awful." He dropped his head. "Poor Ben. What they say in ninety percent of the cases where a man or wife is murdered, it's the spouse that's guilty. That's what started 'em in thinking about Ben."

I could understand how it might have *started* them, but not how they could have *ended* with thinking it was Ben Queen. The Sheriff once told me that when you've got a homicide staring you in the face, you begin by going for the most obvious explanation, for nearly all homicides can be explained that way. You don't do what mystery writers do: you don't hit on the *least* obvious, or one that's so all-fired complicated only a damned fool would try it. So here we were: the police hit on what struck me as the least obvious explanation. Ben was in Hebrides, but others were here. So why not Sheba Queen, who was known to have taken a powerful dislike to Rose? Why not Fern Queen, who was in a rage over being sent to an institution and who was kind of crazy anyway? As far as I was concerned, Fern was the obvious choice. She had a motive; Ben didn't.

I guessed in the end you couldn't blame the investigation if Ben Queen never denied he'd done it. But you'd have thought his own lawyer could have worked out that he was protecting someone. Then, again, maybe the lawyer did figure it out, only Ben Queen told him to keep his mouth shut. There's only one kind of person you'd do that for and that's someone you feel responsible for. It leaves out, of course, how good Ben Queen's judgment was to let a homicidal killer run around free.

But I just couldn't tackle the matter of Ben Queen's judgment right now. Right now I wanted to know what he'd done in Hebrides. "You said your brother always went into Hebrides on Thursdays. Was it some kind of regular thing he had to do?"

George said, "Well, he always picked up the feed Thursdays. Always went to Smitty's outside town."

"Did he get it that day? I mean with the truck acting up, did he have time?"

George frowned, concentrating. "Yeah, I think he did."

Sheba had to butt in again with her thoughts. "That day, that day will live in infamy."

She could live in infamy with it as far as I was concerned. Why hadn't they done something? If they'd believed their brother Ben's innocence so much, why hadn't they questioned the times? Maybe it was from hanging out with the Sheriff so much and listening to him talk about past investigations that made me suspicious of conclusions. *You've got to be sure you have every scrap of available evidence before you can draw your conclusion.* (I wish he'd reminded himself of this in *my* case.)

I asked, "How long after it happened did he come back?"

"Couple hours, I guess. Of course, police said he came back *before*. You recall, Sheba?"

"Three o'clock. I remember because I noted the time that sheriff came."

"So she was killed like around noon?"

"Well, police put it at between eleven and three. But of course we knew closer than that. I saw her at noon when she went to the barn. George here went out to the barn around one-thirty."

George nodded. "That was the time all right. I never saw such a scene in my life. It was terrible, terrible. I tried to keep you from goin' out there, Sheba, but you would insist."

"Well," was all Sheba said as she rocked more intensely.

"He got the truck fixed okay, though?"

"Yeah. Carl's one of the best mechanics around."

Carl. "My mother's in need of a good mechanic. I guess he's not there any more. It's been so long."

"Sure is. Carl's had that Sinclair station for fifty years and his dad before that. But you got Slaw's over in Spirit Lake. That Wayne . . . what's his name?"

"Dwayne Hayden?"

"That's the one. Nobody's better'n him. Not in Hebrides, Cloverly, or any place in a hundred miles."

"I'll sure tell my mother about him. We're looking for a good feed store, too. We've got a mess of chickens out back." We did have four, actually.

"What you been feedin' 'em?"

"Ah, corn. And stuff. See, I don't actually do it myself."

Sheba said, "Well, you should. It's good for youngsters to get a start on finding out what the real world's like."

They thought this was the real world?

Solace

54

I stood on Louise Landis's porch thinking up a reason for coming. How I wished I'd chosen the history project I had told Imogene about. But couldn't the project have started after my first visit to Louise Landis? No. I had to stick with what I had.

"Hello, Miss Landis," I said, when she opened the door.

She seemed really pleased I'd come. "Emma! Come in, come in."

"Thank you. I just wanted to tell you about the entertainment for the orphans' lunch." I said this as I followed her through the cool, dark hall and into the living room. It was exactly the same as it had been when I'd left, down to the last detail, which included the length of orange yarn I'd been using to make a cat's cradle. Did I suppose she'd move all the furniture around and hang wallpaper after I left? (This question was asked by my sarcastic self.) No, of course not (my more patient self answered). Perhaps it was more that everything seemed to have stopped and had just started in ticking now, like the mantel clock.

I sank into the deep armchair and considered curling up and going to sleep, it was so comfortable. Instead, I said, "My brother Will and his friend Brownmiller—he's a real musician—would be happy to entertain the orphans." Was I crazy? Why hadn't I asked them yet? But wait! There was another way to approach this. "Now, what they said was they weren't sure if they could come to the lunch, but they thought you could all come to their production. As their guests, of course. (They never charged anybody anyway unless it was someone they didn't like.) They put one on every year in summer."

"How nice of them to suggest it. What day is the performance?"

"The day's not quite certain, but it'll be in the next couple of weeks. Usually they do two or three performances. I have a part in it; I'm to be the *deus ex machina.*"

She looked truly surprised. No wonder. How many people had ever heard of a *deus ex machina,* much less could pronounce it? "How ambitious of them! Is it Sophocles? Euripides? Is it *Oedipus?*"

I'd forgotten to find out who wrote it, though I imagine what Will and Mill were putting on didn't have a lot of the original in it. "*Medea.* I mean it's *about* Medea."

"A Greek tragedy. My word, but your brother and his friend must be very well read."

I could have argued that, based on the comic books and magazines under his bed. "It's a lot different than most Greek plays because it's a musical. That's what Brownmiller is an expert at. He writes lyrics and is a musician. He plays just about every instrument you can imagine."

Louise Landis's expression didn't give away much of what she was thinking and I supposed that came from teaching all these years, making your expression coolly polite like that. I went on: "Brownmiller writes all the words for the songs and just borrows the music from over there at the camp meeting or from other composers." I sat forward a little to make my position clear: "I don't think you should really do that—I mean, it doesn't seem exactly right, *morally* right (how nice to toss that word in!) to have this woman that's just killed or is going to kill her kids sing, " 'I'm Medea. Mama mia'." I sat back.

She coughed and said, "Why—Emma, would you like some tea?"

"Yes, thanks."

She rose rather carefully, as if trying to hold herself in check and walked out, just as carefully. I hoped I hadn't upset her, though I couldn't imagine why Medea would. I got out of my chair and turned to the wall of bookcases. I didn't see *Light in August,* but there were a couple of others by William Faulkner I wasn't familiar with. I wondered if he spent his whole life writing books and how he managed to do that, what with life being as busy as it is. I looked for Greek plays she might have, but didn't see any. I would like to see a *deus ex machina* in action, instead of just hearing it described. (I certainly couldn't depend on the one in Will's play to be a good example.)

Miss Landis was back with our tea. As she poured I watched and commented on all of her books. Then we both sat down and I added three spoons of sugar to my tea. "There's a lot of killing of family members down through the years in Greek plays. They're always after revenge, it seems to me."

"Well, the Greeks were certainly caught up in the notion of retribution."

I blew on my tea (a habit my mother didn't encourage), then said, "Do you think, if you wrote a play and needed a *deus ex machina* at the end that it's a very good play? I mean, shouldn't you have to get out of the mess on your own?"

"In some circumstances, perhaps you can't."

But that was just saying it again, it seemed to me. "How come?"

"It might be like running a fever. Eventually, it either breaks or it kills you. You can't do much about it. Except to wait."

I thought about this. "But—" I tried to put words to what I was thinking. Sometimes words just walked out on you and left you stranded. I went back to the murder. "What about that murder that happened here forty years ago?"

"Rose Queen?"

I nodded. "And then somebody comes along and kills this Fern? Her daughter?"

"Yes."

"Well . . . you don't think it was him do you?"

We seemed both to know who I meant.

"No. No, I don't."

There was a silence. I tried fashioning a cat's cradle again and said, "At the diner I had lunch, and I overheard people talking about this Fern Queen's murder. The Sheriff in La Porte thinks her father did it, but he can't see any motive. Why would her father murder her?"

"He wouldn't; Ben Queen would be incapable of such a thing. As your sheriff says, there's no motive."

"He doesn't like coincidences."

Miss Landis raised an eyebrow. " 'Coincidences'?"

I tried snapping the yarn taut, but I hadn't done it right. "Like Ben Queen getting out of jail just days before the murder of Fern."

She looked over my head at the wall of books behind me, so long that I turned to see what she was seeing. "Sorry. I was just thinking that it might not be a *coincidence;* at the same time it doesn't mean Ben Queen did it."

I thought about that, frowning at the orange thread as if it had some part in the matter. "Have you lived here all your life?"

"Yes, I have."

"What about your mother? And father?" I sometimes forgot fathers, as I didn't have one. I wondered if that made me, as a person, lopsided.

"This house goes back to my great-grandparents. I think he's the one who built it."

"Nobody else has lived here, then? Nobody came along to interfere, did they?"

She didn't answer for a moment, then she said, "You mean—?"

"To move in, to try and take it away."

"Oh, no. I can't imagine that happening."

"I can." I concentrated on my hands. Finding something to do with them, like the cat's cradle, helps you not look at the other person.

"Interlopers?"

That was a good word, good enough to repeat. "Interlopers." I smiled.

"You must be referring to the Davidow woman."

"You know her?"

"Yes. I've often seen her in La Porte. I go there to buy groceries and things."

"Well, I mean, more her daughter is the interloper." I pulled the cat's cradle as if both ends were Ree-Jane's arms.

"Interlopers are extremely hard to take."

Well, *that* didn't tell me anything new. I said, "But you should be able to do something about them."

"There should, you mean, be a *deus ex machina?*"

I looked over at her. She was not being sarcastic. And it suddenly came to me that a *deus ex machina* was exactly what I thought should come along. "Yes."

"But remember what you said."

I frowned. What had I said? I said so many things it hardly bore remembering.

To my blank (or perhaps surly) look, she said, "You said the playwright must not be very good if he couldn't find a way for his characters to get out of the mess on their own."

I wished I hadn't said it; now I was stuck with it. Still, it was nice to have your words remembered. "Yes, but this isn't a play."

"All the more reason to be able to depend upon yourself. And wouldn't you rather, in the long run?"

I slipped down in the chair, something I had a habit of doing if talk got around to my character. I didn't want to talk about depending on myself. For one thing, it made me lonesome. I changed the subject. "Have you read all of these books?"

"No. A lot of them, but not all."

"Do you like William Faulkner? Right now I'm reading *Light in August.*" Actually, I hadn't picked it up after it came in handy for getting Dwayne to go with me to White's Bridge.

"That's wonderful. You must like words."

" 'Words'?" But I right away knew what she meant. For I loved sitting in the Abigail Butte County Library with an open book, or several books, feeling they were consoling me, somehow. "I guess I do, yes."

"They're an idea of home, I think. Words are. It really is like opening a door, isn't it, to open a book. If that's not too sentimental to say. Books, words, stories are a kind of solace."

I frowned, taking it in. This was definitely a new idea, one worth coming back to, when I didn't havc this mystcry to solvc.

Words, stories, solace.

Smitty

55

Instead of going to Spirit Lake on the 4:32 from Cold Flat Junction, I got off in La Porte. I figured Delbert would be waiting in his cab, hoping for a fare.

He was, but not for me. "You goin' to the hotel?" he asked in a hopeful tone, suggesting he didn't want to take another unscheduled trip with me.

"No." I slammed the door. "I need to go to Hebrides." It wasn't yet five o'clock and that meant businesses would still be open, as I was sure a feed store would stay open until five-thirty or six. I'd try the feed store first, and then Carl's garage, though I didn't think Carl would do much toward establishing an alibi, since the police knew about the truck being fixed.

"Hebrides?"

Did he have to make out that any destination outside of La Porte and Spirit Lake meant he'd have to trudge over sand dunes and mountains for a year? "You know where it is, don't you?"

He half turned in his seat to present a worried face to me, to let me know just how much he didn't want to do this. "That's like a twenty-minute, even a half-hour drive."

I sighed. "Delbert, why do you always have to argue about where your customer wants to go. This is a *taxicab.* Axel has this business to drive people where they want to go. Not where you want them to go." I fell back against the seat. "So, go."

He let out this enormous sigh, then grunted a little, then began pulling away from the depot. "Where at in Hebrides?"

"The feed store. It's called Smitty's, I think."

This was so outlandish to him, he turned to look at me and nearly got hit by Helen Baum's yellow Cadillac. I enjoyed this, for she was really mad and waving her fist at him. After we crawled out of the depot and turned left, he said, "There's a Smith's. J. L. Smith's Feed and something. Is that the one? On the outskirts?"

"I guess. I wouldn't imagine there's more than one in Hebrides."

"Yeah, I think J. L. Smith is called Smitty by people."

I wondered how much more conversation we'd have before he was confident we had the same place in mind. "How far is it from Cold Flat Junction?"

"Why?"

I raised my hands, clawlike, to the back of his head as if to rip his neck open, but simply said, "I just want to know."

"You plannin' goin' to Cold Flat Junction, too?" He sounded affrighted. "I ain't got the time for that."

"No, I don't want to go there; it's just a *question,* Delbert."

"Oh. Well, it's about the same as from here. Same distance. We're south of Hebrides and Cold Flat Junction's west."

"Like a half-hour from either place?"

"Yeah. I guess."

I settled back in my seat and rode northward. If you were the police, you'd time it exactly to see if an alibi held up. There didn't seem to be all that much exactness to the investigation of the Rose Queen murder, though.

Out of my window, farmland slipped by like a length of green silk unrolling. Barns, farmhouses, fences. Horses, their tails swishing away flies, came up to a white-painted rail fence to watch. I wondered why the cab interested them. The farmhouse sat way back, maybe a half mile from the highway, on a straight-as-a-die dirt road, hemmed on both sides by more of the white rail fence. More horses grazed within its boundaries and I guessed it was a horse farm. By this time it was behind us and I could see it only in my head (where I saw most things).

I decided Henrietta Simple and her family lived on just such a farm. I wished I hadn't told the Windy Run crowd that Henrietta had a retarded brother, for I now felt he might disturb the tranquility of what I saw as a peaceful scene. But it was too late, too late to get rid of the brother unless I just killed him off. He could be up in a tree, maybe swinging from a limb, and fall into the creek below.

Then I started wondering if William Faulkner had similar problems with his characters. Once he'd created one, if he decided he didn't like him, could he just go back and erase the person altogether? Most people would say "Sure," but I wondered. It might appear that if a writer was making the person up anyway, then he should be able to go back and unmake him. Maybe it wasn't that simple; maybe it was more complicated than that. Once William Faulkner (who was an incredibly powerful writer—look at the effect he'd had on Dwayne and me: I still thought of Lena even after only a dozen or so pages)—once he made you up, you stayed made up. Yes, you stayed and stayed and if you were yanked out of the story, you'd just come back as somebody else. There must have been characters William Faulkner was sorry he invented. Take that "Flem" person. How disgusting. But I also imagine William Faulkner's disgust threshold was a lot higher than mine. The idea, though, was worth thinking about when I had more time: that a person could peel right off the page and go wandering around (causing trouble, mainly) until William Faulkner found another place for him. Even the name of the character couldn't be changed after a certain point of getting used to. Names were like barnacles and limpets, crusted to you so it would need a saw or ax or something to get the name off.

"Why you goin' to the feed store? You ain't got animals at the Hotel Paradise, last time I looked."

Delbert must have been trying to work this out all the while we'd been driving. It really annoyed me, as I'd been having a nice time until he broke in. "I just want to talk to him."

"Smith?"

"Yes."

"We're goin' all this way just to talk? Well, my goodness, girl, why not just call him up on the phone?"

"Because I want to talk in person. There's a difference."

Delbert grunted. "Beats me. Words is words far as I'm concerned."

I was sorely tempted to grab his neck and squeeze. *Words is words.* William Faulkner turned over in his grave. I could feel it.

"We're in Hebrides," Delbert called like we'd just landed on the moon.

Houses flashed by, big trees lining wide streets, and driveways, cars, bicycles, basketball hoops—all let us know Hebrides was a thriving city, which it was, about as far from Cold Flat Junction as you could get in prosperity. We waited at a traffic light that marked the town's center where my favorite store stood. This was the Emporium. I loved this store, the way the headless mannequins posed with their hip bones jutting. We turned right and were soon passing the Nickelodeon, which showed the latest movies a week before our own Orion got them (if it ever did). Across from the movie house was Barb's Beach House, although there weren't any beaches around; the nearest one might even be in Florida. Barb's was where Ree-Jane had come in her white convertible to get her bright new swimsuits. (Too bad she lost them in Miami Beach and had to wear that old brown one.) The windows of Barb's were always covered with sand and shells and whatever else caught her fancy as she dressed them. I bet she had a fake palm tree somewhere I could have borrowed.

I really liked Barb; she seemed to live in a sun-and-sand fantasy land, which was swell with me. In the window today was a huge blue and green striped beach umbrella with nothing but four feet jutting from under it, one set wearing flippers. Barb sold water-sport equipment too. Indeed, except for boats themselves, she had furnished out her shop (and her mind, I guessed) with just about everything relating to beaches and cruises.

We were now past the Hebrides town limit, going east, and Delbert was asking me if I wanted to drive back with him.

"Of course, what did you think?"

"There's a charge for waiting time, you recall."

"I know because you must have told me twenty times when you waited at the library the other day. There it is!" I pointed to our left. Delbert turned into the big parking lot of J. L. Smith's Feed and Garden Supply.

I got out and walked to the wide open garagelike door, thinking that I should have been spending my time during the ride rehearsing what I was going to say instead of thinking about William Faulkner. What *was* I going to say? *Mr. Smith, I would like you to search your memory . . . Mr. Smith, twenty or so years ago . . . Hi! Mr. Smith. You don't remember me—I'm kin of Ben Queen . . .*

I stood stalk still in front of bags of fertilizer and pruning shears, thinking.

"Hello, little lady!"

I wanted to snub whoever'd said that. I squeezed my eyes shut to get control of myself.

"What can I do you for?"

He seemed to be all teeth. The teeth glistened white above his red apron. Oh, how I hated expressions like that old tired "do you for" phrase, supposed to be funny. But I put on my phony smile and asked him if Mr. Smith was here. (Mr. Smith, I suddenly realized, could easily be dead.)

"Which one?" he asked, and laughed as if he were just the funniest person on God's green earth (as my mother likes to say). "I'm one of 'em. Then there's Pa and Grampa. All three of us in business like beans in a row."

I stretched my mouth in a wider smile imitation. "It's not you, but it might be your dad, if he was here twenty years ago."

This really stumped him, not whether his dad had been here, but that he didn't have a set response to fit the occasion. He was worse than Delbert. "Why'd you want to see someone from back then?" He struggled with the question as if he were just learning to read.

"I just do, Buddy." That was the name stitched in blue on the bib of his red apron.

Buddy scratched his neck as if I'd just given him a rash and finally said, "Yeah. They both were. Store's been in the family for over seventy-five years. Yeah, they were both here back then. He's over there."

I got the impression that Buddy felt he came up lacking because he himself hadn't been here, and wasn't of interest even to a twelve-year-old kid. I guessed I should feel sorry for him, being this insecure, but I didn't. He was standing here wasting my time. Then he turned and walked off, and I went over to where his father was standing, passing the time with another man who looked like a farmer in his feed hat. This Mr. Smith wasn't wearing an apron (probably thinking it against his dignity to do so, which I agreed it was), but his name was stitched on the pocket of his shirt: *Smitty.* This definitely was the right person. And he was obviously old enough to have been here twenty years ago, or thirty, even.

It was kind of hard to browse in a feed store. I wandered over to the wall behind him and looked at some gardening tools. Every once in a while, Lola Davidow would don some of these "Green-thumb" gardening gloves and go down to our big garden along the gravel road that went by the Pink Elephant. It was usually after a brunch of several Bloody Marys that she did this and would bring back a cabbage or runner beans. Once she even got Ree-Jane to go with her and I tagged along just to see what would happen. What happened was Mrs. Davidow would pull up potatoes or snap off beans and hand them up to Ree-Jane, who just stood there being bored.

I don't know how long I stopped there, running over this scene in my mind, but in a while a voice said, "Hello, there."

Mr. Smith—Smitty—I liked immediately. He asked "Can I help you" in exactly the same voice he'd use talking to an adult, instead of that stilted, slow-paced, singsongy manner adults use for retarded people and children.

I said, "Yes, sir. The Queens over in Cold Flat Junction asked me to pick up about fifty pounds of fertilizer? But I'm not sure what kind, and you seem to have several kinds here? Something else they wanted, too, but I can't remember it right now." I squinted up at him as if they'd told him, too.

"Fertilizer's easy. Maybe you'll recall what the item was after we've dealt with the fertilizer."

This was a very sensible and relaxed person, I thought. I was immediately calmer. It could be nerve-racking, thinking up ways to get information.

Mr. Smith looked the fertilizer over, searching, I guessed, for a certain kind. He found it and said, "Here we are. Fifty pounds, you'd want two twenty-pound and a ten-pound bag." He started hauling the bags out to the aisle.

This was going too fast and I better think quick. "Maybe there was other stuff they usually get you might know about?"

I was trying to think of a way to introduce Ben Queen into the fertilizer pickup when he said, "Well, when George picks up he gets chicken feed, usually. Could that be what they wanted?"

I smiled widely and said, "That's it. Thank you. I guess you know the Queens pretty well."

"Oh, yes. Known Ben and George for years and years. Ben'd come in every other Thursday like clockwork. Right here's the feed. It's good quality."

Like clockwork. That's what I was interested in. "I never knew him. Of course, now he's out of jail, maybe I'll meet him. That all sounded real bad, what happened."

Smitty shook his head and his eyes looked as if a pool of sadness had gathered in them. “Ben Queen. I just could hardly believe all that business. You know, he was in here that day and not a trace of any behavior that would have said he was upset or bad tempered. He was just as usual. We caught up with each other like we always did, could’ve talked the afternoon away.” Smitty laughed. “I’m a terrible talker.”

“That must’ve been the day he had to get his truck fixed?” I kind of held my breath, hoping he’d forgotten I was only twelve and what interest would I have in that day?

“I do believe that’s right; he said he’d had it over to Carl’s shop that morning. Something wrong with the carburetor. I guess I remember pretty good because of what happened.”

He was pulling out the chicken feed and didn’t notice that I was nearly doing a tap dance. *He was here, he was here, I knew he was here.*

“I was mighty puzzled when Ben confessed. You’d never have made me believe it otherwise.”

That was the reason Mr. Smith hadn’t said anything to the police: the so-called “confession”—which hadn’t been a confession at all, but a silence. I looked at him, a very nice man, and wondered how he’d feel, finding out he could have supplied Ben Queen with an alibi.

Mr. Smith called his son over to load the fertilizer into the cab. I could take the sack of chicken feed. I figured Buddy could take Delbert’s one hundred questions as well as I could, about what was being put in his cab and why. I went to the cash register and paid for all the fertilizer and feed. Mr. Smith had said he could just put it on the Queen’s account, but I said, no, I’d rather pay. I told him I’d really enjoyed meeting him and he seemed pleased at that.

Delbert went on and on about the three bags of fertilizer as we drove to La Porte. His talk was more a humming in my ears as I stared out the passenger’s window—I’d slid over to the other side to watch everything go by in reverse. I was so elated that what I’d believed to be true, was true, and now all that remained was to convince the Sheriff. “All”? It wouldn’t be easy.

It was so strange that what Ben Queen had been doing that afternoon had been here all along in Mr. Smith’s mind and no one had known. But Ben Queen knew it, knew he had an alibi and would have used it, I suspected, if he hadn’t thought it would call down even greater harm on someone. So where he had been or *if* he had been anyplace other than at the house made no difference as far as he was concerned. He was determined to take the blame upon himself.

It was almost funny about Mr. Smith. Smitty, a *deus ex machina,* come out of nowhere to finally straighten things out. And he didn't even know it. I wondered, as we again passed the horse farm, if you could be God and not know it. If God didn't know he was God.

Here was a question for Father Freeman.

The fertilizer had taken all my taxi money and then some. Delbert would love that.

Cold Turkey

56

Delbert was really put out that I'd spent all my money on fertilizer. He had to wait until I ran in and took the fare from the cash box in the back office. I asked since he had to wait anyway, why couldn't he unload the fertilizer? He argued it wasn't like suitcases, that suitcases were part of a person's trip, but fertilizer wasn't. I got him to do it by saying I'd give him a big tip (which I wouldn't). Finally, he left, mumbling curses which I would report to Axel, if Axel ever got within speaking distance.

It was time for dinner. I left the fertilizer on the front porch and half walked, half ran to the kitchen, taking the short cut on the wooden walk to the kitchen's side door.

Walter, dependable as always, was just taking Salisbury steak out of the oven, a more dignified version of hamburger. There would be my mother's dark rich gravy to pour over it.

"I took 'em in their first course. Melon balls. I didn't have much to do so I made some."

In a glass dish were perfect little rounds of watermelon, honeydew, and cantaloupe. I congratulated Walter on his inventiveness.

"Miss Jen called, too. They're on their way back. Miss Jen said the sun was something fierce."

"Did you tell her it was Florida?"

Walter hawked a laugh around and shook his head.

Of course, Miss Bertha objected to her Salisbury steak, fussing her fork around her plate as if poking and prodding meat and potatoes would turn them into whatever glamour dish she had in mind.

I told her, "It's not hamburger; it's a high-quality ground beef. Ground round, I think I heard my mother say."

Mrs. Fulbright had taken a bite and proclaimed it delicious. She did this all the time, like a fond parent trying to get a baby in a high chair (a pretty good description of Miss Bertha) to mimic her actions. But Miss Bertha only demanded, as usual, something else besides "this muck" to eat.

Referring to anything my mother cooks as "muck" is the same as calling gold or silver shavings "sawdust," but my day had been so spectacularly successful (at least as far as I was concerned) that I could rise above my daily and ordinary self and offer something else. My mother had left, exclusively for me, some ham pinwheels. These are made of pastry dough spread with perfectly seasoned ground ham, and then rolled up and sliced (something like icebox cookies). After baking they are lathered with rich cheese sauce. This scrumptious dish, beloved by me, is also a favorite of Miss Bertha's, at least as much as she favors anything.

So this dinnertime I offered Miss Bertha a ham pinwheel in place of the Salisbury steak. This was such an instant success that I decided not to mix a lot of fiery English mustard into her cheese sauce as I was tempted to do. And I reminded myself to divide the cheese sauce three ways (for I was also going to let Walter have a pinwheel), which did not mean an equal three ways, for my portion would be biggest. (Now, I will say this for Aurora Paradise, and that is she eats just about everything. I mean, unless she throws it at you instead, like the chicken wing and the stuffed tomato.)

The two old ladies' meal proceeded in relative peace after Miss Bertha got her ham pinwheel. My own and Walter's dinners were also peaceful. I had the largest pinwheel, half a Salisbury steak with my mother's lucious gravy, the au gratin potatoes, and peas as green as an Irish meadow. I saw to it Walter got just the same meal, except for not as much cheese sauce.

Following dinner, I stayed in the Pink Elephant saying goodbye to all of my new friends at the Rony Plaza, who pleaded with me to come back next year, telling me I was the most entertaining guest they had ever had. The manager said he would hold "my room" and was even considering putting a bronze plaque on the door with my name. I think he would even have offered to hold a sunset.

What a day, what a day.

I wrapped the cord around the fan and lay the palm tree against the wall and scooped sand back in the bucket. Will and Mill had been agitating to get their fan back, needing it (they said) to "create a disturbance." I told them please to keep it away from me.

I hauled the fan up to the Big Garage and knocked at the door. The noise behind it quickly subsided as if someone had shot it dead. When Will finally came to the door, he refused to open it more than an inch or two, as usual.

"Here's your fan."

"Good. Leave it."

"Why not open the door and take it inside."

"Just leave it."

"This is *really* stupid. I've already *seen* what you're doing, haven't I?"

"Leave it. Good-bye."

I heard laughter. There was a girl's voice, probably June's, and Paul's crazy laugh. As I walked away, I thought it wasn't *what* the secret was but the whole nature of secretive-ism that Will and Mill loved. It didn't matter that I'd seen some of the "production." Simply leaving it behind restored the secret of it.

When I went back to the kitchen Walter told me Aurora Paradise had been hollering down the dumbwaiter when he went into the back office. "It was way past the cocktail hour is what she said and she wants her Cold Comfort."

I sighed. Then I went to the office to sort through the bottles, and found no Southern Comfort, only gin and vodka and Wild Turkey. Well, the Wild Turkey would do, so I took it and miniatures of crème de menthe and brandy. Back in the kitchen I mixed up a couple of juices and ice in the blender, then dumped in the liquor. I poured it, frothing, into a tall glass, speared some melon balls on a long swizzle stick and held it up for Walter to inspect.

"Cold Turkey," I said.

We laughed.

Ghosts

57

First thing after breakfast I got a taxi into La Porte. Because of yesterday, Delbert was in a really sour mood, which would have been fine with me if only it kept him from talking.

"Courthouse don't open till nine-fifteen; it ain't even nine yet."

"The Sheriff will be there. He goes in early."

"Maybe. But that don't mean the sheriff's *office* is open. I know for a fact Maureen ain't there yet, for I just got a call to pick her up over in Spikersville."

His bad mood was evaporating in the face of his need to disagree. I didn't comment. I refused to say anything else in our trip to the courthouse. Now I was in a sour mood, but it faded as soon as I was out of the cab.

The Sheriff was there, as I thought he would be, looking as if he hadn't shaved in a couple of days and hadn't slept in a week. I felt sorry for him.

Donny was also there. "Uh-oh," he said, "here's trouble."

Actually, that was a compliment, but he couldn't see it. I ignored him and said to the Sheriff. "Could I talk to you for a few minutes? Please?"

Donny answered: "Sam's got enough to do without you dragging in more—"

The Sheriff leveled him with a look, I was pleased to see. Then he said to me, as he unhitched his jacket from the back of his chair, "Come on."

"Where?" I picked up my folder and wondered if I was under arrest for file-drawer theft.

"Over to the Rainbow. Donny can hold down the fort." He turned at the door. "Donny, you hear *anything,* let me know."

"Well, sure, Sam," he said, as if to say, *Don't I always?*

As we walked down the steps of the courthouse, I said, "What I have to tell you is kind of private."

"The best place for telling that kind of story's in the midst of a crowd. People are so busy listening to themselves they can't be bothered with somebody else. "Of course, there's Maud—?"

He meant she might sit down with us at some point, and did that bother me? "No. Maud's okay."

We had started across the street, but had to wait for a car to pass that had just rounded the corner. The Sheriff would never hold up his hand to stop a car just so he could cross a street.

The regulars were pretty much settled at the counter, having their morning coffee. Morning coffee sometimes ran into early lunch and I wondered how people like Dodge Haines ever did any business. As we passed them, they said hi to the Sheriff, who said hi back again. Maud was taking a breakfast order from some man who was probably just passing through. She winked. And Patsy Cline was kind of presiding over all of this, as she often did, singing "I Fall to Pieces," one of my all-time favorites.

We sat down in the back booth and I lay my folder on the table. I still hadn't shown him anything in it, but that would come as I told my story. I said, now, "I'll make a bargain with you if you hear me out before you get mad, for I know you will, at least on the inside."

Smiling, he settled back in the booth. "I'll try and reign in my temper."

"Because part of this is about Ben Queen. There's evidence he never murdered his wife Rose. It's not just my imagining things."

The Sheriff started in: "That old case isn't mine and I don't see how it's important—"

I held up my hand. "The reason it's important is because you think Ben Queen killed Fern and you think that because you think he killed Rose."

"Wait a minute, that's not altogether true—"

"What's not true? Altogether?" Maud was standing there with her order book and a Coke, which she set before me.

"It's true you're looking for him. Why are you looking for him?"

Maud said, "So he can help the police with their inquiries. That's always what they say. Sam?" She sort of waved her order book back and forth. "Breakfast?"

"No, and sit down as long as you don't interrupt."

"Well! Emma?"

I didn't know if she was asking if she could, or if I wanted something. But she sat down beside the Sheriff.

"What's this proof you've got, Emma?"

"Ben Queen was somewhere else when Rose got killed."

Maud raised her eyebrows, but didn't interrupt.

"Where?" asked the Sheriff.

"He was in Hebrides. He went to Smith's Feed Store, it's out on 219 the other side of Hebrides. I was hoping you'd go and talk to Mr. Smith because he's the alibi. The old one, not his son, who's kind of dumb. If Ben Queen didn't do it, don't you think his name should be cleared? Twenty years in prison for nothing; I think he should get back his good name."

"Absolutely. But what's your part of this bargain?"

"I'll tell you what I know about Ben Queen." It struck me, though, that for a person who wasn't there that night and hadn't heard him, I didn't know much. Ben Queen hadn't out-and-out denied killing Fern. It was like the murder of Rose all over again. And he did have that gun with him. If the Sheriff had been there, he might have agreed with me.

Maud had her chin propped in both hands. She turned her head to look at the Sheriff, who was surprised.

"That's fair. Tell me what you know."

I shook my head. "Not until you go talk to this Mr. Smith."

"You don't trust me?"

"Of course not," said Maud. "Why would she? You haven't believed anything she's said up to now."

The Sheriff looked, I can only say, crestfallen as he studied Maud's face, as if he couldn't imagine she'd think he was untrustworthy.

The thing was, it wasn't because I didn't trust him to keep his part of the bargain, it was because I knew if I told him about Ben

Queen being at the Devereau house, he'd be out of here like a shot. I couldn't have that. "That's one part of your bargain. The other is to go back and look at what happened to Mary-Evelyn Devereau. It wasn't any accident. That sheriff back then was an idiot, or plain lazy, or was cowed by the Devereaus. Even Dr. McComb thinks the whole thing was peculiar and maybe hushed up. The way she died?"

The Sheriff said, trying not to sound impatient, "I haven't got the reports on that case, so how could I—?"

I opened the folder and took out the police report.

"Where'd you get this?" The Sheriff was astonished.

"It's all in your files. I just took this stuff out."

"Did you get this out of the files?"

"Sam—"

"When Donny took one of his seven-hour coffee breaks."

"Sam—" Maud said again, her hand closing on his arm.

"I'm sorry," I said. "But you weren't paying any attention to me."

"I *wasn't?* Well, who went looking for you when you *disappeared?* Who took—"

So he *did* know the missing girl was me! Well, I hadn't time to bother about that.

"*Sam!* Stop being ridiculous!"

The Sheriff turned to look at Maud, and somehow, some way, the anger seemed to drain out of him.

"Listen," I said, trying to get my story back on course. "The way Mary-Evelyn died, why would anyone *not* think it's peculiar for a little girl to take a boat out at night. If it'd been *you,* wouldn't you have investigated?"

"Of course he would have," said Maud.

The Sheriff's face was down, but he held up both hands in a silencing gesture. "That case is forty years old, Emma."

"What difference does *that* make? They shouldn't be allowed to get away with it. Mary-Evelyn's good name is be-, be-" I couldn't think of the word.

"Besmirched," said Maud, indignantly.

"Right. They were so spiteful toward each other, those three sisters, they took it all out on Mary-Evelyn. You should go and talk to Imogene Calhoun that lives over in Cold Flat Junction, too. She actually went to that house when she was a kid, and she'll tell you. They hated each other. Isabel and Iris hated each other because of *him.*" I slapped down the photo of Jamie Makepiece.

The Sheriff picked it up. "Who is this?"

"His name is Jamie Makepiece. And this letter—" I took out the letter the Sheriff had already seen. "—is a goodbye letter to Iris Devereau." The "I" could have meant Isabel, but what reason would he have to write it? He no longer cared about Isabel. I didn't go into this for it would just complicate things more. "That's reason enough for Iris and Isabel to hate each another. And for both to hate Elizabeth for breaking up the romance. And listen to *this*—Mary-Evelyn wasn't their little niece, I bet you. Mary-Evelyn was probably Iris's *daughter. Now* do you see why they'd hate the sight of her?"

Maud had a paper napkin scrunched in the hands she held up to her mouth. She was wide-eyed. The Sheriff's frown I can only describe as exquisite. Exquisitely wondering. Boy, I really had their attention. "Just look at her." I pushed the picture of Mary-Evelyn around so both could give it a good, hard look. I also took out my one snapshot of the Devereaus under the porte cochere. "Look at her, then him, then them. Everything about her looks is like him, especially the hair. You can't tell in the police picture because her hair's wet and looks dark. But you can certainly tell in the other picture." I tapped it with my finger.

We were all silent for a moment. Then Maud asked, "What about Brokedown House, Emma? These things were there. Where does that come into your story?" All she had heard, I could tell by her look, by her voice, had seeped into her as if, like Mary-Evelyn, she might be drowning.

I thought of that light shining in my face. "Somebody's there."

"Ben Queen," said the Sheriff, always ready to blame the man for the state of the whole world. "It's Ben Queen, isn't it? That's where you saw him."

"No!" I said. "But there's someone. You know from being there that night. Remember?"

"Dwayne Hicks said there was somebody, but—"

"You think Dwayne was making it up?" asked Maud, irritated. "You want to bend everything to fit your own theory?"

"No, Maud, I didn't say he was making it up. I'm only thinking he might have been mistaken." He drummed his fingers on the table, looking at me all the while. "Who would have a motive for killing Fern Queen? I've got to say, it doesn't sound like her father would. Unless maybe Fern killed her mother."

"Revenge?" said Maud. "That doesn't make any sense if he'd gone to prison himself to protect Fern."

"Fern must've killed her mother. That's the only thing I can see would account for it." Ben Queen wouldn't have any motive. But the

Girl might, since her mother had abandoned and betrayed her. "There's a Girl—"

Maud leaned forward as if not wanting to miss a single drop of this story, and I thought, even more than the Sheriff, she was the person to tell it to.

"What girl?" asked the Sheriff.

I started to remind him about that afternoon a few weeks ago when I'd seen her through the window of Souder's Drug Store and run after her. I'd collided with the Sheriff and asked him if he'd seen her. I started to say this, but didn't. After those few words I'd uttered, it was like I got stuck. Was I afraid he'd go after her? Was I afraid she wouldn't come back if I talked about her? I studied my hands folded on the table, then my untouched Coke glass. My mind just seemed too empty of words. Words can abandon you just like people can. I had to get my mind going again. I said, "She looks like Rose Devereau. She looks *exactly* like Rose Devereau." I opened my mouth to say more, but fell silent again.

"Where?" asked the Sheriff. "Where have you seen her?"

"In Cold Flat Junction. At the railroad station. And here." But I didn't want to say where here. I had told Dr. McComb more than anybody and that was precious little, but I had told him about seeing her across Spirit Lake, in front of the Devereau house. And I saw her again, when I was in the house, outside, standing just within the rim of pines out there. I did not want to tell anybody that I believed she was getting closer. For a moment, I thought she might know about being lost, know the secret of lostness. It all sounded crazy, even to me it sounded crazy, the whole story—wild, weird, nightmarish when you heard it like this all at once. I can't say how far away my mind had traveled from the Rainbow Café, for Maud's voice pierced me like an arrow.

"You look," she said, "as if you've seen a ghost."

Dead man walking

58

Two hours was plenty of time to get to the Devereau house and tell Ben Queen, if he was there, what had happened. Warn him off, only he didn't strike me as the sort of person that needed warning off, the sort who would hightail it out of town when trouble came his way. The Sheriff's pursuit of Ben Queen would still continue, even if the reason for it had changed, even if the reason were only to ask him some questions. For there was still the murder of Fern and she was still, after all, Ben Queen's daughter.

But I had to lie down for a few minutes; I was more tired from telling my story to them than from all the running around I'd been doing. Maybe what tired me was the end of it. Or maybe what tired me was knowing the Davidows would be back soon to flatten everything. Or maybe I was just afraid my story was just a story, full of what William Faulkner said was sound and fury. (Or at least what Dwayne said he said.)

I lay in bed, thinking all this while holding my bear who, I discovered, did have a very small hole in its stomach that could leak stuffing if I didn't pinch it closed as I was doing. I found a tiny safety pin and closed the tear with that.

To make up for being so lackadaisical, I ran down the back stairs, taking care to use the route that bypassed the dining room. Miss Bertha and Mrs. Fulbright would be heading in for their dinner, if they weren't already seated at their table.

I took the wooden walk to the kitchen and announced to Walter I had to do something really important and would he mind waiting on the two for dinner? I also told him where I was going just to be on the safe side although I wasn't sure the safe side of what.

I didn't mean to be dramatic about things; I left the drama to Will and Mill who were dramatic enough for all of us. I wanted to be more like Lena, who was the most *un*dramatic person I had ever come across (except maybe for Walter), considering everything wrong in her life, and being about to have a baby and looking for the father (and even inexperienced me could see *that* disappointment coming a mile away). Imagine walking all the way from Alabama to Mississippi, taking a whole month to do it. Imagine having that kind of faith in your feet.

My own feet were carrying me down the half mile of dirt road to Spirit Lake and another quarter mile or more to Crystal Spring. I stopped to look at the old boathouse and remember back to when my father brought us here and further back to the night of Mary-Evelyn's drowning. At Crystal Spring I stopped to get a drink of water. The tin cup was where it always was, shoved back in against the rock by me so no one could see it except the ones who knew it was there. I drank and looked off into the woods where a look didn't penetrate very far. I figured I had been through there eight times already, coming and going, so there was no reason I couldn't do it the ninth and tenth times. It was still daylight, but however light out here, the woods were closer to midnight. And it had begun to rain, not much, but enough to veil the available light.

In the woods the rain did not penetrate any more than the light. I was glad there was this rutted old road, even though it was mostly overgrown, narrowed to just the ridge of earth between tire tracks. A lot of tires and a lot of feet had trampled it down. The Devereau sisters had passed this way the night they had brought Mary-Evelyn through. Brought her, not gone looking for her. I believed that now.

My feet scuffed up cold wet leaves, making as much of a squelch as they could for comradely noise. I had picked up a sturdy stick and battered and whacked the beeches and pines as I passed, again, I guess, to make noise, as if to scare something off. I moved as fast as I could and as noisily as I could through the laurel bushes and tangled vines, through pines and heavily laden oaks that littered the ground with acorns, past ash trees whose bark was like cold gray marble, through patches of wildflowers I couldn't name, but which my mother could.

I even stopped and thought of my mother as something more than my cook, as a person making her way through the Carolinas with crazy people, almost as crazy as Aurora Paradise could ever be. I marveled that my mother had been brazen enough or had enough starch in her to put up with them for all of these years without much help from Will or me.

I tore bark from my stick as I thrashed along, getting it down to white bone. An uneven runnel of light showed above me where thin branches fretted the sky that was nearly canceled out. Then the trees opened up ahead and I was at the dark line of pines that edged this end of the wood and the Devereau yard.

I crossed it and went around to the rear, to the kitchen door. The kitchen had been used again, which made me think Ben Queen was around. In the sink were a couple of plates, a bowl, and two cups. On one plate were the remnants of egg and toast. If only Walter were here! He could tell me not only when all of these dishes had been eaten off of, but what kind of person had done the eating! The drying baked beans that had been a careless puddle? "Ain't Miss Bertha, she's too mean to leave them beans behind." Or the asparagus spear sheared cleanly in half? "Someone got a grudge on, it's Aurora Paradise, most likely." Yes, Walter could tell more from the state of uneaten food than an Irish famine. (I should tell the Sheriff to add Walter to his list of crime-scene people.)

On the stove there was a frying pan in which the eggs had been fried, a quart of milk and bread standing by it. Crumbs lay on the white enamel counter and a bread knife, such as my mother uses, with a serrated edge. My mother is horribly particular about which knives cut what. Vera once used her meat-cutting knife to slice lemons. It's the only time I recall my mother giving Vera hell (which she very often deserves, as far as I'm concerned). What I was seeing here looked like the remains of a breakfast. It must have been Ben Queen's.

I walked through the dining room without stopping as I doubted the intruder would have set himself a place. With a table setting I would probably be as good as Walter was with food when it came to figuring out what kind of person had been sitting at the table. Cutlery shoved all anyhow? Miss Bertha, for sure. Knife and fork aligned perfectly on a plate? The Poor Soul, definitely.

The living room produced in me the same mixture of gloom and nostalgia I had felt before, only now it was weightier, as if the room itself were inconsolable. I stood looking at the picture of the sisters that hung on the wall near a sideboard, the only picture there. Three of them with their dark hair worn loose or in plaits, and Rose herself, not more than a child and much younger then the Girl was now, but still with that light bright hair, incandescent if the sun hit it, otherwise shining with a cool and moonish glow. The sisters must have been in their late teens; it was hard to think of them that way, so solemn they looked, their dark hair against their black clothes.

The piano and a small table were studded with candles stuck to small plates in their own wax, as if there had been a power outage. I looked at the sofa where Ben Queen had dropped the gun like a toy. I could see him doing it, as if tossing it off himself. He seemed himself almost affrighted by coming face-to-face with a little kid, no more dangerous to him than one of Dwayne's rabbits. I could only think now he was afraid of my fear of him. I had never known an adult to react so quickly to something in a child, not even Maud or the Sheriff.

I looked through the screen door that opened out onto the porch, across the yard for any sign of either of them, the Girl or Ben Queen. The rain fell sluggishly, or that was just me seeing my own tiredness in the rain.

I climbed the stairs. I wanted particularly to see the relation between those two rooms, the one I thought to be Iris's, since there was a sewing machine, and the one I knew was Mary-Evelyn's. The doors were opposite one another, as I had thought. And there was a rocking chair in Iris's room in direct line with the door. I sat in it and looked across the hall into Mary-Evelyn's room at Mary-Evelyn's bed. Had she been lying in it, I could have seen her clearly; had she been sitting by her toy chest, I also could have seen her. There was no way she could have left without Iris seeing her. I suppose Mary-Evelyn could have said she was going downstairs to get a glass of milk or something, but that was not in any of the sisters' statements. There were other possibilities, such as her sneaking out when they were all asleep, but with the open doors upstairs and locked and bolted doors down, I doubted it. This house, after all, was geared to imprisonment.

I left the rocking chair and Iris's room and went across to Mary-Evelyn's. She might still have lived here, for the white iron bed was made up with its yellow and white chenille bedspread and her beautiful dresses hung in the mahogany wardrobe.

I really was in awe of these dresses and the fine workmanship that had gone into their making. But had they scared her into a carefulness of behavior she wouldn't have felt if she'd had my old clothes to wear? Ice-blue taffeta, pale yellow cotton with tiny pleats and satin-covered buttons, rose-colored wool, as soft as cashmere.

Then I went to the toy chest, opened it, and rummaged through puzzles, stuffed animals, cotton dolls, and a Ouija board until I found the Mr. Ree game. I removed the board and the cards and the tiny weapons and lined up the hollow tubes with their molded plastic heads, marveling at the care that had gone into the making of this game, as much care as had gone into the sewing of the dresses. I lined up the tubes: Mr. Perrin, Butler Higgins, Aunt Cora, Miss Lee. The tubes were used by the players to conceal the tiny weapons which you had to have in your possession to murder somebody. It was the best game I knew of.

Niece Rhoda, of course, was missing. Dwayne had found her on the path. It brought up the same question I asked about Mary-Evelyn's doll and Jamie's photograph: how had they got to Brokedown House? The Artist George piece had been in the alcove in the wall of Crystal Spring where the tin cup was kept. There hadn't been any message because—I thought this now, but hadn't then—it might fall into the wrong hands. All of the character cards were here, though. Mary-Evelyn had cut the faces of her aunts from some old snapshot and pasted them over the card faces. I had discovered this the first time I'd looked in the toy chest. Somehow, I found that a totally terrifying act on the part of Mary-Evelyn.

I sat absorbed, trying to make something of all this, and probably making too much, as I guess I tend to do about everything. I was not facing the door, but sitting sideways to it on the floor. I felt a kind of shadow hovering over the room and though there had been not the slightest noise, not even a disturbance of the air, I knew someone was in the hall. If I moved my head scarcely an inch outward, I would see the person. I moved nothing, not a scrap, as if my stillness might void the shape that I knew was filling the doorway. Whoever it was had been in the house all the while, and had kept quiet, which was the scariest thing of all.

In seconds my mind would collapse under a weight of fear if I didn't stave it off by just going blank. Blank. Any thought I had ran before my inner eye as if it were coming by ticker tape, from outside.

"Why are you here?"

It was a woman's voice. There was no way I could pretend I was deaf. I was shaking, I couldn't help it, but I could try and cover it up by pretending stupidity. I did turn my head then and said "Huh?"

"Get up from there."

She was tall, gaunt, and plain, as plain as the dark wool dress she was wearing. It was an ugly plum color. She was fifty years older than she was in the picture with Jamie Makepiece, but she was still unmistakably Isabel Devereau.

I had stared at the pictures of the sisters and Jamie long enough to know to a fault who was who. But her question was strange. Shouldn't it have been "Who are you?" and not "Why are you here?"

I could not hold the cards because my hands shook, but I could handle the tubes. I dropped the miniature gun and knife into the Miss Lee tube, as if I were continuing to play, and when it rattled, no one would know it was my shaking hand causing it. It wasn't until then that I saw the gun. She was holding the gun Ben Queen had dropped on the couch, loosely, as if it were an afterthought.

She appeared to look over my head and take direction from something or somebody. I resisted the urge to follow her look. The "huh" which had registered as stupidity or emptiness was frozen there, which probably made it that much more convincing. If I could keep her from doing anything for another minute I might come up with something from the mental ticker tape. One thing on it was that question, "Why are you here?" What threatened to upset me from this tightrope walk was the terrifying notion that Isabel Devereau took me for Mary-Evelyn. Here I was, the same age and size. My face wasn't Mary-Evelyn's, but I didn't think that would matter to Isabel. After all, here I was in Mary-Evelyn's room, with Mary-Evelyn's things.

She was crazy. I don't mean the Davidow craziness or even the Aurora Paradise kind. I mean *crazy* crazy. Insane. A craziness perhaps shared by a few of the old people in Weeks's Nursing Home, the ones who talked to the air and hit whatever was around to hit, even empty space. No, Lola and Aurora weren't even in the running if it was Isabel Devereau they had to beat; they weren't even close. She seemed to be listening to something. Although I knew nothing was there, still it was an effort not to turn and make sure nothing was coming up behind me. Her eyes widened and narrowed.

Then she was standing over me and reaching down to grab my arm. "Get up! We have to go." Pulling me to my feet, she shook me as if I were one of Mary-Evelyn's cotton dolls, the gun at my back.

I couldn't have put up any resistance even if I hadn't been numbed by the fear I was trying to hold at bay. It would flood in like the news of a death if I so much as opened my mind for a moment to it. My blank self was pushed and prodded down the stairs. My hand was all this time glued around the Miss Lee tube.

I mustered up some will to act as if this were just one more occasion of angry-adult-disciplining-willful-child. "What are you *doing?*" My feet clattered on the stairs. She didn't answer; I hadn't really expected her to. I wanted to hear the sound of my own voice.

The screen door was at the bottom of the stairs and on the last step I gave a terrific yank, freed my arm of her grip and rushed the door. But she was just as quick, pulling me back, and this time her iron grip was on my neck.

"Isabel!" I yelled.

Her hand fell from my neck. I hadn't the vaguest idea what to add to the shouted name. I turned and looked at her and wished I hadn't. She was standing with the gun raised.

"Go on," she said, prodding me forward.

With the gun at my back we came to the living room screen door. That I had managed to control her actions by calling out her name made me feel momentarily elated. If I had done it once, maybe I could do it again. Right now, I saw myself running. *All you need to do is break the point of contact.* No, I thought, running was instinct, and instinct was too dangerous. Anything without cold reasoning behind it was too dangerous. I realized right then that the enormous practice I'd had all these years in controlling my feelings would be to my advantage. I *had,* after all, controlled Isabel for a few seconds when I'd said her name. If I was patient, I could do it again.

But patience with a gun at your back isn't an easy thing to practice. I did what the gun wanted and it wanted me to cross the yard and enter the woods. Into the thick darkness we went. It was not the time to think of Donny Mooma and what he had said about the last mile.

For here I was, dead girl walking.

The boathouse

59

I wondered how much time had passed, for it felt like half my life. As I went by the few landmarks I knew, I thought the woods had never seemed such a friendly and familiar place, one I really would hate to leave. Something life-threatening does that I suppose, throws up a different face to things. I looked up briefly to that narrow bit of sky and saw that there was still a scrap of light and was relieved.

Out of it, we came to the spring. We had to pass the little stone alcove where the cup sat, and, without knowing why, I reached out my stubborn fist and shoved Miss Lee into it.

Why did I do this? Did I think someone would find it, like a message in a bottle, and come like a lightning bolt to knock mad Isabel down? Why had I taken the chance, when any sudden movement could have got me shot in my back? I think it was because of that fairy tale I told myself when I was little, that there are certain places that can't be got at by the wrong people. That stone alcove was a charmed place. I think that's why Artist George had ended up there. I knew it was why the tin cup was there in the first place. I had told myself back then a drink from that cup would arm me against evil. That was back when I knew what it was.

But Isabel hadn't noticed; she was too intent on getting where we were going. I was sure we were headed for the boathouse. The gun had dropped farther down my back as we walked; it was now at my waist. I imagined it as some tiny burrowing creature looking for a hiding place.

Behind me, she spoke not a word. All I could hear was her ragged breathing, as if she'd run a race. Quick, short jabs of breath. I think I knew what she intended to do, and it was certainly preferable to the gun at my back, although it carried its own hazards with it. We had come to the boathouse.

As in those old stories of pirate ships and mutinies, I was being made to "walk the plank"—the boardwalk to the boathouse. The boats, some of them, were still there, though I hadn't seen anyone ever using them. Whether the one that had carried Mary-Evelyn like some old Eskimo woman sent out to sea to die was among them. I counted four rowboats, all of them old as the hills, none of them looking like it could bear any weight, but I hoped they could, even though they were oarless. My heart hammered; my stomach fell another foot as we left the boardwalk that stretched out over Spirit Lake, which I saw now, as I had the woods, with a fresh vision. I seemed to grasp the story all at once, as if my mind closed around it as my fist had closed around the Miss Lee tube.

In my heart-hammering dread, I was surprised I could still talk, surprised I could still make out language. It wasn't talk; it was more like an echo of talk, more like a memory of it.

"She was dead before you put her in the boat, wasn't she?"

"Elizabeth drowned her first. Not I. I hate death up close."

"Why did you kill Fern Queen?" I choked this out, feeling as if a wasp were in my throat, stinging it closed.

"She murdered our Rose."

"Our Rose? *Our* Rose? You hated Rose Queen!"

Isabel smiled and her smile was dreadful, a blackened crescent, moon lava. Once she had been a handsome woman, cold but dignified. Her mind had ravaged her face, now. "Rose was under his spell. It wasn't her fault."

I knew how much of a lie all of this was. But the Devereau sisters had managed to shore up each other's beliefs with lies. There were things she wanted to believe, most of all in Jamie's love for her.

The gun touched my chest. Her tone was actually friendly as she talked about how I was a bastard child, how they had to get rid of me, even Iris thought so. (I had nearly forgotten that to her I was Mary-Evelyn and so was a hateful thing. I was proof of Jamie's and Iris's betrayal.) Her smile was impenetrable, as if me being a bastard child was of no consequence. She said Iris blinded Jamie with her beauty and then stole him away. It was then it occurred to me that she wanted to believe in Jamie, that there are things each of us wants to believe and could believe in spite of there being no evidence for it. If this weren't so, she wouldn't be doing all of this talking; it was nervous talking, the kind that keeps things at bay. What I thought was it wouldn't be too hard to convince her of what she wanted to be convinced of.

"Jamie. What about that letter Jamie wrote you?"

She paused, uncertain. "What letter?"

By now I had read it or heard it read enough times I could almost recite it. I did, coming down hard on the "I" of "My dear I."

"Iris is who he meant."

"How do you know if it only said 'I'?"

"Because Iris told me—"

"She told you it was to her." My teeth had finally stopped chattering. I was almost beginning to believe myself. Even with that gun pointed at me, I had a taste of power, which was what people usually had over me. Now I saw why they used it. It felt good. "You believed her and you shouldn't have. He came back. He must have gone to that old Calhoun house where you've been living. Where you brought the photograph. Where you brought the doll."

"Jamie's gone. Elizabeth sent him packing. She controlled all of us, excepting Rose. Rose was the lucky one—she ran off. Even though it was with that no-account Queen fellow. Too bad he got blamed for what his awful daughter did. But I fixed her."

For that minute she'd been seeing events in her mind. Now, she was seeing me. She shifted the gun. I could not look at it any longer. The moon was caught behind cloud cover and the stars were hidden. There was usually such a bright rash of them I could hardly believe they'd retreated on me, too. I thought of a hand shutting the eyes of the dead. I felt as if we were talking underwater, where words scarcely rose to the surface. Maybe I was drowning in the wake of a boat. I could hardly keep my head above all of this imaginary water.

It's as though all these years never were. Had she said that? Or had I thought it? I felt I was getting farther and farther away, drifting away across Spirit Lake, out of reach of everyone. I felt this more strongly even than fear, fear had almost nothing to do with it. It was loneliness, pure and simple. It was the blue devils.

Yet I thought all of this while I was talking, telling things I could only guess at, but kept on talking, for that fixed her mind on that long-ago summer when for a while she had the power that happiness lent her: with Jamie she could have done anything.

"My own sister." That's what she kept saying, in a dead voice, over and over again, *My own sister.*

My mind tried to race to a way out of this, but it could only plod. Then I thought, *Wait:* she knew I—or Mary-Evelyn—was Iris's child, but she didn't know I was Jamie's, not for certain.

"I'm not his; I'm not Jamie's. Iris lied."

At this the gun dropped to her side, but she still had a quick enough hold on it that I didn't dare move. She was mad, but she wasn't addled.

"Lies."

"No. Iris was really bad. There were other men besides Jamie." Then for some reason I came upon this lucid patch in my mind that said: You're twelve years old and here you are trying to take charge of your own life and maybe death. I would sooner be sitting in the Orion with my bag of popcorn and my eyes silvered by the reflection of the silver screen, as if I were up there too in that fantasy land of men and women going mad for love or lack of it.

It made more sense than this. I should have been merely an observer of life that I couldn't possibly understand, instead of stuck down in the midst of it as an actor, a player, a participant. It wasn't fair. *Whine, whine,* my player-self said. *Nobody twisted your arm, did they?* Then my mind rushed past this lucid place and I felt its weight again, trying, trying to get myself out of here.

She had been uttering a storm of epithets, heaping abuse on Iris's head, apparently partly convinced that what I'd said was true. She raised the gun again. "Just you back up, now."

I did.

"Get down into that boat." She pointed to the one closest, bobbing slightly, though Spirit Lake seemed deathly quiet.

There were no oars and I was a poor swimmer, but any place was better than here.

A short wooden ladder that was used to get to the boats was attached to the dock on both sides. I climbed down into at least six inches of water sloshing around in the bottom; it looked pretty old, and I'm sure it was. I can't recall ever having seen anyone using this dock in the last several years. I could swim to shore from here, as it wasn't more than fifty or sixty feet. Certainly, I could, except she could get there quicker than I and I'd just be back to where I was. So I watched her undo the rope from the post it was tied to, toss it into the boat, then pick up one of the oars lying on the dock and shove the boat. I floated on quietly moving water toward the center of the lake. She stood on the dock, watching, and I had no idea, none, what she meant by all of this. What I felt was the most incredible relief I'd ever known, getting away from her. Even though there was water in the bottom of the boat, I think it had come perhaps from rain, or disturbance of the lake which had sloshed over the side. For it didn't get any deeper, and although I had nothing to scoop it up with, I could do a little with my hands, and nothing came to fill it up again. I didn't see any sign of leaks. I kept bailing water with my hands, feeling if I had to bail all the rest of the night, I'd still be lucky. Shore got farther away; I wouldn't want to have to swim from where I was now.

I was looking down and bailing when I heard a shot and beside the boat the water caved as if someone were skipping big stones. I looked toward the dock. She was firing at me. I dropped down, terrified, my face in the water. So this was what she had in mind. I put my hands over my ears, which did no good for I heard the second shot as clearly as the first. More clearly, because it was closer. The frightening thing was, she didn't even have to hit *me.* All she had to do was hit the boat and then it *would* sink. Able or not, I might have to swim toward shore, and I could imagine the shots in the water. How many bullets did that gun hold?

I was a sitting duck. I couldn't stand it, just to have thought I was safe from her, and now I find that this was what she had in mind all along. *I hate death up close.* It was Elizabeth who'd had to hold Mary-Evelyn down. I could just picture vicious Isabel walking away from the scene, hands over her eyes.

Another shot that didn't split the water, but came with a cry. I raised my head just enough to see over the bow. What I saw astonished me more than anything else that night: Isabel fell, flailing, into the water. A figure emerged from the brush along the road and walked the boardwalk to the dock.

It was Ben Queen. Even from this distance, and in the dark, I could tell it was him. He had a certain way, a certain walk. He shouted something, but I couldn't understand it. I had come to save Ben Queen, and here he was, saving me.

I tried to use my hands as oars, but made precious little progress.

I could see her, floating there near the dock, her ugly purple dress turned black by the water. Holding one of the old white lifesavers stacked on the dock, Ben Queen jumped into the water and started toward me. He swam like a sewing needle running up a seam, scarcely parting the water, dragging the lifesaver with him. When he got close enough he shoved it to me.

He was treading water and raking his wet hair out of his face. "Glad I happened along."

"Me too."

"You can swim some?"

"Some."

"Paddle with one hand and give me the other and let's get the hell outta here."

When I'd spotted the police car fast arriving along the road, my main concern was not for Ben Queen's welfare, but whether I looked like a drowned rat. You'd think being held at gunpoint would overcome a person's self-consciousness and vanity, but not mine.

"Emma, long as you're all right, I think it might be best for me to vamoose."

I insisted I was all right. I thanked him and thanked him.

"I owed you, Emma. Looks like I might again." He was looking at the car a short distance down the road, its red bulb flashing, aimed here. Ben Queen picked up his shotgun and vamoosed.

The two of them were out of the car, and the Sheriff was running along the boardwalk, calling out my name. I'd forgotten: Walter knew where I was and the Sheriff would have come looking for me once he got back from Hebrides.

He sounded really worried—Good! *And just wait until you hear about what you failed to save me from!* I wish the body of Isabel Devereau hadn't chosen that moment to float up and bang against the dock. I nearly screamed, but caught myself.

"Hi," I said, casually. "She's down there."

The Sheriff kept an arm around me, saying things like *My God, Jesus Christ, holy hell,* and a few other blasphemies which I might have to report to Father Freeman. Donny swaggered around with his thumbs hooked in his Sam Brown, chewing gum and generally giving the impression that he knew right away nobody was in danger. The Sheriff told him to get the hell back to the car and call in for an ambulance and the coroner. Get things going. Donny reluctantly left.

The Sheriff kept his arm around me and asked me if I was okay. I said, grandly, of course, hating that I looked soggy and caked with water and lily-pad muck. But I was flattered that he asked me about me before he asked about the body floating in the water, whom he didn't recognize.

I said, "You've got a really bad memory, considering all those pictures I showed you." But he hadn't spent as much time as I had looking at them. "Isabel Devereau," I said, shivering, while trying to look blasé and modest but only managing to look dripping wet. The Sheriff saw me shiver and immediately removed his uniform jacket and whirled it around my shoulders.

Well! I thought. This was worth getting wet for! Was it worth almost dying for?

I guess not.

Ree-Jane goes spastic

60

I was a celebrity. Glasses were being raised to me so much and so often, you'd think I was Tangerine. There were all these reporters come from newspapers for miles around, from our nearest big city a hundred miles away, and someone even suggested the New York papers would pick it up.

I was a celebrity not just in Spirit Lake and La Porte, but in Cloverly, Hebrides, and you-name-it. My fame was spreading.

The three returned to find me rocking on the front porch, in the company of reporters from three newspapers also rocking on the front porch, and all drinking Cold Comforts and having an hilarious time interviewing me. I thought perhaps their laughter and clear enjoyment of the assignment might have been suppressed in view of the danger I had been placed in, but then I put that down to my mixing too much Jack Daniel's and Wild Turkey in their drinks. (I had ransacked Mrs. Davidow's storeroom.)

Now: imagine Ree-Jane.

Imagine Ree-Jane getting out of the car (hideously sunburned) and walking up the front steps into this scene. For here I was at the very center of her own daydream. Her daydream become waking reality, not for her, but for me: Famous Adventurer, Famous Heroine, Famous Actress (for Hollywood must be on its way). Famous.

Famous, Famous, Famous, Famous, Famous.

Me. It was all happening to *me,* Emma Graham, not to *her,* Ree-Jane Davidow.

Even Walter was there, leaning against the porch railing, smiling to beat the band, for he had been interviewed and photographed, too. It was Walter, after all, who had sent the police car to Spirit Lake.

Walter! Walter, who was so low on the totem pole. Walter, who was mere background music. Walter had stepped out of the shadows into the story of a lifetime.

"Now, be sure you tell them, Walter," I'd said when I was whipping up the Cold Comforts for the reporters, "you be sure to tell them that *you* were the only one who knew where I was and that *you* would have come looking for me if the Sheriff hadn't turned up."

"Well, it's true, ain't it? I woulda."

Ree-Jane stayed spastic for two days. Lola, who took her fame where she found it, even if it was being lit by reflected glory (and extra martinis), had me in the back office going over the story again and again. Laughing in the wrong places, of course, but who cares? One of the funniest things was watching Lola and Ree-Jane compete for the most "print" (as the reporters called it). Elbowing Ree-Jane aside, Lola told the reporters she had always said I had more gumption than anyone and that she had raised me always to assert myself. To another reporter, with whom she was sharing martinis, she came very close to adopting me—I was as good as her daughter.

The only ones not jumping on the bandwagon were Will and Mill, who could have got a lot of free publicity for their production out of it, but who didn't seem to care. When I mentioned this, Will put his hand on my shoulder and said he wouldn't want to intrude upon my success. That was the *biggest* lie. They'd intrude all over the place if they thought it would get them something they wanted, and publicity wasn't it. But why would it be, if everything they did was a secret?

I was there when a reporter approached the two—searching them out in the Big Garage, which was nervy—and to her questions, they both said, "No comment."

No *comment!* Oh, for heaven's sake!

"But aren't you thrilled that your little sister has done this?"

Will favored her with a tilted smile. "Like a *deus ex machina,* you mean?" He even pronounced it right.

The reporter stumbled over that. "A *what?*"

Mill answered: "You really ought to bone up on your Greek tragedies."

They turned, unconcerned, and walked away. Back to Paul and the bucket of flour.

But Ree-Jane went wandering around in her new blue dress like a wilting delphinium. I knew she would make a nasty recovery, though, and she did.

She started laughing when she saw me, pointing and laughing, fit to kill as if she knew a version of my exciting story that others didn't. It was that silent fake laughter she'd got down so well.

But it didn't last long.

One morning shortly after their return, Mr. Gumbrel called me up and asked me if I'd mind coming into the *Conservative* office; I said I'd be glad to, and did not ask him what this was all about. But I had an inkling something else was about to be added to the list of Me.

Famous Reporter.

Poor Ree-Jane.

Star reporter

61

"What I'd like you to do, Emma, is write this up for me." Mr. Gumbrel held up his palm as if I'd been going to object. "Don't say it's already been written up until we're blue in the face, because it hasn't. Don't tell me that you don't have a lot more to add, and don't tell me these reporters didn't include a pile of misquotes and mistakes—*including Suzie Whitelaw!*" She was passing by his little glassed-in cubicle, and he wanted to make sure she heard this.

She did. Her face went cherry red. She'd been walking by just to find out what he had me in there for.

"Oh, yes, there were mistakes all right." I did not give as an example the city paper that had spelled Regina Jane ReeJane (as suggested by me), this spelling having been picked up and flaunted by a dozen other papers. "But I'll correct them." Except for that particular mistake, I didn't add.

"Good! Wonderful! What I have in mind is your in-depth history of this whole affair. Maybe begin with telling how you came in here over a month ago, wanting to read our report on the death of the Devereau girl. It's stuff like that, it's the details I want. And I want it spread—" His hands measured off a width of air. "—through at least three and maybe even four or five issues."

I was really excited, but kept it in check. "Yes, I can see a story like this could take a lot of print."

"You betcha! I'm going to sell more papers with this than I have in the last two years!"

"I wonder," I said suavely, "if it'll go on the wire?"

Mr. Gumbrel said undoubtedly, as he lit his cold cigar. "You know, ReeJane—"

(Would *everyone* now be calling her this? Would it turn up on her headstone? How wonderful!)

"—she'll take offense I turned her down," Mr. Gumbrel went on. "But obviously she can't write it."

"You mean—she *asked* to write this story?"

"Oh, my goodness, yes. Came in here like the Queen of the Nile, telling me she was a lot nearer the source than Suzie Whitelaw and so could do a better job." He plugged the cigar into his mouth, took it out again. "I had to remind her the one little thing she wrote a couple years ago didn't constitute 'experience.' Which is what she says she has. There's a girl could turn a silk purse right back into a sow's ear."

"Can I quote you?"

He guffawed.

My progress from the *Conservative* up Valley Road was marked by bursts of jumping and laughing. I guess anyone who might see me would conclude that fame had driven me mad.

No one did see me, though, for both Valley Road and Red Bird Road were so empty of houses. On Red Bird Road, the mobile home with its half-moon garden had set a plastic goose family among the zinnias and petunias. A pink flamingo had been added to this plastic family, and I had to admire the owners' attempt to draw what color out of life they could.

Dr. McComb's house seemed, as always, to be drowsing in its acres of tall grass, weeds, gladioli, and Queen Anne's lace. The lack of a front porch or a cellar gave it this submerged and sleeping look. The front door stood open, so I didn't have to knock, which might have summoned the strange, tall, voiceless woman, who I personally thought was as crazy as a loon, but then I'd been too long among stories of the Devereau sisters to have a good slant on madness.

I walked through the kitchen to see if any baking was going on. It was; from the oven wafted the smell of lemons. I went out to the back.

"Hi, Dr. McComb," I called.

His head came up and he waved, "Over here!"

I plowed through buffalo grass and strange tall winged flowers until I got to him. He was wearing his floppy broad-brimmed straw hat the color of burnt grass, which he swept off as he made me a courtly bow amid the butterfly bushes. "Brilliant! Brilliant! How'd you do it?"

"Thank you. That's what I came for—to thank you for the autopsy information you gave me."

"Autopsy information?" He looked swiftly around as if he had overlooked a dead body. "Did I dig someone up?"

I gave an exaggerated sigh. "You know. About drowning."

Slapping his straw hat back on his head, he said, "Emma, as I recall, all I did was *confirm* what you'd already figured out. That the child could have been drowned beforehand and someplace else." Then he put his arm around my shoulders. "This is at least a two-brownie topic. Let's go." He picked up the net and we walked back to the house.

"I didn't smell any brownies," I said. "I smelled lemon. Is it cookies?"

"Good grief! Does your investigative prowess never take a holiday? Right now what's baking is a citron pound cake. I already made the brownies, especially for your visit."

As we pushed through the weeds and Queen Anne's lace I said, "There's something else I wanted to thank you for, though."

"Um? What's that?"

"For not laughing."

Hearsayist

62

As I walked up the street to the Rainbow Café, I saw, of all people, Ree-Jane coming down the steps of the courthouse. Upon seeing me, she stopped. She did not cross the street to say anything; she merely stood there, pointing at me and laughing. Even as far away as she was, I could tell it was one of her fake, soundless laughs, but she really acted as if she would split in two with it. She had done this before, of course, but she hadn't done it coming out of the courthouse. What was going on? Who had she been talking to?

Shirl gave me a blistered look when I walked into the Rainbow (she being another one unaffected by my fame). I made my way to the back booth, slower than usual, as the counter sitters kept stopping me to comment. Mayor Sims enjoyed telling me that maybe I should be sheriff instead of Sam (ha ha ha), whereupon Ulub, sitting next to him, gave him a verbal thrashing, or as near as Ulub could get to it. We were so pleased with ourselves we nearly knocked Ubub off his stool with all of our friendly pats and punches. Patsy Cline was singing "Crazy."

Maud brought me a Coke. It was nice, always being fed by people. It almost made me want to be a wandering orphan or a matchstick girl, for then I would really have appreciated it.

I hadn't seen much of Maud in the last several days because the reporters (and the police) had kept me so busy answering questions, and because there'd been this big increase in business at the hotel. Today, I had been let off serving lunch when I'd told my mother I had really important business to attend to. Such are the benefits of being a celebrity that my mother had neither questioned the business nor why it was important.

Will certainly questioned it, since I would be missing another rehearsal. "You'll never get anywhere in the theater if you can't be serious about it."

"Why do I have to rehearse, for heaven's sake? All I *do* is come down on that swing thing."

"It's the *timing,* for fuck's sake."

I refused to lower myself to tell him he'd just said the f-word. That was really more because I wanted to say it myself and waited for him to pave the way. Yet, he said it so calmly, and without emphasis, that you'd think it was just another old word. Maybe it was.

"What timing? Mill just lowers the contraption with me on it. That's all."

Will put his hand to his head and groaned a little as if weary of dealing with amateurs.

"You producers are all alike," I said. "Temperamental, egotists, rude. Really fucking rude."

I turned away and marched off, the tart taste of the word on my tongue.

Maud said, putting down my Coke and her cigarettes, "You look as if you're holding up pretty well."

"Outside I ran into Ree-Jane."

"Everyone calls her that, now." Maud lit up a cigarette. "It's hysterical."

"That's what she was. Hysterical, I mean. She was laughing at me, pointing and laughing. It's like she knew something. And she was coming out of the courthouse."

"But she does that—I mean, you've said she laughs at you just to make you think the way you're thinking now: that she knows something, when she doesn't at all."

"Still, I'd like to see the Sheriff."

"Well, honey, your prayers are answered, for here he comes now." She looked toward the counter, where the Sheriff was stopping to talk to the Mayor.

The Sheriff broke out a smile so beaming it was like my Florida vacation all over again, but I was too suspicious of what Ree-Jane had been doing in the courthouse to appreciate it.

"Why was Ree-Jane in the courthouse? Were you talking to her?"

He frowned. "Nope. All I did was pass her outside, just a minute ago. I'd say she was talking to herself. Laughing to herself. Does she act like that often?"

I could have gone on at length about her actions, but I was focused on the most recent. "Well, if she wasn't talking to you, was she to Donny?"

"Donny knows better than to discuss police business." The Sheriff looked a little concerned, now.

Why would he think about "police business" in relation to Ree-Jane's weird behavior? I didn't like the sound of this.

Neither, apparently, did Maud. "And just what 'police business' does Donny know not to discuss, which he would discuss anyway, if it made him look at all good to discuss it?"

I leaned up against the edge of the table hard enough it dented my chest, waiting to hear him answer.

"Nothing. There's no new evidence. Nothing."

"*Evidence?* Evidence of *what?*" I demanded. "You know *everything,* more or less, and I can repeat every single word to you of what Isabel said. She admitted she shot Fern Queen. She admitted they murdered Mary-Evelyn. You said her prints are all over that gun."

It was rare for the Sheriff to look uncomfortable, but he did now. "That's right. Of course, so are Ben Queen's prints. We still haven't found him, even though—"

Wide-eyed, I literally fell back in the booth with a thud. "Ben Queen's *prints?* Why are you concerned about Ben Queen's prints?"

The Sheriff looked down, frowning, as if he'd expected to see a cup of coffee there.

Maud said, "Sam?"

She knew. So did I. "But it's *over.* It's solved! I *told* you—" Then it hit me square in the face and I stood up in the booth, jammed between table and seat. "You don't believe me. I told you everything. *You don't believe me!*"

"Listen, Emma—" the Sheriff began.

I said to Maud, "Let me out, please."

Immediately, she rose and I all but threw myself out of the booth.

The Sheriff looked really unhappy. "Emma. It's not that I don't believe you. It's just that in police work there's something called hearsay—"

Maud shook and shook her head. "Oh, for God's sake, Sam."

I glared at him. "You're telling *me* about police work?" I turned and walked off.

But I heard Maud say to the Sheriff something I couldn't imagine her ever saying to him. She said it calmly, without accent, the way Will had said "fuck."

"Asshole."

I had a coin out and as I passed the jukebox, now silent, I plugged it in and stabbed a button for Patsy Cline.

Let *him* fall to pieces for a change.

Ree-Jane rousted

63

I told Delbert to drop me off not at the hotel but at Slaw's Garage. Of course he wanted to know "what-all" kind of business I had at a garage, but I ignored the question. I didn't tip him either because he'd asked it. I was not in a good mood as I walked into the garage, where Dwayne was working by himself on the engine of some big old car. The hood was up and he was leaning over the engine. He didn't see me come in and I said hello.

"Well, Lord, look who's here," said Dwayne, standing up and wiping his hands on an oily rag. "That's some story, girl. I read all about it in the paper."

I hoisted myself up on a pile of new tires, as there were no chairs. I said, in an offhand manner, "Don't believe everything you read."

"Okay," he said, shoving the rag back in his pocket.

I sighed. It was just like him to say that; he irritated me to death sometimes. "I didn't *mean* that nothing was *true* in that newspaper story. A lot was. Maybe most was. Just, you know how reporters exaggerate. I mean, I wouldn't call myself 'courageous' or even 'spunky.' " Of course, I would.

"Okay, neither will I." He was leaning over the engine. He adjusted his caged lightbulb to see into its depths.

"The *way* it happened was right. I mean, with Isabel Devereau's turning a gun on me and forcing me to walk through that dark, cold wood. It was like a death march."

"Wasn't that bad, was it?" He studied a spark plug.

"Yes. *Yes.* It was worse, if you must know. And there was *nobody* to help me."

He held the spark plug up toward the light and seemed to be regarding it as if it were a jewel. "I guessed I'd of helped, if I'd known." Then he hummed something. "You want to go rabbit hunting tonight?"

This took me completely by surprise. "With you?"

His head was lowered, half in shadow. "No, I figured maybe you could hook up with a couple foxes and the three of you go."

"Ha ha ha ha." I hated when I couldn't think of a clever response and had to resort to childish ha ha ha's. I shrugged to suggest I could take it or leave it, then quickly de-shrugged, thinking of his retort a moment ago. "Yes, I would." Besides, I wanted to talk to him about what the Sheriff had said. Even thinking about that now made me want to hit something.

"What's wrong?" He was looking at me through the triangle of light made by the raised hood of the car.

"Nothing. What time are we going?"

"I'm through here in a couple hours. I need to finish this. I can come pick you up at the hotel. In that." He nodded toward a fancy little car.

"*This?* Are you saying this's yours?"

"No. I'm saying Abel's loaning it to me because my truck's outta commission. It's Abel's."

"*This?* But it's . . . foreign, isn't it?"

"Lotus Elan. Really nice to drive."

How I pictured the reaction when he spun to a stop in this car under the porte cochere. I mean, of course, how Ree-Jane would react, since she's been flirting with Dwayne—or trying to—and he pays her no attention. Dwayne is handsome enough he doesn't have to be an earl to get Ree-Jane's interest.

"Okay, I'll be ready." I had been released from waiting tables that night, again, because I was famous.

As I walked lazily up the dirt path on the hotel grounds, I entertained myself with thoughts of Ree-Jane's reaction to the sight of me getting into that foreign car and purring off into the evening. This pleased me so much, I forgot for a moment the Sheriff's giving me that hearsay insult. How did I know but what he'd have me up on a murder charge? As if I'd shoved Isabel Devereau into the lake on general principle? Oh, it was all too infuriating.

When I left the leafy walk for our circular drive, I saw a smart little car that looked mildly familiar parked beneath the porte cochere, and when I neared the porch, I saw someone sitting, talking to Lola Davidow, who was rocking, drinking, and laughing—three of her favorite pastimes, at least the drinking and rocking part. The other person I was astonished to see was Louise Landis!

I stopped dead. The *orphans!* The orphans' lunch! For what day had I arranged it? Well, but I hadn't arranged it except between the two of us. I hadn't said a thing to my mother or Mrs. Davidow and here Louise Landis would be assuming they knew all about it. Thank heavens it was the cocktail hour and Lola had a pitcher of martinis close by.

Now, I figured that what Lola would think was that my mother had made the arrangements and forgotten to mention it. And if she was on her fourth martini (and by the look of the pitcher's contents she was), she wouldn't even care.

I bounded up the steps and said a bright hello to Miss Landis, who looked as happy as a lark to see me. Indeed, she did something seldom done: she hugged me. It wasn't that no one ever hugged me (Maud did a while back), but I was certainly not the most hugged person around.

"Emma!" She said, giving my shoulder an extra squeeze, "you are absolutely wonderful. You know you saved Ben Queen's reputation, to say nothing of probably saving his life!"

Now, it was just too bad that Ree-Jane chose that moment to sashay out and drop her little bomb. "Are you talking about that Queen person the police are looking for?" She arranged her pale blue dressed-up self in a green wicker chair. "But they're *still* looking for him." She gave one of her mirthless laughs.

Louise Landis asked her what she meant. It was such an innocent question, I felt like socking Ree-Jane in the teeth before she said what I knew she would.

"The police need more to go on than just the story of a twelve-year-old *child.*" Ree-Jane glanced my way, laughing as if the mere idea of my story being useful was the funniest *thing.* "She might just have been imagining the whole thing. And as far as the law is concerned, what she says the Devereau woman said to her is only *hearsay.*"

The "h" word. I clenched my teeth to keep from yelling at her, but my hands made fists of themselves without any help from my brain.

Remarkably, Miss Landis's expression didn't alter one whit. She stayed slightly smiling. She was one cool customer, I was delighted to see. She said, "How do you know that?"

"You mean about the police?" Ree-Jane looked surprised, unused to having her words questioned. "Why, the deputy *sheriff* told me. Donny Mooma."

Louise Landis's smile deepened. "But that," she said, "is only hearsay, too. So I'll just go on believing Emma's the heroine of the story."

My mouth dropped open. To be hugged and made a heroine all in ten minutes' time was almost more than I could bear. To have someone stand *up* for me was a novel experience, too.

At that moment two things happened: my mother walked out on the porch and the foreign sports car crunched to a stop on the gravel under the porte cochere. My mother, surprised to see Louise Landis, gave her a friendly hello. They were glad to see each other again. And me, I was even more glad to watch Dwayne getting out of the car.

Ree-Jane twisted herself around so that her chin rested on the back of her chair in a coy sort of way, and called, "Dwayne! Hel-*lo*!" Dwayne's appearance got her over the retort from Louise Landis.

In the background, my mother was hearing all about the orphans' lunch, apparently thinking Lola Davidow and Louise Landis had just been arranging it, while Mrs. Davidow (as I thought she would) assumed my mother knew about it all along but didn't care one way or the other, having poured herself another martini.

Of course, Ree-Jane thought Dwayne had come to see her wonderful self and smiled lavishly at him as he walked up the porch steps. He nodded to her (coolly, I was happy to see), then, more energetically, put out his hand to shake my mother's, then Lola's, then Louise Landis's. I had no idea Dwayne was so very mannerly. I could see in my mother's eyes he had climbed a rung or two up the breeding ladder. Of course, it might not get him a seat in what I sometimes believed my mother fantasized was her Paris *salon* life, but he was still a cut above most of the uncouth inhabitants of Spirit Lake.

Ree-Jane was craned around, staring at the red car. "I haven't seen your *car* before, Dwayne. It's really something!"

He smiled a little. "Not mine; it's a borrower. I drive a broke-down truck."

It was then I knew Dwayne was a man who didn't need the world's favor. Most men would have let us think the fancy car was his. Not Dwayne. He didn't need to impress us, he didn't need our approval. I thought of how rare this quality was. *I* sure didn't have it; no one on this porch had it with the possible exception of Louise Landis.

Dwayne was turning down—very politely—the offer of a drink, as Ree-Jane asked him what brought him here, certain it was her baby-blue self.

He smiled at me. "To pick up Emma."

Oh, for a snapshot of Ree-Jane's open mouth! Wondering if I could stand another moment of glory, I crimped my mouth shut against shouts of glee and tried to look nonchalant.

My mother, understandably, I guess, raised an eyebrow. Mrs. Davidow would've too, except her eyebrows were engaged in looking sober. "Emma? What for? Where are you going?"

As if he were looking at cue cards written by God, Dwayne gave the perfect answer. "Scene of the Crime. Emma has to look it over again."

Ree-Jane, who wasn't getting cue cards, worked her mouth, but couldn't come up with anything, and just sat twisting a lock of her blond hair so madly I thought she'd pull it out. Goody.

Between Louise Landis and Dwayne, my day had really improved. If tomorrow I said "Dwayne Hayden came by in his red Lotus Elan to drive me to the scene of the crime," it would not be hearsay.

My mother was discussing the food Louise Landis would like for the orphans' lunch. Neither she nor Lola had figured out the source of this. Of course, Miss Landis now was pretty sure no one had sent me to Flyback Hollow to check on the details, but if she did, she wasn't talking.

So, before any of them could ask me any embarrassing questions, I said to Dwayne it was time to get going, and we got. Ree-Jane did not want to stare at the car disappearing down the drive, or me turning and waving to her, but she couldn't help herself, and I almost felt sorry for her.

But it's a long way from "almost" to "most," as long a way as from here to the Rony Plaza.

Bugswirled, stumppocked

64

"That is one helluva story, Emma."

We were sitting on the wide smooth rock on the path near White's Bridge Road where Dwayne always stopped for his cigarette break. The air was soft and cool and the moon had risen as we sat there.

I was leaning over, my chin resting on my knees, pulling up grass and weeds. It helped me think. "Well, but do you *believe* it? Because the Sheriff I don't think does." I told him about our talk in the Rainbow. "He said it was hearsay; I'm a hearsayist."

"It's probably a lot more complicated than that. You know what the law's like."

"No, I don't."

Dwayne pulled over the small insulated cooler he'd brought along. It was one of those six-pack-sized ones. "Want a beer?"

That made me *so* impatient, when here I was, telling my story. *"No.* You know you wouldn't give me one even if I did."

"Want a Coke?"

"Yes, thank you." It surprised me that Dwayne must've thought about me when I wasn't around. Although a lot of people probably would have preferred me that way.

He flipped off the caps with a bottle-opener he took from his back pocket. He handed me the Coke. "Maybe you should've heard DeGheyn out, instead of stomping off like you did."

"I did not *stomp* off!"

"Uh-huh." Dwayne tilted the bottle of Rolling Rock and drank off nearly half.

"I *didn't!*"

"Sure you did. Takes one to know one." He turned and smiled. "I'm a prime stomper."

"You? But you always act like nothing ever bothers you."

"Well, it does." Dwayne exhaled a big smoke ring and then sent smaller ones through it.

Smoke could do so many things, I thought. I watched the rings dissolve and said, "But you never answered my question. Do you believe it? You think I'm making it all up?"

"Did I say that? What the sheriff is probably thinking is the only witness to all of this is Ben Queen, and he can't be found."

"The *only* witness? What about me? That's what I mean; you think I'm making it up!"

"You're not a witness; you're the victim."

Victim. I liked the sound of that. It was so much more than being just a "witness." I leaned my head against the stumppocked stump and thought about it. "Well, how do I know but what he thinks *I* shot her?" The idea excited me, though I didn't believe a word of it. "Shot her, and then just threw the gun in the water?"

Dwayne scratched the back of his neck, thoughtfully. "Well, I wouldn't let it worry me. You'd be tried as a juvenile and probably get off with ten, fifteen years."

"Du-*waaaayne!* Stop that!"

"This Queen fella—he's probably fled the coop, what with everybody looking for him."

"No, he hasn't." I said this without thinking. "He's looking for someone, too."

"Oh, yeah? Who?"

"I think she's his granddaughter." I told him about the Girl, about the five times I'd seen her. For some reason he seemed to be the right person to tell it to.

He shook his head. "My Lord."

I was glad he was impressed. "It's like a Greek tragedy." I stashed my Coke by the stump.

"What about this girl? Anyone else know she exists at all? Anyone else seen her?" He turned to look at me in a way that could be described as "meaningful." The look was full of it, I was annoyed to see.

"Don't look at me like that. She *exists*. I *saw* her those five times."

"Oh, I'm not contradicting you saw her."

"Then what? *What?* You think she's a figment of my imagination?"

"That's what you said Ben Queen said."

"But he didn't mean it! He was only *pretending*." I was really irritated. "William Faulkner would believe it. He would. Maybe she's a shape to fill a lack."

Dwayne looked from the sky down to me. "A word? Yeah, but maybe Faulkner meant it the other way. That a word itself don't amount to a hill of beans. Like the word "love" can't take the place of the feeling. The word's a shape, a husk, an empty shell."

I was absolutely astounded he'd think such a thing. "But of course he believed in words. He was a writer, after all. How could he not?" I recalled Louise Landis talking. "Words are home."

Dwayne stopped in the act of setting his beer down to finger out another cigarette. "That's pretty deep. Where'd you hear that?"

"Oh, I just made it up," I lied.

Before he put the cigarette in his mouth, he said, "One of the deepest things I ever heard."

"Actually, I didn't. Someone else said it." Whatever provoked me to tell the truth? "That lady you met, up on the porch. Louise Landis."

"She must be interesting. She's sure good-looking for a woman that age."

Quickly, I said, "Well, she's too old for you. A lot too old."

"Yeah? Well, you're too young for me, yet here we are."

I put my chin on my knees again, for I was blushing, and he, being a poacher, could probably see straight through the dark to my insides. "Don't be stupid."

He was handing me a cigarette. "Hate smoking all alone."

My jaw dropped as I took it. I sat up and watched him light his and then pinch out the match. I wiggled my cigarette at him. "Well?"

"You can just pretend. You could go through a whole carton just pretending."

I think that was a compliment, but, knowing Dwayne, I thought I'd better leave well enough alone and not ask.

We were silent now, both looking up at the moon. "Hunter's moon," he said. "That's because of the brightness."

"Poacher's moon, you mean."

Dwayne laughed. "That's pretty good. It looks silvery, looks the color of a gun barrel tonight."

We were silent again. I disliked the wet taste of the tobacco in my cigarette. "I've smoked before, you know. You can't get to my age without doing it at least once."

"Oh, I can see that."

We grew silent again, and I thought about my story. Mr. Gumbrel believed it. All those reporters believed it. Even Ree-Jane believed it, for heaven's sake. So I could stop worrying about that. I went over everything that had happened, thinking about what to put in and what to leave out for my newspaper write-up. I wondered where the beginning began. Was it down in the Pink Elephant, going through my Whitman's candy box? Was it my first glimpse of Cold Flat Junction and that horizon of dark trees? Or was it even further back? Was it back before our playhouse burned down? Or when my dog got run down out on the highway? Was it back with the Waitresses?

I said, "I wish the past weren't dead and gone; I wish things weren't over."

Dwayne smiled. "The past ain't dead; it ain't even past. Billy Faulkner."

I thought for a moment, and then I smiled too. "This is *my* story, and it's not over till I say it's over. Emma Graham."

We laughed.

I watched Dwayne's real smoke and my pretend twine upward toward the gunmetal poacher's moon.